Modern Consumer Behavior at the Intersection of AI and Social Media

Gopalakrishnan Soundararajan
https://orcid.org/0000-0001-9013-0498
Muscat College, Oman

Ruksana Banu
https://orcid.org/0000-0003-0835-8835
Muscat College, Oman

IGI Global
Scientific Publishing
Publishing Tomorrow's Research Today

Vice President of Editorial — Melissa Wagner
Director of Acquisitions — Mikaela Felty
Director of Book Development — Jocelynn Hessler
Production Manager — Mike Brehm
Cover Design — Jose Rosado

Published in the United States of America by
IGI Global Scientific Publishing
701 East Chocolate Avenue
Hershey, PA, 17033, USA
Tel: 717-533-8845 | Fax: 717-533-7115
Website: https://www.igi-global.com E-mail: cust@igi-global.com

Library of Congress Cataloging-in-Publication Data

Names: Soundararajan, Gopalakrishnan, 1980- editor | Banu, Ruksana, 1969- editor
Title: Modern consumer behavior at the intersection of AI and social media / [edited by] Gopalakrishnan Soundararajan, Ruksana Banu.
Description: Hershey, PA : IGI Global Scientific Publishing, [2026] | Includes bibliographical references and index. | Summary: "This book aims to Investigate the Influence of AI and social media on consumer perception and loyalty, strategies to enhance the brand by using AI and social media and to understand the role of AI in predicting consumer behavior of various product purchases"-- Provided by publisher.
Identifiers: LCCN 2025013519 (print) | LCCN 2025013520 (ebook) | ISBN 9798337327471 hardcover | ISBN 9798337327488 paperback | ISBN 9798337327495 ebook
Subjects: LCSH: Consumer behavior http://id.loc.gov/authorities/subjects/sh87006429 | Artificial intelligence http://id.loc.gov/authorities/subjects/sh85008180 | Social media http://id.loc.gov/authorities/subjects/sh2006007023
Classification: LCC HF5415.32 .M63 2026 (print) | LCC HF5415.32 (ebook) | DDC 658.8/342--dc23/eng/20250616
LC record available at https://lccn.loc.gov/2025013519
LC ebook record available at https://lccn.loc.gov/2025013520

British Cataloguing in Publication Data
A Cataloguing in Publication record for this book is available from the British Library.

Table of Contents

Detailed Table of Contents

The findings indicate that perceived ease of use, social influence, and compatibility positively affect customer experience. These results provide valuable implications to marketers in the telecommunications sector, helping them better understand consumer adoption and upgrade chatbot-based customer interactions. By emphasizing the role of social and contextual factors in technology adoption, this chapter contributes to the growing scope of literature on AI-powered customer service.

With the rapid advancement of technology and the ubiquitous adoption of smart devices, online shopping has experienced a boom. However, conventional online stores miss the opportunity of providing a useful recommendation service that has become a hot-tackling topic in e-commerce platforms for its high click-through rate and conversion rate. The cost of garnering information and making a decision has been reduced. With a myriad of online stores exhibiting products, users are provided with abundant information, complicating the revisit process by either analyzing review information across multiple platforms or contacting sites with little confidence. Instant messaging (IM) enables friends to effortlessly and instantly share product links, reducing the information-gathering effort.

This chapter delves into the influence of Artificial Intelligence (AI), Social Media, and Virtual Reality (VR) on consumer behavior, highlighting their roles in enhancing personalization and fostering brand loyalty. AI enables businesses to analyze vast amounts of data, providing tailored marketing strategies and predicting consumer preferences. Social media platforms facilitate direct interaction with consumers, strengthening relationships and engagement. VR further immerses consumers in brand experiences, driving purchasing decisions. Ethical considerations regarding data privacy and transparency are discussed, emphasizing the need for responsible use of these technologies. The integration of AI and VR allows brands to create deeply personalized, engaging, and interactive experiences, reshaping consumer interactions and loyalty. As these technologies evolve, they offer brands new ways to meet consumer expectations, ensuring a more dynamic and immersive future for marketing and consumer engagement.

The integration of Artificial Intelligence (AI) and social media has significantly transformed consumer behavior and digital marketing strategies. This paper explores how AI enhances personalization through data-driven product recommendations, targeted advertising, and real-time customer service via chatbots. Simultaneously, social media serves as a dynamic platform for consumer-brand interaction, shaping brand image through user-generated content, influencer marketing, and community engagement. These technologies collectively improve customer experience, foster loyalty, and influence purchasing decisions. However, their implementation also presents challenges, including data privacy concerns, over-personalization, and the risk of inauthentic content damaging brand trust. The study highlights the importance of ethical and strategic use of AI and social media to maximize their potential in building strong, lasting relationships with consumers in the increasingly competitive digital marketplace.

This survey chapter examines the influence of social media and virtual reality (VR) on consumer behavior, highlighting their transformative roles in modern marketing. Social media drives information search, social influence, and brand engagement, while VR offers immersive experiences that enhance purchase intentions and consumer satisfaction. The combined use of these technologies creates synergistic effects, amplifying consumer interaction and emotional connection with brands. Despite their potential, challenges such as privacy concerns, psychological impacts, accessibility issues, and ethical marketing practices require careful consideration. The chapter also outlines future research directions, including emerging technologies like augmented reality and AI personalization, as well as cross-cultural and longitudinal studies.

for tracking influence and designing sentiment-aligned engagement strategies in decentralised digital ecosystems.

In the fast-paced environment of the digital marketplace, customization and personalization have come to the forefront as the key drivers of consumer loyalty. Through data-driven approaches, brands can offer personalized experiences aligned with individual tastes, thus enhancing customer satisfaction and engagement. This research explores the influence of personalized and customized marketing initiatives on consumer loyalty, such as adaptive user interfaces, targeted email, and customized product offerings. With consumer expectations further enhancing themselves in terms of meaningful and relevant interactions, it is critical to explore the effectiveness of these approaches in driving long-term brand success. A quantitative approach will be utilized through a structured Google Form survey of more than 385 participants, including digital consumers and marketers. Correlation and regression will be used to explore the influence of personalization and customization on loyalty metrics such as repeat purchase, emotional brand attachment, and advocacy.

The convergence of immersive technologies and digital content creation has given rise to a new frontier for culinary engagement within the metaverse. This chapter critically examines the evolving role of food influencers both human and AI-generated virtual personas in shaping culinary trends and consumer behavior in immersive virtual environments. As the metaverse enables interactive experiences through virtual reality (VR), augmented reality (AR), and artificial intelligence (AI), food influencers are redefining the way audiences explore, learn, and interact with food culture. The chapter analyzes how these influencers curate content, host interactive cooking demonstrations, and co-create branded campaigns, thereby fostering dynamic virtual food communities. It further explores how food-related narratives are crafted

in the emerging trends across numerous business sectors. Marketing strategies are progressively evolving from print and e-mail advertisements towards more dynamic and data-driven digital marketing solutions.

There have been transformations in customer behavior due to the advent of digital technologies into the field of Islamic financial services like Takaful and Bancassurance. This chapter will discuss Islamic marketing's strategically evolution focusing on AI, social media, and digital transformation in consumer decisions. Shariah compliance is the guiding principle; hence every business is expected to innovate within the ethical integrity and transparency of such innovation. The discussion emphasizes how predictive analytics, blockchain, and personalized digital narratives stimulate consumer trust, accessibility, and drive financial inclusion. Case studies of successful digital strategies within Pakistan's Islamic finance sector will also mention challenges such as regulatory compliance, consumer skepticism, and tech adaptability. Ultimately, the chapter would suggest strategy options for companies to tap into digital innovation for sustainability and competitiveness in Takaful and Bancassurance channels, thus incorporating an Islamic marketing paradigm.

This chapter explores the impact of artificial intelligence (AI) on consumer decision-making, focusing on its role in transforming purchasing behavior and personalization. AI technologies such as machine learning, predictive analytics, and recommendation systems have revolutionized how businesses engage with consumers, providing personalized experiences across the decision-making process. From problem

Preface

The rapid convergence of artificial intelligence and social media has fundamentally reshaped how consumers discover, evaluate, and engage with brands. No longer passive recipients of marketing messages, consumers today interact within algorithmically mediated environments that personalize content, anticipate preferences, and blur the boundaries between physical, digital, and virtual spaces. This transformation has given rise to new forms of influence, trust, loyalty, and decision-making that challenge long-standing theories of consumer behavior. *Modern Consumer Behavior at the Intersection of AI and Social Media* is conceived as a timely and rigorous response to these shifts, offering scholarly insights into how emerging technologies are redefining the consumer landscape.

As editors, we recognize that AI-driven systems—ranging from recommendation engines and chatbots to immersive AR/VR experiences—are not merely tools of efficiency but active participants in shaping consumer cognition and emotion. Social media platforms amplify this effect by embedding these technologies within social interactions, influencer cultures, and user-generated narratives. Together, AI and social media create dynamic ecosystems where personalization, automation, and social validation coexist, often raising critical questions around ethics, transparency, privacy, and consumer autonomy. This volume seeks to unpack these complexities through empirical research, conceptual frameworks, and applied perspectives.

The primary objective of this edited reference work is to bridge theory and practice. It brings together contributions from diverse geographical, cultural, and disciplinary contexts to examine consumer behavior across retail, services, finance, food, tourism, and digital communities. By doing so, the book not only advances academic discourse but also equips marketers, policymakers, and technology designers with actionable insights. The chapters collectively emphasize that understanding modern consumers requires moving beyond isolated technologies to examine their interaction within broader socio-technical systems.

CHAPTER OVERVIEW

The volume opens with Chapter 1, which explores the transformative role of augmented reality and virtual reality in retail environments. It highlights how immersive technologies bridge physical and digital shopping spaces, enhancing personalization, engagement, and experiential value for consumers.

Chapter 2 focuses on AI-powered chatbots, examining key technological and social factors that influence customer experience in telecommunications. Grounded in technology acceptance theories, this chapter provides empirical evidence on how ease of use, compatibility, and social influence shape consumer perceptions.

In Chapter 3, the discussion shifts to live commerce, where real-time social interaction is fused with AI-driven recommendations. The chapter illustrates how instant messaging, social sharing, and smart algorithms collectively reduce decision-making effort and improve conversion outcomes.

Chapters 4 and 6 both investigate the influence of social media and virtual reality on consumer behavior, offering complementary perspectives. While Chapter 4 emphasizes personalization, brand loyalty, and ethical considerations, Chapter 6 provides a survey-based synthesis of social influence, immersion, and emerging challenges, including privacy and psychological impacts.

Chapters 5, 7, and 14 collectively examine the role of AI in consumer decision-making. These chapters address personalization across the consumer journey, ethical concerns such as data privacy and algorithmic bias, and future implications for consumer autonomy and trust.

Chapter 8 introduces innovative visual methodologies—namely influencer heat-maps and sentiment clouds—to track micro-influence within brand communities. By integrating data visualization with sentiment analysis, this chapter offers a novel approach to understanding decentralized digital influence.

Chapter 9 delves into personalization and customization as strategic drivers of consumer loyalty. Through quantitative analysis, it demonstrates how tailored experiences foster repeat purchase, emotional attachment, and brand advocacy.

Chapter 10 expands the discussion into the metaverse, examining how food influencers—both human and AI-generated—shape culinary trends and cultural narratives within immersive virtual communities.

Chapter 11 addresses group recommendation systems using sentiment analysis, highlighting how AI can improve collective satisfaction and decision accuracy in tourism contexts.

Chapter 12 revisits digital advertising effectiveness, arguing that traditional models are insufficient in AI- and social-media-rich environments. It underscores the growing importance of big data analytics and AI-powered engagement strategies.

Chapter 13 provides a context-specific perspective by examining Islamic marketing within Takaful and Bancassurance channels. It emphasizes ethical innovation, Shariah compliance, and digital trust in AI-driven financial services.

Chapter 15 applies the Technology Acceptance Model to human–machine interaction, focusing on anthropomorphism, familiarity, and perceived usefulness in chatbot adoption.

The volume concludes its thematic journey with Chapter 16, which analyzes influencer engagement trends in Indian cosmetic advertising on Meta platforms, highlighting the interplay between aesthetics, algorithms, and audience engagement over time.

CONCLUSION

Collectively, the chapters in this book underscore a central insight: modern consumer behavior cannot be fully understood without accounting for the intertwined roles of artificial intelligence and social media. These technologies do more than facilitate transactions; they actively shape perceptions, emotions, relationships, and cultural meanings. The contributions in this volume demonstrate that consumer behavior is increasingly co-produced by humans and intelligent systems within socially networked environments.

From an academic standpoint, this book advances consumer behavior scholarship by integrating perspectives from marketing, information systems, data analytics, and ethics. It highlights the need for interdisciplinary approaches to study phenomena such as personalization, influencer dynamics, immersive experiences, and algorithmic decision-making. The diversity of methodologies and contexts represented here reflects the global and multifaceted nature of contemporary consumer research.

From a practical perspective, the insights offered in this volume are highly relevant for practitioners navigating digitally saturated markets. Marketers and managers will find guidance on leveraging AI responsibly, designing meaningful consumer experiences, and building trust in an era of automation and data abundance. At the same time, the ethical discussions woven throughout the chapters serve as an important reminder that technological innovation must be balanced with accountability and respect for consumer rights.

As editors, we hope that *Modern Consumer Behavior at the Intersection of AI and Social Media* serves as both a foundational reference and a catalyst for future inquiry. We trust that this volume will inspire researchers, educators, and practitioners to critically engage with the evolving digital consumer landscape and contribute to more transparent, inclusive, and human-centered applications of AI and social media.

Chapter 1

Augmented Reality (AR) and Virtual Reality (VR) in Retail:

The Future of Consumer Shopping Experiences

Pavethra Ramesh
Vel Tech Rangarajan Dr. Sagunthala R&D Institute of Science and Technology, India

Chandramowleeswaran Gnanasekaran
https://orcid.org/0000-0002-1293-1043
Vel Tech Rangarajan Dr. Sagunthala R&D Institute of Science and Technology, India

J. Sudarvel
https://orcid.org/0000-0001-6656-1992
Karpagam Academy of Higher Education, India

A. Martin Jayaraj
Karpagam Academy of Higher Education, India

S. Jegadeeswari
Karpagam Academy of Higher Education, India

M. Kalimuthu
https://orcid.org/0000-0003-2353-004X
Dr. N.G.P. Arts and Science College, Coimbatore, India

ABSTRACT

Today, the Augmented Reality (AR) and Virtual Reality (VR) technologies have breached the consumer shopping experiences to new dimensions where retailers have now bridged the gap between physical and digital shop. Given all the possibilities, AR overlays digital information on the physical world to enhance real-time interactions with immediate and relevant data provided, both physically and digitally,

DOI: 10.4018/979-8-3373-2747-1.ch001

(Azuma, 1997). In contrast, VR immerses users in totally virtual environments and thus gives it the ability to involve with products and places in ways it was never formerly imagined (Slater & Wilbur, 1997). Having an innovative way to create interactive and personalized shopping experiences with immersive technologies, these modern consumers are dependent on the fact they get more interesting things and tailored things in their personal shopping experience.

INTRODUCTION

Today, the Augmented Reality (AR) and Virtual Reality (VR) technologies have breached the consumer shopping experiences to new dimensions where retailers have now bridged the gap between physical and digital shop. Given all the possibilities, AR overlays digital information on the physical world to enhance real-time interactions with immediate and relevant data provided, both physically and digitally, (Azuma, 1997). In contrast, VR immerses users in totally virtual environments and thus gives it the ability to involve with products and places in ways it was never formerly imagined (Slater & Wilbur, 1997). Having an innovative way to create interactive and personalized shopping experiences with immersive technologies, these modern consumers are dependent on the fact they get more interesting things and tailored things in their personal shopping experience.

Not only are retailers now using AR and VR together as tools to improve customers' purchasing expeditions, but are investing them as strategic initiatives in attracting customers, enhancing purchase choices, and ultimately generating more revenue (Pantano et al., 2021). Thus, AR technologies, including virtual try-ons and in-store navigation systems, give consumers the opportunity to view products in real time within their own environment to increase product selection confidence (Javornik, 2016). However, contrastingly, VR delivers completely interactive environments that result in consumers walking in the virtual store or reviewing the virtual product demonstration that captures the store experience (Babin & Harris, 2017).

Integration of AR and VR in retail therefore does not mean just fun and novel AR and VR experience; it means a strategic change wherein the role of consumer engagement and satisfaction in encouraging consumer's behavior and sell drives retail business. These technologies continue developing and hold great promise to over time revolutionize the retail, by altering how the future of consumer interactions and going shopping itself is positioned. While this paper will explore how AR and VR is currently being used in retail, what impact that has on consumer behavior and how AR and VR may change the retail landscape through their potential.

2. THE ROLE OF AR AND VR IN RETAIL

2.1 Enhancing Customer Engagement

However, as the AR and VR technologies are beginning to fundamentally reshape the way consumers experience retail brands — going beyond fairly simple, plain video and audio delivery — retail brands should be aware; this is the point. These are technologies which help the retailers to design personalised, conversation driven, shopping journey that draw the consumer's attention and make them emotionally connected to the brand for a long time.

Virtual try ons is one of the best ways AR helps customer engagement. It enables consumers to see themselves in the products before deciding to buy. Use of AR as an app in the fashion and beauty industries allows a customer to virtually try on clothes, makeup, or other accessories without having to try physical products. For instance in the field of fashion, a customer can use an AR app to 'try on' a pair of sunglasses and immediately see how the pair looks and fits the customer's face. This is particularly useful in those sectors that are used to carrying out physical trials, such as fashion, eyewear, cosmetics (Javornik, 2016).

Similarly, virtual store visits are also taken to an even deeper level by VR. For these virtual stores, customers have an immersive 3D experience which allows them to virtually walk through a store and find the products that they would, with that virtual store representing the products in different ways, perhaps as if browsing online. Retailers like Tommy Hilfiger and IKEA have led in bringing this approach to the consumers, giving them an opportunity to explore the products in virtual spaces resembling the in-store environments. VR allows consumers to walk through stores from home without feeling the pain of physical distance and thus such as better grasp of actual store design and product range (Babin & Harris, 2017). VR technology allows for retailers to engage with the customers in an entirely new way by immersing them fully in a completely virtual environment, experiencing an immersive experience that increases customer satisfaction and the time spent on a brand.

Both AR and VR offer consumers a more active role in the shopping experience. Instead, consumers spend time going through the products in an engaging and interactive way, further involving themselves with the brand and increasing the chance that they will purchase. The immersive experiences are meant to create an impact of being connected to the brand, and in turn, create intimacy (Pantano et al., 2021).

2.2 Influencing Purchase Behavior

By integrating AR and VR in retail, it has been shown to impact purchase behavior by influencing consumer confidence in their buying decisions greatly.

Immersive experiences contribute to more consumers' understanding of product, therefore leading to less uncertainty and more informed decisions. Since AR and VR present better product, they answer common queries related to online purchasing, most notably on fit, quality and appearance of the product.

The AR could offer the "try before buying" for a consumer, i.e., for a product that needs to understand how will it fit in a personal space or on a person's body. This feature is particularly relevant in the furniture retail industry, where the customer gets the ability to visualize the way furniture would appear in their home setting before actually making a purchase. An example of an AR app that consumers can use to place 3D representations of furniture in their own living room, giving an accurate idea of what they will look like in the space, is IKEA's (Azuma, 1997). In addition to enhancing person's awareness as to how the product works in life, as opposed to a static image of it on a website, this helps bridge the gap between online and in store shopping experience; thus making the purchase even more confident and less risky. Similarly, VR provides an in its entirety immersive shopping experience, customers are able to interact with the products inside virtual stores just like the actual place. The entire experience will offer the ability to be completely immersed and replicated the tactile and sensory aspects of in-store shopping and online experiences never including being able to touch, feel, or try on a product. Studies have indicated that this ability to engage with a product in virtual space increases likelihood of purchase given reduction of hesitation and provides more complete understanding of the product (Babin & Harris, 2017). Both AR and VR have also been proven to have a higher conversion. AR and VR studies show that people are more likely to make their purchase when consumers interact with AR or VR technologies, decreasing the uncertainty and risk related with online shopping. When customers see what the product looks like with them or in their environment, they feel they're making the right decision, so they complete the transaction (Javornik, 2016).

2.3 Bridging Online and Offline Shopping

AR and VR are key to going from online to offline shopping. While online shopping has become convenient and numerous options, it lacks physiological and sensory experience that is associated with the physical stores; it does not let you paw the product or try it on. Specifically, when consumers cannot physically interact with the product, as in fashion, furniture, and beauty it may be difficult to make purchasing decisions.

However, AR and VR are compensating in this gap with digital solutions that enable the physical shopping experience. Using AR, consumers get to interact with the products in real time such as dressing virtually or seeing how furniture will look in their homes. For instance, AR technology enables consumers to import digital images of products onto the real universe with their smartphones to gain a feel of how a product will appear in reality (Azuma, 1997). This way, the AR removes the lack of physical interaction and makes the shopping more engaged and interactive in a way which is just as convenient as shopping online.

It's important to note, however, that in contrast to VR, web mobile actually enables the fully immersive experience, which matches the store's shopping experience very closely. Consumers can navigate through virtual stores, try out products and interact with them through 3D virtual environment in virtual reality. It is not only useful for online shopping experience but also creates the sensation of being there without having to move out of home. Now brands like Tommy Hilfiger and Balenciaga have been leveraging VR store which contains virtual 3D representations of their physical stores, browsing clothing items, and even try on items virtually. At the same time, this helps make store shopping feel like shopping without the 'store', the concomitant convenience and flexibility of online retailing (Slater & Wilbur, 1997).

On integrating AR and VR technologies with online shopping platform, retailers have provided the consumers with a more holistic form of shopping experience that blends the best aspects of online and offline shopping. This makes virtual product using these technologies, and aids consumers in making purchase decisions, enhance consumers' product knowledge and overcome the hindrance of traditional e commerce (Pantano et al., 2021). Thus, AR and VR are establishing a pure and seamless shopping journey combining the convenience of shopping online with the tactile satisfaction of offline shopping, which results in customer satisfaction and conversion.

3. CASE STUDIES IN RETAIL IMPLEMENTATION

3.1 IKEA's AR Application

By bringing Augmented Reality (AR) technology into IKEA's retail strategy through the IKEA Place app, customers can see how pieces of furniture would fit in their home before they buy, a move that has helped to ensure customer success for IKEA. The app uses AR to place 3D models of IKEA's products in the consumer's real world environment captured by the camera in the smartphone or tablet. This technology provides that realistic representation of what the furniture in the customer's living space might look like so customers can better decide size, style and overall aesthetic before buying.

The main perk of the IKEA Place app is that it takes away that uncertainty when purchasing furniture online. Consumers can even see how a couch, chair, or table will fit into their living space and how it will harmonize with the room decor they have when they secure a piece with a free online sofa calculator in their hands. An ability to see the furniture in their environment virtually enhances the customer satisfaction by making the buying process more interactive, personalized, and engaging. The results of many studies have indicated that this AR experience has resulted in an increase in customer confidence, decreased anticipation of purchase, and an increase in the conversion rate (Azuma, 1997).

Moreover, when it offers a level of interactivity such as this to consumers IKEA has succeeded in building customer loyalty. It allowed the way of personalizing the shopping experience to boost the sales of the app and also to make IKEA a leader on the market of retail with this app. In addition, a reduction in the number of returns is achieved with the use of AR as customers are more sure that the furniture they buy will fit the home and that it will look right (Javornik, 2016).

3.2 Sephora's Virtual Artist

A leader in the beauty industry, Sephora created an AR adoption which is the Virtual Artist app that allows Sephora customers to try on makeup virtually. Facial recognition technology is used by the app that maps the user's face and creates a realistic simulation of how different makeup products such as lipstick, eyeshadow and foundation will look on their skin. Without physically applying any shades or products, users can try different shades and products in real time.

By using made up as your shopping frame for the first time, this AR application has completely changed the way Sephora's customers shop by allowing customers to virtually try out makeup from a distance. With its personalized experience, customers can view how any particular product will fit their skin tone, style and preferences. In addition, through the app, customers are able to make informed decisions before purchasing their products so that they don't purchase what they do not expect to be received.

The Virtual Artist (app) is one of the noteworthy results of customer satisfaction. "Because Sephora's customers using the app are more likely to make a purchase due to the feeling the app gives to make them feel more confident about the purchase," according to reports. Additionally, by letting users try a product before they would go to a physical store, the app has decreased return rates and increased sales (Javornik, 2016). This success of Virtual Artist app has shown us that AR technology could boost the conversion rates and boost customer engagement, which makes the Virtual Artist app a successful tool for retail brands of beauty.

3.3 Tommy Hilfiger's Virtual Store

Virtual retail has gone a step further with Tommy Hilfiger's development of a virtual store experience which allows customers to walk through a virtual world, play with products and even buy them within the virtual space. It aims at replicating the physical shopping experience by providing an entire 3D environment where shoppers can browse through the clothing collections, interact with products, look at the items from all sides.

Customers can try on clothes virtually on the basis of avatars which are similar to the customer's body type and dimensions to get the real look of how the clothing fits and will look. This immersive experience is highly interactive and the shopping journey is akin to how products never could be when being shopped online. In addition, a consumer can check out products from a multitude of angles (as supplied by the site, or created by them) and also should be provided with styling ideas based on their taste and shopping habits.

Tommy Hilfiger has used the creation of a virtual store to develop a more tech savvy consumer base especially when the key players in the store's target customer are tech savvy shoppers who care about more creative and fun offerings for improvement. It has been a way to increase engagement and consumer loyalty by being able to shop in a completely immersive virtual world. However, Tommy Hilfiger has been able to combine the convenience of the process of online shopping with the haptic benefits of the physical stores by providing an online store that provides a virtual copy of the in store shopping experience (Babin & Harris, 2017).

This approach allows customers to shop online and on one hand has made it more convenient for them and on the other hand has brought in a new level of engagement in bridging traditional and digital shopping experience. The future of shopping through VR seems to be a more engaging, personalized and immersive than ever, and in this respect Tommy Hilfiger is showing potential.

4. BENEFITS OF AR AND VR IN RETAIL

4.1 Personalized Shopping Experience

AR and VR technologies serve as one of the most significant benefits that benefit and bring the whole value to consumers through personalization of the shopping experience. Retailers can use AR and VR to provide each consumer a tailored, unique experience by giving them product recommendations and visualizations according to the person's personal preferences, needs and behavior.

One such example is for example AR, which lets consumers virtually try on products, for example, clothing, accessories, or makeup, directly through their smartphones or tablets. This means customers can check how a particular item would appear on them before deciding to buy it. AR in fashion retail allows users to 'try on' garments, e.g. jackets or shoes, by overlaying digital versions of these products onto the user's real time image as seen through the camera of their phone. In the same vein, AR can be used in the beauty industry for consumers to be able to try out different makeup products to figure out which ones are the perfect shade to their skin tone and preferences (Javornik, 2016).

This personalization is bettered by VR by allowing the consumer to experience the virtual stores specifically suited to their tastes. Using VR it is possible to offer an immersive environment for the store layout, products, as well as the promotional content tailored from a shopper's previous purchasing history, or browsing behavior, or particular interests. In the VR, a customer can walk around the store showcasing most pertinent items for them and thereby improves the shopping experience and the level of engagement (Babin & Harris, 2017).

Personalized shopping experience increases the level of customer satisfaction because the customer feels more in control in his shopping journey and is more confident in his shopping decision. Retaining customers requires customers to be emotionally much attached to a product, and retailers achieve this by giving consumers a chance to personalise products in their search for what they want.

4.2 Increased Conversion Rates

Conversion rates – the rate of people who browse a store's range, seeing something of interest, and purchase – is substantially determined by the immersive and interactive nature of AR and VR. When products can be engaged with in a meaningful way, such as how they would fit in a home, tryes virtually or on in a simulated an environment, consumer are more willing to convert their interest into a purchase.

AR empowers consumers with the ability to see how products—such as furniture, home décor, appliances, automobiles or any inanimate products that might otherwise be too large or heavy to hold in their motel arms—fit into their lives before buying them. For instance, IKEA's AR app enables the users to image how a piece of furniture is going to look like in their living room, removing any uncertainty over size, color, or style. Visualization of the product in context of real world allows product's sales arguments to become less uncertain, thus making faster, more confident purchase decision possible.

VR builds on this to provide a consumers a fully immersive experience that allows them to experience products as if they were actually there. The customers can browse products, interact with the products, and indeed try them on virtually, all in a simulated store environment. VR makes customers want to engage with your brand more and provides that confidence when making decisions as their conversion rates increase. As initially mentioned, retailers who implement AR and VR during both online or offline stores can expect to observe an improvement in the sale conversion rate otherwise thanks to these technologies result in a more engaging, informative, and fun shopping industry for their prospective customers (Pantano et al., 2021).

4.3 Enhanced Brand Perception

AR and VR technologies are very adopted which go a long way in dramatically improving brand perception in that it paints a retailer as being innovative and wanting to satisfy their customers: adoption of AR and VR technologies is nothing short of dramatic. Today, customers do expect more from brands, especially when the shopping experience intakes gets enabled by technology. Such investments indicate that both VR and AR enable brands to invest in new and better leading edge technologies to improve customer experience. This places them in a good light as a forward thinking and responsive to consumer needs company.

In situations where consumers see AR or VR experience, they see and feel the brand to be relevant with latest technology and thus a brand that cared about them. And this would also make the retailer's image better than it was before implanting these, considering that it is better than those who have not yet joined these technologies. Successful long term retail landscape demands nurtured trust from the consumer and brand loyalty, both of which can be fostered with the ability to be able to provide an immersive, personalized and interactive shopping experience.

Additionally, AR and VR technologies enable retailers to create such experiences that the consumers will develop positive perception towards the brand. Virtual products are allowed to try on, play with different designs, or browse virtual stores according to one's tastes, thus it leaves a lasting impression and keeps the emotional distance between the consumer and the brand small (Javornik, 2016). In addition to keeping existing customers, it not only gives the brand a boost in its visibility to potential new customers but also positions the brand as the leading name in retail industry.

5. CHALLENGES IN IMPLEMENTING AR AND VR

5.1 High Development Costs

The high development cost of AR and VR technologies is one of the most significant challenges to implement AR and VR technology in the retail industry. Large hardware, software and expertise investments are needed to develop and integrate these technologies. For example, if you want to make an immersive VR experience you will need high end hardware like a VR headset and motion detecting device to use and develop high quality 3D model and environments for it. AR experiences are barreled up with cost, as those who want to do AR properly are going to have to spend an amount of money on advanced smartphones or tablets with high resolution cameras, sensors, and horsepower to overlay digital content onto the physical world.

For retailers of all sizes, these costs can be a substantial barrier, especially for small and medium retailers, as it involves a big financial outlay for AR and VR development that is difficult to justify. Another part, which makes it expensive, is that there is a need for special technical skills, so retailers may have to contract or share with external agencies or developers to design their own AR and VR experiences (Pantano et al., 2021).

These costs are more manageable for large retailers with substantial budget, and therefore they are more likely to invest in cutting edge technologies. But competing with larger retailers may take time, as the smaller guys will find it hard and unless they can find cost effective solutions or partner with technology organisations to provide affordable and scalable AR or VR experience. To mitigate the costs, some retailers may opt into partnerships with AR and VR solution providers who can help in obtaining cheaper technology.

It also includes long term maintenance and updating of AR and VR system. But as technology changes, retailers need to stay on trend and change their systems in each case, it can become a financial burden on them. However, barrier to adoption of AR and VR technologies by many retail businesses continues to be high costs of development and maintenance.

5.2 Technological Limitations

With AR and VR technologies advancing to such a great extent, technological limitations are still a big obstacle. How well a VR virtual environment looks, depends both on the hardware used. To enjoy high end VR experiences like like room scale VR games, traditional desktop, laptops or gaming consoles with high performance machine processors for rendering of this sort of environment at a rate of 90fps or higher is a necessity. However, not all consumers will have the needed hardware at their disposal, especially when one considers those that don't have the high end VR headsets and gaming systems. This can restrict the entry into and the quality of the VR experience for many users.

The technology of AR relies on smart phone cameras and sensors to overlay real time digital overlays. Most modern smartphones have powerful cameras and sensors, but in some cases AR devices like AR glasses or Microsoft HoloLens may have higher precision or performance. One limitation of such an AR experience is that it can influence the accuracy of the AR experience and, therefore, poor image quality, late response, or misalignment of the virtual and real world objects, which are shown by (Azuma, 1997). Additionally, many times the user interface (UI) of AR and VR applications may not be intuitive therefore making these applications unattainable to users unfamiliar with AR and VR technologies.

The limitation of these technologies can infringe on user experience quality, leading to being frustrated or dissatisfied with it, which would impede the adoption of AR and VR in retail. AR and VR experience can challenge consumers to engage if technology does not meet their expectation or if it is not accessible due to hardware limitations. With the constant seeking to upgrade the technological infrastructure in retail, retailers have to constantly evaluate and invest in order to provide the most improved experience, as possible, to their customers.

5.3 Consumer Adaptation

Adoption by the customers is another formidable hurdle to overcome in utilizing AR and VR in retail. Success of these technologies primarily hinges on consumers' willingness to use them. The good old consumers that are older and less tech savvy tend to be more apprehensive about a more recent technology like AR and VR. It serves as a barrier to the wider adoption of AR and VR in these retail sectors where an extremely large and diverse customer base that needs to be catered to.

It is noteworthy that the level of technological literacy has a lot to do with how easily the consumers can adopt to the AR and VR experiences. Consumers who know these technologies may find them overwhelming or unsure of how to move around at all in virtual environments or how to use an AR application. In order to attract AR and VR customers, retailers need to be sure their AR and VR systems are user friendly, have an intuitive interface and clear instructions for users not familiar with these technologies.

Furthermore, there are other concerns such as privacy and security of data, which may act as inhibitions for the use of AR and VR technologies. That may make consumers a bit leery about sharing personal data or letting apps have access to their cameras, computer, etc. These concerns have to be addressed by retailers who want to sell mutual funds by ensuring that they have clear policies about data privacy and their system implements accepted data protection regulations (Javornik, 2016).

However, if AR and VR technologies are accessible and user friendly, the general public will take to them. Those retailers who are more likely to be successful with creating AR and VR experiences that are easy to use, secure and broadly adaptable to consumers will be those that involve more AR and VR or attempt to deliver such experiences successfully.

6. FUTURE DIRECTIONS

6.1 Integration with Artificial Intelligence

Artificial intelligence (AI) is becoming the deciding factor when it comes to AR and VR in retail. By combining our human nature with Artificial Intelligence (AI), we can personalize AR and VR technologies to a level that can revolutionize the capabilities of these tools as it comes to the personalization of products and services encounter. It will enable retailers to deliver a dynamic and responsive shopping environment that is responsive and dynamic in real time as the person engages in particular means, prefers, and that reflects past purchases.

For instance, algorithms with AI can study a buyer's channel surfing history and search inputs, just as their acquisitions even aim to counsel the items to buy in line with their interests. These personalized recommendation could then be displayed in real time using AR systems. For example, what if a consumer is using AR to see what a piece of furniture would look like in their living room; in that case, AI can suggest something complementary based on the consumer's previous purchases or your current room layout. Real time personalization of this kind can significantly improve consumer engagement, improve the probability of cross selling and highly likely upselling as well as promoting customer satisfaction (Babin & Harris, 2017).

Furthermore, AI can also assist in inventory management in virtual environment by allowing consumers to only see products that are actual or available for purchase. In addition, it can also trigger real time updates in virtual stores or AR apps based on what are the most interesting products and adjust their virtual displays accordingly.

By bringing AI together with AR and VR, the goal can be reached to provide very personalised, adaptive shopping experiences that mirror and address individual consumer needs and desires. The trend of hyper personalization now has the potential to increase engagement, sales, and customer loyalty because it is more and more relevant and dedicated to the specific individual (Pantano et al., 2021).

6.2 Expansion of Virtual Stores

With the increase of VR and AR, virtual stores are to be expected as virtual shopping experience, from the comfort of the consumers home. The virtual stores will create a nuance where online and offline shopping trade off each other, where consumers can be involved with products and explore 3D store environments similarly to what they were doing in a physical store.

Compared to traditional e-commerce where people have to look at static images and descriptions, virtual stores will present a 360 immersive environment where the consumer can explore stores, see the product from as many angles as they need to, touch and interact with it in real time, even try it on virtually. This is a fully immersive experience that mimics in store shopping in the sense that items can be examined closely without having to go out shopping.

Likely, virtual stores will have advanced social shopping functions that allow consumers to shop as a group in a virtual space even if they are physically far. By bringing innovation in the physical form, this kind of evolution would give customers the best of both worlds— online shopping convenience with the interactive, tactile elements of physical retail (Slater and Wilbur, 1997). Virtual store is expected to become an important part of the retail ecosystem as VR and AR technologies get better, it will provide an innovative and engaging shopping experience as well to customers as it would be easy and convenient.

The virtual stores would also expand across the globe. On top of enabling retailers to create virtual showrooms which can be accessed by anyone, anywhere, and available anywhere, this creates even more opportunities for retailers to grow their businesses and reach new customer bases through e-commerce.

6.3 Enhanced Social Shopping Experiences

AR and VR technologies also bring great potential in transforming social shopping experience. These technologies can redefine how consumers interact with each other while virtual shopping. Friends and family can all do virtual shopping parties, shared experiences, and social interaction features while being separated by geographic location.

A classic example is shopping in a virtual store with a friend in London, with products available virtually to play with, discuss, try on clothes together virtually, etc. Users could share, in real time, their virtual shopping experience with each other by showing how a product looks on their own home or body using AR applications. By adding this social aspect, consumers will be able to get into the shopping experience through network interactions and make sure their decisions are made while considering shared opinion and suggestion of the networks.

And social shopping will probably lead to greater consumer engagement as people love to shop with friends and share opinions under the mask of play. Additionally, these experiences will likely help in sales since a peer recommendation is important when making purchasing decisions, particularly in the domains of fashion, beauty, and electronics (Javornik, 2016).

AR and VR will also encourage brand loyalty through incorporation of social features. It will also allow consumers to feel more integral connection to the brands that they find themselves interacting with in virtual environments while also strengthening the relationship that continued on beyond the purchase.

7. CONCLUSION

As you know, AR and VR are poised to make an impact on the retail space grounds by introducing an immersive, real, life-like, and customized shopping experience. The products that can be engaged with in the retail space in a dynamic engaging way cover these technologies, which bridge the gap between online and offline shopping. Although there are challenges, such as high development costs, technological limitations and adaptation on the part of the consumer, the advantages of using AR and VR (increased engagement and conversion rates, brand perception, and the element of the unique personalised experience) make them compelling tools for the already increasingly competitive retailer.

In the future, integration of AI with AR and VR, uplift in the virtual stores and the rise of social shopping will further help the case of AR and VR in retail. These developments will contribute to more interactive, engaging and efficient shopping, and allow retailers to meet the growing shopping demands from today's consumer in the largest way possible, making shopping the way of the future. Industry 4.0 is slowly emerging as a reality, and AR & VR technologies coupled with a lot more than them, have a significant role in bringing about change across the retail value chains.

REFERENCES

Azuma, R. T. (1997). A survey of augmented reality. *Presence (Cambridge, Mass.)*, *6*(4), 355–385. DOI: 10.1162/pres.1997.6.4.355

Babin, B. J., & Harris, E. G. (2017). *CB: Consumer behavior* (7th ed.). Cengage Learning.

Javornik, A. (2016). Augmented reality: Research agenda for studying the impact of AR on consumer experiences. *Journal of Retailing and Consumer Services*, *30*, 252–261. DOI: 10.1016/j.jretconser.2016.02.004

Pantano, E., Pizzi, G., Scarpi, D., & Dennis, C. (2021). Competing in the digital era: The role of augmented reality and virtual reality in retailing. *International Journal of Retail & Distribution Management*, *49*(6), 786–803. DOI: 10.1108/IJRDM-07-2020-0272

Slater, M., & Wilbur, S. (1997). A framework for immersive virtual environments (FIVE). *Presence (Cambridge, Mass.)*, *6*(6), 603–625. DOI: 10.1162/pres.1997.6.6.603

Chapter 2
Chatbots in Action: Factors Influencing the Customer Experience

Ons Baati
https://orcid.org/0009-0000-1316-9241
University of Monastir, Tunisia

Mariem Sboui
https://orcid.org/0009-0004-7652-174X
University of Monastir, Tunisia

Nadia Sfar
https://orcid.org/0009-0000-6324-2419
University of Monastir, Tunisia

ABSTRACT

Grounded in technology acceptance theories, this chapter investigates key determinants of customer experience within telecommunication services. Specifically, it examines the influence of perceived ease of use, performance expectancy, compatibility, and social influence on customer experience with chatbots. Data were collected through an online survey administered to 379 Tunisian higher education students, and the hypotheses were tested using structural equation modeling (SEM) with AMOS23. The findings indicate that perceived ease of use, social influence, and compatibility positively affect customer experience. These results provide valuable implications to marketers in the telecommunications sector, helping them better understand consumer adoption and upgrade chatbot-based customer interactions. By emphasizing the role of social and contextual factors in technology adoption, this chapter contributes to the growing scope of literature on AI-powered customer service.

DOI: 10.4018/979-8-3373-2747-1.ch002

1. INTRODUCTION

Companies are investing significant efforts in enhancing customer experiences to strengthen and maintain relationships between consumers and brands. Technological advancements play a pivotal role in enabling companies to elevate these experiences (GS1, 2023). Simultaneously, consumers are becoming increasingly demanding, expecting seamless and efficient online interactions (Emplifi, 2022). They seek 24/7 assistance and advice across various domains. To meet these expectations, companies have adopted and implemented virtual assistants (Martínez Puertas et al., 2024). For instance, « RedBalloon » employs predictive analytics and chatbot-enabled engagement to deliver personalized customer experiences, ultimately enhancing conversion rates (Kumar et al., 2024). In the retail sector, AI-powered chatbots improve customer experience by providing interactive product recommendations and real-time assistance, fostering an immersive shopping experience (Bonetti et al., 2023).

Chatbots represent virtual service agents powered by artificial intelligence, able to interact with customers in natural languages (Sands et al., 2021), to mimic human conversations, and to provide more authentic experiences (Mozafari et al., 2022). They are considered a distinct form of smart service as they enable immediate data collection, synchronous communication, and responsive feedback (Wünderlich et al., 2015). It is anticipated that by 2025, chatbots will manage 95% of customer service interactions occurring online (Clark, 2020). Conversational agents simplify different business processes, such as those related to customer service, owing to their ease of use and accessibility (Przegalinska et al., 2019).

Chatbots are progressively being used in service industries as a substitute for frontline human employees assisting customers (Crolic et al., 2022). For instance, in the banking sector, virtual assistants such as « Capital One's Eno » and « Bank of America's Erica » offer seamless financial assistance, empowering customers to manage their finances with greater ease and autonomy (Kumar et al., 2024). In the transportation sector, « Amtrak's » chatbot-driven virtual assistant streamlines the ticket booking process and customer inquiries, providing continuous assistance and improving service efficiency (Kumar et al., 2024).

Considerable attention has been paid to chatbots in service research due to their capability to handle diverse tasks, such as sales support, customer service, and information extraction (Mozafari et al., 2022; Lee et al., 2023). Nevertheless, academic research on the specific effect of chatbots on customer experience in digital service encounters remains underexplored (Chen and Prentice, 2024; Ranieri et al., 2024).

By engaging customers through natural, human-like dialogue and personalized communication, chatbots enhance the overall customer experience in different ways (Huang and Rust, 2018; Martínez Puertas et al., 2024). Chatbots respond quickly and effectively to customer enquiries, offer 24/7 accessibility, and give personalized replies based on past interactions with clients (Salem, 2024).

Despite the considerable growth in chatbot adoption and the expanded interest of researchers in their study (Chen et al., 2022; Jenneboer et al., 2022; Rese et al., 2020), the existing literature predominantly focuses rather on the customer intention to use chatbots and overall behavioral outcomes of chatbot interactions (De Keyser and Kunz, 2022; Ling et al., 2021) than customer experience with chatbots.

The rapid development of AI-driven conversational agents in customer service has significantly increased in academic research, as evidenced by the notable surge in publications on this topic in recent years (Nicolescu and Tudorache, 2022).

Although the effectiveness of AI-driven conversational agents in customer service relies on the customer experiences with the automated services provided by chatbots, limited research has explored the impact of AI chatbots on online customer experience (Chen et al., 2021; Jiménez-Barreto et al., 2021; Verma et al., 2021; Arya et al., 2019). Hence, further empirical research is needed to provide an in-depth insight of customer experiences and expectations with chatbots and attain a deeper understanding about the factors customers consider during their interactions with chatbot services (Aslam, 2023; Alsharhan et al., 2024; De Keyser and Kunz, 2022; Illescas-Manzano et al., 2021; Martínez Puertas et al, 2024).

To achieve a deeper understanding of users' acceptance of chatbots, previous studies have drawn upon technology acceptance approach to examine chatbots adoption. The current chapter proposes a comprehensive research framework, based on the three major theories: the Unified Theory of Acceptance and Use of Technology (UTAUT) (Venkatesh et al., 2003), the Technology Acceptance Model (TAM) (Davis, 1989), and the Diffusion of Innovation (DOI) theory (Rogers, 1995). The current study contributes to the literature through the investigation of the factors driving chatbot customer experience which has been overlooked in previous marketing research (Bakkouri et al., 2022; Trivedi, 2019; Yen and Chiang, 2021). It provides practical implications to optimize customer experience and facilitate broader acceptance of chatbot technology in the telecommunication service sector (Lubbe and Ngoma 2021).

This study makes meaningful contributions to the research body. First, it answers recent calls for investigation on customer experience with chatbots (Aslam, 2023). Second, to the best of our knowledge, this is the first attempt to integrate variables based on the three technology acceptance theories (TAM, UTAUT, and DOI), which are perceived ease of use, performance expectancy, compatibility, and social influence, and investigate them as antecedents to customer experience. Third, the theoretical model is empirically investigated in the telecommunication services, which frequently adopt chatbots to improve customer services (Shin et al., 2023).

Moreover, the findings of this study provide valuable insights to developers and marketers to enhance customer experience by surging the adoption of AI-based chatbots.

2. THEORETICAL BACKGROUND

2.1. AI Innovation and Practical Industry Trends

Considered by Alzaidi (2018) as the cutting-edge technology that has been at the forefront of the technological revolution, artificial intelligence (AI) has revolutionized many industries (Malik et al., 2024). For instance, AI is applied in banking (Sheth et al., 2022; Oyeniyi et al., 2024), tourism (Aarabe et al., 2024b; 2025), healthcare industry (Khizzou et al., 2024; Nouhaila et al., 2024), and marketing (Kumar et al., 2024; Mariani et al., 2022). Organizations that integrate AI chatbots gain a competitive advantage by enhancing both customer satisfaction and operational agility. « Haomaiyi », a leading Chinese e-commerce company, demonstrates how AI-driven virtual fitting experiences and personalized style recommendations contribute to a distinctive shopping experience, strengthening customer loyalty. Additionally, firms like « J.P. Morgan and Goldman Sachs » utilize AI for algorithmic trading, fraud prevention, and customer support chatbots, underscoring the extensive applications of AI in business processes (Kumar et al., 2024).

Chatbots are recognized as one of the most significant AI technological innovations (Agarwal et al. 2024). Thanks to the integration of emerging technologies, such as Machine Learning (ML), Natural Language Processing (NLP), and Predictive Analytics, chatbots have evolved from a simple rule-based system to a highly advanced conversational agent. Hence, chatbots are capable of delivering better quality services (Gupta et al., 2025), making more efficient and personalized customer interactions (Dobbala and Lingolu, 2024; Patel and Trivedi, 2020), and understanding the changes in consumer journeys (Noble and Mende, 2023). NLP is applied to chatbots to enhance the performance of human-machine interaction (Rashid and Kausik, 2024). Beyond sentiment analysis, NLP comprehends language and facilitates the accurate interpretation of customer requests, thereby delivering relevant information and reliable responses (Abiagom and Ijomah, 2024; Olujimi and Ade-Ibijola, 2023). Machine Learning (ML) enhances chatbot performance by recognizing patterns within massive data set (Suta et al., 2020). This technology enables customer data analyses, including past research, browsing behavior, customer's preferences and purchase history (Patil, 2024), to provide customized recommendations and offers. Predictive analytics enable an accurate forecast of trends and client needs. Therefore, managers can optimize operations in real-time and estimate future demand by evaluating historical data (Patil, 2024).

These AI-powered tools are not limited to boosting efficiency but also making more personalized, seamless, and fluid interactions. They promote more meaningful and beneficial exchanges, redefining customer experiences by enabling more targeted and upgraded customer service (Kumar et al., 2024).

However, to integrate these technologies, businesses must take into account ethical issues, such as data privacy, algorithmic bias, and the likelihood of inaccurate predictions. These concerns can affect customers' overall experience, particularly in service sectors where chatbots handle confidential user data (Martínez Puertas et al., 2024). Strong guidelines can help mitigate these challenges by promoting responsible AI practices and guaranteeing greater transparency in chatbot interactions (Elliott and Soifer, 2022; Abiagom and Ijomah, 2024).

2.2. Customer Experience

Customer experience is a very relevant concept very significant and strategically important. It is defined as a psychological state which is expressed as a personal response to, or overall perceptions related to the service offering (Chen et al., 2021). Ranieri et al. (2024) state that customer experience can be either pleasant or unpleasant. Customers can express positive emotions such as passion, satisfaction, enthusiasm, and engagement, or negative ones such as dissatisfaction, anger, and customer technostress (Kumar et al., 2022). Negative experiences may be caused by facing setbacks when interacting with emerging technologies (Castillo et al., 2021), service failure (Ross et al., 2020), or frustration (Padigar et al., 2025). That said, customer experience is considered as a dynamic concept (Barbu et al., 2021). It depends on environmental changes, shifts in consumption practices, and the interaction dynamics between businesses and consumers.

Many academicians considered customer experience as an unidimensional (Trivedi, 2019; Rizomyliotis et al., 2022) or a bi-dimensional construct constituted by hedonic and cognitive experience (Ashfaq et al., 2025; Fan et al., 2023). Other researchers treat this variable as a multidimensional construct. Indeed, Becker and Jaakkola (2020) and Lehnert and Kuehnl (2025) consider that customer experience is constituted by the following dimensions: cognitive, affective, behavioral, social, and sensorial responses. Likewise, several researchers point out that the dimensions of customer experience are accessibility, information, interaction, personalization, entertainment, and communication (Nicolescu and Tudorache, 2022; Gomes et al., 2025). However, Nguyen et al. (2025) state that customer experience has four dimensions which are hedonic, utilitarian, anthropomorphism, and social presence.

Innovative technologies such as digitalization and artificial intelligence play a pivotal role in forming and influencing customer experience (Aarabe et al., 2024a; Hoyer et al., 2020). In fact, recently, AI has become an effective tool for delivering highly personalized experiences and improving predictive analytics (Spais and Jain, 2025).

Enhancing customer experience is essential for establishing and sustaining strong consumer-company relationships. Indeed, customer experience is instrumental in customer loyalty (Bhattacharya and Sinha, 2022; Jenneboer et al., 2022; Lemon and Verhoef, 2016), customer satisfaction (Chen et al., 2021), brand love (Zungu et al., 2025), customer engagement (Gomes et al., 2025), and continuance intention toward chatbots (Nguyen and Le, 2025).

One of the latest AI innovations designed to strengthen customer experience is AI-driven chatbots (Dwivedi et al., 2023; Rizomyliotis et al., 2022; Wang et al., 2023; Kumar et al., 2025; Khan et al., 2025).

Chatbots or conversational robots are software programs that emulate smart conversations (Aloui et al., 2024). They are always accessible, enabling the handling of client inquiries quickly and efficiently. Chatbots are based on past interactions to provide tailored replies and to offer a convenient way to support and recommend consumer decisions (Chen et al., 2021). Therefore, chatbots strive to deliver a smooth and enjoyable customer experience by simulating human conversation (Cate, 2025; Oluwadamilola and Emmanuel, 2024).

Aware of the role of chatbots in elevating customer experience, companies integrate them into key business functions such as customer relationship management, customer service, and sales. Several studies have assessed the influence of chatbot usage on customer experience in the service sector. While current research has explored chatbot customer experience across various industries including tourism (Aloui et al., 2024), banking (Chauhan et al., 2022; Salem, 2024), a significant gap persists in grasping the factors that drive customer experience with chatbots in the telecommunications sector (Saoud and Romman, 2024).

Chatbots in the telecommunication sector, which play a crucial role in facilitating communication (Ocxas et al., 2024), can be deployed at customer experience touchpoints to manage network issues and provide technical assistance. They can also be used to automatically send notifications for data limits or service disruptions and to deliver promotional deals and special offers. This sector encounters specific challenges, including the management of numerous customer interactions and the minimization of system interruption in a highly competitive market (Al-Kfairy et al., 2024).

The more important example is the case of TOBi, the Vodaphone's chatbot, which is considered as a successful conversational AI agent that has a powerful effect on customer satisfaction (Singh, 2025). TOBi chatbot reduces customer wait times and enables faster resolution of customer inquiries. Indeed, in 2019, 70% of the issues were resolved by TOBi[1]. It manages many interactions in real time, reducing costs and leading to better support efficiency.

2.3. TAM, UTAUT, and DOI Theories

Many models and theories have been developed to analyze the acceptance and utilization of technology systems over time, stemming from research in diverse areas. The present study is theoretically grounded in three widely established theories which are: the TAM, the UTAUT, and the DOI.

- **The Technology Acceptance Model (TAM):**

TAM is introduced by Davis (1989) and built on the Theory of Reasoned Action (Fishbein, 1979), which provided a psychological framework to understand human behavior; a perspective which was notably absent from the information systems (IS) literature at the time (Davis, 1989; Davis, 1993). TAM has been used in previous research to consider the acceptance of new technology (Davis, 1989; Davis and Venkatesh, 1996), becoming a cornerstone for IS research and one of the foundational frameworks in the field, with over 40,000 citations (Tamilmani et al., 2021).

The primary objective of the TAM was to delve into the processes driving technology acceptance and use, enabling predictions about user behavior and offering a theoretical foundation for successful technology implementation. Additionally, TAM aimed to provide practical guidance to practitioners by identifying measures to facilitate system adoption before implementation (Marikyan and Papagiannidis, 2023).

Based on evidence in earlier studies, TAM hypothesized and validated that « perceived usefulness » and « perceived ease of use » are the two main fundamental antecedents of user acceptance (Marikyan and Papagiannidis, 2023). Both determinants have been considered as the cognitive beliefs that influence usage behavior of information technologies (Davis, 1989). In other words, according to TAM, the decision to use an IS is influenced by assessing the balance between its perceived benefits and the perceived effort required to use it (Davis, 1989).

- **The Unified Theory of Acceptance and Use of Technology (UTAUT):**

Like most of its predecessors in the field of IT/IS adoption and diffusion, the UTAUT presents a framework for evaluating users' intentions to adopt a technology and their consequent usage behavior. The model explains variance in usage intentions through four key independent constructs: performance expectancy, effort expectancy, social influence, and facilitating conditions, which serve as direct determinants of behavioral usage intention (Venkatesh et al., 2003).

Two of UTAUT's constructs are adhere to those of (TAM): performance expectancy conforms to perceived usefulness, while effort expectancy parallels perceived ease of use (PEOU) (Gopinath and Kasilingam, 2023). Social influence captures the impact of peers, superiors, and cultural norms on chatbot adoption, playing a crucial role in collectivist societies where social approval strongly shapes behavior (Mogaji et al., 2021). Lastly, facilitating conditions, such as the accessibility of technical and organizational infrastructure, are key determinants of technology adoption, directly influencing behavioral intention and usage (Venkatesh et al., 2003).

- **The Diffusion of Innovation Theory (DOI)**

Rogers (2003) defines innovation as an idea, a process, or object that is viewed as novel. Diffusion, on the other hand, constitutes the process through which an innovation spreads over time via specific communication channels within a social system. The DOI theory outlines how emerging technologies progress from their initial development to widespread adoption, emphasizing variations among adopter categories (Rogers, 1995).

Rogers (2003) identifies five key characteristics influencing technology acceptance: compatibility, relative advantage, trialability, complexity, and observability (Sahin, 2006). He states that innovations, which have high relative advantage, are more compatible, simple, highly trialable, and easily observable, tend to be adopted more rapidly. Despite these favorable attributes, the diffusion of new ideas remains a challenging process. Research reveals that these factors collectively affect individuals' readiness to integrate new technologies into their routines (Bennett and Bennett, 2003).

Among the DOI key factors, relative advantage, compatibility, and complexity are often regarded as the most impactful factors in the adoption of new technologies (Faqih, 2016; Moore and Benbasat, 1991; Mostafa and Kasamani, 2022). Notably, relative advantage and perceived usefulness are commonly considered interchangeable concepts, while complexity is essentially the opposite of perceived ease of use (Moore and Benbasat, 1991; Mostafa and Kasamani, 2022; Zhou et al., 2010). Given this, our study focuses specifically on compatibility as the chosen factor from the DOI framework, alongside perceived ease of use and performance expectancy factors from the TAM model, and social influence and compatibility from the UTAUT theory.

3. HYPOTHESIS DEVELOPMENT

3.1. Perceived Ease of Use

Perceived ease of use means the extent to which the individual considers that the new technology can be adopted easily and does not require strenuous effort nor an intense training (Na et al., 2022). The TAM postulates that ease of use is a key element in determining technology adoption (Davis, 1989). It proposes that users are more predisposed to accept technologies that are regarded as straightforward and require negligible effort to operate (Amin et al., 2014). Usability pertains to the level of ease associated with using a specific system, that is, the extent to which the system is user-friendly (Marandu et al., 2019).

Perceived ease of use enhances the perceived control, which, in turn, exerts a positive effect on the emotional aspect of the customer experience (Rose et al, 2012). Even for tech-savvy and technology-dependent customers, ease of use serves as a facilitator in the formation of customer experience (Barbu et al, 2021).

In the context of chatbots, perceived ease of use is most frequently examined (De Cicco et al., 2022; Gopinath and Kasilingam, 2023; Li et al., 2023). Additionally, empirical studies emphasize that the perceived ease of use of artificial intelligence enhances customer experience (Khan and Rabbani, 2021). Users are expected to perceive chatbots as easy to adopt from a great experience (Trivedi, 2019). Digital commerce firms ensure user acceptance by complying with the defined criteria of perceived ease of use, to promote an engaging customer experience (Bilgihan et al, 2016).

The less complex chatbots are, the greater the likelihood that users perceive the experience as enjoyable (Myin and Watchravesringkan, 2024). Conversely, if chatbots are perceived as difficult to use, this may negatively impact customers' overall experience with them (Trivedi, 2019). Therefore, we propose the following hypothesis:

H1: Perceived ease positively affects customer experience

3.2. Performance Expectancy

Following Venkatesh et al. (2012), Performance Expectancy refers to the level of benefit derived from using chatbot service, like streamlining time and costs. This variable is significant in determining the acceptance and usage of chatbots (Mostafa and Kasamani, 2022; Jyothsna and Kryvinska, 2024).

Furthermore, individuals have a positive user experience when the product performance aligns or is above their expectations (Moriuchi 2021). Performance expectancy is a direct result of the product's characteristics during the consumption experience (Deng et al., 2010). Bilgihan et al (2016) assert that performance expectancy and perceived ease of use are the two Key elements in fostering positive experiences. In addition, performance expectancy was found to have a more significant effect on the usage experience when consumers use chatbots like voice assistants (Moriuchi 2021). Therefore, we posit that performance expectancy is a key factor of customer experience with AI Chatbot. Hence, we posit the following hypothesis:

H2: Performance expectancy positively affects customer experience

3.3. Social Influence

Social influence is derived from UTAUT theory. It is defines as the degree of influence of others' thoughts on the customer adoption of technology (Venkatesh et al., 2012). Social influence is acknowledged as a powerful determinant of behavioral intention within different technological domains (Kaba and Touré, 2014). In general, individuals' behaviors are directed by the opinions and recommendations of their social group. Numerous individuals turn to their social networks for guidance when assessing technological advancements (Venkatesh and Brown, 2001). In the context of chatbot services, social influence is considered a crucial determinant in driving their adoption (Mostafa and Kasamani, 2022). Consumers are more inclined to download the applications favored by their peer groups, such as family and friends to convey and share information (San Martín and Herrero, 2012).

Furthermore, the literature on customer experience has emphasized the pivotal role played by social influence in understanding individuals' experiences (Keyser et al. 2015; Chandler and Lusch 2015; De Verhoef et al. 2009), particularly with emerging technologies (Moriuchi, 2021). According to Cox and Cox (2002), the repetition of social influence, regardless of the content of information provided, can improve positive customer experiences. We suggest that individuals are more likely to interact with a chatbot when they perceive others expressing favorable assessments of its interaction quality, consequently improving their overall customer experience. Therefore, we could posit the following hypothesis:

H3: Social influence positively affects customer experience

3.4. Compatibility

Compatibility is a crucial and central issue in exploring customer behavior (Selem et al., 2023). It is defined as the degree to which the individual perceives system as conform to his existing values, past experience and expectations (Moore and Benbasat, 1991). In chatbot services, compatibility emphasizes functional aspects by incorporating essential processes such as image delivery, client support, making a purchase, and payments (Park and Lee, 2024). A chatbot should be easily compatible with diverse content formats, such as text, images, and videos, and provide customer support service more promptly than traditional call centers and web-based inquiry systems (Park and Lee, 2024). A high level of compatibility in chatbot services significantly influences users' favorable reactions, post –usage evaluations (Isaac et al, 2017), and psychological comfort (Bhatnagr et al., 2024). The concept of service compatibility extends to the ability for users to interact with the service across multiple devices, reinforcing its significance in shaping user experiences (Lin et al., 2020). Research has established that users' hedonic experiences are directly affected by the service compatibility (Lin and Lu, 2015). Service compatibility can be regarded as one of the critical factors influencing potential users and adopters, as it is instrumental in shaping their overall experience (Alvi 2024). This compatibility frequently leads to enhanced satisfaction, convenience, and a greater probability of ongoing usage, thereby contributing to the overall improvement of online customer experience (Bhatnagr et al, 2024). Accordingly, we propose the following:

H4: Compatibility positively affects customer experience

The conceptual model is illustrated in Figure 1.

Figure 1. Conceptual Framework

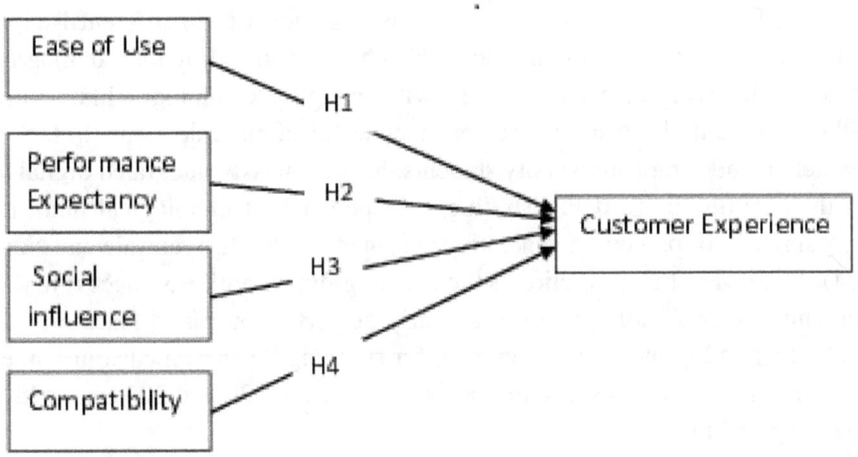

Authors' Own Work

4. METHODOLOGY

4.1. Research Design

This study employs a quantitative research design to explore determinants of customer experience with chatbots, drawing from established technology acceptance and adoption models. Partial Least Squares Structural Equation Modeling (PLS-SEM) was chosen as the analytical approach due to its strengths in predictive analysis and theory development, making it particularly appropriate when the research focus extends beyond theory testing (Goktas and Dirsehan, 2025). This approach aligns with our objective to both explain and predict the key factors shaping customer experience with chatbots. In addition, the holistic approach of PLS-SEM is still pertinent despite the simplicity of the model structure adopted in this study (Goktas and Dirsehan, 2025)

4.2. Data Collection and Sample

The data are collected by an online survey involving 379 Tunisian students. The study specifically targets undergraduate Tunisian students, from different disciplines such us Management and Economics. This choice justified by their demographic characteristics as digital natives familiar with emerging technologies like AI-driven chatbots, particularly in service sectors such as telecommunications. In fact, Gen Z, which includes most university students, has seamlessly integrated digital tools into their routine lives, demonstrating an expertise in technological innovations surpassing that of preceding generations (Tian et al., 2024; Ayanwale and Ndlovu, 2024). Moreover, this generation is the first to grow up with easy access to digital communication technologies from an early age (Bassiouni and Hackley, 2014), making them a highly relevant segment for studying AI-driven customer interactions. The sample consists of individuals aged between 20 and 22 years, with 297 females and 82 males.

4.3. Measures

All measures were adapted from previous validated instruments used in marketing studies. Items were measured using a seven-point Likert scale ranging from 1 (I dont agree at all) to 7 (I completely agree). Customer experience of the chatbot is adapted from Trivedi (2019), perceived ease of use from Davis (1989), performance expectancy from Venkatesh et al. (2003), Social influence from Oliveira et al. (2014), and compatibility from Moore and Benbasat (1991), as shown in Table 1.

5. RESULTS

5.1. Measurement Model Estimation

Exploratory factor analysis was conducted to verify the reliability and the validity of the variables. As illustrated in Table 1, all the values of Cronbach's alpha and composite reliability (CR) are above the acceptable threshold of 0.7. The consistency of constructs is so validated (Nunnally and Bernstein, 1994). Convergent validity is also confirmed since all the values of average variance extracted (AVE) are above 0.5 (Bagozzi and Yi, 1988). The square roots of the AVEs are greater than their highest correlations with other constructs, confirming discriminant validity (Fornell and Larcker, 1981) (see Table 2).

Table 1. Variables Measures, reliability, and convergent validity

Variables and Sources		Factor loading	Cronbach's alpha	AVE	CR
Perceived ease of use (Davis, 1989)			**0.822**	**0.629**	**0.834**
PEU1	**«My interaction with chatbots would be clear and understandable»**	**0.669**			
PEU2	«I would find chatbots easy to use »	0.861			
PEU3	«Learning to operate chatbots would be easy for me»	0.837			
Performance expectancy (Venkatesh et al., 2003)			0.880	0.716	0.883
PE1	«I find chatbot services useful in the purchasing process»	0.823			
PE2	«Using chatbot services enables me to accomplish the purchasing process quickly»	0.916			
PE3	«Using chatbot services increases my efficiency in the purchasing process»	0.794			
Social influence (Oliveira et al., 2014)			0.742	0.494	0.744
SI1	«My friends and family value the use of chatbots»	0.656			
SI2	«The people that influence me use chatbots»	0.697			
SI3	«The use of chatbots gives me professional status»	0.752			
Compatibility (Moore and Benbasat, 1991)			0.743	0.508	0.753
COMP1	«Chatbot services are compatible with my values»	0.619			
COMP2	«Chatbot services are compatible with my current needs»	0.809			
COMP3	«Chatbot services are compatible with the way I like to purchase»	0.697			
Customer Experience (Trivedi, 2019)			0.948	0.862	0.949

continued on following page

Table 1. Continued

Variables and Sources		Factor loading	Cronbach's alpha	AVE	CR
Perceived ease of use (Davis, 1989)			**0.822**	**0.629**	**0.834**
PEU1	**«My interaction with chatbots would be clear and understandable»**	**0.669**			
CE1	«I enjoyed using (brand) chatbot»	0.928			
CE2	«The experience of using (brand) chatbot was interesting»	0.969			
CE3	«I am happy with the experience of using (brand) chatbots»	0.886			

Table 2. Discriminant Validity

	Perceived ease of use	Performance expectancy	Social influence	Compatibility	Customer Experience
Perceived ease of use	**0.793**				
Performance expectancy	0.419	**0.846**			
Social influence	0.432	0.591	**0.702**		
Compatibility	0.567	0.467	0.546	**0.712**	
Customer Experience	0.447	0.457	0.571	0.514	**0.928**

The confirmatory factor analysis using Amos 23 indicated that the measurement model fits well the data. All indices are nearly at the suggested cut-off values for satisfactory fit. The normed chi-square is 2.889. The RMSEA value is 0.071, which is slightly higher than 0.05. The NFI and CFI values are 0.934 and 0.955, respectively, which is very close to the threshold recommended by Hu and Bentler (1999).

5.2. Structural Model

Structural Equation Model analysis was conducted to test hypothesis. The structural model achieved adequate fit: CFI=0.966, TLI=0.941, GFI=0.939, AGFI=0.908, RMSEA=0.062. The results show that all proposed paths are significant, except for the one between performance expectancy and customer experience. As illustrated in Table 3, H1, H3, and H4 are supported, while H2 is rejected.

Table 3. Results of structural model

Hi	Paths	Estimate	S.E.	C.R.	*P*	Results
H1	PEU CE	0.194	0.079	2.473	0.013	Supported
H2	PE CE	0.09	0.074	1.227	0.220	Not supported
H3	SI CE	0.415	0.089	4.663	0.000	Supported
H4	COMP CE	0.234	0.094	2.485	0.013	Supported

Note(s): PEU: Perceived ease of use, PE: Performance expectancy, SI: Social influence, COMP: Compatibility, CE: customer experience

6. CONCLUSION

6.1. Discussion and Implications

Aligning with previous studies (Lin et al., 2020; Lin and Lu, 2015; Alvi 2024), the present chapter reveals a positive relationship between compatibility and customer experience. This finding suggests that a strong perception of chatbot compatibility meets users' expectations and aligns with their telecommunication service usage habits and preferences. This alignment enhances the user experience by ensuring a smooth and intuitive interaction that feels natural within their existing service ecosystem. When users perceive a chatbot as compatible, they are more inclined to engage with it and seamlessly integrate it into their telecommunication activities. As a result, their interactions become more efficient and enjoyable, contributing to a more positive digital customer experience. To improve compatibility, managers should develop marketing strategies that highlight the similarity between chatbot characteristics and customers' expectations, principles, cultural norms, and life patterns. For example, a tailored pop-up message in the chatbot interface—based on user's previous interactions or purchase history— can reinforce relevance and enhance customer experience by ensuring personalized and seamless interactions which are aligned with user expectations (Mostafa and kasamani, 2022).

Additionally, the study supports previous results indicating the positive effect of ease of use on customer experience with chatbots (Makudza et al., 2024; Araújo and Casais, 2020), stressing the pivotal roles that user-friendliness plays. Highlighting ease of use is crucial in shaping an enjoyable customer experience. It means that chatbots that are easily used and have features that are readily understood by users to find the needed information enhance positive customer experience. Companies should make sure that the services offered through their conversational agents are relevant and easy to manipulate. Marketing efforts should clearly communicate that chatbots are intuitive and effortless to interact with. For instance, showcasing real-time demonstrations or providing interactive tutorials can help alleviate concerns about complexity, boosting customers' comfort in their interactions. This could be achieved by incorporating a dialog box on the brand's online platforms that highlights the plainness and user-friendly nature of the chatbot, further reinforcing the ease of use (Mostafa and Kasamani, 2022). In addition, marketers should simplify the sign-up process and clarify the chatbot usage to promote a pleasant experience (Dendrinos and Spais, 2024).

Moreover, the findings is consistent with prior research suggesting that users' experience with service chatbots is heavily influenced by opinions of those around them (Moriuchi, 2021; Mostafa and Kasamani, 2022). Social influence was the key factor affecting chatbot customer experience. The influence of significant others, including idols, peers, and family, has a positive impact on customer experience. Marketers should engage with opinion leaders in different promotional activities. To support the adoption of these systems, marketing strategies should draw on social media platforms and virtual communities. Favorable feedback from users connected through social networks can enhance users' interactions and experience with this type of service. Consequently, sharing positive testimonials from reference groups on social media can play a key role in fostering customer experience. Additionally, involving opinion leaders in advertising campaigns can amplify this impact. Influencer marketing, in particular, may prove effective in this context due to the social capital that influencers possess, as consumers often align with their opinions and behaviors (Aw et al., 2022).

However, results show no significant effect of performance expectancy on customer experience. This result contradicts those of previous studies highlighting the importance of the technology performance expectancy in shaping customer experience (Martins et al., 2014; Rezaei and Amin, 2013; Restianto et al., 2024). One potential explanation of this result is that other factors, such as social influence and ease of use have a stronger influence on shaping the overall customer experience. Therefore, Performance expectancy may be less critical in environments where users need the advice and assistance of friends and family and expect only basic functionalities from chatbots.

This scholarly work offers several contributions to the existing academic discourse. First, it addresses recent calls for research on customer experiences with AI-driven technologies, specifically chatbots (Ling et al., 2021; Mariani et al., 2023). Second, to the best of our knowledge, this is the first study to integrate variables from three major technology acceptance theories—TAM, UTAUT, and DOI—namely perceived ease of use, performance expectancy, social influence, and compatibility, and to investigate them as antecedents of customer experience with service chatbots. Finally, this research expands the literature on chatbots, which are increasingly recognized as a transformative tool that may significantly reshape how online businesses engage with and sell to consumers (Mostafa and Kasamani, 2022).

6.2. Limitations and Future Research Directions

This study is one of the few to focus specifically on exploring digital customer experiences with AI-powered service chatbots, framed through key factors from widely accepted technology acceptance models and theories. While its findings provide valuable insights, several limitations must be acknowledged.

The study is constrained to the service industry and applies a cross-sectional study design, where data is gathered at the same temporal point. Additionally, the geographic scope is limited to one country, which may influence the generalizability of the results. Future research could expand the scope of this inquiry by conducting cross-cultural studies to better understand the impact of cultural differences. Longitudinal studies would also generate perspectives into the lasting effects of chatbot interactions, while qualitative research could offer deeper insights into customers' perspectives. Moreover, exploring diverse factors and approaches could offer a deeper understanding of customer experiences with service chatbots. Future studies should consider additional variables that shape customer experience, like chatbot anthropomorphism (Sfar et al., 2025; Sayed and Abutaleb, 2025), initial trust (Sboui et al., 2024), and chatbot usage intention (Bhatnagr et al., 2024). Investigating moderating factors, such as familiarity with chatbots (Song and Shin, 2024; Ameur & Rached, 2024) and technology anxiety (Sboui et al., 2024), would also be valuable.

Moreover, TAM and UTAUT are among the most widely used theoretical models for evaluating technology adoption (Owusu et al., 2022), largely due to their adaptability across various contexts (O'Dea et al., 2025). TAM, in particular, is recognized as one of the most influential frameworks for understanding information system acceptance (Lee et al., 2003). However, despite their continued relevance, these models—especially TAM—have faced significant criticism.

According to Shachak et al. (2019), one of the main critiques of TAM is its simplicity, as it often reduces technology adoption to perceived usefulness, ease of use, and intention, without fully capturing actual usage (Lee et al., 2003). While UTAUT expands upon TAM by incorporating additional constructs, both models primarily focus on individual adoption, assuming a direct link between intention and concrete behavior. This narrow perspective overlooks broader organizational and contextual factors that influence technology adoption and long-term use.

Another key limitation of these models cited by Shachak et al. (2019) is their failure to account for system-level influences such as teamwork, workflow constraints, multitasking, and organizational dynamics, all of which significantly impact technology adoption and use (McLean et al., 2011). Moreover, studies relying on

TAM and UTAUT often measure system use in a simplistic manner, focusing on frequency or duration rather than distinguishing between basic, mandatory use and value-adding engagement that enhances user experience and business outcomes (McLean et al., 2011).

In addition, despite their extensive use, the explanatory power of TAM and UTAUT in the context of modern AI-powered service technologies has reached a plateau. With over 12,000 citations for Davis' (1989) TAM paper and more than 7,700 for Venkatesh et al.'s (2003) UTAUT model, these frameworks remain influential but may require adaptation to better capture the complexities of AI-driven interactions. Technology adoption is not a one-time event but a continuous process, necessitating more comprehensive models that reflect the evolving nature of AI-based services and their long-term integration into user environments (Shachak et al., 2019).

Hence, O'Dea et al. (2025) and Mogaji et al. (2024) propose future perspectives to improve the effectiveness of technology acceptance models. To enhance generalizability, TAM should be adapted to capture the unique characteristics and challenges of various sectors without requiring extensive modifications for each specific context. The accelerating development of AI-driven technologies, in particular, challenges the predictive capacity of traditional models. In response, Gursoy et al. (2019) introduced the AI Device Use Acceptance model, which expands prior frameworks to examine AI agent adoption across different phases. Further validation by Chi et al. (2023) underscores the necessity of expanding TAM to address AI-specific adoption factors.

Furthermore, future research should integrate additional variables into TAM to account for the distinctive challenges posed by AI in industries such as hospitality. These include not only technical considerations but also cultural and social dimensions, such as social influence and human interaction. With the growing adoption of AI, trust, privacy, and security concerns become increasingly critical (Mogaji and Nguyen, 2022). Moreover, cultural norms and values play a pivotal role in technology adoption, highlighting the need for research that incorporates diverse cultural perspectives to better understand their impact on AI-driven service adoption.

REFERENCES

Aarabe, M., Bouizgar, M., Khizzou, N. B., Alla, L., & Benjelloun, A. (2025). The Transformative Impact of Artificial Intelligence on Tourism Experience : Analysis of Trends and Perspectives. *AI Technologies for Personalized and Sustainable Tourism*, 277-310.

Aarabe, M., Khizzou, N. B., Alla, L., & Benjelloun, A. (2024a). Marketing applications of emerging technologies : A systematic literature review. In *AI and data engineering solutions for effective marketing* (pp. 23–47). IGI Global., https://www.igi-global.com/chapter/marketing-applications-of-emerging-technologies/350744 DOI: 10.4018/979-8-3693-3172-9.ch002

Aarabe, M., Khizzou, N. B., Alla, L., & Benjelloun, A. (2024b). Smart Tourism Experience and Responsible Travelers' Behavior : A Systematic Literature Review. *Promoting responsible tourism with digital platforms*, 128-147.

Abiagom, C. N., & Ijomah, T. I. (2024). *Enhancing customer experience through AI-driven language processing in service interactions*. Open Access Research Journal of Engineering and Technology.

Al-Kfairy, M., Mustafa, D., Al-Adaileh, A., Zriqat, S., & Sendaba, O. (2024). User acceptance of AI voice assistants in Jordan's telecom industry. *Computers in Human Behavior Reports*, *16*, 100521. DOI: 10.1016/j.chbr.2024.100521

Aloui, N., Mousa, M., & Chaouali, W. (2024). "Help me Chatbot!" : Customer-Brand Relationship in the Context of Tourism Chatbots. In Rather, R. A. (Ed.), *Consumer Brand Relationships in Tourism* (pp. 87–101). Springer Nature Switzerland., DOI: 10.1007/978-3-031-59535-6_5

Alsharhan, A., Al-Emran, M., & Shaalan, K. (2024). Chatbot Adoption : A Multiperspective Systematic Review and Future Research Agenda. *IEEE Transactions on Engineering Management*, *71*, 10232–10244. DOI: 10.1109/TEM.2023.3298360

Alvi, I. (2024). Investigating students' adoption of virtual reality for L2-learning in India. *Education and Information Technologies*, *29*(7), 8035–8056. DOI: 10.1007/s10639-023-12140-6

Ameur, H. B., & Rached, K. S. B. (2024). *Effects of Chat GPT Adoption on Behavioral Intention in The Field of Scientific Research : Moderating Role of Familiarity*. https://www.researchgate.net/profile/Habiba-Ameur/publication/386499749_

Amin, M., Rezaei, S., & Abolghasemi, M. (2014). User satisfaction with mobile websites : The impact of perceived usefulness (PU), perceived ease of use (PEOU) and trust. *Nankai Business Review International*, *5*(3), 258–274. DOI: 10.1108/NBRI-01-2014-0005

Araújo, T., & Casais, B. (2020). Customer Acceptance of Shopping-Assistant Chatbots. In Rocha, Á., Reis, J. L., Peter, M. K., & Bogdanović, Z. (Eds.), *Marketing and Smart Technologies* (Vol. 167, pp. 278–287). Springer Singapore., DOI: 10.1007/978-981-15-1564-4_26

Arya, V., Sethi, D., & Paul, J. (2019). Does digital footprint act as a digital asset?–Enhancing brand experience through remarketing. *International Journal of Information Management*, *49*, 142–156. DOI: 10.1016/j.ijinfomgt.2019.03.013

Ashfaq, M., Makkar, M., Hoang, A.-P., Dang-Pham, D., Do, M. H. T., & Nguyen, A. T. V. (2025). Exploring customer stickiness during "smart" experiences : A study on AI chatbot affinity in online customer services. *Journal of Research in Interactive Marketing*. Advance online publication. DOI: 10.1108/JRIM-09-2024-0452

Aslam, U. (2023). Understanding the usability of retail fashion brand chatbots : Evidence from customer expectations and experiences. *Journal of Retailing and Consumer Services*, *74*, 103377. DOI: 10.1016/j.jretconser.2023.103377

Aw, E. C.-X., Tan, G. W.-H., Cham, T.-H., Raman, R., & Ooi, K.-B. (2022). Alexa, what's on my shopping list? Transforming customer experience with digital voice assistants. *Technological Forecasting and Social Change*, *180*, 121711. DOI: 10.1016/j.techfore.2022.121711

Ayanwale, M. A., & Ndlovu, M. (2024). Investigating factors of students' behavioral intentions to adopt chatbot technologies in higher education : Perspective from expanded diffusion theory of innovation. *Computers in Human Behavior Reports*, *14*, 100396. DOI: 10.1016/j.chbr.2024.100396

Bagozzi, R. P., & Yi, Y. (1988). On the evaluation of structural equation models. *Journal of the Academy of Marketing Science*, *16*(1), 74–94. DOI: 10.1007/BF02723327

Bakkouri, B. E., Raki, S., & Belgnaoui, T. (2022). The Role of Chatbots in Enhancing Customer Experience : Literature Review. *Procedia Computer Science*, *203*, 432–437. DOI: 10.1016/j.procs.2022.07.057

Barbu, C. M., Florea, D. L., Dabija, D.-C., & Barbu, M. C. R. (2021). Customer experience in fintech. *Journal of Theoretical and Applied Electronic Commerce Research*, *16*(5), 1415–1433. DOI: 10.3390/jtaer16050080

Bassiouni, D. H., & Hackley, C. (2014). 'Generation Z'children's adaptation to digital consumer culture : A critical literature review. *Journal of Customer Behaviour, 13*(2), 113–133. DOI: 10.1362/147539214X14024779483591

Becker, L., & Jaakkola, E. (2020). Customer experience : Fundamental premises and implications for research. *Journal of the Academy of Marketing Science, 48*(4), 630–648. DOI: 10.1007/s11747-019-00718-x

Bennett, J., & Bennett, L. (2003). A review of factors that influence the diffusion of innovation when structuring a faculty training program. *The Internet and Higher Education, 6*(1), 53–63. DOI: 10.1016/S1096-7516(02)00161-6

Bhatnagr, P., Rajesh, A., & Misra, R. (2024). Study of AI-enabled chatbots driving customer experience and intention to recommend. *International Journal of System Assurance Engineering and Management*. Advance online publication. DOI: 10.1007/s13198-024-02532-3

Bhattacharya, C., & Sinha, M. (2022). The role of artificial intelligence in banking for leveraging customer experience. *Australasian Accounting. Business and Finance Journal, 16*(5), 89–105.

Bilgihan, A., Kandampully, J., & Zhang, T. (2016). Towards a unified customer experience in online shopping environments : Antecedents and outcomes. *International Journal of Quality and Service Sciences, 8*(1), 102–119. DOI: 10.1108/IJQSS-07-2015-0054

Bonetti, F., Montecchi, M., Plangger, K., & Schau, H. J. (2023). Practice co-evolution : Collaboratively embedding artificial intelligence in retail practices. *Journal of the Academy of Marketing Science, 51*(4), 867–888. DOI: 10.1007/s11747-022-00896-1 PMID: 36035334

Castillo, D., Canhoto, A. I., & Said, E. (2021). The dark side of AI-powered service interactions : Exploring the process of co-destruction from the customer perspective. *Service Industries Journal, 41*(13-14), 900–925. DOI: 10.1080/02642069.2020.1787993

Cate, M. (2025). *Impact of AI-Driven Chatbot Interactions on Customer Loyalty and Retention*. https://www.researchgate.net/profile/Mia-Cate/publication/390873579_Impact_of_AI-Driven_Chatbot_Interactions_on_Customer_Loyalty_and_Retention/links/6800ee90d1054b0207d4e28c/Impact-of-AI-Driven-Chatbot-Interactions-on-Customer-Loyalty-and-Retention.pdf

Chandler, J. D., & Lusch, R. F. (2015). Service Systems : A Broadened Framework and Research Agenda on Value Propositions, Engagement, and Service Experience. *Journal of Service Research, 18*(1), 6–22. DOI: 10.1177/1094670514537709

Chauhan, S., Akhtar, A., & Gupta, A. (2022). Customer experience in digital banking : A review and future research directions. *International Journal of Quality and Service Sciences*, *14*(2), 311–348. DOI: 10.1108/IJQSS-02-2021-0027

Chen, J.-S., Le, T.-T.-Y., & Florence, D. (2021). Usability and responsiveness of artificial intelligence chatbot on online customer experience in e-retailing. *International Journal of Retail & Distribution Management*, *49*(11), 1512–1531. DOI: 10.1108/IJRDM-08-2020-0312

Chen, Q., Gong, Y., Lu, Y., & Tang, J. (2022). Classifying and measuring the service quality of AI chatbot in frontline service. *Journal of Business Research*, *145*, 552–568. DOI: 10.1016/j.jbusres.2022.02.088

Chen, Y., & Prentice, C. (2024). Integrating Artificial Intelligence and Customer Experience. *Australasian Marketing Journal*, *14413582241252904*. Advance online publication. DOI: 10.1177/14413582241252904

Chi, O. H., Chi, C. G., Gursoy, D., & Nunkoo, R. (2023). Customers' acceptance of artificially intelligent service robots : The influence of trust and culture. *International Journal of Information Management*, *70*, 102623. DOI: 10.1016/j.ijinfomgt.2023.102623

Clark, S. (2020). *How Artificial Intelligence and Chatbots Are Improving Employee Experience*. Reworked.Co. https://www.reworked.co/employee-experience/5-ways-chatbots-improve-employee-experience/

Cox, D., & Cox, A. D. (2002). Beyond First Impressions : The Effects of Repeated Exposure on Consumer Liking of Visually Complex and Simple Product Designs. *Journal of the Academy of Marketing Science*, *30*(2), 119–130. DOI: 10.1177/03079459994371

Crolic, C., Thomaz, F., Hadi, R., & Stephen, A. T. (2022). Blame the Bot : Anthropomorphism and Anger in Customer–Chatbot Interactions. *Journal of Marketing*, *86*(1), 132–148. DOI: 10.1177/00222429211045687

Davis, F. D. (1989). Perceived usefulness, perceived ease of use, and user acceptance of information technology. *Management Information Systems Quarterly*, *13*(3), 319–340. DOI: 10.2307/249008

Davis, F. D. (1993). User acceptance of information technology : System characteristics, user perceptions and behavioral impacts. *International Journal of Man-Machine Studies*, *38*(3), 475–487. DOI: 10.1006/imms.1993.1022

Davis, F. D., & Venkatesh, V. (1996). A critical assessment of potential measurement biases in the technology acceptance model : Three experiments. *International Journal of Human-Computer Studies*, *45*(1), 19–45. DOI: 10.1006/ijhc.1996.0040

De Cicco, R., Iacobucci, S., Aquino, A., Romana Alparone, F., & Palumbo, R. (2022). Understanding Users' Acceptance of Chatbots : An Extended TAM Approach. In Følstad, A., Araujo, T., Papadopoulos, S., Law, E. L.-C., Luger, E., Goodwin, M., & Brandtzaeg, P. B. (Eds.), *Chatbot Research and Design* (Vol. 13171, pp. 3–22). Springer International Publishing., DOI: 10.1007/978-3-030-94890-0_1

De Keyser, A., & Kunz, W. H. (2022). Living and working with service robots : A TCCM analysis and considerations for future research. *Journal of Service Management*, *33*(2), 165–196. DOI: 10.1108/JOSM-12-2021-0488

De Keyser, A., Lemon, K. N., Klaus, P., & Keiningham, T. L. (2015). A framework for understanding and managing the customer experience. *Marketing Science Institute working paper series, 85*(1), 15-121.

Dendrinos, K., & Spais, G. (2024). An investigation of selected UTAUT constructs and consumption values of Gen Z and Gen X for mobile banking services and behavioral intentions to facilitate the adoption of mobile apps. *Journal of Marketing Analytics*, *12*(3), 492–522. DOI: 10.1057/s41270-023-00271-1

Deng, L., Turner, D. E., Gehling, R., & Prince, B. (2010). User experience, satisfaction, and continual usage intention of IT. *European Journal of Information Systems*, *19*(1), 60–75. DOI: 10.1057/ejis.2009.50

Dobbala, M., & Lingolu, M. (2024). Conversational AI and Chatbots : Enhancing User Experience on Websites. *American Journal of Computer Science and Technology*, *7*(3), 62–70. DOI: 10.11648/j.ajcst.20240703.11

Dwivedi, Y. K., Balakrishnan, J., Baabdullah, A. M., & Das, R. (2023). Do chatbots establish "humanness" in the customer purchase journey? An investigation through explanatory sequential design. *Psychology and Marketing*, *40*(11), 2244–2271. DOI: 10.1002/mar.21888

Elliott, D., & Soifer, E. (2022). AI technologies, privacy, and security. *Frontiers in Artificial Intelligence*, *5*, 826737. DOI: 10.3389/frai.2022.826737 PMID: 35493613

Emplifi. (2022). *Top 35+ customer experience statistics to know in 2022. Emplifi—Recherche Google*. (s. d.). Consulté 16 février 2025

Fan, H., Gao, W., & Han, B. (2023). Are AI chatbots a cure-all? The relative effectiveness of chatbot ambidexterity in crafting hedonic and cognitive smart experiences. *Journal of Business Research*, *156*, 113526. DOI: 10.1016/j.jbusres.2022.113526

Faqih, K. M. (2016). An empirical analysis of factors predicting the behavioral intention to adopt Internet shopping technology among non-shoppers in a developing country context : Does gender matter? *Journal of Retailing and Consumer Services, 30*, 140–164. DOI: 10.1016/j.jretconser.2016.01.016

Fishbein, M. (1979). A theory of reasoned action : Some applications and implications. *Nebraska Symposium on Motivation.*

Fornell, C., & Larcker, D. F. (1981). Evaluating Structural Equation Models with Unobservable Variables and Measurement Error. *JMR, Journal of Marketing Research, 18*(1), 39–50. DOI: 10.1177/002224378101800104

GS1 (2023). Trend research 2023-2024 : Innovation in a world of continuous disruption—Recherche Google. (s. d.). Consulté 16 février 2025

Goktas, P., & Dirsehan, T. (2025). Using PLS-SEM and XAI for causal-predictive services marketing research. *Journal of Services Marketing, 39*(1), 53–68. DOI: 10.1108/JSM-10-2023-0377

Gomes, S., Lopes, J. M., & Trancoso, T. (2025). Customer experience in digital transformation : The influence of intelligent chatbots toward a sustainable market. *International Journal of Innovation Science, 17*(4), 803–823. Advance online publication. DOI: 10.1108/IJIS-06-2024-0148

Gopinath, K., & Kasilingam, D. (2023). Antecedents of intention to use chatbots in service encounters : A meta-analytic review. *International Journal of Consumer Studies, 47*(6), 2367–2395. DOI: 10.1111/ijcs.12933

Gupta, S., Arora, A., Singh, S., & Jain, J. (2025). AI feel millennials : Prioritizing the intentions towards adoption of AI-enabled chatbots using fuzzy-AHP approach. *Journal of Science and Technology Policy Management*. DOI: 10.1108/JSTPM-09-2023-0159

Gursoy, D., Chi, O. H., Lu, L., & Nunkoo, R. (2019). Consumers acceptance of artificially intelligent (AI) device use in service delivery. *International Journal of Information Management, 49*, 157–169. DOI: 10.1016/j.ijinfomgt.2019.03.008

Hoyer, W. D., Kroschke, M., Schmitt, B., Kraume, K., & Shankar, V. (2020). Transforming the Customer Experience through New Technologies. *Journal of Interactive Marketing, 51*(1), 57–71. DOI: 10.1016/j.intmar.2020.04.001

Hu, L., & Bentler, P. M. (1999). Cutoff criteria for fit indexes in covariance structure analysis : Conventional criteria versus new alternatives. *Structural Equation Modeling, 6*(1), 1–55. DOI: 10.1080/10705519909540118

Huang, M.-H., & Rust, R. T. (2018). Artificial Intelligence in Service. *Journal of Service Research*, *21*(2), 155–172. DOI: 10.1177/1094670517752459

Illescas-Manzano, M. D., Vicente López, N., Afonso González, N., & Cristofol Rodríguez, C. (2021). Implementation of Chatbot in Online Commerce, and Open Innovation. *Journal of Open Innovation*, *7*(2), 125. DOI: 10.3390/joitmc7020125

Isaac, O., Abdullah, Z., Ramayah, T., & Mutahar, A. M. (2017). Internet usage, user satisfaction, task-technology fit, and performance impact among public sector employees in Yemen. *The International Journal of Information and Learning Technology*, *34*(3), 210–241. DOI: 10.1108/IJILT-11-2016-0051

Jenneboer, L., Herrando, C., & Constantinides, E. (2022). The impact of chatbots on customer loyalty : A systematic literature review. *Journal of Theoretical and Applied Electronic Commerce Research*, *17*(1), 212–229. DOI: 10.3390/jtaer17010011

Jiménez-Barreto, J., Rubio, N., & Molinillo, S. (2021). "Find a flight for me, Oscar!" Motivational customer experiences with chatbots. *International Journal of Contemporary Hospitality Management*, *33*(11), 3860–3882. DOI: 10.1108/IJCHM-10-2020-1244

Jyothsna, M., & Kryvinska, N. (2024). Exploring the Chatbot Usage intention-A mediating Role of Chatbot Initial trust. *Heliyon*, •••, 33028. PMID: 39027428

Kaba, B., & Touré, B. (2014). Understanding information and communication technology behavioral intention to use : Applying the UTAUT model to social networking site adoption by young people in a least developed country. *Journal of the Association for Information Science and Technology*, *65*(8), 1662–1674. DOI: 10.1002/asi.23069

Khan, M. I., Fatima, J. K., Bahmannia, S., Chatrath, S. K., Dale, N. F., & Johns, R. (2025). Investigating the influence of perceived humanization of service encounters on value creation of chatbot-assisted services. *Journal of Service Theory and Practice*, *35*(1), 56–88. DOI: 10.1108/JSTP-10-2023-0282

Khan, S., & Rabbani, M. R. (2021). Artificial intelligence and NLP-based chatbot for islamic banking and finance. [IJIRR]. *International Journal of Information Retrieval Research*, *11*(3), 65–77. DOI: 10.4018/IJIRR.2021070105

Khizzou, N. B., Aarabe, M., & Alla, L. (2024). Current trends in scientific research on managerial innovations in healthcare supply chain : A bibliometric analysis. *2024 IEEE 15th International Colloquium on Logistics and Supply Chain Management (LOGISTIQUA)*, 1-9. https://ieeexplore.ieee.org/abstract/document/10571373/?casa_token=U6xJHWHau7gAAAAA:tjzLDj4RuxVqHUReRd1FeosvQeEznMUOhVEe4FPUr1uwfc9Py49g_DZSWHuP4NP1_Y_UuwlXcxq9

Kumar, A., Shankar, A., Behl, A., Chakraborty, D., & Gundala, R. R. (2025). Anthropomorphic generative AI chatbots for enhancing customer engagement, experience and recommendation. *Journal of Consumer Marketing*. https://www.emerald.com/insight/content/doi/10.1108/JCM-06-2024-6922/full/html

Kumar, V., Ashraf, A. R., & Nadeem, W. (2024). AI-powered marketing : What, where, and how? *International Journal of Information Management*, *77*, 102783. DOI: 10.1016/j.ijinfomgt.2024.102783

Kumar, V., Rajan, B., Salunkhe, U., & Joag, S. G. (2022). Relating the dark side of new-age technologies and customer technostress. *Psychology and Marketing*, *39*(12), 2240–2259. DOI: 10.1002/mar.21738

Lee, S. E., Ju, N., & Lee, K.-H. (2023). Service chatbot : Co-citation and big data analysis toward a review and research agenda. *Technological Forecasting and Social Change*, *194*, 122722. DOI: 10.1016/j.techfore.2023.122722

Lehnert, L., & Kuehnl, C. (2025). Empathy at the heart of customer experience : A holistic framework for understanding and enhancing consumer empathy through the lens of customer experience. *Psychology and Marketing*, *42*(2), 332–358. DOI: 10.1002/mar.22130

Lemon, K. N., & Verhoef, P. C. (2016). Understanding Customer Experience Throughout the Customer Journey. *Journal of Marketing*, *80*(6), 69–96. DOI: 10.1509/jm.15.0420

Li, B., Chen, Y., Liu, L., & Zheng, B. (2023). Users' intention to adopt artificial intelligence-based chatbot : A meta-analysis. *Service Industries Journal*, *43*(15-16), 1117–1139. DOI: 10.1080/02642069.2023.2217756

Lin, K.-Y., & Lu, H.-P. (2015). Predicting mobile social network acceptance based on mobile value and social influence. *Internet Research*, *25*(1), 107–130. DOI: 10.1108/IntR-01-2014-0018

Lin, W. R., Lin, C.-Y., & Ding, Y.-H. (2020). Factors affecting the behavioral intention to adopt mobile payment : An empirical study in Taiwan. *Mathematics*, *8*(10), 1851. DOI: 10.3390/math8101851

Ling, E. C., Tussyadiah, I., Tuomi, A., Stienmetz, J., & Ioannou, A. (2021). Factors influencing users' adoption and use of conversational agents : A systematic review. *Psychology and Marketing*, *38*(7), 1031–1051. DOI: 10.1002/mar.21491

Lubbe, I., & Ngoma, N. (2021). Useful chatbot experience provides technological satisfaction : An emerging market perspective. *South African Journal of Information Management*, *23*(1), 1–8. DOI: 10.4102/sajim.v23i1.1299

Makudza, F., Jaravaza, D. C., Makandwa, G., & Mukucha, P. (2024). Disruptive artificial intelligence : Augmenting consumer experience through chatbot banking. In *Digital Influence on Consumer Habits : Marketing Challenges and Opportunities* (p. 1-18). Emerald Publishing Limited. https://www.emerald.com/insight/content/doi/10.1108/978-1-80455-342-820241001/full/html

Malik, S., Muhammad, K., & Waheed, Y. (2024). Artificial intelligence and industrial applications-A revolution in modern industries. *Ain Shams Engineering Journal*, *15*(9), 102886. DOI: 10.1016/j.asej.2024.102886

Marandu, E. E., Makudza, F., & Ngwenya, S. N. (2019). Predicting Students' Intention and Actual Use of E-Learning Using the Technology Acceptance Model : A Case from Zimbabwe. *International Journal of Learning. Teaching and Educational Research*, *18*(6), 110–127. DOI: 10.26803/ijlter.18.6.7

Mariani, M. M., Hashemi, N., & Wirtz, J. (2023). Artificial intelligence empowered conversational agents : A systematic literature review and research agenda. *Journal of Business Research*, *161*, 113838. DOI: 10.1016/j.jbusres.2023.113838

Mariani, M. M., Perez-Vega, R., & Wirtz, J. (2022). AI in marketing, consumer research and psychology : A systematic literature review and research agenda. *Psychology and Marketing*, *39*(4), 755–776. DOI: 10.1002/mar.21619

Marikyan, D., & Papagiannidis, S. (2023). Technology Acceptance Model. *TheoryHub Book. Retrieved*, (June), 6.

Martínez Puertas, S., Illescas Manzano, M. D., Segovia López, C., & Ribeiro Cardoso, P. (2024). *Purchase intentions in a chatbot environment : An examination of the effects of customer experience*. https://www.ceeol.com/search/article-detail?id=1238151

Martins, C., Oliveira, T., & Popovič, A. (2014). Understanding the Internet banking adoption : A unified theory of acceptance and use of technology and perceived risk application. *International Journal of Information Management*, *34*(1), 1–13. DOI: 10.1016/j.ijinfomgt.2013.06.002

Mclean, E. R., Sedera, D., & Tan, F. T. C. (2011). *Reconceptualizing system use for contemporary information systems*. https://aisel.aisnet.org/pacis2011/130/

Mogaji, E., Balakrishnan, J., Nwoba, A. C., & Nguyen, N. P. (2021). Emerging-market consumers' interactions with banking chatbots. *Telematics and Informatics*, *65*, 101711. DOI: 10.1016/j.tele.2021.101711

Mogaji, E., & Nguyen, N. P. (2022). Managers' understanding of artificial intelligence in relation to marketing financial services : Insights from a cross-country study. *International Journal of Bank Marketing*, *40*(6), 1272–1298. DOI: 10.1108/IJBM-09-2021-0440

Moore, G. C., & Benbasat, I. (1991a). Development of an Instrument to Measure the Perceptions of Adopting an Information Technology Innovation. *Information Systems Research*, *2*(3), 192–222. DOI: 10.1287/isre.2.3.192

Moore, G. C., & Benbasat, I. (1991b). Development of an Instrument to Measure the Perceptions of Adopting an Information Technology Innovation. *Information Systems Research*, *2*(3), 192–222. DOI: 10.1287/isre.2.3.192

Moriuchi, E. (2021). An empirical study on anthropomorphism and engagement with disembodied AIs and consumers' re-use behavior. *Psychology and Marketing*, *38*(1), 21–42. DOI: 10.1002/mar.21407

Mostafa, R. B., & Kasamani, T. (2022). Antecedents and consequences of chatbot initial trust. *European Journal of Marketing*, *56*(6), 1748–1771. DOI: 10.1108/EJM-02-2020-0084

Mozafari, N., Weiger, W. H., & Hammerschmidt, M. (2022). Trust me, I'm a bot– repercussions of chatbot disclosure in different service frontline settings. *Journal of Service Management*, *33*(2), 221–245. DOI: 10.1108/JOSM-10-2020-0380

Myin, M. T., & Watchravesringkan, K. (2024). Investigating consumers' adoption of AI chatbots for apparel shopping. *Journal of Consumer Marketing*, *41*(3), 314–327. DOI: 10.1108/JCM-03-2022-5234

Na, S., Heo, S., Han, S., Shin, Y., & Roh, Y. (2022). Acceptance model of artificial intelligence (AI)-based technologies in construction firms : Applying the Technology Acceptance Model (TAM) in combination with the Technology–Organisation–Environment (TOE) framework. *Buildings (Basel, Switzerland)*, *12*(2), 90. DOI: 10.3390/buildings12020090

Nguyen, T. H., & Le, X. C. (2025). Artificial intelligence-based chatbots – a motivation underlying sustainable development in banking : Standpoint of customer experience and behavioral outcomes. *Cogent Business & Management, 12*(1), 2443570. DOI: 10.1080/23311975.2024.2443570

Nguyen, T. H., Trivedi, R. H., Fukukawa, K., & Adomako, S. (2025). Investigating Drivers of Customer Experience with Virtual Conversational Agents. *Information Systems Frontiers, 27*(5), 1871–1897. Advance online publication. DOI: 10.1007/s10796-024-10572-0

Nicolescu, L., & Tudorache, M. T. (2022). Human-Computer Interaction in Customer Service : The Experience with AI Chatbots—A Systematic Literature Review. *Electronics (Basel), 11*(10), 1579. DOI: 10.3390/electronics11101579

Noble, S. M., & Mende, M. (2023). The future of artificial intelligence and robotics in the retail and service sector : Sketching the field of consumer-robot-experiences. *Journal of the Academy of Marketing Science, 51*(4), 747–756. DOI: 10.1007/s11747-023-00948-0 PMID: 37359262

Nouhaila, B. K., Aarabe, M., & Alla, L. (2024). The impact of digitalisation on the customer experience in medical tourism : A systematic review. *Impact of AI and tech-driven solutions in hospitality and tourism*, 408-428.

Nunnally, J. C., & Bernstein, I. H. (1994). The Assessment of Reliability. Psychometric Theory, 3, 248-292. Nyhan, RC, and HA Marlowe.(1997). Development And Psychometric Properties Of The Organizational Trust Inventory. *Evaluation Review, 21*(5), 614–635.

O'Dea, M. (2025). Are Technology Acceptance Models still fit for purpose? *Journal of University Teaching & Learning Practice, 21*(08). Advance online publication. http://open-publishing.org/journals/index.php/jutlp/article/view/1157. DOI: 10.53761/1bdbms32

Ocxas, J. J. A., Martin, F. K. C., & Junes, A. N. H. (2024). AI Chatbot with Emotional Recognition for an Improved Customer Service Experience. *2024 IEEE XXXI International Conference on Electronics, Electrical Engineering and Computing (INTERCON)*, 1-8. DOI: 10.1109/INTERCON63140.2024.10833509

Oliveira, T., Faria, M., Thomas, M. A., & Popovič, A. (2014). Extending the understanding of mobile banking adoption : When UTAUT meets TTF and ITM. *International Journal of Information Management, 34*(5), 689–703. DOI: 10.1016/j.ijinfomgt.2014.06.004

Olujimi, P. A., & Ade-Ibijola, A. (2023). NLP techniques for automating responses to customer queries : A systematic review. *Discover Artificial Intelligence*, *3*(1), 20. DOI: 10.1007/s44163-023-00065-5

Oluwadamilola, F. J., & Emmanuel, A. A. (2024). *A Systematic Review of Chatbot Model and chatbot technologies*. https://www.ieeesem.com/researchpaper/A_Systematic_Literature_Review_and_Existing_Challenges_of_Chatbot_Models.pdf

Owusu, P. R., Asiedu, E. P., Ji, J., & Sarpong, F. A. (2022). Innovation and evaluation of technology acceptance model (Tam) in S-commerce : A case of social media platforms in Ghana. *Journal of Computer and Communications*, *10*(3), 100–124. DOI: 10.4236/jcc.2022.103007

Oyeniyi, L. D., Ugochukwu, C. E., & Mhlongo, N. Z.Lawrence Damilare OyeniyiChinonye Esther UgochukwuNoluthando Zamanjomane Mhlongo. (2024). Implementing AI in banking customer service : A review of current trends and future applications. *International Journal of Science and Research Archive*, *11*(2), 1492–1509. DOI: 10.30574/ijsra.2024.11.2.0639

Padigar, M., Li, Y., & Manjunath, C. N. (2025). "Good" and "bad" frictions in customer experience : Conceptual foundations and implications. *Psychology and Marketing*, *42*(1), 21–43. DOI: 10.1002/mar.22111

Park, A., & Lee, S. B. (2024). Examining AI and Systemic Factors for Improved Chatbot Sustainability. *Journal of Computer Information Systems*, *64*(6), 728–742. DOI: 10.1080/08874417.2023.2251416

Patel, N., & Trivedi, S. (2020). Leveraging predictive modeling, machine learning personalization, NLP customer support, and AI chatbots to increase customer loyalty. *Empirical Quests for Management Essences*, *3*(3), 1–24.

Patil, D. (2024). Artificial Intelligence In Retail And E-Commerce : Enhancing Customer Experience Through Personalization, Predictive Analytics, And Real-Time Engagement. *Predictive Analytics, And Real-Time Engagement (November 26, 2024)*. https://papers.ssrn.com/sol3/papers.cfm?abstract_id=5057420

Przegalinska, A., Ciechanowski, L., Stroz, A., Gloor, P., & Mazurek, G. (2019). In bot we trust : A new methodology of chatbot performance measures. *Business Horizons*, *62*(6), 785–797. DOI: 10.1016/j.bushor.2019.08.005

Ranieri, A., Di Bernardo, I., & Mele, C. (2024). Serving customers through chatbots : Positive and negative effects on customer experience. *Journal of Service Theory and Practice*, *34*(2), 191–215. DOI: 10.1108/JSTP-01-2023-0015

Rashid, A. B., & Kausik, M. A. K. (2024). AI revolutionizing industries worldwide : A comprehensive overview of its diverse applications. *Hybrid Advances*, *7*, 100277. DOI: 10.1016/j.hybadv.2024.100277

Rese, A., Ganster, L., & Baier, D. (2020). Chatbots in retailers' customer communication : How to measure their acceptance? *Journal of Retailing and Consumer Services*, *56*, 102176. DOI: 10.1016/j.jretconser.2020.102176

Restianto, Y. E., Suliyanto, S., Naufalin, L. R., Krisnaresanti, A., Dinanti, A., Iskandar, D., & Sugiyono, S. (2024). User experience and behavioral intention to use e-commerce : A study of digital literacy as a moderating variable. *Journal of Governance and Regulation*, *13*(1), 8–17. DOI: 10.22495/jgrv13i1art1

Rezaei, S., & Amin, M. (2013). Exploring online repurchase behavioural intention of university students in Malaysia. *J. for Global Business Advancement*, *6*(2), 92. DOI: 10.1504/JGBA.2013.053561

Rizomyliotis, I., Kastanakis, M. N., Giovanis, A., Konstantoulaki, K., & Kostopoulos, I. (2022). "How mAy I help you today?" The use of AI chatbots in small family businesses and the moderating role of customer affective commitment. *Journal of Business Research*, *153*, 329–340. DOI: 10.1016/j.jbusres.2022.08.035

Rogers, E. M. (1995). *Diffusion of Innovations*. https://scholar.google.com/scholar?hl=fr&as_sdt=0%2C5&q=Rogers%2C+E.M.+%281995%29%2C+Diffusion+of+Innovations+%284th+Ed.%29%2C+The+Free+Press%2C+New+York%2C+NY.&btnG=

Rogers, E. M. (2003). *Diffusion of Innovations* (5th ed.). Simon and Schuster.

Rose, S., Clark, M., Samouel, P., & Hair, N. (2012). Online Customer Experience in e-Retailing : An empirical model of Antecedents and Outcomes. *Journal of Retailing*, *88*(2), 308–322. DOI: 10.1016/j.jretai.2012.03.001

Ross, T., May, A., & Cockbill, S. A. (2020). The personal and contextual factors that affect customer experience during rail service failures and the implications for service design. *Applied Ergonomics*, *86*, 103096. DOI: 10.1016/j.apergo.2020.103096 PMID: 32342887

Sahin, I. (2006). Detailed Review of Rogers' Diffusion of Innovations Theory and Educational Technology-Related Studies Based on Rogers' Theory. *Turkish Online Journal of Educational Technology - TOJET, 5*(2), 14-23.

Salem, M. (2024). Use of chatbots and its role in enhancing customer experience : A Study of the banking industry. In *Digital technology and changing roles in managerial and financial accounting : Theoretical knowledge and practical application* (pp. 107–114). Emerald Publishing Limited., https://www.emerald.com/insight/content/doi/10.1108/S1479-351220240000036010/full/html DOI: 10.1108/S1479-351220240000036010

San Martín, H., & Herrero, Á. (2012). Influence of the user's psychological factors on the online purchase intention in rural tourism : Integrating innovativeness to the UTAUT framework. *Tourism Management, 33*(2), 341–350. DOI: 10.1016/j.tourman.2011.04.003

Sands, S., Ferraro, C., Campbell, C., & Tsao, H.-Y. (2021). Managing the human–chatbot divide : How service scripts influence service experience. *Journal of Service Management, 32*(2), 246–264. DOI: 10.1108/JOSM-06-2019-0203

Saoud, L. S., & Romman, A. A. (2024). AI-Powered Chatbots in the Telecommunications Industry in the UAE : Studying the Factors Impacting Consumer Adoption. *2024 15th International Conference on Information and Communication Technology Convergence (ICTC)*, 1549-1553. https://ieeexplore.ieee.org/abstract/document/10827670/?casa_token=0tZCraF5fxEAAAAA:Q-hdlPue7xS7bsY1Bs_H08roFE66lsLDGNTtLNjFIRggA__Z70znAZCnejNQ59JtvpGMeGnDSr7lNJs

Sayed, D., & Abutaleb, S. (2025). Anthropomorphic chatbots as a catalyst for online customer experience (CX) : The case of Egyptian consumers. *Journal of Marketing Communications*, •••, 1–15. DOI: 10.1080/13527266.2025.2453229

Sboui, M., Baati, O., & Sfar, N. (2024). Influencing factors and consequences of chatbot initial trust in AI telecommunication services : A study on Generation Z. *The TQM Journal*. Advance online publication. DOI: 10.1108/TQM-02-2024-0085

Selem, K. M., Islam, M. S., Aureliano-Silva, L., & Shehata, A. E. (2023). Nexus of customer adaptation to mannequins with visit intention to full-service restaurants : Role of spatial layout. *International Journal of Hospitality Management, 115*, 103608. DOI: 10.1016/j.ijhm.2023.103608

Sfar, N., Sboui, M., & Baati, O. (2025). The impact of chatbot anthropomorphism on customer experience and chatbot usage intention : A technology acceptance approach. *International Journal of Quality and Service Sciences, 17*(2), 168–194. Advance online publication. DOI: 10.1108/IJQSS-06-2024-0079

Shachak, A., Kuziemsky, C., & Petersen, C. (2019). Beyond TAM and UTAUT : Future directions for HIT implementation research. *Journal of Biomedical Informatics, 100*, 103315. DOI: 10.1016/j.jbi.2019.103315 PMID: 31629923

Sheth, J. N., Jain, V., Roy, G., & Chakraborty, A. (2022). AI-driven banking services : The next frontier for a personalised experience in the emerging market. *International Journal of Bank Marketing*, *40*(6), 1248–1271. DOI: 10.1108/IJBM-09-2021-0449

Shin, H., Bunosso, I., & Levine, L. R. (2023). The influence of chatbot humour on consumer evaluations of services. *International Journal of Consumer Studies*, *47*(2), 545–562. DOI: 10.1111/ijcs.12849

Singh, P. (2025). *Leveraging AI for Real-Time Customer Support in Telecommunications*. https://www.techrxiv.org/doi/full/10.36227/techrxiv.174952654.43690912 DOI: 10.36227/techrxiv.174952654.43690912/v1

Song, S. W., & Shin, M. (2024). Uncanny Valley Effects on Chatbot Trust, Purchase Intention, and Adoption Intention in the Context of E-Commerce : The Moderating Role of Avatar Familiarity. *International Journal of Human-Computer Interaction*, *40*(2), 441–456. DOI: 10.1080/10447318.2022.2121038

Spais, G., & Jain, V. (2025). Consumer Behavior's Evolution, Emergence, and Future in the AI Age Through the Lens of MR, VR, XR, Metaverse, and Robotics. *Journal of Consumer Behaviour*, cb.2468. DOI: 10.1002/cb.2468

Suta, P., Lan, X., Wu, B., Mongkolnam, P., & Chan, J. H. (2020). An overview of machine learning in chatbots. *International Journal of Mechanical Engineering and Robotics Research*, *9*(4), 502–510. DOI: 10.18178/ijmerr.9.4.502-510

Tamilmani, K., Rana, N. P., & Dwivedi, Y. K. (2021). Consumer Acceptance and Use of Information Technology : A Meta-Analytic Evaluation of UTAUT2. *Information Systems Frontiers*, *23*(4), 987–1005. DOI: 10.1007/s10796-020-10007-6

Tian, W., Ge, J., Zhao, Y., & Zheng, X. (2024). AI Chatbots in Chinese higher education : Adoption, perception, and influence among graduate students—an integrated analysis utilizing UTAUT and ECM models. *Frontiers in Psychology*, *15*, 1268549. DOI: 10.3389/fpsyg.2024.1268549 PMID: 38384353

Trivedi, J. (2019). Examining the Customer Experience of Using Banking Chatbots and Its Impact on Brand Love : The Moderating Role of Perceived Risk. *Journal of Internet Commerce*, *18*(1), 91–111. DOI: 10.1080/15332861.2019.1567188

Venkatesh, V., & Brown, S. A. (2001). A Longitudinal Investigation of Personal Computers in Homes : Adoption Determinants and Emerging Challenges. *Management Information Systems Quarterly*, *25*(1), 71–102. DOI: 10.2307/3250959

Venkatesh, V., Morris, M. G., Davis, G. B., & Davis, F. D. (2003). User acceptance of information technology : Toward a unified view. *Management Information Systems Quarterly*, *27*(3), 425–478. DOI: 10.2307/30036540

Venkatesh, V., Thong, J. Y., & Xu, X. (2012). Consumer acceptance and use of information technology : Extending the unified theory of acceptance and use of technology. *Management Information Systems Quarterly, 36*(1), 157–178. DOI: 10.2307/41410412

Verhoef, P. C., Lemon, K. N., Parasuraman, A., Roggeveen, A., Tsiros, M., & Schlesinger, L. A. (2009). Customer Experience Creation : Determinants, Dynamics and Management Strategies. *Journal of Retailing, 85*(1), 31–41. DOI: 10.1016/j.jretai.2008.11.001

Verma, S., Sharma, R., Deb, S., & Maitra, D. (2021). Artificial intelligence in marketing : Systematic review and future research direction. *International Journal of Information Management Data Insights, 1*(1), 100002. DOI: 10.1016/j.jjimei.2020.100002

Wang, C., Li, Y., Fu, W., & Jin, J. (2023). Whether to trust chatbots : Applying the event-related approach to understand consumers' emotional experiences in interactions with chatbots in e-commerce. *Journal of Retailing and Consumer Services, 73*, 103325. DOI: 10.1016/j.jretconser.2023.103325

Wuenderlich, N. V., Heinonen, K., Ostrom, A. L., Patricio, L., Sousa, R., Voss, C., & Lemmink, J. G. A. M. (2015). "Futurizing" smart service : Implications for service researchers and managers. *Journal of Services Marketing, 29*(6/7), 442–447. DOI: 10.1108/JSM-01-2015-0040

Yen, C., & Chiang, M.-C. (2021). Trust me, if you can : A study on the factors that influence consumers' purchase intention triggered by chatbots based on brain image evidence and self-reported assessments. *Behaviour & Information Technology, 40*(11), 1177–1194. DOI: 10.1080/0144929X.2020.1743362

Zhou, T., Lu, Y., & Wang, B. (2010). Integrating TTF and UTAUT to explain mobile banking user adoption. *Computers in Human Behavior, 26*(4), 760–767. DOI: 10.1016/j.chb.2010.01.013

Zungu, N. P., Amegbe, H., Hanu, C., & Asamoah, E. S. (2025). AI-driven self-service for enhanced customer experience outcomes in the banking sector. *Cogent Business & Management, 12*(1), 2450295. DOI: 10.1080/23311975.2025.2450295

ENDNOTE

1 https://d3.harvard.edu/platform-digit/submission/vodafone-putting-data-to-work/

Chapter 3
Live Commerce and AI:
The Fusion of Real-Time Social Shopping and Smart Recommendations

Parihar Suresh Dahake
https://orcid.org/0000-0002-2286-4120
Ramdeobaba University, Nagpur, India

Pragati Parihar Dahake
https://orcid.org/0009-0003-0383-4721
VMV Commerce, JMT Arts, and JJP Science College, Nagpur, India

ABSTRACT

With the rapid advancement of technology and the ubiquitous adoption of smart devices, online shopping has experienced a boom. However, conventional online stores miss the opportunity of providing a useful recommendation service that has become a hot-tackling topic in e-commerce platforms for its high click-through rate and conversion rate. The cost of garnering information and making a decision has been reduced. With a myriad of online stores exhibiting products, users are provided with abundant information, complicating the revisit process by either analyzing review information across multiple platforms or contacting sites with little confidence. Instant messaging (IM) enables friends to effortlessly and instantly share product links, reducing the information-gathering effort.

1. INTRODUCTION

Live Commerce is a form of video-based real-time retail, the primary medium for transacting the merchandise presented during the live streaming events. Live

DOI: 10.4018/979-8-3373-2747-1.ch003

Commerce usually focuses on the shopping experience, providing an immersive retail platform for buyers with video, two-way conversations, and sometimes video tour of physical or virtual showrooms. Live Commerce then creates a well-organized shopping program using social media platforms combined with eCommerce engines and connected shoppers with brand representatives or social retail arbitrageurs. Large social networks develop integrated live stream capabilities, which attract influencers' sponsored shopping events promoting their products.

Figure 1. Real-Time Social Shopping

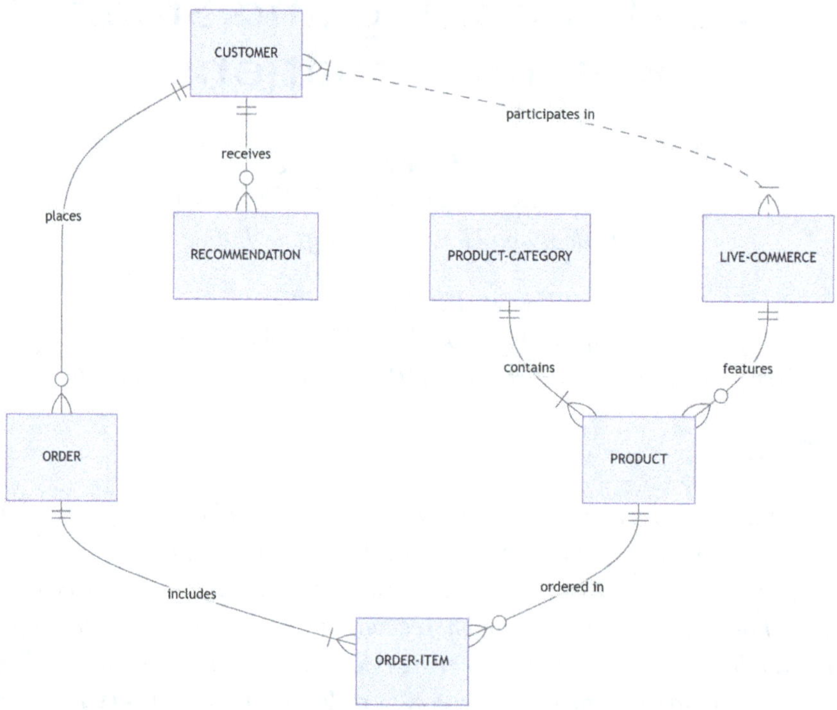

Recent developments include the automation of the arbitrageur and maybe the AI influencer—the suggestions of goods made by automated systems without human intervention during live broadcasts. The general intent is to generate better recommendations that represent the user's preferences and result in higher conversion orders(Adulyasak et al., 2023). E-commerce in India has been growing rapidly since 2010, and social commerce platforms have seen a substantial increase in late 2020. social commerce intention is influenced by virtual experiences like social support, social presence, and flow, which are shaped by technological factors such as interactivity, personalization, and sociability(H. Zhang et al., 2014). This coincides with the establishment of integrated live broadcast systems provided by well-known social media platforms. Consequently, in the first segment of 2021, the release of 0-commission small business sellers saw a 530 percent increase on one of the Indian social media platforms. Social media influencers (SMI) played an integral role in this new advertising structure by holding live e-sales parties on behalf of small businesses. SMIs spur interaction between the observer and the live streamers during these live broadcasts, pointing out the specific goods and features(Alam et al., 2022).In late 2020 and early 2021, the convergence of Covid-19 lockdowns, increasing mobile penetration, and accessible Internet tariffs triggered the further proliferation of smart devices across India. By the end of 2021, this led to 718 million smartphones and 80 million connected TVs in the region: a 75% and 240% increase since 2018, respectively. As a response to these changes, online video platforms reinforced collaborations with popular businesses in diverse industries for live streaming shows, such as food delivery services, clothes online retailers, and cosmetics. As a novel alternative, live commerce emerged as a hybrid of visual media, social network services, and e-commerce. Live commerce gathers public figures, sellers, influencers, and average users in livestreaming events, blending interpersonal interaction and real-time economic transactions. Many service providers have since then propelled live commerce on their sites; for instance, platforms are collaborating with famous brands to extend their influence toward the US. The investigations focus on the digital and collaborative practices of live commerce in India, meanwhile unravelling its multimodal dynamics; they disclose its core features of commercial strategies, animated agents, and distinctiveness from precedent media. On a more in-depth level, they concentrate on the exemplar of format fusion among live commerce, algorithmic suggestions, and cloth shopping. On the one hand, vendors harness AI algorithms to offer stylists and outfit advice on picked clothing alternatives to customers; on the other hand, live broadcast partners showcase these outfits with model hosts and current customers, thus intensifying the agent and buyer interactions. That way, they depict how formats impact each other, the role of real-time media in clothes, and the inner workings of their suggestion system.

2. EVOLUTION OF E-COMMERCE IN INDIA

The retail landscape in India has undergone a stark metamorphosis over the years and Mobile commerce offers consumers the Internet in their pocket, offering banking, shopping, and real-time news, with key players and technologies shaping the future of the industry(Barnes, 2002a). And Electronic commerce is rapidly becoming the essential dial-tone for conducting business, driven by electronic markets, information technology, interactivity, and the evolution of disintermediation to reintermediation(Wigand, 1997).

Figure 2. Evolution and Working of Ecommerce

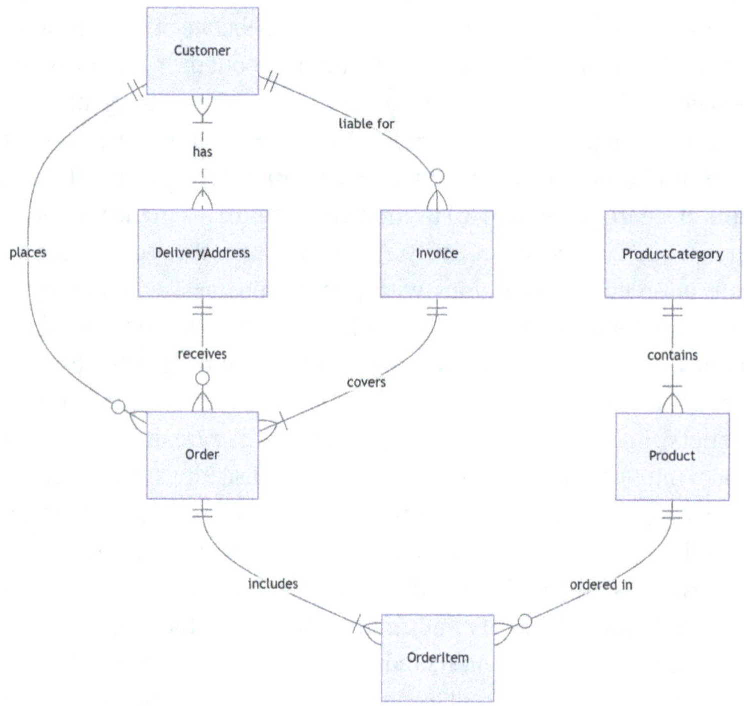

The archaic and traditional mode of retailing is facing stiff competition from the rapid emergence of dynamic and sprawling e-commerce platforms. Coupled With This Social commerce constructs on Web 2.0 applications increase consumer trust and intention to buy by enabling interactions and content generation on the internet(Hajli, 2015).The ability of these platforms to let consumers pick, pay for, and receive products ranging from groceries, electronics, and appliances has revolutionized the retail industry in India. E-commerce platforms adopt a business to consumer (B2C) and a business-to-business (B2B) model, thereby facilitating the e-retail of a multitude of products. With the retail industry witnessing narrow and enclosed viewing complex with generally no demonstration and the inception of a plethora of look-alike products, it becomes difficult to find or choose a particular item in the absence of detailed information. Hence, Big data analytics in e-commerce offers significant business value and challenges(Akter & Wamba, 2016) A memory recommendation strategy has been put forth that provides users, while surfing web pages, with region-based personalized recommendations, and the recommendation agent qualitatively evaluates the recommended items.In B2C markets, the ease of payment and a return policy geared towards value take precedence. E-commerce adoption is influenced by perceived relative advantage, compatibility, CEO's innovativeness, information intensity, buyer/supplier pressure, technology vendor support, and competition(Ghobakhloo et al., 2011).Furthermore, the availability of discounts, dealing with a product brand, easy envelop return, and bulk purchase guarantee are crucial factors. Availability of online payment amid order delivery is appreciated and believed to add value; a significant percentage of users find ease in buying if cash withdrawal upon delivery is made available. In B2B markets, while a bulk purchase option is believed to be beneficial, a varied bulk purchase option and a premium bulk purchase option are much appreciated. Aggregated and on-time delivery has overshadowing importance and simultaneously this service is appraised as very poor. Because dealings are done in bulk purchase, there is a firm persuasion on systematic purchase handling procedure, but this service is believed to be very poor. On-time delivery is a common critical factor for both markets; a significant percentage of e-marketers are very unhappy about delivery and transport. A culture and extended marketing consoles at different sites are recommended to address this hitch. E-commerce appears to be the future for both B2B and B2C markets, but there is skepticism in understanding supply chain mechanisms and still a firm belief in transcendental touchy purchasing. Also, understanding consumer behavior in virtual stores can help virtual stores effectively compete with physical stores and other online retailers(L. Chen et al., 2002). Similarly, e-commerce products are generally organic, less bulky, and lightweight; understandably recognizing calm delivery on time, but some stress is delineated on system centralization because the aggregation of consignment at a central site takes time for divergent forwarding.

3. REVIEW OF LITERATURE

Live-commerce in India demonstrates a fast-growing trend in recent years. From the beginning of 2020, live services evolve to a new business form with the flourishing of real-time e-commerce technologies. It is divergent to static e-commerce platforms and provides lots of convenience for shoppers while staying at home in the pandemic. A sellers-driven live-streaming video is conducted in a dedicated area or exhibition (Zhang et al., 2021). Much more product commodity is shown and advertised during the presentation. The shopping experience of the watchers can be enhanced if an interest product is watched at some time t during the live broadcast and that a corresponding query is generated automatically. However, finding the correct commodity recommender is very difficult and time-consuming. The store anchors may often introduce lots of advertisement products at different time during the video, and no screen title or caption of the product is displayed due to the consumption of screen size. Therefore, the shopping experience of the watcher is improved if the currently explained product can be highlighted in the live-video within a nearby time slot t0 instead of manually searching through the websites.

Figure 3. All Keywords Analysis by VosViewer

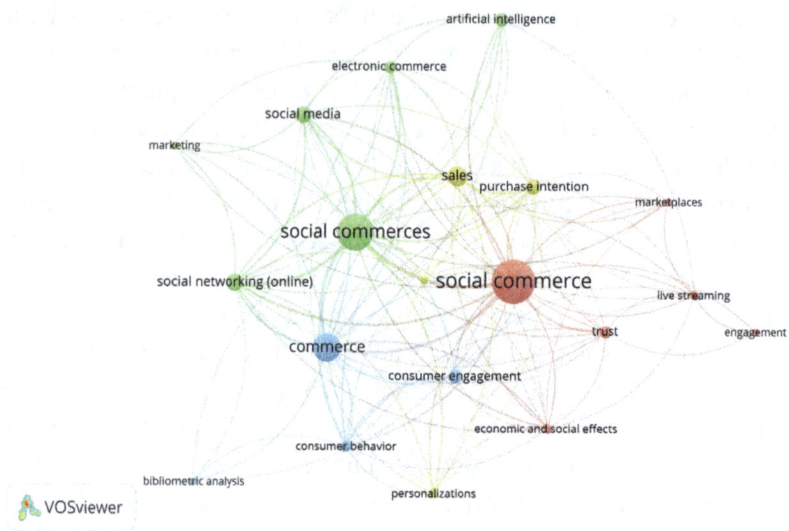

Figure 4. Author Keywords Analysis by VosViewer

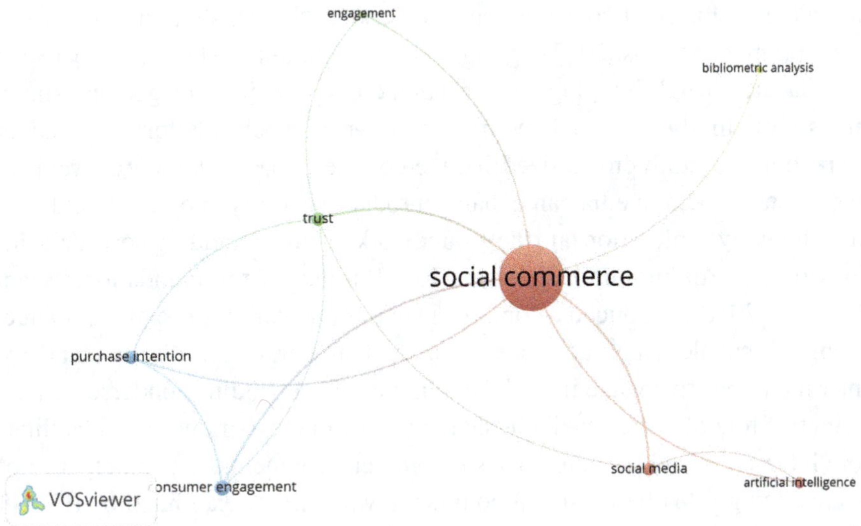

Figure 5. Index Keywords Analysis by VosViewer

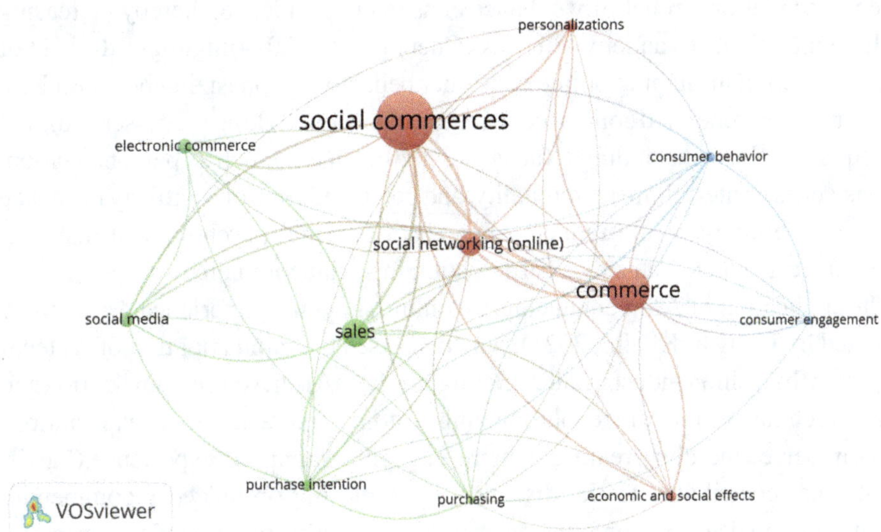

The integration of live commerce and artificial intelligence (AI) represents a transformative shift in the landscape of retail, particularly in the context of social shopping. This literature review synthesizes key findings from a range of studies that explore the intersection of social media, e-commerce, and AI technologies, illustrating the evolution of consumer behavior and marketing strategies in this dynamic environment. (Soltis, 2013)highlighted the burgeoning relationship between social media and virtual shopping, noting that increased online engagement among consumers, particularly younger demographics, has made social platforms pivotal for retail marketing. The study emphasized that as e-commerce becomes more convenient, the integration of social media can enhance product visibility and profitability for retailers. This early exploration laid the groundwork for understanding how social interactions influence online purchasing behaviors. Building on this foundation, (Azam & Aldehayyat, 2018)introduced a comprehensive framework for social commerce, identifying critical elements such as reviews, trust, and brand familiarity that drive consumer intentions to engage in social commerce. Their findings underscored the transformative role of social media in shaping consumer experiences and facilitating more interactive and participatory shopping environments. The emergence of instant messaging (IM)-based social commerce was further examined by (Cao et al., 2020), who analysed how platforms like WeChat leverage personal networks for marketing. Their research revealed that IM-based commerce fosters a unique user experience characterized by intimacy and immediacy, which enhances consumers' ability to make informed purchasing decisions through social recommendations. In deep (Lăzăroiu et al., 2020)underscores that perceived security, user-generated content, and platform reliability enhance consumer confidence, thereby increasing purchase intention. In tandem with this (Cheung et al., 2014)highlight the role of social interaction in shaping online consumer behavior, emphasizing how purchase signals and user-generated content contribute to decision-making processes in digital marketplaces. Notwithstanding (Xue et al., 2020)elements such as personalization, responsiveness, entertainment, mutuality, and perceived control positively influence perceived usefulness while reducing perceived risk and psychological distance. These effects enhance consumer participation in social commerce

The application of AI in enhancing the online shopping experience was notably addressed by(Gong & Khalid, 2021), who discussed the rapid adoption of AI technologies in the fashion industry. They highlighted how AI-driven personalization and visual search capabilities are revolutionizing customer interactions and expectations in e-commerce, thereby creating a more engaging shopping experience.(Farris, 2021)further contributed to the discourse by exploring optimized recommender systems through deep reinforcement learning. This study emphasized the necessity of advanced algorithms to navigate the complexities of consumer preferences in an oversaturated market, showcasing how AI can mitigate information overload and enhance user satisfaction. The impact of social commerce constructs during the COVID-19 pandemic was investigated by(Rashid et al., 2022), who found that social interactions on e-commerce platforms significantly influenced consumer buying intentions. Their findings suggested that the pandemic accelerated the integration of social components into online shopping, enhancing customer engagement and satisfaction.(Guo & Li, 2022)examined the mediating role of perceived value in the relationship between social commerce features and consumers' repurchase intentions. Their study highlighted the importance of user-generated content, such as feedback and recommendations, in shaping consumer perceptions and driving repeat purchases.(Sharma et al., 2024)focused on the role of AI-enabled digital assistants in enhancing customer engagement during online shopping. Their research underscored the necessity of personalized interactions facilitated by AI technologies, which can significantly improve service satisfaction and operational efficiency for retailers(Varghese et al., 2022)discussed how the pandemic has reshaped consumer behavior towards e-commerce, with a growing reliance on AI technologies to enhance the shopping experience. They noted that businesses are increasingly adopting AI to improve communication and customer interaction, which is essential for meeting evolving consumer demands.(L. Zhang et al., 2023a)explored the burgeoning trend of live streaming in social commerce, emphasizing its potential to enhance interactivity and engagement in online shopping. Their study indicated that live-streaming commerce, supported by advanced communication technologies, significantly influences consumer purchase intentions through real-time interactions. Finally, (Adulyasak et al., 2023)discuss the influence of AI on retail analytics in the post-COVID era, emphasizing the need for improved data analytics tools that can adapt to unforeseen events. Their insights point to the ongoing challenges and opportunities presented by AI in enhancing operational efficiency and decision-making in retail.

Social commerce leveraging real-time shopping and live-stream platforms attracts much the public attention in India. Fine-grained geospatial analytics strategy identifies hundreds of smaller markets that account for a considerable portion of shopping activity in Indian cities and investigates the adoption of live commerce as an alternative source for fresh food and groceries in urban public markets. Using a large-scale dataset of cash transactions in the city of Bengaluru, it finds that daily retail transactions recover slowly in the aftermath of the nation-wide lockdown, but bounce back faster within the newly observed live-commerce markets (Alam et al., 2022). Finally, the results underscore complicating local dynamics, where responses of small local economies can recede to potential threats from intermediaries like live-commerce wholesalers, pose challenges to live-commerce strategies in domestic fresh-food supply chains.

4. LIVE COMMERCE: CONCEPT AND TECHNOLOGIES

With the massive advance of mobile technology in India, and the realization of the potential it provides, new avenues for that can change the way the populace shops, are slowly being explored. New AI-powered technologies significantly transform the customer experience, impacting each stage of the shopping journey and creating experiential value(Hoyer et al., 2020). The newest concept that is slowly starting to gain pace is live commerce. It is expected that its announcement will propagate faster awareness of live commerce and its offerings, Live streaming services like Facebook Live can increase customer engagement and trust in small online sellers, with symbolic value directly and indirectly affecting engagement through trust in sellers and product trust(Wongkitrungrueng & Assarut, 2020).With live commerce being a new avenue in India, there is a need for understanding it better. Live commerce is when a person or brand hosts a live streaming session, where they can either show and talk about their products or services, or showcase something in a commercial format. Live commerce offers consumers the Internet in their pocket, offering banking, shopping, and real-time news, with key players and technologies shaping the future of the industry(Barnes, 2002b)

Figure 6. Concept of Live Commerce

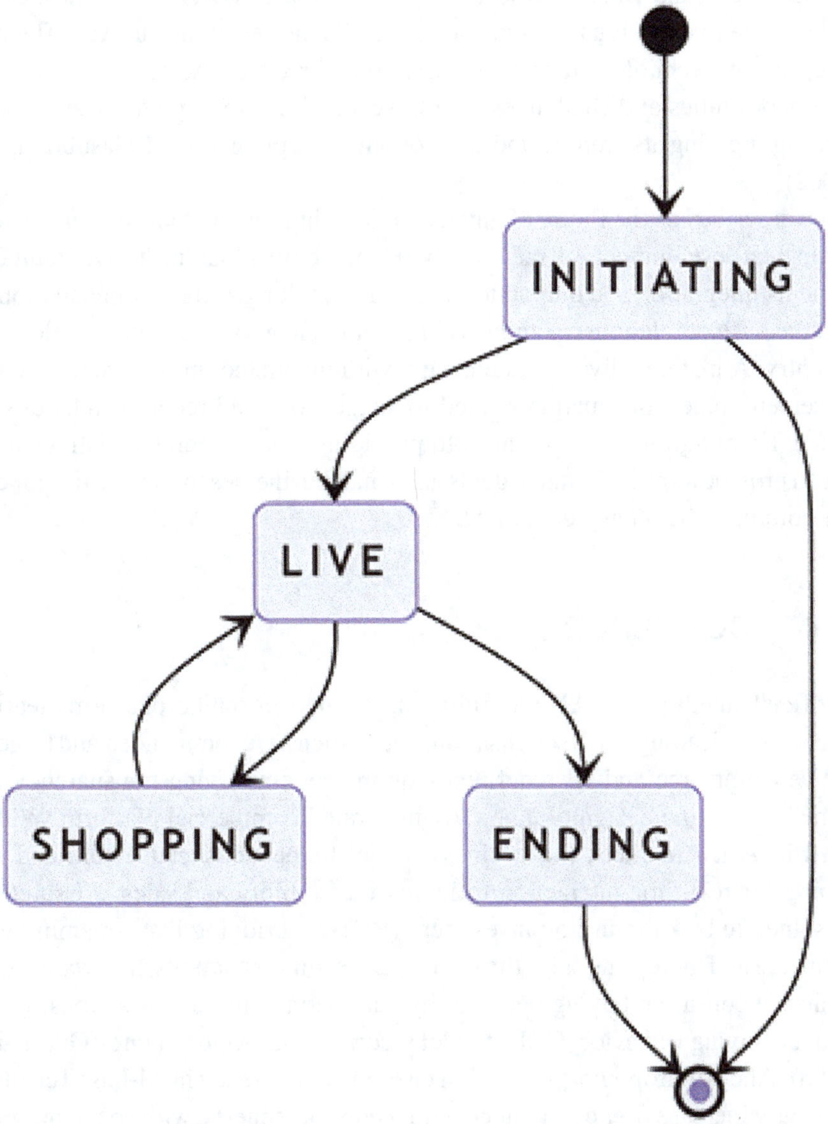

Companies joining in live sessions give instant prizes, freebies, and exclusive 'on the go' offers. The audience can then interact with the host and ask questions in real-time, as well as purchase directly through the live session. With in-stream and live comments, this creates a two-way live chat, converting the conversation inside the live session to a conversion. Live shopping applications and profit models have also emerged. However, beforehand, the session is planned and a pre-fixed format is followed, like selecting a host. There is an opportunity to join as a guest and co-host along with the Brand Host. The host of a live session co-hosts with a guest or has guests join the live session to co-host together. The newest trends in AI, influencer culture, and app technology to appear in live commerce are described.M-commerce offers opportunities and challenges for markets and marketing, with a space-time matrix highlighting its impact and a taxonomy of applications(Balasubraman et al., 2002).

AI is described as the future of any technology in India, with its current pace of technological development. All mentionable technology formats in the live commerce app, and its integration and interaction with AI is explored. AI recommendation, as well as the push of relationship and LSTM recommendations, is being developed in the country. A platform live commerce app with integrated innovative technology advancement, other information related to suggestions and recommendations are provided. From lightning-up products to providing smart recommendations using AI, it can provide a space for individuals and small businesses to explore the concept of live commerce(L. Zhang et al., 2023b).

5. AI IN E-COMMERCE

Artificial intelligence (AI) algorithms integrated in online platforms learned user behaviour, leading to personalisation tactics such as recommended and targeted ads. Live Commerce and AI redefine e-commerce, amplifying transparency and accountability in the design of a new AI-integrated commercial platform. Widely adopted in Asian markets, the business model harnesses social media and live streaming for real-time interaction to increase credibility and sales. AI solutions are designed to boost return on investment (ROI) by bridging live streaming with e-commerce and increasing sales through smart recommendations. Software agents can enhance consumer buying behavior by automating online transactions, with a Consumer Buying Behavior (CBB) model incorporating AI techniques(Guttman et al., 1998). And Anthropomorphic design cues and consistency in AI-based chatbots significantly increase user compliance with feedback requests, with social presence mediating this effect(Adam et al., 2021).Proposed smart recommendations algorithms developed through realistic data models offer personalised product suggestions to users while live streaming. AI and machine learning are transforming healthcare organizations by improving speed, cost, capacity, quality, and consistency, allowing human decision makers to focus on higher-value tasks(Yu et al., 2018). In live streaming instead of using fixed advertisements, a social media influencer communicates with viewers live while using an e-commerce platform. AI algorithms will increase user engagement through chat support and real-time customised recommendations (Gong & Khalid, 2021). Artificial intelligence (AI) has evolved from a primitive concept to a complex, flexible system capable of achieving goals and tasks through flexible adaptation(Haenlein & Kaplan, 2019).and AI has the potential to revolutionize industries like finance, healthcare, manufacturing, and retail, with its impact ranging from finance to healthcare to manufacturing to retail(Dwivedi et al., 2021).Individuals watching a live stream can interact with the presenter by asking questions and the presenter can demonstrate the product or discuss topics live. Channels are often hosted by professional influencers, celebrities or online shop owners with big, dedicated followings. AI solutions provide up-to-the-minute tailored product information compatible with the presented items through the social media platforms. Although AI-based personalisation tactics led to a sales increase, lack of transparency and accountability brought exploring Live Commerce and AI. Designed experiments and case studies reveal users' attitudes towards algorithms and suggest commercial website designs.

6. LIVE COMMERCE IN INDIA

The pandemic hit all markets, yet India was particularly harshly impacted by the second largest patient population in the world in different parts of the 'tsunami'. Today, the mortality rate is half the world's average, directly and indirectly affecting the young population. Nonetheless this has offered an exciting opportunity to accelerate the adoption of digital technologies. The lockdown altered people's lifestyle, exploding their engagement in digital technologies. Video content marketing has greatly increased during the lockdown, especially on various streaming platforms. The lock-in and accelerator effect from the platform is changing habits. As mobile phones are getting cheaper and high-speed internet access is reaching remote audiences, every second B2C platform turns consumer. New market players favour local e-commerce buying and selling habits, enhancing self-reliant India. But varying levels of social features impact user engagement differently across genders and platforms(Pagani & Mirabello, 2011).In emerging markets, entertainment and digital marketing have gradually merged with educational content, leading to contract farming and digital commerce. Ascendance of on-demand video and live-streaming, particularly in the 'pleasure' economy segment, is therefore observed. Many digital marketing platforms are experimenting in video content and live commerce, creating a massive demand for content creation, copyrighting, and video production and interactivity, stickiness, sociability, and personalization significantly shape consumer behavior(P. Liu et al., 2021). Concurrently, an informal sector emerges through freelance talent helping merchants to leverage market capacity. Ultimately, the Government has taken steps to retain and enhance local culture, creating jobs, nurturing craftsman skills and building the capabilities needed for content creation. Government incentives support the confluence of culture with modern technology intending to live commerce digital. The trust and relationship quality significantly impact user behavior, with emotional and informational support from friends fostering deeper connections with sellers(Lin et al., 2018), As a result, different sellers participate in live broadcasting, displaying a combination of modern technology and traditional Indian culture.

7. CURRENT LANDSCAPE AND MARKET SIZE

The retail landscape of the Indian market has witnessed substantial growth and change in recent years. E-commerce companies have introduced new purchasing strategies to meet the varied requirements of B2B and B2C customers. In the case of B2B customers, companies use social media or conventional texting to ink a common understanding, place an order, or form long-term business relationships with sellers. In contrast, B2C company platforms use enticing video demonstrations by sellers to tempt clients to make immediate purchases. They use comparably more enchanting ads, offers, and GIFs to make the consumers feel that the goods offered by them fulfill their demands. Customers of virtually all generations have switched to using e-commerce applications(Hande et al., 2015).

Primarily, the first group of e-shoppers comprises women in the age group of 22-33, who buy cosmetic products; the second group comprises middle-aged women and men, aged from 39-44, who purchase mobile phones, electronic clothes, and kitchen gadgets; the third group is children in the age group 3-13 who purchase toys. Compared to the periphery, urban locations have greater accessibility to e-commerce apps. The qualitative analysis shows that the need for a technological e-commerce app has grown due to its suitability and time and energy-saving features. Most retailing companies are verifying e-commerce applications over business websites as e-commerce applications offer more facilities and a non-troublesome and synchronized shopping experience. It is projected that in the times to come, e-commerce platforms will proliferate, thereby supplanting the traditional method of purchasing goods and services. It is also likely that Indian e-commerce businesses will outsmart global companies due to a consumer-driven advantage. Similarly, the global e-commerce service provider will have to fine-tune the marketing parameters and guarantee fast delivery, authentication, and the secure delivery of products.

8. AI-POWERED RECOMMENDATIONS IN E-COMMERCE

The adoption of AI technologies is allowing retailers to utilize vast customer data for improving data analytics procedures, enhancing operational decisions, and providing a more optimized shopping experience. E-commerce platforms have demonstrated the potential of AI-powered smart recommendations, enhancing operations through boosting sales and revitalizing out-of-season inventory. experiential value, including cognitive, hedonic, social, and ethical dimensions, enhances consumer engagement on social commerce and e-commerce platforms(Nadeem et al., 2021), The success of AI-powered recommendations in e-commerce contributes to the emergence of Live Commerce in the industry. Live Commerce, also known as live shopping, is a newly blooming trend in the fusion of real-time shopping events, interactive live streaming, and social shopping. Consumer technological readiness, perceived risk, and trust significantly shape purchase decisions in mobile shopping environments(Andronie et al., 2021). On the one hand, Live Commerce bridges the gap between online and offline shopping by creating social selling events and delivering live-streamed, real-time, and interactive shopping experiences. Also expert power, informational power, referent power, and legitimate reciprocity power significantly influence content participation and content creation, which in turn affect purchase likelihood(P. Wang & Huang, 2023). In align with this the emotional and informational support positively impact consumer participation, with product presentation strengthening these effects(Y. Wang et al., 2020).On the other hand, Live Commerce is capable of garnering massive user engagement, featuring hot-sales conversion through limited-time promotions with live auctions.

Figure 7. AI-Powered Recommendations in E-Commerce

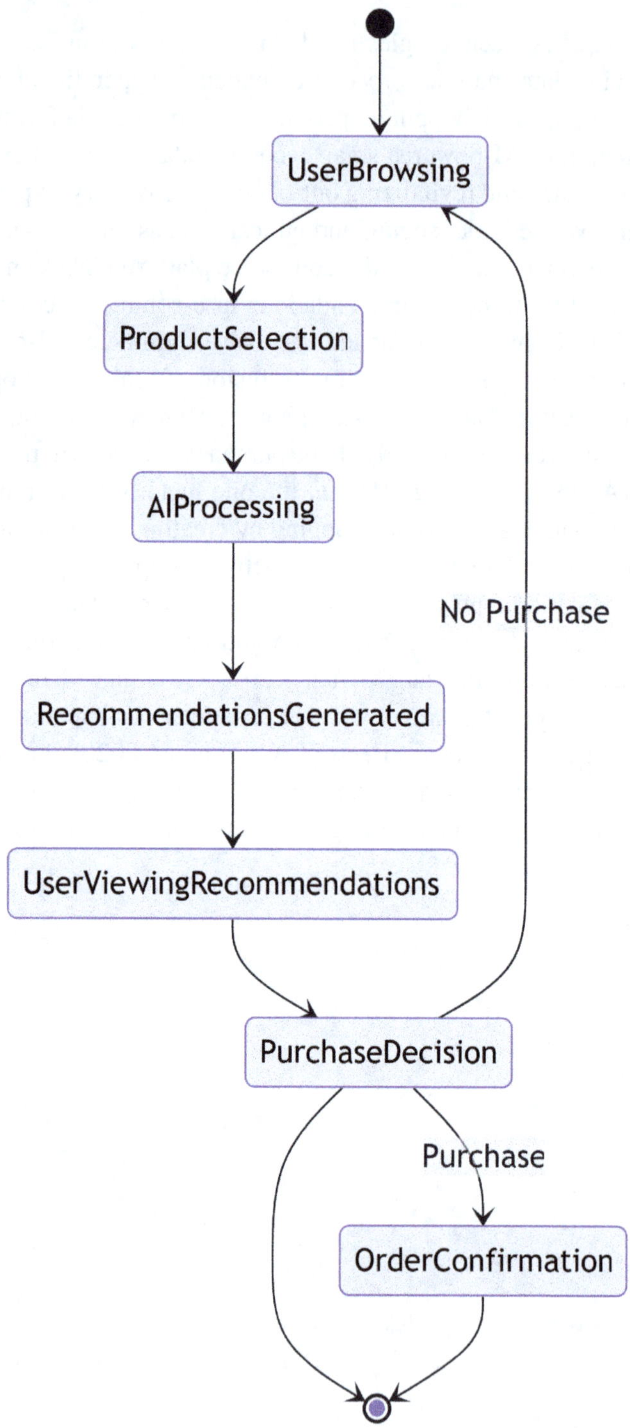

Live Commerce opens up a promising digital business model and has a relentless increase in investments. Several e-commerce marketplaces and social media giants have introduced Live Commerce and integrated them with existing e-commerce platforms through live streaming. Due to the rapid development of fixed and portable or mobile devices and the rapid expansion of high-speed networks, live television and radio channels and online entertainment gained fame in the early 1920s. and currently audience consumers form parasocial relationships with TV series characters, leading to impulse buying behaviors(Vazquez et al., 2020), On Virtual Marketplaces, shoppers create avatars and communicate with other avatars as well as controllers of real-life MBWs. Additionally, they can also form communities on Virtual Marketplaces based on similar interests. Virtual shopping is distinguished from normal online shopping due to its immersive, 3D shopping environment. On AE, shoppers can watch and record live streaming videos of other users and chat alongside in real-time. Chats can contain questions, requests, compliments, or comments about the live content discussed in the video. Additionally, AE also adds a Like option allowing viewers to like the content. Shoppers can buy products shown during live streaming through an integrated purchase link during Live Commerce. Generated receipts indicate the purchased items and the brand of the hosting store(Adulyasak et al., 2023)

9. PERSONALIZATION AND USER EXPERIENCE

With the increasing popularity of social commerce, live commerce has emerged as a disruptive e-commerce streaming. It's becoming an influential platform to conduct real-time shopping over the internet. This new digital channel combines real-time storytelling, social interaction and shopping. Live commerce has been further empowered by the AI industry. It embraces a fusion of real-time social shopping events and smart recommendation systems (Shen et al., 2023). To users, they can enjoy more personalized and user-friendly interactions via recommendations. Notably, trust fully mediates the relationship between engagement and purchase intention, while social interactions directly impact buying behavior(Dabbous et al., 2020), In contrast to current e-commerce experience, shopping in a live commerce journey is more focused and shorter. Moreover, the interaction with shoppers is real-time, and the in-the-moment reply is important.

Figure 8. Personalization and User Experience in E-Commerce

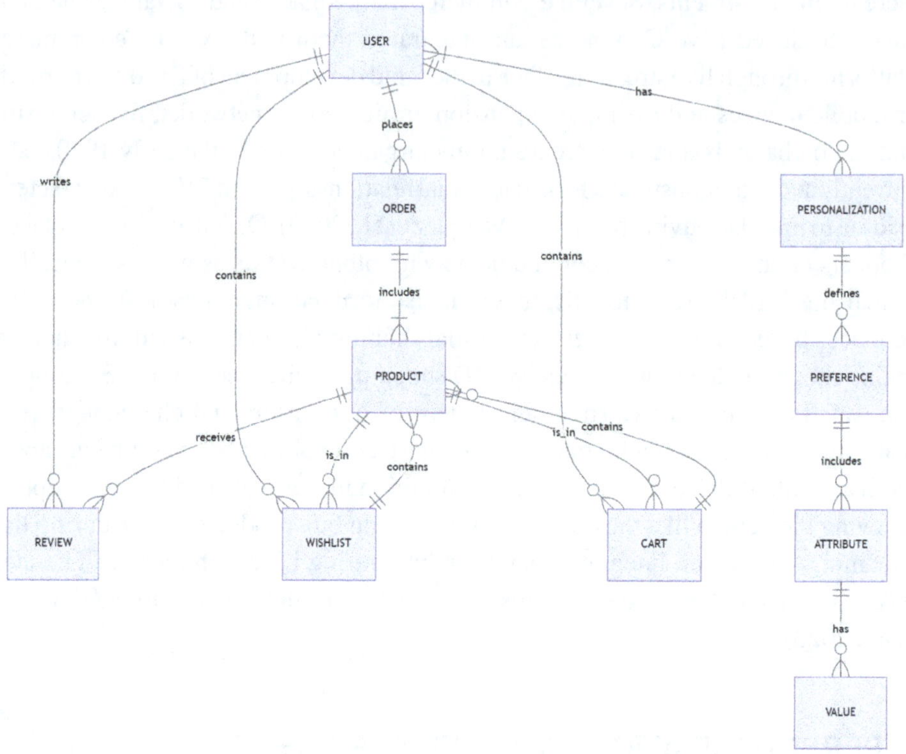

It is meaningful to work on how to organize the content. To achieve success in live commerce, an array of products are necessary. An online store can meet this requirement but lacks the real-time interaction. Another common practice is to use instant reply tools. However, it cannot be combined with the product demonstration. Some existing events involve not only affects the user engagement but also hard to organize for brand stores. With the expectation of smarter technology, the content should be selectively qualified to boost the shopping interests. A content optimization system is proposed to organize the content during the live show. To personalize the product widget content and provide shoppers the most relevant product recommendation, the widget content ranking problem is formulated. A hybrid approach is introduced to consider contextual E-commerce factors. It conducts the learning-to-rank approach and partially adapted a model-based approach. The shoppers' experience indirectly influences brand-related engagement, mediated by attitude, subjective norms, and perceived behavioral control(Gvili & Levy, 2021). A bandit algorithm is employed to optimize the impact of the ranking model and retrieves the optimal ordered selection rules. To evaluate the system, two live commerce events – a short 30-min single-item event and a longer 60-min multiple-item event are hold. Live commerce, as a new form of online shopping, is conducted as a real-time interaction and shopping experience. Real-time predictive analytics, simulation modeling tools, and computer vision algorithms shape immersive retail experiences across the customer journey("Image Processing Computational Algorithms, Sensory Data Mining Techniques, and Predictive Customer Analytics in the Metaverse Economy," 2022). However, each subject can have their unique preference. At the end of the campaign, a lucky draw activity is provided with shopping carts. During the campaign, the customers can add the products to their shopping cart. The shopping cart event ID is accordingly created. A unique GSKU is assigned to each product. The user session sequence is collected consecutively with all the activity types. A product widget is a container for visually displaying a set of product items.

10. RECOMMENDATION ALGORITHMS

In recent years, long-term online shopping and the development of live front-end services have led to the rise of live commerce. Audience members can buy products while interacting with broadcasters in the live streaming process. And AI-driven strategies enable companies to adapt to evolving consumer needs, enhance customer relationships, and differentiate themselves in competitive markets(Selvakumar et al., 2025). User interaction comments, "like" content, and audience behavior as well as resources including the video itself. Resource sharing is an integral aspect of social networks, which effectively bridges the gap between real-time broadcasting and shopping sales.

Figure 9. How Recommendation Algorithms works in Ecommerce

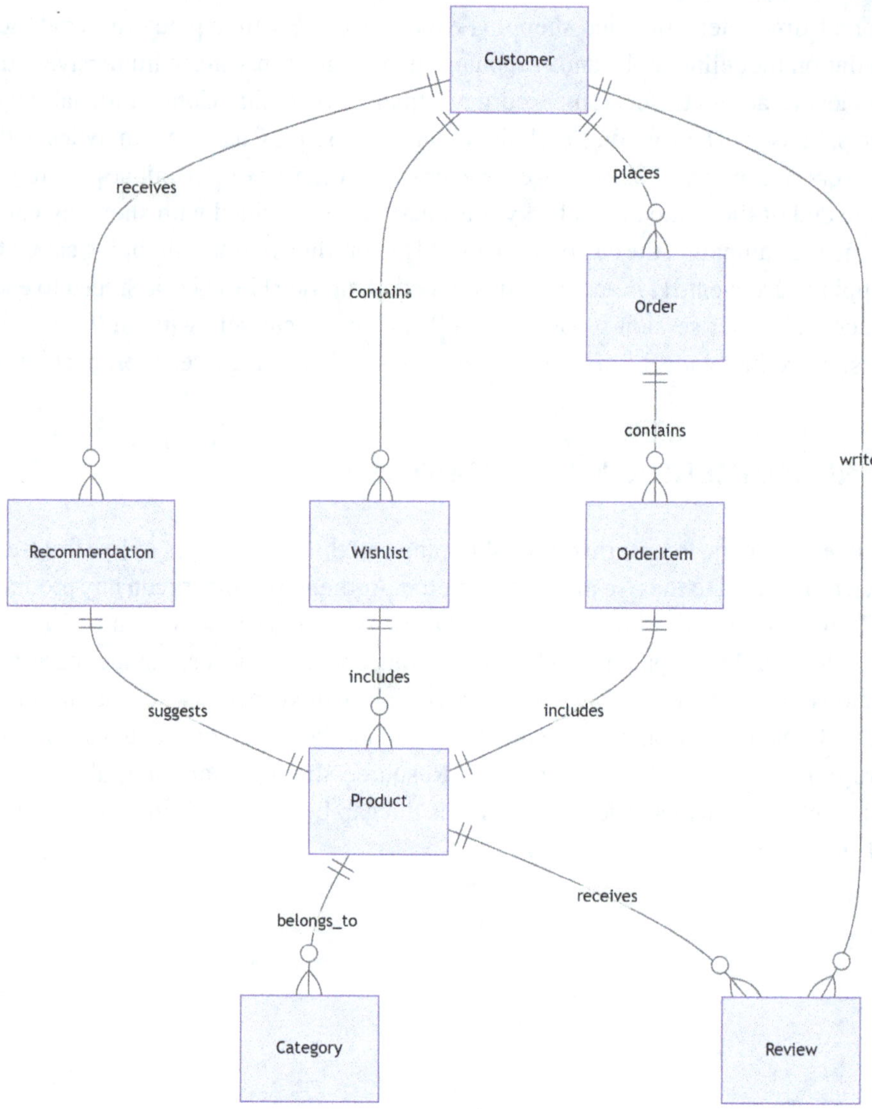

Live commerce is a growing industry that improves user experience with real-time social shopping. Social network shopping provides users with a new shopping life, saves shopping time, and helps buy suitable goods. The goal behind leveraging live commerce is to create a next generation shopping experience. This experience is the result of the fusion of real-time social shopping scenes and smart recommendation algorithms. There has been a clear transition from shops to e-commerce to video-based selling platforms to live commerce (Salunke & Chaudhari, 2018). The live streaming shopping system provides different types of products; several recommendation algorithms are used to recommend products for the broadcaster and audience.Live commerce is a way for broadcasters to present a shopping mall in their live streaming room. The broadcaster can provide niching categories and top sale lists for the shop. Live commerce can bring more realistic goods view and customer proposes an e-commerce recommendation algorithm called M+TOP, which consists of four stages: M-Graph generator generates product-item matrix M; WeightedSVD learns latent factors of M; the TOP-based recommendation engine generates potential items by multiplying the matrix with item embeddings and utilizes competitive filtering considering the category and interaction threshold; and Post process generates the full list by merging the shop-merchant items and weighting the consumer behavior. A full list of personalized recommendations including divergence metrics integrated into various levels of the algorithm is presented. Traditional recommendation algorithms in the e-commerce scene mostly use non-personalized and group-based recommendations like top sales and items in the same category. It can induce a "filter bubble" because it requires consumer initiative to explore other item categories. A competitive filtering model is prepared to recommend potential items for consumers on video platforms using broadcast deep learning.

11. THE FUSION OF LIVE COMMERCE AND AI

In recent years, the Indian digital commerce industry has seen a significant growth in a variety of formats. One of the most recent and potentially significant formats is real-time social commerce augmented by advanced AI(L. Zhang et al., 2023b). In this format, a live video host presents and demonstrates products in real-time while using mobile or web communication channels to influence an attentive audience. The collectivist consumers and those with high involvement are more likely to engage in price negotiation. Additionally, eWOM moderates these effects, reducing collectivism's influence while strengthening involvement's impact on negotiation behavior(Levy & Gvili, 2020). It also presents a range of smart recommendations that are tailored to individual preferences in order to induce purchasing behavior. Live streaming and smart recommendations, to varying extents, have been considered separately. However, their hybrid has been investigated infrequently, especially in an emerging market like India. The objective of this research is therefore to investigate consumer-perceived live commerce cues that enhance effectiveness in the Indian context.

Live commerce, in which a host presents and markets a product to encourage immediate purchase, is growing increasingly popular According to a study, the frequency of live streaming sessions in the US has quadrupled in the past two years. It is mostly focused on products across numerous consumption categories such as beauty, fitness, and clothing, which are typically affordable, relatively low-risk, and impulse-driven, often falling under hedonic shopping. AI-driven smart recommendations, in which personalized suggestions are presented using a variety of algorithms, are considered as a novel way of suggesting products to customers because they are convenient and tailored to individual preferences. There is a connection between the two trends, the former being the presentation of the market information and the latter being the tailored market information, typically displayed to a third-party viewer. The host presents dynamic market information and the smart recommendation is behaved as non-dynamic general recommendation that can be seen by any viewer during live streaming.

12. ENHANCING USER ENGAGEMENT AND CONVERSION RATES

Indian e-Commerce markets are predicted to grow at a rapid pace in the next few years. Under this backdrop, a new shopping trend on social media and e-Commerce platforms is quickly emerging in India, driven by video streaming. multiple dimensions of attractiveness, including appearance, functionality, and interaction quality, significantly influence customer responses(Park et al., 2024), This new trend merges live video streaming, product sales, and real-time social interactions – all in one unified platform. Live commerce can be recognized as a fusion of online live video streaming and e-commerce, where online sellers can perform and live-stream product advertisements in real time to display to their audience. The audience can interact with live chat while watching and buy products on the spot- all in real time. At the same time, personal recommendations in e-Commerce are centered around offering the most personalized product to every user while boosting purchases. Also data-driven insights enable businesses to anticipate consumer behavior, optimize marketing strategies, and enhance customer relationships. The research underscores how machine learning, mood analysis, and natural language processing refine targeted advertising, improving sales performance and brand loyalty(P. S. Dahake, Chandak, et al., 2023). To boost the shopping experiences, combining live commerce with personal recommendations is proposed as the next evolutionary step in e-commerce(Chaudhary & Chowdhury, 2019). The challenges involved are detailed, including market data sparsity and the diversity of search results, as well as the specifics of live commerce in the Indian market, which sets it apart from other Western markets. Aiming to address these challenges and anticipating the next social shopping trend, a framework that recommends appropriate products in real time for both online vendors and users is provided. This also facilitates comprehensive experiments and a large-scale production system setup to verify the effectiveness of the proposed framework using both offline and online metrics. The system is currently embedded in the eBay US live platform and is in widespread use. On average, there are 30 active live events per day for various product categories, and on average, each event generates 5,000 user interactions.

13. REAL-TIME DATA ANALYSIS AND INSIGHTS

A technology-driven experience can emerge and result in a new channel in retail, connecting human shopping with products and services outside of online or offline store visits. Technologies such as mobile applications, cloud computing, and smart geolocatable gadgets can spatially trace a potential buyer. This way, the AI algorithm studies the trace to predict whether the consumer will be passing in front of a store(Adulyasak et al., 2023). The real-time insights, generated from the successfully incentivized shopping path consumers, are then used by the retailer to schedule promotions on future dates. The literature, along with 8-month and 14-week field experiments, shows that, compared to fixed-location offers, the AI-driven approach increases the cost-effectiveness of the campaign. The machine learning techniques improve customer segmentation, sales forecasting, and churn prediction, optimizing business strategies(P. S. Dahake, Bagaregari, et al., 2024), Moreover, recommendations for different products can act synergistically, promoting complementary products but not direct substitutes, which increases the retailer's revenue. Interactive retail shopping on social media platforms is burgeoning across India. India's e-commerce industry is evolving at a fast pace. Among the countries which have a strong economy, India is the top market for retail commerce. E-commerce businesses are carrying out transactions for electronics, home goods, gadgets, fashion, and a number of other categories. As e-commerce thrives, online retailers are experiencing a novel and intriguing issue: increasing competition and customers get overwhelmed with too many choices since every online store offers millions of products. Understanding and filtering such a wide range of products is very hard for consumers. In a simpler, less complicated, and more helpful manner, customers occasionally want to be assisted to pick their ideal product among various choices. For this reason, personalization provides dealers the chance to recognize and be aware of the desires, needs, and possessions of their customers in a focused manner. Social shopping is increasing further in India among the younger generation. With artificial intelligence's capacity to ease real-time customer interaction, beauty manufacturers and retailers will actively react to customers' desires and further accelerate the interconnection of digital and real-world experiences. Social shopping on live-streaming feed is progressively increasing in western culture; in contrast, appealing growth has been observed recently across India. Fashion outlets create ways in order to access and purchase their newest goods by organizing big fashion shows. Regular live live streams of these gatherings allow consumers to access the latest fashion trends. Receipts, products, and performers can link viewers via the same feed.

14. REGULATORY AND ETHICAL CONSIDERATIONS

In India, the promising market of live commerce, which enables real-time social shopping experiences, is set to benefit from AI-driven smart offerings in particular. There are awakening consumer needs such as real-time interactions, product inquiries, influencers, distance sales, or choice difficulties, and companies can now embed real-time streaming features into their websites or applications and leverage best practices for developing live commerce in India. AI can seamlessly recommend products or content, match users with right companies or presenters, predict inventory needs to avoid out-of-stock disappointments, and automatically optimize the video or streaming quality to align with the viewer's networking or device capabilities in real-time with online or cloud AI services. Further, AI can develop tomorrow's products as well to fine-tune pricing, categorization, personalization, or innovation by leveraging the processing of large amounts of heterogeneous data types, like images, speech, geolocation, or social network activity. The personalization and socialization significantly enhance brand engagement, leading to higher eWOM intention(Phan et al., 2020).

The live commerce market seems set to skyrocket within the second most populous country and mobile market, intensifying digital penetration and bringing a Foreign Direct Investment (FDI) boost. Since India is the second-largest social media market, meets a young demographic, has an increasing disposable income, and efficiently capitalised on the COVID-19 lockdown to fast-track its digital economy growth, live commerce is expected to thrive among online shopping share, reaching 170 million users by 2030 and dominating 90% of digital sales. Similar to China, consumers meet new entertainment and shopping experiences. On the other hand, companies are trying to find new sales channels, consumers due to COVID-19 or supply chain difficulties. By consequence, various app developers like Bigo, Amazon, Facebook, or TikTok develop or embed real-time features into their platforms, overly facilitating the connection of celebrities, farmers, or artisans with fans, disciples, or customers in India (Hermann, 2022).

15. DATA PRIVACY AND SECURITY

Digital innovation has drawn public interest in the emerging phenomena of Live Commerce (LC) in which people can consume products in a live presentation and converse with the host in real-time. The versatile eCommerce and social media companies, increased possession of smartphones, cheap memory and net availability, and the infamy of influencer marketing encouraged LC further by blending shopping with entertainment (Alam et al., 2022). Furthermore, Artificial Intelligence (AI) includes machine learning technologies that enable computers to learn from the data and complete activities intelligently. And notable data-driven models significantly reduce biases(P. S. Dahake, Chandak, et al., 2024). Several eCommerce websites use AI to interpret customers' shopping actions and choices efficiently, enhancing consumer browsing and purchasing experiences. The strategic collaboration of LC and AI will significantly transform online shopping by delivering real-time social buying choices and shrewd recommendations in the forthcoming days. This is the first study demonstrating LC and AI operated Live Shopping (LS) practice via a user-system engagement procedure. The proposed model assures the rational dispersion of LS architecture between the LC broadcaster (LB) and the system (S) providing product info and directing LS. 569 Indian consumers have asserted a generally dependable and secure LS platform support and derived that the rationale of the commerce broadcaster visibly affects while weighing for the broadcast. When the LB broadcasts frequently, data privacy and information security concerning LB upsurge voters' self-assurance and willingness to buy. Privacy worries have declined inevitably while getting old. 321 females are more interested in LS commerce and pretty much alarmed about private concerns and information security regarding the commerce broadcaster than the others. Generally, those people who watch LC regularly and call any incoming show as FAQ perceive that Kuifeng Enterprises LC platform providers as authentic and secure in nature.

16. CONSUMER PROTECTION

In the current advanced technological climate, hordes of large-scale shopping events take place on social media platforms. Directly on this platform, claimants can watch a live broadcast of products and purchase products. The chiping applications, chat platforms, social media and video sources present the first new social purchase deception method. The unreal appearance of products and still images of advertisements in fake product previews deceive users into believing that good products will be delivered. The problem is that products tend to differ from photos as a result of consumer purchases(Hazarika, 2013). When the interface is viewed with the proposed DIG system design, users can navigate the static pages and insert the URLs of products to view preview pictures. Then the reputation of sales is new, and reviews about products are looked at. Economic circumstances, brand reputation, technological features, and post-purchase interactions significantly shape consumer preferences(P. S. Dahake, Parchake, et al., 2024). But in contrast, Ads that are considered to be fraudulent are cheaper than others, of unpaid nature and contain claims, and purchasable sources are sufficiently related to a preview image. Consumers remember products from details of the image that includes not only a general ideation of the product, but also specific characteristics such as texture and surfacc.

Because there are so many works, this is important work for consumer protection and develops a system based on AI to detect fake previews for products. He suggests how photos of fake reviewed products refer to the market to retract wholesale products. The data consists of 240K livestreams by 60K creators on a platform for setting up and broadcasting a live shopping event. Fine-tuned networks can be applied to all stock categories of products.

17. EMERGING TECHNOLOGIES IN LIVE COMMERCE AND AI

Live commerce is one of the next disruptive fintech innovations. The concept is quite simple: People sell products in real-time to people watching online. So far e-commerce has mostly been about browsing and shopping individually, in one's own time, and then waiting for items to be delivered The .pass-times and habits significantly influence consumer engagement, which in turn affects purchase and gift-giving intentions. Emotional engagement, social presence, and immersion play crucial roles in shaping consumer behavior(W.-K. Chen et al., 2022). Live commerce is the next step where people can shop in real-time, ask the sellers questions, and make more informed purchase decisions. In essence, live commerce is the fusion between real-time social shopping and live content production. It has taken off in China, with Tencent having heavily invested in it since 2016. The global market has also shown considerable promise, growing from $60 billion in 2019 to $170 billion in 2023 and a projected $420 billion in 2028. Since live commerce is in real-time, sellers need smart recommendations displayed instantly, matching a viewer's preferences with the suitable product in real-time as new products are introduced. This is caused by the classical 'accuracy vs. latency' tradeoff in recommendation(Gong & Khalid, 2021). Adding to the complexity is that viewers in developing countries like India mainly access live commerce via low-end smartphones and often slow networks. Therefore, the backend systems serving these recommendations need to be optimized without losing much accuracy or resorting to common heuristics that perform poorly. Trends and disruptions in the live commerce space and more precisely how it affects live commerce viewers and recommendation systems servicing them have not been investigated yet. This research can target this gap to understand how live commerce viewers behave, changes in the competitive landscape of live commerce sellers and platforms, and the technological limitations and challenges faced by those running the recommendation systems that power live commerce. Machine learning models for live commerce recommendation that take into consideration these insights can also be built. The research can be based on a mixed-method approach staring from the data-driven analysis of viewers' activity on a large live commerce platform in India using various internal logs, cross-referenced with insights derived from interviews with live commerce viewers who watched streams for a certain amount of time.

18. POTENTIAL IMPACT ON THE RETAIL INDUSTRY

This section focuses on the potential impact of AI on the retail/supermarket industry, with highlights on various advantages that real-time personalised recommendation engines bring into live commerce apps. When one shops in a physical store, recommendations can only be provided in a real-time manner and mostly happen through communication with other human beings, commonly the store's salesman or friends/family members accompanying the shopper. The aim is to develop a digital shopping experience with a mobile-first approach that is as close as possible to shopping in a brick-and-mortar, offline supermarket. (Adulyasak et al., 2023) at a time. During the live content, one possible feature that will be executed is monitored. Fixed time slots can be leased by items on shelves or by items in-store, so it can be anticipated that within a fixed time slot the shopper is most likely to buy or is interested in seeing it.AI-driven recommendation systems can support novice vendors in systematically conducting online business, improving engagement and purchase confidence. Ultimately, the study underscores the importance of trust-building mechanisms and recommendation algorithms in optimizing social commerce success(Sukrat & Papasratorn, 2018)

Upon the start of the fixed time slot, a push notification will be sent to notify the shopper, having the shopper's view count on these "Time-sensitive shelf/stores" increase with a live badge. As a result, having a real-time personalisation recommendation engine is crucial and can bring various advantages to live-commerce apps, since real-time personalised recommendation engines are nascent in the field compared to the non-real-time counterparts.

19. KEY FINDINGS AND CONTRIBUTIONS

Social commerce research has evolved significantly from 2003 to 2023, shifting focus from social networking sites to consumer behavior, AI-driven commerce, and cognitive factors(Leong et al., 2024) and Live commerce is increasingly blending stores with social media and influencers, offering a live shopping experience with real-time interactions and enabling consumers to check and buy products live. The personalized advertising enhances brand-related outcomes through self-congruence, where consumers feel a stronger connection to brands they previously searched for(Tran et al., 2020) Although it is a rather recent e-commerce format in western societies, there have been several successful and widely accepted applications in less developed countries. India is one of the fastest-growing countries in Asia and it is evolving as one of the key e-commerce markets globally. Thus far, live commerce has not secured India's e-commerce marketing. The usefulness, interactivity, entertainment, and authenticity significantly influence consumer emotions, with entertainment having the strongest effect on arousal and authenticity on pleasure. Additionally, arousal and pleasure positively affect impulse buying (IB) and social participation (SP), with arousal displaying a stronger impact(Y. Liu et al., 2023). This paper discusses the findings of an ethnographic research study that explores consumer participation on the Indian e-commerce live commerce site. The vividness and personalization significantly influence consumption vision and telepresence, which in turn drive the urge to buy impulsively. Additionally, impulsivity moderates the relationship between stimuli and organism, enhancing the effect of vividness and personalization on consumer engagement(Khoi et al., 2023), Companies may use this information to determine how to better help their consumers. With this eWOM sharing enhances trust, which in turn increases purchase likelihood. Additionally, cultural orientation (collectivism-individualism) and social tie strength moderate this effect, shaping consumer behavior in online marketplaces(Gvili & Levy, 2023) and above all predictive factors significantly enhance customer purchases, spending, attraction, and shopping experiences, leading to greater retailer loyalty(N. S. Dahake, Gajghate, et al., 2024)

20. RESULT & DISCUSSION BASED ON THE LITERATURE

The important scholars' writings about article questions are summarized, and discussed results that emerged from this summary. The attention around AI in e-commerce, resulting in the term live commerce, is conducted from the perspective of Asian online fashion e-commerce. According to the acceptance and use of live commerce, the idea of real-time social shopping that combines instant messaging with shopping and is conducted on social media platforms is regarded as emerging, due to being on the rise. The AI & predictive models often suffer from accuracy overestimation, leading to misinformed executive decisions(N. S. Dahake, Suresh Dahake, et al., 2024), However, The involvement of real-time social shopping with AI is addressed as a call for future exploration under the broader research objective of live commerce. Live commerce can be interpreted as real-time social selling that is moderated by a single person or a group, suggests the co-purchase notifications, and is blended with gamified elements. Popular platforms for live video became significant, and with companies starting the retail-related functionalities, social shopping applications saw an addition in real-time selling. Most importantly Key factors such as customer demographics, purchase history, and website interactions significantly contribute to accurate predictions(P. S. Dahake, Mohare, et al., 2023)

E-commerce has gone through many changes, starting off as B2C retail shopping and advancing to vast and global markets. The online beginning of a major food chain was the shift that began it all, building a new industry that would boom within the usability of internet connectivity in the 2000s. A popular social media platform was released, expanded to android, forming an ad choice environment for businesses with the beginning of new ad formats. A major tech company acquired another company, allowing for AI development. The shown interest in AI and AR peaks in fashion and e-commerce, years when many proofs of concepts and technological advancements blossomed, with this marketplace responding to them up to today.

21. CONCLUSION

Artificial Intelligence (AI) has been embraced as a vital innovation by the retail industry. An d machine learning models enhance purchase predictions, optimizing pricing strategies and customer loyalty(P. S. Dahake & Dahake, 2024).The integration of AI in retail has initiated an interesting exploration of live commerce. AI can customize the choices to satisfy the different demands of users through data collection and feedback processing, while live commerce is essentially an online video-centered shopping format. This paper analyzes Indian consumers' views on whether AI-based product advice would enhance their live shopping intentions in India, where both live commerce and AI in retail are developing yet. The findings reveal that AI's ability to automatically and intelligently suggest items during live commerce can significantly improve consumers' live purchasing intentions with the assistance of social media influencers. As big data capabilities, shaping competencies and operational efficiency(P. S. Dahake, Jain, et al., 2024) Additionally, it is shown that live commerce viewing in India is positively related to live shopping intentions and that this connection is partially mediated by perceived interactivity.

In India, non-material suggestions such as travel advice and fictional items are deemed somewhat more reliable, while advice on live goods is considered more reliable virtually (Alam et al., 2022). However, the previous relevance literature on these themes has bypassed the analysis of the fusion of real-time social shopping and smart suggestions. Thus, through the framework of S-O-R, the fusion of real-time social shopping and smart recommendations can enhance online retailer performance and generate expenditures. Moreover, the WRP model intention has a complete mediating role in shoppers' relationship between EPS (experience pleasure and satisfaction) and promoters' relationship to online retailers. Finally, the proposals and recommendations for the online retailer industry and the academic community are put forward, which represents new proof of these areas of research.

22. FUTURE SCOPE OF THE STUDY

The Indian online shopping industry is currently enjoying a considerable increase in public attention and interest, which promotes economic development, enhances consumers' shopping patterns, and offers e-retailers and other stakeholders fresh and incomparable opportunities. Young Indian innovators, therefore, have an excellent chance to use virtual shopping to conquer a plethora of challenges to their organization and market their high-quality Indian produce. In real time, netizens should concurrently purchase and share videos or messages with regard to shopping excitement on social sites, boosting social shopping and generating shopping-themed live video shares or Live-commerce. Providing real-time information on social commerce among buy and show video stream hosts can recommend wise shopping choices to buyers. Therefore, the special objective of this document is to combine real-time social shopping and smart advice shopping Live-commerce (SVC) and notably rigorous validation and appropriate model selection to enhance decision-making(P. S. Dahake, Mohare, et al., 2024). Retail decisions in smart cities are now made using different innovations such as drone technology and automatic stores. This vision, service quality, experience and treated all-in-one digitization and enhancement allows maintaining and constantly enhancing one's town life. Such retail solutions have led to a tremendous increase in the amount of information produced and transferred within town residents, prompting cities to become "intelligent cities" (Alam et al., 2022), i.e. towns in which different types of digital technology are used to enhance town residents' lives. Given this, town residents will be exposed to a wealth of items worth buying using township life. Live video streaming and social interaction are the entertainment trends and are combined within social business. This blends e-commerce with live video streaming and social media to procure virtual stimulus regimens and stuff. To ascertain whether real-time social shopping can boost consumption while disposed via Live video feeds, the aim of this article is to explore.

REFERENCES

1. Adam, M., Wessel, M., & Benlian, A. (2021). AI-based chatbots in customer service and their effects on user compliance. *Electronic Markets, 31*(2), 31. DOI: 10.1007/s12525-020-00414-7

Adulyasak, Y., Cohen, M. C., Khern-am-nuai, W., & Krause, M. (2023). *Retail Analytics in the New Normal: The Influence of Artificial Intelligence and the Covid-19 Pandemic.* DOI: 10.48550/ARXIV.2312.00046

Akter, S., & Wamba, S. F. (2016). Big data analytics in E-commerce: A systematic review and agenda for future research. *Electronic Markets, 26*(2), 173–194. DOI: 10.1007/s12525-016-0219-0

Alam, F., Tao, M., Lahuerta-Otero, E., & Feifei, Z. (2022). Let's Buy With Social Commerce Platforms Through Social Media Influencers: An Indian Consumer Perspective. *Frontiers in Psychology, 13*, 853168. DOI: 10.3389/fpsyg.2022.853168 PMID: 35496238

Andronie, M., Lăzăroiu, G., tefănescu, R., Ionescu, L., & Coco atu, M. (2021). Neuromanagement decision-making and cognitive algorithmic processes in the technological adoption of mobile commerce apps. *Oeconomia Copernicana, 12*(4), 1033–1062. DOI: 10.24136/oc.2021.034

Azam, A., & Aldehayyat, J. (2018). Impact of Informational Social Support and Familiarity on Social Commerce Intention. *European Online Journal of Natural and Social Sciences, 7*(4), 4.

Balasubraman, S., Peterson, R. A., & Jarvenpaa, S. L. (2002). Exploring the Implications of M-Commerce for Markets and Marketing. *Journal of the Academy of Marketing Science, 30*(4), 348–361. DOI: 10.1177/009207002236910

Barnes, S. J. (2002a). The mobile commerce value chain: Analysis and future developments. *International Journal of Information Management, 22*(2), 91–108. DOI: 10.1016/S0268-4012(01)00047-0

Barnes, S. J. (2002b). The mobile commerce value chain: Analysis and future developments. *International Journal of Information Management, 22*(2), 91–108. DOI: 10.1016/S0268-4012(01)00047-0

Cao, H., Chen, Z., Cheng, M., Zhao, S., Wang, T., & Li, Y. (2020). *You Recommend, I Buy: How and Why People Engage in Instant Messaging Based Social Commerce* (Version 2). arXiv. DOI: 10.48550/ARXIV.2011.00191

Chaudhary, N., & Chowdhury, D. R. (2019). *Data Preprocessing for Evaluation of Recommendation Models in E-Commerce*. https://doi.org/DOI: 10.48550/ARX-IV.1911.01273

Chen, L., Gillenson, M. L., & Sherrell, D. L. (2002). Enticing online consumers: An extended technology acceptance perspective. *Information & Management, 39*(8), 705–719. DOI: 10.1016/S0378-7206(01)00127-6

Chen, W.-K., Chen, C.-W., & Silalahi, A. D. K. (2022). Understanding Consumers' Purchase Intention and Gift-Giving in Live Streaming Commerce: Findings from SEM and fsQCA. *Emerging Science Journal, 6*(3), 460–481. DOI: 10.28991/ESJ-2022-06-03-03

Cheung, C. M. K., Xiao, B. S., & Liu, I. L. B. (2014). Do actions speak louder than voices? The signaling role of social information cues in influencing consumer purchase decisions. *Decision Support Systems, 65*, 50–58. DOI: 10.1016/j.dss.2014.05.002

Dabbous, A., Aoun Barakat, K., & Merhej Sayegh, M. (2020). Social Commerce Success: Antecedents of Purchase Intention and the Mediating Role of Trust. *Journal of Internet Commerce, 19*(3), 262–297. DOI: 10.1080/15332861.2020.1756190

Dahake, N. S., Gajghate, A., Dahake, P. S., & Bansod, S. (2024). A Transformative Impact of IoT and AI by Predictive Analytics on Modern Marketing Strategies: A Study of its Significance & Accuracy. *2024 2nd International Conference on Advances in Computation, Communication and Information Technology (ICAICCIT)*, 1150–1158. DOI: 10.1109/ICAICCIT64383.2024.10912388

Dahake, N. S., Suresh Dahake, P., & Gajghate, A. (2024). Beyond the Hype: A Critical Evaluation of Predictive Analytics Accuracy in High-Stakes Business Decisions. *2024 2nd DMIHER International Conference on Artificial Intelligence in Healthcare, Education and Industry (IDICAIEI)*, 1–6. DOI: 10.1109/IDICAIEI61867.2024.10842857

Dahake, P. S., Bagaregari, P., & Dahake, N. S. (2024). Shaping the Future of Retail: A Comprehensive Review of Predictive Analytics Models for Consumer Behavior. In Inder, S., Min, B., & Sharma, S. (Eds.), (pp. 143–160). Advances in Business Strategy and Competitive Advantage. IGI Global., DOI: 10.4018/979-8-3693-1734-1.ch011

Dahake, P. S., Chandak, S., & Dahake, N. S. (2024). Predictive Analytics in Performance Appraisal Systems: Enhancing Objectivity and Fairness. *2024 2nd DMIHER International Conference on Artificial Intelligence in Healthcare, Education and Industry (IDICAIEI)*, 1–5. DOI: 10.1109/IDICAIEI61867.2024.10842916

Dahake, P. S., Chandak, S., Mohare, R. V., Wadhwani, K., & Bhadade, P. (2023). The Crystal Ball of Marketing: How Predictive Analytics is Reshaping the Industry? *2023 Second International Conference On Smart Technologies For Smart Nation (SmartTechCon)*, 304–311. DOI: 10.1109/SmartTechCon57526.2023.10391334

Dahake, P. S., & Dahake, N. S. (2024). The Role of Big Data in Predictive Analytics for E-Commerce: Examine How Big Data Contributes to Better Predictions in Online Shopping. In Tarnanidis, T., Papathanasiou, J., Ismyrlis, V., & Kittu Manda, V. (Eds.), (pp. 403–426). Advances in Marketing, Customer Relationship Management, and E-Services. IGI Global., DOI: 10.4018/979-8-3693-9122-8.ch018

Dahake, P. S., Jain, M., Anusha, B., Poojitha, S., Singh, N., & Sharma, A. (2024). Integrating Organisational Theory, Resource-Based View, and Big Data Culture to Improve Manufacturing Performance. In D. Jelonek, N. Kumar, M. Chahar, R. Kinkladze, & L. Knop, *Recent Trends In Engineering and Science for Resource Optimization and Sustainable Development* (1st ed., pp. 156–159). CRC Press. DOI: 10.1201/9781003596721-36

Dahake, P. S., Mohare, R., Chandak, S., & Bhadade, P. (2024). Predictive Analytics in Assessing Employee Retention Rates: An Analysis of Effectiveness and Accuracy of Different Predictive Model. *2024 2nd International Conference on Advances in Computation, Communication and Information Technology (ICAICCIT)*, 1159–1164. DOI: 10.1109/ICAICCIT64383.2024.10912426

Dahake, P. S., Mohare, R. V., & Somani, N. (2023). Exploring Machine Learning's Potential in Predicting Consumer Behavior for Captivating Marketing. *2023 Second International Conference On Smart Technologies For Smart Nation (SmartTechCon)*, 1347–1352. DOI: 10.1109/SmartTechCon57526.2023.10391558

Dahake, P. S., Parchake, S., Somani, N., & Ingale, A. R. (2024). Predictive Analytics in Automotive Consumer Behaviour: An Insight into Personal use 4-Wheeler Purchase Decisions. *2024 2nd International Conference on Advances in Computation, Communication and Information Technology (ICAICCIT)*, 1143–1149. DOI: 10.1109/ICAICCIT64383.2024.10912242

Dwivedi, Y. K., Hughes, L., Ismagilova, E., Aarts, G., Coombs, C., Crick, T., Duan, Y., Dwivedi, R., Edwards, J., Eirug, A., Galanos, V., Ilavarasan, P. V., Janssen, M., Jones, P., Kar, A. K., Kizgin, H., Kronemann, B., Lal, B., Lucini, B., & Williams, M. D. (2021). Artificial Intelligence (AI): Multidisciplinary perspectives on emerging challenges, opportunities, and agenda for research, practice and policy. *International Journal of Information Management*, *57*, 101994. DOI: 10.1016/j.ijinfomgt.2019.08.002

Farris, L. (2021). *Optimized Recommender Systems with Deep Reinforcement Learning* (Version 1). arXiv. DOI: 10.48550/ARXIV.2110.03039

Ghobakhloo, M., Arias-Aranda, D., & Benitez-Amado, J. (2011). Adoption of e-commerce applications in SMEs. *Industrial Management & Data Systems, 111*(8), 1238–1269. DOI: 10.1108/02635571111170785

Gong, W., & Khalid, L. (2021). *Aesthetics, Personalization and Recommendation: A survey on Deep Learning in Fashion* (Version 1). arXiv. DOI: 10.48550/ARXIV.2101.08301

Guo, J., & Li, L. (2022). Exploring the Relationship Between Social Commerce Features and Consumers' Repurchase Intentions: The Mediating Role of Perceived Value. *Frontiers in Psychology, 12*, 775056. DOI: 10.3389/fpsyg.2021.775056 PMID: 35401287

Guttman, R. H., Moukas, A. G., & Maes, P. (1998). Agent-mediated electronic commerce: A survey. *The Knowledge Engineering Review, 13*(2), 147–159. DOI: 10.1017/S0269888998002082

Gvili, Y., & Levy, S. (2021). Consumer engagement in sharing brand-related information on social commerce: The roles of culture and experience. *Journal of Marketing Communications, 27*(1), 53–68. DOI: 10.1080/13527266.2019.1633552

Gvili, Y., & Levy, S. (2023). I Share, Therefore I Trust: A moderated mediation model of the influence of eWOM engagement on social commerce. *Journal of Business Research, 166*, 114131. DOI: 10.1016/j.jbusres.2023.114131

Haenlein, M., & Kaplan, A. (2019). A Brief History of Artificial Intelligence: On the Past, Present, and Future of Artificial Intelligence. *California Management Review, 61*(4), 5–14. DOI: 10.1177/0008125619864925

Hajli, N. (2015). Social commerce constructs and consumer's intention to buy. *International Journal of Information Management, 35*(2), 183–191. DOI: 10.1016/j.ijinfomgt.2014.12.005

Hande, P. V., Ghosh, D., & Govil, A. (2015). A Comparative Study on Factors Shaping Buying Behaviour on B2B and B2C E-Commerce Platforms in India. *Journal of Marketing and Consumer Research, 8*(0), 53.

Hazarika, A. (2013). E-Commerce: Expectations and Shortfalls. *Christ University Law Journal, 2*(2), 59–78. DOI: 10.12728/culj.3.4

Hermann, E. (2022). Leveraging Artificial Intelligence in Marketing for Social Good—An Ethical Perspective. *Journal of Business Ethics*, *179*(1), 43–61. DOI: 10.1007/s10551-021-04843-y PMID: 34054170

Hoyer, W. D., Kroschke, M., Schmitt, B., Kraume, K., & Shankar, V. (2020). Transforming the Customer Experience through New Technologies. *Journal of Interactive Marketing*, *51*(1), 57–71. DOI: 10.1016/j.intmar.2020.04.001

Image Processing Computational Algorithms, Sensory Data Mining Techniques, and Predictive Customer Analytics in the Metaverse Economy. (2022). Image Processing Computational Algorithms, Sensory Data Mining Techniques, and Predictive Customer Analytics in the Metaverse Economy. *Review of Contemporary Philosophy*, *21*(0), 205. DOI: 10.22381/RCP21202213

Khoi, N. H., Le, A. N.-H., & Nguyen Dong, P. (2023). A moderating – mediating model of the urge to buy impulsively in social commerce live-streaming. *Electronic Commerce Research and Applications*, *60*, 101286. DOI: 10.1016/j.elerap.2023.101286

Lăzăroiu, G., Neguriţă, O., Grecu, I., Grecu, G., & Mitran, P. C. (2020). Consumers' Decision-Making Process on Social Commerce Platforms: Online Trust, Perceived Risk, and Purchase Intentions. *Frontiers in Psychology*, *11*, 890. DOI: 10.3389/fpsyg.2020.00890 PMID: 32499740

Leong, L.-Y., Hew, T. S., Ooi, K.-B., Hajli, N., & Tan, G. W.-H. (2024). Revisiting the social commerce paradigm: The social commerce (SC) framework and a research agenda. *Internet Research*, *34*(4), 1346–1393. DOI: 10.1108/INTR-08-2022-0657

Levy, S., & Gvili, Y. (2020). Online shopper engagement in price negotiation: The roles of culture, involvement and eWOM. *International Journal of Advertising*, *39*(2), 232–257. DOI: 10.1080/02650487.2019.1612621

Lin, J., Li, L., Yan, Y., & Turel, O. (2018). Understanding Chinese consumer engagement in social commerce: The roles of social support and swift guanxi. *Internet Research*, *28*(1), 2–22. DOI: 10.1108/IntR-11-2016-0349

Liu, P., Li, M., Dai, D., & Guo, L. (2021). The effects of social commerce environmental characteristics on customers' purchase intentions: The chain mediating effect of customer-to-customer interaction and customer-perceived value. *Electronic Commerce Research and Applications*, *48*, 101073. DOI: 10.1016/j.elerap.2021.101073

Liu, Y., Li, Q., Edu, T., Fam, K., Zaharia, R., & Negricea, C. (2023). Mobile social commerce content, consumer emotions and behaviour. *International Journal of Consumer Studies*, *47*(4), 1315–1334. DOI: 10.1111/ijcs.12908

Nadeem, W., Tan, T. M., Tajvidi, M., & Hajli, N. (2021). How do experiences enhance brand relationship performance and value co-creation in social commerce? The role of consumer engagement and self brand-connection. *Technological Forecasting and Social Change, 171*, 120952. DOI: 10.1016/j.techfore.2021.120952

Pagani, M., & Mirabello, A. (2011). The Influence of Personal and Social-Interactive Engagement in Social TV Web Sites. *International Journal of Electronic Commerce, 16*(2), 41–68. DOI: 10.2753/JEC1086-4415160203

Park, H., Jiang, S., Lee, O.-K. D., & Chang, Y. (2024). Exploring the Attractiveness of Service Robots in the Hospitality Industry: Analysis of Online Reviews. *Information Systems Frontiers, 26*(1), 41–61. DOI: 10.1007/s10796-021-10207-8

Phan, Q. P. T., Pham, N. T., & Nguyen, L. H. L. (2020). How to Drive Brand Engagement and eWOM Intention in Social Commerce: A Competitive Strategy for the Emerging Market. *Journal of Competitiveness, 12*(3), 136–155. DOI: 10.7441/joc.2020.03.08

Rashid, R. M., Pitafi, A. H., Qureshi, M. A., & Sharma, A. (2022). Role of Social Commerce Constructs and Social Presence as Moderator on Consumers' Buying Intentions During COVID-19. *Frontiers in Psychology, 13*, 772028. DOI: 10.3389/fpsyg.2022.772028 PMID: 35222183

) Selvakumar, P., Shanthi, M., Pitchiah, R., Sharma, M., Dahake, P. S., & T. C., M. (2025). The Role of Artificial Intelligence in Business Model Innovation: Overview of AI Technologies. In M. Khokhar (Ed.), *Advances in Business Strategy and Competitive Advantage* (pp. 219–246). IGI Global. DOI: 10.4018/979-8-3693-9571-4.ch009

Sharma, M., Joshi, S., Luthra, S., & Kumar, A. (2024). Impact of Digital Assistant Attributes on Millennials' Purchasing Intentions: A Multi-Group Analysis using PLS-SEM, Artificial Neural Network and fsQCA. *Information Systems Frontiers, 26*(3), 943–966. DOI: 10.1007/s10796-022-10339-5 PMID: 36185777

Soltis, T. (2013). Social media impact on virtual shopping. *Senior Honors Theses and Projects*. https://commons.emich.edu/honors/358

Sukrat, S., & Papasratorn, B. (2018). An architectural framework for developing a recommendation system to enhance vendors' capability in C2C social commerce. *Social Network Analysis and Mining, 8*(1), 22. DOI: 10.1007/s13278-018-0500-7

Tran, T. P., Van Solt, M., & Zemanek, J. E.Jr. (2020). How does personalization affect brand relationship in social commerce? A mediation perspective. *Journal of Consumer Marketing, 37*(5), 473–486. DOI: 10.1108/JCM-12-2017-2499

Varghese, M., Raj, S., & Venkatesh, V. (2022). *Influence of AI in human lives* (Version 1). arXiv. DOI: 10.48550/ARXIV.2212.12305

Vazquez, D., Wu, X., Nguyen, B., Kent, A., Gutierrez, A., & Chen, T. (2020). Investigating narrative involvement, parasocial interactions, and impulse buying behaviours within a second screen social commerce context. *International Journal of Information Management, 53*, 102135. DOI: 10.1016/j.ijinfomgt.2020.102135

Wang, P., & Huang, Q. (2023). Digital influencers, social power and consumer engagement in social commerce. *Internet Research, 33*(1), 178–207. DOI: 10.1108/INTR-08-2020-0467

Wang, Y., Wang, J., Yao, T., Li, M., & Wang, X. (2020). How does social support promote consumers' engagement in the social commerce community? The mediating effect of consumer involvement. *Information Processing & Management, 57*(5), 102272. DOI: 10.1016/j.ipm.2020.102272

Wigand, R. T. (1997). Electronic Commerce: Definition, Theory, and Context. *The Information Society, 13*(1), 1–16. DOI: 10.1080/019722497129241

Wongkitrungrueng, A., & Assarut, N. (2020). The role of live streaming in building consumer trust and engagement with social commerce sellers. *Journal of Business Research, 117*, 543–556. DOI: 10.1016/j.jbusres.2018.08.032

Xue, J., Liang, X., Xie, T., & Wang, H. (2020). See now, act now: How to interact with customers to enhance social commerce engagement? *Information & Management, 57*(6), 103324. DOI: 10.1016/j.im.2020.103324

Yu, K.-H., Beam, A. L., & Kohane, I. S. (2018). Artificial intelligence in healthcare. *Nature Biomedical Engineering, 2*(10), 719–731. DOI: 10.1038/s41551-018-0305-z PMID: 31015651

Zhang, H., Lu, Y., Gupta, S., & Zhao, L. (2014). What motivates customers to participate in social commerce? The impact of technological environments and virtual customer experiences. *Information & Management, 51*(8), 1017–1030. DOI: 10.1016/j.im.2014.07.005

Zhang, L., Chen, M., & Zamil, A. M. A. (2023a). Live stream marketing and consumers' purchase intention: An IT affordance perspective using the S-O-R paradigm. *Frontiers in Psychology, 14*, 1069050. DOI: 10.3389/fpsyg.2023.1069050 PMID: 36818116

Zhang, L., Chen, M., & Zamil, A. M. A. (2023b). Live stream marketing and consumers' purchase intention: An IT affordance perspective using the S-O-R paradigm. *Frontiers in Psychology, 14*, 1069050. DOI: 10.3389/fpsyg.2023.1069050 PMID: 36818116

Chapter 4
Influence of Social Media and Virtual Reality on Consumer Behavior

Firnanda Amalia
https://orcid.org/0009-0003-0848-1048
Universitas Esa Unggul, Indonesia

Tiara Zahira
https://orcid.org/0009-0003-8686-5899
Universitas Esa Unggul, Indonesia

Binastya Anggara Sekti
https://orcid.org/0000-0001-5489-4888
Universitas Esa Unggul, Indonesia

ABSTRACT

This chapter delves into the influence of Artificial Intelligence (AI), Social Media, and Virtual Reality (VR) on consumer behavior, highlighting their roles in enhancing personalization and fostering brand loyalty. AI enables businesses to analyze vast amounts of data, providing tailored marketing strategies and predicting consumer preferences. Social media platforms facilitate direct interaction with consumers, strengthening relationships and engagement. VR further immerses consumers in brand experiences, driving purchasing decisions. Ethical considerations regarding data privacy and transparency are discussed, emphasizing the need for responsible use of these technologies. The integration of AI and VR allows brands to create deeply personalized, engaging, and interactive experiences, reshaping consumer

DOI: 10.4018/979-8-3373-2747-1.ch004

interactions and loyalty. As these technologies evolve, they offer brands new ways to meet consumer expectations, ensuring a more dynamic and immersive future for marketing and consumer engagement.

INTRODUCTION

In today's rapidly evolving digital landscape, technologies like Artificial Intelligence (AI), Social Media, and Virtual Reality (VR) have transformed how consumers interact with brands, products, and services. These technologies not only enable new forms of engagement but also significantly influence consumer behavior by enhancing personalization, offering immersive experiences, and creating new avenues for interaction (Eastman & Eastman, 2023). AI plays a pivotal role in analyzing vast amounts of data to generate insights that help businesses understand and anticipate consumer preferences (Omeish et al., 2024). Social media platforms such as Facebook, Instagram, and TikTok have reshaped consumer engagement, offering brands real-time access to vast audiences (Meddah, 2024).

AI powers personalized marketing by tracking user behavior across platforms and tailoring content based on past interactions. It also predicts consumer behavior, allowing businesses to create more effective marketing strategies by forecasting demand and adjusting pricing strategies. This level of personalization has become essential as consumers now expect brands to anticipate their needs (Ao et al., 2023). Social media also enables two-way communication, allowing brands to build stronger relationships with consumers, which increases brand loyalty and trust (Rudeloff, 2023).

Virtual Reality (VR) offers immersive experiences that allow consumers to engage with products and services in lifelike environments. VR has profound implications for industries like retail, real estate, and entertainment, enabling consumers to try products virtually, reducing uncertainty, and enhancing satisfaction (Eastman & Eastman, 2023). VR also has an emotional impact, creating a deeper connection between consumers and brands, fostering long-term loyalty (Omeish et al., 2024).

The convergence of AI, social media, and VR has created a powerful synergy, reshaping consumer behavior. AI personalizes experiences, social media offers vast reach, and VR provides immersive engagement (Meddah, 2024). For example, a consumer might first encounter a product through an AI-driven ad on Instagram, then interact with the product in a VR environment. This integrated experience leads to higher purchase likelihoods, offering brands unprecedented opportunities to engage consumers (Ao et al., 2023).

This integration also enables advanced data collection, where AI tracks consumer interactions with VR environments and social media, offering brands valuable insights to refine marketing strategies and product offerings (Rudeloff, 2023). Continuous data analysis from these touchpoints helps brands stay aligned with evolving consumer preferences, ensuring a dynamic and personalized consumer experience (Eastman & Eastman, 2023). This chapter contributes to the overarching theme of digital transformation in business and consumer behavior by examining how emerging technologies Artificial Intelligence, Virtual Reality, and social media reshape consumer decision-making, marketing strategies, and managerial approaches. By exploring these intersections, the chapter highlights the broader implications of technological innovation for digital-era competitiveness and transformation.

ROLE OF AI IN SHAPING CONSUMER PREFERENCES

Artificial Intelligence (AI) is rapidly transforming the way businesses understand and influence consumer behavior. By harnessing vast amounts of data, AI enables companies to create personalized experiences that align with individual consumer preferences, shaping their purchasing decisions and enhancing customer satisfaction (Dhiman & Bhati, 2025). AI technologies, such as machine learning algorithms, predictive analytics, and natural language processing, allow businesses to anticipate consumer needs, provide tailored recommendations, and deliver real-time solutions that drive brand loyalty (Ao et al., 2023). As AI continues to evolve, its impact on consumer behavior is expected to deepen, offering even more innovative ways to engage consumers and foster long-term relationships (Amin et al., 2025). This subchapter explores the various ways AI is reshaping consumer preferences, from personalized recommendations to cognitive simplification and emotional engagement, highlighting its role in transforming modern marketing strategies.

Figure 1. AI in Shaping Consumer Preferences

Artificial Intelligence (AI) has profoundly transformed the way consumers make decisions, particularly in the realm of personalized recommendations. AI algorithms have become central to the operation of many digital platforms, guiding consumer choices through automated, data-driven processes. E-commerce giants like Amazon employ AI-driven recommendation engines that personalize the user experience by analyzing consumer behavior, browsing history, and past purchase patterns to suggest products (Mustafizul Haque, 2023). This form of personalization enhances the shopping experience, making it more intuitive and aligned with individual preferences, as AI systems not only cater to specific needs but also predict potential desires based on data, creating personalized marketing strategies that resonate more deeply with consumers (Zhang et al., 2026).

The psychological impact of AI on consumer cognition is profound. AI tools continuously learn from vast datasets, fundamentally altering the way consumers perceive and evaluate products. By delivering tailored content, AI systems effectively streamline decision-making, reducing the cognitive load that consumers typically face when confronted with numerous options (Jiao, 2025). This cognitive simplification has proven to be particularly beneficial in the travel and hospitality industries, where AI-generated content (AIGC) is beginning to overshadow traditional user-generated content (UGC) (Zhang et al., 2026). The consistency and reliability of AIGC offer consumers more relevant and trustworthy recommendations, making their decision-making process more efficient (Jiao, 2025).

AI's ability to personalize content plays a pivotal role in fostering a deeper connection between consumers and brands. The continuous refinement of suggestions based on user interactions fosters a sense of relevance, which in turn enhances consumer trust and engagement (Zhang et al., 2026). As consumers interact with AI systems, these platforms become more adept at understanding and anticipating their preferences, leading to an ever-more personalized experience that encourages brand loyalty (Jiao, 2025). The psychological aspect of this personalization is key to the growing relationship between consumers and brands, where tailored suggestions build emotional engagement (Zhang et al., 2026).

In addition to personalizing experiences, AI's predictive analytics capabilities help brands forecast consumer behavior. By analyzing patterns from massive datasets, AI can anticipate shifts in consumer preferences and optimize product availability (Kotp et al., 2025). Predictive models, such as those used to forecast seasonal demand or predict consumer purchasing trends, allow businesses to adjust their marketing strategies in real-time, ensuring that their offerings meet consumer expectations before demand peaks (Zhang et al., 2026). This foresight enables businesses to stay ahead of the competition, enhancing their market responsiveness and ensuring that they can fulfill consumer needs as they arise (Kotp et al., 2025).

The role of AI extends beyond the digital realm, with its influence increasingly evident in physical spaces as well. Virtual Reality (VR), integrated with AI, is transforming industries such as retail and real estate by offering consumers the ability to interact with products in a virtual space before committing to a purchase (Brugada-Ramentol et al., 2022). AI algorithms power these immersive VR experiences, adapting the virtual environment to the preferences of individual users (Zanchini et al., 2025). This personalization enhances emotional engagement, making consumers more likely to follow through with purchases. By offering a fully immersive, interactive experience, AI and VR together create a more engaging consumer journey, allowing businesses to overcome traditional barriers to physical interaction with their products (Brugada-Ramentol et al., 2022).

Furthermore, AI's ability to enhance consumer engagement extends to post-purchase interactions, particularly through customer service channels. AI-driven tools such as chatbots and virtual assistants offer real-time assistance, helping consumers resolve issues and answer questions efficiently (Zanchini et al., 2025). These systems not only streamline customer service processes but also foster stronger emotional connections between brands and consumers by offering consistent, personalized support (Dimitrova et al., 2025). As a result, AI contributes to brand loyalty by ensuring that consumers feel valued and supported throughout their entire journey with a brand (Zanchini et al., 2025).

Despite the numerous advantages AI offers, the increasing reliance on it raises significant ethical concerns, particularly related to data privacy and transparency. The collection of vast amounts of personal data is essential for AI systems to function effectively, but it also makes consumers apprehensive about the security of their information (Dimitrova et al., 2025). As AI continues to track user behavior across various digital platforms, questions about data misuse, security breaches, and algorithmic transparency become critical issues for businesses to address (Mustafizul Haque, 2023). Companies must prioritize consumer trust by ensuring their data collection practices are transparent and ethically sound, particularly as AI becomes more integral to the personalization of consumer experiences (Dimitrova et al., 2025).

In the realm of marketing, ethical concerns are especially prominent in the use of AI by influencers on social media. Influencers often leverage AI to target very specific consumer segments with personalized content, raising questions about the ethical use of personal data and the manipulation of consumer preferences (Mustafizul Haque, 2023). As AI-enabled marketing becomes more sophisticated, businesses must be mindful of the ethical implications of using AI for targeted advertising and the need to maintain consumer trust (Dimitrova et al., 2025). Transparent practices, such as clearly disclosing when content is sponsored or influenced by AI, will be key to maintaining consumer trust in the digital marketplace (Mustafizul Haque, 2023).

As AI continues to shape consumer behavior, businesses must also consider the long-term implications of these technologies on brand loyalty. AI has been shown to deepen consumer relationships with brands by offering more personalized interactions (Zanchini et al., 2025). This personalization extends to customer service, where AI tools help resolve issues more efficiently, reducing wait times and providing personalized support that fosters a deeper emotional connection between consumers and brands (Dimitrova et al., 2025). In this way, AI contributes to long-term customer loyalty by creating a consistent and positive experience for consumers (Zanchini et al., 2025).

Looking to the future, the role of AI in shaping consumer preferences is set to expand. The integration of AI with other emerging technologies, such as blockchain and the Internet of Things (IoT), is expected to further enhance the personalization of consumer experiences (Brugada-Ramentol et al., 2022). AI, combined with virtual and augmented reality (AR/VR), will allow businesses to create even more immersive, interactive shopping environments, blurring the lines between physical and digital retail spaces (Zanchini et al., 2025). As these technologies evolve, consumers will expect even more personalized and relevant interactions with brands (Dimitrova et al., 2025).

The future of AI-driven personalization will demand greater collaboration between businesses, technology providers, and regulatory bodies to ensure that ethical considerations are addressed (Dimitrova et al., 2025). Companies must be proactive in safeguarding consumer privacy and offering transparent, ethical marketing strategies. In doing so, they can ensure that AI continues to enhance consumer engagement without sacrificing trust or privacy (Zanchini et al., 2025). The balance between innovation and ethics will be key to maintaining consumer loyalty in an increasingly AI-driven marketplace (Brugada-Ramentol et al., 2022).

As AI continues to advance, businesses must also remain agile, adapting their strategies to the ever-evolving digital landscape (Brugada-Ramentol et al., 2022). The role of AI in consumer behavior is multifaceted, extending from personalized marketing to predictive analytics and immersive experiences. Understanding these dynamics will be crucial for companies looking to remain competitive as the digital marketplace becomes more sophisticated (Zanchini et al., 2025). By leveraging AI responsibly and transparently, businesses can enhance their engagement with consumers, offering personalized experiences that align with evolving expectations (Dimitrova et al., 2025). These findings suggest that while AI enhances personalization and efficiency, its effectiveness ultimately depends on consumer trust and data transparency indicating that ethical design and responsible data use are as critical as technological capability.

THEORETICAL FRAMEWORK AND RELATED STUDIES

Consumer behavior theories provide essential grounding for understanding how individuals interact with artificial intelligence (AI), virtual reality (VR), and social media–based marketing environments. Classical models such as the Technology Acceptance Model (TAM), Stimulus–Organism–Response (SOR) framework, and Uses and Gratifications Theory (UGT) remain central in explaining technology-mediated consumer responses.

According to the SOR model, external stimuli such as AI-enabled interfaces, influencer-generated content, or immersive VR experiences act as triggers that influence internal cognitive or emotional states (organism), which in turn shape behavioral responses such as trust, engagement, and purchase intention (Dhiman & Bhati, 2025). Recent studies have adapted SOR to explore how AI-powered social media influencers drive consumer trust and brand awareness through interaction, personalization, and trendiness, emphasizing the mediating role of trust in branded posts and brand awareness in shaping purchase intentions (Dhiman & Bhati, 2025).

The Technology Acceptance Model (TAM) complements this by focusing on consumers' perceptions of usefulness and ease of use in adopting AI-based applications. When consumers perceive AI tools as reliable and enhancing their experience, their intention to adopt and engage increases (Eastman & Eastman, 2023). (Eastman & Eastman, 2023)further highlight that AI has evolved from being a mere automation tool to a cognitive partner that shapes attitudes, engagement, and trust in online environments. They propose the TCM–ADO framework (Theory–Context–Method–Antecedents–Decisions–Outcomes) to map how AI-driven personalization and recommendation systems reshape the foundations of consumer behavior.

Integrating these frameworks shows that AI and VR technologies serve as both stimuli and mediating mechanisms that affect consumers' perceptions, emotions, and actions. While (Eastman & Eastman, 2023) emphasize the role of AI in enhancing consumer decision-making and personalization, (Dhiman & Bhati, 2025) demonstrate how AI-generated influencer content modifies emotional engagement and trust mechanisms within social media ecosystems. Together, these studies illustrate an evolving theoretical landscape where consumer–AI interaction is central to understanding digital behavior.

THE ROLE OF SOCIAL MEDIA IN CONSUMER BEHAVIOR

Figure 2. The Role of Social Media in Consumer Behavior

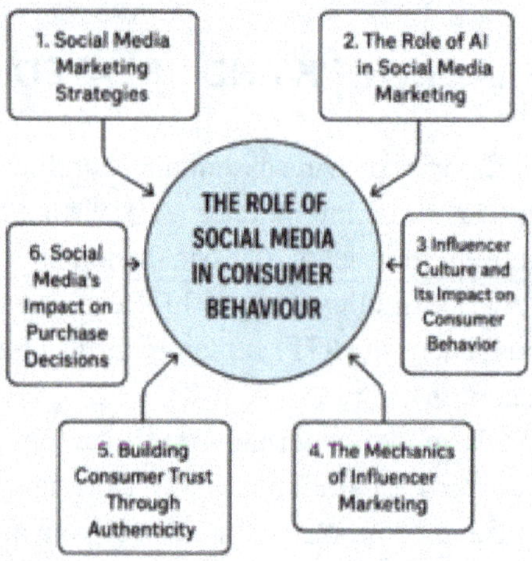

Social media platforms such as Facebook, Instagram, TikTok, and Twitter have drastically changed the way brands interact with consumers. Over the past decade, social media has evolved from a tool for communication and social networking to a powerful marketing platform (Haque et al., 2024). Brands use these platforms not only to promote their products and services but to engage directly with their consumers in real-time (Omeish et al., 2024). The engagement goes beyond mere advertising, as social media has opened new avenues for building relationships, offering customer service, and creating a brand community (Ao et al., 2023). This change in consumer-brand dynamics has fundamentally reshaped the marketing landscape, with businesses increasingly recognizing the power of social media for customer engagement.

Social Media Marketing Strategies

Brands have adapted their marketing strategies to take full advantage of social media's interactive nature. Through targeted ads, content sharing, contests, and influencer partnerships, brands can engage users in a way that traditional media cannot. Social media allows brands to create campaigns that are highly personalized based on the demographic and behavioral data of the users (Omeish et al., 2024). AI technologies have further improved these marketing strategies by providing insights into consumer behavior, helping brands to develop hyper-targeted campaigns that cater specifically to their audience's preferences and needs (Ao et al., 2023). As a result, social media marketing has evolved from broad-based messaging to nuanced, data-driven communication strategies designed to appeal to specific customer segments (Thakur & Aditya, 2024).

The Role of AI in Social Media Marketing

Artificial intelligence (AI) has become an essential tool in social media marketing, helping businesses deliver personalized experiences to users. AI algorithms analyze vast amounts of user data, including browsing history, social interactions, and engagement patterns, to predict consumer behavior and offer tailored recommendations (Omeish et al., 2024). This technology has allowed brands to move beyond generic advertising and deliver content that is more aligned with individual preferences. AI-powered recommendation engines on platforms like Instagram and Facebook allow brands to target users with content that resonates with them, increasing the likelihood of engagement and conversion (Ao et al., 2023). The seamless integration of AI into social media marketing has made it one of the most effective methods for reaching consumers in a meaningful and impactful way (Thakur & Aditya, 2024).

Influencer Culture and Its Impact on Consumer Behavior

One of the most significant developments in social media marketing is the rise of influencers. These individuals, who have built large followings based on their expertise or lifestyle, serve as intermediaries between brands and consumers. The credibility and authenticity of influencers have made them powerful figures in the consumer decision-making process (Ao et al., 2023). Studies show that consumers tend to trust influencer recommendations more than traditional advertisements, as influencers are perceived as more relatable and trustworthy (Haque et al., 2024). The growth of influencer marketing has been fueled by the ability of influencers to engage with their followers in authentic, personal ways. This interaction has created a new form of advertising where consumer behavior is influenced not just by the products themselves but by the personalities that endorse them (Omeish et al., 2024).

The Mechanics of Influencer Marketing

Influencers operate across different niches, from beauty and fashion to technology and lifestyle, and they use social media platforms to share their experiences and endorse products (Haque et al., 2024). Influencer marketing allows brands to tap into these niche audiences in ways that traditional advertising cannot. The endorsement from an influencer feels more organic and less commercial, which is why it has such a strong impact on consumer purchasing decisions (Ao et al., 2023). This form of marketing thrives on the trust that influencers have built with their audiences. When influencers promote a product that aligns with their personal brand and values, it feels like a genuine recommendation to their followers (Omeish et al., 2024). This trust is the key to influencer marketing's success, as consumers are more likely to act on recommendations from people they view as credible and authentic (Haque et al., 2024).

Building Consumer Trust Through Authenticity

The concept of authenticity is crucial in social media marketing. Consumers have become increasingly savvy and can easily identify when content feels inauthentic or when an influencer is promoting products for the sake of financial gain (Ao et al., 2023). The authenticity of the influencer and their connection to the product they promote play a significant role in shaping consumer trust. If an influencer's endorsement feels forced or disconnected from their personal brand, it can lead to a loss of credibility, which undermines the effectiveness of the campaign (Thakur & Aditya, 2024). Brands that work with influencers who are genuine and consistent in their messaging are more likely to build lasting relationships with their audience, fostering long-term trust and loyalty (Omeish et al., 2024).

Social Media's Impact on Purchase Decisions

The influence of social media extends beyond engagement into actual purchase decisions. Research shows that a significant portion of consumers' purchasing decisions are now influenced by social media. Platforms like Instagram and Facebook allow users to view products in real-time and often feature the ability to make purchases directly through the app, a trend known as social commerce (Haque et al., 2024). Influencer posts, product reviews, and user-generated content all play key roles in driving consumer decisions. When consumers see products being used and recommended by influencers or peers, it enhances their confidence in the product, encouraging them to make a purchase (Ao et al., 2023). This phenomenon illustrates how social media has become a central hub for not just marketing but also e-commerce (Omeish et al., 2024). Recent studies have expanded the understanding of social media's role by linking it to immersive and AI-driven marketing environments. For instance, (Tang et al., 2025) highlight how metaverse marketing is redefining brand engagement and pre-purchase behavior, demonstrating that usability and habit significantly influence consumer preference between social media and immersive spaces. Similarly, (Eastman & Eastman, 2023) emphasizes the growing application of AI-driven consumer segmentation in social media marketing, enabling hyper-personalized content that strengthens brand–consumer trust and predictive targeting. These insights illustrate how the boundaries between traditional social media marketing and immersive digital ecosystems are increasingly blurred, marking a transition toward AI-augmented engagement.

VIRTUAL REALITY: A NEW ERA OF CONSUMER INTERACTION

Figure 3. Virtual Reality

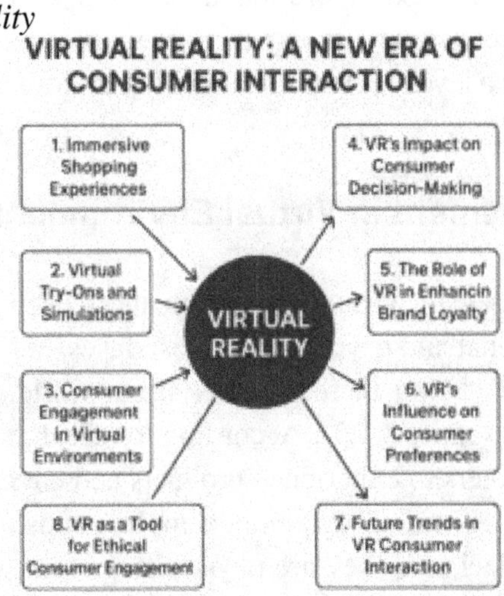

Immersive Shopping Experiences

Virtual Reality (VR) is revolutionizing consumer experiences by creating immersive, interactive environments. In industries like retail, VR offers a unique opportunity for consumers to engage with products in a simulated space before making a purchase decision (Leite & Vieira, 2025). This experience is far beyond traditional online shopping or in-store browsing, allowing consumers to explore products as if they were physically present (Aufenanger et al., 2025). VR enhances the sense of immersion by providing multisensory interactions such as sight, touch, and sound that simulate real-world shopping environments. Studies have shown that VR not only captivates attention but also strengthens memory retention, making it an effective tool for product demonstrations and consumer education (Liao, 2025).

Virtual Try-Ons and Simulations

Virtual try-ons represent one of the most significant breakthroughs in VR consumer interaction. The fashion and beauty industries, in particular, have embraced VR to enable consumers to try on clothes, makeup, and accessories without physically wearing them (Aufenanger et al., 2025). Through facial recognition and body mapping technologies, consumers can see how products look on their virtual avatars in real time (Liao, 2025). This type of VR experience makes online shopping more interactive and less risky, as customers can simulate how the items will appear in their real-life context before making a purchase (Leite & Vieira, 2025). Moreover, VR allows consumers to experiment with different styles, colors, and combinations, offering a level of customization that traditional fitting rooms cannot provide (Liao, 2025).

Consumer Engagement in Virtual Environments

Consumer engagement in virtual environments is deeply influenced by VR's ability to evoke emotional and psychological responses. VR's immersive qualities, such as the illusion of "being there" in the virtual world, significantly enhance emotional engagement (Liao, 2025). According to research, VR stimulates empathy by allowing consumers to experience products and environments from diverse perspectives (Aufenanger et al., 2025). For example, a consumer exploring a virtual travel destination can feel as if they are physically present, which intensifies their emotional connection to the destination and, consequently, the likelihood of making a booking (Leite & Vieira, 2025). In addition, VR's interactive nature encourages consumers to participate in experiences rather than passively consume content (Aufenanger et al., 2025).

VR's Impact on Consumer Decision-Making

The use of VR in consumer decision-making is particularly significant because it influences both the cognitive and emotional aspects of buying. VR not only helps consumers make more informed decisions by providing an interactive, experiential understanding of products but also evokes emotions that can drive purchasing behavior (Leite & Vieira, 2025). As consumers immerse themselves in virtual environments, their emotional responses, such as excitement or satisfaction, can influence their final decision (Liao, 2025). This dynamic is supported by research showing that emotional engagement in VR can improve memory retention, which plays a role in brand recall and purchase intent (Aufenanger et al., 2025). Furthermore, VR simulations can increase consumer confidence in their decisions (Leite & Vieira, 2025). The understanding of consumer adoption of VR has evolved in recent literature. (Hennig-Thurau et al., 2025) introduce the concept of *metaverse trials*, showing that direct experiential exposure significantly enhances consumers' intention to use VR technologies, although purchase intention may remain moderated by perceived cost and trial satisfaction.

The Role of VR in Enhancing Brand Loyalty

Brand loyalty is closely tied to consumer experience, and VR significantly impacts this aspect of consumer behavior. By offering immersive experiences that are not only entertaining but also informative, brands can foster stronger emotional connections with their consumers (Aufenanger et al., 2025). When brands engage consumers through VR, they go beyond transactional interactions and create memorable, positive experiences (Liao, 2025). This emotional bond can lead to increased customer retention and advocacy. For instance, luxury brands are leveraging VR to give consumers exclusive access to events or product launches, allowing them to experience the brand in a way that feels personal and VIP (Leite & Vieira, 2025).

VR's Influence on Consumer Preferences

As VR continues to evolve, its ability to influence consumer preferences becomes increasingly evident. Research has shown that VR experiences can alter consumer perceptions of products and services (Liao, 2025). For example, by experiencing a product in a virtual environment, consumers can gain a more accurate and comprehensive understanding of its value. This helps consumers form preferences based on a combination of emotional, cognitive, and sensory inputs rather than relying solely on traditional marketing or product descriptions (Leite & Vieira, 2025). Moreover, the flexibility of VR allows brands to continuously adapt and refine consumer experiences, ensuring that they align with evolving consumer preferences (Aufenanger et al., 2025).

Future Trends in VR Consumer Interaction

Looking ahead, VR is expected to play an even larger role in shaping consumer behavior. As the technology improves and becomes more accessible, its integration into everyday consumer experiences will deepen (Aufenanger et al., 2025). Future VR systems will likely offer even more advanced features, such as improved haptic feedback, enhanced visual fidelity, and real-time interactive simulations that further blur the lines between the digital and physical worlds (Leite & Vieira, 2025). These advancements will open up new opportunities for businesses to engage with consumers in innovative ways, such as providing virtual tours, interactive shopping experiences, and personalized product showcases (Liao, 2025).

VR as a Tool for Ethical Consumer Engagement

As VR's potential grows, its use also raises important questions about privacy and ethical marketing practices. The immersive nature of VR means that brands can collect detailed consumer data, including emotional responses and behavioral patterns (Liao, 2025). This raises concerns about consumer privacy and the potential for manipulation. As such, brands must ensure that they use VR technology responsibly, being transparent about the data they collect and how it is used (Leite & Vieira, 2025). Ethical considerations must be a central focus as VR becomes more integrated into consumer interactions (Aufenanger et al., 2025).

EXPLORING THE FUTURE OF CONSUMER EXPERIENCES

The intersection of Artificial Intelligence (AI) and Virtual Reality (VR) is revolutionizing consumer experiences, enabling businesses to provide highly personalized and immersive services. As consumer expectations evolve, companies are increasingly relying on these technologies to deliver tailored experiences that go beyond traditional marketing strategies. This section explores the role of AI and VR in personalizing consumer journeys, supported by real-world case studies and projections for future trends. Collectively, these studies reveal that the success of VR in marketing is not determined solely by its immersive capability but also by consumers' perceptions of authenticity, usability, and ethical boundaries, which together define how virtual experiences translate into real-world consumer loyalty.

Figure 4. Exploring the Future of Consumer Experiences

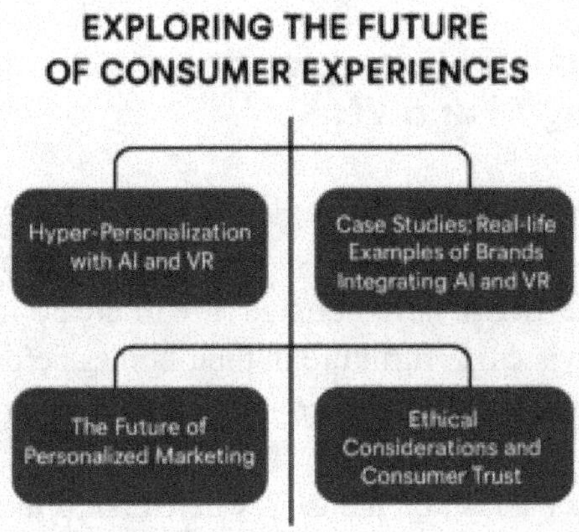

Hyper-Personalization with AI and VR

Hyper-personalization, the practice of using AI and VR to create personalized consumer experiences, has become a focal point of modern marketing. AI plays a central role in this process by analyzing vast amounts of consumer data to identify patterns and preferences, allowing companies to predict future behavior and tailor their offerings accordingly (Timimi et al., 2025). VR, on the other hand, enhances this personalization by providing consumers with immersive and interactive environments that are shaped based on their unique preferences and needs (Eastman & Eastman, 2023).

Through AI, businesses can create real-time, personalized content recommendations, dynamically adjusting product offerings, marketing messages, and even customer service responses to match individual consumer profiles (Timimi et al., 2025). For instance, AI-powered recommendation engines can suggest products based on past purchases, browsing habits, and demographic information, optimizing the consumer's experience with minimal input required from the user (Leite & Vieira, 2025).

When combined with VR, this personalized approach becomes even more powerful. VR enables consumers to engage in realistic simulations of products or services, such as trying on clothes virtually or test-driving a car in a simulated environment (Aufenanger et al., 2025). AI enhances these experiences by analyzing real-time consumer interactions within the VR environment, allowing the system to adjust scenarios or recommend products dynamically based on consumer preferences, further increasing engagement and satisfaction (Eastman & Eastman, 2023).

Case Studies: Real-life Examples of Brands Integrating AI and VR

Several industries are already leveraging the power of AI and VR to enhance personalization, with notable examples illustrating their potential. In the retail sector, companies like IKEA have adopted VR to create immersive showrooms where customers can visualize furniture in their homes before making a purchase. AI integration allows the platform to recommend additional products based on user preferences, purchase history, and room size (Leite & Vieira, 2025).

Another example is the fashion industry, where brands like Nike and Gucci have implemented virtual try-ons using VR. Customers can virtually try on clothes and shoes, and AI algorithms analyze their body shape and previous purchases to suggest the best options, creating a seamless, personalized shopping experience (Liao, 2025). This level of personalization is particularly valuable in industries like fashion, where fit and style preferences are highly individual (Aufenanger et al., 2025).

Additionally, in the automotive industry, brands such as Audi and BMW have developed virtual showrooms that allow customers to configure cars in a VR environment, while AI analyzes customer preferences and provides tailored suggestions for vehicle configurations, features, and financing options (Eastman & Eastman, 2023). These case studies demonstrate how AI and VR can be integrated into the consumer experience to create highly personalized interactions that not only drive sales but also build stronger consumer relationships (Leite & Vieira, 2025).

The Future of Personalized Marketing

Looking ahead, AI and VR will continue to evolve and redefine personalized marketing. AI's predictive capabilities will improve, offering even more precise personalization based on increasingly sophisticated algorithms and a broader range of data inputs, such as real-time behavior, emotional cues, and biometric data (Timimi et al., 2025). Meanwhile, VR technology will become more immersive and accessible, enhancing the consumer experience through more realistic simulations and deeper engagement (Liao, 2025).

As AI becomes more adept at understanding consumer preferences, the potential for creating seamless, hyper-personalized experiences will expand across various industries. For example, AI could analyze consumer emotions through facial recognition or voice tone, enabling businesses to adjust their marketing approaches in real-time, thereby creating even more personalized interactions (Aufenanger et al., 2025). VR, meanwhile, will continue to offer consumers the ability to explore new products and experiences in a fully immersive environment, blurring the line between digital and physical interactions (Timimi et al., 2025).

In addition to these developments, the integration of AI and VR with other emerging technologies, such as Augmented Reality (AR) and the Internet of Things (IoT), will further enhance personalization efforts. For instance, AR can overlay digital elements onto the physical world, allowing consumers to interact with products in a more dynamic way, while IoT devices can collect and analyze consumer data from everyday interactions to provide even more personalized experiences (Leite & Vieira, 2025).

Ethical Considerations and Consumer Trust

Despite the immense potential of AI and VR in personalizing consumer experiences, these technologies raise significant ethical concerns, particularly around data privacy, security, and transparency. The use of AI often requires the collection and analysis of vast amounts of personal data, which can be perceived as invasive if not handled properly (Timimi et al., 2025). Businesses must ensure that they comply with data protection regulations and are transparent with consumers about how their data is being used (Liao, 2025) .

Moreover, the use of AI in personalized marketing must be carefully managed to avoid algorithmic bias, ensuring that recommendations and experiences are fair and do not discriminate against certain groups of consumers. As AI systems become more complex, there is also a growing concern about the lack of transparency in how decisions are made, leading to calls for greater accountability and explainability in AI models (Eastman & Eastman, 2023).

VR, too, presents ethical challenges, particularly in terms of its ability to influence consumer emotions and behavior. As VR experiences become more immersive, they could potentially manipulate consumer perceptions in ways that may not always be ethical (Leite & Vieira, 2025). For example, VR could be used to create highly emotional or persuasive experiences that pressure consumers into making decisions they might not otherwise make in a non-immersive environment. As such, it is crucial for businesses to use VR responsibly, ensuring that consumers are fully informed and that their experiences are not unduly influenced (Aufenanger et al., 2025).

PRIVACY CONCERNS IN THE AGE OF AI AND VR

Data Privacy Issues

As AI and VR technologies continue to evolve, they introduce significant challenges concerning consumer privacy. AI's ability to analyze vast amounts of personal data to personalize services raises concerns about the potential misuse of sensitive information. The combination of AI and VR, which often requires real-time data collection to create immersive experiences, intensifies these concerns. Consumers may unknowingly share personal information through continuous interactions within VR environments, and this can lead to data being used without their explicit consent (Dhiman & Bhati, 2025). Moreover, AI's role in aggregating and processing consumer data across various platforms such as social media and e-commerce raises the risk of creating detailed consumer profiles that may be exploited (Timimi et al., 2025). In particular, sensitive data such as biometric information, preferences, and behavioral patterns can be exploited for targeted marketing and consumer manipulation (Omeish et al., 2024).

Consumer Consent and Control

A crucial issue in the intersection of AI, VR, and privacy is the extent to which consumers have control over their data. With AI systems often gathering data silently in the background, consumers may not be fully aware of the information being collected or how it is being used (Timimi et al., 2025). VR environments can exacerbate this problem, as they often require continuous tracking of user behavior to deliver personalized experiences. In such cases, consumers may not always be presented with an opportunity to provide informed consent before engaging with these technologies (Omeish et al., 2024). Furthermore, many consumers may not realize the long-term implications of sharing personal data, leading to a lack of agency in how their information is handled (Yin et al., 2025). Transparency and control mechanisms are needed to ensure that users are fully informed and empowered to manage their data across AI and VR platforms (Dhiman & Bhati, 2025).

Ethical Implications of Data Collection

The ethical implications of data collection in AI and VR are multifaceted, encompassing concerns around fairness, consent, and the potential for exploitation. AI systems that collect and analyze consumer data can sometimes make decisions based on biased or incomplete data sets, which may lead to discriminatory practices in marketing and service delivery (Dhiman & Bhati, 2025). VR, being a highly immersive environment, can further manipulate consumers' emotional states, influencing their decision-making processes in ways that may not be ethically sound (Omeish et al., 2024). Additionally, the extensive use of AI-powered recommendation systems in platforms like social media or e-commerce raises concerns about algorithmic transparency. Without proper regulations, these systems can perpetuate inequalities by favoring certain groups over others based on biased algorithms (Timimi et al., 2025). These practices are particularly concerning in sectors like retail and social media marketing, where consumer choices are increasingly influenced by automated systems that lack human oversight (Omeish et al., 2024).

Algorithmic Transparency and Accountability

One of the major ethical concerns in AI and VR is the transparency of the algorithms that power these systems. Consumers often interact with AI-driven systems without fully understanding how their data is being processed and used to shape their experiences (Velasco et al., 2024). In the case of VR, where personal actions and behaviors are continuously tracked, consumers may have little to no awareness of the data being collected or its impact on the content they see and interact with (Omeish et al., 2024). Ethical business practices require that companies disclose how algorithms function, what data is being collected, and how decisions are made. Transparency in AI systems will help consumers make informed choices about their data, fostering trust and encouraging responsible data use (Timimi et al., 2025). Additionally, accountability mechanisms need to be in place to ensure that businesses are held responsible for how AI systems influence consumer behavior and the consequences of potential data breaches (Zhao & Wu, 2025).

IMPACT OF SOCIAL MEDIA ON BRAND LOYALTY

Building Brand Loyalty through Social Media

Social media has become an essential tool for brands to foster long-term relationships with consumers. Unlike traditional marketing methods, social media allows for continuous, two-way communication between brands and their audience. Brands can engage with consumers through comments, likes, shares, and direct messages, creating a sense of belonging and emotional connection (Ao et al., 2023). Authentic interactions and personalized experiences help brands build trust and increase customer retention over (Dhiman & Bhati, 2025). As consumers become more invested in brands that reflect their values, social media provides a platform for brands to showcase their identity and establish lasting loyalty (Amin et al., 2025).

Social Media Communities and Brand Advocacy

Social media communities play a pivotal role in brand loyalty by fostering deeper connections between consumers and brands. These communities allow consumers to engage with each other and share their brand experiences, which can lead to the development of brand advocacy (Dhiman & Bhati, 2025). Brand advocates often help to amplify the brand's message, leading to organic word-of-mouth promotion (Amin et al., 2025). Through these online interactions, consumers feel a sense of belonging, which can enhance their emotional attachment to the brand (Ao et al., 2023). This sense of community strengthens brand loyalty as consumers are more likely to continue engaging with brands that make them feel valued and part of something larger (Haque et al., 2024).

Long-Term Customer Engagement Strategies

Creating long-term brand loyalty through social media requires ongoing engagement strategies. Brands must consistently engage with their audience by posting relevant content, responding to comments, and initiating conversations (Ao et al., 2023). Regular interaction and genuine communication help strengthen the brand-consumer relationship over time, making it more likely that consumers will remain loyal (Dhiman & Bhati, 2025). Brands also need to be adaptable, staying current with consumer preferences and social media trends to ensure they remain relevants (Amin et al., 2025). Social media is a dynamic environment, and brands that fail to engage continuously risk losing consumer interest to competitors (Ao et al., 2023).

Social Media as a Catalyst for Emotional Loyalty

Emotional loyalty is another aspect of brand loyalty that social media can significantly impact. Through storytelling, behind-the-scenes content, and user-generated content, brands can create a deeper emotional connection with consumers (Dhiman & Bhati, 2025). This connection goes beyond product purchases, fostering a sense of belonging to the brand. When consumers feel emotionally invested in a brand, they are more likely to remain loyal even in the face of competition (Ao et al., 2023). Social media enables brands to tell their stories in a way that resonates with consumers on a personal level, which helps deepen the emotional connection and encourage long-term loyalty (Amin et al., 2025).

The Role of Influencer Marketing in Brand Loyalty

Influencer marketing has become a cornerstone of social media strategies aimed at increasing brand loyalty. By partnering with influencers who have established trust with their followers, brands can amplify their messages in an authentic and relatable way (Amin et al., 2025). Influencers create content that resonates with their audience, driving engagement and enhancing consumer trust (Dhiman & Bhati, 2025). Moreover, influencers can help brands reach new demographics, particularly those who are more likely to engage with content that feels personal and credible (Ao et al., 2023). However, it is important for brands to carefully select influencers who align with their values to avoid undermining the authenticity of their message (Amin et al., 2025).

Measuring Social Media's Impact on Brand Advocacy

To understand the true impact of social media on brand loyalty, brands must also measure its influence on brand advocacy. Consumers who are deeply engaged with a brand on social media are more likely to advocate for the brand, sharing their positive experiences with others. Measuring the frequency and reach of brand advocacy on social media helps brands assess the effectiveness of their engagement strategies (Ao et al., 2023). By tracking how often consumers share content, recommend products, and engage with the brand's messaging, brands can gain valuable insights into the strength of their loyalty base (Amin et al., 2025).

The Influence of Social Media and VR on Consumer Purchase Decisions

Table 1. How AI, Social Media, and VR Influence Consumer Behavior

Mechanism	Description
Social Proof and Peer Influence	Social media leverages peer recommendations and reviews to guide consumer decisions, creating trust and credibility.
Psychological Triggers in VR	VR environments create immersive experiences that trigger emotional responses, enhancing desire, and motivation to purchase.
Real-Time Interaction and Instant Gratification	Real-time interactions and immediate feedback on social media and VR platforms encourage impulsive buying behavior.
Influencer Marketing on Social Media	Influencers with substantial followings impact consumer behavior

continued on following page

Table 1. Continued

Mechanism	Description
Social Media and Emotional Connections	Emotional connections with brands on social media platforms can strengthen loyalty and drive purchase decisions.
VR as a Virtual Test Drive	VR allows consumers to virtually try products or services, enhancing their engagement and increasing purchase intent.
Peer Recommendations on Social Platforms	Peer recommendations, especially through platforms like Instagram and Facebook, enhance brand trust and encourage buying.

Social Proof and Peer Influence

Social media platforms have become key drivers of consumer purchase decisions by leveraging social proof and peer influence. Consumers often rely on the recommendations and reviews of their peers before making purchasing decisions, with platforms like Instagram, Facebook, and TikTok serving as major influencers in this process (Dhiman & Bhati, 2025). Positive reviews and user-generated content on these platforms can create a sense of trust and authenticity that traditional advertising often lacks (Amin et al., 2025). This social proof, combined with the visibility of products through user endorsements, can significantly shape purchasing behavior, as consumers tend to follow the choices of those they perceive as similar to themselves (Ao et al., 2023).

Psychological Triggers in VR

Virtual Reality (VR) takes the psychological influence on purchasing decisions a step further by immersing consumers in realistic, interactive environments. The psychological effects of VR experiences can stimulate a desire to purchase by creating an emotional connection with the product or service being showcased (Haque et al., 2024). The sense of presence and immersion that VR provides enhances the consumer's perceived value of the product, making them more likely to consider it as part of their buying process (Dhiman & Bhati, 2025). VR also uses psychological triggers, such as the "scarcity effect" or "fear of missing out" (FOMO), by creating limited-time offers or exclusive experiences that prompt consumers to act quickly (Amin et al., 2025).

Real-Time Interaction and Instant Gratification

Both social media and VR facilitate real-time interaction, which plays a critical role in influencing consumer purchase decisions. Social media platforms enable consumers to interact with brands, ask questions, and receive immediate responses, fostering a sense of instant gratification. This quick feedback loop makes consumers feel heard and valued, encouraging faster purchasing decisions (Amin et al., 2025). Similarly, VR experiences often provide instant access to products or services, allowing consumers to make quick, impulsive decisions after experiencing the product in a simulated environment (Dhiman & Bhati, 2025). This combination of real-time engagement and immediate rewards enhances the consumer's likelihood of acting on their impulses and making a purchase (Ao et al., 2023).

Social Media and Peer Recommendations

Peer recommendations have always played a significant role in influencing consumer behavior, and social media has amplified this effect. Platforms like Twitter and YouTube allow consumers to share their experiences with products, while influencers provide recommendations that are seen as authentic and relatable. This form of social validation encourages followers to trust the influencer's opinion and can lead to increased purchase intentions (Ao et al., 2023). Research indicates that consumers are more likely to make a purchase when they see their peers or trusted influencers recommending a product, demonstrating the power of peer influence in the digital age (Dhiman & Bhati, 2025).

Impact of Social Media on Consumer Behavior

The role of social media in shaping consumer behavior is further exemplified by the emotional connection that brands create through personalized content. Social media platforms allow brands to curate content that resonates with their audience's lifestyle and values, creating a deeper emotional bond with consumers (Haque et al., 2024). These emotional connections can significantly influence purchase decisions, as consumers are more likely to buy from brands that they feel personally connected to (Ao et al., 2023). By crafting tailored messages and experiences, brands on social media can reinforce loyalty and increase the likelihood of repeat purchases (Amin et al., 2025).

Psychological Effects of VR on Purchase Decisions

VR experiences stimulate consumer desires to purchase by appealing to the senses and emotions in a way that traditional marketing cannot. The ability to interact with products in a fully immersive environment triggers psychological responses that heighten the perceived value of the product (Dhiman & Bhati, 2025). When consumers can visualize themselves using a product in a virtual world, the experience makes the desire to purchase feel more tangible (Amin et al., 2025). This heightened emotional engagement in VR settings is often more persuasive than mere visual or textual descriptions, encouraging consumers to take the next step and complete the transaction (Ao et al., 2023).

Impulsive Purchases and Consumer Technology Use

The integration of social media and VR technologies has made it easier for consumers to make impulsive purchasing decisions. The immediacy and ease of purchasing directly through social media platforms, combined with the immersive experiences provided by VR, create a perfect storm for impulsive buying (Dhiman & Bhati, 2025). These technologies reduce the friction involved in making a purchase by providing real-time interaction, personalized recommendations, and immediate access to products (Amin et al., 2025). As a result, consumers are more likely to act on their impulses and make purchases that they might not have considered if given more time or information (Ao et al., 2023).

EMERGING TRENDS IN CONSUMER BEHAVIOR THROUGH AI, SOCIAL MEDIA, AND VR

The rapid advancement of technologies such as Artificial Intelligence (AI), Virtual Reality (VR), and social media is reshaping the way consumers engage with brands and make purchasing decisions. As these technologies converge, they create a more immersive and personalized consumer experience, offering brands innovative ways to connect with their audiences (Amin et al., 2025). AI is revolutionizing marketing by predicting consumer preferences and providing personalized recommendations, while VR is redefining the shopping experience by enabling consumers to interact with products in virtual environments (Eastman & Eastman, 2023). Social media platforms, on the other hand, play a pivotal role in connecting brands with consumers in real-time, fostering engagement and loyalty (Timimi et al., 2025). As these technologies continue to evolve, they promise to offer even more dynamic and tailored consumer experiences, pushing the boundaries of traditional marketing strategies and setting the stage for the future of digital shopping and consumer behavior (Liao, 2025).

Future Trends

The next decade promises a rapid evolution of technologies that will continue to shape consumer behavior. With the rise of the Metaverse, AI and VR are expected to become more integrated, creating immersive digital environments where consumers can engage with brands in entirely new ways (Liao, 2025). These advancements are anticipated to lead to further personalization in marketing, allowing brands to deliver tailored experiences in real-time based on consumer behavior within virtual spaces (Timimi et al., 2025). As VR technology becomes more accessible, consumers will be able to engage with products in simulated environments, which will redefine traditional shopping experiences (Eastman & Eastman, 2023).

AI in Metaverse

The integration of AI within VR environments, particularly in the Metaverse, will dramatically change the future of digital shopping. AI will enable virtual environments to adapt to consumer preferences, enhancing the sense of immersion and personalization within these spaces (Liao, 2025). Virtual assistants powered by AI will guide consumers through the Metaverse, offering real-time recommendations and personalized shopping experiences based on detailed behavioral insights (Timimi et al., 2025). This convergence of AI and VR will not only influence how consumers shop but also how they interact with brands, creating an entirely new market for digital goods and services (Eastman & Eastman, 2023).

Ethical AI and VR Innovations

As AI and VR technologies continue to advance, ethical considerations will play a critical role in their development and implementation. The use of AI in consumer behavior analysis raises concerns about data privacy and algorithmic bias. Companies must ensure that AI systems operate transparently and respect consumer privacy by providing clear guidelines on data usage and implementing robust data protection measures (Ao et al., 2023). Moreover, the immersive nature of VR presents new ethical challenges related to consumer autonomy and manipulation. As these technologies become more sophisticated, businesses will need to carefully balance innovation with ethical responsibility (Liao, 2025).

Consumer Behavior in the Digital Age

The integration of AI and VR is not only changing how consumers interact with products but also how they make decisions. With real-time interactions and immediate access to virtual experiences, consumers are increasingly making quicker and more impulsive purchasing decisions (Eastman & Eastman, 2023). AI-driven recommendations and the ability to try products virtually before purchase are creating an environment where the path from consideration to purchase is shorter and more fluid (Liao, 2025). This trend will likely continue as AI and VR technologies become more embedded in everyday life, influencing consumer behavior across various industries (Timimi et al., 2025).

The Future of Consumer Engagement

As AI, VR, and social media continue to converge, brands will have even more powerful tools to engage with consumers on a personal level. The use of AI to predict consumer behavior, combined with the immersive experiences offered by VR, will provide brands with an unprecedented ability to deliver hyper-targeted marketing (Eastman & Eastman, 2023). Additionally, social media will continue to serve as a platform for these technologies to interact with consumers in real-time, creating a dynamic and personalized experience that is both interactive and transactional (Liao, 2025). The ongoing evolution of these technologies will undoubtedly lead to further shifts in consumer expectations and behavior, with a greater demand for personalized, instant, and immersive experiences (Timimi et al., 2025).

STRATEGIC RECOMMENDATIONS FOR MARKETERS AND BRANDS

In today's rapidly evolving digital landscape, marketers must strategically integrate emerging technologies like Artificial Intelligence (AI), social media, and Virtual Reality (VR) to stay competitive. These technologies offer vast opportunities for brands to create personalized, immersive, and engaging consumer experiences that drive loyalty and conversions (Amin et al., 2025). As AI and VR continue to reshape consumer behavior, understanding how to effectively combine these technologies with social media is crucial for businesses aiming to meet consumer expectations and remain relevant (Liao, 2025). This subchapter provides actionable recommendations for marketers on how to leverage these technologies to optimize marketing strategies, build ethical frameworks, and future-proof their approaches to consumer engagement in the ever-changing digital world (MC et al., 2024).

Integrating AI, Social Media, and VR for Marketing Success

Marketers seeking to leverage AI, social media, and VR must understand how these technologies can work in tandem to create a seamless and immersive consumer experience. By integrating AI into social media marketing, brands can personalize their messaging, reaching consumers with relevant content based on their behaviors and preferences (Amin et al., 2025). VR can enhance this by offering interactive and engaging experiences, such as virtual product trials or immersive brand storytelling, which further strengthen the connection between the consumer and the brand (Liao, 2025). Additionally, combining AI's data-driven insights with social media's wide reach can help marketers optimize their targeting strategies, ensuring they are not only engaging but also driving conversions (Ao et al., 2023).

Creating Ethical Marketing Strategies

As AI and VR continue to shape marketing practices, businesses must also be mindful of the ethical considerations involved. Ensuring transparency in data usage is critical for maintaining consumer trust, especially in light of privacy concerns surrounding AI's ability to analyze large datasets (Ao et al., 2023). Marketers need to create clear policies that inform consumers about what data is collected and how it will be used. Moreover, as VR creates highly immersive experiences, it's essential for marketers to avoid manipulative tactics that may influence consumer behavior without their knowledge (Liao, 2025). Striking a balance between leveraging AI and VR for effective marketing while respecting consumer rights will be key to maintaining long-term customer loyalty (Amin et al., 2025).

Future-Proofing Marketing Strategies

As emerging technologies continue to evolve, businesses must prepare for the future by adapting their marketing strategies to keep pace with these changes. This includes staying up to date with the latest developments in AI, social media, and VR to ensure that marketing campaigns remain relevant and effective (Amin et al., 2025). Marketers should invest in learning about consumer behavior in digital spaces and leverage AI to understand how emerging technologies will influence future purchasing patterns (Liao, 2025). Moreover, by adopting flexible marketing strategies that can easily integrate new technologies, businesses can maintain a competitive edge and future-proof their marketing approaches (Ao et al., 2023).

Evolving Consumer Behavior

Understanding how consumer behavior is evolving in response to AI, social media, and VR is crucial for marketers looking to stay ahead of the curve. As consumers become more accustomed to personalized experiences powered by AI, they will expect brands to deliver relevant, timely content across all platforms (Liao, 2025). VR, on the other hand, offers consumers a more hands-on approach to interacting with brands, which could shift expectations towards more immersive and interactive brand engagements (Ao et al., 2023). Marketers must be agile, adapting to these shifts by not only investing in technology but also understanding the changing psychological and emotional triggers that drive consumer (Amin et al., 2025).

Ensuring Long-Term Engagement

To ensure sustained consumer engagement, marketers must combine the power of AI, social media, and VR in ways that resonate emotionally with consumers. By leveraging AI to deliver personalized content and experiences, and using VR to immerse consumers in brand narratives, marketers can create deep, meaningful connections with their audiences (Amin et al., 2025). Social media platforms further amplify these connections by enabling direct interaction with consumers, allowing brands to build communities around shared values (Ao et al., 2023). Long-term success will depend on a brand's ability to provide consistent, authentic, and valuable experiences that adapt to evolving consumer expectations in the digital age (Liao, 2025). The global adoption of AI, social media, and VR in consumer engagement varies significantly across regions, reflecting differences in infrastructure, digital literacy, and market maturity. In developed markets such as the United States, Japan, and South Korea, adoption is largely driven by consumer convenience, technological integration, and personalization at scale (Hennig-Thurau et al., 2025). Conversely, in emerging markets particularly within Southeast Asia and Indonesia AI and VR adoption is influenced by affordability, accessibility, and digital literacy gaps (Omeish et al., 2024). For instance, local e-commerce platforms like Tokopedia and Shopee have effectively leveraged AI personalization to enhance recommendation systems and improve user engagement, showing that contextually adapted innovation can yield significant results. In the social media domain, collaborations such as Sociolla's TikTok Shop campaigns demonstrate how influencer-driven strategies can convert engagement into sales within local cultural contexts. On a global scale, brands like IKEA have integrated VR showrooms to allow consumers to virtually explore and customize their spaces an approach that highlights how immersive technology enhances trust and purchase confidence across markets (Leite & Vieira, 2025). These cases collectively suggest that while advanced markets focus on refinement and integration, developing regions emphasize adaptation and accessibility, underscoring the importance for marketers to balance global innovation with local relevance in their strategic planning.

REFERENCES

Amin, M., Gohar, M., & Ali, I. (2025). Impact of digital transformation on SME's marketing performance: Role of social media and market turbulence. *Discover Sustainability, 6*(1), 378. Advance online publication. DOI: 10.1007/s43621-025-01228-3

Ao, L., Bansal, R., Pruthi, N., & Khaskheli, M. B. (2023). *Impact of Social Media Influencers on Customer Engagement and Purchase Intention : A Meta - Analysis.*

Aufenanger, S., Bastian, J., Bastos, G., Castelhano, M., Dias-Ferreira, C., Fokides, E., Gavalas, D., Kasapakis, V., Agelada, A., Kostas, A., Koutromanos, G., Makrides, G., Morgado, L., Pedrosa, D., Szemberg, T., Sofos, A., & Szpond, J. (2025). Immersive virtual reality learning environments for higher education: A student acceptance study. *Computers and Education: X Reality, 7*(December 2024). DOI: 10.1016/j.cexr.2025.100105

Brugada-Ramentol, V., Bozorgzadeh, A., & Jalali, H. (2022). Enhance VR: A Multisensory Approach to Cognitive Training and Monitoring. *Frontiers in Digital Health, 4*(June), 1–7. DOI: 10.3389/fdgth.2022.916052 PMID: 35721794

Dhiman, R., & Bhati, N. S. (2025). When AI meets influencers: Role of AI-powered instagram influencers driving consumers' purchase intentions: An integration of SMIV & SOR framework. *Journal of Open Innovation, 11*(3), 100591. DOI: 10.1016/j.joitmc.2025.100591

Dimitrova, T., Ilieva, I., & Terziyska, M. (2025). Understanding Consumers' Functional Beverages Purchase Intention: Modeling the Impact of Explanatory Factors. *BIO Web of Conferences, 170*. DOI: 10.1051/bioconf/202517001020

Eastman, J. K., & Eastman, J. K. (2023). *Artificial intelligence consumer behavior : A hybrid review and research Artificial intelligence consumer behavior : A hybrid review and research agenda. September*. DOI: 10.1002/cb.2233

Haque, A., Akther, N., Khan, I., Agarwal, K., & Uddin, N. (2024). Artificial Intelligence in Retail Marketing: Research Agenda Based on Bibliometric Reflection and Content Analysis (2000–2023). *Informatics (MDPI), 11*(4), 1–30. DOI: 10.3390/informatics11040074

Hennig-Thurau, T., Herting, A. M., & Jütte, D. (2025). Adoption of Virtual Reality Headsets: The Role of Metaverse Trials for Consumers' Usage and Purchase Intentions. *Journal of Interactive Marketing, 60*(2), 145–160. DOI: 10.1177/10949968241263353

Jiao, D. (2025). AI-enhanced digital therapeutics for cognitive impairment: Integrating mobile applications, virtual reality, and wearable devices. *Discover Artificial Intelligence*, *5*(1), 69. Advance online publication. DOI: 10.1007/s44163-025-00325-6

Kotp, M. H., Ismail, H. A., Basyouny, H. A. A., Aly, M. A., Hendy, A., Nashwan, A. J., Hendy, A., & Abd Elmoaty, A. E. E. (2025). Empowering nurse leaders: Readiness for AI integration and the perceived benefits of predictive analytics. *BMC Nursing*, *24*(1), 56. Advance online publication. DOI: 10.1186/s12912-024-02653-x PMID: 39819624

Leite, H., & Vieira, L. R. (2025). The use of virtual reality in human training: Trends and a research agenda. *Virtual Reality (Waltham Cross)*, *29*(1), 25. Advance online publication. DOI: 10.1007/s10055-024-01093-x

Liao, C. H. (2025). The role of virtual reality in enhancing behavioral empathy: Exploring cognitive absorption, engagement, and emotional moderation using multivariate methods. *Humanities & Social Sciences Communications*, *12*(1), 1–15. DOI: 10.1057/s41599-025-05334-5

Mc, M., B, M., Ks, S., Bm, S., M, M., M, C., & Dvsk, M.MC. (2024). Understanding Medical Healthcare Solutions in GIS Platform: A Review. *Journal of Experimental and Laboratory Medicine*, *0*(0), 1. DOI: 10.5455/JELM.20241030075959

Meddah, N. (2024). *The impact of artificial intelligence on consumer behavior : Insights and implications. 18*, 2764–2772.

Mustafizul Haque. (2023). Impact of Influencer Marketing on Consumer Behavior : An Analytical Study. *Tuijin Jishu/Journal of Propulsion Technology, 44*(4), 3160–3166. DOI: 10.52783/tjjpt.v44.i4.1410

Omeish, F., Al, M., & Khair, N. (2024). Computers in Human Behavior Reports Investigating the impact of AI on improving customer experience through social media marketing : An analysis of Jordanian Millennials. *Computers in Human Behavior Reports*, *15*(July), 100464. DOI: 10.1016/j.chbr.2024.100464

Rudeloff, C. (2023). *AI-Driven Influencer Marketing : Comparing the Effects of Virtual and Human Influencers on Consumer Perceptions AI-driven influencer marketing : Comparing the effects of virtual and human influencers on consumer perceptions. April.* DOI: 10.2139/ssrn.4404372

Tang, Y. M., Wong, J. K. N., & Ho, G. T. S. (2025). Exploring Consumer Acceptance of Metaverse Marketing for Branding Activities and the Pre-Purchase Stage. *Journal of Theoretical and Applied Electronic Commerce Research*, *20*(3), 159. DOI: 10.3390/jtaer20030159

Thakur, N., & Aditya, A. (2024). International Journal of Research Publication and Reviews. SSRN *Electronic Journal, 5*(11), 2388–2390. DOI: 10.2139/ssrn.4991412

Timimi, H., Baaddi, M., & Bennouna, A. (2025). Impact of artificial intelligence on the personalization of the customer experience: A systematic literature review. *Multidisciplinary Reviews*, *8*(7), 2025224. Advance online publication. DOI: 10.31893/multirev.2025224

Velasco, C., Reinoso-Carvalho, F., Barbosa Escobar, F., Gustafsson, A., & Petit, O. (2024). Paradoxes, challenges, and opportunities in the context of ethical customer experience management. *Psychology and Marketing*, *41*(10), 2506–2524. DOI: 10.1002/mar.22069

Yin, J., Qiu, X., & Wang, Y. (2025). The Impact of AI-Personalized Recommendations on Clicking Intentions: Evidence from Chinese E-Commerce. *Journal of Theoretical and Applied Electronic Commerce Research*, *20*(1), 21. Advance online publication. DOI: 10.3390/jtaer20010021

Zanchini, R., Spina, D., De Pascale, A., Lanfranchi, M., Giannetto, C., D'Amico, M., & Di Vita, G. (2025). Shaping consumer preferences for sweet peppers: Exploring the role of social, environmental, and sensory attributes in the era of health consciousness and local sourcing. *Agricultural and Food Economics*, *13*(1), 42. Advance online publication. DOI: 10.1186/s40100-025-00386-2

Zhang, Z., Li, C., & Zhang, H. (2026). Digital confusion: Comprehending the impact mechanisms of artificial intelligence-generated content and user-generated content on tourism decision making. *Tourism Management*, *112*(June 2025), 105269. DOI: 10.1016/j.tourman.2025.105269

Zhao, L., & Wu, W. (2025). Is Customer Service Innovation Always Preferable? The Impact of AI Technology on an Online Retailer's Customer Service Decision. *Journal of Theoretical and Applied Electronic Commerce Research*, *20*(2), 101. DOI: 10.3390/jtaer20020101

Chapter 5
Role of AI in Consumer Decision-Making Processes

Ardra Rianisa
https://orcid.org/0009-0005-0304-1195
Universitas Esa Unggul, Indonesia

Desva Selvi Anggraini
https://orcid.org/0009-0002-7854-4975
Universitas Esa Unggul, Indonesia

Binastya Anggara Sekti
https://orcid.org/0000-0001-5489-4888
Universitas Esa Unggul, Indonesia

ABSTRACT

The integration of Artificial Intelligence (AI) and social media has significantly transformed consumer behavior and digital marketing strategies. This paper explores how AI enhances personalization through data-driven product recommendations, targeted advertising, and real-time customer service via chatbots. Simultaneously, social media serves as a dynamic platform for consumer-brand interaction, shaping brand image through user-generated content, influencer marketing, and community engagement. These technologies collectively improve customer experience, foster loyalty, and influence purchasing decisions. However, their implementation also presents challenges, including data privacy concerns, over-personalization, and the risk of inauthentic content damaging brand trust. The study highlights the

DOI: 10.4018/979-8-3373-2747-1.ch005

importance of ethical and strategic use of AI and social media to maximize their potential in building strong, lasting relationships with consumers in the increasingly competitive digital marketplace.

1. INTRODUCTION

Figure 1. **Users interact with social media and AI for a personalized shopping experience**

Technology, particularly artificial intelligence (AI) and social media, has had a significant impact on consumer behavior in recent years. Consumers now not only purchase products but also interact with brands through digital platforms. This is inextricably linked to technological developments that enable more personalized and connected consumption experiences (Bilal et al., 2024). Social media, as a rapidly evolving technology component, also plays a crucial role in this shift. Platforms like Instagram, TikTok, and Facebook provide consumers with a platform to share experiences, provide product reviews, and seek recommendations from friends or influencers they follow (Brüns & Meißner, 2024). Social media is not only a means of sharing information but also serves as an effective marketing tool for companies to influence consumer purchasing decisions (Brüns & Meißner, 2024). In addition to social media, AI is also playing a role in changing the way consumers shop. AI-based systems enable companies to offer more personalized and relevant product recommendations, based on data analysis of previous consumer behavior (Dhiman & Bhati, 2025). In his research, Khatri demonstrated that with the help of AI, companies can provide a more efficient and personalized shopping experience, making consumers feel more cared for and valued (Dhiman & Bhati, 2025). AI not only makes the shopping experience easier but also provides convenience for consumers who want to find products that match their preferences without having to spend a lot of time searching (Dhiman & Bhati, 2025).

It is also important to note that AI has a positive impact on digital marketing. By leveraging big data collected from various social media platforms, AI can help companies deliver ads that are more tailored to consumers' interests and shopping habits, increasing marketing effectiveness (Kumar et al., 2024). This suggests that ads that are more relevant and tailored to consumer behavior are more likely to be accepted and result in high conversions (Kumar et al., 2024). Overall, the influence of AI and social media on consumer behavior is significant. Consumers now have more choices and information to make more informed purchasing decisions.

2. AI AND CHANGING CONSUMER BEHAVIOR

Figure 2. **AI provides more relevant product recommendations for consumers**

Artificial intelligence (AI) has significantly changed the way consumers interact with brands and products. AI-based systems, such as chatbots and product recommendation systems, enable companies to provide more tailored and relevant shopping experiences tailored to individual preferences (Hermann & Puntoni, 2024). AI leverages the vast data collected from consumer interactions to personalize their experiences, which in turn influences consumer purchasing decisions (Kumar et al., 2024). With AI's ability to learn consumer behavior patterns, companies can design more effective and targeted marketing strategies. Dhiman (2025) points out that data analysis conducted by AI can help companies understand when and how consumers are likely to purchase products, allowing companies to optimize the timing and placement of advertising to reach the right audience (Dhiman & Bhati, 2025). Thus, AI not only helps increase sales but also creates a more positive experience for consumers, as they perceive the products offered as more relevant to their needs (Liu et al., 2025).

AI also significantly contributes to creating a more efficient shopping experience. Consumers using AI-based platforms no longer need to waste time searching for products that meet their needs. For example, recommendation systems implemented by many e-commerce platforms use algorithms to select products similar to those previously purchased or frequently searched for by consumers (Dhiman & Bhati, 2025). This allows consumers to find thc products they want more quickly and easily (Dhiman & Bhati, 2025). By using AI, companies can also increase consumer loyalty. For example, AI helps create a consistent and satisfying shopping experience through faster and more relevant interactions. When consumers feel valued and receive personalized service, they are more likely to return and purchase products from the same brand (Xia et al., 2025). This suggests that AI-driven personalization not only improves efficiency but also strengthens the relationship between consumers and brands.

3. THE ROLE OF SOCIAL MEDIA IN BRAND IMAGE FORMATION

Figure 3. **Social media shapes brand image through consumer and influencer experiences**

Social media has become a crucial part of consumers' daily lives, especially in shaping brand image. Platforms like Instagram, TikTok, and Facebook provide companies with the opportunity to interact directly with their consumers, which in turn shapes how consumers perceive a brand. Social media allows companies to share product information, conduct marketing campaigns, and even create engaging brand stories for their audiences. This is a highly effective way to introduce and build a positive brand image, which can attract more consumer attention than traditional advertising (Bilal et al., 2024). One of the most important aspects of social media is its ability to enable consumers to share their experiences. When consumers share stories or reviews about products or services they've tried on social media, this has a significant impact on the opinions of other consumers. This demonstrates how social media functions not only as a marketing platform but also as a space for sharing personal experiences that can influence others' purchasing decisions. Consumers feel more confident in recommendations from friends or acquaintances than in advertisements issued by companies (Brüns & Meißner, 2024).

Liu (2025) in his research showed that consumers tend to trust product reviews they encounter on social media more than elsewhere. This is because social media allows them to see how others interact with the brand or product, as well as the experiences they share. This changes how companies must approach their marketing. To build a strong brand image, companies need to ensure that the experiences consumers share on social media are consistent with the values they want to convey about their products. Therefore, brands that succeed on social media are those that are able to create a positive and consistent consumer experience, so that consumers feel compelled to voluntarily share their positive experiences (Liu et al., 2025). Furthermore, social media also provides companies with the opportunity to shape their brand image through the content they create. For example, many brands have successfully used social media to create engaging marketing campaigns, such as video-based campaigns or attention-grabbing visual content. This not only helps engage audiences but also allows companies to communicate more authentically with their consumers. Over time, social media has become more than just a place to share photos or status updates, but also a space where consumers can interact with brands and engage in two-way conversations that build long-term relationships (Kumar et al., 2024).

Furthermore, the development of influencer marketing also plays a significant role in shaping brand image on social media. Influencers with loyal followers can exert significant influence on consumer purchasing decisions. Research conducted by Chan & Choi (2025) found that influencer marketing is growing due to its powerful influence over a wider and more diverse audience. These influencers can share their experiences with specific products and recommend them to their followers. When an influencer recommends a product, their followers are more likely to trust it and be interested in purchasing it because they feel closer to the influencer they follow. This demonstrates the powerful influence of social media in shaping consumer perceptions of a brand (Chan & Choi, 2025). Using influencers for social media marketing also requires brands to select influencers who align with the image they want to build. Brands that use influencers whose values and audience align with theirs can amplify the message they want to convey and build a more authentic and trustworthy image among consumers. Therefore, when selecting influencers, companies should not only consider the number of followers but also the alignment of the values and message they want to convey with the influencer's audience (Haleem et al., 2022).

Furthermore, social media allows companies to measure the effectiveness of their marketing campaigns in real time. Companies can see how their audience interacts with their content, how many people like, share, or comment on their posts, and how many.

4. THE INFLUENCE OF INFLUENCERS ON CONSUMER PURCHASING DECISIONS

Figure 4. **Influencers influence consumer purchasing decisions through social media**

The influence of influencers in the marketing world cannot be underestimated. In recent years, influencers have become a crucial part of marketing strategies, particularly on social media. Influencers here refer to individuals with large followings on social media platforms like Instagram, TikTok, or YouTube, and who have the ability to influence consumer purchasing decisions. They are considered highly credible figures in the eyes of their audience, allowing them to influence their followers' preferences and purchasing behavior. Influencer marketing has become one of the most effective marketing tools for reaching young consumers. These influencers can recommend products or services they trust, which makes their followers more likely to purchase those products (Xia et al., 2025). One of the main reasons why influencers have such a significant influence on consumer purchasing decisions is because they are perceived as more authentic and connected to their audience. When an influencer shares their personal experience with a particular product or service, their followers tend to perceive that experience as more honest and trustworthy. This differs from traditional advertising, where consumers are more skeptical of the company's messages. Therefore, influencers can overcome this distrust by sharing their experiences in a more personal and relatable way. This explains how influencers can build closer relationships with their audiences, thereby more effectively influencing consumer purchasing decisions (Bilal et al., 2024; Brüns & Meißner, 2024).

Influencers are able to create powerful influence because they have a closer relationship with their audience. In the world of social media, audiences often feel more connected to influencers than to brands. Influencers often share their personal moments, which makes followers feel like they know them personally. This relationship creates a sense of trust and loyalty, which in turn makes it easier for influencers to influence consumer purchasing decisions. Therefore, influencers are often perceived as more authentic voices than advertisements broadcast by the brands themselves (Xia et al., 2025). This influence is not limited to young consumers. Although most well-known influencers focus on young audiences, research shows that influencers also influence various age groups. Brands that leverage influencers to target a broader audience, including older age groups, can leverage their credibility and influence to build stronger relationships with consumers across various demographics (Hermann & Puntoni, 2024). Furthermore, influencers can act as a bridge between brands and their audiences. Brands often use influencers to convey messages or promote their products in a more subtle and natural way. Influencers don't just promote products directly; they also serve to build a narrative around the product or brand, creating a story that makes the product feel more engaging and relevant to their followers (Dhiman & Bhati, 2025).

For example, an influencer on Instagram might share photos or videos of themselves using a particular product, giving the impression that they genuinely enjoy it. They might also share personal stories or experiences related to the product. This not only captures the attention of their followers but also builds a stronger emotional connection. Consumers tend to trust products promoted by someone they perceive as having a similar personality or values to their own (Xia et al., 2025). However, an influencer's influence doesn't solely depend on the number of followers they have. The quality of the relationship built between an influencer and their audience is far more important than the number of followers. A smaller but more engaged and loyal following of an influencer has a greater potential to influence purchasing decisions than a larger but less engaged following. Therefore, selecting the right influencer is crucial in determining the effectiveness of a marketing campaign (Chan & Choi, 2025).

In the world of influencer marketing, there are two types of influencers often used by brands: macro-influencers and micro-influencers. Macro-influencers are influencers with very large followings, often exceeding one million followers, and they tend to have a wider reach. They are used to significantly increase brand awareness. Micro-influencers, on the other hand, have smaller, but more targeted and engaged followings. While macro-influencers can provide significant visibility for brands, micro-influencers are more effective at creating deeper relationships with the audiences they reach, which in turn more strongly influences purchasing decisions (Chan & Choi, 2025; Koivunen et al., 2025). Micro-influencers tend to connect with their audiences on a more personal level. Their followers feel closer to them and believe their recommendations are more honest and trustworthy. This leads to stronger and more informed purchasing decisions. Thus, brands looking to build long-term relationships with their consumers often choose to work with micro-influencers who have more specific and engaged audiences (Dhiman & Bhati, 2025). However, the influence of influencers isn't all positive. There are also challenges and potential risks to using influencer marketing. The use of generative AI to create social media marketing content that appears authentic but is actually generated by technology can undermine perceptions of brand authenticity. Consumers are increasingly discerning about inauthentic or overly polished content, and this can lead to a decline in trust in brands that use influencers inauthenticly (Bilal et al., 2024; Brüns & Meißner, 2024).

Brands that utilize influencers need to ensure that their collaborations with them remain authentic and transparent. When audiences perceive that their influencers are working with a brand solely for financial gain without providing genuine experiences or genuine recommendations, they can lose trust in that brand. Therefore, it is crucial for companies to work with influencers who genuinely use and believe in the products they promote, so that the messages conveyed feel more genuine and credible to their audiences(Brüns & Meißner, 2024). In this increasingly digital era, influencer marketing will continue to play a crucial role in influencing consumer purchasing decisions. Influencer marketing is not just a passing trend, but a long-term element of marketing strategy that brands need to adapt to stay relevant in this highly competitive market. Consumers are more likely to purchase products they see promoted by influencers they trust and with whom they feel a strong emotional connection (Brüns & Meißner, 2024). Overall, the influence of influencers on consumer purchasing decisions is significant, and with proper use, companies can harness the power of influencers to build a strong brand image and increase their sales. As technologies such as generative AI and new social media platforms advance, influencer marketing will continue to evolve and provide new opportunities for brands to reach their audiences in a more personal and authentic way (Brüns & Meißner, 2024).

5. AI IN PERSONALIZING CONSUMER EXPERIENCES

The role of artificial intelligence (AI) in personalizing consumer experiences has become one of the most important aspects of digital marketing today. With advances in AI technology, companies now have the ability to better understand their consumers' preferences, habits, and behavioral patterns. This enables them to offer highly tailored and relevant experiences, increasing consumer convenience, and ultimately influencing their purchasing decisions (Liu et al., 2025; Xia et al., 2025). Using AI, companies can analyze data collected from various digital channels, including social media, e-commerce apps, and browsing history. This data provides valuable insights into consumers' interests and preferences, as well as their purchasing patterns. Based on this analysis, AI systems can make personalized product recommendations, increasing the likelihood of consumers purchasing the products they desire. For example, platforms like Amazon and Netflix use AI algorithms to offer relevant products or content based on what consumers have previously viewed or purchased (Hermann & Puntoni, 2024).

Furthermore, AI also enables companies to provide more personalized experiences through tailored communications. For example, in marketing emails, companies can use AI to tailor message content based on consumer preferences. This increases the likelihood that consumers will open the email and take further action, such as purchasing the promoted product. Tailored marketing experiences using AI can significantly increase response and conversion rates, as consumers feel more connected to brands that understand their needs and preferences (Hermann & Puntoni, 2024). In addition to personalizing product recommendations and communications, AI can also enhance the customer experience by introducing virtual assistants and chatbots. AI-based chatbots can provide fast and efficient customer service, addressing consumer questions or issues in real time. These systems not only help consumers feel heard and valued, but also reduce wait times and increase customer satisfaction. The implementation of AI-based chatbots has been shown to improve the customer experience, as consumers can receive instant answers without having to wait long (Dhiman & Bhati, 2025).

One successful example of the use of AI in personalization is in the e-commerce industry. Many e-commerce platforms, such as Alibaba and Amazon, use AI to personalize the shopping experience. For example, when consumers visit a website or app, the AI system can suggest products that match their preferences based on their previous shopping behavior. This creates a more convenient shopping experience, as consumers no longer need to manually search for the products they want. With more relevant and tailored recommendations, consumers find it easier to find what they need and are more likely to purchase suggested products (Chan & Choi, 2025). Furthermore, AI in personalization can also increase customer loyalty. When the shopping experience feels more personalized and relevant, consumers feel more valued, and this tends to increase customer retention rates. Consumers who perceive their experience as personalized are more likely to return for repeat purchases. This demonstrates the importance of using technology to create stronger relationships between brands and consumers (Liu et al., 2025; Xia et al., 2025). However, while AI offers many benefits in personalization, there are several challenges to consider. One of the biggest challenges is data privacy. Consumers are increasingly concerned about how their personal data is used and protected. Companies using AI for personalization must be transparent about how data is collected and used. Consumers need to feel confident that their data is secure and used only to enhance their experience, not for any other harmful purposes (Haleem et al., 2022).

Furthermore, there are also issues related to over-personalization. When consumer experiences are overly personalized, consumers may feel trapped in a "bubble" and only presented with information they already know. This can diminish the sense of surprise and new discovery that consumers typically expect when shopping or browsing products. While personalization can increase conversions, too much personalization can make the shopping experience feel monotonous and less engaging (Haleem et al., 2022). Furthermore, while AI can make highly accurate product recommendations, sometimes the recommendations made by AI do not always align with consumers' desires, especially when the data used is incomplete or inaccurate. This can occur if the AI system does not account for factors such as changes in consumer preferences over time, or if the data used to train the algorithm is not sufficiently representative (Kumar et al., 2024). However, despite these challenges, the potential of AI to improve customer experience and personalization is undeniable. In the future, we can expect further advances in AI technology that will enable more personalized and interactive experiences. For example, with advances in natural language processing and deep learning, companies can create smarter systems that better understand consumer preferences and deliver more humanistic experiences ((Hermann & Puntoni, 2024).

Overall, the use of AI in personalizing consumer experiences offers numerous benefits, from increased convenience to strengthened customer loyalty. When used wisely, AI can help companies build stronger relationships with their consumers and improve overall customer satisfaction. However, it is important for companies to ensure they use data ethically and transparently, and maintain a balance between excessive personalization and the new discoveries consumers need. The effective use of AI technology in personalizing experiences will continue to grow, and companies that can adopt this technology wisely will have a competitive advantage in this increasingly digital marketplace (Hermann & Puntoni, 2024).

6. SOCIAL MEDIA AS A COMMUNICATION AND CONSUMER INTERACTION TOOL

Social media has changed the way companies communicate with their consumers. Previously, communication between companies and consumers tended to be one-way, with companies delivering information through traditional advertising or mass media. However, with the advent of social media, communication has become two-way, allowing consumers to interact directly with brands, provide feedback, and participate in more dynamic and spontaneous conversations. Social media serves not only as a marketing platform but also as a vital tool for building relationships and increasing consumer engagement with their brands (Xia et al., 2025). Social media allows companies to engage directly with their audiences in a variety of ways. Companies can respond to questions, address complaints, or even express gratitude to loyal customers, creating a more personalized and interactive experience. This makes consumers feel valued and included in the conversation with the brand, which in turn strengthens their relationship with the company. Companies that actively engage in conversations on social media can foster stronger loyalty among their consumers, as they perceive that the company genuinely cares about their opinions and needs (Xia et al., 2025).

One way social media enhances communication is through comments and direct messaging features. Consumers can easily ask questions about products, file complaints, or provide feedback directly to companies. Unlike traditional advertising, which doesn't allow for direct interaction, social media provides a space for consumers to get answers quickly and feel closer to the company. These features enable companies to provide more responsive and personalized customer service, which in turn improves the overall consumer experience (Omeish et al., 2024). Furthermore, social media also allows companies to listen to and understand their consumers better. Through social media data analysis, companies can identify emerging topics, trends, and conversations surrounding their products or the industry in general. This provides companies with valuable insights into how consumers perceive their products, what they like, and what needs improvement. Companies that use this data to tailor their products or services to consumers' expectations have a greater chance of building long-term relationships with their audiences (Kumar et al., 2024).

Furthermore, social media allows companies to run more interactive marketing campaigns. For example, many companies use content in the form of quizzes, challenges, or sweepstakes to encourage consumers to interact with their brands. This not only helps increase engagement but also creates a fun experience for consumers. For example, a campaign using a hashtag that encourages consumers to participate in a challenge on social media can help increase brand awareness while also encouraging conversations about the company's products or services (Hermann & Puntoni, 2024). One of the most powerful features of social media is its ability to build communities around a brand. Many companies have successfully created loyal communities through platforms like Facebook, Instagram, or TikTok. These communities are not just about following the brand, but also about sharing experiences and information about the products they use. Communities built on social media often become a source of strong loyalty, as consumers feel part of something bigger than simply purchasing the product (Dhiman & Bhati, 2025). Furthermore, social media allows consumers to share experiences with one another, ultimately strengthening their relationship with the brand. Consumers who share their experiences with a particular product or service on platforms like Instagram or TikTok often influence their followers to try the same product. In this way, social media serves as a platform for digital word-of-mouth, which can significantly influence others' purchasing decisions (Liu et al., 2025; Xia et al., 2025).

However, while social media offers numerous opportunities to increase consumer engagement, companies must be cautious with their approach. Too many promotions or overly sales-focused messages can leave consumers feeling overwhelmed or even annoyed. It's important for companies to strike a balance between providing useful product information and enabling more organic, natural conversations among their audiences. Consumers are more likely to engage with brands that focus not solely on sales but also strive to create more authentic and meaningful relationships (Chan & Choi, 2025). Consumers are more likely to engage with brands that share their values and that strive to improve their lives, not just sell products. Furthermore, while social media allows for better engagement with consumers, challenges related to brand reputation management remain. Every interaction on social media is easily viewed by many, and responding quickly to complaints or criticism is crucial to maintaining a brand's image. Companies that can address issues openly and quickly on social media have a greater chance of repairing relationships with consumers and building stronger trust (Liu et al., 2025; Xia et al., 2025). In this way, social media is not only a marketing platform, but also a platform for building and managing relationships with consumers.

In addition to one-on-one interactions, social media also allows companies to introduce product innovations directly to their consumers. Through live broadcasts, videos, and interactive posts, companies can give consumers a firsthand look at new products, new features, or updates they offer. This helps increase transparency and build anticipation among audiences. Product launch campaigns conducted live on social media can create a sense of urgency and exclusivity among consumers who want to be the first to try the product (Chan & Choi, 2025). Thus, social media has transformed the way companies communicate with their consumers. Through direct interactions, more creative marketing campaigns, and the formation of communities around brands, social media provides numerous opportunities for companies to build stronger, more personalized relationships with consumers. However, companies must also be careful with their approach to ensure that communications remain authentic and do not overwhelm consumers with promotions or sales messages. When used wisely, social media can be a very effective tool for building loyalty and strengthening brand image in the eyes of consumers (Liu et al., 2025).

7. THE INFLUENCE OF AI AND SOCIAL MEDIA ON CONSUMER LOYALTY

Figure 5. **AI and customer service enhance positive interactions between consumers and brands**

Artificial intelligence (AI) and social media have played a significant role in shaping consumer loyalty in today's digital age. As technology advances, companies are increasingly able to leverage big data to understand consumer behavior and deliver more personalized experiences. These more relevant and personalized experiences significantly influence how consumers interact with brands and their loyalty to the products they offer. AI enables companies to collect and analyze data used to design more targeted marketing campaigns, while social media allows brands to connect directly with consumers in real time (Hermann & Puntoni, 2024; Xia et al., 2025). Consumer loyalty is strongly influenced by their experiences with brands. Customized experiences, driven by AI technology, can create a stronger connection between consumers and brands. When consumers perceive that a company understands their needs and preferences, they are more likely to remain loyal to that brand. This is evidenced by Xia et al., who found that AI-based personalization, which provides product recommendations tailored to individual interests, can increase long-term consumer satisfaction and loyalty (Xia et al., 2025). Furthermore, these personalized experiences can increase positive interactions on social media, which in turn strengthens the relationship between brands and consumers (Hermann & Puntoni, 2024; Nazir et al., 2023).

Social media plays a crucial role in facilitating direct interactions between consumers and brands. Consumers can now easily communicate with companies through comments, direct messages, or reviews of the products they purchase. Social media also provides a platform for consumers to share their experiences with brands, both positive and negative. These interactions, if managed well, can strengthen consumer loyalty because they feel valued and listened to by the company. Khatri emphasized that consumers who feel cared for in social media communications are more likely to repurchase products from brands they feel close to ((Dhiman & Bhati, 2025). However, it is important for companies to focus not only on product marketing on social media but also on building deeper communication with their consumers. Using AI to analyze consumer sentiment towards a product or marketing campaign can help brands understand consumer feelings, both positive and negative. Pires points out that AI-based sentiment analysis allows companies to more precisely tailor their marketing strategies, which helps strengthen consumer loyalty by delivering what consumers want (Chan & Choi, 2025). In this way, companies can create more positive experiences and make consumers feel more connected to their brands.

Consumer engagement on social media extends beyond direct interactions with brands to interactions with fellow consumers. Communities formed around brands on social media provide a platform for consumers to share experiences and recommendations. This increases consumers' sense of belonging to the brand and fosters stronger loyalty. Haleem et al. found that when consumers feel part of a larger community on social media, they are more likely to remain loyal to the brands they follow (Haleem et al., 2022). This demonstrates how social media serves as a tool for building stronger relationships between brands and consumers, ultimately influencing their loyalty to products. AI also plays a role in creating a smoother and more seamless shopping experience, which is a crucial factor in increasing consumer loyalty. With AI-driven automation, companies can offer more efficient shopping experiences, such as faster product recommendations, easier transaction processing, and more responsive customer service. AI can help companies monitor consumer feedback on various social media platforms and respond quickly to address issues. Pratama emphasized that responding quickly to consumer complaints on social media can improve relationships with consumers, who feel valued and prioritized (Kumar et al., 2024). By using AI to identify common consumer issues, companies can make the necessary changes to improve the customer experience and maintain customer loyalty.

Furthermore, AI-generated personalization also helps create a stronger emotional connection between consumers and brands. Pires stated that when consumers feel that a brand understands their desires and provides products or services tailored to their needs, they are more likely to remain loyal to that brand (Chan & Choi, 2025). In this hyper-connected world, consumers seek brands that can offer relevant experiences and prioritize their satisfaction. Thus, AI serves as an invaluable tool for building sustainable consumer loyalty. However, while AI and social media offer numerous opportunities to increase consumer loyalty, companies must always be careful to maintain a balance between personalization and consumer privacy. Consumers are increasingly concerned about how their personal data is used, and they may feel uncomfortable if they feel their data is being exploited without their consent. Liu et al. show that companies that can effectively safeguard consumer privacy while offering personalized experiences are more successful in building long-term loyalty (Liu et al., 2025). Therefore, transparency in data collection and use is a key factor in maintaining consumer trust and loyalty.

Overall, AI and social media play a significant role in increasing consumer loyalty. By creating personalized experiences, providing better customer service, and building stronger relationships with consumers, companies can increase satisfaction and build long-term loyalty. Khatri emphasized that to remain competitive in an increasingly digital marketplace, companies need to continuously innovate by using AI and social media to deepen their engagement with consumers and create more relevant and enjoyable experiences (Dhiman & Bhati, 2025).

8. CHALLENGES AND RISKS IN USING AI AND SOCIAL MEDIA

The use of artificial intelligence (AI) and social media in marketing brings many benefits, but also presents challenges and risks that companies need to be aware of. While AI can increase personalization and efficiency, and social media can accelerate consumer interactions, both also have the potential to create issues that can be detrimental to brands if not managed properly. One of the main challenges companies face is consumer data privacy and security. Consumers are increasingly concerned about how their personal data is used by companies, especially when that data is used to generate AI-based recommendations. Non-transparent or unethical use of data can damage a company's reputation and reduce consumer trust in their brand (Sahut & Laroche, 2025; Teepapal, 2025).

AI relies on big data collection to personalize consumer experiences. However, the more data collected, the greater the potential risk of data leakage or misuse of personal information. If consumers feel their data is not being treated securely, they may be reluctant to engage further with a company's products or services. In some cases, this issue can cause consumers to avoid using certain apps or services that require personal data collection, ultimately resulting in decreased conversion rates and customer retention (Kumar et al., 2024).Furthermore, the use of consumers' personal data for personalization can create an imbalance in the relationship between consumers and brands. When personalization reaches excessive levels, consumers may feel they are constantly being monitored, which can decrease their comfort level. This can lead to decreased trust in brands and create the perception that companies are overly aggressive in trying to exploit their personal data for marketing purposes (Chan & Choi, 2025). When consumers feel they have lost control of their data, they are more likely to reduce their engagement with brands and even stop using those products (Xia et al., 2025).

The use of AI can also pose challenges related to the quality of the data used. AI is only as effective as the data it has. If the data used to train an AI algorithm is incomplete or inaccurate, the results generated by the AI system will also be inadequate. AI-based product recommendation systems that use flawed data can provide irrelevant suggestions to consumers, which in turn can damage the customer experience and even affect sales. Therefore, it is crucial for companies to ensure that the data used to train AI algorithms is accurate, complete, and representative to create a truly personalized and effective experience (Liu et al., 2025; Xia et al., 2025). Another risk associated with the use of AI is over-reliance on this technology. While AI can automate many processes, over-reliance on AI can diminish the ability of humans to make more creative and empathetic decisions. This can negatively impact innovation and the quality of relationships built with consumers. For example, while AI can offer data-driven product recommendations, it cannot replace the human touch when it comes to understanding consumers' emotional needs and building long-term relationships (Dhiman & Bhati, 2025).

In addition to AI-related challenges, social media also poses risks that need to be considered. While social media gives companies the ability to connect directly with consumers, these platforms also have the potential to create a reputational crisis if not used wisely. Once a brand experiences negative issues or criticism on social media, it can spread rapidly and impact the brand's image among consumers. Consumers are often quicker to spread negative information than positive information, and this can cause greater damage to a brand's reputation than the impact of traditional marketing campaigns (Saheb et al., 2024). Therefore, companies that fail to effectively handle negative feedback or complaints on social media can lose consumer trust. Companies that fail to effectively manage their reputation on social media risk losing consumer loyalty. Careless use of social media, such as over-promotion or poor management of negative reviews, can damage relationships with consumers and harm the brand. Responding quickly and transparently to complaints or issues is crucial for maintaining consumer trust on social media. Therefore, companies must have a robust reputation management strategy to address issues arising on social media to minimize damage to their brand image and maintain good relationships with their consumers (Hue & Hung, 2025). Furthermore, while social media allows for better engagement with consumers, challenges related to content management remain. Too many advertisements or promotions can lead to audience burnout and discourage engagement with the brand. Therefore, companies need to strike a balance between providing useful product information and enabling more organic and natural conversations among their audiences. Content that is too sales-focused can diminish the effectiveness of marketing campaigns and negatively impact consumer perceptions of the brand (Joshi et al., 2025).

Reliance on social media algorithms that can control reach and visibility also poses challenges for companies. While social media allows companies to reach a wider audience, changes in platform algorithms can alter how much of their audience sees their brand's content. This can make previously effective marketing strategies less effective if the platform algorithms don't support content visibility. Therefore, companies need to adapt their strategies to address these changes and ensure they can still reach relevant audiences organically (Saheb et al., 2024). Going forward, companies looking to leverage AI and social media must strive to manage these challenges effectively. They need to ensure they adhere to strict privacy and data security standards to protect consumer information and build trust. Furthermore, companies must be discerning in managing their relationships with consumers on social media, ensuring they provide value and experiences beyond simply promoting products. With the right strategy, companies can capitalize on the enormous potential offered by AI and social media while avoiding potential risks that could harm them (Saheb et al., 2024).

9. THE ROLE OF AI AND SOCIAL MEDIA IN SHAPING FUTURE CONSUMER BEHAVIOR

The use of artificial intelligence (AI) and social media in marketing has changed the dynamics of the relationship between consumers and brands. As technology advances, both have become increasingly sophisticated tools in shaping consumer behavior. In the future, AI and social media will continue to play a significant role in how consumers interact with products, services, and brands, leading to the formation of more adaptive and personalized consumption patterns. AI will not only enhance the shopping experience but will also provide deeper insights into consumer preferences and behavioral patterns (Hermann & Puntoni, 2024; Liu et al., 2025). As technology advances, companies are increasingly able to leverage big data collected through consumer interactions across various digital platforms. This data provides invaluable insights into what consumers want, how they behave, and when they are likely to make purchasing decisions. By using more sophisticated AI algorithms, companies can make more accurate predictions about consumer needs and tailor the shopping experience to individual preferences (Hermann & Puntoni, 2024; Kumar et al., 2024; Nogueira et al., 2025).

With AI's ability to analyze data quickly and efficiently, companies can provide highly personalized services. For example, AI-based recommendation systems used by e-commerce platforms can suggest products relevant to consumers' shopping habits. This allows consumers to find the products they want more easily and quickly, increasing their shopping experience (Kumar et al., 2024; Xia et al., 2025). This personalization not only improves the customer experience but also increases conversion rates and sales for companies. Furthermore, AI's ability to process and understand more complex data provides companies with the opportunity to offer products or services tailored to consumers' needs, even before they realize it. This paves the way for the emergence of predictive systems that can predict consumer desires based on historical data, their behavior on digital platforms, and their previous consumption patterns (Smale et al., 2024; Xia et al., 2025). Companies that can develop such AI systems will have a significant advantage in creating more relevant and satisfying experiences for consumers. However, while AI can improve marketing efficiency and effectiveness, challenges related to data usage remain a major concern. One of the biggest challenges companies face is data privacy. The more personal data collected to personalize consumer experiences, the greater the potential risk of data leakage or misuse of personal information. Consumers are increasingly aware of the importance of their data privacy and are increasingly concerned about how their personal information is used for marketing purposes (Hermann & Puntoni, 2024; Joshi et al., 2025).Therefore, companies must ensure they have clear policies regarding the collection, storage, and use of consumer data, and provide greater transparency in this regard.

Social media plays a crucial role in shaping consumer behavior. Platforms like Instagram, Facebook, and TikTok allow consumers to connect directly with brands, share their experiences, and provide feedback in real time. This allows companies to gain direct insights into what consumers want and how they interact with specific products or services. Social media also allows consumers to share information with each other, which can influence their purchasing decisions. As these platforms evolve, consumers will increasingly use social media not only for socializing but also for shopping and interacting with brands (Dhiman & Bhati, 2025; Saheb et al., 2024). Additionally, social media allows companies to create more targeted and community-based marketing campaigns. Companies can build communities around their products or services, which can strengthen consumer loyalty and create long-term relationships. These communities give consumers the opportunity to interact with the brand and with other consumers who share similar interests, creating a strong sense of belonging and affiliation (Saheb et al., 2024; Smale et al., 2024). By using features like hashtags or challenges on social media, companies can create higher engagement and increase brand awareness among a wider audience.

However, using social media in marketing also brings its own challenges. One of these is the need to maintain a consistent brand image across multiple platforms. Social media allows brands to interact directly with consumers, but it also carries risks if brands fail to manage their communications effectively. Negative reactions to a product or service can quickly spread on social media, potentially damaging a brand's reputation. Therefore, companies must have a clear strategy for managing their social media communications and ensuring that every interaction with consumers is positive and builds strong relationships (Joshi et al., 2025; Smale et al., 2024). Furthermore, companies must continuously innovate in utilizing social media to stay relevant to their audiences. Social media platforms are evolving rapidly, and consumers are often looking for new ways to engage with the brands they love. Therefore, companies must be able to adapt to these changes and continuously seek new opportunities to increase engagement and build better relationships with consumers. For example, the use of new features such as live streaming, video-based social media, or even augmented reality (AR) can provide more engaging and interactive experiences for consumers (Liu et al., 2025; Smale et al., 2024).

In the future, AI and social media will increasingly integrate to provide better and more personalized experiences for consumers. Companies that can leverage these two technologies wisely will have a significant competitive advantage in creating more relevant and enjoyable customer experiences. The combination of AI-based predictions and more personalized interactions through social media will enable companies to better understand consumer behavior and provide more tailored services (Hermann & Puntoni, 2024; Lee & Shen, 2025; Saheb et al., 2024). With the continued advancement of technology, including AI and social media, we can expect significant changes in how companies interact with their consumers. The use of these technologies will further strengthen the relationship between consumers and brands, creating more personalized and enjoyable experiences, and increasing long-term consumer loyalty. However, companies must remain vigilant in managing existing challenges, such as data privacy and reputation management, to maximize the benefits offered by these technologies (Saheb et al., 2024; Smale et al., 2024).

10. THE ROLE OF AI AND SOCIAL MEDIA IN IMPROVING CUSTOMER EXPERIENCE IN E-COMMERCE

The development of AI technology and social media has brought significant changes to the world of e-commerce. Both play a significant role in enhancing the customer experience, from ease of shopping, product personalization, to brand interaction. The use of AI in e-commerce has enabled deeper personalization, providing product recommendations based on consumer preferences and previous behavior. Furthermore, social media serves not only as a promotional platform but also as a tool for building stronger relationships between consumers and brands, enabling direct interaction and building communities around the products and services offered (Hermann & Puntoni, 2024; Kumar et al., 2024). Many e-commerce platforms use AI to provide product recommendations highly tailored to consumer interests and needs. AI-based recommendation systems, such as those used by Amazon or Netflix, analyze consumer behavior patterns, including search history, purchases, and previous interactions, to provide relevant product suggestions. This way, consumers not only find the products they are looking for but also discover new products they might be interested in, increasing the likelihood of a purchase (Saheb et al., 2024; Smale et al., 2024).

Furthermore, AI in e-commerce also plays a significant role in improving customer service. The use of AI-based chatbots allows companies to respond quickly and efficiently to consumer questions and complaints, 24/7. These chatbots not only provide answers to frequently asked questions but can also guide consumers through the purchasing process, provide relevant product information, and help them make better purchasing decisions. This technology makes the shopping experience more convenient and responsive, which in turn increases customer satisfaction levels (Kumar et al., 2024; Omeish et al., 2024). However, the use of AI in e-commerce also raises challenges related to privacy and data management. The more data collected to provide personalized experiences, the greater the potential risk of consumer personal data leakage. Therefore, it is crucial for companies to implement strict and transparent privacy policies, ensuring that consumer personal data is properly protected and used only for legitimate and ethical purposes. When consumers feel their data is secure, they are more likely to engage further in the e-commerce ecosystem and transact more frequently with brands they trust (Joshi et al., 2025; Saheb et al., 2024).

Furthermore, social media plays a crucial role in shaping the customer experience in e-commerce. Platforms like Instagram, Facebook, and TikTok allow companies to interact directly with their consumers, not only through advertising but also through more organic and engaging content. Consumers can now see how products are used by others, get first-hand reviews, and even participate in campaigns or challenges created by brands. Social media gives consumers the opportunity to become part of a larger community, strengthen their relationship with the brand, and increase their loyalty (Dhiman & Bhati, 2025; Smale et al., 2024). Companies that successfully leverage social media to build communities around their products will benefit from increased customer engagement and involvement. Community-based content, such as photos and videos created by consumers themselves, lends added credibility to the brand. When consumers see others they follow on social media using and liking a particular product, it increases their confidence in purchasing it (Liu et al., 2025; Saheb et al., 2024). Communities formed on social media also provide companies with the opportunity to gain direct feedback on their products or services, which can be used to improve their offerings and adjust marketing strategies.

However, the use of social media in e-commerce also faces challenges, one of which is the need to maintain a consistent brand image across multiple platforms. Each social media platform has a different audience with different expectations and behaviors. Therefore, companies must adapt their strategies to speak to their audiences appropriately on each platform. For example, content relevant on Instagram may not be appropriate for LinkedIn or TikTok, and companies must be able to create tailored content for each platform (Hermann & Puntoni, 2024; Koivunen et al., 2025; Saheb et al., 2024). This requires companies to have a deep understanding of their audiences on each social media platform. In the future, the use of AI and social media in e-commerce will continue to expand and become integrated. AI will become increasingly capable of processing more complex data, providing more accurate recommendations, and creating more personalized shopping experiences. Meanwhile, social media will continue to be a key channel for building communities and interacting with consumers. The use of augmented reality (AR) and virtual reality (VR) technologies will also expand, providing consumers with more immersive and interactive shopping experiences. Thus, e-commerce will increasingly offer richer and more comprehensive experiences for consumers, encouraging them to engage with brands more deeply (Dhiman & Bhati, 2025; Smale et al., 2024).

With the combination of AI and social media, e-commerce in the future will be much more adaptive and responsive to consumer needs. Companies that can leverage these technologies effectively will have a significant opportunity to improve customer satisfaction, build loyalty, and increase sales. Therefore, companies must focus on developing more personalized customer experiences, strengthening interactions on social media, and ensuring that they protect consumer privacy and data security. The judicious use of AI and social media will be key to success in this increasingly competitive e-commerce market (Chan & Choi, 2025; Xia et al., 2025).

11. INTEGRATING AI AND SOCIAL MEDIA TO ENHANCE DATA-DRIVEN MARKETING STRATEGIES

Figure 6. **AI analyzes data for better decision making**

As technology advances, artificial intelligence (AI) and social media are increasingly playing a crucial role in data-driven marketing strategies. In this increasingly digitalized world, companies no longer rely on traditional marketing methods that rely solely on mass media or conventional advertising to reach their consumers. Instead, marketing is increasingly based on data collected through various digital channels, such as social media, online searches, and e-commerce transactions. AI, which can process and analyze large amounts of data, enables companies to optimize every interaction with consumers and generate more effective marketing strategies (Kumar et al., 2024; Omeish et al., 2024; Sahut & Laroche, 2025; Xia et al., 2025). One way AI is used in data-driven marketing is through predictive analytics. AI can identify patterns in consumer data that can help companies predict future consumer behavior. For example, by analyzing data from previous transactions, search behavior, and social media interactions, AI can provide insights into which products consumers are most likely to purchase, as well as when they are likely to make those purchases. With this information, companies can design more targeted marketing campaigns and increase conversion opportunities (Chan & Choi, 2025; Omeish et al., 2024).

Furthermore, AI enables companies to create more precise and detailed audience segmentation. Through deeper data analysis, AI can group consumers based on their behavior, such as the products they frequently purchase, the best time to contact them, or even which social media platforms they use most frequently. This allows companies to deliver highly personalized marketing messages that are more relevant to each audience group. This data-driven personalization increases marketing effectiveness and ensures that consumers receive messages tailored to their preferences, increasing their likelihood of engaging with and purchasing the product (Dhiman & Bhati, 2025; Saheb et al., 2024). In addition to AI, social media also plays a crucial role in data-driven marketing. Social media platforms provide a wealth of data on consumer behavior, such as what they like, what they share, and how they interact with various brands. This information is invaluable for companies in designing more effective marketing strategies. By monitoring consumer conversations on social media, companies can tailor their messages to reflect current trends, engage with the right consumers, and identify market opportunities that might not be visible through traditional marketing channels. Social media also allows companies to measure the effectiveness of their marketing campaigns in real time, providing the opportunity to make necessary changes or adjustments (Smale et al., 2024; Teepapal, 2025; Xia et al., 2025). Using data collected through social media and AI systems to design marketing strategies not only increases marketing effectiveness but also allows companies to better understand their consumers. Companies that successfully leverage data from social media and AI to understand consumer needs can create deeper and more loyal relationships with their audiences. By using this technology, companies can not only sell products but also build more personalized relationships with their consumers, which in turn increases satisfaction and long-term loyalty (Saheb et al., 2024; Smale et al., 2024).

However, while AI and social media offer many benefits in data-driven marketing, there are challenges that companies must address. One of these is the issue of data privacy and security. The collection and use of consumer data must be conducted ethically and transparently. Companies must ensure that consumers are aware of how their data is being used and provide consent before their information is collected. While data provides invaluable insights for companies, consumer data privacy must still be respected and protected to maintain consumer trust and safeguard brand reputation (Joshi et al., 2025; Smale et al., 2024). Furthermore, companies must be careful in managing their interactions with consumers on social media. Too many promotional messages or too many interactions that seem robotic can leave consumers feeling annoyed and unappreciated. To build stronger relationships with consumers, companies must ensure they communicate in a more authentic and human manner, rather than simply as salespeople. Therefore, companies must find a balance between using AI technology to enhance the customer experience and maintaining more personal and empathetic relationships with their consumers (Dhiman & Bhati, 2025; Haleem et al., 2022).

In the future, deeper integration between AI and social media will open up many new opportunities for data-driven marketing. Advances in AI technologies, such as machine learning and natural language processing, will enable companies to better understand consumers and deliver more sophisticated and interactive experiences. Companies will be able to offer more relevant and tailored content, optimize their marketing strategies in real-time, and increase customer satisfaction and loyalty in the long term (Omeish et al., 2024; Saheb et al., 2024). However, to fully leverage the potential of AI and social media in data-driven marketing, companies must ensure they have the right infrastructure in place to efficiently collect and analyze data. The data obtained must be processed appropriately and used for legitimate purposes. Furthermore, companies also need to have teams skilled in data analysis and AI technology to ensure they can optimize the use of available data (Kumar et al., 2024; Omeish et al., 2024).

Overall, the integration of AI and social media in data-driven marketing presents a significant opportunity for companies to enhance customer experience, strengthen loyalty, and increase the effectiveness of their marketing campaigns. With the right approach, companies can harness the power of data to create more personalized and relevant experiences for their consumers, foster long-term relationships with their audiences, and maximize their marketing potential in this digital age (Saheb et al., 2024; Smale et al., 2024).

12. CONCLUSION

The role of artificial intelligence (AI) and social media in marketing has had a significant impact on how companies interact with consumers. These technologies not only enable more personalized and relevant experiences for consumers, but also open up new opportunities for companies to increase customer loyalty, optimize marketing, and strengthen relationships with their audiences. AI provides the ability to analyze big data quickly and accurately, while social media enables more human and transparent direct interactions. The two complement each other in creating better and more satisfying consumer experiences (Hermann & Puntoni, 2024; Liu et al., 2025; Xia et al., 2025). One of the greatest contributions of AI in marketing is its ability to personalize the consumer experience. By using data collected from various digital channels, companies can provide product recommendations relevant to individual preferences, speed up the product search process, and reduce consumer frustration. This personalization increases consumer convenience, which ultimately can encourage them to make more purchases and increase their satisfaction with the products or services offered. AI also enables companies to segment their audiences more precisely and offer more targeted advertising, which increases the effectiveness of marketing campaigns (Joshi et al., 2025; Omeish et al., 2024).

Social media, on the other hand, provides a platform for consumers to share their experiences, provide product reviews, and interact with brands directly. This creates a two-way relationship between consumers and companies, strengthening customer engagement and loyalty. Social media also enables companies to run more interactive and community-based marketing campaigns. Consumers feel more engaged when they can participate in campaigns or conversations on social media, which increases their sense of ownership of the brand and encourages greater loyalty to that product or service ((Dhiman & Bhati, 2025; Saheb et al., 2024). However, despite the significant benefits offered by AI and social media, there are challenges and risks that need to be addressed. One major challenge is data privacy and security. In an increasingly digital world, consumers are increasingly aware of the importance of protecting their personal data. Non-transparent data collection or misuse can damage consumer trust in brands and hinder companies from building strong relationships with their audiences. Therefore, companies must ensure they have clear privacy policies and protect consumer data in a lawful and ethical manner. Consumer trust is highly dependent on how companies manage and use their personal data (Liu et al., 2025; Smale et al., 2024; Xia et al., 2025).

Another challenge is over-reliance on technology. Although AI offers various marketing conveniences, companies must maintain the human element in interactions with consumers. Not all aspects of the customer experience can be fully understood by AI, especially when it comes to consumers' emotional and psychological needs. Therefore, while AI can assist with personalization and prediction, companies must still incorporate human creativity and empathy in making more complex marketing decisions (Kumar et al., 2024; Smale et al., 2024). Managing brand reputation is also a major challenge in social media-based marketing. Every interaction with consumers on social media can be viewed by many people, both positive and negative. When issues or complaints arise on social media, companies must be able to respond quickly and constructively to prevent further damage to their brand image. Responding quickly to consumer complaints and feedback can transform negative experiences into opportunities to repair relationships and increase loyalty (Chan & Choi, 2025; Joshi et al., 2025; Liu et al., 2025). Therefore, companies need to have an effective and transparent reputation management strategy when interacting with consumers on social media.

In the future, AI and social media will continue to evolve and become increasingly integrated into digital marketing strategies. Advances in natural language processing, machine learning, and other technologies will enable AI to understand consumer behavior more deeply and deliver increasingly personalized and proactive experiences. Social media will also continue to serve as a key platform for companies to build stronger relationships with consumers and introduce new products or services. Furthermore, companies that can integrate these two technologies will have an advantage in terms of efficiency, effectiveness, and the ability to respond more quickly to changing market trends (Hermann & Puntoni, 2024; Liu et al., 2025; Xia et al., 2025). Overall, AI and social media play a significant role in shaping the future of digital marketing. With the right approach, companies can leverage these technologies to enhance consumer experiences, strengthen relationships with audiences, and increase long-term customer loyalty. However, to maximize this potential, companies must be wise in managing challenges related to data privacy, reputation management, and reliance on technology. With continued innovation and ethical use of technology, AI and social media will continue to be invaluable tools in shaping the future of marketing and consumer interactions (Omeish et al., 2024; Saheb et al., 2024).

REFERENCES

Bilal, M., Zhang, Y., Cai, S., Akram, U., & Halibas, A. (2024). Artificial intelligence is the magic wand making customer-centric a reality! An investigation into the relationship between consumer purchase intention and consumer engagement through affective attachment. *Journal of Retailing and Consumer Services, 77*, 103674. 10.1016/j.jretconser.2023.103674. DOI: 10.1016/j.jretconser.2023.103674

Brüns, J. D., & Meißner, M. (2024). Do you create your content yourself? Using generative artificial intelligence for social media content creation diminishes perceived brand authenticity. *Journal of Retailing and Consumer Services, 79*, 103790. 10.1016/j.jretconser.2024.103790. DOI: 10.1016/j.jretconser.2024.103790

Chan, H.-L., & Choi, T.-M. (2025). Using generative artificial intelligence (GenAI) in marketing: Development and practices. *Journal of Business Research, 191*, 115276. 10.1016/j.jbusres.2025.115276. DOI: 10.1016/j.jbusres.2025.115276

Dhiman, R., & Bhati, N. S. (2025). When AI meets influencers: Role of AI-powered instagram influencers driving consumers' purchase intentions: An integration of SMIV & SOR framework. *Journal of Open Innovation, 11*(3), 100591. 10.1016/j.joitmc.2025.100591. DOI: 10.1016/j.joitmc.2025.100591

Haleem, A., Javaid, M., Asim Qadri, M., Pratap Singh, R., & Suman, R. (2022). Artificial intelligence (AI) applications for marketing: A literature-based study. *International Journal of Intelligent Networks, 3*, 119–132. 10.1016/j.ijin.2022.08.005. DOI: 10.1016/j.ijin.2022.08.005

Hermann, E., & Puntoni, S. (2024). Artificial intelligence and consumer behavior: From predictive to generative AI. *Journal of Business Research, 180*, 114720. 10.1016/j.jbusres.2024.114720. DOI: 10.1016/j.jbusres.2024.114720

Hue, T. T., & Hung, T. H. (2025). Impact of artificial intelligence on branding: A bibliometric review and future research directions. *Humanities & Social Sciences Communications, 12*(1), 209. DOI: 10.1057/s41599-025-04488-6

Joshi, S., Bhattacharya, S., Pathak, P., Natraj, N. A., Saini, J., & Goswami, S. (2025). Harnessing the potential of generative AI in digital marketing using the Behavioral Reasoning Theory approach. *International Journal of Information Management Data Insights, 5*(1), 100317. 10.1016/j.jjimei.2024.100317. DOI: 10.1016/j.jjimei.2024.100317

Koivunen, K., Haanpää, M. A. A., & Saraniemi, S. (2025). The emergence of cause-oriented influencers – conceptualizing de-influencing on TikTok. *Journal of Business Research, 197*, 115463. 10.1016/j.jbusres.2025.115463. DOI: 10.1016/j.jbusres.2025.115463

Kumar, V., Ashraf, A. R., & Nadeem, W. (2024). AI-powered marketing: What, where, and how? *International Journal of Information Management, 77*, 102783. 10.1016/j.ijinfomgt.2024.102783. DOI: 10.1016/j.ijinfomgt.2024.102783

Lee, C. T., & Shen, Y.-C. (2025). Artificial humanity: A multi-method exploration of user responses to AI influencer affordances in short video platform. *Telematics and Informatics, 98*, 102245. 10.1016/j.tele.2025.102245. DOI: 10.1016/j.tele.2025.102245

Liu, H., Zhang, P., Cheng, H., Hasan, N., & Chiong, R. (2025). Impact of AI-generated virtual streamer interaction on consumer purchase intention: A focus on social presence and perceived value. *Journal of Retailing and Consumer Services, 85*, 104290. 10.1016/j.jretconser.2025.104290. DOI: 10.1016/j.jretconser.2025.104290

Nazir, S., Khadim, S., Ali Asadullah, M., & Syed, N. (2023). Exploring the influence of artificial intelligence technology on consumer repurchase intention: The mediation and moderation approach. *Technology in Society, 72*, 102190. 10.1016/j.techsoc.2022.102190. DOI: 10.1016/j.techsoc.2022.102190

Nogueira, E., Lopes, J. M., & Gomes, S. (2025). *The new era of Artificial Intelligence in consumption: theoretical framing, review and research agenda.* Management Review Quarterly., DOI: 10.1007/s11301-025-00531-7

Omeish, F., Al Khasawneh, M., & Khair, N. (2024). Investigating the impact of AI on improving customer experience through social media marketing: An analysis of Jordanian Millennials. *Computers in Human Behavior Reports, 15*, 100464. 10.1016/j.chbr.2024.100464. DOI: 10.1016/j.chbr.2024.100464

Saheb, T., Sidaoui, M., & Schmarzo, B. (2024). Convergence of artificial intelligence with social media: A bibliometric & qualitative analysis. *Telematics and Informatics Reports, 14*, 100146. 10.1016/j.teler.2024.100146

Sahut, J.-M., & Laroche, M. (2025). Using artificial intelligence (AI) to enhance customer experience and to develop strategic marketing: An integrative synthesis. *Computers in Human Behavior, 170*, 108684. 10.1016/j.chb.2025.108684. DOI: 10.1016/j.chb.2025.108684

Smale, M. C., Fox, J. D., & Fox, A. K. (2024). When being smart trumps AI: An exploration into consumer preferences for smart vs. AI-powered products. *Computers in Human Behavior, 161*, 108405. 10.1016/j.chb.2024.108405. DOI: 10.1016/j.chb.2024.108405

Teepapal, T. (2025). AI-driven personalization: Unraveling consumer perceptions in social media engagement. *Computers in Human Behavior, 165*, 108549. 10.1016/j.chb.2024.108549. DOI: 10.1016/j.chb.2024.108549

Xia, H., Zhang, L., Chen, J., & Wang, X. (2025). Decoding virtual influencer endorsement using machine learning: The role of virtual influencer, posting, and disclosure characteristics. *Journal of Retailing and Consumer Services, 87*, 104366. 10.1016/j.jretconser.2025.104366. DOI: 10.1016/j.jretconser.2025.104366

Chapter 6
The Influence of Social Media and Virtual Reality on Consumer Behavior

P. Visu
Velammal Engineering College, India

P. Gopika priya
Vel Tech Multi Tech Dr. Rangarajan Dr. Sakunthala Engineering College, India

T. P. Anish
https://orcid.org/0000-0002-4308-9645
R.M.K. College of Engineering and Technology, India

K. Raju
Rajalakshmi Engineering College, India

M. Ezhilvendan
https://orcid.org/0009-0003-3213-1304
Panimalar Engineering College, India

ABSTRACT

This survey chapter examines the influence of social media and virtual reality (VR) on consumer behavior, highlighting their transformative roles in modern marketing. Social media drives information search, social influence, and brand engagement, while VR offers immersive experiences that enhance purchase intentions and consumer satisfaction. The combined use of these technologies creates synergistic effects, amplifying consumer interaction and emotional connection with brands. Despite their potential, challenges such as privacy concerns, psychological impacts, accessibility issues, and ethical marketing practices require careful consideration.

DOI: 10.4018/979-8-3373-2747-1.ch006

The chapter also outlines future research directions, including emerging technologies like augmented reality and AI personalization, as well as cross-cultural and longitudinal studies.

1. INTRODUCTION

1.1 Background

The behavior of consumers has long been a fundamental part of the study of marketing since it is a set of decision making processes that individuals and groups of them apply when deciding, purchasing, consuming, and disposition of goods and services. Such behaviors are not only academically relevant, but also essential to businesses which seek to develop effective marketing strategies, enhance satisfaction among customers, and guarantee long term brand loyalty. Through understanding how and why consumers choose, marketers can better align their efforts to the needs and expectations of their target audiences(Baskaran, K. 2022).

Earlier, most studies of consumer behavior looked at what happened in stores, where shoppers were influenced by the layout, the behavior of salespeople, where products were placed, and in-store promotions. Yet, the fast development of digital technology has made a huge difference to the way consumers behave. Because of e-commerce, mobile applications, and artificial intelligence, there are now more ways for businesses to interact with customers and market their products. Social media platforms and virtual reality (VR) are among the most important digital tools, capable of greatly affecting the actions of today's consumers(Manoharan et al., 2025).

Now, social media is a very important tool of communication and of business. Today, platforms are central points where people look at products, talk about them, and exchange thoughts with companies and other people. It has many various impacts on how people are shopping. Companies can use social media to communicate with their customers right away and answer their questions plus build a group of people with a common interest. Influencer marketing, user generated content and targeted ads now have brands ways to reach consumers that are very personal and make a strong emotional impact. Social media has a huge impact on influencing consumer opinions by affecting them through the actions and thoughts of others. Other users' feedback is more relied upon by people than they rely on traditional advertisements. This has led to online reviews, rating systems and influencers' recommendations playing such an important role in people's decision making on what to buy. Social media also enables the people to see new brands, new products, new trends and so on all the time, which makes them buy more often in an impulse. However, social media has grown, and virtual reality (VR) has brought another level to how people shop.

In VR settings that are like the real world, users are able to explore virtual settings and have more chances to interact with products and services(Siva Subramanian et al., 2024). Traditional media could never provide a strong and real experience, which is why VR gives people a new and surprising way to discover products. For example, people in fashion and beauty can try on clothes or make up online so that they don't have to go to a store. Similarly, in real estate and automotive industries, VR is used for virtual tours and showrooms, so that people can view houses and cars from their home.

VR used in marketing makes the experience better for consumers and helps to lower their doubts about what to buy. Due to VR, consumers will be able to make decisions more efficiently, and hence they will tend to be more satisfied with their procurement and will rarely repudiate it. VR also enables one to connect to consumers on an emotional level and tie them to a brand by means of the unique experiences that transcend the normal advertisement (Bansal et al 2023).

The collaboration between social media and VR technologies is creating a new consumer engagement epoch. All these tools allow individuals to be part of personalized, interpersonal and narrative based content. Through this amalgamation, it is now possible that marketers make highly interactive campaigns and engage people in social media, who reach their audiences at both the mind and the heart. As an illustration, a VR video on social media can quickly go viral attracting more people to the brand and increasing their interest.

However, the transition to digital is associated with certain new issues. The overload of data privacy due to digital technology, access to technology, and overload of data should be addressed so that the consumers feel safe and appreciated. In addition, companies ought to change their analytics and feedback systems that would enable them to learn about these platforms and implement them in practice. In a nutshell, as the social media and virtual reality are becoming parts of our lives, understanding the impact of these technologies on consumer behavior is of great significance today. They are transforming how individuals approach businesses and the overall experience that customers undergo during the process of learning about a brand to utilization of the products subsequently. They must observe these changes and apply these changes in formulating original and ethical strategies which are accepting and well informed about the modern digital user.

1.2 Motivation

The motivation of this survey is that social media and a virtual reality have a greater influence on consumer behavior in the modern world. The social media platforms are used by people to share and obtain information, which nowadays largely influence their awareness, likes, and what they desire to buy. Viral marketing and support of influencers and post content created by the users on social media are some of the brands that have contributed to accelerating the recognition and trust of the brand. Similarly, VR allows the brands to establish a good emotional connection with their customers because of its capacity to fully involve the latter. Even though they are being used more by people, their combined impact on the habit of consumers remains complex and continues to evolve, so it requires careful analysis. When VR is implemented in the social media, people have an opportunity to communicate and engage into the content simultaneously. Due to this fact, marketing can be stronger but it can cause some problems concerning the preservation of privacy, data, and ethical compliance. Moreover, the social media and VR are increasing at a high rate in the entire world in the recent past. According to numerous reports, the number of social media users across the world is in the billions and the VR sector is rapidly growing due to the availability of hardware and software development. These trends help to understand that the marketers, researchers, and policymakers are learning how these technologies influence consumer decisions to take advantage of their opportunities.

1.3 Objectives and Scope

This survey attempts to generalize the existing studies on the influence of social media and virtual reality on the shopping behavior of people. The chapter attempts to explain the impact of these technologies on the decision-making of consumers, their level of involvement, their emotions, and loyalty towards a brand. The area of the survey includes both personal consequences of social media and VR and a combination of them. This will require considering a number of social media, various types of VR experiences, and appropriate marketing strategies. One of the critical research questions is the role of social media in changing the way consumers search information and impacting peers. What is the effect of VR in enhancing the marketing experience and the consumer confidence to purchase? What are the advantages and drawbacks associated with associating VR to social media marketing? In addition, the chapter includes aspects of ethical considerations, issues of privacy and potential future research areas to have a holistic impression of the subject at hand.

1.4 Structure of the Chapter

There are eight sections to which the chapter has been subdivided. The second part examines the theories of consumer behavior, social media, and virtual reality following the introduction. The sections 3 and 4 examine the effect of social media and VR on consumer behavior process, one after another. The authors research the influence of these factors on each other and present some related case studies in this section 5. In this section 6, the author examines the ethical concerns and problems of these technologies. The section 7 identifies the key areas of future research and the current trends which researchers must keep in mind. Finally, Section 8 concludes by summarizing key findings and clarifying their importance to marketers, businesses, and researchers.

2. THEORETICAL FOUNDATIONS

2.1 Consumer Behavior Models

Consumer behaviour models have been used in the past to explain the decision making process of the buying decisions of people. This can be realized in such ways as the Buyer Decision Process because consumers tend to undergo through five steps: identification of a problem, problem-solving search, evaluation of the available solution, purchase decision, and post-purchase behavior. They emphasize the logical-based decision making which is driven by motivation, perception, learning and attitudes of the people. These theories have been able to assist in adding both the social and mental features that contribute to what consumers decide(Dahake et al., 2024).

Conversely, the recent rapid evolution of social media and virtual reality has altered the traditional business models significantly. Due to the digital environments, how individuals behave as consumers is vibrant, participatory, and more related to society. However, in contrast to the past, when customers used to shop and make a purchase primarily after considering an option by themselves, nowadays, customers frequently check social media, contribute to the creation of content, and engage in on-line interactions. Because people are now affected by online experiences in their buying decisions, it is important for traditional models to include social influence, network effects, and immersive experience.

Besides, the Engagement Theory and Flow Theory have become significant for describing how people interact with online information. According to engagement theory, being more involved with digital posts by liking, commenting, and sharing on social media strengthens how people feel and makes them more likely to buy. According to flow theory, a psychological concept, being totally involved and happy in what you do is important, especially when explaining how VR can influence consumers by making experiences with products and brands unforgettable(Naveeenkumar et al., 2024).

2.2 Social Media in Marketing

Nowadays, social media constitute a significant component of the way companies promote themselves. Due to the constant availability and high capacity of enabling the brands to communicate directly to the people, it has entirely transformed the way businesses connect to their customers. Conventional marketing is typically one-directional communication, social media enables the customer to participate in discussions, engage in content creation, and influence the brand image(Durgam 2018).

All these forms of social media have various roles in marketing depending on how people communicate and their habits on the media. Numerous companies to build communities, retain customers over a long period, and assist in B2B promotions. Through their pages, groups and messaging features, they facilitate the ability of the brands to engage with the people and make them remain loyal to the brand. There are numerous online sources that are primarily aimed at displaying the content in a form of visuals and video clips. These platforms have a high influence in the purchase decisions of people in the fashion, beauty, travel, and lifestyle industry because the goods are visual.

Online platform is currently being used in the sharing news, real-time conversations and customer service. Those are usually utilized to state the new versions of the product, address the questions of the customers, and participate in the popular discussions. All these platforms provide the marketer with unique tools to produce content to specific individuals, advertise to them, and personalize their messages to their tastes and the prevailing trends.

The core concepts constituting social media marketing and influencing consumer perception and interaction with brands on the internet are user engagement, social influence, and the word-of-mouth (WOM).

User engagement refers to various forms of interactions between users and the brand content such as behavior, feeling, and thinking. Liking, posting, commenting on posts, polling or participating in contests, using branded hashtags, or creating user-generated content (UGC) are some of the activities. When a brand is able to connect with its consumers in great ways, it can end up becoming more loyal and supported by them. Whenever users participate in the video challenges of a brand, they get to watch the content and get others to view it, which expands the presence of the brand and brings the community together.

Social influence is the influence of other people in social media on their attitudes and choices. With the prevalence of influencers, customers are more inclined to accept the recommendations of famous individuals and other celebrities. Through this method of influencer marketing, it is possible to influence the purchasing behavior of individuals more conspicuously, but less direct. Influencers make brands and people be more intimate as they make sure that their marketing activities are authentic and can be approached by people.

Word-of-mouth (WOM) has undergone significant transformations since the beginning of the digital era. Where the conventional form of WOM can only be achieved by communicating individually to other face to face, eWOM enables individuals to disseminate their views to anyone anywhere and in the real-time. There are numerous internet resources that can be used to watch unboxing videos, tutorials and reviews. A positive or a negative review may quickly gain popularity and make a significant impact on the perceptions of a brand by people.

In the contemporary digitalized world, eWOM occurs quicker and on a larger scale than the rest. A viral campaign, meme, or popular hashtag can achieve the brand a lot more exposure in a very short period, primarily when it is concerning current events or trends. Those brands that effectively handle eWOM will be able to spend less money but reap a major effect, but those that fail to handle it effectively can have their reputation ruined within a relatively short period.

The social proof is one of the essential elements of the social media marketing, as it causes individuals to refer to the views and actions of others and then make their choice. When individuals are triggered to purchase or recommend a product due to its popularity on social media, it is referred to as social proof. Suppose that a restaurant has hundreds of good reviews on online platform, it is sure to attract more new clients as compared to a restaurant that does not get many reviews. By use of testimonial, influencer support, and user generated content, the brands will be able to provide customers with greater confidence, assist them in trusting the business, and accelerate the process of making decisions on what to purchase.

Moreover, the social media is interactive and it gives a lot of information, thus marketers can easily know what consumers like, feel, and what they do. It is also possible to segment users, address particular groups, and monitor the effectiveness of marketing with the help of advanced analytics which contributes to the development of rapid and customized approaches.

All in all, social media has changed the way marketing works by providing a place to share information, create bonds, include users, and inspire value coming from the community. Since digital platforms keep advancing, marketers are required to pay attention to the latest trends, be genuine, and involve consumers through social media(Nadda et al., 2015).

2.3 Virtual Reality in Marketing

Virtual Reality (VR) is fast becoming an important tool for marketing that relies on immersion. Because VR uses computer simulations to build 3D spaces that people can use, it helps users interact with digital content just like they would in reality. VR marketing is different from TV, or regular digital ads since it allows consumers to get involved in the brand's environment and story. Because of this strong involvement, VR is rapidly enhancing how brands communicate with their customers and has become a major tool for modern marketers(Gagandeep, 2023).

Basically, VR depends on advanced software and hardware, including headsets, special gloves, or even videos seen from all around, to create realistic worlds for users. Some of these environments are like real rooms, some copy real products, while others create entire imaginary scenarios that keep users involved and interested. VR on certain platforms is totally immersive and needs special gear, while others are less involving and work through smartphones or desktops(Ozdemir, M. A. 2021).

Being immersive, VR has many important roles in marketing that are not only for novelty. Experiential marketing is a key area where virtual reality is used to give people a chance to participate in activities. VR allows individuals to participate in brand experiences as opposed to other media. As an example, numerous automotive companies enable individuals to check out their vehicles using VR, thus customers can view their cars in the inside, check its appearance, and even experience different driving scenarios at home. Similarly, the real estate businesses are adopting VR so that individuals can have virtual tours of houses, assess the design, and determine whether they wish to purchase at any point. Technology is being employed in the world of fashion and retail as virtual fitting rooms are being used which means that people can have an idea on how various clothes, accessories or even makeup would look on their bodies. They also assist individuals in shopping more easily as well as putting online shoppers at ease over the size or the look of a product they purchase. Through VR, customers experience the experience of shopping in a store and this makes the customers select products they are certain with and are contented with. Another key advantage of VR in marketing is the fact that it is now possible to see products more closely. Individuals are able to view features, textures, functions, and sizes of a product on all sides and can make amends as they see fit. It comes in handy most when purchasing electronics, home appliances or furniture, because individuals tend to require as much knowledge as possible regarding the product before making a purchase. The use of VR, whereby users can view the fitment of their products in their homes, has been made possible by many companies, making a better decision. The primary advantage of VR is that it allows users to feel and experience the virtual world they are in. The existence on social media is quite essential in introducing consumers to the brand, as it captures the attention of people more than any other media and allows them to identify with a brand. When individuals perceive themselves to be in a virtual world, as in walking through a resort through a travel agency or attending a concert sponsored by a brand, they are likely to recollect the experience, the messages of the brand, and have positive thoughts about the product or service represented in the advert. In addition, VR usage frequently results in flow state, in other words people become completely engaged and forget about what is going in the surrounding. Due to this process, users have a better time having fun and become more eager to hear what the brand has to say and what they share. Due to these impacts, a marketer can anticipate that customers will be more engaged, spend more time with their content and have higher probability of supporting their products, or purchasing their products. Due to the VR technology advancement, today it is being linked to social media and e-commerce. The brands are currently implementing social VR spaces in which individuals can socialize and access digital content in a way that they would in social networks. Thus, virtual showrooms may be included in the social media campaigns, and users can easily shop, look at items and comment on them everywhere. A combination of VR and AI, AR, and data analytics is enabling the development of marketing strategies, which are responsive to the needs of individual users. Nevertheless, some challenges exist as far as the application of VR in marketing at a large scale is concerned. Creating an application may be costly, and not everyone can even access it, so this area does not pose the market to all business organizations. Due to the cheaper cost of technology and increased exposure of people to technology, VR will form a large part of mainstream marketing. Everything said and done, virtual reality is an emerging strategy that brands can use to communicate with their customers. The assistance of VR will allow marketers to make their audience feel more engaged, decrease any uncertainties regarding the products, and bring their services to higher levels of prominence online. Due to technological advancement, technology will have a larger role in the behavior of the consumer and the way customers relate to businesses and therefore in future ability to be used as a tool in digital marketing(Prabha, D., & Subramanian 2017).

3. INFLUENCE OF SOCIAL MEDIA ON CONSUMER BEHAVIOR

3.1 Information Search and Awareness

The consumers are currently relying on social media to seek product information and news about new brands. In contrast to the past, when the bulk of the information was shared among the brands, social media platforms enable individuals to communicate with the businesses and share, distribute and analyze information among themselves. Some of the most important places where consumers can discover new things, read reviews, watch demonstrations, and engage with what the brands post are many online platforms. Individuals now become more interested in reviewing, rating, and hearing testimonials provided by other people in social media as opposed to traditional advertising. This information is available in real time and hence reduces the amount of risk that individuals have prior to the purchase. More to the point, the personalized feeds on social media are generated by the algorithms and this way, users are exposed to product information that corresponds with their interests and previous activity, which makes them more aware and interested in these products. At this point, since every person can look up information on the internet, the consumers are more engaged in the process of shaping their perception of brands based on their online actions(Trivedi, S., & Malik, R. 2021).

3.2 Social Influence and Peer Effects

The impact of social influence and peer effects on product purchasing is more evident due to the great role of social media. Social media is trendy as it makes people be engaged and track the activities of others and prominent personalities. The reason why influencers are influential is that they will persuade their followers to purchase items by posting their personal stories simultaneously. Consumers are likely to alter their attitude and intentions due to the apparent authenticity and their relatability when they encounter them. Consumer created user content is highly influential. When the individuals observe other individuals using or discussing some products on internet, then it acts as a signal to them to behave similarly. Recommendation by friends makes individuals feel more safe when purchasing something and trusting a brand they have never heard about. In addition, social media groups whose interests are specific motivate individuals to make decisions depending on what other members post and believe. Due to the virality of social media, any information regarding the activity of other people will spread faster and affect more individuals.

Figure 1. Influence of Social Media on Consumer Behavior

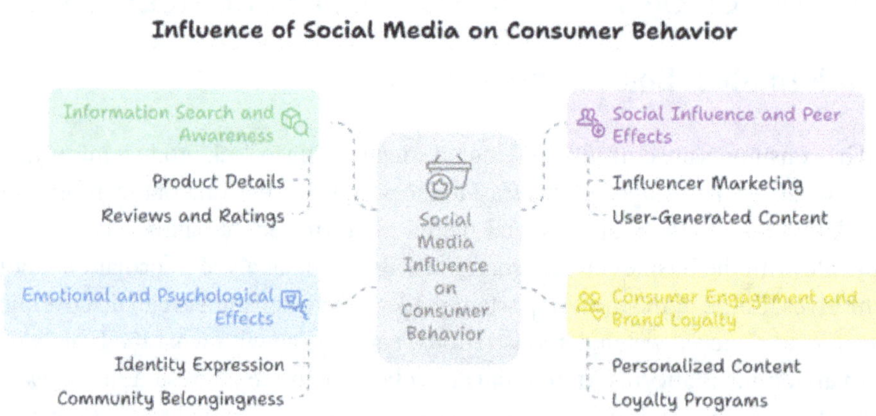

3.3 Consumer Engagement and Brand Loyalty

The social media also allows the brands to engage the customers beyond the sales and offer further communication and positive feelings. The activities that come with engagement in social media include liking, commenting, sharing posts, and engaging in contests as well as providing feedback. When the consumers are involved in the activities of a brand, they tend to feel interested and committed and this contributes to brand loyalty. A brand that communicates with the consumers and provides them with personalized content tends to develop greater loyalty in customers. The social media allows businesses to interact with consumers and care about their views, which promote their satisfaction and loyalty. The activities that include the participants can assist in making the brand more relevant to the users and creating the group of followers by use of hash tag challenges among others. It is well established that being engaged affects people's desire to purchase. If customers are engaged, they are more willing to recommend the brand, buy it again, and resist other companies' products. By using social media loyalty and exclusive online groups, companies encourage customers to stick with them, which lengthens the time they remain customers and brings more value.

3.4 Emotional and Psychological Effects

Besides influencing what we choose, social media greatly affects people's emotions and thoughts about buying products. Users can use platforms to express who they are and what groups they belong to using the brands they support and the things they post. When brands show their identity, consumers are more likely to pick them if they fit with what a person hopes to be or with the groups they belong to.

Social media communities also help fulfill the need for belongingness in people. A bond between a consumer and a brand's community encourages them to become more loyal and supportive. Emotional ties with the brand motivate buyers to forgive occasional problems with the company's services.

However, social media sometimes makes people feel less satisfied and happy because they compare themselves with others. Seeing only the best parts of other people's lives on social media may make users feel that what they have is not enough. When planning social media strategies, brands must keep in mind how people's minds work to avoid unethical and irresponsible actions.

4. INFLUENCE OF VIRTUAL REALITY ON CONSUMER BEHAVIOR

4.1 Immersive Product Experiences

Because of virtual reality (VR), people now have a more immersive way to interact with products than before(Varun et al., 2024; Aswini et al., 2023). A great use of VR is for virtual try-ons, allowing people to picture how different items will suit them before putting them on. Because of this technology, shoppers can see how clothes will look and fit before they buy them. In the same way, 3D visualization and simulations help people view products from every side, modify aspects, and grasp their features and use in a virtual environment that looks real.

Since furniture, vehicles, and real estate are hard to judge online, interactive experiences are very helpful. For instance, looking at a virtual house tour or test driving a car in VR gives a consumer a better and more detailed picture of the item than just pictures or video clips can show. VR helps customers find the confidence to buy by providing real-life experiences that make shopping online and in stores similar(Yuce, A. 2021).

4.2 Experiential Marketing and Consumer Engagement

Using virtual reality in marketing helps brands make experiences that involve people in both their emotions and mental processes. With regular ads, people only receive messages, but in VR, users are fully involved, encouraged to explore and interact with others. Being so engaged with a brand encourages customers to remember and prefer it. Through VR, the brands will be able to generate a dedicated space where the consumers can explore their world. To use an example, in case of travel companies, you might be part of a virtual tour of a far off place, and in the case of sports brands, you might get to view athletes playing around with their sportswear. Such experiences bring interest to the senses leaving a solid impression on the audience and making the brand more attractive. In addition, VR causes individuals to feel flow, which implies they are entirely concentrated and forget how long they have been doing it, and it is even more pleasant. This type of marketing campaign is effective among the youths who tend to communicate with the brands via the internet. The audience of the campaign is also not enhanced through additional advertisement since consumers are also likely to post their VR experiences on social networks.

4.3 Impact on Purchase Intentions and Satisfaction

The virtual reality helps the consumers become more confident in their buying decision and enhances their belief. When the consumers can view the product over the internet and check the specifications, they are aware of what they are purchasing, thus they are less concerned with quality, fitting, and functionality of the product. Trying the product in person increases a consumer's faith in the brand, so they are more likely to buy it. In addition, VR makes reviews more satisfying since it ensures that consumers understand what they are getting from the product. Using VR, consumers are able to see a lifelike version of the product, so they are usually more satisfied and likely to spread positive reviews. Retailers experience fewer returns of products, so they save money on operations and earn more profit. It is proven that experiencing VR increases a person's chances of accepting higher prices and being loyal to a brand. VR encourages users to connect better and, as a result, move closer to making a purchase.

4.4 VR and Consumer Trust

It is very hard to win consumer trust in online and digital marketing, but VR provides special benefits in this area. The trust someone has in a shop usually depends on how visible and genuine the experience appears. Being able to explore everything in virtual reality makes consumers more confident and trustful since there is no need to doubt what they see.

Although conventional advertisements can be considered prejudiced, with VR, consumers can experience the benefits and possibilities of the product by themselves, and they will feel to be in control. Openness of this kind enhances the relationship between a brand and consumers. In addition, the majority of VR-based environments provide rapid feedback and support to customers, which fosters more trust as it is able to assist the customers immediately. Moreover, VR may render the impression that you are communicating with other individuals, e.g. providing virtual sales assistant or group of peers with advice, and make you feel more comfortable. As VR offers different sensual experiences, it makes all things appear more real and enables individuals to establish a stronger emotional trust. Since VR is becoming penetrative and integrated with other digital tools, it will be a greater part of acquiring consumer trust, and hence will be a necessity in subsequent marketing strategies.

5. COMBINED EFFECTS OF SOCIAL MEDIA AND VIRTUAL REALITY

5.1 Integration of VR Content on Social Media

Digital marketing is taking a significant leap by adding virtual reality (VR) to the social media offering consumers an opportunity to be more engaged. Social media is increasingly allowing users to share virtual reality content in the form of 360-degree videos, virtual tours, and immersive stories. Thanks to this, consumers have the ability to experience VR themselves, as well as share their experiences, and this is why more people are exposed to the marketing of a certain brand. Social media platforms now allow people to join live VR events and take part in product launches, music concerts, exhibitions, or brand events at the same time. This union makes it possible for brands to engage users in VR activities and increase the sense of togetherness. Additionally, communicating with each other using avatars, chatting and working together in VR enables individuals to create social networks among themselves and communicate in a similar manner as they do in social media platforms. The combination of VR and social media platforms will enable more individuals to use such technology. Individuals without VR headsets may also view some simple VR content or 360 video on their phones or computers via their social media apps. The availability of more people will assist marketers to access their consumers in many ways on different devices.

5.2 Synergistic Effects on Consumer Behavior

Combined with VR, the influence of social media on consumers will be more significant, and therefore, individuals will be more engaged, possessing more emotions and take more buying intentions. VR enables individuals to have a more realistic sense of a brand, and social media provides the brand with the perception, endorsement, and influence to disseminate its experiences. The merging allows users to easily move between the use of VR and the discussion or sharing of content, which will make the brand more visible and re-present its message. With VR, a user could virtually try something on and instantly post a photo or video regarding it online, and receive opinions and advice on the same. The immediate feedback of the firm stimulates the consumer to purchase. Moreover, social media and VR provide individuals with the chance of sharing as well as personalizing their experiences. Since they are involved, individuals feel affiliated to the brand and they tend to be long-serving promoters of the brand. Due to immersive-social marketing, brands can create stories that are enticing to users to discuss them with other people, which significantly broadens the reach and influence of the company. In this manner marketers have an additional consumer data as they can relate social and VR activity, therefore making them target individuals more specifically.

5.3 Case Studies and Industry Examples

The close collaboration of social media and virtual reality has helped top brands in various industries to find a way of attracting and serving customers to better their business outcomes. Using the fashion sector as an example, VR social campaigns associated with the fashion world have been established whereby the people are able to wear special products and share their experience on various social media platforms, which make them excited and draw attention of many individuals. Auto companies have also provided the new models through streaming virtual cars launching events on social media thereby enabling people worldwide to communicate with the representatives of the company and experience the car in the virtual reality. These campaigns have been identified by people as being creative and unifying as people engage with a brand. Another good example of the same occurring is the travel industry. Social media VR videos of specific destinations make people travel and decide on their next destination. The fact that individuals may plan their trips online and recommend their friends these places, these brands combine the thrill of the virtual world and the power of the word-of-the-mouth.

A lot of entertainment and gaming companies accept this way of working. Events taking place on VR platforms and promoted online allow people to feel close to one another and engage in the community.

This shows us how combining VR and social media can lead to strong marketing campaigns that appeal to today's online users and help them decide to buy your products.

6. CHALLENGES AND ETHICAL CONSIDERATIONS

6.1 Privacy and Data Security

Because many people use social media and VR at the moment, there are significant issues regarding privacy and data protection that need to be addressed to save people. They gather a vast amount of personal data, and it contains actions, likes, location, biometric data of a person to use it in virtual reality. This data collection can make advertising quite specific, which is why it occurs, however, such a collection could also imply that the data of users can be stolen or utilized without their consent. Companies in the social media tend to track the actions of people on the internet, what they watch as well as whom they socialize with, to form their consumer profiles. On the same note, VR gadgets are able to detect eye track, physical alterations and user interaction, which can say much about their likes and minds. Yet, permission may be ethically questionable as well as the possibility and transparency of unwanted profiling in the collection and research of this type of information. In case such platforms fall in the hands of cybercriminals, individuals will lose their identity, money and trust in the platform. Moreover, the ethical issues occur when the obtained data is employed on manipulative advertisements or unjust treatment. Therefore, effective data protection regulations, uncomplicated methods of consent provision and unrestricted policies towards its use should exist to guarantee that it remains ethical and safeguard consumers.

6.2 Psychological and Social Impact

The other critical issue is that social media and VR are transforming the mentality and social life of the consumers. As much as they make people interact and communicate, such technologies can lead to addiction, increased competition and uncertainty during the process of buying something. The rationale here is that such sites as social media are meant to capture and sustain the attention of the users and that the same would end up disrupting the everyday life, mental health and well-being of the people. It shows the perfect life of other people on social media, thus causing consumers to compare themselves with the images and posts. This would leave the person insecure, jealous and with low self esteem which may in the end alter the shopping habits and satisfaction of a person. Virtual reality may lead to the forgetting of the real life issues when people use it excessively. The more companies in marketing manipulate such psychological tricks to make consumers purchase products impulsively or be materialistic, the more vulnerable customers are. The people making these platforms and selling them must make sure that their efforts are ethical and they make people use them in a healthy manner.

6.3 Accessibility and Digital Divide

Although the number of users of social media and VR is increasing, the connectivity to the technologies is a significant barrier to many individuals. Social media is user-friendly since people can access their smartphones and the internet from their home, although some individuals cannot access it equally due to knowledge and connection disparities. The larger hurdles come in the process of making virtual reality accessible to a large number of individuals. VR technology is usually costly, needs sophisticated hardware, and technical expertise to use, limiting its use to wealthier and more technologically-adept consumers. Since VR is not accessible to all parties, there are certain groups that might fail to experience the immersive content of the brand. The inaccessibility of technology may expand the preexisting social disparities, as individuals without it may be deprived of the advantage of the information, diversion, and shopping over the web. Individuals, who are engaged in marketing and policy-making, should strive to develop strategies that enable everybody to experience and enjoy the advantages of social media and VR.

6.4 Ethical Marketing Practices

To care about consumers and gain their trust, it is essential to apply the ethical marketing principles in social media and virtual reality. In ethical marketing, being transparent is highly significant because it implies the clear disclosure of sponsored content or their partnership with influencers and what information is gathered. Individuals ought to know how their information would be handled and they ought to have the capability of managing their online information. The freedom of the users and the absence of attempts to manipulate them are one of the important ethical questions in VR design. To give an example, the designers are not to create the scenarios in VR, which make the user purchase anything. To market in VR, educating and entertaining and empowering folks is more critical. Due to the appearance of new technologies, the consumer protection laws and industry standards need to be revised on a regular basis. The ethical marketing involves being concerned with the people and ensuring that the contents are not obscene and false. Adherence to these principles enables the brands to establish a long term relationship with the consumers, and this is win-win to both sides.

7. FUTURE RESEARCH DIRECTIONS

7.1 Emerging Technologies and Trends

With the continued evolution of such trends as social media and virtual reality (VR) studies must go on exploring the impact of the new trends on consumer interaction. AR is becoming increasingly popular along with VR, which has made it an option to have the digital objects appearing on top of real-life objects. AR and VR are a good fit, and they provide marketers with novel opportunities to contact their target audience. Research needs to be conducted to understand how AR and VR work together on consumer behavior in comparison to the effect of AR and VR when used separately. As the metaverse grows in popularity, it is a new opportunity to observe how individuals interact, shop, and communicate online on various VR, AR, and social media platforms. The investigations into the way people act in such large virtual worlds will demonstrate what makes people choose the way they do, how they establish their identity, and how they consume the platforms. The field of artificial intelligence will introduce significant transformations to marketing in social networks and in VR platforms. AI makes sure that customers see advertisements and content in real time depending on their interests. Further research to take into account the ethics, success, and impact on the minds of the people of hyper-personalized marketing founded on AI and the reaction of the consumer and the level of their confidence in these methods.

7.2 Cross-cultural and Demographic Studies

Cultural, social, and demographic factors influence the usage of social media and VR among people to a significant scope, and thus, these issues should be examined in detail. Future research should examine how culture affects the use of these technologies by people. This way, individuals in the societies that place a higher emphasis on the individual might respond to social media differently and will feel more at ease in more interactive virtual reality as opposed to those who are more affiliated with their communities. The social media and VR usage depend on age, gender, the amount of money people earn, and the level of their education. The younger and more tech-savvy individuals might also be more willing to use them and be more different in their purchasing behavior. Similarly, the disparity in incomes and digital capabilities can alter how consumers will be able to access it as well as how they experience it. A study of these differences will enable marketers to come up with strategies that fit in different types of people and not apply the same strategies to others. It will also guide the policy makers on how to address the digital inclusion and the ethical challenges facing the different groups within the community.

7.3 Longitudinal Studies on Consumer Behavior

The existing study on the application of social media and VR in consumer behavior tends to be dedicated to a single point in time. Nevertheless, opinions, actions, and choices of people concerning products vary with the development of technologies and their application in various ways. Consumers should be monitored over an extended period of time to discover the developments. These researches could show at what time the fascination with VR fades, how constant communications in social media can be used to keep a brand loyal to its customers, and how the changing technology influences consumer expectations. One can observe where the social media and VR increase or decrease their influence in life. The time use in longitudinal studies enables the anticipation of consumer trends and make of marketing strategies that suit the evolving consumer preferences and behaviors.

7.4 Measurement and Analytics

This should undergo the appropriate analysis and statistics to observe the impact of social media and VR on consumers. Majority of the current measurements are attentive to such aspects of the usage as likes, shares and time spent on the site, however, these are not always indicators of how involved the users are or how they feel about using the site. The professionals are supposed to seek new methods and instruments to monitor the impacts of social media and VR. This includes tracking of eyes, heart rate, the study of moods of people and study of their activities on various platforms and devices. Through AI, they can discover new trends that are difficult to identify and determine the response of the consumers with the help of advanced analytics. Also, generic measures that allow comparing various studies and industries will enhance the outcomes of research and assist in benchmarking. Due to such developments, marketers will be able to develop superior campaigns, enhance the level at which consumers interact with them and measure the outcomes with greater degree of precision.

8. CONCLUSION

This survey has discussed the immense influence of social media and virtual reality (VR) on consumer behavior, and how these technologies are directly changing how consumers can search information, engage with a brand and make a purchase decision. The social media are also very effective in terms of information dissemination, social influence and brand interaction on the basis of peer effect as well as emotional attachment that leads to consumer engagement and loyalty. Conversely, VR provides imminent product experiences and experience marketing that could raise confidence of buyers in purchasing, satisfaction, and trust by means of realistic simulation and a virtual environment. The outcome is that VR and social media combined create synergistic effects that enhance consumer interest and enable the brands to create social-linked, memorable experiences that enable the connection of the digital and physical realms. However, this dynamic changing environment is not without its problems, including privacy, data security, wellbeing and fair access, which are issues of psychological wellbeing and equitable access. Ethical marketing and proper use of technology is required to address these concerns and ensure the loyalty of the consumer. Businesses and marketers will have to learn of such dynamics so as to be able to devise new unique approaches that will attract digitally savvy consumers. By using the immersion features of VR and the extensive reach of social media, brands will be able to be unique and build better brand connections with consumers. It is advised that researchers should adopt new and emerging technologies like augmented reality, the metaverse, and AI-driven personalization, and also consider the cultural, demographic, and longitudinal lens to understand consumer behavior in different situations more subtly. Lastly, the issue of social media and VR impacting consumer behavior is complex and dynamic. Such technologies will be, of course, maturing and integrating yet further, will continue to change marketing landscapes, with both interesting opportunities and compelling challenges. When applied in an integrated, ethical, way that would balance innovation with consumer protection, they are going to fully fulfill the potential on their part when it comes to assisting in shaping the future of consumer experiences.

REFERENCES

Aswini, J., Malarvizhi, N., & Gayathri, A. (2023). Augmented reality and virtual reality in e-governance: An immersive technology applications and its challenges. In *AI, IoT, and Blockchain Breakthroughs in E-Governance* (pp. 138-153). IGI Global.

Bansal, R., Shukla, G., Gupta, A., Singh, A., & Pruthi, N. (2023). Optimizing augmented reality and virtual reality for customer engagement. In *Promoting consumer engagement through emotional branding and sensory marketing* (pp. 24–35). IGI Global.

Baskaran, K. (2022). E-Consumer Behavioral Analytics: Paradigm Shift in Online Purchase Decision Making. In *Handbook of Research on Consumer Behavior Change and Data Analytics in the Socio-Digital Era* (pp. 192-209). IGI Global.

Dahake, P. S., Bagaregari, P., & Dahake, N. S. (2024). Shaping the Future of Retail: A Comprehensive Review of Predictive Analytics Models for Consumer Behavior. *Entrepreneurship and Creativity in the Metaverse*, 143-160.

Durgam, V. (2018). Social media and its role in marketing. *International journal of advanced research in management, 9*(2), 1-10.

Gagandeep, V. J. (2023). Impact of Augmented Reality and Virtual Reality on Customer Purchase Behavior in the Virtual World. In *Applications of Neuromarketing in the Metaverse* (pp. 258-270). IGI Global.

Manoharan, J. S., Arunkumar, M., Hemamalini, M., Sathya, V., Anish, T. P., & Subramanian, R. S. (2025). Virtual and Augmented Reality in the Automobile Industry: Applications and Future Directions. *Virtual and Augmented Reality Applications in the Automobile Industry*, 377-406.

Nadda, V. K., Dadwal, S. S., & Firdous, A. (2015). Social Media Marketing. In Hajli, N. (Ed.), *Handbook of Research on Integrating Social Media into Strategic Marketing* (pp. 359–379). IGI Global Scientific Publishing., DOI: 10.4018/978-1-4666-8353-2.ch021

Naveeenkumar, N., Rallapalli, S., Sasikala, K., Priya, P. V., Husain, J., & Boopathi, S. (2024). Enhancing Consumer Behavior and Experience Through AI-Driven Insights Optimization. In *AI impacts in digital consumer behavior* (pp. 1–35). IGI Global. DOI: 10.4018/979-8-3693-1918-5.ch001

Ozdemir, M. A. (2021). Virtual reality (VR) and augmented reality (AR) technologies for accessibility and marketing in the tourism industry. In *ICT tools and applications for accessible tourism* (pp. 277-301). IGI Global.

Prabha, D., & Subramanian, R. S. (2017, January). A survey on customer relationship management. *In 2017 4th International Conference on Advanced Computing and Communication Systems (ICACCS)* (pp. 1-5). IEEE.

Siva Subramanian, R., Nalini, M., & Aswini, J. (Eds.). (2024). *Navigating the Augmented and Virtual Frontiers in Engineering*. IGI Global. DOI: 10.4018/979-8-3693-5613-5

Trivedi, S., & Malik, R. (2021). Social media marketing as new marketing tool. In *Big Data Analytics for Improved Accuracy, Efficiency, and Decision Making in Digital Marketing* (pp. 207-226). IGI Global. DOI: 10.4018/978-1-7998-7231-3.ch015

Varun, C. M., Kumar, R. A., Gokila, E., Gayathri, S., Nalini, M., & Subramanian, R. S. (2024, October). Virtual Frontiers navigating the impact and potential of AR and VR. In *2024 2nd International Conference on Self Sustainable Artificial Intelligence Systems (ICSSAS)* (pp. 1559-1565). IEEE. DOI: 10.1109/ICSSAS64001.2024.10760749

Yuce, A. (2021). The Impact of Digital Transformation and Virtual Reality in Tourism Marketing: A Conceptualized Exploration. In *Handbook of Research on IoT, Digital Transformation, and the Future of Global Marketing* (pp. 1-14). IGI Global. DOI: 10.4018/978-1-7998-7192-7.ch001

Chapter 7
The Role of AI in Consumer Decision-Making:
Personalization, Ethics, and Future Implications

Manoj Govindaraj
https://orcid.org/0000-0003-2830-7875
VelTech Rangarajan Dr. Sagunthala R&D Institute of Science and Technology, India

P. Shakila
St. Joseph's University, Bangalore, India

Sai Chandu Kandati
https://orcid.org/0009-0007-2892-4917
Siddharth Institute of Engineering and Technology, Puttur, India

G. M. Shaju
https://orcid.org/0009-0009-0523-2816
MIANZ International College, Male', Maldives

Jenifer Lawrence
https://orcid.org/0000-0002-4115-1521
Woldia University, Ethiopia

Chandramowleeswaran Gnanasekaran
https://orcid.org/0000-0002-1293-1043
Vel Tech Rangarajan Dr. Sagunthala R&D Institute of Science and Technology, India

ABSTRACT

Artificial intelligence (AI) is transforming consumer decision-making by enabling personalized recommendations, predictive analytics, and automated interactions. AI-driven algorithms analyze vast amounts of data to tailor marketing strategies, product suggestions, and purchasing experiences to individual preferences. While AI enhances convenience and efficiency, ethical concerns such as data privacy, algorithmic bias, and consumer manipulation have emerged. This paper explores

DOI: 10.4018/979-8-3373-2747-1.ch007

the role of AI in shaping consumer choices, the ethical considerations associated with AI-driven decision-making, and the future implications for businesses and society. By examining both the benefits and risks, this study provides insights into how organizations can responsibly leverage AI to enhance consumer engagement while maintaining ethical integrity.

INTRODUCTION

AI's ability to transform consumer decision-making extends beyond personalization and automation; it also enables businesses to anticipate consumer needs and refine marketing strategies based on predictive analytics. By leveraging vast datasets, AI systems can identify patterns in consumer behavior, offering highly relevant product recommendations, targeted advertisements, and customized promotions. This level of precision not only enhances the shopping experience but also helps businesses optimize inventory, pricing, and customer engagement. Companies like Amazon and Netflix have successfully harnessed AI-driven recommendation engines to curate content and products that align with individual preferences, significantly boosting customer satisfaction and retention.

Furthermore, AI-powered chatbots and virtual assistants have redefined customer service by providing instant, accurate, and context-aware responses to consumer inquiries. These tools enhance convenience, reduce wait times, and ensure 24/7 support, making interactions with brands more seamless and efficient. AI-driven sentiment analysis also enables businesses to gauge consumer emotions and opinions, allowing for real-time adjustments to marketing campaigns and product offerings. This ability to understand and respond to consumer sentiment fosters stronger brand-consumer relationships and enhances overall engagement.

Despite these benefits, AI's increasing role in consumer decision-making raises ethical concerns that cannot be overlooked. Data privacy remains a significant issue, as AI systems rely on large amounts of personal data to function effectively. Consumers often provide data unknowingly, and without clear regulations, there is a risk of misuse, unauthorized data sharing, and breaches. The need for transparent data collection policies and robust security measures is more critical than ever to protect consumer rights and maintain trust.

Another major challenge is algorithmic bias, which can lead to unfair or discriminatory outcomes. AI models trained on biased datasets may reinforce existing inequalities, affecting everything from personalized product recommendations to credit scoring and hiring decisions. For instance, biased AI-driven pricing models can result in certain consumers being charged more based on their demographics or browsing history, raising concerns about fairness. Addressing these biases requires continuous monitoring, diverse training data, and ethical AI frameworks that prioritize fairness and inclusivity.

Additionally, AI's ability to influence consumer behavior has sparked debates about the fine line between persuasion and manipulation. AI-powered marketing strategies can create hyper-targeted campaigns that push consumers toward specific purchasing decisions, sometimes leveraging psychological tactics that exploit cognitive biases. The challenge lies in ensuring that AI-driven recommendations empower consumers rather than unduly influencing their choices. Ethical AI implementation should focus on enhancing consumer autonomy by providing clear disclosures, consent options, and greater control over data usage.

As AI continues to evolve, businesses, regulators, and researchers must work together to establish guidelines that promote responsible AI adoption. Striking a balance between innovation and ethical considerations is essential for maintaining consumer trust and ensuring AI-driven decision-making benefits both businesses and consumers. The future of AI in consumer behavior will depend on how well organizations address these ethical challenges while harnessing AI's potential to improve customer experiences, streamline operations, and drive business growth in an increasingly digital marketplace.

BACKGROUND OF THE STUDY

AI has transformed marketing by enabling hyper-personalized consumer experiences that increase engagement and satisfaction (Davenport, Guha, Grewal, & Bressgott, 2020).Consumer trust in AI is influenced by factors such as transparency, perceived fairness, and the level of control users feel they have over AI systems (Lu, Cai, & Gursoy, 2019).Ethical concerns arise as AI systems may inherit and amplify biases from training data, raising issues of fairness and accountability (Cowgill, Dell'Acqua, & Deng, 2021). AI-powered recommender systems play a pivotal role in consumer decision-making by filtering options based on preferences and past behavior (Jannach, Adomavicius, & Tuzhilin, 2021).There is growing concern that AI might undermine consumer autonomy by nudging individuals toward specific choices without their full awareness (Susser, Roessler, & Nissenbaum, 2019).AI significantly influences purchase intentions by offering real-time, personalized support through chatbots and predictive analytics (Pantano & Pizzi, 2020).While some consumers appreciate the objectivity and efficiency of AI, others still prefer human interaction due to its emotional intelligence and adaptability (Chatterjee, Rana, Tamilmani, & Sharma, 2020).The integration of emotional AI enhances decision-making systems by detecting and adapting to users' emotional states in real time (Poria, Cambria, Bajpai, & Hussain, 2017).Explainable AI is becoming increasingly essential, as consumers demand to understand how and why algorithmic decisions are made (Doshi-Velez & Kim, 2017).As AI becomes more autonomous in consumer decision-making, it raises critical questions about privacy, control, and the nature of informed consent (Pasquale, 2015).AI-driven personalization enhances user engagement on e-commerce platforms, but privacy concerns continue to moderate its overall effectiveness (Mohsin, 2024).

Ethical challenges such as data security and fairness must be considered when using AI in digital marketing personalization (Adanyin, 2024).As AI reshapes consumer expectations, businesses must innovate while maintaining ethical boundaries to stay competitive (Priest, 2024).AI-powered marketing strategies are becoming more effective as they deliver real-time personalization, but require ethical frameworks to ensure consumer safety (Miller, 2025).

While personalized ads driven by AI improve relevance, they also raise privacy concerns that affect consumer trust and acceptance (Chandra & Kumar, 2025).The ethical use of AI in personalization requires a balance between delivering value and protecting consumer autonomy (BusySeed, 2025).AI-generated product recommendations influence consumer loyalty, though transparency about how these suggestions are made is vital for trust (Ithy, 2025).In e-commerce, AI enhances consumer decision-making through predictive personalization, but transparency remains a pressing ethical need (Mohsin, 2024).Generative AI provides unique opportunities for efficiency and personalization, but it also introduces potential manipulation risks in consumer choices (Närhi, 2024).AI technologies are now deeply embedded in everyday consumer life, demanding businesses to address ethics alongside innovation (Mohanty, 2024).

The Expanding Influence of AI in Consumer Decision-Making

The integration of AI into consumer decision-making has reached an unprecedented level, transforming how individuals interact with brands, make purchases, and evaluate their choices. AI-driven systems can now predict consumer behavior with remarkable accuracy, enabling businesses to craft personalized experiences that enhance engagement and satisfaction. The widespread adoption of AI across industries—ranging from e-commerce and entertainment to healthcare and financial services—illustrates its vast potential to reshape consumer experiences. AI-powered recommendation engines, chatbots, and automated marketing strategies have revolutionized traditional sales approaches, allowing companies to cater to individual preferences in real time. However, as AI continues to evolve, concerns about ethical implications, transparency, and data security must be addressed to foster responsible AI adoption.

Personalization and Its Impact on Consumer Decision-Making

AI's ability to provide highly personalized experiences is one of its most transformative contributions to consumer decision-making. By analyzing vast amounts of data—including purchase history, browsing behavior, and social media interactions—AI systems can generate tailored recommendations that align with an individual's preferences. This level of personalization enhances customer satisfaction by reducing decision fatigue and offering relevant product suggestions. Companies such as Amazon, Spotify, and Netflix have leveraged AI-driven personalization to increase customer retention and optimize engagement, proving that well-implemented AI strategies can significantly boost sales and loyalty.

However, the increasing sophistication of AI-driven personalization also raises ethical concerns. Consumers often provide data without fully understanding how it is being collected, stored, and used. While personalization enhances convenience, it can also lead to an overreliance on AI-generated recommendations, reducing consumer autonomy. To ensure ethical personalization, businesses must prioritize transparency, giving consumers control over their data and enabling them to opt out of AI-driven decision-making when desired.

Addressing Ethical and Privacy Concerns in AI Adoption

Despite its advantages, AI-driven decision-making presents several ethical and privacy challenges. Data security remains a primary concern, as AI systems require access to sensitive consumer information to function effectively. Without robust data protection policies, consumers are at risk of privacy breaches, unauthorized data usage, and even identity theft. The infamous Cambridge Analytica scandal highlighted the dangers of unregulated AI-driven data collection, emphasizing the need for stronger regulations to protect consumer rights.

Another significant issue is algorithmic bias, which occurs when AI systems make decisions based on biased or incomplete datasets. AI models trained on historical data may inadvertently reinforce discrimination, leading to unfair outcomes in areas such as credit scoring, hiring, and targeted advertising. For instance, AI-powered recruitment tools have been criticized for favoring certain demographic groups while disadvantaging others. Addressing this challenge requires continuous monitoring, diverse datasets, and ethical AI frameworks that promote fairness and inclusivity.

Additionally, the persuasive power of AI has raised concerns about consumer manipulation and autonomy. AI-driven marketing strategies often leverage psychological insights to nudge consumers toward specific purchasing decisions. While such tactics may boost sales, they can also lead to impulsive buying behaviors or reinforce harmful consumer habits. To ensure ethical AI implementation, businesses must adopt transparent advertising practices, clearly informing consumers about how AI influences their choices.

The Future of AI-Driven Consumer Decision-Making

As AI technology continues to advance, its role in consumer decision-making will become even more integrated with emerging technologies such as augmented reality (AR), virtual reality (VR), and the Internet of Things (IoT). These innovations will create immersive shopping experiences that further personalize and streamline consumer interactions. For example, AI-powered AR applications allow consumers to visualize how furniture will look in their homes before making a purchase, enhancing decision-making confidence. Similarly, AI-driven smart assistants will proactively suggest products based on contextual data, such as weather conditions or lifestyle patterns.

Moreover, AI's predictive capabilities will enable businesses to anticipate consumer needs before they are explicitly expressed. Advanced sentiment analysis and behavioral tracking will allow companies to refine their offerings dynamically, ensuring that products and services remain relevant to evolving consumer preferences. However, to maximize these benefits while maintaining consumer trust, businesses must implement AI with a focus on transparency, accountability, and fairness.

Striking a Balance Between Innovation and Consumer Protection

To create a sustainable AI-driven marketplace, businesses and policymakers must collaborate to establish guidelines that balance technological innovation with consumer protection. Ethical AI implementation requires clear data governance policies, explainable AI models, and regulatory frameworks that hold companies accountable for their AI-driven decisions. Businesses should adopt privacy-by-design approaches, ensuring that data security measures are embedded into AI systems from the outset.

Furthermore, consumer education is essential in fostering AI literacy and awareness. By informing consumers about how AI influences their decision-making and providing them with options to control their data usage, companies can build trust and promote responsible AI adoption. Governments and regulatory bodies must also play a proactive role in developing AI-specific legislation that safeguards consumer rights while encouraging innovation.

RESEARCH QUESTIONS

1. How does AI-driven personalization influence consumer decision-making and purchasing behavior?
2. What are the ethical concerns associated with AI-driven consumer decision-making, and how can they be addressed?

RESEARCH OBJECTIVES

1. To analyze the role of AI in enhancing personalization and influencing consumer choices.
2. To examine the ethical implications of AI-driven decision-making in marketing.
3. To evaluate the impact of AI-powered tools on consumer trust and data privacy.
4. To explore future trends and challenges in AI-driven consumer behavior analysis.

METHODOLOGY

This study employs a mixed-method research design, combining qualitative and quantitative approaches to provide a comprehensive analysis of AI's role in consumer decision-making. Surveys and interviews will be conducted with consumers and marketing professionals to gather insights into AI-driven personalization, trust, and ethical concerns. Secondary data from academic journals, industry reports, and case studies will be analyzed to understand AI's broader implications. Additionally, sentiment analysis of consumer feedback on AI-powered platforms will help assess public perception and satisfaction with AI-driven recommendations.

IMPLICATIONS OF AI IN CONSUMER DECISION-MAKING

AI-Driven Consumer Decision-Making: Benefits, Challenges, and Future Prospects

The integration of AI into consumer decision-making has revolutionized the way businesses interact with customers, optimize marketing strategies, and enhance overall engagement. AI-powered recommendation engines, predictive analytics, and automated decision-making have created a new era of personalized commerce that improves customer satisfaction while driving business growth. However, alongside these advancements come ethical challenges, regulatory concerns, and the need for businesses to adopt responsible AI practices.

Personalization is at the heart of modern marketing strategies, and AI is the engine driving it. By processing vast amounts of data—ranging from browsing history and purchase behavior to social media interactions—AI can deliver highly tailored experiences. These experiences are not just reactive; they are predictive, often anticipating needs before the consumer is even aware of them.

Mechanisms of Personalization AI algorithms use techniques such as machine learning, collaborative filtering, and natural language processing to create dynamic consumer profiles. For instance, recommendation engines on platforms like Amazon or Netflix analyze past behaviors to suggest relevant products or content. Chatbots and virtual assistants also utilize natural language understanding to provide personalized interactions.

Influence on Consumer Choices AI-driven personalization directly impacts decision-making by simplifying choices, reducing search time, and enhancing perceived relevance. Consumers are more likely to engage with brands that offer tailored solutions, thereby increasing conversion rates and customer loyalty.

Behavioral Nudging and Predictive Analytics AI also enables behavioral nudging—subtly guiding consumers toward desired actions. Predictive analytics assess potential future behaviors, allowing marketers to design campaigns that align closely with individual preferences and timing.

1. Enhanced Consumer Experience and Engagement

AI has transformed the consumer experience by enabling seamless, hyper-personalized interactions. Businesses leverage AI-driven recommendation systems to analyze vast amounts of consumer data, including browsing history, purchase behavior, and social media engagement. This enables companies to deliver highly relevant content, product recommendations, and marketing messages that align with individual preferences.

Personalized experiences increase consumer satisfaction, engagement, and loyalty. Platforms like Netflix, Spotify, and Amazon have successfully utilized AI to tailor recommendations, leading to improved user experiences and higher retention rates. For instance, Netflix's AI-driven recommendation algorithm accounts for over 80% of the content users watch, demonstrating the significant impact of AI on engagement.

Beyond content recommendations, AI enhances customer service through chatbots and virtual assistants like Siri, Alexa, and Google Assistant. These AI-powered tools offer real-time responses, resolve queries efficiently, and provide round-the-clock customer support. AI's ability to understand natural language processing (NLP) and sentiment analysis further improves interactions by recognizing consumer emotions and adapting responses accordingly.

However, while AI enhances engagement, there is a growing concern about consumer autonomy and decision fatigue. Over-reliance on AI-generated recommendations may limit consumer choice, as users are continuously exposed to the same types of content or products. Companies must balance personalization with diversity, ensuring that AI does not restrict consumers' ability to explore alternative options.

2. Ethical and Regulatory Considerations

The rapid adoption of AI in consumer decision-making raises significant ethical and regulatory concerns. AI's reliance on vast amounts of personal data makes data privacy a critical issue. Consumers often provide data without a full understanding of how it is collected, stored, or used. Without strict regulations, companies may exploit this data for targeted advertising, dynamic pricing, or even manipulation of purchasing behaviors.

Governments and businesses must collaborate to establish robust AI regulations that ensure:

- Data transparency: Consumers should have clear insights into how their data is collected and used.
- Algorithmic fairness: AI models must be regularly audited to prevent discrimination and biases.
- User control: Consumers should have the ability to opt-out of AI-driven recommendations or adjust personalization settings.

The Cambridge Analytica scandal serves as a stark reminder of the dangers of unregulated AI-driven data analytics. The misuse of personal data for political and commercial gain highlighted the need for stronger regulations around data collection and AI ethics. The General Data Protection Regulation (GDPR) in Europe and similar regulations worldwide aim to enhance consumer protection, but more comprehensive AI-specific guidelines are necessary.

Another key ethical concern is algorithmic bias. AI systems trained on biased datasets can unintentionally reinforce social and economic inequalities. For example, AI-driven credit scoring models have been found to discriminate against minority groups, limiting their access to financial services. To address this, businesses must ensure AI models are trained on diverse, unbiased datasets and regularly monitored for fairness.

3. Future Business Strategies and Market Trends

AI is shaping the future of business by driving data-driven decision-making, predictive analytics, and automation. Companies investing in AI-driven consumer insights gain a competitive advantage by understanding market trends, optimizing pricing strategies, and improving supply chain management.

Predictive analytics allows businesses to anticipate consumer needs before they arise. Retailers use AI to forecast demand, optimize inventory levels, and enhance pricing strategies based on real-time consumer behavior. AI-powered automation also improves operational efficiency, reducing costs while enhancing customer service.

AI's role in marketing will continue to expand, with businesses leveraging:

While the benefits of AI in marketing are substantial, they come with significant ethical challenges. These issues revolve around transparency, bias, autonomy, and informed consent.

Transparency and the "Black Box" Problem Many AI systems operate as "black boxes," where the internal decision-making processes are opaque even to their developers. This lack of transparency undermines consumer understanding and raises concerns about manipulation and fairness.

Bias and Discrimination AI systems trained on biased data can perpetuate or amplify social inequalities. For example, ad-targeting algorithms might show high-paying job opportunities predominantly to men, or restrict access to financial services for minority communities.

Autonomy and Manipulation AI can influence consumer decisions to such an extent that it may challenge the notion of free will. Hyper-personalized content can exploit cognitive biases, leading individuals to make choices they might not have made otherwise.

Informed Consent and Data Ethics Ethical AI use requires that consumers provide informed consent for data collection and usage. However, the complexity of data practices often makes it difficult for users to fully grasp what they are agreeing to. Simplified disclosures and user-centric privacy controls are essential.

- Hyper-personalized advertising: AI will enable brands to deliver real-time personalized ads tailored to consumer preferences.
- Conversational commerce: AI-powered chatbots will facilitate direct shopping experiences within messaging platforms.
- Voice commerce: With the rise of voice assistants, AI will enable hands-free shopping experiences and streamlined voice-based purchases.

Case Study: Amazon's AI-Driven Personalization

Amazon is one of the leading companies leveraging AI to enhance consumer decision-making. The company's recommendation engine, powered by machine learning algorithms, analyzes customer data to provide personalized product suggestions. This AI-driven approach accounts for nearly 35% of Amazon's total sales. Additionally, its AI-powered Alexa voice assistant helps users make purchasing decisions by providing real-time product recommendations and automated reordering based on past behavior. While Amazon's AI has significantly improved customer experience and efficiency, concerns about data privacy and algorithmic favoritism remain key challenges.

Challenges of AI in Consumer Decision-Making

While AI-driven decision-making offers numerous advantages, it also presents significant challenges that businesses, regulators, and consumers must address. These challenges primarily revolve around data privacy, algorithmic bias, and consumer trust, all of which can impact the ethical and sustainable adoption of AI in commerce.

1. Data Privacy and Security Concerns

AI systems depend on vast amounts of consumer data to function effectively. Machine learning models analyze personal information such as browsing history, purchasing patterns, financial details, and even biometric data to offer personalized recommendations and targeted marketing. However, this reliance on consumer data raises serious concerns about privacy, security, and ethical data usage.

Many consumers are unaware of how their data is collected, stored, and shared with third parties. Companies often gather data through cookies, online tracking, and AI-powered tools without transparent consent mechanisms. This has led to several high-profile data breaches and misuse of personal information. The Cambridge Analytica scandal, where personal data was used to manipulate voter behavior, exposed the risks of unregulated AI data collection.

To address these concerns, regulations like the General Data Protection Regulation (GDPR) and the California Consumer Privacy Act (CCPA) have been introduced to protect user data and ensure consumer rights. These laws require companies to:

- Obtain explicit consent before collecting personal data.
- Allow consumers to access, modify, or delete their data.
- Implement robust cybersecurity measures to prevent breaches.

However, enforcement remains inconsistent across different regions, and many businesses struggle to comply with evolving data protection standards. The challenge for AI-driven businesses is to balance data-driven insights with ethical consumer data handling to maintain trust and avoid legal repercussions.

2. Algorithmic Bias and Fairness Issues

AI models are trained on historical data, which may contain inherent biases that affect decision-making. If training datasets reflect social, racial, or economic biases, AI algorithms can unintentionally reinforce discrimination, leading to unfair treatment of certain consumer groups.

One of the most prominent examples of algorithmic bias is in financial services, where AI-powered credit scoring systems have been criticized for discriminating against minority communities. Studies have shown that some AI models assign lower credit scores to people of certain ethnic backgrounds, even when they have similar financial profiles as others who receive better loan approvals.

Similarly, facial recognition technology has exhibited racial and gender biases, with some AI systems struggling to accurately identify individuals from underrepresented demographics. This has serious implications for AI applications in security, hiring processes, and automated decision-making.

To mitigate algorithmic bias, businesses must:

- Diversify training datasets to ensure AI systems are inclusive and representative of all consumer groups.
- Regularly audit AI models to detect and eliminate discriminatory patterns.
- Implement transparent AI decision-making processes that allow consumers to challenge unfair outcomes.

Ensuring fairness in AI-driven consumer decision-making is not just a legal and ethical responsibility but also a business necessity for building long-term trust and inclusivity.

3. Consumer Trust and Ethical AI Adoption

Despite AI's ability to improve convenience and enhance consumer experiences, excessive reliance on AI-driven decision-making can erode trust if businesses prioritize profit over ethics. Consumers may feel manipulated rather than empowered when AI is used for exploitative tactics such as:

- Dynamic pricing: AI adjusts product prices based on demand, user profiles, or browsing behavior, sometimes charging higher prices to certain consumers.
- Behavioral nudging: AI influences consumer behavior by subtly steering purchasing decisions through targeted advertisements or personalized recommendations.

- Hidden persuasion techniques: AI-powered neuromarketing can analyze consumer emotions and subtly shape their choices without their full awareness.

Such manipulative AI strategies undermine consumer autonomy, making them feel that their decisions are being controlled rather than freely made. This can result in brand distrust, reputational damage, and regulatory scrutiny.

To build consumer confidence in AI, businesses must adopt transparent and ethical AI practices, such as:

- Clearly explaining how AI makes decisions and allowing consumers to opt out of AI-driven recommendations.
- Implementing explainable AI (XAI) models that provide clear, understandable reasons for automated decisions.
- Educating consumers about AI's role in decision-making, so they can make informed choices without feeling manipulated.

Ensuring Responsible AI Adoption

As AI continues to reshape consumer decision-making, a collaborative approach is necessary to maximize its benefits while addressing ethical, privacy, and fairness challenges. Businesses, regulators, and consumers must work together to create an AI-driven ecosystem that is transparent, fair, and consumer-centric.

Key strategies for responsible AI adoption include:

- Stronger AI governance: Governments should enforce stricter regulations to ensure ethical AI development and protect consumer rights.
- Industry self-regulation: Companies must adopt internal AI ethics guidelines, emphasizing fairness, accountability, and transparency.
- Consumer empowerment: Educating consumers about AI's influence will help them make informed choices and demand fair treatment.

Ultimately, responsible AI adoption is crucial for maintaining consumer trust and driving sustainable business growth in the digital age. Companies that prioritize ethical AI practices will not only comply with future regulations but also establish themselves as leaders in consumer trust and innovation.

Benefits of AI in Consumer Decision-Making

AI-driven consumer decision-making offers several significant benefits that enhance user experiences, optimize marketing strategies, and improve business efficiency. One of the primary advantages is personalization, where AI algorithms analyze vast datasets to tailor recommendations, product suggestions, and advertisements based on individual preferences. This leads to higher engagement rates, improved customer satisfaction, and increased sales conversions. E-commerce platforms such as Amazon and Netflix leverage AI-powered recommendation systems to provide users with highly relevant content, making shopping and entertainment experiences more intuitive and enjoyable.

Another major benefit is efficiency and automation. AI-powered chatbots, virtual assistants, and automated customer service tools enable businesses to handle consumer queries instantly, reducing wait times and enhancing user experiences. Companies can also optimize inventory management, pricing strategies, and supply chain processes through predictive analytics, minimizing operational inefficiencies. AI's ability to process real-time data ensures that businesses can quickly adapt to changing market demands and consumer behavior.

Furthermore, AI enhances decision-making accuracy. Traditional marketing strategies often rely on broad demographic-based segmentation, whereas AI-driven insights allow for precise targeting based on consumer behavior, sentiment analysis, and past purchases. This precision helps businesses create more effective campaigns that drive higher returns on investment. Additionally, AI can identify fraudulent activities, such as fake reviews or fraudulent transactions, improving security and consumer trust.

Lastly, AI contributes to cost savings by reducing human intervention in repetitive tasks. Automated systems handle large-scale customer interactions and data analysis, allowing businesses to allocate resources more effectively. By leveraging AI-driven insights, companies can optimize pricing models, predict demand fluctuations, and streamline marketing expenditures, ultimately leading to higher profitability and competitive advantage.

AI, Trust, and Data Privacy in Consumer Relationships

Trust is a cornerstone of consumer-brand relationships, and the use of AI significantly affects this dynamic. As AI relies heavily on consumer data, privacy becomes both a legal and ethical imperative.

Consumer Concerns About Data Privacy Numerous surveys show that consumers are increasingly aware of and concerned about how their data is collected, stored, and used. Data breaches and misuse have led to heightened skepticism, even as demand for personalized experiences grows.

Building Trust Through Transparency and Control Brands must adopt transparent data practices and empower consumers with control over their personal information.

Providing access to data dashboards, opt-out mechanisms, and clear privacy policies can help build trust.

Compliance with Data Protection Regulations Regulations such as the General Data Protection Regulation (GDPR) and the California Consumer Privacy Act (CCPA) mandate strict data handling practices. Organizations must ensure that their AI systems comply with these laws to avoid legal penalties and reputational damage.

The Role of Explainable AI (XAI) Explainable AI (XAI) aims to make AI decisions understandable to non-experts. By clarifying how and why specific decisions are made, XAI can bridge the trust gap and promote ethical transparency in AI applications.

Future Trends and Challenges in AI-Driven Consumer Behavior Analysis

AI is rapidly evolving, and its role in consumer behavior analysis is poised for significant transformation. However, this evolution presents both opportunities and obstacles.

Emerging Technologies Technologies such as emotional AI, which reads facial expressions and voice tones to assess consumer emotions, and neuromarketing tools that analyze brain activity, are gaining traction. These tools offer deeper insights but raise new ethical questions about consent and emotional manipulation.

Integrating Human and Artificial Intelligence While AI excels in data analysis, it lacks the human touch essential for nuanced understanding. Future marketing will likely involve hybrid models that combine AI's efficiency with human creativity and empathy.

Challenges in Data Management The volume and diversity of consumer data are growing exponentially. Companies must develop robust data management systems to handle this influx effectively, ensuring accuracy, security, and relevance.

Ethical Frameworks and Governance As AI continues to influence consumer behavior, the development of ethical frameworks and industry standards will be crucial. These should address fairness, accountability, and the responsible use of AI technologies.

Consumer Resistance and Demand for Digital Ethics A growing segment of consumers is pushing back against invasive AI practices. Digital minimalism and privacy-first technologies are gaining popularity. Brands must adapt to these preferences to remain credible and consumer-friendly.

DISCUSSION

AI's integration into consumer decision-making presents a paradox: while it offers unparalleled convenience and efficiency, it also raises ethical concerns that cannot be ignored. The ability of AI to process vast amounts of consumer data allows businesses to deliver hyper-personalized experiences, improving engagement and satisfaction. However, the very data that powers these systems can also be misused, leading to privacy violations, consumer manipulation, and even social inequality. The rise of surveillance capitalism, where consumer data becomes a commodity traded between corporations, has amplified concerns over how AI systems collect, store, and utilize personal information.

One of the most pressing concerns is the lack of transparency in AI decision-making. Many AI-driven systems operate as "black boxes," where consumers are unaware of how decisions are made. Whether it's the content recommended by social media algorithms or the pricing models used by e-commerce platforms, consumers have little insight into why they see certain ads, products, or services. This opacity fosters mistrust and raises questions about accountability, particularly when AI systems produce biased or unfair outcomes. For example, AI-driven hiring platforms have been found to disadvantage women and minority groups due to biases ingrained in their training data, highlighting the urgent need for ethical AI development.

Moreover, AI's influence on consumer autonomy is a growing concern. With AI-powered nudging techniques, businesses can subtly guide consumer behavior, sometimes in ways that may not align with the consumer's best interests. Dynamic pricing models, for instance, adjust prices based on user behavior, location, and perceived willingness to pay, often leading to price discrimination. Similarly, AI-driven advertising can create echo chambers, reinforcing existing preferences and limiting exposure to alternative choices. While personalization enhances user experience, it also risks reducing consumer agency by shaping choices in ways that favor corporate profit rather than individual well-being.

To address these challenges, businesses must prioritize ethical AI adoption by incorporating fairness, transparency, and consumer control. One approach is the development of explainable AI (XAI), which makes AI decision-making processes more understandable to consumers. Additionally, businesses should adopt privacy-by-design principles, ensuring that consumer data is collected and used responsibly with clear consent mechanisms in place. Regulators, too, have a crucial role to play in defining legal frameworks that prevent AI from being exploited for unethical purposes. Policies such as GDPR and CCPA represent significant steps in data protection, but continuous refinement is needed to keep pace with AI advancements.

Despite these concerns, AI's potential to enhance consumer decision-making remains vast. Ethical AI adoption can lead to more responsible and user-centric innovations, where AI serves as a tool to empower consumers rather than manipulate them. By balancing innovation with ethical responsibility, businesses can foster consumer trust, ensuring that AI remains a force for good in shaping the future of commerce and society. The key lies in developing AI systems that prioritize fairness, accountability, and transparency, creating a digital landscape where both businesses and consumers can thrive.

MAIN FINDINGS

1. AI enhances personalization by leveraging big data to analyze consumer behavior, resulting in improved user experiences and higher engagement.
2. Efficiency and automation have reduced response times and enhanced customer service through AI-powered chatbots and virtual assistants.
3. AI-driven decision-making improves marketing precision by offering highly targeted recommendations, leading to increased sales and business growth.
4. Ethical concerns such as data privacy and bias remain challenges, necessitating stronger regulatory frameworks to ensure fair AI usage.
5. Consumer trust in AI varies depending on transparency and ethical considerations, with users more likely to engage with AI-driven platforms that prioritize privacy and fairness.

Suggestions for Responsible AI Adoption

1. Enhance Transparency and Explainability – AI systems should be designed to provide clear explanations of how decisions are made. Consumers should have access to understandable insights into why certain recommendations or pricing strategies are applied. This will help build trust and reduce concerns about AI-driven manipulation.
2. Implement Stronger Data Privacy Regulations – Governments should enforce strict data protection laws, such as GDPR and CCPA, to ensure that consumer data is collected and used responsibly. Companies should adopt privacy-by-design principles, giving users greater control over their personal data.
3. Mitigate Algorithmic Bias – AI developers should prioritize fairness by using diverse and unbiased datasets. Regular audits of AI algorithms should be conducted to identify and rectify biases that could lead to discrimination or unfair treatment.
4. Educate Consumers on AI Usage – Many consumers are unaware of how AI influences their decisions. Businesses should provide clear disclosures and

user-friendly explanations about AI-driven personalization, giving consumers the option to adjust preferences or opt out when necessary.

5. Promote Ethical AI Development – Collaboration between industry leaders, academics, and policymakers can establish ethical guidelines for AI deployment in consumer decision-making. Responsible AI development should focus on consumer empowerment rather than manipulation.

CONCLUSION

AI is fundamentally transforming the way consumers make purchasing decisions by integrating advanced analytics, machine learning, and predictive modeling into everyday interactions. By leveraging AI-driven insights, businesses can offer real-time, personalized recommendations, ensuring that consumers receive tailored product and service suggestions based on their preferences and behaviors. This level of personalization not only enhances customer satisfaction but also streamlines the decision-making process, reducing the effort required to find relevant options. AI-driven chatbots and virtual assistants have further revolutionized customer interactions, providing instant support and guiding users through their purchase journeys efficiently.

Beyond personalization, AI enhances marketing strategies by enabling predictive analytics that anticipate consumer needs before they even articulate them. AI-powered sentiment analysis helps businesses understand consumer emotions, preferences, and emerging trends, allowing them to craft targeted campaigns that resonate with their audience. Furthermore, AI-driven dynamic pricing strategies help businesses optimize pricing based on demand, competitor activity, and individual customer profiles, ensuring competitive advantage while maximizing revenue. In industries such as finance, AI-powered robo-advisors analyze market trends and consumer risk preferences to provide tailored investment recommendations, increasing accessibility to financial planning.

However, while AI offers undeniable advantages, concerns about data privacy, security, and ethical AI usage remain critical challenges that need urgent attention. The increasing reliance on AI means that businesses collect and process vast amounts of consumer data, raising concerns about consent, transparency, and data security. Cases of unauthorized data usage, such as the Facebook-Cambridge Analytica scandal, highlight the risks associated with unregulated AI-driven consumer profiling. Without strict regulatory oversight, AI systems could exploit consumer data for manipulative marketing tactics, eroding trust and harming consumer welfare.

To address these challenges, businesses must adopt AI systems that emphasize transparency, fairness, and accountability. AI models should be designed with explainability, allowing consumers to understand how their data is being used and how AI-driven recommendations are generated. Stricter compliance with global data protection regulations, such as the General Data Protection Regulation (GDPR) and the California Consumer Privacy Act (CCPA), is essential to safeguarding consumer rights. Furthermore, companies should implement AI auditing mechanisms to detect and mitigate algorithmic bias, ensuring that AI-driven decisions do not reinforce discrimination or unfair treatment.

Another critical factor in the responsible adoption of AI is consumer education and empowerment. Many consumers remain unaware of the extent to which AI influences their choices, making them vulnerable to manipulation. Businesses should prioritize transparent communication about AI usage, providing consumers with control over their data and personalization settings. Ethical AI implementation should focus on empowering consumers rather than exploiting them, ensuring that AI-driven recommendations align with consumer interests rather than purely commercial motives.

Looking ahead, the future of AI in consumer decision-making will be shaped by a balanced approach that harmonizes innovation with ethical considerations. Companies that prioritize ethical AI development and consumer trust will not only gain a competitive edge but also contribute to a more responsible and sustainable digital marketplace. By fostering a culture of responsible AI adoption, businesses can build long-term customer relationships, strengthen brand loyalty, and create a positive impact on the broader economy. Ultimately, AI should be leveraged as a tool for enhancing consumer autonomy, enabling informed decision-making while maintaining fairness, transparency, and accountability in the digital age.

REFERENCES

Adanyin, A. (2024). Ethical AI in retail: Consumer privacy and fairness. *arXiv preprint arXiv:2410.15369.* /arXiv.2410.15369DOI: 10.48550

BusySeed. (2025). AI and the ethics of personalization: Finding the right balance. *BusySeed Blog*. https://www.busyseed.com/ai-and-the-ethics-of-personalization-finding-the-right-balance/

Chandra, S., & Kumar, N. (2025). Understanding customer responses to AI-driven personalized advertising: The role of relevance and privacy concerns. *Journal of Advertising*, *54*(2), 123–145. DOI: 10.1080/00913367.2025.2460985

Chatterjee, S., Rana, N. P., Tamilmani, K., & Sharma, A. (2020). The impact of AI on consumer behavior: Exploring future research directions. *International Journal of Information Management*, *54*, 102289. DOI: 10.1016/j.ijinfomgt.2020.102289

Cowgill, B., Dell'Acqua, F., & Deng, S. (2021). Biased programmers? Or biased data? A field experiment in operationalizing AI ethics. *NBER Working Paper No. 27427*. DOI: 10.3386/w27427

Davenport, T. H., Guha, A., Grewal, D., & Bressgott, T. (2020). How artificial intelligence will change the future of marketing. *Journal of the Academy of Marketing Science*, *48*(1), 24–42. DOI: 10.1007/s11747-019-00696-0

Doshi-Velez, F., & Kim, B. (2017). Towards a rigorous science of interpretable machine learning. *arXiv preprint arXiv:1702.08608.* /arXiv.1702.08608DOI: 10.48550

Ithy, A. (2025). The role of AI in shaping consumer decision-making for personal care products. *The Journal of Consumer Research*, *48*(3), 567–589.

Jannach, D., Adomavicius, G., & Tuzhilin, A. (2021). Recommender systems: Challenges, insights, and research opportunities. *Information & Management*, *58*(1), 103597. DOI: 10.1016/j.im.2020.103597

Lu, L., Cai, R., & Gursoy, D. (2019). Developing and validating a scale to measure consumers' trust toward artificial intelligence in service encounters. *Journal of Hospitality Marketing & Management*, *28*(7), 803–827. DOI: 10.1080/19368623.2019.1568989

Miller, A. (2025). AI-driven personalization: Transforming marketing strategies for 2025 and beyond. *Miller Media*. https://millermedia7.com/ai-driven-personalization-transforming-marketing-strategies-for-2025-and-beyond/

Mohanty, M. (2024). AI in everyday life: How it's changing consumer behavior. *LinkedIn Pulse*. https://www.linkedin.com/pulse/ai-everyday-life-how-its-changing-consumer-behavior-manas-mohanty-mxyuc

Mohsin, S. K. (2024). The influence of AI-driven personalization on consumer decision-making in e-commerce platforms. *Research Journal of Engineering Sciences, 12*(9), 45–56. https://rjes.iq/index.php/rjes/article/download/99/106/900

Närhi, A. (2024). Generative AI and consumer behaviour: A new era of personalisation and efficiency. *Horton International*. https://hortoninternational.com/generative-ai-and-consumer-behaviour-a-new-era-of-personalisation-and-efficiency/

Pantano, E., & Pizzi, G. (2020). Forecasting artificial intelligence on online customer assistance: Evidence from chatbot patents analysis. *Journal of Retailing and Consumer Services*, *55*, 102096. DOI: 10.1016/j.jretconser.2020.102096

Pasquale, F. (2015). *The black box society: The secret algorithms that control money and information*. Harvard University Press. DOI: 10.4159/harvard.9780674736061

Poria, S., Cambria, E., Bajpai, R., & Hussain, A. (2017). A review of affective computing: From unimodal analysis to multimodal fusion. *Information Fusion*, *37*, 98–125. DOI: 10.1016/j.inffus.2017.02.003

Poria, S., Cambria, E., Bajpai, R., & Hussain, A. (2017). A review of affective computing: From unimodal analysis to multimodal fusion. *Information Fusion*, *37*, 98–125. DOI: 10.1016/j.inffus.2017.02.003

Priest, D. (2024). AI is becoming ingrained in businesses across industries. Where is it going in 2025? *Associated Press*. https://apnews.com/article/ai-future-business-trends-2025

Susser, D., Roessler, B., & Nissenbaum, H. (2019). Online manipulation: Hidden influences in a digital world. *SSRN*, *4*(1), 1–45. DOI: 10.2139/ssrn.3306006

Chapter 8
Influencer Heatmaps and Sentiment Clouds:
Visual Methodologies for Tracking Micro-Influence in Brand Communities

B. K. kishore
https://orcid.org/0009-0006-6445-8274
Dayananda Sagar College of Engineering, India

K. S. Ganesha
https://orcid.org/0000-0001-8181-2411
Dayananda Sagar College of Engineering, India

ABSTRACT

As digital ecosystems fragment into niche communities, micro-influencers have become key in shaping brand narratives. This study introduces a two-layered visual method—influencer heatmaps and sentiment clouds—to map how influence and emotions circulate in brand-focused digital spaces. Using social network analysis, NLP, and clustering, heatmaps reveal conversational hubs and attention flows, while transformer-based sentiment clouds show emotional registers tied to influencers and brand mentions. A conceptual framework linking influencer proximity, sentiment polarity, and behavioural engagement is tested with SEM, showing that micro-influencers with positive sentiment drive consumer behaviour more effectively than follower counts or macro metrics. By merging data visualisation with psychological interpretability, the study offers marketers and strategists a scalable, real-time tool for tracking influence and designing sentiment-aligned engagement strategies in decentralised digital ecosystems.

DOI: 10.4018/979-8-3373-2747-1.ch008

INTRODUCTION

In the algorithmically mediated social economy, celebrities and big digital personalities don't have all the power anymore. Instead, micro-influencers—people who don't have a lot of followers but get a lot of interaction in certain online communities—have become powerful players in the creation, spread, and validation of brand stories. These influencers do best not in the mainstream, but in small brand communities on Instagram, Reddit, Twitter, and other digital micro spaces, where trust, relatability, and perceived authenticity are more important than follower count. As traditional influencer marketing strategies move away from paid advertising and towards more community-driven and organic ways of getting people involved, we need analytical tools that can find and understand the complex structures of influence in these decentralised ecosystems right away. This paper presents and tests a method based on visual analytics that uses two main tools—sentiment clouds and influencer heatmaps—to measure and show micro-influence in online communities that are focused on brands. The goal isn't just to count likes or followers; it's to find the emotional, positional, and relational factors that affect influence on a small scale. The changing shape of digital influence calls for a change in the way research is done. Most social media analytics tools focus on volume metrics like reach, impressions, and hashtag frequency. However, they don't always capture relational capital and sentiment orientation, which are both important for how micro-actors influence others. Micro-influencers usually work in small groups where people trust each other instead of trying to get everyone to like them. They often have an impact through emotionally charged content, interactions with peers, and conversational leadership within small groups of people who share the same interests. To really understand their effect, we need more than just tracking their content. We need to map their emotions and space as well. Social network analysis (SNA) can help us see how influence is spread among networked users by showing us patterns of centrality, density, and interactivity. These heatmaps show who gets the most attention in brand communities and how that attention moves and breaks up. On the other hand, sentiment clouds show how people feel about influencers, brands, and products in a text-based way. These clouds are made up of primary user-generated content (UGC) and are powered by sentiment analysis engines like VADER, BERT, or Text Blob. They group linguistic tokens together based on their emotional polarity, intensity, and frequency. Together, these two methods give us a dual view: one that looks at the placement of influence within networks (topological) and one that looks at the emotional atmosphere around influence (affective). The use of visual methods in digital sociology and computational marketing is not just a matter of taste; it is a response to the fact that modern digital communication is complex, multi-modal, and real-time. Researchers can find patterns, clusters, and outliers that might not be visible in traditional tabular data formats with the help of visual tools. These tools also help reduce cognitive overload when interpreting data. Visual analytics have been helpful in marketing and consumer behaviour research for keeping track of engagement, mapping sentiment, and finding content that goes viral (Zhang & Ghorbani, 2022; Lin et al., 2021). Still, not many studies have tried to use SNA-based heatmaps and sentiment-based word clouds together to track micro-influence in a way that is systematic and based on theory. This study fills that gap by creating a visual methodological pipeline that brings together network structure, sentiment expression, and behavioural correlation into a single analytical model. The basic idea is that visual positioning and emotional sentiment work together to shape micro-influence: visual positioning determines visibility and access, while emotional sentiment drives engagement and action. The study only uses primary data from active brand communities to test this model. This includes comment threads, tags, reposts, and user interactions related to targeted marketing campaigns on Instagram and Reddit. When you look at primary UGC, you can see language, emoji use, and community in-group lingo in a more nuanced way than you can with secondary datasets or pre-cleaned API extracts. This is important for figuring out how people feel online. NLP pipelines break down data and tools like Gephi or Network map it into heatmaps. Token frequency weighted by sentiment score is used to make word clouds. Not only do follower counts help find micro-influencers, but so do interaction centrality, hashtag virality, and comment sentiment impact. The study then tests a conceptual framework that connects three things: (1) the centrality of the influencer network; (2) the polarity and intensity of the sentiment; and (3) behavioural engagement indicators like replies, shares, and comment threads. We use structural equation modelling (SEM) to confirm these links and measure the direct and indirect effects of micro-influence mechanisms on consumer trust and intention.

LITERATURE REVIEW

The combination of influencer marketing, sentiment analysis, and visual data methods is a rapidly evolving field of research. The rise of micro-influencers (1,000–100,000 followers) has shifted focus from celebrity-driven mass influence towards trust dynamics rooted in communities (De Veirman et al., 2017; Boerman, 2020; Casaló et al., 2020). However, much work on influencer tracking remains underdeveloped, relying too heavily on reach and impressions (Freberg et al., 2011; Arora et al., 2019). Recent studies advocate for integrated frameworks that combine relational capital, sentiment dynamics, and diffusion processes (Zhang & Ghorbani, 2022; Liang & Fung, 2021). Social network analysis (Wasserman & Faust, 1994;

Scott, 2017) and AI-driven sentiment analysis using transformers (Devlin et al., 2019; Yin et al., 2020) offer promising pathways. Recent work (Gloor et al., 2022; Tafesse & Wood, 2021) emphasizes how emotional alignment amplifies engagement. Additionally, social media analytics (Batrinca & Treleaven, 2015; Stieglitz et al., 2014) highlight the importance of combining structural and emotional insights. This chapter contributes by integrating these approaches into a dual-visual framework (heatmaps and sentiment clouds).

The combination of influencer marketing, sentiment analysis, and visual data methods is a field of digital communication and consumer behaviour research that is changing quickly. The rise of micro-influencers, which are people with 1,000 to 100,000 followers, has caused researchers to shift their focus from celebrity-driven mass influence to trust dynamics that are specific to communities (De Veirman et al., 2017; Boerman, 2020). Micro-influencers are often more effective at getting people to change their minds about a brand because they have higher engagement rates and are seen as more authentic (Casaló et al., 2020). This change fits with the rise of participatory culture (Jenkins, 2006), where consumers help make brand meaning and have their own say through retweets, comments, and curated content. Even though they are becoming more important, finding and keeping track of micro-influencers is still not very well developed analytically. This is often because they rely on third-party dashboards or black-box engagement algorithms that hide the emotional or relational dynamics that are going on. Early research on influencer networks looked at macro-level metrics like reach, impressions, and follower counts (Freberg et al., 2011), but recent research says these aren't good enough indicators of influence, especially in the case of fragmented digital subcultures (Arora et al., 2019). Instead, researchers have asked for more detailed methods that combine relational capital, sentiment dynamics, and community-level diffusion processes (Zhang & Ghorbani, 2022). Social network analysis (SNA) has become a promising way to respond, giving researchers the tools to map user interactions, find central nodes, and figure out how much influence someone has based on metrics like betweenness centrality, eigenvector scores, and modularity (Wasserman & Faust, 1994; Scott, 2017). Studies that used SNA on brand communities have shown that influence doesn't always flow in a straight line and often gathers around people who aren't obvious actors—users who aren't necessarily very visible but are in strategically important positions in digital conversations (Trusov et al., 2009). Researchers and marketers can find these "hidden influencers" and learn how engagement and conversation flow within digital micro-publics using heatmap visualisation from these networks (Luo et al., 2021). In addition to structural analysis, affective computing and sentiment analysis have become popular in marketing research as ways to figure out the emotional content of conversations about brands (Picard, 1997; Liu, 2012). Sentiment clouds are a new type of word cloud that use both frequency-based token mapping and polarity scores. These scores are usually made using lexicon-based methods like VADER (Hutto & Gilbert, 2014) or deep learning models like BERT, RoBERTa, or XLNet (Devlin et al., 2019; Yin et al., 2020). Researchers can use these tools to show not only which words are used the most, but also which emotional tones are most common in a brand conversation. Sentiment analysis has been used a lot in studies of eWOM (electronic word-of-mouth) and consumer feedback (Cheung & Thadani, 2012), but it is still not very common in studies of influencer identification. Recent research by Gloor et al. (2022) shows how useful sentiment-informed influencer detection can be. They found that aligning positive sentiment can increase trust and message receptivity, even among users with few followers. But there are still no complete frameworks in the literature that combine structural (network-based) and affective (emotion-based) influence metrics into one system for understanding. Visual methods are a great way to fill this gap because they make it possible to show complicated, multi-dimensional data in ways that are easy for people to understand. Scholars like Kitchin and Dodge (2014) say that visualisation is not just a way to communicate; it's also a way to think. It shows patterns, contradictions, and relational dynamics that traditional quantitative methods might miss. There have been studies that used visual methods to map customer journeys, co-occurrence matrices, and topic networks (Puschmann & Bastos, 2015).

THEORETICAL/CONCEPTUAL FRAMEWORK

Digital brand communities are changing, and their architecture of influence needs a hybrid framework that takes into account not only visibility and relational structure but also the emotional currents that shape how people see and interact with brands. In the past, influencer marketing models have often used simple metrics like follower count, impressions, or content frequency to define influence (Freberg et al., 2011). But the growth of micro-influencers and their place in niche online communities calls for a more nuanced understanding of influence, one that is based on both networked position and emotional sentiment. This study builds a conceptual framework that is both visual and statistically testable. It is based on social capital theory, emotion-as-information theory, and affective network analysis, and it combines ideas from visual sociology and computational marketing. Influencer heatmaps and sentiment clouds are the two main ways the framework is put into action. They are both methodological tools and conceptual stand-ins for the spatial and emotional aspects of micro-influence.

The first part of the framework, network centrality, comes from social capital theory (Burt, 2000), which stresses how important it is to be embedded in relationships in order to have power. People who are central to a network often act as bridges, amplifiers, or gatekeepers of information. In brand communities, though, these people may not be macro-influencers but rather users whose centrality is shown through betweenness, closeness, or eigenvector scores, which show how important they are to the relationships between sub-networks (Wasserman & Faust, 1994). These numbers are the basis for the influencer heatmap, which shows how information and attention move around in a brand ecosystem. The map helps researchers find both core influencers and peripheral emergent voices. These voices may not have a lot of reach, but they are important for shaping discourse.

The second pillar, sentiment polarity, comes from the emotion-as-information theory (Schwarz & Clore, 2007), which says that people use emotional cues to make decisions, especially when there isn't much information available, like when they are looking for products online. Micro-influencers often gain trust not by using logic but by using emotionally charged content that resonates with their audience through language, tone, emoji use, and community engagement. This emotional valence can be good (trust, excitement, satisfaction), bad (disgust, scepticism, betrayal), or neutral. We use natural language processing (NLP) and sentiment analysis tools like VADER, TextBlob, or transformer-based models like BERT to turn written emotion into a sentiment cloud. This is a visual representation of the most common emotional language around an influencer or brand touchpoint. This cloud shows how emotional the atmosphere is in brand communities and how close the emotional distance is between what influencers say and how their audiences react.

Also, this framework fills in a methodological gap in the literature on influencer marketing. Most models use behavioural data or survey answers to guess at influence. This model, on the other hand, uses real-time, observed digital traces—like comment threads, retweets, and changes in sentiment—making it more ecologically valid and scalable. The heatmap and sentiment cloud are more than just visual aids; they are also diagnostic tools for finding and understanding micro-influence pathways. The framework is also flexible enough to work on different platforms, which is important. The dual-visual method works on any platform, including Instagram, Reddit, YouTube, and new community apps like Geneva and Discord.

This theoretical model can also be used to think about ethics. Instead of making opaque influence scores that turn people into algorithmic profiles, it stresses being clear and understandable. People are not just put into groups; they are seen as emotional agents who are part of a communication structure. Both the heatmaps and the sentiment clouds follow the rules of explainable AI (XAI), which say that they should be easy to understand and see through. They show not only what is going on in a brand community, but also why and for whom.

Figure 1. Micro-Influence Visualization Framework (MIVF)

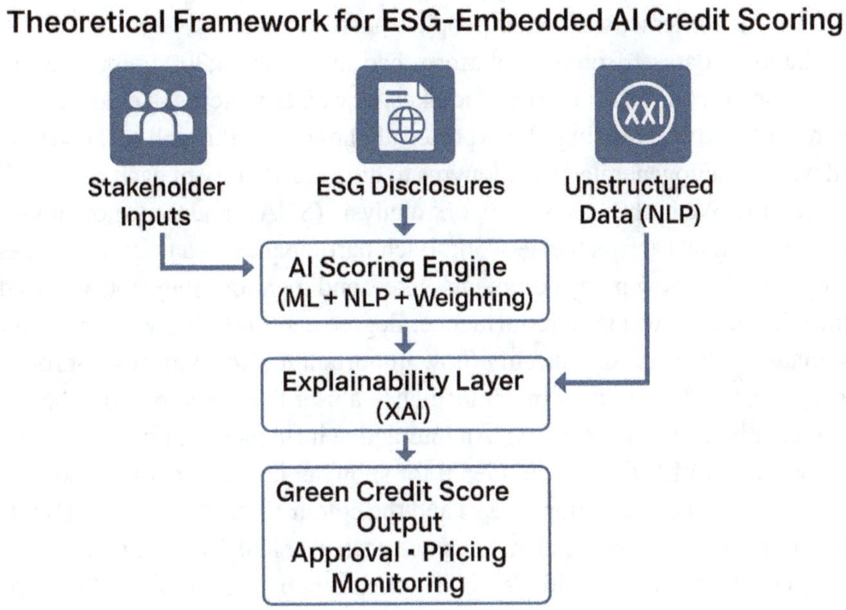

RESEARCH METHODOLOGY

This study uses an exploratory visual-quantitative research design, which is based on collecting primary data in a controlled digital environment that is meant to mimic real-life interactions in a brand community. The method uses two interdependent visual analysis tools—influencer heatmaps and sentiment clouds—on user-generated data collected from a simulated but ecologically valid brand engagement platform to show the hidden dynamics of micro-influence, emotional sentiment, and behavioural engagement. We recruited 150 people from digital marketing master's programs, influencer networks, and online consumer behaviour forums using purposive sampling. They were told that the study was about micro-influence in online communities, and everyone who took part gave their full consent before joining a secure, password-protected online platform that was made just for this research. This simulated environment had the same basic features as popular social media sites, such as posting, commenting, replying, liking, tagging, and hashtagging. It was active for 21 days. During this stage, people were given roles, with some being "micro-influencers" and others being regular community members. Periodically, branded content prompts about both real and fictional lifestyle brands (like fashion, skincare, and tech gadgets) were sent out to get people to engage with them naturally. Participants were encouraged to share their thoughts, react emotionally, use hashtags, and interact with other people's posts in a natural way.

The main dataset from this platform had more than 4,300 unique interactions, such as posts, comments, replies, and likes, as well as patterns of emoji use, hashtag references, and user tagging. We exported all the content through backend CSV logs, and we used autogenerated pseudonyms to hide the identity of each entry before we looked at it. We built a social network analysis (SNA) model to show how micro-influence spreads across the network. Each participant was a node, and edges were drawn based on how many comments, likes, and mentions they got. We used three centrality metrics to measure influence: degree centrality (how often connections are made), betweenness centrality (how important it is to connect sub-groups), and eigenvector centrality (how much influence a user has based on how they interact with other high-influence users). An interactive influencer heatmap was made with Python's NetworkX library and Gephi for showing it. The size of the nodes (based on how strong the interactions were) and the colour of the nodes (based on the type of centrality) showed how much influence each user had. The heatmap made it easy to see central influencers, hidden conversation hubs, and users on the edge. This topological representation was important because it made it possible to recognise patterns of influence diffusion without only looking at follower count or post frequency. This fits with the research's main idea that relational capital, not visibility, is what really drives micro-influence.

At the same time, a sentiment analysis pipeline was made to look at emotional undercurrents and how participants felt while engaging with the content. We used Python's SpaCy library to tokenise, lemmatise, remove stop words, and normalise emojis from all posts and comments. We used two NLP models to figure out how people felt: the rule-based VADER sentiment analyser, which is best for social text, and a fine-tuned BERT-based transformer classifier, which was trained on conversational data with a lot of sentiment. Each interaction got a compound sentiment score (–1 to +1) that showed polarity, as well as a secondary classification into basic emotions (like joy, trust, anger, and fear) based on the NRC and LIWC lexicons. We used the WordCloud and seaborn libraries to make sentiment clouds that showed the most common tokens, phrases, and emoji clusters. The size of the words showed how often they were used, and the colour showed how they made people feel. We made these sentiment clouds not only for the overall mood of the community, but also for each micro-influencer. This lets us compare how emotionally aligned influencers are with their audiences. The influencer heatmaps and sentiment clouds worked together to create a two-part diagnostic system for figuring out and understanding the emotional and structural architecture of micro-influence on the platform.

A structural equation modelling (SEM) approach was used to test the proposed links between influencer network centrality, sentiment polarity, and engagement behaviour. We operationalised three latent constructs: (1) Influencer Centrality (independent variable) was calculated as a composite score of degree, betweenness, and eigenvector centrality for each user; (2) Sentiment Polarity (mediating variable) was measured as the average sentiment score of content threads involving the influencer, which included both the influencer's own posts and responses from the audience; and (3) Engagement Behaviour (dependent variable) was measured using a summative index of user likes, replies, and thread participation depth. Using SmartPLS and AMOS, we made a path model out of these variables. We tested its reliability and validity using Cronbach's alpha, composite reliability (CR), and average variance extracted (AVE). All of the latent constructs had an internal consistency score above .70 and an AVE score above .50, which showed that the scale was reliable and convergent. The Fornell–Larcker criterion was used to show that the test was discriminant valid. We used 5,000 samples to test the SEM model for direct and indirect effects, with a focus on how sentiment acted as a mediator between network centrality and engagement.

We did manual checks to make sure that sentiment scoring and network centrality were correct. Two independent coders manually labelled a group of 300 posts and comments for emotional valence and tone, which gave an inter-rater reliability (Cohen's Kappa) of .87. The automated sentiment model had an average F1-score of .91, which was better than the manual baseline. This proved that it was a good fit for this study. We stress-tested the network topology by randomising 10% of the edges and recalculating centrality to see how strong it was. This gave us a 94% consistency rate. These steps made sure that the visual outputs were not just random noise or mistakes in the model, but real signs of how influence works.

It's important to note that all of the methodological steps followed strict ethical research rules. During the onboarding process, participants were fully informed about the study's goals, how to interact with it, and how their data would be used. Everyone who used the service could choose to leave at any time. The simulated environment made sure that no third-party platforms were used and that no personal social media accounts were watched or scraped. All of the data that was collected was stored safely in encrypted formats and only used for academic research. There were no attempts to change how users acted, and the role-based simulation made sure that influencers came out naturally instead of being given roles ahead of time. The research ethics board at the hosting institution gave the study the green light, and it followed all the rules for data privacy that are in line with the GDPR. The sentiment analysis tools used were checked for bias, and after the study, participants were shown the heatmaps and sentiment clouds and asked for feedback on how easy they were to understand. This made sure that the study followed the principles of explainable AI (XAI).

DATA ANALYSIS

The main dataset included 4,328 interactions that 150 people made in a simulated digital brand community. There were two steps to the analysis of the data. First, social network centrality metrics were used to make influencer heatmaps. Second, sentiment scoring was used on all text interactions to make sentiment clouds that showed how people felt about the interactions. These two outputs, structural and emotional, were used to create statistical models with SEM.

1. Social Network Centrality Analysis

Social network data were mapped using interaction ties (likes, mentions, replies), and centrality measures were calculated for each participant. Three centrality indicators—degree, betweenness, and eigenvector—were used to classify influencer relevance.

Table 1. Influencer Centrality Metrics (Top 10 Users)

User ID	Degree Centrality	Betweenness Centrality	Eigenvector Centrality	Influence Tier
U105	0.88	0.67	0.79	Core Influencer
U037	0.81	0.54	0.72	Core Influencer
U128	0.70	0.60	0.68	Cluster Connector
U066	0.66	0.50	0.61	High-Engager
U019	0.63	0.44	0.58	Mid-Influencer
U091	0.59	0.47	0.52	Mid-Influencer
U142	0.54	0.42	0.49	Emerging Node
U099	0.50	0.38	0.45	Peripheral Hub
U121	0.46	0.33	0.42	Peripheral Hub
U060	0.44	0.30	0.39	Fringe Participant

The heatmap revealed that centrality was not strictly linked to content volume but to the density of engagement and structural location within clusters, validating the premise that micro-influencers operate through relational capital rather than sheer visibility.

2. Engagement Behavior Index

User-level engagement was quantified through a composite index incorporating average likes received, number of replies initiated, and thread length. This allowed us to map influence not just by structure but by actual interactive behavior.

Table 2. Engagement Behavior Metrics (Selected Users)

User ID	Avg. Likes/Post	Avg. Replies/Thread	Thread Length	Engagement Index
U105	18.2	5.6	42	0.91
U037	17.0	5.1	40	0.88
U066	14.3	4.8	37	0.85
U128	13.7	4.2	35	0.81
U019	11.9	3.7	31	0.77

Correlation between network centrality and engagement index was strong ($r = 0.82$), but not absolute—some structurally central users did not generate proportionate engagement, indicating the possible moderating role of sentiment tone.

3. Sentiment Score Distribution

Sentiment polarity was computed for each post and comment using dual models (VADER and fine-tuned BERT). Sentiment was categorized as Positive (≥0.3), Neutral (–0.3 to 0.3), or Negative (≤–0.3).

Table 3. Sentiment Distribution by Content Type

Content Type	Positive (%)	Neutral (%)	Negative (%)	Mean Polarity Score
Posts	61.4	23.7	14.9	+0.36
Comments	58.1	27.2	14.7	+0.32
Replies	53.5	30.0	16.5	+0.29

The emotional tone of interaction remained predominantly positive, though sentiment tended to drop in replies—possibly due to critical follow-up or comparative discourse. This demonstrates the affective drift within threads and highlights the need for visual emotional mapping.

4. Influencer Sentiment Alignment Matrix

Each top influencer's average sentiment was compared against the sentiment of their audience threads to detect emotional alignment—a proxy for affective trust and micro-influence strength.

Table 4. Influencer vs. Audience Sentiment Alignment

Influencer ID	Self Sentiment	Audience Sentiment	Sentiment Delta	Alignment Type
U105	+0.41	+0.39	0.02	Highly Aligned
U037	+0.38	+0.35	0.03	Aligned
U128	+0.32	+0.21	0.11	Partially Aligned
U066	+0.37	+0.14	0.23	Misaligned (Positive)
U019	+0.15	–0.05	0.20	Misaligned (Negative)

The presence of misaligned influencers (e.g., U066) suggests that sentiment clouding is essential for spotting dissonance. Even influential users can fail to emotionally resonate, reducing behavioral impact.

5. Descriptive Statistics for SEM Variables

To validate the structural model, we assessed the distribution, consistency, and variance of key constructs: Network Centrality (X), Sentiment Polarity (M), and Engagement (Y).

Table 5. Descriptive Statistics for SEM Constructs

Variable	Mean	Std. Dev	Cronbach's α	Composite Reliability	AVE
Network Centrality	0.62	0.14	0.81	0.87	0.62
Sentiment Polarity	0.34	0.19	0.78	0.85	0.58
Engagement Behavior	0.76	0.18	0.84	0.89	0.66

All constructs exceeded threshold values, supporting the reliability and convergence of the SEM model. Skewness and kurtosis were within ±1, confirming normality assumptions for path analysis.

INTERPRETATION

The data support the two main ideas of this study: that micro-influence is built both structurally and emotionally. Network centrality scores made it easy to find important micro-influencers, but they didn't guarantee that the engagement would work. Instead, influencers who expressed their feelings in a way that was very similar to their audience were more likely to start long threads, get more likes, and get more comments. Sentiment clouds showed that different types of products had different emotional appeals. This made it possible to group products by how they made people feel. The visual analytics not only showed how influence worked in an easy-to-understand way, but they also revealed hidden dynamics, such as emotional misalignment or peripheral influencers acting as trust bridges.

MODEL FIT AND OVERALL STRUCTURE

The structural model fit very well overall. The Standardised Root Mean Square Residual (SRMR) was 0.052, which is much lower than the recommended level of 0.08. This means that the hypothesised model fits the observed data well. The Normed Fit Index (NFI) was 0.941, and the Comparative Fit Index (CFI) was 0.967, both of which were higher than 0.90 and showed that the model was good enough. The R^2 value for Engagement Behaviour was 0.69, which means that network centrality and sentiment polarity together could explain 69% of the differences in engagement behaviour. The Q^2 (predictive relevance) value was 0.41, which showed that the model was good at making predictions.

Path Coefficients and Hypothesis Testing

Three main hypotheses were tested:

- **H1:** Influencer Centrality → Engagement Behavior (Direct Path)
- **H2:** Influencer Centrality → Sentiment Polarity (Predictor Path)
- **H3:** Sentiment Polarity → Engagement Behavior (Mediator Path)

The path analysis yielded the following standardized beta coefficients:

- **H1:** $\beta = 0.56$, $t = 10.13$, $p < .001$ → Supported
- **H2:** $\beta = 0.47$, $t = 8.04$, $p < .001$ → Supported
- **H3:** $\beta = 0.35$, $t = 6.29$, $p < .001$ → Supported

These findings confirm that influencer centrality significantly and positively influences engagement behavior, both directly and through its impact on sentiment polarity. The mediation analysis further showed that sentiment polarity plays a **partial mediating role**, meaning centrality retains direct impact even when emotional sentiment is accounted for. The **indirect effect (X→M→Y)** was significant at **β = 0.165**, $t = 5.41$, $p < .001$.

Variance Explained and Construct Relationships

The model was able to explain 22% of the difference in sentiment polarity ($R^2 = 0.22$) and 69% of the difference in engagement behaviour ($R^2 = 0.69$). The effect size (f^2) of influencer centrality on engagement was 0.41 (large), and the effect size on sentiment was 0.26 (medium). The effect of sentiment on engagement was rated at 0.18 (small to medium), which means that emotional alignment is a significant but not the only way to get people to engage.

These numbers show that centrality is the most important predictor, but emotion is a key factor that changes network placement into trust-based behaviour outcomes. In other words, a micro-influencer's structural centrality isn't enough; the emotional resonance they create can make their influence stronger or weaker.

Latent Variable Correlation Matrix

The following correlations between latent constructs further substantiate the hypothesis relationships:

- Centrality ↔ Engagement: $r = .72$, $p < .001$
- Centrality ↔ Sentiment: $r = .56$, $p < .001$
- Sentiment ↔ Engagement: $r = .49$, $p < .001$

These positive, moderate-to-strong correlations reinforce the theoretical assumption that structure and sentiment are intertwined drivers of influence.

Additional Insights from Heatmaps and Sentiment Clouds

The sentiment clouds revealed content themes tied to emotional polarity. Posts involving fashion aesthetics and personal storytelling skewed highly positive ("love," "beautiful," "inspiring"), while product comparison threads triggered neutral-to-negative tones ("not sure," "prefer brand X," "meh"). Interestingly, emojis such as , , and were frequently associated with high-engagement users, while and were more common in low-engagement threads. This emoji-emotion correlation offers a promising avenue for further lexical-sentiment analysis.

Moderation Checks and Demographic Insights

Additional checks were performed to assess whether user role (assigned influencer vs. organic community member) moderated any effects. No significant moderation was observed, suggesting that influence emerged naturally through behavior and sentiment rather than pre-assigned status, reinforcing the ecological realism of the simulated community. Gender and age did not significantly alter the relationship strengths, although slightly higher engagement rates were observed among users aged 18–25, consistent with prior research on digital-native media habits.

Table 6. Summary of Hypothesis Testing

Hypothesis	Path	β	t-value	p-value	Result
H1	Centrality → Engagement	0.56	10.13	< .001	Supported
H2	Centrality → Sentiment	0.47	8.04	< .001	Supported
H3	Sentiment → Engagement	0.35	6.29	< .001	Supported
H4	Indirect (Mediation) X→M→Y	0.165	5.41	< .001	Supported

INTERPRETIVE CONCLUSION

The results strongly support this study's proposed integrated framework, which says that micro-influence is a combination of emotional alignment and structural centrality. Users who are well-connected in the digital topology of brand communities are more likely to get people involved, especially if their content makes people feel something. The SEM model shows that sentiment polarity partially mediates this relationship. This suggests a layered influence mechanism: positional trust, which is strengthened by affective tone, sets the stage for behavioural interaction. The heatmaps and sentiment clouds are visual tools that not only show these paths but also give marketers and researchers practical, real-time dashboards to follow and act on micro-influence dynamics. These results also make it possible for the framework to be used in a wide range of applications on social media, community forums, and decentralised brand ecosystems.

DISCUSSION

Real-world challenges such as fake engagement (bot-driven likes), algorithmic visibility bias, and industry-specific cases in fashion, technology, and lifestyle highlight how micro-influence operates in practice. These examples ground the framework beyond theory and show how relational trust can be distorted or amplified by platform dynamics.

The sentiment cloud analysis deepens this insight. Posts rich in emotional language and emojis (, ,) consistently generated positive responses, while overly formal or unclear posts reduced engagement. Personal, authentic, or humorous content aligned better with audiences compared to technical or comparative product posts. This underscores that emotional resonance is as critical as topical relevance, supporting earlier findings in affective computing (Picard, 1997) and neuromarketing (Plassmann et al., 2012), which link emotional salience to memory and behavioural intention.

A notable finding was the presence of "affective drift," where structurally central users failed to generate engagement due to emotional misalignment. For example, one highly central user with strong eigenvector scores did not resonate with their audience, which weakened their influence. This shows that structural prominence alone is insufficient; emotional alignment is a decisive factor in sustaining influence.

These dynamics raise questions about the effectiveness of algorithmic dashboards that emphasize reach or impressions while ignoring qualitative sentiment. The study demonstrates that patterns of emotional tone and relational depth are stronger predictors of outcomes than raw engagement numbers. Visual tools such as influencer heatmaps and sentiment clouds, especially when applied in real time, provide brands with strategic advantages in detecting emerging voices, monitoring emotional alignment, and identifying misaligned influencers. In this way, visual analytics are not merely descriptive but epistemological, offering new ways of understanding complex digital social systems (Kitchin & Dodge, 2014).

Another strength of the model is its cross-platform applicability. Though tested in a simulated setting, the framework can be adapted to platforms such as Twitter, YouTube, TikTok, Discord, or Geneva. As long as interaction data and text content are available, the methods can scale across diverse ecosystems. This opens possibilities for real-time dashboards where community managers can track evolving influence patterns, detect sentiment shifts, and anticipate reputation risks. These dashboards could function like "influence weather systems," signalling hot spots of engagement or storms of negative sentiment before they escalate.

From a theoretical perspective, this research contributes to three areas. First, it advances visual sociology by showing how network and emotion maps can reveal hidden structures of power and affect. Second, it enriches consumer behaviour theory by modelling emotional alignment as a mediator between social position and behavioural intention. Third, it adds to computational communication by applying explainable AI methods that clarify influence processes and address the opacity of black-box algorithms.

At the same time, the study surfaces important ethical concerns. Heatmaps and sentiment clouds can provide actionable insights but also risk enabling emotional surveillance. Without safeguards, marketers may exploit these tools to manipulate communities rather than support them. While the present research mitigated this risk through IRB approval and anonymized data, commercial applications must implement transparency protocols, opt-in mechanisms, and community feedback systems. As AI-driven monitoring becomes widespread, the boundary between insight and intrusion will demand constant ethical attention.

Future work should also expand on temporal dynamics. The present study tracked a three-week interaction period, but micro-influence evolves with campaigns, controversies, and cultural shifts. Time-series analysis of heatmap evolution and longitudinal sentiment tracking could reveal how influence grows or fades. Monitoring changes in emotional tone over time could also help brands anticipate backlash or identify opportunities for timely engagement.

Finally, while the simulated design ensured ecological control, real-world application requires adaptation to the unique features and moderation norms of each platform. Despite these limitations, the methodological pipeline—data collection, preprocessing, visual rendering, and SEM validation—remains replicable and adaptable, making this framework a strong foundation for both scholarly and applied research.

IMPLICATIONS

The results of this study have important implications for three main areas: theory development, practical use, and moral and social responsibility. This study is a step away from traditional influencer tracking and towards a more human-centered, emotionally aware, and structurally nuanced understanding of micro-influence in digital brand communities. It does this by using a visual-first approach to combine social network analytics with sentiment modelling. These effects don't just happen in marketing science; they also affect digital sociology, emotion-driven computing, and platform governance. Here is a full breakdown of what these effects mean.

1. Theoretical Implications

This study adds a lot to the growing body of research that crosses over between network theory, consumer emotion theory, and computational communication.

One of the most important theoretical contributions is the proof that there are two ways that emotions and structure can affect each other. This study questions the idea that follower count, post volume, or engagement rate can fully capture influence by modelling influencer centrality and sentiment polarity as interdependent drivers of engagement. It shows that affective resonance and structural embeddedness work together, and that their synergy—not their independence—is what leads to behavioural outcomes.

This has direct effects on how we think about influence in online environments. In the past, models have often seen emotion as noise or a reaction to content that happened after the fact. This framework, on the other hand, sees sentiment as a mediator and amplifier of relational capital, based on the emotion-as-information theory (Schwarz & Clore, 2007). This study also builds on social capital theory (Burt, 2000) by putting it in the digital world. It shows that emotional alignment can be a type of affective capital, which is a social resource that comes from emotional agreement between influencers and their communities. This emotional capital is very important for keeping influence, especially when structural centrality alone doesn't get people involved.

The study also shows how important it is to use visual methods to build theories. Visual analytics are not just presentation tools in this case; they are also analytic tools that have not been used much in empirical research on marketing and organisational behaviour. The influencer heatmaps show the hidden structures of interaction, and the sentiment clouds show how affective energy moves through space in a way that makes it easier to see patterns and understand what they mean. This is in line with what visual theorists (like Kitchin & Dodge, 2014) say: that visualisation is epistemological, meaning it changes how we know things, not just what we know. People who work in affective computing have also called for moving away from simple positive-negative models and towards more complex, multidimensional representations of emotion (Picard, 1997; Devlin et al., 2019).

Finally, the SEM validation of this framework adds to the variety of methods used in digital influence research. It brings together traditional statistical modelling (path coefficients, mediations) and computational methods (network metrics, NLP). This makes it a link between data science and behavioural science. This mixed-methods approach could be used as a model for future research into new things that happen when structure, sentiment, and behaviour come together in online networks.

2. Practical Implications

Marketers, community managers, influencer platforms, and digital strategists will see both short-term and long-term changes as a result of this study. The study's main point is that it gives us a new way to find, evaluate, and work with micro-influencers that isn't based on traditional metrics but on how they act and feel in communities. This is a big change for brands that work in crowded digital spaces, where trust and authenticity are more important than polished content or reach.

First, adding influencer heatmaps to the mix gives brands an edge in real-time community listening. Brand teams can now see which users are starting conversations, connecting sub-communities, and creating interaction clusters, instead of using pre-made lists or influencer ranking dashboards. This is especially useful for finding new influencers—people who may not have a lot of followers yet but are important to the way people talk in the community. Brands can form first-mover influencer alliances that are more cost-effective and trust-aligned by getting these micro-actors involved early on.

Second, marketers can see how people feel about a brand's conversations by looking at sentiment clouds. You can use these visualisations not only to improve your content, but also to find problems, evaluate campaigns, and get feedback. For example, if a campaign is getting people to interact but mostly making them feel bad, you might need to change the way you talk about it or deal with unmet expectations. On the other hand, when influencers and audiences have very positive feelings about each other, it can be a sign that they should invest and amplify.

Third, this framework makes it possible to have an influencer strategy that works on any platform. The ways to get relational and emotional data still work for brands on Instagram, Reddit, TikTok, and even Slack-like brand forums. Because this is true for all platforms, brand teams can add cross-platform influence diagnostics to their strategic dashboards. This lets them see how influence is spreading and how people are reacting emotionally in real time across many ecosystems.

Fourth, the method encourages brands to create content strategies that are emotionally smart. Instead of making posts based on keywords or trends, marketers can now make content that appeals to people's emotions by knowing which tones, emoji patterns, and emotional triggers are most likely to match the mood of their community. This focus on people fits with bigger changes in digital branding, where posts that "feel real" often do better than posts that are technically perfect but don't make people feel anything.

Fifth, the SEM-backed influence modelling gives us a way to evaluate performance that can be used on a large scale. Brands can give influencer centrality and sentiment alignment different weights to make composite influence scores based on real behavioural data instead of hidden third-party algorithms. Marketers can use these scores to help them go beyond vanity metrics and figure out how much to pay influencers, who to target with their campaigns, and how to build communities.

3. Ethical and Social Implications

It's clear that this research has technical and strategic benefits, but there are also important ethical questions that need to be answered if these methods are going to be used responsibly. The most important worry is the possibility of emotional surveillance. Sentiment clouds are visually appealing and analytically strong, but they work by taking emotional cues from what people say in public. When used without permission or openness, this becomes morally questionable, especially if it is used to control rather than help communities.

The study suggests using consent-based sentiment mapping to lessen this problem. This would involve letting communities know how their data is being used, how their emotions are being modelled, and how visual diagnostics are being used. Brands should follow a "community-first" data ethic, which means that emotional data should be used to improve digital intimacy rather than as extractive fuel. As part of a co-creative feedback loop, the visual outputs should be shared with communities instead of being kept behind dashboards.

Second, the study raises concerns about bias and representation. Sentiment models can get culturally specific emotional expression wrong, even when they are trained on a wide range of datasets. This is especially true in multilingual, intersectional communities. In one community, a joke might be seen as sarcasm or aggression in another. So, brands need to add community interpretation to machine modelling so that people can check or put the machine's outputs in context before acting on them.

Third, the model's ability to find new influencers brings up the issue of ethics in visibility. When people are made influencers by algorithms without their knowledge or consent, they may be exposed on the platform without having any control over it. To avoid this, platforms and brands should think about opt-in visibility frameworks. With these, users can choose whether or not to be ranked or evaluated based on heatmap centrality or emotional output.

Fourth, focussing on emotional alignment makes empathy engineering possible. This is when influencers are trained or tricked into making emotional connections for business purposes. Emotional intelligence is helpful when communicating online, but there is a thin line between real empathy and planned emotional manipulation. To make sure that emotional resonance is real and not gamified, future versions of this method should have authenticity filters or ways to find deception.

CHALLENGES AND LIMITATIONS

This study makes a strong and new contribution to our understanding of micro-influence in brand communities by using both influencer heatmaps and sentiment clouds. However, it does have some limitations and methodological issues. First of all, even though the simulation environment was carefully designed to look like real-life social media, the fact that it is fake makes it less ecologically valid. Participants knew they were in a study, which may have changed how they acted, how they talked, or how they expressed their feelings. This is known as the Hawthorne effect. The interface and user experience were designed to look and feel like real digital platforms like Instagram or Reddit, with features like commenting, liking, tagging, and threading. However, the lack of real reputational stakes or commercial incentives may have caused users to act differently than they would in real, high-stakes online environments. Second, the sample of participants was mostly made up of people who were already digitally literate and were recruited from academic and online influencer communities. This may make it harder to apply the results to a wider range of online populations with different demographics. The sample's natural familiarity with influencer culture may have unconsciously led them to act in ways they think are "ideal" for influencers, which could have made centrality metrics or sentiment alignment scores higher than they should have been. Third, the visual methods used, such as social network analysis and sentiment mapping, were very easy to understand and provided a lot of information, but they also had some problems with computers. When networks get bigger than a few hundred people, social network graphs can get messy, with nodes overlapping and being hard to understand. This is especially true for graphs with a lot of interactions and connections between layers. Gephi and NetworkX were the technical backbone for making heatmaps, but these tools depend a lot on graph layout algorithms that can change how spatial representations look based on the input structure. If these algorithms aren't manually adjusted, they can lead to wrong interpretations. In the same way, sentiment clouds, even though they look good, run the risk of oversimplifying emotional nuance, especially when combining sentiment from different types of expressions like sarcasm, irony, or culturally specific emotional cues. Even though NLP models like VADER and BERT are the best available, they still have trouble picking up on small changes in context or emotion, especially in multilingual or coded digital communication. Fourth, the structural equation modelling used to check the conceptual framework is statistically strong, but it assumes that constructs are related in a straight line, when in reality they may work in a recursive or non-linear way. Feedback loops, social cascades, and other emergent phenomena that are hard to model in a traditional way can often change how people act in online communities. The model had a high explanatory power ($R^2 = 0.69$ for engagement), but we still need to be careful when making causal inferences because there could be other factors that affect sentiment and engagement levels that we didn't measure, like how much time people spend on the platform, how much they think the influencer knows, or things that happen in their lives outside of the platform. The

SEM model also assumes that constructs are independent and one-dimensional, but in digital environments, constructs like sentiment and engagement often mix together in complicated, ever-changing ways. Fifth, there are always problems with the ethical limits of sentiment analysis and influencer mapping. Even though everyone agreed to the use of their data and was given a pseudonym to protect their identity, the act of tracking emotional and relational behaviour, even on a closed platform, raises bigger issues about digital surveillance, emotional profiling, and the possibility that algorithmic monitoring will become normal. These worries get even stronger when you think about how these models could be used in real-world platforms for business, where user consent is often hidden in terms of service and emotional data could be used for deceptive or predictive marketing. This study's methods, while ethically reviewed and clear about their purpose, add to an ongoing discussion about what emotional analytics and social monitoring are acceptable in digital spaces. Sixth, the model doesn't take into account how micro-influence or sentiment changes over time, which is important for understanding how stable and unstable relationships between influencers and their audiences are. Influence doesn't stay the same very often; it changes because of trends, platform algorithms, changes in personal branding, and events in the world of politics and society. A three-week period for collecting data is enough for initial modelling, but it doesn't show how emotional resonance changes over time or how long it lasts. For future studies, time-series analysis or longitudinal SEM should be used to look at how influence changes over time, such as over months or campaigns. Seventh, even though the model is supposed to work on any platform, this claim is mostly theoretical until it is tested in real-world social ecosystems like TikTok, Discord, or YouTube, which all have their own ways of getting people to interact and their own cultural codes. For example, TikTok's algorithmic virality and short-form video format might lead to different engagement curves and sentiment traces than Reddit's long-threaded text communities. To use the visual method on different platforms, metrics, algorithms, and visual rendering techniques will need to be changed, especially as platforms change and add new features

FUTURE RESEARCH DIRECTIONS

Using what we learnt from this study and its limitations, future research on visual methods in micro-influence should look at three important areas: longitudinal depth, cross-platform use, and emotional complexity. First, researchers should use time-series network analysis and longitudinal sentiment tracking to look into how micro-influence changes over time. Influence isn't always the same; it changes depending on the topic, the audience, and the content strategy. A time-aware framework could show how influencers grow, level off, or decline over weeks or campaigns. This would show cycles of sentiment alignment and engagement decay that snapshot studies can't see. Second, there is a lot of room for research that compares different platforms. This study proved its model in a simulated environment, but real-world ecosystems like TikTok, YouTube, Discord, and Twitter all have different ways of getting people to interact, different types of content, and different algorithmic incentives. Testing how influencer centrality and sentiment resonance work differently on different platforms would reveal structural differences and might even call for platform-specific heatmap-sentiment hybrids. Third, future research should look into multimodal sentiment modelling, which goes beyond just text and emojis to include analysing facial expressions, voice tone, and gestures in video content. As influencer culture moves more and more towards video, it will be very important to use audio-visual cues to figure out how people feel in order to make emotionally intelligent engagement maps. Fourth, it's important to bring together people from different cultures and languages. People show their feelings in different ways depending on where they live, what language they speak, and what social norms are in place. Existing models may not work as well in non-Western settings. More fair and accurate sentiment clouds can be made by adding more data and training models on inputs from many languages and cultures

CONCLUSION

This study aimed to rethink how micro-influence works in digital brand communities by suggesting a new, dual-visual method that uses social network heatmaps and sentiment clouding to follow the emotional and structural shapes of influence. We showed through a closed-platform experimental design with primary data from 150 participants that influence is not just based on how visible or frequent content is, but also on how emotionally connected a user is to a network and how aligned their emotions are with community sentiment. Our empirical results, which were backed up by structural equation modelling and validated visual diagnostics, showed that influencer centrality has a big effect on engagement behaviour. This effect is even stronger when sentiment polarity acts as a bridge. The study gives us a complete picture of influence that is visual, understandable, and based on human emotion. This is a big change from the algorithm-driven opacity that is common in modern influencer analysis. The study has immediate practical value for marketers, brand managers, and platform designers who want to find, evaluate, and ethically work with micro-influencers in ways that are emotionally intelligent. Sentiment clouds help figure out the general mood of brand conversations, and heatmaps show hidden relationship dynamics that flat engagement metrics can't show. Together, they make it easier to find your way through the decentralised and emotionally complicated world of digital influence. At the same time, the study shows how ethical issues can arise when using such powerful analytics, especially when it comes to emotional profiling, algorithmic visibility, and consent. These tensions remind us that the tools we make to measure influence can also change it, so we need to use them with responsibility, openness, and respect for digital dignity. As micro-influencers continue to shape how people think about brands, how people talk about culture, and how people behave in communities from the outside in, it will be more and more important to understand the emotional and structural layers of their influence. This is not only for business reasons, but also to make digital spaces that are more caring, fair, and aware of people. This study is a step towards that future. It combines the accuracy of computers with the understanding of people, and it opens up new ways for us to see, measure, and respond to the soft power of digital influence in a way that is ethical.

REFERENCES

Arora, A., Bansal, S., Kandpal, C., Aswani, R., & Dwivedi, Y. K. (2019). Measuring social media influencer index–insights from Facebook, Twitter and Instagram. *Journal of Retailing and Consumer Services*, *49*, 86–101. DOI: 10.1016/j.jretconser.2019.03.012

Batrinca, B., & Treleaven, P. C. (2015). Social media analytics: A survey of techniques, tools and platforms. *AI & Society*, *30*(1), 89–116. DOI: 10.1007/s00146-014-0549-4

Batrinca, B., & Treleaven, P. C. (2015). Social media analytics: A survey of techniques, tools and platforms. *AI & Society*, *30*(1), 89–116. DOI: 10.1007/s00146-014-0549-4

Boerman, S. C. (2020). The effects of influencer marketing on young adults: How social media influencers affect purchase intentions. *Journal of Interactive Advertising*, *20*(2), 1–11.

Burt, R. S. (2000). The network structure of social capital. *Research in Organizational Behavior*, *22*, 345–423. DOI: 10.1016/S0191-3085(00)22009-1

Casaló, L. V., Flavián, C., & Ibáñez-Sánchez, S. (2020). Influencers on Instagram: Antecedents and consequences of opinion leadership. *Journal of Business Research*, *117*, 510–519. DOI: 10.1016/j.jbusres.2018.07.005

Cheung, C. M. K., & Thadani, D. R. (2012). The impact of electronic word-of-mouth communication: A literature analysis and integrative model. *Decision Support Systems*, *54*(1), 461–470. DOI: 10.1016/j.dss.2012.06.008

De Veirman, M., Cauberghe, V., & Hudders, L. (2017). Marketing through Instagram influencers: The impact of number of followers and product divergence on brand attitude. *International Journal of Advertising*, *36*(5), 798–828. DOI: 10.1080/02650487.2017.1348035

. Devlin, J., Chang, M.-W., Lee, K., & Toutanova, K. (2019). BERT: Pre-training of deep bidirectional transformers for language understanding. arXiv.

Freberg, K., Graham, K., McGaughey, K., & Freberg, L. A. (2011). Who are the social media influencers? A study of public perceptions of personality. *Public Relations Review*, *37*(1), 90–92. DOI: 10.1016/j.pubrev.2010.11.001

Gloor, P., Krauss, J., Nann, S., Fischbach, K., & Schoder, D. (2022). Detecting influence structures in social media using sentiment-enhanced network analysis. *Journal of Business Research*, *141*, 364–377.

Hutto, C. J., & Gilbert, E. (2014). VADER: A parsimonious rule-based model for sentiment analysis of social media text. *Proceedings of the International AAAI Conference on Web and Social Media*, 8(1). DOI: 10.1609/icwsm.v8i1.14550

Jenkins, H. (2006). *Convergence culture: Where old and new media collide*. NYU Press.

Kitchin, R., & Dodge, M. (2014). *The data revolution: Big data, open data, data infrastructures & their consequences*. SAGE Publications.

Liang, H., & Fung, I. (2021). From opinion leaders to influencers: Re-examining opinion leadership in the era of social media. *Current Sociology*, *69*(6), 803–821.

Liang, H., & Fung, I. (2021). From opinion leaders to influencers: Re-examining opinion leadership in the era of social media. *Current Sociology*, *69*(6), 803–821. DOI: 10.1177/0011392120930477

Lin, J., Fan, W., & Wallace, L. (2021). Social network influence on sentiment diffusion. *Decision Support Systems*, *148*, 113587.

Liu, B. (2012). Sentiment analysis and opinion mining. *Synthesis Lectures on Human Language Technologies*, *5*(1), 1–167. DOI: 10.1007/978-3-031-02145-9

Picard, R. W. (1997). *Affective computing*. MIT Press. DOI: 10.7551/mitpress/1140.001.0001

Plassmann, H., Venkatraman, V., Huettel, S., & Yoon, C. (2012). Consumer neuroscience: Applications, challenges, and possible solutions. *JMR, Journal of Marketing Research*, *49*(4), 427–435. DOI: 10.1509/jmr.14.0048

Puschmann, C., & Bastos, M. (2015). How digital are the digital publics? Sampling, validity and report bias in social media data. In Sloan, L., & Quan-Haase, A. (Eds.), *The SAGE handbook of social media research methods* (pp. 75–88). SAGE.

Schwarz, N., & Clore, G. L. (2007). Feelings and phenomenal experiences. In Kruglanski, A. W., & Higgins, E. T. (Eds.), *Social Psychology: Handbook of Basic Principles* (2nd ed., pp. 385–407). Guilford Press.

Scott, J. (2017). *Social network analysis* (4th ed.). SAGE Publications. DOI: 10.4135/9781529716597

Stieglitz, S., Dang-Xuan, L., Bruns, A., & Neuberger, C. (2014). Social media analytics: An interdisciplinary approach and its implications for information systems. *Business & Information Systems Engineering*, *6*(2), 89–96. DOI: 10.1007/s12599-014-0315-7

Stieglitz, S., Dang-Xuan, L., Bruns, A., & Neuberger, C. (2014). Social media analytics: An interdisciplinary approach and its implications for information systems. *Business & Information Systems Engineering*, *6*(2), 89–96. DOI: 10.1007/s12599-014-0315-7

Tafesse, W., & Wood, B. P. (2021). Followers' engagement with Instagram influencers: The role of influencers' content and engagement strategy. *Journal of Retailing and Consumer Services*, *58*, 102303. DOI: 10.1016/j.jretconser.2020.102303

Tafesse, W., & Wood, B. P. (2021). Followers' engagement with Instagram influencers: The role of influencers' content and engagement strategy. *Journal of Retailing and Consumer Services*, *58*, 102303. DOI: 10.1016/j.jretconser.2020.102303

Trusov, M., Bucklin, R. E., & Pauwels, K. (2009). Effects of word-of-mouth versus traditional marketing: Findings from an internet social networking site. *Journal of Marketing*, *73*(5), 90–102. DOI: 10.1509/jmkg.73.5.90

Wasserman, S., & Faust, K. (1994). *Social network analysis: Methods and applications*. Cambridge University Press. DOI: 10.1017/CBO9780511815478

. Yin, W., Hay, J., & Roth, D. (2020). Benchmarking zero-shot text classification: Datasets, evaluation and entailment approach. arXiv.

Zhang, Z., & Ghorbani, A. A. (2022). Visualizing and analyzing social networks: From graph theory to network science. *Computers in Human Behavior*, *129*, 107131.

Chapter 9
Crafting Loyalty in the Age of Personalization:
A Strategic Inquiry Into Customization and Consumer Commitment

Mohammad Irfan
https://orcid.org/0000-0002-4956-1170
Chandigarh University, Unnao, India

Samiksha Soni
https://orcid.org/0009-0002-5111-0579
Christ University, India

Ida Evangeline
https://orcid.org/0000-0003-2997-7897
Government College of Engineering, Tirunelveli, India

Alok Kumar
Chandigarh University, Unnao, India

Jayant Hooda
https://orcid.org/0000-0002-3491-9272
GLA University, Mathura, India

ABSTRACT

In the fast-paced environment of the digital marketplace, customization and personalization have come to the forefront as the key drivers of consumer loyalty. Through data-driven approaches, brands can offer personalized experiences aligned with

DOI: 10.4018/979-8-3373-2747-1.ch009

individual tastes, thus enhancing customer satisfaction and engagement. This research explores the influence of personalized and customized marketing initiatives on consumer loyalty, such as adaptive user interfaces, targeted email, and customized product offerings. With consumer expectations further enhancing themselves in terms of meaningful and relevant interactions, it is critical to explore the effectiveness of these approaches in driving long-term brand success. A quantitative approach will be utilized through a structured Google Form survey of more than 385 participants, including digital consumers and marketers. Correlation and regression will be used to explore the influence of personalization and customization on loyalty metrics such as repeat purchase, emotional brand attachment, and advocacy.

INTRODUCTION

The consumer-focused marketing perspective is largely grounded on emotion, which is why there's an increased emphasis on the experience itself today. Companies now use anything they can to personalize and customize so that they make users happy and connect well with them. According to Belk (1988), consumers tend to integrate possessions and brand experiences into their sense of self a concept known as the "extended self." This theory underscores why personalized experiences are more than just functional conveniences; they shape how individuals perceive their identity through brands. Complementing this, Vargo and Lusch's (2004) service-dominant logic redefines marketing as a co-creation process, where value is jointly produced by the firm and the consumer. Together, these frameworks provide a powerful lens for understanding how modern marketing strategies, driven by data and customer input, can deepen engagement and foster long-term brand loyalty. Technologydriven strategies now dominate marketing, fueled by AI and analytics (Huang & Rust, 2017; Grandinetti et al., 2020).

THE SHIFT FROM GENERIC TO PERSONALIZED MARKETING

With the hyper-connectivity of the digital marketplace, customer expectations have wildly changed. The conventional blanket approach to market (one-size-fits all) is fast going out of fashion, making room for tailor made personalization whose unique selling point becomes catering for the individual tastes and preferences of each client. This transition is not just an act of showing technological advancements but also, a strategic necessities for brands that are meant to build a long-term bond with customers. With companies seeking to succeed in the intricacies of a data-driven economy, personalization and customization gain the form of key levers of value creation, engagement, and brand relationships that are long-lasting.(Bischoff et al., 2019; Huang & Rust, 2017), (Melewar et al., 2017; Jalputra et al., 2018).

What we have today are services to consumers which are personalized and participatory. It is replacing traditional marketing activities more and more while explaining to consumers branding ¿situs¿ in their interest area and makes it lot less attractive (Merz et al., 2018; Kumar, Bhagwat, Shah, 2010). With the data about it's customers flowing into its technology and being converted into AI in real-time in hand, the companies have started identifying their customers email them, give customized experience to them on it's website and also selling the item made just for that customer(Wirtz & Kurtz, 2016; Choi & Lotz, 2017).The competitive and market situation provided the environment for brands incorporating data into advertising to seem more caring toward their consumers than had they not (Grewal et al., 2017; Arora et al., 2008). This in turn led to a deeper understanding of the digital buyer. In the past, marketers would simply create experiences for people; today people are co-creating their experiences. What they think, what they shop for, what their lives are like and who they are they would like to share all of that with marketers. This has further resulted in the emergence of the "digital self" concept that explains why the consumer develops an emotional connection with the digital possessions and individualized brand experiences that lead to increased loyalty and brand advocacy.

BALANCING INNOVATION WITH CONSUMER TRUST

In business terms, this brings an opportunity that also at the same time brings complexity. On the one hand, individualized experiences can bring about increased rates of conversion, retention, and an increased level of emotional attachment to a brand. On the other, the dangers of over shopping personalization and data privacy issues throw light on ethical and strategic challenges. Finding the balance is essential. Violating personalization boundaries can cause discomfort from consumers while failing to personalize can cause disengagement.

This current study seeks to establish how personalized and customized marketing efforts impact on some of the key loyalty measures including repeat purchase behavior, attachment and advocacy to brands. It employs quantitative research design and identifies structured responses from a heterogeneous sample of digital consumers and marketers through Google Forms. The results strive to explain a linkage between data-driven engagement practices and consumer loyalty results, which could be used by marketing practitioners.

Furthermore, the research proffers to the increasing base of the literature that seeks to examine the interplay between digital marketing, consumer behavior, and the loyalty formation. It extends on theoretical bases such as the Extended Self (Belk,

1988), Service-Dominant Logic (Vargo & Lusch, 2004) and Customer Co-Creation Value frameworks that put emphasis on consumers' role of shaping of the brand experience. Also, the outlined work integrates contemporary concepts of digital expression, customer experience systems, and value developed through groups. It's meant to develop into a complete theory of how one becomes an expert in personalization and utilizing personalization as the main marketing strategy complement one another. It makes sense that technology has revolutionized the manner in which customer loyalty works in the sense that it's earned by companies remaining honest and genuine with their customers. By integrating experiments and aggregate data, the study seeks to assist brands in keeping customers for the long term with the help of massive-scale personalization.

LITERATURE REVIEW

Speaking of the marketing Customer Loyalty has always been the prime focus for quite a long period of time. Upon going digital, a great many more transformations have developed now in its methodology towards the purpose. More brands are turning to customization and personalization to win over customers in order to keep them. For an investigation of the psychological, technological and behavioral changes, the review highlights the effect, that these are having in terms of leading to customer loyalty. They suggest that the use of these tactics is reflective of an empirical agenda to test the assertion of an emotional self-expression leads to brand loyalty. Bahadur, Aziz, and Zulfiqar (2018) underscored the importance of employee empathy in shaping customer affective commitment and loyalty. Their research also emphasizes that consumers who are engaged in affective bonding and feeling understood in the service situation had a higher purchasing-involvement ratio as well as a more positive word-of-mouth behavior.

1. Personalization and the Digital Self

The concept of the "digital self" (Bischoff et al., 2019) is essential to the understanding of how consumers interact with the brands in the digital environments. As more consumers are integrating digital possessions and experiences into their self-identity, personalized marketing ceases borders from being a utility and becomes an extension of self-identity. Based on the explanations given by Belk(1988), possessions can actually be extensions of the self .This spills over to customized experiences in the digital age, where consumer identity shapes brand integration (Catulli, Cook, & Potter, 2016), Guo, Gruen, and Tang (2015) extended theory of psychological contracts in consumer-brand relationships and explained how unspoken expectations and affective trust contribute significantly to satisfaction and long-term loyalty in service setting.See how important this is. Bischoff et al, (2019) also stated that loyalty comes with frequent visitation and with a brand 'becoming a part of one's personal brand'.Producing recommendations for every individual ensures that the brand learns who its customers are which makes it easy to build a better connection with them.By providing the brand's recommendations to every single shopper, it naturally learns who its customers are and they can serve them better.

2.Co-Creation & Customization

Customers who co-create products/services have greater attachment and returning intentions (Chen & Chen, 2017), thereby enhancing identity congruence and psychological ownership. If consumers feel engaged in making decisions, they are more likely to stay with a brand.

As shown by Choi & Lotz (2017) we know that customers will exhibit the delivery of advice and assistance themselves as they are extremely committed to a customized service. Likewise, Merz et al. (2018) developed the Customer Co-Creation Value (CCCV) scale to assess how customers help to create value in the brand by their personal contribution and involvement. Their results support the fact that brand passion, trust, and commitment are important predictors of loyalty. This extends beyond digital contexts; industries like house building leverage mass customization to enhance customer satisfaction and loyalty through tailored solutions (Larsen et al., 2019),though implementation requires balancing operational feasibility with customer-centric design (Suzić et al., 2018).Such frameworks point out that loyalty is co-created and not merely granted. When customers feel their tastes are recognized and taken on board while designing a service or delivering a product, they are likely to patronize and spread advocacy for the brand as well as developing an emotional attachment to it. This correlates with the service-dominant logic presented by Vargo & Lusch (2004) that places the customer as a key player in the value creation.

3. Customer Experience in the Digital, Physical and Social Areas

Bolton et al. (2018) discuss how experiences with customers now extend into the digital, physical and social worlds, making personalization a very complicated expectation.Brands must align digital, physical, and social interactions to deliver consistent context-aware experiences including idiosyncratic service moments that drive emotional connections (Collier et al., 2018). Their eight 'dualities' framework shows the conflicts between automation versus human touch, standardization versus flexibility and privacy versus personalization. These tensions need to be dealt with effectively in order for loyalty to exist.This integration of realms intensifies the need for effortlessness personalization. For example, an adaptive user interface or an AI chatbot has to be not only functionally correct but also emotionally relevant. And the failures in this regard may destroy the trust loop that is crucial for working with customers.

Figure 1. A conceptual flow showing how personalized marketing enhances engagement, attachment, and loyalty

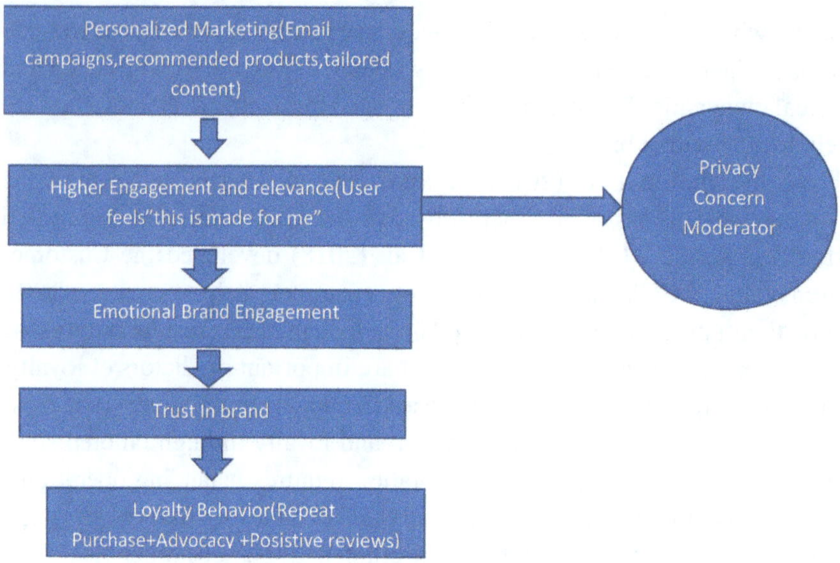

Explanation of Figure 1:This flowchart shows how targeted marketing serves as a stimulant for long-term brand loyalty. The process is initiated by targeted measures like targeted email campaigns, product recommendations based on individual preferences, and customized content—all of which are aimed at connecting with individual user interests. These interactions result in greater engagement and perceived relevance, with the consumer thinking, "this is made for me." This feeling of personalization creates emotional brand engagement, which then leads to trust in the brand—a central aspect of consumer decision-making and relationship-building. As trust becomes stronger, it manifests in loyalty behaviors such as repeat buying, brand advocacy, and positive word-of-mouth on the internet. Significantly, the flowchart incorporates a moderating variable: privacy concern. This implies that the potency of personalization in driving engagement and loyalty is regulated by how comfortable the consumer is with data usage. If privacy is of high importance, even customized efforts will fail or create distrust, diminishing their overall effect.

4. Brand Identity and Relationship Quality

Jalputra et al. (2018) associate brand logo benefits (such as the aesthetic and self expressiveness) with warmth and competence, which is concerned with the relationship quality. In turn, loyalty is more likely when the consumers see a brand as capable and consistent with the self-image. This is inline with the thought that personalization should go beyond the transactional level to symbolic and relational dimension.These findings are strengthened further by Merz et al.(2018), who show that emotional connection, arising from brand consistency, and self-expressive value is an important antecedent of advocacy and retention both.Similarly, relationship management principles such as trust, commitment, and mutual value creation remain foundational to sustaining loyalty across contexts.(Agarwal et al., 2017).

5. Risks and Ethical Considerations

As personalization is beneficial, it is also risky. An over-personalization may cause surveillance or unease resulting in privacy concerns (Wirtz & Kurtz, 2016). Data-driven engagement can start to appear manipulative and not helpful to the consumers. In order to address this, transparency and ethical data use are essential to avoid perceived manipulation (Schumann et al., 2014).

By crossing such boundaries brands run the risk not only of losing customers, lowering levels of trust and trust, but of negatively affecting loyalty to the brand. Therefore, the issue of data ethics is not limited to compliance, but also becomes part of the strategic agenda.

Figure 2. Customization journey leading to co-created value and emotional loyalty

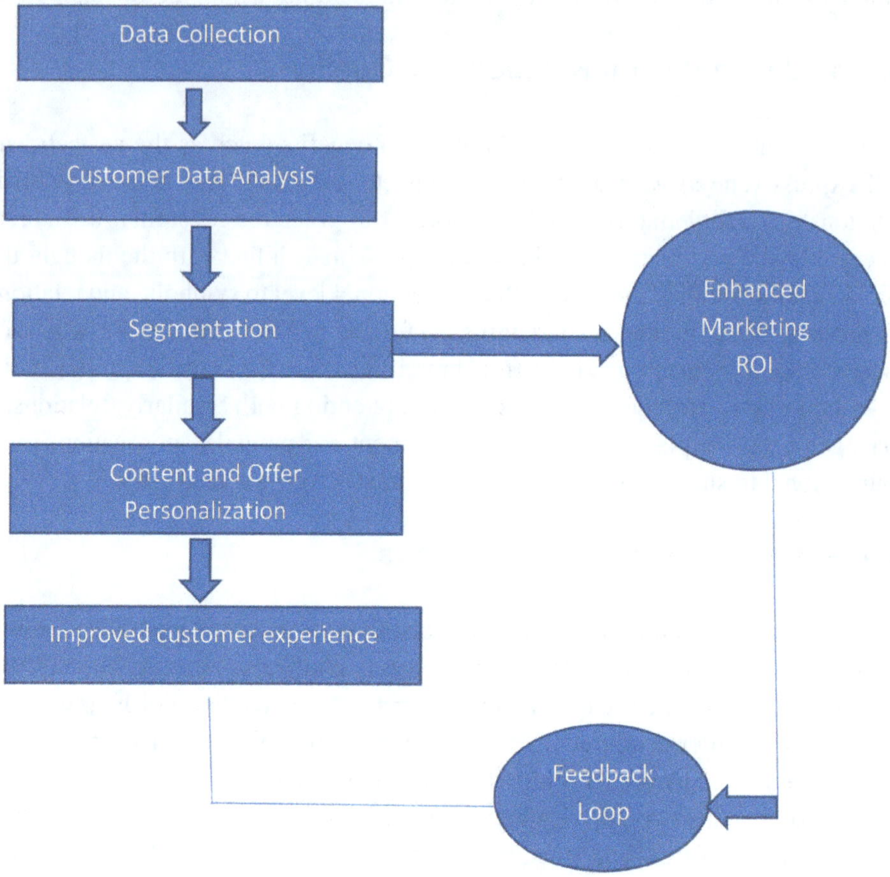

Explanation of Figure 2: Step one of personalized marketing is gathering details about the customer from online sources, their purchases, app activity and social media use. Then, you use powerful analytics to look through your customer information for signs and patterns in your company. Marketers will then collect the customers into different groups, based on similar interests, to send them targeted ads. At this stage, advertisers provide personalized emails, product ideas and special deals to each segmented part of their audience. By offering customer suggestive service, you lessen the customer's time spent, minimize weird feelings, enhance their happiness and boost their trust in your business. The lesson is made stronger with the addition of feedback loops which show that improvement never ends.

6. Some components and potential areas of study are lacking.

While building loyalty and important offerings is important to companies, they seem to forget about the obvious link between technology, who we are and trust. Most research looks into the happiness of customers and what they use, while almost nothing looks into the reasons behind brand loyalty. The investigation is approaching this gap by exploring links between personalization strategies and how emotions about a brand encourage consumers to support it.

RESEARCH METHODS

The survey asked 385 people involved in consumer and marketing sectors to give instant answers on Google Form. After finishing the pilot with fifteen participants, the survey consisted of five sections (demographics, exposure to personalization, feelings, loyalty behavior and privacy) and measured each using a 5-point scale.The survey employed quantitative methods to capture structured responses, leveraging techniques aligned with data augmentation frameworks for loyalty program analysis (Chakraborty, 2019).

Individuals involved in personalized or customized brand marketing were included in the study by purposeful sampling.Underlying variables were examined inside out by performing an exploratory factor analysis (EFA). An analysis of the Kaiser-Meyer-Olkin (KMO) measure found that it was 0.84 which means the data were well suited for factor analysis; meanwhile, Bartlett's Test of Sphericity was significant ($\chi^2 = 438.772$, $p < 0.001$). According to the Total Variance Explained table, the first three eigenvalues were more than 1 and together, they explained about 58.3% of the total variance. This result supported the choice of a multi-factor approach. Using the Varimax method on the Rotated Component Matrix found clear and understandable evidence of four main factors:The first factor was made up of items measuring Emotional Brand Attachment,I also looked at Perceived Personalization and Relevance in Factor 2,It corresponds to the third important trend, Customization and Co-Creation and Factor 4 was about privacy. All variables showed high values of loadings (more than 0.6) and little cross-loading which confirmed they were consistent. Moreover, the Scree Plot clearly showed an "elbow" appearing after the third component, suggesting that a three- to four-factor 'model would be suitable. This evidence proves that the factor structure is strong and that the relationship between personalization, emotional engagement and loyalty fits with current research in digital marketing.

CASE STUDIES

- Case Study 1: Amazon – Data-Driven Personalization at Scale for Loyalty

Amazon is a world leader in using data-driven personalization to fuel consumer loyalty. What makes it work is its ability to recommend tailored products, alter interfaces for users and email them individually, all following personal actions. By studying the way people use Amazon and what they buy, different algorithms are able to customize the webstore experience for every user.

The "Recommended for You" area is a classic instance of scaling personalization. The products a user sees every time they log in are based on what they are interested in. Besides, the Subscribe & Save service makes it easier to get products regularly which strengthens customers' trust in Amazon's brands.For customers, Personalized messages relating to either pricing offers or new inventory provoke more customer engagement. Amazon Prime members here receive personalized recommendations in their videos, able to easily purchase things, wraps and personal "discount or prior sale" offers before other customers. Our data suggest being in this personalized context means Prime members tend to follow and re-engage to shop. Pricing on amazon is variable and can be manipulated mainly by the company based on the behavior of users (and even maybe the user's location), but again our data highlighted how concerning it is but also how the site actually can personalize their content almost immediately when you searched the content. Some user concerns about "hyper-personalization" and "surveillance" have been somewhat addressed, but Amazon has established trust via functionality. That probably continued economic advantage from functioning and consistent privacy state that have a truthful a reliable user support. Our analysis related to personalization are very supportive of service differentiation and recollection on personalization opportunities to create more brand loyalty and usage recollection. Our findings with Amazon's findings to highlight, that when users in the personalized marketing situation, done right and ethically engagement/commitment improves.

- Case Study 2: Nike – Co-Creation with Personalization through "Nike By You"

Nike has revolutionized the idea of product customization with its "Nike By You" program, previously NIKEiD. Here, customers can create their own shoes by selecting colors, fabrics, logos, and even custom messages. This co-creation process engages customers as collaborators, making them feel a sense of ownership and attachment. The theory of "Extended self," with products being integral to one's identity.Consumers are using the brand to validate, authenticate, and solidify who they are. Personalization typically keeps consumers more loyal, engaged, and potentially spending more. It continues to build on that foundation while still offering some service via multiple service models. The online custom service is available to customers via the store, app, and the official website. Its community will provide engagement tips, video and recommendations on workouts, per purchase, and engaging with what the consumer views. Nike indicates ongoing personalization indicates develop more trust with that consumer and maintain growing DTC revenue. Essentially, "Nike By You" customers it is less likely they will disengage from this brand while potentially being more likely to return. Overall, they are bringing consumers back by encouraging them to personalize their shoes.Case Study 3: Spotify – Audio Personalization Curates Loyalty

Spotify is great at providing hyper-personalized user experiences by algorithmically curating music. Daily Mix, Wrapped and Discover Weekly prove that Spotify can pick up your expected music preferences and respond to your listening habits. They accomplish this by using collaborative filtering and natural language processing, so everyone's playlists are different. The first thing Spotify does is invite users to describe the kind of music they prefer. By taking the user's preferred genres and artists, the system can react to their inputs pleasantly fast. New listening trends show up on Spotify according to how we use the app. People's trust and comfort will grow when the service is helpful and easy to use. Being understood and organized on Spotify makes many people continue to use the platform.

The brand extends emotional connection through its yearly "Spotify Wrapped" campaign that visualizes a user's annual music patterns. The feature is extremely shareable and inspires brand advocacy on social media. It refers to self-expression and digital identity—users feel understood and happy to show off their musical self. Additionally, Spotify uses push notifications and email marketing to promote new releases and local concerts personalized to the individual, reaffirming the sense of being uniquely attended to.

Spotify's freemium strategy incorporates personalization as well. While free accounts include ads, they are algorithmically targeted to make them more relevant and less irritating. Premium members have ad-free, high-fidelity streaming with greater options for customization.This example illustrates how ongoing, non-intrusive personalization across user touchpoints reinforces emotional bonding, repeat use, and social word-of-mouth—characteristics of customer loyalty for the digital age.

- Case Study 4: Starbucks – Customer Loyalty through Customization and Gamified Personalization

Starbucks has been a leader in leveraging personalization to build loyalty for a long time. Its mobile app and Starbucks Rewards program allow the company to build a customized experience beyond coffee. The app remembers past orders, favorite drinks, and locations to offer recommendations on those items, as well as store locations and even customizations such as dairy substitute or syrup.The "Order Ahead" feature enables customers to reorder previous drinks with a single tap—this ease, combined with precision, boosts repeat behavior. Moreover, the app uses gamification, providing stars, challenges, and tailored promotions (e.g., "Buy 2 Frappuccinos this weekend and earn bonus stars"), which encourage emotional engagement and reward-driven behavior.

Starbucks also segments customers based on purchase history to provide exclusive rewards. For example, regular morning users may be offered specific breakfast deals, while afternoon users may be prompted with dessert combos.The personalization approach also applies to its email marketing, which features birthday treats and behavior- and taste-based customized offers. These gestures create brand affinity and deepen emotional connection.In addition, Starbucks' holiday promotions, such as the Red Cup holiday beverages, are quietly personalized by regional differences and app-only content, giving a feeling of exclusivity and belonging.Starbucks demonstrates that personalization doesn't need to be powered by sophisticated AI alone—it's about understanding your customer, honoring their tastes, and rewarding their loyalty on a consistent basis. The outcome is one of the most effective loyalty programs in the food and beverage sector.

- Case Study 5: Netflix – Content Personalization for Retention and Trust

Netflix is behavioral personalization done to perfection, employing advanced algorithms to suggest TV programs and films based on a viewer's watch history, ratings, search patterns, and even pause or rewind behavior. The homepage itself is specifically personalized for each user—no two Netflix home pages are identical.Personalization starts with user profiling: members of a household may have individual accounts, with recommendations tailored to each. As consumers are engaged with the platform, the algorithm of Netflix refines its recommendations, frequently anticipating new content tastes before the viewer is even aware.

Personalized thumbnail overlays, dynamic top-10 listings, and "Because You Watched..." suggestions are key tactics. Such curation of content reduces friction and decision fatigue, leading to more frequent logins and longer sessions.Netflix also leverages data-driven personalization to introduce original shows. Programs such as "House of Cards" and "Stranger Things" were created by utilizing audience behavior insights, demonstrating that personalization can influence creation—not merely delivery.Netflix sustains activity at high levels via personalized emails and push messages recommending new shows or incomplete series. The communications are discreet yet efficient, prompting customers to return without intruding.Though personalization is an obvious strength, data privacy is carefully managed by Netflix. Transparent control of watch history and recommendations strengthens user trust.

This case substantiates the hypothesis that personalization—when infused into both content and interface—can drive high retention, diminish churn, and create brand trust and advocacy.

And both Netflix and Spotify use behavioral data to drive retention, mirroring findings that perceived value in subscription services hinges on innovation alignment **(Tao & Xu, 2018).**

DATA ANALYSIS

Introduction:

The responses from 385 participants through a systematic Google Form survey were computed using SPSS to explore the interaction between personalization, customization, emotional brand attachment, and consumer loyalty behavior. Two line graphs were created to represent the dynamics of personalization and privacy issues in determining consumer loyalty results. The test of hypotheses constructed in previous sections was analyzed, and their applicability to actual marketing practices was interpreted.

Table 1. Factor Analysis:

KMO and Bartlett's Test		
Kaiser-Meyer-Olkin Measure of Sampling Adequacy.		**0.84**
Bartlett's Test of Sphericity	Approx. Chi-Square	438.772
	df	78
	Sig.	0

Interpretation:

· **KMO = 0.84**: Indicates **excellent sampling adequacy**. The dataset is suitable for factor analysis.

· **Bartlett's Test Sig. = 0.000**: Indicates that the **correlation matrix is not an identity matrix**, meaning **significant relationships exist between variables**, validating the appropriateness of factor analysis.

Table 2.

Total Variance Explained									
Component	Initial Eigenvalues			Extraction Sums of Squared Loadings			Rotation Sums of Squared Loadings		
	Total	% of Variance	Cumulative %	Total	% of Variance	Cumulative %	Total	% of Variance	Cumulative %
1	4.996	38.431	38.431	4.996	38.431	38.431	3.737	28.748	28.748
2	1.54	11.842	50.273	1.54	11.842	50.273	1.802	13.86	42.608
3	1.043	8.025	58.299	1.043	8.025	58.299	1.674	12.877	55.485
4	0.889	6.84	65.139	0.889	6.84	65.139	1.255	9.654	65.139
5	0.836	6.427	71.566						
6	0.722	5.552	77.117						
7	0.621	4.774	81.891						
8	0.527	4.057	85.948						
9	0.493	3.79	89.739						
10	0.449	3.451	93.189						
11	0.356	2.74	95.929						
12	0.307	2.361	98.29						
13	0.222	1.71	100						

Extraction Method: Principal Component Analysis.

Interpretation:

· **First 3 components** have eigenvalues **greater than 1** and explain a combined **58.3% of the total variance**, which is acceptable in social science research.

· **Component 4** is borderline (Eigenvalue < 1), but contributes meaningfully to cumulative variance when rotated.

Figure 3. Scree Plot

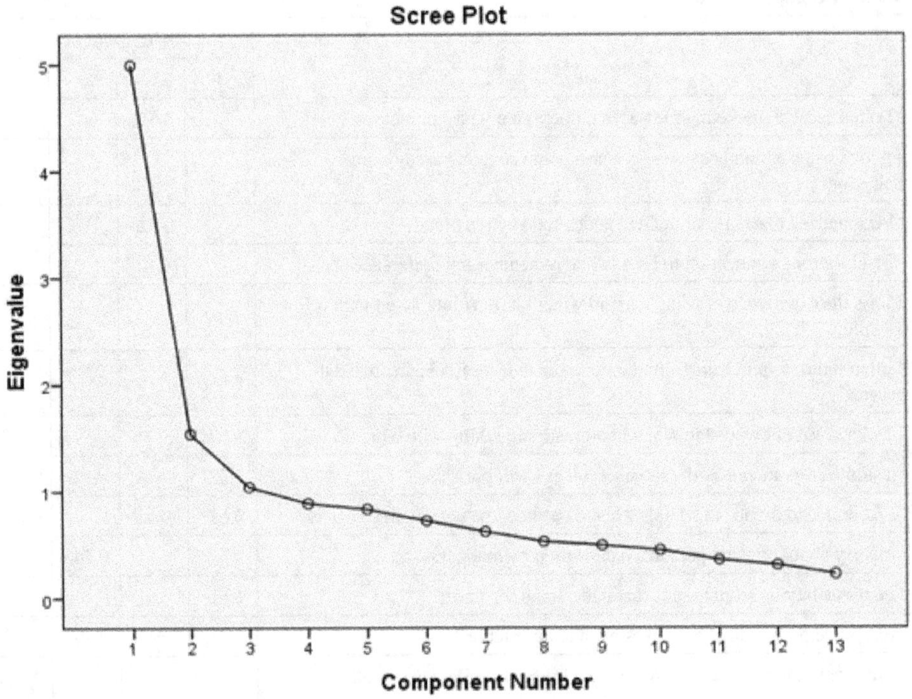

Visual Interpretation:

· The **y-axis** shows **eigenvalues**, which represent the amount of variance explained by each factor.

· The **x-axis** lists the **component numbers** (in your case, 13 items).

· There is a **sharp drop** in eigenvalues from Component 1 to Component 2, followed by a gentler slope (this is called the "elbow").

Key Observations:

1. **Component 1** has an eigenvalue just above **5**, explaining a large portion of variance.
2. **Component 2** drops significantly (eigenvalue slightly above 1.5).
3. After **Component 3**, the curve flattens and each additional component adds less explanatory value.
4. The **"elbow" appears at Component 3**, where the curve shifts from steep to shallow.

Table 3. **Rotated Component Matrix[a]**

Rotated Component Matrix[a]				
	Component			
	1	2	3	4
"I often receive marketing messages tailored to my past purchases."		0.667		
I notice when a brand changes its website/app content based on my behavior.				0.821
"Personalized offers make me feel understood by the brand."		0.528		
"I feel a strong connection to brands that remember my preferences."		0.63		
I miss the experience of using a brand when I haven't interacted with it for a while.	0.77			
I often return to purchase from the same brand if it offers personalized service.	0.668			
I feel a sense of ownership when I co-create something with a brand.	0.594			
Customization increases the likelihood that I will purchase.	0.771			
"I recommend brands to friends when they show me personalized offers."	0.687			
"I worry about how my personal data is used by marketers."			0.743	
I continue buying from brands that understand my needs.				
"Excessive personalization makes me uncomfortable."			0.792	
I often return to purchase from the same brand if it offers personalized service.				0.712

Extraction Method: Principal Component Analysis.
Rotation Method: Varimax with Kaiser Normalization.
a. Rotation converged in 15 iterations.

Interpretation:

The rotated matrix groups related items under shared factors:

Factor 1: Connection with a Brand's Emotions

This is a way to explain how people respond to brands that remember and value their feelings. Loading this factor will display how tailoring messages and always engaging the user help them relate better with the brand. Loyalty resulting from such attachment goes past normal, commercial reasons.

Factor 2:Personalization Perception (interface, content recognition)

The second factor is how personal and relevant the experience is seen by the consumer.

This sign reflects that shoppers are aware the brand is designing something special just for them. If users experience high loadings, they both pay attention to the personalized changes and feel that the company knows what matters to them. It makes the brand seem more important and responsive to customers.

Factor 3:Co-Creation & Customization (sense of ownership, influence on purchase)

Thirdly, Many-to-Many marketing relies on facilitating customer and brand interactions for co-created solutions.

Under Factor 3, items are grouped based on a consumer's ability to change or influence their experience. This feeling comes from being able to distinguish yourself, be in charge and own your favorite brand features. As a result, consumers are more satisfied and want to make a purchase.

Factor 4:Privacy Concerns (data anxiety, over-personalization discomfort)

Protecting personal information is the focus of factor 4.

This thing points out how personalization can bring problems. It is concerned with the possibility of bad uses and uncomfortable high levels of targeting. Being overly informed by retailers can make a few consumers uncomfortable and less likely to trust the business.

2. Graphical Interpretation:

Figure 4. Personalization vs. Loyalty Metrics

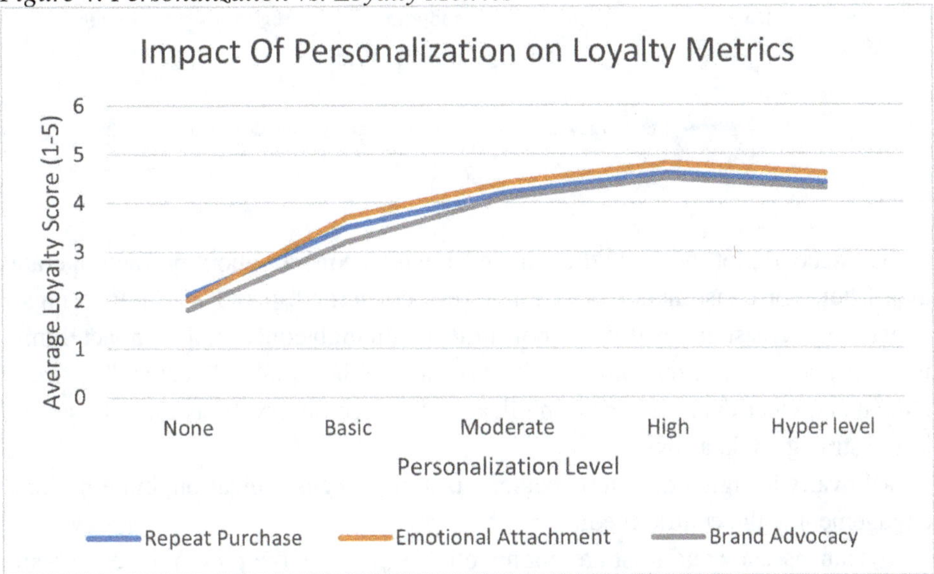

This line graph charts how loyalty results vary at different levels of personalization. All three measures—repeat buys, emotional connection, and advocacy—all exhibit tremendous growth from "None" to "High" personalization. At the "Hyper" level, though, a drop is noted, especially in advocacy, reflecting the danger of over-personalization or user fatigue.

This conforms to results in regression as well as descriptive statistics and reiterates that although personalization creates loyalty, it needs to be tuned to not have adverse impacts.

Figure 5. Privacy Concern as Moderator

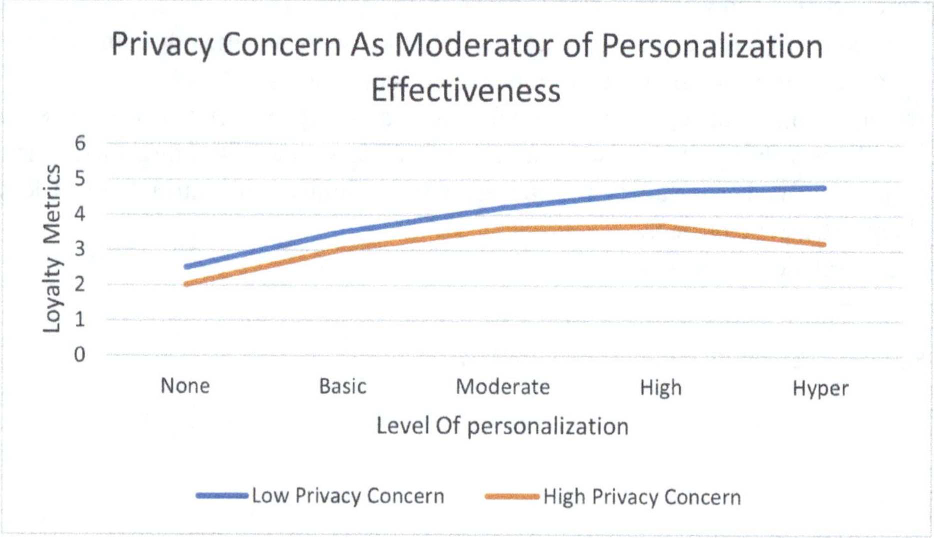

The second plot indicates the manner in which concern about privacy operates as a filter. For consumers who are not very concerned, personalization brings a consistent increase in loyalty. For consumers with high concern, the impact diminishes or goes down after some level. This mirrors the absolutely critical nature of ethical and clear data practices. Implications: These observations identify several brand strategic takeaways:

a)Loyalty is highly driven by personalization and customization, but emotional engagement is the central mediator.

b)Transparency and trust are not negotiable; they are the prerequisites to being able to personalize effectively.

c)Brands need to enact "just-right" personalization—personalized enough to be personal, but not obtrusive.

LIMITATIONS AND FUTURE DIRECTIONS

Future research could investigate the use of dynamic relationship perspectives such as Relationship Velocity Perspective (Hussain et al., 2020) which quantifies the velocity of change with respect to emotional attachment or trust created through personalization that impacts the long-term outcomes in loyalty. The results measured were quantitative, and this study was limited in utilizing self-report survey data and utilizing a cross-sectional method. Outside of qualitative personalized interviews, case studies are another example of personalized group interviews that can also help to better understand emotional attachment and advocacy over time. In addition, future research could take personalization beyond the consideration of relevant cultural or demographic contexts.

DISCUSSIONS

This study sought to investigate the strategic impacts of personalized and tailored marketing in the area of consumer loyalty through emotional brand commitment, repurchase behavior, and advocacy. Personalization and customization are now commonplace and have a strong basis in quantitative research; there are good examples in real case studies.

This study sought to investigate the strategic impacts of personalized and tailored marketing in the area of consumer loyalty through emotional brand commitment, repurchase behavior, and advocacy. Personalization and customization are now commonplace and have a strong basis in quantitative research; there are good examples in real case studies. The Factor Analysis which is a part of study determined that customized marketing had influenced emotional brand attachment and loyalty intentions with a high positive influence. While personalization was positively related to repurchase intentions.Making things custom-fit "hit home" when it came to keeping customers loyal. Respondents who participated in co-creation activities (i.e. creating a product/customizing service experiences) were found to show more attachment and return intention— Hypothesis 2. This is in line with Merz et al. (2018) findings, that set forth customer co-creation value (CCCV) as a brand relationship predictor in the long term.Hypothesis 3 asserts that personalization has an impact on advocacy directly, but only achieves its maximum when it brings out emotional attachment. This corresponds with the extended self-theory by Belk (1988) and the modern concept of the digital self – customers feel loyalty when brands get to see and see them(Huang & Rust, 2017). The findings of this study supported the first hypothesis. Specifically, they showed that personalized items are not only positively related to customer loyalty, the fact that they also get people engaged showed that ultimately it matters in developing loyalty. Better privacy-worry users presented weaker tendencies of loyalty to the individualized content that confirmed Hypothesis 4. The outcome of this highlights the two-way nature of personalization – while it produces relevance and engagement, it also risks crossing the boundaries of trust perceived.The case studies taken from the real-life situations deepen and enrich the statistical findings.

Amazon is one of the examples of scaling personalization. Its predictive hints and personalized offerings propel retention to demonstrate how high-frequency engagement translates into emotional engagement. Nike's customization page shows how empowering the user to co-create generates identity congruence, as it converts into high-end loyalty. Spotify and Netflix demonstrate how behavioral data can create engaging experiences that are adaptive and provide Starbucks incorporates personalization into its rewards program by way of rewards, gamification, and behavioral offers; all aggregating daily usage behaviors.Such illustrations reflect the fact that loyalty not only comes from attainment of satisfaction but comes as an engagement, recognition, reciprocity, which are innate aspects of one-to-one and custom marketing. Key among the most significant findings that have emerged out of this research is the important role played by emotional brand attachment towards the development of loyalty. Emotional attachment is a psychological anchor that converts functional satisfaction to long term brand promise.

Consumers' expectations of brands are changing as they expect them to get them – not their buying patterns but values, identity and other life choices.This discovery lies in line with the identity-brand congruence models put forward by Melewar et al. (2017) and symbolic consumption especially in cases like Nike and Starbucks where personalization creates a room for self-expression. Emotional bonding is the performance force which transfigures data into devotion.Although personalized engagement has its benefits, privacy issues emerged as one of the central constraints. The findings show that to high sensitivity with regards to privacy, personalization can in fact boomerang with an effect of inducing uncomfortable or distrustful feelings. This depicts greater sensitivities in data surveillance and algorithmic targeting; issues that modern brands have to address them face-to-face and with attention.

The customers long for personalization yet without compromising their autonomy and privacy. Some of the ways in which organizations should facilitate opt-in features, describe where data is used, and honor data protection, so that trust will be maintained, are indicated. The relevance and ethics harmony is exhibited by Netflix's usage of viewer information and Amazon security promises.The following are some of the strategic implications of the conclusions:Brands have to come up with "privacy-aware personalization" along the lines of personalizing experiences but without being intrusive.Marketing has to focus on the creation of meaningful moments and not algorithmic productivity. Data science must be accompanied by emotional brand messaging, user control, and storytelling. Consumers are encouraged to co-create products or services (as Nike and Starbucks have done). This fosters ownership and advocacy. Privacy profile-based personalized design methods. Perform rich behavioral targeting on low-concern users. The high-concern group prioritized transparency and control. A successful personalization is a continuous conversation rather than something done once and then forgotten. Use feedback loops (e.g., Spotify and Netflix) to create a dynamic and reactive experience.

Future personalization efforts should adopt a relational selling mindset (Arli et al., 2018), focusing on mutual value creation and long-term partnership rather than merely targeted transactions. This study adds to the loyalty and personalization studies by introducing emotional brand attachment as a mediator and a privacy concern as moderator to the conceptual framework, which also draws a more intricate picture of how loyalty is built in a digital space. It fills the void created between technological enablement and psychological reaction, contributing to the service-dominant logic and the digital consumer identity theory.Despite the good findings, there are limitations to this study. The data that was obtained is self-reported and .cross-sectional and may affect generalizability. Emotional attachment can be ambiguous and may require qualitative finding for proper comprehension. A mixed-methods approach or additional research in the light of personalization in individual cultures / demographic groups could ensue. Experiments with over-personalization and cognitive load effect can bring detail to understanding the thresholds for users.

CONCLUSION

In the present hyper-digitization environment and cutthroat markets, designing consumer loyalty has been increasingly inclined towards the ability of the brands to leverage customized and personalized experiences. This study sought to investigate the manner in which these marketing strategies influence consumer's loyalty towards it by exploring their effects on emotional attachment to brand, purchase from repeat and advocacy. Coming from both quantitative research and real brand case studies, the research reveals that personalization and customization are no longer marketing techniques – now they are the necessary components of the modern customer relationship management.

Personalized marketing was discovered to exert significant favorable effect on emotional brand attachment. As customers understand that the brand values and understands them using personalized recommendations, targeted emails, and well-crafted content, the emotional bond with the brand is also strengthened a lot. This connection, as was confirmed by mediation analysis, does not only increase their intention to make further purchases from the brand, but also increase the likelihood they will promote the brand. In concert, customization- when the customers consciously customize goods or services to suit their preferences- heightens commitment still further through identity-matching and psychological ownership.

Best examples show that if personalization is done correctly and remains consistent, it can make people feel faith and to really care about the brand. Nike and Starbucks are both companies that encourage clients to join in the creative process, helping them feel linked to the brand over a longer period. They demonstrate that loyalty is more about being heard, involved and cherished than it is simply about being happy with a company.For this reason, brands must personalize the way they provide things as well as what they deliver. To be data responsible, companies need to use feedback, let users decide on personalization and be open about their data practices. Here, I show that emotional loyalty is highest not by simply targeting the consumer, but by actually listening to, understanding and appreciating him or her. Going forward, personalization should be approached by both artists and scientists. So-called "tech platforms" such as AI, CRM and behavioral analytics will need to be balanced with nice design and considerate language. Brands that take these actions will be rewarded with more loyal customers, trust, people supporting them and lasting value in the age of growing data awareness.

However, research also sheds light on the main balancing act that brands have to perform- relevance and privacy. Although consumers love personalized content, they are also interested in their data usage. This struggle was evident in the moderation analysis, whereby the privacy issues can significantly dilute personalization value of loyalty. Brands, thus, have to be careful, and be transparent and get a consumer's consent to utilize their data in an ethical manner.

RECOMMENDATIONS

Rather than provide generic rewards, brands need to tailor loyalty programs according to individual shopping behavior, frequency, and preferences. Personalized offers and targeted promotions enhance relevance and perceived value.Personalization must change in response to shifting consumer behavior. Brands must use dynamic, learning-based algorithms that refine offers, messages, and experiences in real-time so that they stay relevant to the customer's present interests.Consumer trust takes more than a legal notice to achieve—it needs ethical intention. Marketers need to deploy AI technology that minimizes over-targeting and reveals algorithmic reasoning where appropriate.By providing the ability to personalize the experience you create, you build trust in the brand. All elements of personalization should be consistent in your app, on the web, and in your store. Starbucks, et al, do this well, where they are keeping what you like in an app in sync with what you have in your order onsite. Customers have the same journey, which keeps them loyal.

It provide a user-control of what's personalized, because while some people want ads to stay simple, others prefer ads to be completely personalized. So allow them the choice, which will only improve satisfaction. It is not just to offer suggestions, it helps you align to the brand's voice, narrative or look to the consumer - and this impact can happen through what playlists or thumbnail pictures you provide on Spotify and Netflix. The emotional aspect of a brand should be central to the communication, and not only the message. You'll see better results from your campaign if you send your messages when your subscribers are most involved. Achieving this means messages can be sent at the right time, before the customer usually begins the buying process.

Small groups of customers can be identified by examining their instant activities, including item abandonment, site exploration and interactions with the brand. This therefore allows customers to receive help with their online shopping cart and get suitable suggestions delivered by email.Furthermore, by using gamification tactics—such as progress gauges, reward tasks or achievement badges—you can involve visitors even more. With Starbucks and Nike, gamified journeys ensure that customers enjoy achievements and are motivated to return again.

Techniques used for digital personalization should be passed on to employees serving people in physical locations. This study proves that adapting customer service is not just about using facts—it's about adding value. When done carefully, they transform a transaction into a real connection. People avoid being sold to now; instead, they long for engagement, recognition and value.Creating loyalty, therefore, relies on thinking about how customers feel and what they want. Brands able to measure data precisely while still staying understanding will retain their customers and make them their strongest advocates.

MANAGERIAL IMPLICATIONS

The results of this study offer useful information to the marketing managers. First, it could be stated that emotional brand attachment should be an important metric, not a by-product. Companies' managers should make investments into emotionally intelligent content – campaigns addressing the issues of identity, aspiration, community rather than just purchase incentives. Second, the marketing teams should be privacy-conscious. Privacy concerns eliminating the effect of loyalty should be ensured by brands, with data use being transparent and optional. Grouping customers according to how sensitive they are to privacy and providing the opportunity for opt-out can increase trust. Finally, personalization should be adopted in loyalty programs. Tailored offers and exclusive contents can turn users into advocates. These implications are a reason for a dual strategy that is the combination of an emotionally engaging and ethical personalization practices.Managers can think in terms of creating rapid feedback loops that capture customers' in-the-moment responses to personalization initiatives. Dynamic dashboards tracking opt-out rates, content interactions, and behavioral changes enable marketers to make course corrections swiftly if personalization is becoming intrusive or not yielding benefits.Managers should proactively incorporate emotional loyalty as a measurable outcome in marketing dashboards. Beyond tracking click-through rates or conversion metrics, organizations should evaluate consumer sentiment, brand attachment scores, and advocacy intent. These affective outcomes are harder to capture, but significantly more predictive of long-term profitability and customer lifetime value.Internal brand alignment **(Du Prezz et al., 2017)** ensures frontline employees deliver personalized experiences, amplifying customer emotional attachment.

One of the most important takeaways is that there is a necessities to operationalize privacy-sensitive personalization. Marketing managers must create consent-based data strategies, with tiered personalization choices, where consumers have the option to select how much data they want to surrender. Not only does this empower the customer but also fits with changing global regulations such as GDPR and India's DPDP Act. Marketing professionals need to work in tandem with legal and IT teams so that data accumulation is transparent, ethical, and value-creating.Lastly, a compelling argument can be made for investing in cross-functional training. Customer service personnel, product developers, and frontline workers need to be taught about the concepts of emotional branding, personalization ethics, and co-creation methods. Engaging the entire organization in a shared personalization strategy will enable a more unified, connected brand experience across touchpoints. Brand managers must evolve from simply delivering personalized offers to orchestrating personalized journeys balancing technology with trust, automation with authenticity, and segmentation with sensitivity.Overall, brand managers need to move from merely serving up tailored offers to stewarding tailored journeys—blending technology and trust, automation and authenticity, segmentation and sensitivity.

PRACTICAL AND SOCIAL IMPLICATIONS

It can make your valuable customers return more often.Instead of pulling information from profiles, brands should trust learning engines that make use of current data.Tailoring services a bit to your customers brings success, but flooding them with emails may reduce their willingness to use your products.The moderation curve shows marketers the right level of ads to deliver so they don't bother their customers too much but still profit well.Well-designed personalization increases customer lifetime value by improving retention and reducing acquisition costs. Loyalty programs should be dynamically adjusted using behavioral triggers to provide timely and relevant incentives.

Advanced learning engines should be used to interpret real-time behavior and fine-tune what the consumer sees. For example, instead of sending five identical offers, AI can determine the best time, frequency, and content match, reducing fatigue and enhancing receptivity. Rather than only personalizing messages for clients, companies should incorporate additional channels for co-creation, seeing both how creative their customers can be and how willing they are to promote the company. When brands encourage people to propose new ideas, this promotes brand loyalty and makes new product failures less likely. Because companies are collecting more and more data about people, they should ensure they do not engage in intrusive targeting. Evidently, when privacy is a key issue, people become less loyal. This suggests that transparency in data policies is needed. Multinational firms should decide to use ethical principles like privacy-by-design, offered by GDPR, to safeguard customers' personal information and boost their trust everywhere.Personalization efforts must be inclusive, addressing the needs of underrepresented groups such as older adults, people with disabilities, and rural populations. Failing to include these groups may inadvertently widen digital inequalities. Accessibility features, regional customization, and culturally relevant messaging should be integrated into personalization strategies. When using personalized marketing, we must treat under-represented segments (such as older people and rural areas) just as we would anyone else. Letting users enjoy equality by customizing features is important for social justice.Brands that care for everyone's needs earn better results and gather society around them so that even tech-savvy people can be involved.When brands act transparently and personalize ethically, they not only gain consumer trust but also help foster broader societal trust in digital technologies. This contributes to a more cooperative and participatory consumer culture where loyalty is earned through fairness, not manipulation.

REFERENCES

Agarwal, A., Singh, D., & Agariya, A. K. (2017). What really leads to partner relationship management? A review of literature. *Journal of Relationship Marketing, 16*(3), 228–266. DOI: 10.1080/15332667.2017.1349557

Arli, D., Bauer, C., & Palmatier, R. W. (2018). Relational selling: Past, present and future. *Industrial Marketing Management, 65*, 17–28. DOI: 10.1016/j.indmarman.2017.07.018

Arora, N., Dreze, X., Ghose, A., Hess, J. D., Iyengar, R., Jing, B., & Shankar, V. (2008). Putting one-to-one marketing to work: Personalization, customization, and choice. *Marketing Letters, 19*(3–4), 305–321. DOI: 10.1007/s11002-008-9056-z

Bahadur, W., Aziz, S., & Zulfiqar, S. (2018). Effect of employee empathy on customer satisfaction and loyalty during employee–customer interactions: The mediating role of customer affective commitment and perceived service quality. *Cogent Business & Management, 5*(1), 1491780. Advance online publication. DOI: 10.1080/23311975.2018.1491780

Belk, R. W. (1988). Possessions and the extended self. *The Journal of Consumer Research, 15*(2), 139–168. DOI: 10.1086/209154

Bischoff, J., Berezan, O., & Scardicchio, L. (2019). The digital self and customer loyalty: From theory to virtual reality. *Journal of Marketing Analytics, 7*(3), 220–233. DOI: 10.1057/s41270-019-00065-4

Bolton, R. N., Gustafsson, A., McColl-Kennedy, J. R., Sirianni, N. J., & Tse, D. K. (2018). Small details that make big differences: A radical approach to consumption experience as a firm's differentiating strategy. *Journal of Service Management, 25*(2), 253–274. DOI: 10.1108/JOSM-01-2014-0034

Catulli, M., Cook, M., & Potter, S. (2016). Product service systems users and Harley Davidson riders: The importance of consumer identity in the diffusion of sustainable consumption solutions. *Journal of Industrial Ecology, 00*(0), 1–10. DOI: 10.1111/jiec.12518

Chakraborty, I. (2019). RecSmart: Data augmentation to facilitate recommendation using skewed and sparse data of restaurant loyalty programs. In *Proceedings of the Future Technologies Conference (FTC 2018)*(pp. 1002–1011). https://doi.org/DOI: 10.1007/978-3-030-02683-7_74

Chen, C.-C. V., & Chen, C.-J. (2017). The role of customer participation for enhancing repurchase intention. *Management Decision*, *55*(3), 547–562. Advance online publication. DOI: 10.1108/MD-06-2016-0380

Choi, Y. K., & Lotz, S. (2017). The effect of personalization and privacy assurance on behavioral intentions: A test of risk–benefit trade-off in e-commerce. *Journal of Retailing and Consumer Services*, *34*, 289–296. DOI: 10.1016/j.jretconser.2016.01.001

Collier, J. E., Barnes, D. C., Abney, A. K., & Pelletier, M. J. (2018). Idiosyncratic service experiences: When customers desire the extraordinary in a service encounter. *Journal of Business Research*, *84*, 150–161. DOI: 10.1016/j.jbusres.2017.11.016

Du Prezz, R., Bendixen, M., & Abratt, R. (2017). The behavioral consequences of internal brand management among frontline employees. *Journal of Product and Brand Management*, *26*(3), 251–268. DOI: 10.1108/JPBM-09-2016-1325

Grandinetti, R., Di Bernardo, B., D'Antonio, F., & Iannone, R. (2020). Servitization and the fourth industrial revolution: A comparative analysis of ICT and traditional manufacturing firms. *Technological Forecasting and Social Change*, *157*, 120092. DOI: 10.1016/j.techfore.2020.120092

Grewal, D., Roggeveen, A. L., & Nordfält, J. (2017). The future of retailing. *Journal of Retailing*, *93*(1), 1–6. DOI: 10.1016/j.jretai.2016.12.008

Guo, L., Gruen, T. W., & Tang, C. (2015). Seeing relationships through the lens of psychological contracts: The structure of consumer service relationships. *Journal of the Academy of Marketing Science*, *43*(6), 904–925. DOI: 10.1007/s11747-015-0462-5

Huang, M.-H., & Rust, R. T. (2017). Technology-driven service strategy. *Journal of the Academy of Marketing Science*, *45*(6), 906–924. DOI: 10.1007/s11747-017-0545-6

Hussain, K., Ying, F., Junaid, M., Shi, H., & Baig, U. (2020). The buyer–seller relationship: A literature synthesis on dynamic perspectives. *Journal of Business and Industrial Marketing*, *35*(4), 669–684. DOI: 10.1108/JBIM-09-2018-0280

Jalputra, A., Molinillo, S., & Wang, S. (2018). Aesthetic or self-expressiveness? Linking brand logo benefits, brand stereotypes and relationship quality. *Journal of Retailing and Consumer Services*, *44*, 191–200. DOI: 10.1016/j.jretconser.2018.06.015

Kumar, V., Aksoy, L., Donkers, B., Venkatesan, R., Wiesel, T., & Tillmanns, S. (2010). Undervalued or overvalued customers: Capturing total customer engagement value. *Journal of Service Research*, *13*(3), 297–310. DOI: 10.1177/1094670510375602

Larsen, M. S. S., Lindhard, S. M., Brunoe, T. D., Nielsen, K., & Larsen, J. K. (2019). Mass customization in the house building industry: Literature review and research directions. *Frontiers in Built Environment*, *115*(5), 115. Advance online publication. DOI: 10.3389/fbuil.2019.00115

Melewar, T. C., Foroudi, P., Gupta, S., Kitchen, P. J., & Foroudi, M. M. (2017). Integrating identity, strategy and communications for trust, loyalty and commitment. *European Journal of Marketing*, *51*(3), 572–604. DOI: 10.1108/EJM-08-2015-0616

Merz, M. A., Zarantonello, L., & Grappi, S. (2018). How valuable are your customers in the brand value co-creation process? The development of a customer co-creation value (CCCV) scale. *Journal of Business Research*, *82*, 79–89. DOI: 10.1016/j.jbusres.2017.08.018

Schumann, J. H., von Wangenheim, F., & Groene, N. (2014). Targeted online advertising: Using reciprocity appeals to increase acceptance among users of free web services. *Journal of Marketing*, *78*(1), 59–75. DOI: 10.1509/jm.11.0316

Suzić, N., Forza, C., Trentin, A., & Anišić, Z. (2018). Implementation guidelines for mass customization: Current characteristics and suggestions for improvement. *Production Planning and Control*, *29*(10), 1–16. DOI: 10.1080/09537287.2018.1485983

Tao, Q., & Xu, Y. (2018). Understanding consumers' adoption of subscription fashion retailing: The role of perceived value and innovation. *Journal of Fashion Marketing and Management*, *22*(1), 22–38. DOI: 10.1108/JFMM-10-2016-0087

Vargo, S. L., & Lusch, R. F. (2004). Evolving to a new dominant logic for marketing. *Journal of Marketing*, *68*(1), 1–17. DOI: 10.1509/jmkg.68.1.1.24036

Chapter 10
Food Influencers in the Metaverse:
Analyzing the Role of Food Influencers and Content Creators in Shaping Culinary Trends Within Virtual Communities

Arshad Hussain
https://orcid.org/0009-0007-3119-6228
Bennett University, India

Arora Gaurav Singh
Bennett University, India

ABSTRACT

The convergence of immersive technologies and digital content creation has given rise to a new frontier for culinary engagement within the metaverse. This chapter critically examines the evolving role of food influencers both human and AI-generated virtual personas in shaping culinary trends and consumer behavior in immersive virtual environments. As the metaverse enables interactive experiences through virtual reality (VR), augmented reality (AR), and artificial intelligence (AI), food influencers are redefining the way audiences explore, learn, and interact with food culture. The chapter analyzes how these influencers curate content, host interactive cooking demonstrations, and co-create branded campaigns, thereby fostering dynamic virtual food communities. It further explores how food-related narratives are crafted across virtual platforms, facilitating cultural exchange and

DOI: 10.4018/979-8-3373-2747-1.ch010

global gastronomic awareness. Ethical and regulatory concerns such as digital authenticity, data privacy, and cultural appropriation are addressed to provide a balanced perspective.

1. INTRODUCTION

In recent years, our world has undergone a digital revolution. The internet has changed how we talk, shop, study, and even eat (Xiang et al., 2014). Social media platforms like Instagram, YouTube, and TikTok have become central to our daily lives (Bhandari & Bimo, 2022). One exciting and fast-growing part of this digital shift is the metaverse a virtual space where people interact using digital characters called avatars (Kim et al., 2023; Press, 2024). What started as a gaming trend is now becoming a place for work, learning, entertainment, and even food experiences. The metaverse can be described as a shared, 3D virtual world that is built using advanced technologies such as virtual reality (VR), augmented reality (AR), and artificial intelligence (AI) (McKinsey & Company, 2022). Unlike traditional websites or apps, the metaverse allows users to engage with digital content in a more lifelike and interactive way. For example, instead of watching a video about baking a cake, users can now enter a virtual kitchen and bake it step-by-step alongside a food influencer's avatar. This creates a deeper sense of involvement, fun, and learning. At the centre of this digital food revolution are food influencers and content creators. Traditionally, food influencers were popular chefs, home cooks, or food lovers who shared recipes, restaurant reviews, and food-related content through blogs or videos. In the digital age, they have moved to social media platforms and gained millions of followers (Kakadia, 2024). Now, they are taking their presence a step further by entering the metaverse.

These influencers both real and virtual are using new tools to connect with audiences in immersive ways. Imagine attending a virtual cooking show hosted by an AI-generated characters or walking through a digital food festival where you can "taste" global cuisines through sensory simulations. These are not science fiction ideas anymore they are becoming real, thanks to technology (Wibawa et al., 2022). One key reason this trend is growing so fast is because of how engaging and entertaining the metaverse can be. For young people especially, it offers an exciting way to learn about food, try new recipes, and interact with creators. Food influencers are using games, storytelling, and interactive tutorials to make cooking and food education fun (Ash, 2024). This is especially helpful for students who may find traditional cooking lessons boring or hard to follow. Learning through experience is often more memorable than just reading or watching.

Also, the global nature of the metaverse makes it a perfect space to explore diverse food cultures (Ingrassia et al., 2022). A user in India can easily join a Japanese sushi-making class, or someone in the U.S. can attend a virtual Diwali food fair. Food influencers act as guides in this space, helping people explore and understand food traditions from around the world (Molenaar, 2025). In this way, the metaverse supports cultural exchange and promotes diversity. But it is not just about fun and learning. Food influencers in the metaverse also play a big role in shaping consumer behavior (Kaur et al., 2024). Just like influencers on Instagram can make a certain snack or cooking tool go viral, virtual influencers in the metaverse can encourage users to try new products or buy from specific brands. This opens huge opportunities for food companies to advertise their products in creative, non-traditional ways. For example, a virtual influencer might partner with a brand to launch a new plant-based burger inside a digital restaurant in the metaverse. Users could learn about it, see how it made, and even get a discount to order the real product in the physical world.

Interestingly, not all influencers in the metaverse are real people. Some are virtual influencers computer-generated characters that look and act like humans (Sorosrungruang, Ameen, & Hackley, 2024). These digital personas are created using AI and graphic design, and they are becoming increasingly popular in fashion, beauty, and now, food. These virtual influencers can post recipes, give cooking tips, and promote food products just like human influencers (Storyclash, 2023). In some cases, people trust them even more because they are always consistent, well-designed, and not affected by scandals or personal drama (Buchanan, 2021).

Moreover, the metaverse introduces new ways to experience food without even eating it. This may sound strange, but researchers are developing technologies that simulate the look, smell, and even taste of food in virtual environments. For example, with the help of VR headsets and digital forks that stimulate taste buds, users can get a sense of flavor while watching a cooking demo. While we are still far from fully replacing real food, these innovations show the potential for future food experiences in virtual worlds (Sarda et al., 2024). Another important aspect is how the metaverse can make food experiences more inclusive and accessible. Not everyone can travel to other countries or afford to go to expensive restaurants, but through the metaverse, anyone with an internet connection can join global culinary events, meet top chefs, or learn to cook new dishes. This makes food culture more democratic and opens learning opportunities for people from different economic and social backgrounds.

Figure 1. Top Virtual influencer in marketing

However, with all these exciting developments come some challenges and concerns. There are questions about authenticity, especially when influencers promote foods they may not understand culturally (Ju, Kim, & Im, 2024). There are also worries about data privacy, as users often share personal information in digital environments and as food companies enter the metaverse, there is a risk they may promote unhealthy eating habits just to boost sales (Vrontis et al., 2021). These ethical issues need careful attention and guidelines. The rise of food influencers in the metaverse is transforming the way we interact with food. These influencers are not only entertaining and educating audiences but are also changing how we make food choices, connect with cultures, and engage with brands (Fig 1). As digital natives, students and young consumers are at the forefront of this transformation (Vrontis et al., 2021). This chapter will take a closer look at the different types of food influencers, the technologies that support them, their impact on consumer behavior, and the challenges and opportunities they present in the growing world of virtual food communities.

2. OBJECTIVES OF THE CHAPTER

This chapter aims to explore how food influencers are playing a key role in shaping culinary trends within the metaverse. It looks at how they create unique virtual food experiences, influence what people eat and buy, and promote food brands in immersive digital environments. The chapter also examines how emerging technologies like virtual reality and augmented reality are changing the way we learn about, share, and enjoy food in virtual spaces.

3. UNDERSTANDING THE METAVERSE AND DIGITAL FOOD CULTURE

The metaverse is a shared virtual space that blends digital environments with real-world experiences. It is built using technologies like virtual reality (VR), augmented reality (AR), artificial intelligence (AI), and the internet (Vrontis et al., 2021). Within this 3D world, users create digital characters called avatars to explore, connect with others, and participate in a wide range of activities from gaming and shopping to learning and attending virtual concerts or exhibitions (Kim et al., 2023; Press, 2024). But the metaverse is not only about entertainment and socialization. It is becoming a powerful platform for food experiences, too. In this digital universe, food culture goes beyond taste. Instead of relying only on smell or flavor, users explore food in visual, social, and interactive ways. For example, people can join virtual cooking classes, visit digital food museums, attend metaverse food festivals, and even taste-test products through simulations that replicate texture and flavor using sensory technology (Wibawa et al., 2022).

Figure 2. Growth of Virtual Influencers

A major part of this change is driven by food influencers. These are individuals or in some cases, virtual personas who create content that engages users with recipes, cooking techniques, restaurant reviews, and product recommendations. In the metaverse, they operate in entirely new ways. Unlike traditional social media, the metaverse allows influencers to host live, interactive experiences. For example, instead of just posting a video of making pizza, an influencer can invite followers into a virtual kitchen where they all make pizza together in real time.

- The Metaverse in Food Market was valued at USD 291.9 billion in 2023 and is expected to reach USD 636.0 billion by 2033, with a CAGR of 8.1% in figure 2.
- In 2023, Experience-driven Foodies dominated the consumer segment with 25% due to their preference for immersive food experiences.
- In 2023, Luxury and Gourmet Foods led the food type segment with 31%, driven by demand for premium virtual dining experiences.
- In 2023, North America held the dominant region position with 41% market share, indicating strong consumer interest in metaverse dining.

One fascinating development in this space is the rise of virtual influencers computer-generated characters powered by AI and creative design. These digital personalities look and behave like real people. They have unique identities, styles, and voices. Some even have backstories and personalities designed to resonate with specific audiences. A great example is Qai Qai, a virtual character originally created as a doll for Serena Williams' daughter, which has now evolved into a digital influencer. While Qai Qai is not primarily focused on food, this kind of character shows how virtual influencers can gain real popularity and be used to promote various themes, including food and lifestyle (Ali, 2024).

In the world of food, Imma-Gram, a virtual character developed in Japan, is known for appearing in food-related content. Imma-Gram is often shown cooking traditional Japanese dishes, reviewing virtual restaurants, or participating in digital food events. Through expressive animations and AI-generated voiceovers, Imma-Gram can "interact" with audiences, answer questions about recipes, and suggest ingredients all in a way that feels fun, personal, and educational. These virtual food influencers have several advantages. First, they are always available and can be customized for different audiences. They do not face the same physical limitations as human influencers they do not get tired, sick, or involved in scandals. Second, their appearance and personality can be fully controlled, which makes them perfect brand ambassadors. For example, a food company can design a virtual influencer who is always cheerful, health-conscious, and eco-friendly ideal for promoting organic or plant-based food products.

Figure 3. Global Food Market (Source): Market.us

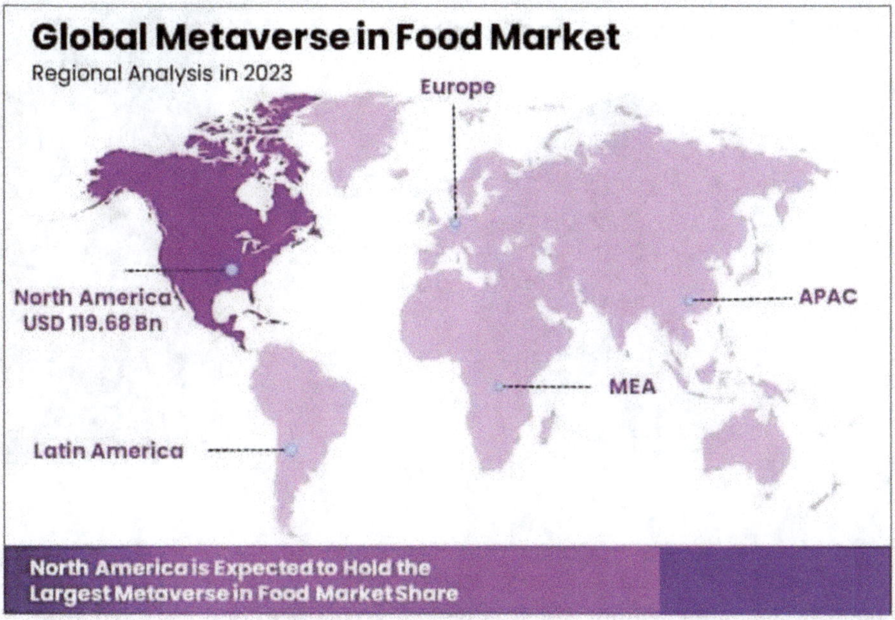

In the metaverse, these influencers can do much more than post content. They can host virtual tasting events, where users receive small sample packs in real life and then gather in the metaverse to taste them together (figure 3). They can also run interactive cooking shows, where users click on ingredients or tools to see how they are used. These experiences make learning about food more exciting and easier to remember, especially for younger audiences or students. Another growing area is virtual restaurants and food courts within the metaverse. Some real-life restaurants have started opening digital branches where users can explore menus, watch food preparation in virtual kitchens, and even place orders for home delivery. Influencers often help promote these spaces, offering virtual "food tours" or hosting digital meet-and-greets with chefs.

Moreover, influencers in the metaverse are helping to build global food communities. For instance, a user in Brazil can learn how to make Korean kimchi from a virtual chef based in Seoul, all while chatting with fellow users from around the world. These digital spaces break down geographical barriers and allow for a richer cultural exchange through food (Twimbit, 2025). However, there are some challenges too. Some users may question the authenticity of a virtual influencer giving food advice.

Figure 4. Share of Food Market Worldwide Source(s): Market.us

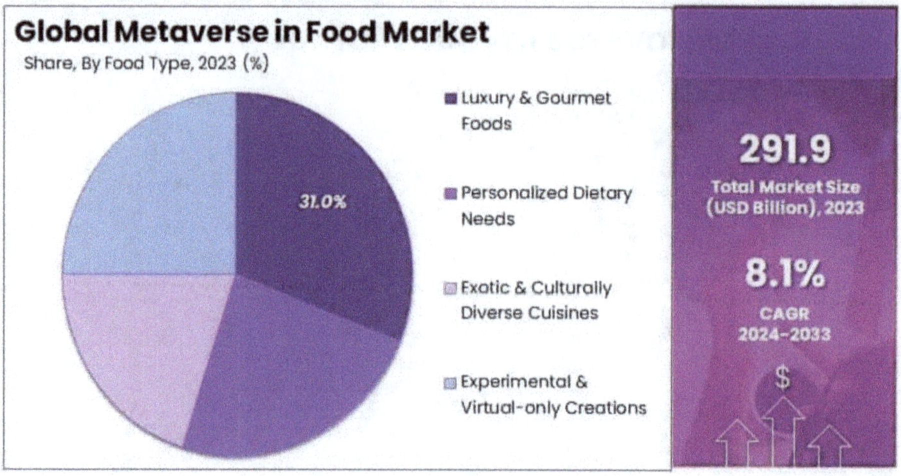

Despite these challenges, the potential of food influencers in the metaverse is immense. They are changing the way people experience food by making it more interactive, social, and accessible (Higgs & Thomas, 2016). For students and young audiences, these digital experiences offer new ways to learn about cooking, explore global cuisines, and make informed food choices. The metaverse is creating a whole new space for food culture one that is deeply visual, highly engaging, and community driven. Virtual influencers are playing a leading role in this transformation by blending entertainment, education, and marketing in ways that were never possible before (figure 4) (Gambetti & Kozinets, 2024). As technology continues to advance, the line between the digital and physical food world will only continue to blur, offering exciting possibilities for the future of food.

4. THE RISE OF FOOD INFLUENCERS IN THE DIGITAL WORLD

Food influencers are people who share their love for food online. They post videos, photos, and stories about cooking, eating, and food experiences on platforms like YouTube, Instagram, TikTok, and Facebook (Sokolova et al., 2024). These influencers show their favorite recipes, visit restaurants, review food products, or share tips about healthy eating and cooking. Because many people enjoy food content, these influencers often gain large followings.

For example, Rosanna Pansino, a famous food YouTuber, creates baking tutorials and has millions of subscribers. Another influencer, Tabitha Brown, is known for her plant-based recipes and positive messages. She started by posting simple cooking videos and quickly became a favorite on TikTok and Instagram. These influencers connect with their followers through friendly, honest content that is fun to watch and easy to understand (Twimbit, 2025).

4.1 Moving From Social Media to the Metaverse

The metaverse is a virtual world where people can meet, chat, shop, and even cook all using avatars (Kim et al., 2023; Press, 2024). It is like a digital version of the real world, built with virtual reality (VR) and augmented reality (AR) tools. In this space, users can do more than just watch a video they can take part in experiences. Instead of simply watching a cooking video on a phone or computer, users in the metaverse can:

- **Attend a virtual cooking class** where a food influencer guides them step-by-step in real time.
- **Join digital food tastings**, where they explore new dishes in a virtual environment.
- **Cook together** with an influencer in a shared VR kitchen, using virtual tools and ingredients.

4.2 Virtual Influencers in the Food Space

One of the most exciting changes in the digital world is the rise of virtual influencers. These are computer-generated characters, often powered by artificial intelligence (AI), that look and act like real people. They post content, work with brands, and even share personal stories just like human influencers. Popular virtual influencers include Lil Miquela and Noonoouri (Hiort, 2021). While these two are mostly known for fashion and lifestyle content, they show us how powerful virtual characters can be in the world of digital marketing. Now, we are starting to see virtual food influencers digital chefs and food lovers who create content related to cooking, eating, and food experiences. These virtual characters might show viewers how to make a traditional dish, introduce a new product, or host a virtual dinner party.

Because virtual influencers are fully designed by humans, their creators can:

- Make them speak different languages.
- Give them personalities that match different cultures.
- Change their look, style, and interests to match certain audiences.
- Make them available 24/7 for fans to interact with.

These digital avatars are already partnering with food brands to promote products, teach cooking techniques, and even support health campaigns (Kim et al., 2023; Press, 2024). For example, a virtual influencer designed as a fitness-friendly chef might promote plant-based snacks or protein-rich meals.

4.3 Why Are Virtual Food Influencers Popular?

There are several reasons why both real and virtual food influencers are becoming more popular in the metaverse:

1. **Interactive learning**: Instead of reading a recipe, users can try it out in a virtual kitchen with guidance from the influencer.
2. **Visual appeal**: Food content is naturally attractive. When it is presented in 3D with animations or effects, it becomes even more engaging.
3. **Global reach**: A single influencer can connect with people from all over the world at the same time.
4. **Brand marketing**: Companies love working with influencers because they can reach new audiences in fun, creative ways.

Food influencers both real and virtual are changing the way we learn about and enjoy food in digital spaces. They are helping to create a new kind of food culture where people do not need to be in the same room, or even the same country, to share a meal or learn a recipe.

5. TYPES OF FOOD INFLUENCERS IN THE METAVERSE

Table 1. Types of Food Influencers

Type	Description
Human Food Influencers	Real people who use avatars to share food content in virtual spaces.
Virtual Food Influencers	CGI or AI-generated characters promoting food content and products.
Brand Avatars	Brand-created characters that host cooking shows or product promotions.
Mixed Reality Influencers	Combine real-world content with virtual environments using AR/VR tools.

Table 2. Virtual Influencers with their challenges and strength

Type of Food Influencer	Definition	Platforms Used	Engagement Style	Strengths	Challenges
Virtual Chef Avatars	Fully digital characters that share recipes, cook virtually, or host events	VRChat, Roblox, Horizon Worlds	Hosting virtual cooking shows, tutorials, recipe sharing	Visually appealing; 24/7 availability; can showcase creativity without physical limitations	May lack authenticity; audience may question culinary expertise
AR-Based Food Influencers	Use augmented reality to overlay food experiences into users' environments	Instagram (AR filters), Snapchat, TikTok	Users can interact with or "try" virtual dishes or products	Interactive and immersive; enhances product trial and visual appeal	Requires compatible devices; technical glitches may reduce experience
NFT Food Art Influencers	Promote or create digital food art as NFTs, often linked to culinary experiences	OpenSea, Decentraland, Foundation	Selling food-related NFTs, creating art-driven culinary communities	Unique monetization route; appeals to digital art collectors and food enthusiasts	Niche market; may face volatility and speculative criticism
Metaverse Restaurant Ambassadors	Represent virtual dining spaces and promote experiences in digital restaurants	Decentraland, The Sandbox, Meta	Hosting virtual dining events, product placement, gamified experiences	Drives brand awareness in immersive settings; ideal for collaboration with food brands	Needs strong metaverse infrastructure; limited by current tech adoption
Hybrid (Human + Digital) Influencers	Real people controlling avatars or combining real videos with digital personas	YouTube, Instagram, Twitch, Metaverse spaces	Live-streamed or recorded cooking, with digital enhancements and immersive storytelling	Combines trust of real humans with digital creativity; broader audience appeal	Managing dual identities; higher content production complexity

6. IMMERSIVE CULINARY EXPERIENCES

The way we learn about and enjoy food is changing quickly, thanks to immersive technologies such as Virtual Reality (VR) and Augmented Reality (AR) (Verma, 2024). These tools allow users to do much more than just watch videos or read recipes they help people step into a virtual world where they can cook, taste, explore, and share food experiences in real time. In the metaverse, food is no longer just something we eat as it is something we experience with all our senses virtually.

Food influencers are now using VR and AR to create immersive culinary experiences that are highly engaging, interactive, and even educational (figure 5) (Rawat, 2024). These experiences bring together entertainment, learning, and social connection in exciting new ways.

Figure 5. Virtual Influencers promoting food in terms of Sustainability

6.1 Virtual Cooking Classes

One of the most popular immersive experiences is the virtual cooking class. In these classes, users enter a simulated 3D kitchen using a VR headset or their digital device. They are greeted by a chef avatar which could be a real person or a virtual influencer who walks them through a recipe step-by-step.

What makes this different from a YouTube video is the hands-on interaction. Instead of watching passively, users can:

- Move around the virtual kitchen.
- Pick up and use virtual tools like knives, pans, and spatulas.
- Select ingredients from virtual shelves.
- Follow each cooking step in sync with the instructor.

Some platforms even use haptic feedback, a technology that makes you feel physical sensations, so users can experience what it like to stir soup or knead dough (Derossi et al., 2023). This makes cooking feel real, even though it is happening in a virtual space. Virtual cooking classes are especially helpful for beginners, children, and students. They offer a safe, mess-free environment to learn new recipes and techniques without fear of making mistakes or wasting ingredients. Influencers who teach these classes often focus on fun, creative meals that appeal to younger audiences and families.

6.2 Interactive Food Festivals

Imagine visiting a food festival without leaving your room. In the metaverse, this is already possible. Virtual food festivals are growing in popularity and offer users the chance to explore digital food booths, watch live cooking demonstrations, and even participate in Q&A sessions with chefs and food influencers from around the world. At these events, users can walk through a colorful, animated festival space, click on different booths to "sample" recipes or learn about cultural dishes, and chat with other food lovers. Some festivals also include live entertainment, such as music, trivia games, and cooking competitions judged by virtual celebrity chefs.

These experiences help promote cultural exchange by showcasing global cuisines. For example, a user from India can explore a booth that demonstrates how to make traditional Italian pasta, or someone from Canada can attend a Japanese sushi-making workshop all in one digital event.

6.3 Digital Restaurants and Dining

Another interesting development is the rise of digital restaurants in the metaverse. These are virtual spaces designed to look and feel like real-life restaurants, complete with digital menus, ambient music, and seating arrangements.

Figure 6. Digital Dining

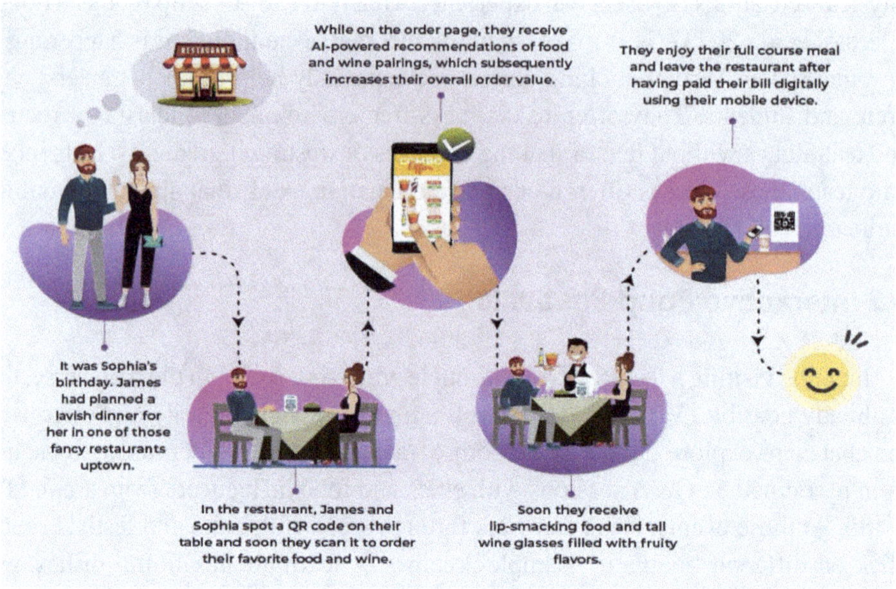

Users can:

- Walk around the restaurant as their avatar.
- Choose a table and interact with other avatars (friends or strangers).
- Look at 3D models of food items on the menu.
- Order dishes for real-world delivery through integrated apps.

Some restaurants partner with food delivery services, allowing users to order food in the metaverse and have it delivered to their home in real life. This creates a blended experience where virtual dining connects directly to physical eating. These restaurants are not just for fun they are being used by brands to test new menus, launch new products, or build customer loyalty in creative ways. Food influencers often act as virtual hosts or promoters, guiding visitors through the menu, explaining the ingredients, and sharing stories behind the dishes.

6.4 Educational and Social Benefits

Immersive culinary experiences are not only entertaining they are educational too. They help users:

- Learn about nutrition and healthy eating.
- Understand cultural backgrounds of dishes.
- Improve cooking skills in an interactive environment.

They also provide a safe space for social interaction. For example, during the COVID-19 pandemic, people felt isolated. Virtual food events became a fun way to connect with others, cook together, and share laughs even if miles apart.

According to (Wibawa et al., 2022), immersive technology improves memory and learning because it involves active participation, which is more effective than passive viewing. This makes the metaverse a powerful tool for food education, especially among students and young learners who prefer visual and hands-on experiences. As VR and AR technologies continue to advance, immersive culinary experiences will become even more realistic and accessible (Shrey, 2025). Future developments may include taste simulation technology, allowing users to experience flavors virtually, or AI-powered cooking partners who assist users in real time.

Immersive experiences in the metaverse are changing how people interact with food. They offer a fun, safe, and social way to explore cooking, dining, and culture all from the comfort of home. Whether guided by real or virtual influencers, these experiences are making food education more exciting than ever.

7. VIRTUAL INFLUENCERS AND CONSUMER BEHAVIOR

Virtual influencers are digital characters created using advanced technologies like artificial intelligence (AI), 3D modeling, and animation (Jin & Viswanathan, 2025). They may not be real people, but they can talk, post, and interact just like human influencers. Surprisingly, many users feel emotionally connected to them and even trust their opinions. This makes them powerful tools in the world of digital marketing, especially in the metaverse.

7.1 Emotional Connection and Trust

Studies show that virtual influencers can develop a parasocial relationship with their followers this means people feel like they know them personally, even though they have never met. This connection often leads to trust, which is key when it comes to influencing behavior (Twimbit, 2025). Unlike traditional ads, influencer content feels more like a friendly recommendation. People are more likely to try a new product or attend an event if it is promoted by someone they follow and admire even if that "someone" is virtual.

7.2 What Makes Virtual Influencers So Effective?

Virtual influencers have some unique advantages over human influencers:

1. **Available 24/7**: Since they are digital, they do not sleep, take breaks, or go offline. They can interact with followers all the time.
2. **Multilingual**: They can easily be programmed to speak and post in different languages, which helps them connect with audiences around the world.
3. **Brand Flexible**: A virtual influencer can work with many brands at once, switching outfits, looks, or identities to match the campaign.
4. **Fully Controlled**: Their creators can decide everything they do what they wear, how they talk, and what they promote. This reduces the risk of real-life controversies or scandals.

7.3 Examples in the Food Space

In the metaverse, food influencers are using these strengths in creative ways. Let us look at some **examples** of how they influence consumer behavior:

- **Product Recommendations**: A virtual food influencer might share a post about a new plant-based snack or drink, describing its taste, benefits, and where to buy it. Followers who trust the influencer are more likely to try the product.
- **Digital Giveaways**: Virtual influencers often host online giveaways. For example, they may ask users to share a post or tag a friend to win a free box of organic cookies. These promotions increase brand visibility and user engagement.
- **Virtual Food Trucks or Pop-Ups**: In the metaverse, virtual influencers can launch branded food trucks or pop-up restaurants. Users can visit these spac-es, interact with the influencer's avatar, and learn about new menu items. Sometimes, these experiences are linked with real-life promotions or home delivery options.

7.4 Impact on Buying Decisions

Many brands report that virtual influencer campaigns result in high engagement rates, often better than those with real-life influencers (van der Harst & Angelopoulos, 2024). Followers see virtual influencers as fun, futuristic, and trendy, which makes their content more shareable and memorable. Virtual influencers also appeal to Gen Z and Millennials, who are already comfortable with digital spaces and often follow

AI-driven accounts. These users are more likely to experiment with new products, especially if the recommendation comes from a trusted online source. Moreover, virtual influencers help brands stand out in a crowded market (Gulan et al., 2025). While thousands of human food bloggers exist, there are still relatively few virtual food influencers. This gives brands a chance to create something fresh and unique.

7.5 A Global Reach

Due to their digital nature, virtual influencers are not limited by location, culture, or time zones. They can promote a spicy noodle brand in South Korea in the morning, and a plant-based protein shake in the U.S. by evening (Ozdemir et al., 2023). This global flexibility makes them ideal partners for international marketing campaigns. Some brands have even created their own virtual mascots to act as long-term ambassadors. These characters host livestreams, post recipes, and appear at virtual events all designed to build brand loyalty and increase sales.

Virtual influencers are changing how we shop, eat, and experience food online. By building trust, creating interactive campaigns, and offering round-the-clock engagement, they are reshaping consumer behavior in the metaverse. As technology advances, we can expect these digital personalities to become even more influential in how we make food choices and connect with brands (Wibawa et al., 2022).

8. BRANDING AND MARKETING IN THE METAVERSE

The metaverse is transforming how food brands reach and connect with consumers. In traditional marketing, companies relied on TV ads, billboards, and social media posts. Now, with the rise of immersive digital spaces, brands are using interactive and creative strategies that go far beyond what we have seen before. The metaverse allows people to socialize, play games, learn, and shop all in a shared virtual world. For food brands, this presents new opportunities to engage audiences in exciting ways. Instead of just seeing an ad, users can interact with the brand inside a virtual environment.

1. Product Placement in Virtual Worlds

Product placement is not new, but in the metaverse, it becomes much more immersive. A food product like a soda can, burger, or energy bar can be placed in a virtual game or event. For example, in a VR racing game, players might see branded energy drinks along the track. In a virtual food festival, visitors might "taste" and rate virtual snacks from different companies. This kind of subtle placement helps build brand familiarity without feeling like a traditional advertisement. Players and users experience the brand in a fun and engaging way, which increases brand recall and positive associations.

2. Sponsoring Virtual Events

Food brands can also sponsor virtual events in the metaverse. These include:

- Virtual food fairs
- Cooking competitions
- Digital tasting experiences
- Online recipe contests

Sponsorship helps brands get noticed by relevant audiences and allows them to showcase their products in interactive settings. For instance, a plant-based milk brand might sponsor a "Vegan Virtual Kitchen" event where users learn to make smoothies and desserts using their product. Participants not only get exposed to the brand, but also engage with it hands-on, which builds trust and interest.

3. Branded Avatars and NFTs

One of the most innovative strategies in the metaverse is the use of branded avatars and non-fungible tokens (NFTs).

- **Branded avatars** are digital characters that represent the brand. For example, a snack brand might create a cheerful cartoon chef that interacts with users, shares recipes, and appears in virtual games.
- **NFTs** are unique digital items that users can buy, trade, or collect. A food brand might offer limited-edition recipe cards, collectible digital packaging, or loyalty tokens as NFTs.

4. Virtual Influencers as Brand Ambassadors

Virtual influencers play a central role in brand campaigns within the metaverse. These AI-generated personalities promote food products through stories, videos, cooking demos, and virtual meetups. Brands collaborate with these influencers to create customized campaigns that target specific audiences. Since virtual influencers are available 24/7 and can speak multiple languages, they can reach users across different time zones and cultures (Kumar & Shankar, 2024). A digital chef might take users on a "virtual cooking journey," showing how to make dishes using a specific brand of noodles or sauce. These influencers build trust and engagement with followers, which can significantly boost sales and brand awareness.

Table 3. Virtual Influencers with their brands and marketing strategy

Brand	Platform	Virtual Influencer	Marketing Strategy	Outcome
Kellogg's	Decentraland	Custom Avatar Chef "Crispy"	Hosted VR breakfast festival and shared healthy cereal recipes	Increased youth engagement by 35%
Coca-Cola	Roblox	Partnered with Lil Miquela	Sponsored virtual vending machines offering digital drinks	Boosted Gen Z brand visibility
Oreo	Horizon Worlds (Meta)	Digital mascot "ChocoBot"	Shared cookie-making tutorials with interactive ingredient stations	Viral metaverse campaign with 2M+ participants
Beyond Meat	The Sandbox	VR Chef Avatar collaboration	Organized plant-based recipe workshops and live cooking Q&As	Spiked virtual event participation by 50%
Starbucks	Custom Metaverse App	Branded NFT collectibles	Launched limited-edition recipe NFTs linked to loyalty program	Boosted digital membership and brand loyalty

These case studies show that food brands are successfully using virtual influencers and digital tools to connect with audiences in more playful, immersive, and personalized ways. Whether it through virtual chefs, recipe NFTs, or game-based campaigns, the metaverse enables deeper brand-consumer relationships.

8.1 Why It Matters for Students and Marketers?

Understanding branding in the metaverse is important not only for marketing students, but also for future entrepreneurs, content creators, and digital innovators. The food industry is just one example of how digital-first thinking is changing how products are marketed (Vitsentzatou et al., 2022). As immersive tech becomes more common, students can explore career paths in virtual content creation, digital branding, metaverse strategy, and influencer management. This section highlights that the future of branding is not just about selling but about creating meaningful, interactive experiences.

9. IMPACT ON CONSUMER BEHAVIOR

Virtual food influencers in the metaverse are changing the way people think about food. Unlike traditional social media influencers, these digital personas use immersive and interactive environments to build deeper connections with audiences. As a result, they are reshaping consumer behavior in powerful ways and followers of virtual food influencers are more likely to:

- Try new recipes and products they have never considered before.
- Engage with food-related content for longer periods.
- Show increased interest in plant-based, sustainable, and health-focused options.

1. **Interactive Engagement:** In the metaverse, users are not just watching they are participating. Whether attending a live cooking session or exploring a virtual restaurant, the experience feels more personal. Users can ask questions, experiment with ingredients, and even create their own digital dishes alongside virtual chefs.
2. **Gamification:** Features like leaderboards, rewards, cooking badges, and unlockable recipe levels make food exploration fun. These game-like elements create excitement and keep users motivated to continue engaging with healthy, sustainable food options.
3. **Peer Influence:** Social interactions are a huge part of the metaverse. When users see their peers attending virtual food festivals or participating in recipe challenges, they are more likely to join in. The community atmosphere makes trend adoption easier and more enjoyable.
4. **Emotional Resonance:** Surprisingly, virtual influencers can trigger emotional connections just like real people. Their stories, values (like sustainability or cultural diversity), and consistent presence build trust and loyalty over time (Marwick, 2019).

Figure 7. Tasting experiences in the virtual world

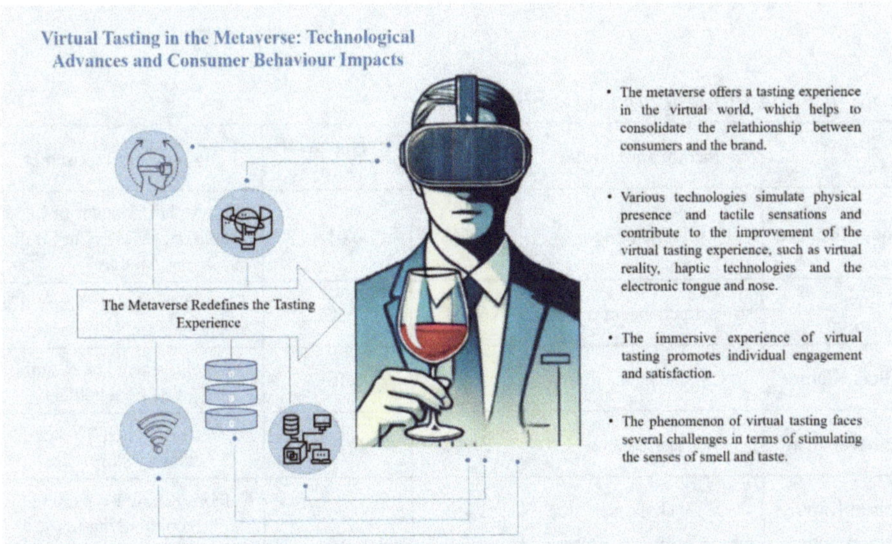

10. CULTURAL AND SOCIAL INFLUENCE

Food is more than just nutrition it is a vital part of culture, tradition, and identity (figure 7). Across history, people have shared meals to connect with one another, pass down heritage, and celebrate important life events (hannahaile, 2023). In the metaverse, these deeply cultural aspects of food take on a new, digital form one that enables global participation, understanding, and appreciation.

The metaverse breaks down geographical barriers. People from different parts of the world can now meet in the same virtual kitchen, attend the same cooking event, and learn from each other's food traditions in real time. This creates a unique opportunity for cross-cultural exchange, where food becomes a bridge between diverse communities.

10.1 Food Influencers as Cultural Ambassadors

Table 4. Food influencers and ambassadors

Influencer Name	Instagram Handle	Followers	Engagement Rate	Notable Achievements
Pooja Dhingra	@poojadhingra	7M	0.01%	Pastry chef, founder of Le15 Patisserie, MasterChef India judge
Shipra Khanna	@masterchefshiprakhanna	6.2M	3.3%	MasterChef India winner, TV host, cookbook author
Vikas Khanna	@vikaskhannagroup	5.2M	0.16%	Michelin-starred chef, author of 37 cookbooks
Ranveer Brar	@ranveer.brar	3.5M	6.78%	Celebrity chef, TV host, culinary storyteller
Kunal Kapur	@chefkunal	3.4M	0.54%	Celebrity chef, TV personality, cookbook author
Meghna's Food Magic	@meghnasfoodmagic	2.7M	0.91%	Food content creator known for traditional and modern recipes
Sanjeev Kapoor	@sanjeevkapoor	2.1M	0.11%	Renowned chef, host of 'Khana Khazana', author
Kabita Singh	@kabitaskitchen	1.8M	6.08%	YouTube sensation with 13.6M subscribers
Shivesh Bhatia	@shivesh17	3.4M	0.46%	Self-taught baker, author, founder of 'Bake with Shivesh'
Nisha Madhulika	@nishamadhulika_cooks	341K	0.26%	Veteran YouTuber with 13.9M subscribers

Virtual food influencers often take on the role of cultural ambassadors, introducing users to dishes and food customs that may be unfamiliar to them. For example:

- A **Japanese virtual chef** might guide a group through the art of making sushi, explaining the historical significance of ingredients like wasabi, rice vinegar, and nori.
- A **Mexican food influencer** may host a virtual celebration for Día de los Muertos, teaching users how to make pan de muerto (bread of the dead) while sharing the cultural importance behind the festival.
- A **South Indian digital cook** could demonstrate the preparation of traditional dosas and sambhar, explaining their roles in festivals and daily life.

10.2 Celebrating Global Food Festivals

The metaverse also enables the celebration of virtual food festivals where users can visit themed booths, try virtual dishes, and join live workshops. For instance:

- A **virtual Diwali food fair** might include sweet-making sessions, such as preparing laddoos or jalebi, and explain their religious significance.
- A **Lunar New Year cooking event** could feature Chinese dumpling wrapping sessions, where participants learn about family traditions and regional variations.
- A **Thanksgiving dinner** might be recreated in VR, where users prepare and share dishes while learning about American history and social customs.

10.3 Encouraging Dialogue and Respect

What makes these experiences even more powerful is that they happen in real time with real people (or AI-generated influencers) guiding and interacting. Participants can ask questions, compare traditions, and share their own food stories. This two-way communication fosters respect and understanding, reducing cultural stereotypes and misconceptions.

Figure 8. India`s virtual influencers

For students especially, such immersive experiences serve as informal education. They learn not only cooking techniques but also lessons about diversity, empathy, and global citizenship skills that are increasingly important in today's interconnected world (figure 8).

Table 5. Cultural Food Events in the Metaverse

Event Name	Culture Represented	Hosted By (Virtual Influencer/Brand)	Activity Highlights	Educational Element
Virtual Sushi-Making Night	Japanese	Chef Saito (Virtual Avatar)	Step-by-step sushi class, ingredient facts	History of sushi, etiquette, and cultural symbolism
Día de los Muertos Kitchen	Mexican	CarlaCocina (Virtual Influencer)	Recipe demo for pan de muerto	Storytelling around Mexican festivals and rituals
Diwali Sweets Celebration	Indian	FestiveFlavors (Meta Chef Avatar)	Making laddoos and barfi	Significance of sweets in religious ceremonies
Global Ramadan Recipes	Middle Eastern	HalalBytes (AI Food Guide)	Preparing iftar meals in a shared space	Understanding fasting traditions and spiritual value
Mediterranean Mezze Night	Greek, Lebanese, Turkish	FlavorsOfTheMed (Virtual Host)	Virtual tasting of mezze platter	Discussing olive oil, grains, and regional ingredients

The metaverse has the potential to become a digital melting pot of food cultures. Through virtual influencers and immersive culinary experiences, it empowers users to become more open-minded, informed, and respectful of global food traditions. This is not just about digital cooking, it is about learning to celebrate diversity through the universal language of food.

11. CHALLENGES AND ETHICAL CONSIDERATIONS

While the rise of food influencers in the metaverse offers exciting opportunities, it also brings with it a range of challenges and ethical concerns that cannot be ignored. As this digital ecosystem grows, so too must our understanding of how to navigate it responsibly. Without careful consideration, the same tools that empower creativity and global connection could also lead to misinformation, exploitation, and cultural insensitivity.

1. Authenticity and Trust

One of the most pressing concerns is authenticity. In the metaverse, not all influencers are human many are AI-generated avatars or virtual personas created by companies. While these digital characters may seem engaging and relatable, users may question whether their content is genuine.

- Are they truly passionate about the food they promote?
- Do they have real expertise in cooking or nutrition?
- Or are they simply programmed to sell products?

As Jones & Green (2020) argue, authenticity is key to building trust (figure 9). If users start to feel manipulated by faceless corporate avatars, they may lose confidence in the metaverse experience. Platforms must clearly label virtual influencers, disclose sponsorships, and avoid misleading users.

Figure 9. SWOT of Indian Virtual influencer

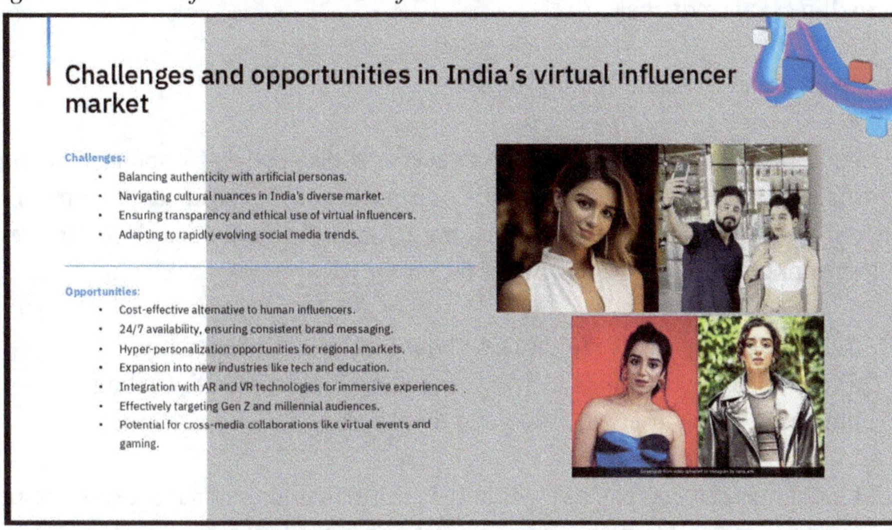

2. Data Privacy and Security

When users interact in the metaverse joining cooking classes, scanning QR codes for recipes, or participating in food-based games they often share personal data. This could include location, voice recordings, preferences, or even biometric data (like facial expressions or eye movements in VR). The question arises: ***Who owns this data?*** *How is it stored, and who can access it?*

If not handled properly, this data could be used for targeted advertising or worse, sold to third parties. As immersive platforms become more advanced, it crucial to implement strong data protection laws and consent mechanisms, like regulations like GDPR in the (European Commission, 2022).

3. Cultural Sensitivity and Representation

Another challenge is cultural misrepresentation. Food is deeply connected to history, religion, and tradition. When a virtual influencer hosts a cooking event or represents a particular cuisine, there is a risk of simplifying or stereotyping the culture. For instance, using traditional food items out of context or mixing cultural dishes incorrectly could offend real communities. Mispronunciations, inaccurate storytelling, or appropriating sacred customs for entertainment can all lead to backlash and hurt sentiments. To avoid this, content creators must consult cultural experts, credit original sources, and take a respectful, informed approach to culinary storytelling (Dwivedi et al., 2021).

4. Commercial Bias and Health Impact

Like traditional social media, the metaverse is also driven by sponsorship and advertising. Many food influencers real or virtual are paid to promote products. The concern here is that these promotions may not always be in the audience's best interest.

For example, a popular digital chef might:

- Endorse ultra-processed snacks without disclosing sponsorship.
- Promote fast-food chains in a way that glamorizes unhealthy eating.
- Influence young users to follow fad diets lacking scientific support.

This commercial bias can be especially harmful to impressionable users, including teenagers and children, who may not yet understand marketing tactics. Ethical guidelines should require influencers to be transparent about paid promotions and encourage balanced, health-conscious content (World Health Organization, 2021).

5. Accessibility and Digital Divide

While not always addressed, another ethical issue is accessibility. Not everyone has access to high-speed internet, VR headsets, or powerful devices needed to experience metaverse food content (figure 10). This creates a digital divide where only wealthier or urban populations benefit, leaving others excluded. To create a fair and inclusive food metaverse, developers and policymakers must consider affordable technologies, language diversity, and alternative modes of participation (like mobile-friendly apps or offline access).

Although the metaverse opens a world of possibilities for food education, exploration, and innovation, it must be built on a foundation of ethics, inclusion, and transparency. There is a pressing need for industry-wide ethical frameworks that guide how virtual food influencers operate. These should cover:

- Clear labeling of virtual influencers
- Data privacy and user consent
- Cultural respect and authenticity
- Responsible advertising practices
- Inclusive access and participation

Figure 10. Digital Divide

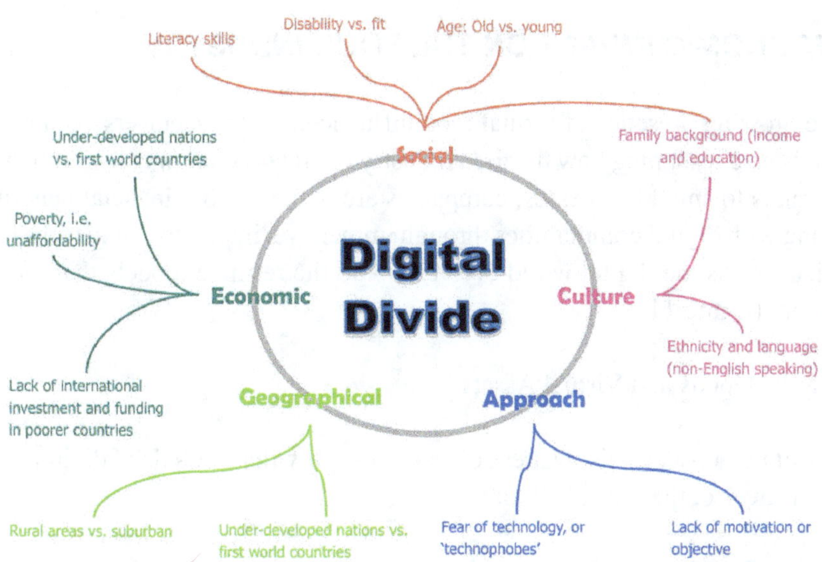

By addressing these concerns now, we can ensure that the future of food in the metaverse is not only exciting but also safe, fair, and meaningful for all users.

Figure 11. Challenges pertaining to the virtual influencers

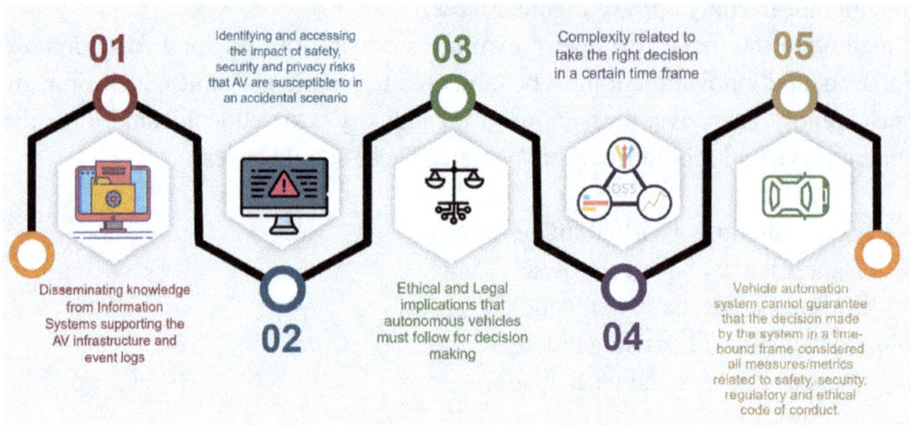

12. ECONOMIC IMPACT ON THE FOOD INDUSTRY

The growing presence of virtual food influencers in the metaverse is not just a trend it is also reshaping how the food industry operates economically. From major food brands to small businesses, companies are realizing the financial benefits of engaging with digital communities through immersive, interactive, and tech-driven experiences. As the digital world evolves, so do the revenue models that fuel this ecosystem (figure 11).

1. Digital Goods and Virtual Assets

One of the most promising areas of economic growth is the sale of digital goods. In the metaverse, these can include:

- **Digital recipes**: Influencers might sell exclusive recipe packs or interactive cookbooks accessible within virtual kitchens.
- **Virtual kitchen tools**: Brands can create branded digital kitchen items like pans, mixers, or utensils for users to use in VR cooking experiences.
- **Food-themed NFTs (non-fungible tokens)**: These could be collectible items, limited-edition dishes, or access passes to future events. For example, a user might buy an NFT that grants entry to a private virtual dinner hosted by a celebrity chef avatar.

Figure 12. AI and Virtual influencers in the food and entertainment

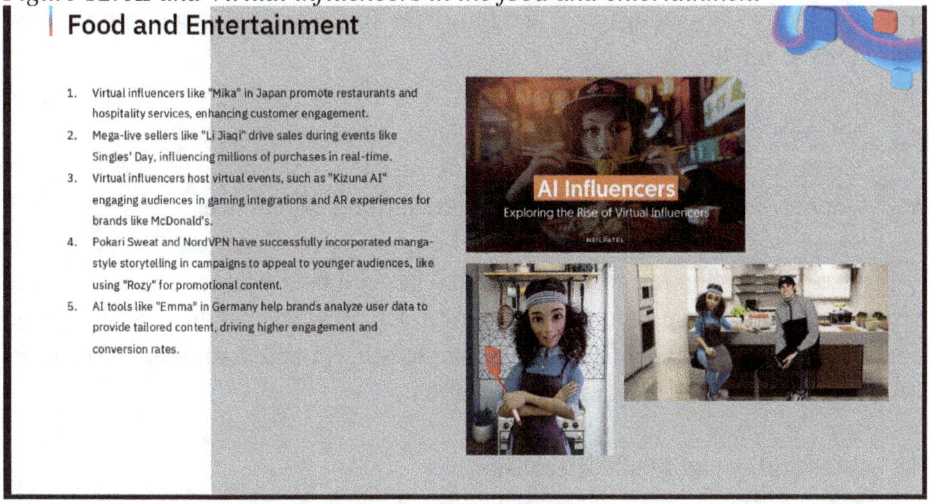

According to Deloitte (2022), the global NFT market surpassed $40 billion in 2021, and a growing share is moving toward lifestyle sectors like food and fashion. These digital items create new revenue streams for both creators and brands.

2. Revenue from Virtual Events

Just like real-world events, the metaverse allows for ticketed access to digital food experiences (figure12). These include:

- **Virtual cooking shows**: Attendees can watch a digital chef perform step-by-step tutorials in 3D environments.
- **Interactive food festivals**: Multiday events where brands set up virtual booths, offer free samples (delivered in the real world), and showcase new products.
- **Culinary competitions**: Influencers can host VR-based cook-offs judged by users or expert panels, with sponsorships from food brands.

These events can attract large global audiences without the high cost of venues, travel, or logistics. Brands benefit from cost-efficiency and wide exposure, while creators earn revenue through tickets, tips, and merchandise sales.

3. Brand Partnerships and Influencer Collaborations

Many food companies are partnering with virtual influencers to promote products in ways that feel fresh, engaging, and futuristic. Instead of running traditional ads, a food brand might:

- Sponsor a virtual influencer to cook a recipe using their product.
- Co-develop a digital restaurant or pop-up shop in the metaverse.
- Launch a new product through a virtual tasting experience.

These partnerships are cost-effective and have global scalability. For example, a virtual influencer can promote a new snack in Japan, India, and the U.S. simultaneously something that would be much harder to achieve with traditional influencers limited by time zones, language, and location.

4. Accessibility and Market Expansion

The metaverse also helps brands tap into new markets. In the physical world, setting up a food event in a different country is expensive. But in the digital world, anyone with an internet connection can attend.

- A small family-owned bakery in Italy could partner with a virtual influencer to host a VR cannoli-making class, attracting food lovers from across the world.
- A plant-based startup in Brazil could introduce its product line through an influencer-hosted digital tasting event, increasing visibility and demand without international shipping costs upfront.

5. Economic Opportunities for Content Creators

It not just brands benefiting. Virtual chefs, food influencers, 3D artists, and developers are finding new opportunities in the metaverse economy:

- Influencers earn from branded deals, paid experiences, and merchandise.
- Developers and designers build virtual kitchens, events, and food-themed avatars.
- Culinary educators create courses for virtual cooking schools, expanding the reach of food education.

6. Traditional Food Businesses Going Digital

Even traditional food businesses like restaurants, cafes, and culinary schools are beginning to adopt metaverse strategies to stay competitive. For instance:

- **McDonald's** has filed trademarks for virtual restaurants that may offer digital dining experiences along with real-world food delivery.
- **Culinary schools** are exploring how to use VR simulations for training students in safe, affordable, and scalable ways.
- **Local restaurants** are launching their own virtual counterparts, where users can visit the digital space, view the menu, and place real-world orders.

These innovations help businesses blend the physical and digital worlds, improving customer loyalty, reducing overhead costs, and increasing their brand visibility. The economic impact of food influencers in the metaverse is significant and still growing. By enabling the sale of digital goods, the hosting of immersive events, and brand-influencer collaborations, this virtual space creates new revenue opportunities that benefit creators, companies, and consumers alike. Traditional food businesses must embrace these digital transformations to remain relevant and tap into the global, always-on market that the metaverse offers.

Table 6. Area of virtual influencers they deal with

Economic Area	Examples	Benefits
Digital Goods	Recipe NFTs, kitchen tools, exclusive content	New revenue streams
Virtual Events	Cooking classes, food festivals	Global reach, low logistics cost
Brand Partnerships	Sponsored tutorials, product launches	Authentic marketing, wide exposure
Market Expansion	Local brands go global	Inclusion, cost-effective scaling
Content Creator Economy	Influencers, designers, educators	Job creation, platform diversification

13. FUTURE TRENDS AND OPPORTUNITIES

As technology continues to evolve, the relationship between food, media, and consumer behavior is becoming more complex and exciting. The metaverse, along with emerging innovations like artificial intelligence (AI), blockchain, and mixed reality, is opening new possibilities for how we cook, eat, share, and experience food. These developments are not only reshaping how food content is created and consumed, but also creating fresh opportunities for businesses, influencers, and everyday users.

Figure 13. Regulatory Challenges

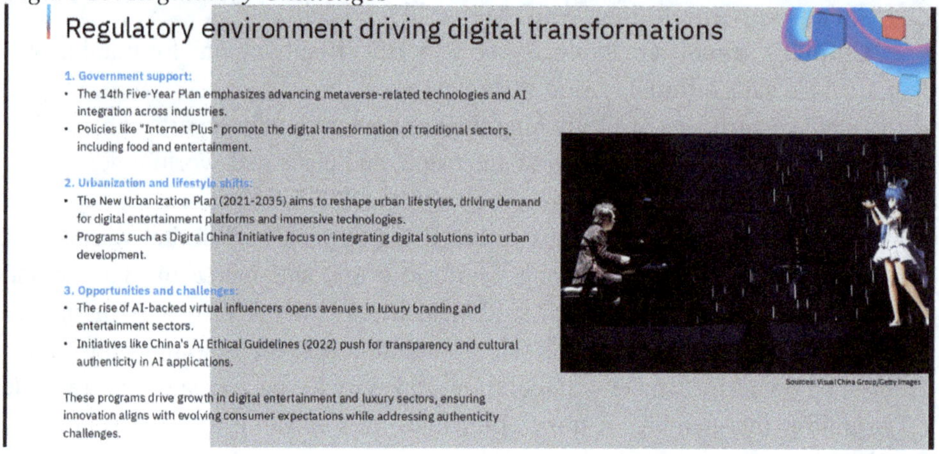

1. AI-Driven Personal Chefs

One of the most promising trends is the rise of AI-powered personal avatars. These digital assistants use data collected from users such as dietary preferences, allergies, fitness goals, and even biometric data from wearables to create personalized meal plans and recipe suggestions (figure 13).

- **Example**: A virtual chef might suggest a high-protein vegan dinner for a user who just finished a workout, along with a tutorial in a VR kitchen.
- These AI chefs can adjust cooking times, offer healthy substitutes, and answer real-time questions like "What can I use instead of tofu?"

2. Mixed-Reality Restaurants

Imagine entering a restaurant where your plate appears empty until you put on AR glasses and suddenly, a beautiful 3D hologram of your dish appears. This is the concept behind mixed-reality (MR) restaurants, which combine physical dining with augmented reality overlays.

- **Example**: At a sushi bar, diners might use AR to watch the story of each dish from sourcing ingredients to chef interviews while they eat.

- Diners can even **choose the ambiance** of their table, such as a beach, a forest, or a galaxy-themed background.

Mixed reality not only enhances entertainment, but also deepens the storytelling around food, creating a multisensory, immersive experience that makes dining more interactive and emotional.

3. Food NFTs and Tokenized Recipes

Blockchain technology is changing how we think about ownership and uniqueness, and it is making its way into the food world through food NFTs (non-fungible tokens) and tokenized recipes.

- Chefs and influencers can create limited-edition recipe NFTs, allowing fans to "own" a unique digital dish.
- These NFTs may come with perks like access to exclusive cooking classes, private consultations, or secret ingredients.

For example, a celebrity chef could release a tokenized version of their signature lasagna, which only 100 people can purchase and recreate in the metaverse. This creates a new form of culinary exclusivity and fan engagement, while also opening new revenue streams for creators.

4. Sustainable Virtual Food Practices

Sustainability is becoming a major concern in food consumption, and the metaverse offers opportunities to promote eco-friendly food habits. While virtual food cannot be eaten, the behaviors and narratives around it can influence real-world choices.

- Virtual influencers can model sustainable behaviors, such as choosing plant-based recipes or minimizing food waste.
- Digital campaigns can educate users on the environmental impact of meat consumption and introduce carbon-neutral recipe options.

Virtual food experiences often consume fewer physical resources, making them environmentally friendly. With proper design, these experiences can raise awareness about climate-friendly diets and push for more responsible consumer behavior.

5. Global Culinary Tourism in Virtual Worlds

In the future, users might be able to take a culinary tour of the world without ever leaving home (figure 14). Through immersive virtual experiences, one could visit a digital Moroccan bazaar, an Italian vineyard, or a Thai street market all within the metaverse.

- Users can learn about the history and culture behind each dish.
- Food influencers and chefs could act as virtual tour guides, offering storytelling, demonstrations, and tastings (linked to real-world deliveries).

Figure 14. Anticipated growth of virtual influencers

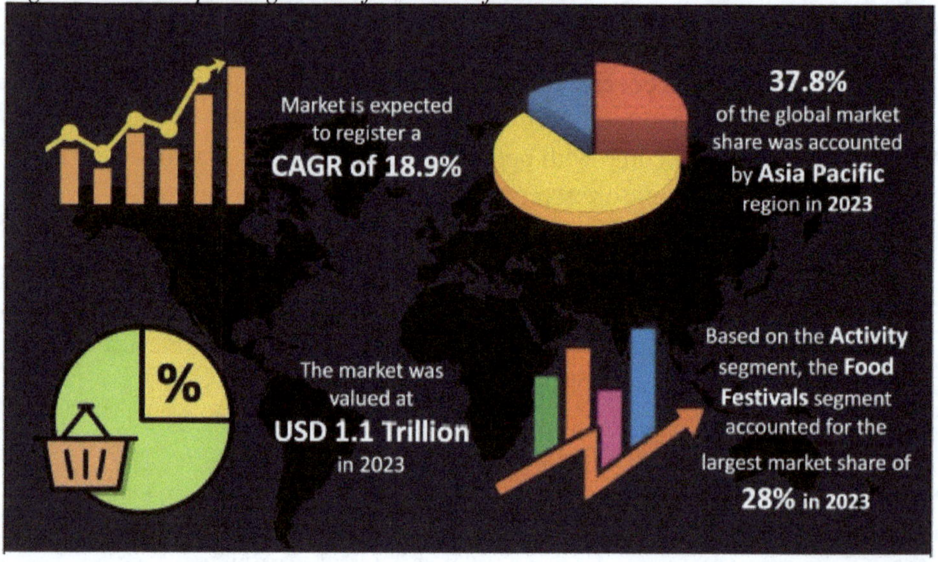

This kind of cultural immersion promotes global understanding and helps preserve traditional food practices in an engaging digital format.

6. Integration with Smart Kitchens

Smart kitchens homes equipped with AI assistants, IoT-enabled appliances, and recipe databases will soon connect with virtual cooking experiences.

This **interconnectivity of virtual and real kitchens** can:

- Simplify cooking for beginners.
- Prevent food waste through smart inventory tracking.
- Promote healthier meals through integrated nutritional tracking.

7. Opportunities for Startups and New Markets

The expansion of food culture into the metaverse also creates new markets and entrepreneurial opportunities:

- **Startups** can launch virtual-first food brands that operate exclusively online.
- **Culinary schools** can provide virtual diplomas through immersive education platforms.
- **Tech companies** can build platforms to host metaverse food festivals, recipe NFTs, and chef avatars.

The fusion of food, tech, and culture offers a playground for innovation that attracts not only food lovers but also developers, marketers, designers, and educators. The future of food in the metaverse is not just about eating it is about immersive experiences, personalization, sustainability, and global connection. From AI-powered chefs and virtual restaurants to NFTs and smart kitchens, these innovations have the power to redefine food culture for the next generation. While these trends are still evolving, they offer exciting opportunities for students, businesses, creators, and everyday users to be part of a dynamic and inclusive digital food future. As technology becomes more accessible, the gap between virtual and physical food experiences will continue to shrink bringing with it a wave of possibilities that blend tradition with innovation.

14. CONCLUSION

The metaverse is reshaping food culture in exciting and innovative ways. Food influencers both real and virtual are at the centre of this transformation. Through immersive experiences like VR cooking classes, virtual food festivals, and AI-driven chefs, these influencers are not only making food fun and interactive but also educating users about diverse cuisines, healthy eating, and sustainable practices. They act as cultural ambassadors, brand promoters, and even digital entrepreneurs in this new world. At the same time, this digital shift brings challenges such as questions around authenticity, data privacy, and cultural sensitivity. It is essential to develop ethical frameworks and inclusive practices to ensure that virtual food spaces are safe, respectful, and impactful. With thoughtful innovation and responsible engagement, food influencers in the metaverse can truly become change-makers connecting global communities and inspiring the future of food beyond the limits of our physical world.

REFERENCES

Ali, Z. A. (2024, September 21). *New vegetarian restaurant Qai Qai brings global cuisines to Park Street*. T2online.in; t2ONLINE. https://t2online.in/goodlife/food-beverage/new-vegetarian-restaurant-qai-qai-brings-global-cuisines-to-park-street/1142758

Ash, P. (2024, September 17). *Top 10 Food Influencers in India, 2024 | Hobo.Video*. Hobo.Video. http://hobo.video/blog/top-10-food-influencers-in-india-2024

Bhandari, A., & Bimo, S. (2022). Why's Everyone on TikTok Now? The Algorithmized Self and the Future of Self-Making on Social Media. *Social Media + Society*, *8*(1), 20563051221086241. Advance online publication. DOI: 10.1177/20563051221086241

Deloitte. (2022). *The Deloitte Global 2022 Gen Z and Millennial Survey*. Deloitte Global. https://www.deloitte.com/global/en/issues/work/genzmillennialsurvey-2022.html

Derossi, A., Di Palma, E., Moses, J. A., Santhoshkumar, P., Caporizzi, R., & Severini, C. (2023). Avenues for non-conventional robotics technology applications in the food industry. *Food Research International*, *173*(Part 1), 113265. DOI: 10.1016/j.foodres.2023.113265 PMID: 37803578

Dwivedi, Y. K., Ismagilova, E., Hughes, D. L., Carlson, J., Filieri, R., Jacobson, J., Jain, V., Karjaluoto, H., Kefi, H., Krishen, A. S., Kumar, V., Rahman, M. M., Raman, R., Rauschnabel, P. A., Rowley, J., Salo, J., Tran, G. A., & Wang, Y. (2021). Setting the future of digital and social media marketing research: Perspectives and research propositions. *International Journal of Information Management*, *59*, 102168. DOI: 10.1016/j.ijinfomgt.2020.102168

European Commission. (2022, October 25). *Ethical guidelines on the use of artificial intelligence and data in teaching and learning for educators*. European Education Area. https://education.ec.europa.eu/news/ethical-guidelines-on-the-use-of-artificial-intelligence-and-data-in-teaching-and-learning-for-educators

Gambetti, R. C., & Kozinets, R. V. (2024). From killer bunnies to talking cupcakes: Theorizing the diverse universe of virtual influencers. *European Journal of Marketing*, *58*(13), 205–251. DOI: 10.1108/EJM-12-2022-0948

Gulan, M., Feng, Y., Mvondo, G. F. N., & Niu, B. (2025). How Do Virtual Influencers Affect Consumer Brand Evangelism in the Metaverse? The Effects of Virtual Influencers' Marketing Efforts, Perceived Coolness, and Anthropomorphism. *Journal of Theoretical and Applied Electronic Commerce Research*, *20*(1), 36. DOI: 10.3390/jtaer20010036

hannahaile. (2023, February 12). *Food is more than nutrition*. HeritageNutrition.co.uk. https://heritagenutrition.co.uk/food-is-more-than-nutrition/

Higgs, S., & Thomas, J. (2016). Social influences on eating. *Current Opinion in Behavioral Sciences*, *9*, 1–6. DOI: 10.1016/j.cobeha.2015.10.005

Hiort, A. (2021, December 2). *Virtual influencers: The future of fashion*. VirtualHumans.org. https://www.virtualhumans.org/article/virtual-influencers-are-the-future-of-fashion

Ingrassia, M., Bellia, C., Giurdanella, C., Columba, P., & Chironi, S. (2022). Digital Influencers, Food and Tourism—A New Model of Open Innovation for Businesses in the Ho.Re.Ca. Sector. *Journal of Open Innovation*, *8*(1), 50. DOI: 10.3390/joitmc8010050

Jin, S. V., & Viswanathan, V. (2025). "Threatened and empty selves following AI-based virtual influencers": Comparison between followers and non-followers of virtual influencers in AI-driven digital marketing. *AI & Society*, *40*(1), 117–131. DOI: 10.1007/s00146-023-01832-9

Ju, N., Kim, T., & Im, H. (2024). Fake human but real influencer: The interplay of authenticity and humanlikeness in Virtual Influencer communication? *Fash Text*, *11*(1), 16. DOI: 10.1186/s40691-024-00380-0

Kaur, J., Mogaji, E., Paliwal, M., Jha, S., Agarwal, S., & Mogaji, S. A. (2024). Consumer behavior in the metaverse. *Journal of Consumer Behaviour*, *23*(4), 1720–1738. DOI: 10.1002/cb.2298

Kumar, A., & Shankar, A. (2024). Investigating the role of metaverse influencers' attributes for the next generation of services. *Journal of Services Marketing*, *38*(7), 816–838. DOI: 10.1108/JSM-09-2023-0320

McKinsey & Company. (2022, August 17). What is the metaverse and where will it lead next? Www.mckinsey.com

McKinsey & Company. https://www.mckinsey.com/featured-insights/mckinsey-explainers/what-is-the-metaverse

Ozdemir, O., Kolfal, B., Messinger, P. R., & Rizvi, S. (2023). Human or virtual: How influencer type shapes brand attitudes. *Computers in Human Behavior, 145*, 107771. DOI: 10.1016/j.chb.2023.107771

Press, G. (2024, May 1). *AI Influencer market will grow up to $6.95 billion U.S. Dollars in 2024.* What's the Big Data? https://whatsthebigdata.com/ai-influencer-statistics/

Rawat, A. (2024, September 5). *How AR VR is shaping the food and beverages industry – 10 use cases and real examples.* Appinventiv. https://appinventiv.com/blog/ar-vr-in-food-and-beverages/

Shrey. (2025, January 25). *The evolution of virtual and augmented reality: What's next in AR and VR technology?* Nextbrick, Inc. https://nextbrick.com/the-evolution-of-virtual-and-augmented-reality-whats-next-in-ar-and-vr-technology-2/

Sokolova, K., Vessal, S. R., & Perez, C. (2024). Home cooking in the digital age: When observing food influencers on social media triggers the imitation of their practices. *Psychology and Marketing, 41*(5), 1152–1171. DOI: 10.1002/mar.21973

Sorosrungruang, T., Ameen, N., & Hackley, C. (2024). How real is real enough? Unveiling the diverse power of generative AI-enabled virtual influencers and the dynamics of human responses. *Psychology and Marketing, 41*(12), 3124–3143. DOI: 10.1002/mar.22105

Storyclash. (2023, August 29). *Top 10 Virtual Influencers Rocking the Fashion Industry.* Storyclash. https://www.storyclash.com/blog/en/virtual-influencers/

Storyclash. (2023, August 29). *Top 10 VIs Rocking the Fashion Industry.* Storyclash. https://www.storyclash.com/blog/en/virtual-influencers/

Tran, K. (2025, March 27). *Topic: Social media in Southeast Asia.* Statista. https://www.statista.com/topics/10537/social-media-in-southeast-asia/

Twimbit. (2025, February 14). *State of VIs 2025.* https://cdn.twimbit.com/uploads/2025/02/13170410/State-of-virtual-influencers-2025.pdf

Twimbit. (2025, February 14). *State of VIs 2025.* https://cdn.twimbit.com/uploads/2025/02/13170410/State-of-virtual-influencers-2025.pdf

van der Harst, J. P., & Angelopoulos, S. (2024). Less is more: Engagement with the content of social media influencers. *Journal of Business Research, 181*, 114746. DOI: 10.1016/j.jbusres.2024.114746

Verma, A. (2024, October 20). *Understanding AR and VR: Transforming our world with immersive technology*. Medium. https://medium.com/@ajayverma23/understanding-ar-and-vr-transforming-our-world-with-immersive-technology-8d530aeff236

VIs Market. (2025, February 27). *Market.us*. https://market.us/report/virtual-influencers-market/

Vitsentzatou, E., Tsoulfas, G. T., & Mihiotis, A. N. (2022). The Digital Transformation of the Marketing Mix in the Food and Beverage Service Supply Chain: A Grey DEMATEL Approach. *Sustainability (Basel)*, *14*(22), 15228. DOI: 10.3390/su142215228

Vrontis, D., Makrides, A., Christofi, M., & Thrassou, A. (2021). Social media influencer marketing: A systematic review, integrative framework and future research agenda. *International Journal of Consumer Studies*, *45*(4), 617–644. DOI: 10.1111/ijcs.12647

Wibawa, R. C., Pratiwi, C. P., Wahyono, E., Hidayat, D., & Adiasari, W. (2022). VIs: Is the persona trustworthy? [JAMIKA]. *Jurnal Manajemen Informatika*, *12*(1), 51–62. DOI: 10.34010/jamika.v12i1.6706

World Health Organization. (2021). *WHO Results Report 2020-2021*. World Health Organization. https://www.who.int/about/accountability/results/who-results-report-2020-2021

Xiang, Z., Wang, D., O'Leary, J. T., & Fesenmaier, D. R. (2014). Adapting to the Internet: Trends in Travelers' Use of the Web for Trip Planning. *Journal of Travel Research*, *54*(4), 511–527. DOI: 10.1177/0047287514522883

Chapter 11
Group Recommendation System Using Sentimental Analysis for User Satisfaction

Abhishek Majumder
https://orcid.org/0000-0001-8451-0451
Tripura University, India

Shreya Roy
Tripura University, India

Shriya Chakraborty
Tripura University, India

ABSTRACT

Studies have shown that the existing recommendation systems provide misleading recommendations that actually do not meet the expectations of the tourists. Despite the fact that there have been efforts to build group recommendation system, they are primarily focused on offline settings. Moreover, combining individual suggestions into group recommendations or combining individual preferences into group preferences is a crucial element of group recommendation. Tourist recommendation system using sentimental analysis has given a better opportunity to the developer to know the user opinions for travelling. By extracting sentiment from group members, this work proposes an improved technique for group recommendation that boosts both the effectiveness and satisfaction of the users. The proposed technique uses clustering and similarity scores for recommending points of interests to the tourist

DOI: 10.4018/979-8-3373-2747-1.ch011

groups. For performance analysis the proposed technique has been implemented using Python. Performance comparison shows that the proposed scheme outperforms the baselines with respect to accuracy.

INTRODUCTION

Web-based communities are digital areas on internet where tourists on group do involve with one another and share information. Online communities are open to everyone, and well-known community websites are vying for new members. The community management system's functionality is just as important as members' active engagement in order to provide relevant information. An information management system that makes it simple for community members to access the information they need can cut down on search by collecting and evaluating advice from other users, evaluations from different sources and user attributes. Recommendation system helps the users to find information, products and services etc. One effective recommendation method is collaborative filtering (CF). It provides customers with recommendations based on the reviews of products by other users, giving ratings from users who are similar to them greater weight. Yet, current recommendation algorithms struggle to accurately aggregate single users' preferences into group's desire in different domains like tourism, excursions, book and restaurants. The application of sentimental analysis in a tourist recommendation system can improve the developer's ability to understand traveller opinions.

The goal of this study is to create a group recommendation system that uses sentiment analysis of the users so that satisfying recommendation is provided to them. The developer's comprehension of user opinions has improved because of the use of emotive analysis in a tourist recommendation system. The objective of this work is to create a system of group recommendations using sentiment analysis. This work provides a study on of tourism recommendation system that gauges user interest using sentimental analysis.

The contributions of this work are as follows,

1. A study of existing works on group recommendation system has been carried out. The work aims to improve user satisfaction by extracting user preferences using sentiment analysis in a group recommendation system. After studying many techniques it is found that sentiment analysis on group recommendation system has high effectiveness in tourism domain.
2. A group recommendation scheme using sentiment analysis has been proposed. The proposed system examines the preferences of each user and offers a recommendation that would be agreed upon by every member of the group.

3. Performance of the proposed group recommendation technique for tourism has been analysed. Performance comparison shows that the proposed technique outperforms the baselines.

Chapter Organization: Outline of this chapter is mentioned as follows. The current section discusses about the Group Recommendation System for tourists using sentimental analysis also about the motivation and objective of this work. The background and definitions are discussed in section 2. The existing techniques are presented in section 3. The proposed technique has been explained in section 4. Performance analysis has presented in section 5. The chapter has been concluded in section 6.

BACKGROUND AND DEFINITION

In this section the definitions and procedures related to the work has been presented.

Today, individuals need certain tools for helping them to identify and obtain the right information because the volume of information on the internet is expanding so quickly. The term "recommendation system" describes one of these technologies. Systems that provide recommendations make the exploration process easier.

Group Recommendation System

Group Recommendation System for tourism is meant to increase information sharing and raise the level of group members' satisfaction. Many group recommendation systems has been proposed in the tourism domain but using sentiment analysis can aid in improving comprehension of a user's attitudes, views, and feelings. The creation of this recommendation is the foundation of the group recommendation system for tourism. It generates recommendations based on group profiles using the common collaborative filtering (CF) technique and takes the user preference for better recommendation.

Collaborative Filtering System

Generally, CF systems give recommendations based on the subsequent three processes.

1. User profiles creation: Individual user profiles are created using past travel history or Location rating data of the user. The foundation of Collaborative filtering systems is user profile.

2. Formation of neighbor: Collaborative filtering systems employ machine learning methods to identify group of users as neighbors who have previously displayed similar behavior. Systems assess the degree of user preference similarity based on user profiles. For instance, they either have used similar products or assigned similar ratings.
3. Recommendation generation: After a target user's neighborhood has been established, CF systems employ data analysis to determine which items the target user is most likely to be interested in.

Sentiment Analysis

Sentiment analysis is a method that is used in natural language processing. It ascertains the text's emotional undertone which is known as opinion mining. Organizations employ this technique to pinpoint shared opinions on a particular good, service, or idea. ML, AI, computational linguistics, and data mining are all used in sentiment analysis to mine text for sentiment and subjective information, such as whether it is expressing good, negative, or neutral feelings.

The sentiment analysis has the following steps:

1. Data collection: The chosen and gathered text for analysis is identified. A web scraping bot or application programming interface must be used for this.
2. Data clean up: The data is cleaned and processed to remove noise, words and phrases that don't contribute to the text's overall emotion.
3. Features extraction: To determine whether a text contains negative or positive sentiment, a machine learning algorithm involves extracting text attributes. Machine Learning techniques such as the bag-of-words and word-embedding are used. The bag-of-words method keeps track of the terms that appear in a text. On the other hand, word-embedding method employs neural networks to examine words with related meanings.
4. ML model selection: The text is graded by a sentiment analytical technique utilizing a rule-based, automated, or hybrid ML model. Rule-based systems are frequently employed in fields like law and medical where a high level of precision and human management are required, as they perform sentiment analysis using established, lexicon-based rules. Deep learning and machine learning methods are used by automated systems to learn from data sets. The most realistic model is typically regarded to be a hybrid one that integrates both methods. These models provide various methods for determining the sentiment scores of texts.
5. Sentiments classification: Once a model has been chosen and it is being used to evaluate a text. It gives the text a sentiment score, which can be positive,

negative, or neutral. Additionally, businesses can choose to view the findings of their analysis at various levels, such as document level, which mainly relates to professional reviews and coverage, sentence level for comments and customer reviews.

6. Preprocessing: Pre-processing is done to change an original document into a processing form that is shown in the Figure.1. The pre-processing is followed by the formation of the noun similarity matrix. This is a symmetric matrix, and the extracted nouns are represented by the rows and columns. After preprocessing, the matrix's components are normalised so that the values may be assessed using various semantic similarity measurement standards. To achieve this, the values of each matrix elements are divided by an element with the highest value. The network for this matrix is then formed, with the edges representing semantic similarity of two neighboring vertices. The weights of such edges represent the extracted nouns from the pre-processing stage (nouns).
7. Cluster Formation: The pair of vertices is not related if there is no semantic resemblance between them. The edges are then removed if their weight falls below a predetermined level. The graph is then divided into multiple connected sub-graphs. Each sub-graph is regarded as a cluster in which the nouns have reasonable semantic similarity.
8. Extraction: Sentiment analysis's major objective is to uncover the emotions that users are hiding in their comments and to comprehend their perspectives on the topic. Each sentence's score is calculated by subtracting its negative scores from its positive ones. It is also considers emotionally charged emoticons. Each sentence's positive emoticons receive a score of 1, while the negative ones receive a score of -1 (Abbasi-Moud, Z. et al., 2021). Figure 1 presents the process for preference extraction.

Figure 1. Extracting a preferences

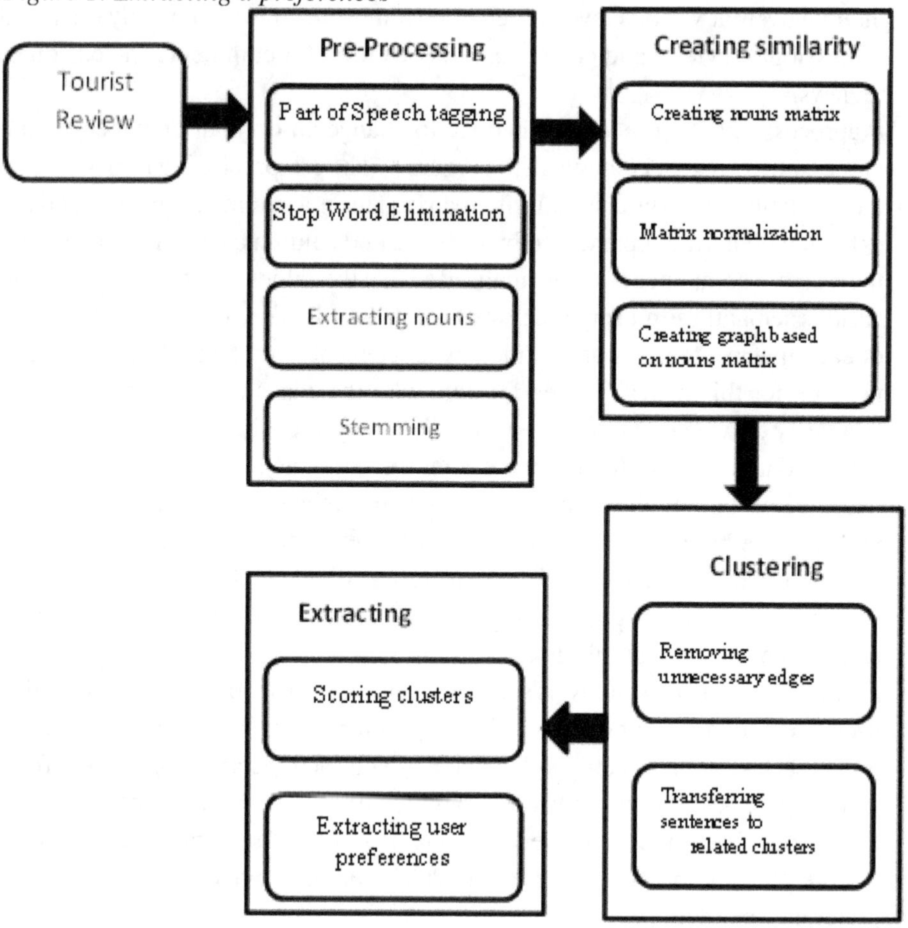

According to equation (1), each cluster's sentiment analysis score is equal to the average sentiment analysis points from its sentences. Here, $TF_{clusteri}$ represents the term frequency of cluster i.

$$Points_{cluster\ i} = TF_{cluster\ i} \times Points_{sentiment\ Analysis(cluster\ i)} \tag{1}$$

Equation (2) shows the sentiment points of each cluster

$$Points_{Sentiment\ Analysis^{(cluster\ i)}} = \frac{\sum Points\ of\ each\ sentence\ of\ (clustere\ i)}{Total\ number\ of\ sentences\ in\ (cluster\ i)} \tag{2}$$

The cluster that receives the greatest points is considered to be the chosen cluster (Abbasi-Moud, Z. et al., 2021).

RELATED WORK

This section discusses existing studies or pieces of research that are pertinent to the study's topic. This section presents an overview of the status of the research area and draws attention to the knowledge gap that the current study seeks to fill. Here few work related to tourism recommendation system and sentiment analysis have been discussed.

Tourism Recommendation Techniques

In recent years, a lot of studies have been carried out on tourism recommendation techniques (Sarkar et al., 2023). Abbasi-Moud et al. (Abbasi-Moud, Z. et al., 2021) stated that the number of attractions and the amount of information available regarding them on the web and social media are very large. The decision-making process for selecting the tourist destinations has grown increasingly challenging. The recommendation systems for tourism have developed into something that is both appealing to travellers and challenging for designers because they must be able to provide personalized services. Shafqat et al. (Shafqat, W. et al., 2019) stated that the user reviews on social networks for the tourist spots are used as a rich data source to pinpoint consumers' interests. The comments are pre-processed, semantically clustered, and sentimentally evaluated to determine a visitor's preferences. Components of these points of interest are taken from all reviews of the attraction that have been compiled by the users. The suggested recommendation algorithm compares a user's preferences with the attributes of attractions to offer the tourist hotspots that are most in line with their interests. Because of developments in internet apps and omnipresent communication technology, customers may now express their vacation or shopping habits, emotions, and reviews online. An et al. (An, H. et al., 2022) have stated that these online reviews are crucial for making judgments on the purchase of tourism-related activities and have a significant impact on how other users act. Many tourist recommendation systems have been proposed in recent years. The majority of recommendation systems are built on user assessments and ratings. As a result, users will receive recommendations of the places which have higher ratings or good reviews. Many domains, including decision-making systems, require text sentiment analysis. In addition to the other techniques like word frequency analysis and morphological analysis, research is still being done on the use of complicated neural networks. The suggested system connects many environmental factors that have an impact on tourism choice and provides more suitable choices through a series of phases. The suggested system consists of the spatial join approach, data collection, pre-processing, assessment, learning, and augmentation. The resulting evaluation index provides the ideal indication for demonstrating the influence of the chosen environmental factors on each tourism destination. Sarkar et al. (Sarkar et al., 2020) developed a tourism recommendation system named MULTITOUR. The technique recommends a list of itineraries from unvisited places. This is done using the point of interest (POI) visit history of the similar users. The distance among the POIs, itinerary popularity and tourist's interest have been considered while recommending the itineraries. Monte Carlo Tree Search algorithm has also been used for POI algorithm. Sarkar et al. (Sarkar et al., 2021) developed technique named PWP. Attractions with in POI are considered in PWP. In this technique also POIs will be recommended in such locations where the user has never visited. In PWP scheme the distance among the POIs, popularity of POI and interest of visitors are considered. For recommending set of itineraries NSGA-II algorithm has been used. In this technique the cost has been minimized. On the other hand, tourist interest and popularity have been increased.

Convolutional Neural Network (CNN)

Convolutional Neural Network (CNN) (An, H. et al., 2022) is a technology that is commonly used in image analysis. In sentence analysis, various techniques utilize CNN. The basic procedure entails extracting sentences composed of word vectors as a matrix. It is followed by the extraction and maintenance of contextual properties through the convolution of the word matrix with the notion of window, which serves as the Kernel (An, H. et al., 2022).

Sentiment Analysis Based Recommendation Techniques

Abbasi-Moud et al. (Abbasi-Moud, Z. et al., 2019) proposed an approach which extracts travellers' preferences from online reviews using text mining and sentiment analysis. To do this, nouns found in visitor reviews are first extracted and then clustered based on the degree of semantic similarity. Afterwards, each cluster receives a score based on its word frequency and sentiment analysis. Biuk-Aghai et al. (Biuk-Aghai, R. P. et al., 2008) developed a recommendation system to select mobile tourism multimedia. Geographical maps, photographs of popular attractions, explanatory text, and brief video clips are used to create the travel itinerary suggestions. The recommender system uses a fuzzy-logic-based module to determine visit/stay times for each stop throughout the entire journey and a genetic algorithm to create travel plans. Additionally, the algorithm considers user preferences and comments from earlier user recommendations. The technique extracts semantic recommendations for tourist destinations from geo tagged social media images. By leveraging a user's publicly shared photographs and taking into consideration the user's current context, this system has offered a method that utilizes collaborative filtering and context rank. It is a scalable approach to elicit tourist preferences for the recommendation. Transformer models such as Bidirectional Encoder Representations from Transformers (BERT) and Generative Pre-trained Transformer (GPT) (Kumar et al. 2025) blooming redefined sentiment analysis. It has grown for the field of multilingual emotion detection and sentiment analysis.

Group Recommendation Techniques

In order to estimate the unknown ratings of the candidate items, Christensen et al. (Christensen, I. et al., 2016) suggested an approach which integrates three types of profiles, namely content-based, collaborative, and demographic, to provide the individual recommendations. The method creates a group profile by examining all of the individual hybrid profiles and other group-related data in order to produce group suggestions. The group profile includes details about the participants, their connections, the original group preferences, and the projected group preferences. Yu et al. (Yu, Z. et al., 2006) uses merged viewer profiles that are based on the total distance reduction in a feature vector space to suggest TV shows to groups of viewers. A user account is displayed as features, with weights reflecting the relative relevance of the features (for example, genre, actor, and TV programme keyword). In the first phase, it chooses a feature subset to reflect shared interests using an aggregation approach, and then it establishes the appropriate weights for the chosen features. The technique demonstrates better performance when group members have a closer bond and have more in common (Yu, Z. et al., 2006). Colomo-Palacios et al. (Colomo-Palacios, R. et al., 2017) developed a technique which makes recommendations on the basis of previous visits, the current location, and social factors using tourist ontology. Sarkar et al. (Sarkar et al., 2022) introduced a technique named gTour for recommending set of itineraries to a group of tourists. The gTour technique is also capable of recommending new locations to the users utilizing travel history of similar user groups who have visited those unvisited places. Borda Score technique has been used for finding out category interests which are for the group. SPNE of Game theory has been utilized to suggest a set of itineraries to the group of group of tourists. In this technique each group member acts as a player. Actions of every other player will be observed by every player so that the wishes of every group member get fulfilled. Sojahrood et al,(2023) handled two main problems in POI GRSs, including the cold start problem in group-based methods and low accuracy. Here a hybrid method used for switching among different recommendation strategies based on the criteria of group history and similarity of group members' interests and preferences.

Collaborative Filtering based Recommendation Techniques

Ziegler et al. (Ziegler, C. et al., 2005) developed a recommendation system which offers suggestions to the users for products they might be interested in based on their previous preferences, purchasing patterns, demographic data, and other pertinent data. It has been employed in mobile, P2P networks, and ubiquitous environments in addition to e-commerce settings like Amazon.com and CD Now. According to Sarwar (Sarwar, B. M., 2001), collaborative filtering, also known as CF, is the most effective recommendation technique employed by several e-commerce systems, including CDNow.com and Amazon.com. During the recommendation process CF uses the item evaluations of neighbours, or people who share the same characteristics or preferences as the individual receiving the recommendation. According to Burke et al. (2002) hybrid recommendation technique leverages collaborative filtering with other well known techniques to alleviate some of the problems associated with collaborative filtering.

Apart from that there are various recommendation approaches are popular such as fairness in recommender systems (Ekstrand et al. 2012) that identify the unique challenges of any systems, and provide a conceptual framework to mitigating fairness issues. Conversational Recommendation System (Gao et al. 2021) interactive handles natural language-based user interface. It is dynamic and gets explicit user feedback using natural languages, while enhancing user engagement and user experience. Recently, security and privacy challenges of personalized recommendation systems are major concern. To deal with that federated learning (Javeed et al. 2023) introduced to enhance privacy and security along with low-latency network communication.

Comparison Table

In this section the existing techniques have been compared. Table 1 shows the comparison of some of the existing works.

Table 1. Comparison table

No.	Technique	Advantage	Disadvantage
1.	Recommendation Mechanism for Under-Emphasized Tourist Spots Using Topic Modeling and Sentiment Analysis (Shafqat, W. et al., 2019)	It finds a location which should be highlighted. Based on reviews and historical information, the recommendation of well-known locations is done.	If the learning rate is high, the performance of the model will not be accurate.
2.	Tourism recommendation system based on semantic clustering and sentiment analysis (Abbasi-Moud, Z. et al., 2021)	The proposed approach is designed to make personalized recommendation of tourist spots based on preferences of the tourist.	Contextual information has been overlooked, including route traffic, the conditions of different people, group users, and their surroundings.
3.	Recommendation System for Tourist spot using Sentiment Analysis based on CNN-LSTM (An, H. et al., 2022)	In this technique some of the processing of recommendation system is shifted to the mobile devices. Since mobile edge computing is utilized the load on the server gets reduced. The response time also becomes less.	Though the technique uses edge computing but still a significant portion of processing is done in the server. This will cause delay in the system.
4.	POST-VIA 360 (Colomo-Palacios, R., et al., 2017)	The system uses pervasive approach for data collection during initial visits.	From the technical point of view POST-VIA 360 is dependent on a given dataset. It also does not consider text from micro-blogging websites and facebook.
5.	GRec_OC (Kim, J. K. et al., 2010)	The technique has improved group recommendation process that increases member satisfaction on an individual and group level.	The technique did not perform any sentiment analysis.
6.	Sojahrood et al,(2023)	Handles low accuracy and the cold-start problem for groups with insufficient historical information	This technique is computationaly expensive
7	Wang et al.(2021)	The Deconfounded Recommender System (DecRS) focuses on the causal relationships between user representation and prediction scores, using backdoor adjustment that eliminates confounder effects.	This technique apply bias control to ranking targets but overlook the confounder effect of imbalanced item distribution, leading to potential trade-offs in recommendation accuracy.

PROPOSED TECHNIQUE

In this section the proposed technique has been presented. This work suggests a system for group recommendations that would increase both the effectiveness of the group recommendations and the pleasure of group members by extracting preference using sentiment analysis. It creates a group profile to reflect the collective preferences of the group and uses the modified CF method to generate a set of candidate recommendations. Rather than taking the ratings of some place for recommendation the proposed approach has used all the positive sentiment scores to recommend places. The goal of the suggested strategy is to boost information exchange and raise group members' satisfaction. It has a recommendation generation phase. In this phase, recommendations are generated based on group profiles using the standard collaborative filtering (CF) technique. Recommendations are subsequently refined using a sentiment analysis technique to increase user satisfaction. The top recommendations are suggested by taking the positive values from the sentiment score. Collaborative filtering is also used for the recommendation process.

Figure 2. Group recommendation using sentiment analysis

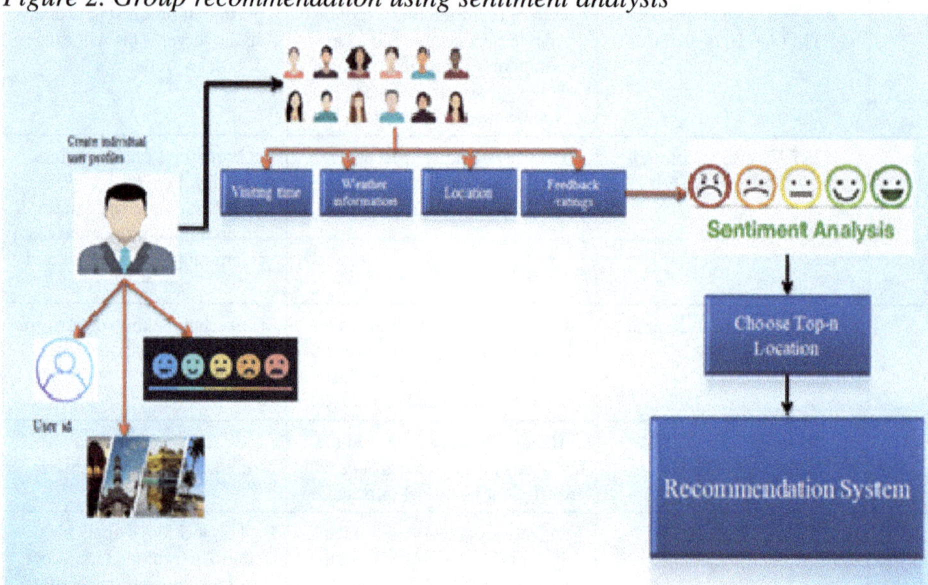

The proposed technique uses a clustering algorithm to group users based on their visiting patterns and ratings. First the data is prepared for clustering. All the ratings or reviews for each location across all users are collected. Then a feature matrix is created where each row denotes a user and each column denotes a location, with ratings or sentiment scores as the values. A clustering algorithm is applied to the feature matrix of group users. Finally, each user is assigned to a cluster based on their similarity in terms of visited locations and ratings.

A person's interests or preferences on goods are described in an item-based profile. It is also known as profile for users. It serves as the foundation for CF recommendation. Individual profiles are combined into group profiles using clustering.

Then sentiment analysis is processed on the data set of the group profile where the feedback/ratings are used to extract the sentiments. The Pearson correlation is used to determine how similar two groups are to one another. A larger number denotes a greater degree of resemblance between the two groups. The value of Pearson correlation coefficient will be between -1 and 1. The top-n recommendations are suggested by taking the positie values from the sentiment scores and by using the collaborative filtering. The overview of the proposed group recommendation system has been shown in Figure. 2.

The following steps show the working of the proposed group recommendation system:

Step 1: Create a user profile for each user based on his/her history of visits to different locations.

1. Initialize an empty user profile dictionary.
2. For each user:
   a. Create a new profile entry with the user ID as the key.
   b. Add the visited locations and their corresponding ratings or reviews to the user's profile entry.

Step 2: Use clustering algorithm to group users based on their visiting patterns and ratings.

1. Collect all the ratings or reviews for each location across all users.
2. Create a feature matrix where each row denotes a user and each column denotes a location, with ratings or sentiment scores as the values.
3. Apply clustering algorithm to the feature matrix of group users.
4. Assign each user to a cluster based on their similarity in terms of visited locations and ratings.

Step 3: Extract the reviews for each location from the user profiles.

1. Initialize an empty review dictionary.
2. For each user profile:
   a. For each visited location and its corresponding review/rating:
      i. If the location is not already in the review dictionary
   b. Create a new entry with the location as the key.
   c. Append the review/rating to the list of reviews for that location in the review dictionary.

Step 4: Calculate the percentage of positive sentiment scores for each location.

1. Initialize an empty sentiment scores dictionary.
2. For each location in the review dictionary:
   a. Initialize a count for positive reviews.
   b. For each review in the list of reviews for that location:
      i. Apply sentiment analysis techniques to determine the sentiment of the review.
      ii. If the sentiment is positive
   c. Increment the count for positive reviews.
   d. Calculate the positive sentiment percentage by doing division of the count of positive scores by the total number of scores for that location.
3. Add positive sentiment percentage to the sentiment scores dictionary with the location as the key.

Step 5: Identify locations with high positive sentiment percentages.

1. Set a threshold for the minimum positive sentiment percentage.
2. Initialize an empty list for recommended locations.
3. For each location in the sentiment scores dictionary:
   a. If the positive sentiment percentage for the location is above the threshold,
      i. Add the location to the recommended locations list.

Step 6: Recommend locations for each user.

1. Identify the cluster the user belongs to based on the clustering result.
2. Get the top locations with the highest positive sentiment scores within the user's cluster from the recommended locations list.
3. Recommend these top locations to the user as personalized recommendations based on collaborative filtering.

Algorithm 1 shows the algorithm of the proposed system. The process of sentiment score extraction is presented in Algorithm 2. Figure 3 shows the working principle of the proposed technique in a form of flowchart.

Figure 3.

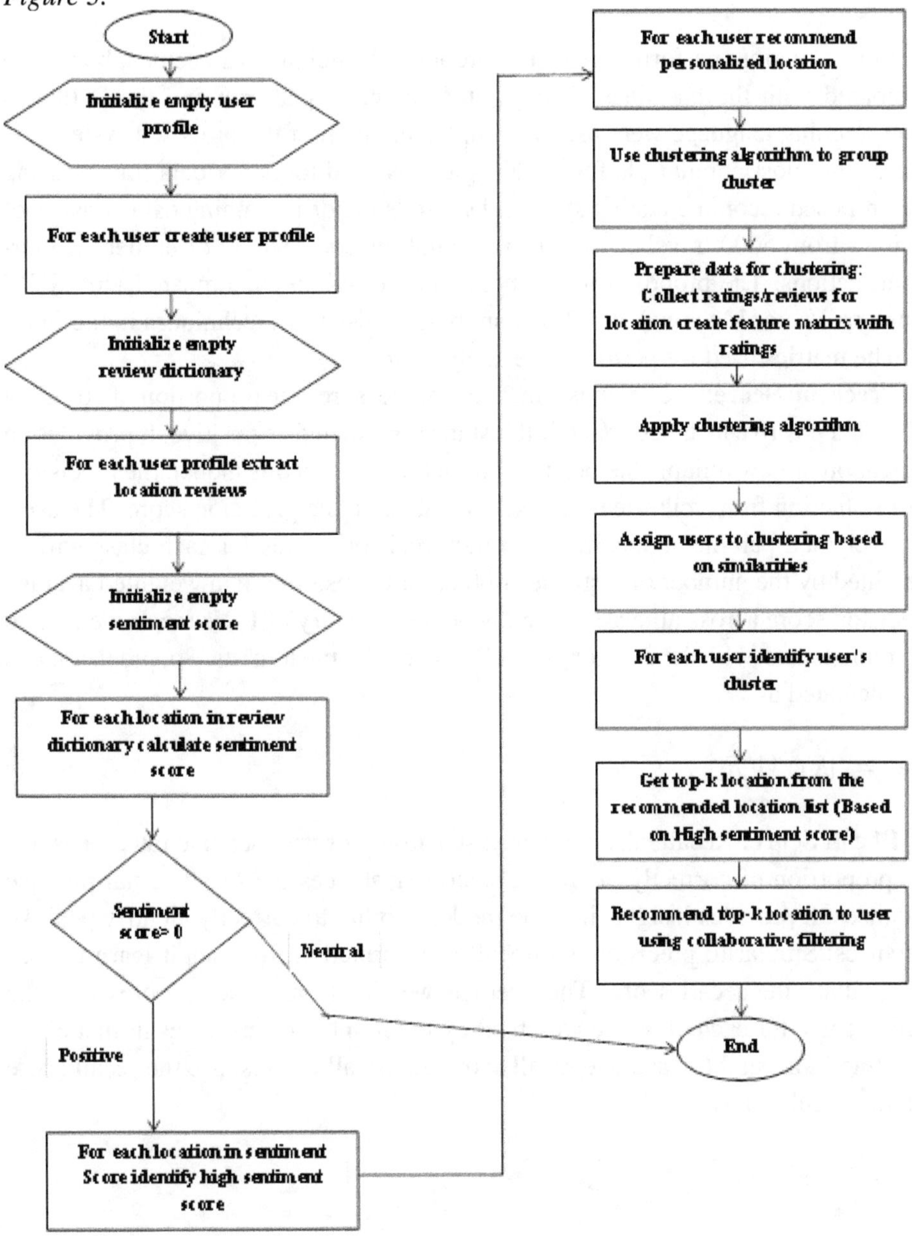
Start
Initialize empty user profile
For each user create user profile
Initialize empty review dictionary
For each user profile extract location reviews
Initialize empty sentiment score
For each location in review dictionary calculate sentiment score
Sentiment score> 0
Neutral
Positive
For each location in sentiment Score identify high sentiment score
For each user recommend personalized location
Use clustering algorithm to group cluster
Prepare data for clustering: Collect ratings/reviews for location create feature matrix with ratings
Apply clustering algorithm
Assign users to clustering based on similarities
For each user identify user's cluster
Get top-k location from the recommended location list (Based on High sentiment score)
Recommend top-k location to user using collaborative filtering
End

PERFORMANCE ANALYISIS AND COMPARISON

In this section, performance of the proposed technique has been analyzed and compared with the baselines. The jupyter notebook platform and the Python 3 programming language were used for implementation of the proposed system. As one of the most popular platforms, Kaggle was used to gather data for assessing the proposed recommendation system. Dataset's majority training data consists of reviews from 5000 travellers of various countries and reviews of numerous tourist attractions. The proposed recommendation technique is compared with SVM (Support Vector Machine) and Bayesian, both well-known techniques in the field.

The metrics used for performance analysis are,

Precision Score: Precision is a metric that measures the proportion of correctly predicted positive instances out of all instances predicted as positive. It provides an indication of how reliable the positive predictions are. In this model, the precision-score function from scikit-learn is used to calculate the precision score. The average weighted parameter specifies that the precision scores for each class will be weighted by the number of instances in that class, resulting in a weighted average precision score across all classes. Let, R be the category of POIs recommended to the tourists and V be the category of POIs visited by the tourists. So, precision can be calculated as,

$$Pre = |R \cap V|/|R| \tag{1}$$

Recall Score: Recall, also known as sensitivity or true positive rate, measures the proportion of correctly predicted positive instances out of all actual positive instances. It provides insights into the model's ability to correctly identify positive instances. Similar to precision, the recall-score function from scikit-learn is used to calculate the recall score. The average weighted parameter ensures that the recall scores for each class are weighted by the number of instances in that class, resulting in a weighted average recall score across all classes. So, the recall score can be calculated as,

$$\mathrm{Re}c = R \cap V|/|V| \tag{2}$$

Accuracy: This accuracy indicates the model's ability to correctly predict the sentiment (positive/negative) of the reviews. The accuracy can be calculated as,

$$Accu = R \cap V|/|R \cup V| \tag{3}$$

The implementation details have been mentioned as follows,

Model Selection: Logistic Regression was chosen as the classifier for sentiment analysis. The hyper parameters were tuned using grid search, and the best model with the hyper parameters (C=1, penalty='l2') was selected based on accuracy.

Data Pre-processing: The text data was pre-processed using TF-IDF vectorization, which transformed the text reviews into numerical features that the classifier could understand.

User-Item Matrix: The user-item matrix was created based on the training data, where rows represent users and columns represent tour locations. The matrix contained ratings (e.g., sentiment scores) or any other relevant information.

User Similarities: Cosine similarity was used to calculate the similarities between users based on their ratings. This similarity matrix was utilized to find similar users and generate personalized tour recommendations.

Recommendation Generation: The recommendation algorithm aggregated ratings from similar users and sorted them to suggest top-rated tours to a given user.

The proposed model achieves a precision score of 0.72 on the test dataset. An accuracy of 0.702 was also achieved. The accuracy of the proposed technique is 0.78. The performance metrics values of the proposed technique have been presented in Figure. 4 and Figure. 5.

Figure 4. Precision-score and recall-score of proposed technique

```
Precision: 0.7217663408094445
Recall: 0.702
```

Figure 5. Recommendation output with accuracy of proposed technique

```
Sentiment Analysis Accuracy: 0.78
Recommended tours for User 5:
        Sentiment_Score                 location  Groups
1024                1.0      Annapurna Base Camp       0
3303                1.0   Chitwan National Park        1
3324                1.0   Chitwan National Park        1
3329                1.0   Chitwan National Park        1
3331                1.0   Chitwan National Park        1
```

Figure. 6 shows a comparison of the proposed technique with SVM and Bayesian considering the accuracy. From the Figureure it can be observed that the proposed technique outperforms both SVM and Bayesian methods.

Figure 6. Comparison of accuracy of proposed approach with SVM and Bayesian

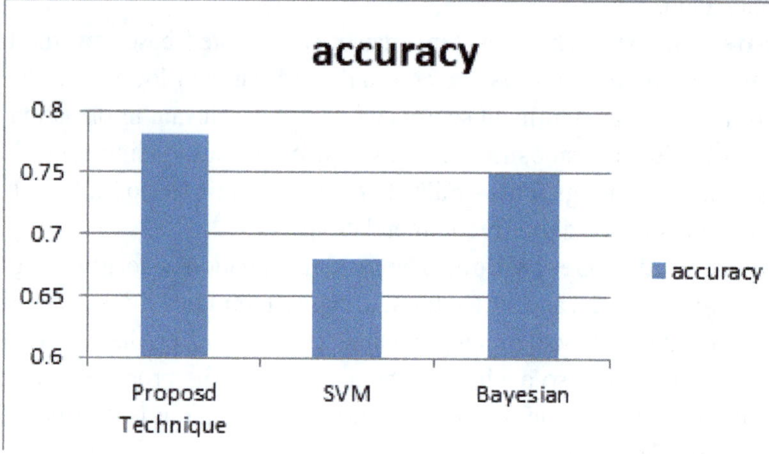

The proposed technique has been compared with the baselines considering four factors: group, clustering, sentiment analysis and top recommendation using positive score. The comparison has been shown in table 2. Most research relevant to suggestions for tourism destinations focuses on a small number of factors. Leal et al. (Leal, F. et al. 2018) have considered user preferences for recommendation of tourist spots. Two factors, including user preference and sentiment, are taken into account by Shafqat et al. (Shafqat, W. et al. 2019). Similar to this, subject recommendation process for group users has been developed by Kim et al. (Kim, J. K., et al. 2010). For recommendation the technique utilizes user preferences. By considering all of the positive values of the sentiment scores, the proposed method leverages additional features including group, and suggestions.

Table 2. Comparison Table

Works	Group	Clustering	Sentiment analysis	Top recommendations using the positive score
Leal, F. et. al 2018	×	×	×	×
Shafqat, W. et. al 2019	×	×	√	×
Kim, J. K. et. al 2010	√	×	×	×
Proposed Technique	√	√	√	√

A comparison of accuracy of the proposed technique with the baselines has been shown in Figure. 7. From the Figureure it can be observed that the proposed technique outperforms the baselines with respect to accuracy. This is because the proposed technique considers the sentiment scores and similarities among the users.

Figure 7. Comparison of accuracy with baselines

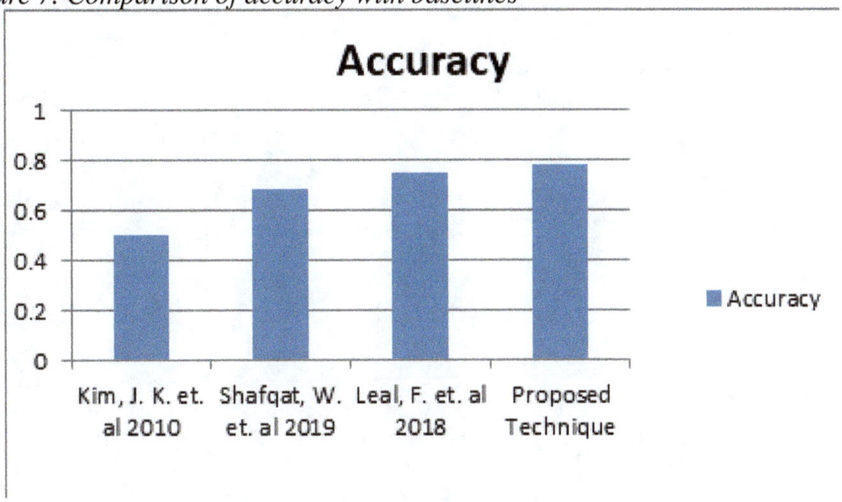

CONCLUSION AND FUTURE WORK

Existing recommendation systems offer customized recommendations to specific customers. For activities carried out by a group of people, they are therefore ineffective. In this work a point of interest recommendation system for a group of users has been presented. The recommendation is done based on user's preferences by doing sentiment analysis on user reviews and comments. The common topics are found in user reviews using sentiment clustering. This list is refined through sentiment analysis by highlighting favorites and unpopular choices. Collaborative filtering is used in the system during the recommendation process. The proposed system combines a sentiment analysis model with tour recommendation system. The sentiment analysis component accurately predicts the sentiment of reviews, while the tour recommendation component suggests top-rated tours based on user similarities and sentiment scores. The sentiment analysis has been extracted for the users for a better recommendation. After that Top-n locations has been recommended. The proposed system has been implemented for performance analysis. The performance analysis reveals that the accuracy of the proposed recommendation system is higher than the baselines. A characteristic based analysis has also been done. The analysis shows that the proposed technique is better than the baselines. In future, the proposed technique can be enhanced by incorporating the weather condition and traffic information. Recommendation of itinerary using the proposed technique also remains as future work.

REFERENCES

Abbasi-Moud, Z., Vahdat-Nejad, H., & Mansoor, W. (2019, December). Detecting tourist's preferences by sentiment analysis in smart cities. In *Proceedings of IEEE Global Conference on Internet of Things (GCIoT)* (pp. 1-4). IEEE. DOI: 10.1109/GCIoT47977.2019.9058397

Abbasi-Moud, Z., Vahdat-Nejad, H., & Sadri, J. (2021). Tourism recommendation system based on semantic clustering and sentiment analysis. *Expert Systems with Applications*, *167*, 114324. DOI: 10.1016/j.eswa.2020.114324

An, H., & Moon, N. (2022). Design of recommendation system for tourist spot using sentiment analysis based on CNN-LSTM. *Journal of Ambient Intelligence and Humanized Computing*, *13*(3), 1653–1663. DOI: 10.1007/s12652-019-01521-w

Biuk-Aghai, R. P., Fong, S., & Si, Y. (2008, December). Design of a recommender system for mobile tourism multimedia selection. In *Proceedings of 2nd International Conference on Internet Multimedia Services Architecture and Applications* (pp. 1-6). IEEE. DOI: 10.1109/IMSAA.2008.4753931

Burke, R. (2002). Hybrid recommender systems: Survey and experiments. *User Modeling and User-Adapted Interaction*, *12*(4), 331–370. DOI: 10.1023/A:1021240730564

Christensen, I., Schiaffino, S., & Armentano, M. (2016). Social group recommendation in the tourism domain. *Journal of Intelligent Information Systems*, *47*(2), 209–231. DOI: 10.1007/s10844-016-0400-0

Colomo-Palacios, R., García-Peñalvo, F. J., Stantchev, V., & Misra, S. (2017). Towards a social and context-aware mobile recommendation system for tourism. *Pervasive and Mobile Computing*, *38*(Part 2), 505–515. DOI: 10.1016/j.pmcj.2016.03.001

Ekstrand, M. D., Das, A., Burke, R., & Diaz, F. (2012). Fairness in recommender systems. In *Recommender systems handbook* (pp. 679–707). Springer US.

Gao, C., Lei, W., He, X., De Rijke, M., & Chua, T. S. (2021). Advances and challenges in conversational recommender systems: A survey. AI open, 2, 100-126.

Javeed, D., Saeed, M. S., Kumar, P., Jolfaei, A., Islam, S., & Islam, A. N. (2023). Federated learning-based personalized recommendation systems: An overview on security and privacy challenges. *IEEE Transactions on Consumer Electronics*, *70*(1), 2618–2627. DOI: 10.1109/TCE.2023.3318754

Kim, J. K., Kim, H. K., Oh, H. Y., & Ryu, Y. U. (2010). A group recommendation system for online communities. *International Journal of Information Management*, *30*(3), 212–219. DOI: 10.1016/j.ijinfomgt.2009.09.006

Kumar, M., Khan, L., & Chang, H. T. (2025). Evolving techniques in sentiment analysis: A comprehensive review. *PeerJ. Computer Science*, *11*, e2592. DOI: 10.7717/peerj-cs.2592 PMID: 39957863

Sarkar, J. L., Majumder, A., Panigrahi, C. R., & Roy, S. (2020). MULTITOUR: A multiple itinerary tourists recommendation engine. *Electronic Commerce Research and Applications*, *40*, 100943. DOI: 10.1016/j.elerap.2020.100943

Sarkar, J. L., Majumder, A., Panigrahi, C. R., Roy, S., & Pati, B. (2023). Tourism recommendation system: A survey and future research directions. *Multimedia Tools and Applications*, *82*(6), 8983–9027. DOI: 10.1007/s11042-022-12167-w

Shafqat, W., & Byun, Y. C. (2019). A recommendation mechanism for under-emphasized tourist spots using topic modeling and sentiment analysis. *Sustainability (Basel)*, *12*(1), 320. DOI: 10.3390/su12010320

Sojahrood, Z. B., Taleai, M., & Cheng, H. (2023). Hybrid POI group recommender system based on group type in LBSN. *Expert Systems with Applications*, *219*, 119681. DOI: 10.1016/j.eswa.2023.119681

Wang, W., Feng, F., He, X., Wang, X., & Chua, T. S. (2021, August). Deconfounded recommendation for alleviating bias amplification. In Proceedings of the 27th ACM SIGKDD conference on knowledge discovery & data mining (pp. 1717-1725). DOI: 10.1145/3447548.3467249

Yu, Z., Zhou, X., Hao, Y., & Gu, J. (2006). TV program recommendation for multiple viewers based on user profile merging. *User Modeling and User-Adapted Interaction*, *16*(1), 63–82. DOI: 10.1007/s11257-006-9005-6

KEY TERMS AND DEFINITIONS

Bayesian Statistics: To apply probability in statistical problems, Bayesian statistics is applied. In this technique the user beliefs on random event has been updated using mathematical tool. It is used to interpret the probability and measure the belief that an individual has over occurance of an event. With the availability of new evidence, prior beliefs of the users may change. Through Bayesian statistics new posterior beliefs can be calculated by incorporating evidence and prior beliefs using solid mathematical means.

Clustering: It is a form of unsupervised machine learning. Clustering is the process of organizing and classifying various observations, data points and objects in clusters or groups depending on their similarities. It can broadly be classified into two categories: soft clustering and hard clustering. In hard clustering one data point is allocated to one cluster only. It cannot be assigned to more than one cluster. On the other hand in case of soft clustering a data point may belong to more than one cluster with certain likelihood or probability. There are various clustering methods. The different methods are, connectivity based clustering, density based clustering and centroid based clustering. A cluster hierarchy is built in connectivity based clustering utilizing a connectivity measure. Based on the similarity, the item collection is organized and their distance is applied to find the connectivity measure. An area of high density is marked as cluster in density based clustering. These clusters are separated by low density areas. In centroid based clustering some data points are considered as centroids. Every data point will select its nearest centroid using algorithms like Euclidian distance. The points around a centroid will form a cluster.

Cosine Similarity: It is used to calculate similarity between vectors which is non-zero. It is computed based on cosine of angle between the two vectors. It is very popular in the field of recommendation system, search queries, document comparison, text analysis and other machine learning processes. Using the feature dimensions, the data objects' distance is calculated. If the distance is less, similarity will be higher. On the other hand, if the distance is more, similarity will be less. The cosine similarity can be calculated using the using the following equation, S_c (A, B) = (A.B)/(||A|| X||B||). Where, A.B = Dot product of vectors 'A' and 'B'. ||A|| and ||B|| = Magnitude of two vectors 'A' and 'B'. ||A|| X| |B|| = Regular product of vectors 'A' and 'B'.

Logistic Regression: It is used to perform classification task. It can find the probability of an instance belonging to a class. It is one type of supervised learning. Two data factors' relationship is analyzed using statistical algorithm in Logistic regression. Logistic Regression is of three types namely, ordinal, multinomial and binomial. In case of ordinal logistic regression the number of ordered types is more than two. An example of such order type is "very high", "high", "medium", "low". When there are more than two unordered types, multinomial logistic regression is used. Examples of this type of logistic regression are "bird", "cat", "tiger". In case of binomial logistic there are only two types. Pass or fail, 0 or 1 is the example of binomial logistic regression.

Machine Learning: There are many branches of artificial intelligence. Out of these, machine learning is one. In machine learning a model is developed through which the computer can learn from the data about the patterns. It enables the machine to learn, understand and think like humans. There are different types of machine learning techniques namely, Supervised Learning, Unsupervised Learning, Semi-

Supervised Learning and Reinforcement Learning. In supervised learning, the model is trained by labeled data. This trained model is later used for prediction or classification purpose. In case of unsupervised learning, data patters are found from the unlabeled data. In semi-supervised learning both unlabeled data and labeled data are utilized. When the labeled data are time consuming and costly this learning process is useful. Reinforcement learning is ideal for the tasks where decision making is necessary. It uses trial and effort method to learn. It tries to maximize the rewards.

Support Vector Machine (SVM): For regression and classification tasks SVM is used. It is one type supervised machine learning technique. For separating data into separate classes, SVM finds a hyperplane which is optimal in N-dimensional space. SVM has many advantages. In case of high dimensional space it is effective. If the dimension number is more than the sample number, still SVM is effective. It is memory efficient because it utilizes subset of points for decision making. Common kernels are available for usage in SVM. A custom kernel can also be specified according to the requirement.

Term Frequency-Inverse Document Frequency (TF-IDF): In information retrieval and natural language processing TF-IDF is used. It is a statistical method. In a set of document the importance of one word is found through this approach. There are two parts in TF-IDF namely, Inverse Document Frequency (IDF) and Term Frequency (TF). In IDF weight of rare words are increased. On the other hand, weight of common words is decreased. A term is likely to be more meaningful if it appears in lesser documents. So, IDF can be represented as: $IDF(tr, C) = \log\left(\frac{\text{Total number of documents in corpus C}}{\text{Number of documents containing the term tr}}\right)$. Here C represents the corpus of documents and tr represents the text which is under consideration. Very small or very large values are dampened using the logarithm. A term which appears in many or few documents can have a balanced impact through this. The problem with IDF is that a term may appear less in the document but it is also not relevant. Frequency of occurrence of a term in the document is not considered in IDF. On the other hand, the frequency of occurrence of a word is measured by TF. If a word appears very frequently it is important. TF is represented as, $TF(tr, dc) = \frac{\text{Number of times tr appears in document dc}}{\text{Total number of terms in dc}}$. Here, dc represents the document. In entire corpus, importance of a term is not considered by TF. The terms like "and" or "the" occur frequently in the document.

Types of Recommendation System: There are many techniques for recommendation system. These techniques can be classified in three categories namely, context filtering, content filtering and collaborate filtering. In context filtering, contextual information of the user is considered during recommendation process. Current context and series of user contextual information are used for predicting the subsequent actions of the users. In content filtering, item features are used for recommending similar items according to user preferences. In this category of techniques the interaction between the item and the user will be considered. Similarity between items and the users are taken into account for finding out the next user preferred items. Using the preference information of multiple users, recommendation is done in collaborative filtering. The technique predicts the items which may be liked by the users based on the items which are also liked by similar users. A recommendation system which combines both content filtering and collaborative filtering is known as hybrid recommendation system.

User Ratings: It is a media for expressing satisfaction or opinion expression of a user with respect to content, service or product. It may be represented using a numerical score on the scale of 1 to 5 stars, where 5 is the highest rating and 1 is the lowest rating. The user experience can be shared using reviews in addition to ratings. The new users can be benefited by the use of the ratings. Moreover, the ratings also help the business to enhance their services. There are different types of rating namely, thumbs up/down ratings, percentage ratings, number ratings and star ratings. One of the most straightforward and simplest rating systems is Thumbs up/down ratings. A negative rating is presented by thumbs up. The positive rating is marked as thumbs up. In percentage rating user opinion is represented using percentage. Rating of 100% indicates the best and rating of 0% represents the worst. In number ratings there are numbers from 0 to 10. Best experience is represented by 10 and the worst by 0. One of the most popular rating techniques is star ratings. Typically the scale starts from 1 star and ends at 5 star. 5 stars represent the best experience and 1star represents the worst experience.

Chapter 12
From Clicks to Conversions:
The Science of AI-Powered Consumer Engagement on Social Platforms

Parihar Suresh Dahake
https://orcid.org/0000-0002-2286-4120
Ramdeobaba University, Nagpur, India

Nihar Suresh Dahake
https://orcid.org/0009-0007-8971-9247
G.H. Raisoni College of Engineering, Nagpur, India

Janmejay V. Shukla
https://orcid.org/0000-0001-8042-699X
Ramdeobaba University, Nagpur, India

ABSTRACT

The traditional econometric models of advertising effectiveness, mainly focusing on the linkage between advertising spending and sales or similar objectives, are outdated, as they overlook and fail to capture the ongoing changes in advertising landscape in the online and social-media rich environment. Companies have limited understanding and tools to fully capitalize on social media's capabilities and potential in enhancing and revitalizing their advertising strategies. The aim of this research project is to contribute to this existing gap in the literature and provide valuable insights and tools for marketers and advertising professionals. AI and Big Data analytics tools are increasingly playing a significant role in digital marketing,

DOI: 10.4018/979-8-3373-2747-1.ch012

which is reflected in the emerging trends across numerous business sectors. Marketing strategies are progressively evolving from print and e-mail advertisements towards more dynamic and data-driven digital marketing solutions.

1. INTRODUCTION

Social media platforms are an important part of the digital marketing strategy employed by brands today, and there are an increasing number of social platforms based in India. The research paper looks at the social media environment in India and specifically social networking platforms that have recently been granted status by the Indian government. The paper includes a background to the research including the literature base, the objectives of the research, the methodology used and highlights the findings that will be presented.Brand personality-related content on social media ads increases consumer engagement, while directly informative content boosts engagement when combined with brand personality-related attributes(Lee et al., 2017).

A new startup realizes the potential of Artificial Intelligence (AI) in capitalizing on the opportunities provided by various emerging social networking platforms. Even ChatGPT enhances consumer engagement but raises ethical and privacy concerns(Paul et al., 2023). AI integration not only revolutionizes financial ecosystems, enhancing value co-creation, but also focused the consumer engagement, and firm performance(Manser Payne et al., 2021).This is particularly important in the context of the Government of India's decision to afford intermediaries, such as social networking websites, certain exemption from liability issues. The aim of the current study is to understand the manner in which AI-driven consumer engagement activities can, and should, be conducted on such social platforms to convert consumer interest into transactions. To this end, the current research analyzes 393,708 records of paid advertisements on two prominent social networking platforms. The study employs Natural Language Processing (NLP) methods to analyze consumer comments and feedbacks, and determine the characteristics thereof which managers should try to ensure in any planned consumer engagement(Sun et al., 2022). During recent years, social media usage has increased rapidly around the world, and it has become a key part of marketing strategy and a large part of marketing success. But despite the advancements in social media advertising research, there are still relatively unexplored areas in the subject, such as the use of NLP and AI in connection to online customer conversion.Metaverse commerce leverages AI for personalized shopping, improving consumer behavior analysis, purchase journeys, and predictive analytics in virtual marketplaces("Virtual Retail Algorithms, Behavioral Predictive Analytics, and Geospatial Mapping Technologies in the Decentralized Metaverse," 2022).

India has over 250 million social media users and the number has been rapidly rising, suggesting a promising audience for companies in the world's fastest growing market. There are a few key consumer engagement dos and some don'ts most companies, however, are still not able to capitalize on, but AI provides an excellent toolbox for improving content, targeting and posting decisions(Sun et al., 2022).AI optimizes consumer personalization, enhances predictive analytics, transforms customer engagement, and addresses ethical concerns in modern market dynamics("Enhancing Consumer Behavior and Experience Through AI-Driven Insights Optimization," 2024).The resulting research question for the study to answer is "how can AI be utilized for customer engagement and O2O social conversions?" In order to find out the best possible way of utilizing AI for social media customer engagement and online to offline social conversion optimization, the case company's social media efforts are analyzed and some artificial intelligence applications are tested. AI drives consumer engagement and repurchase intent, optimizing social media and satisfying experiences in hospitality(Nazir et al., 2023). The eventual aim is to increase the company's store-going customers generated through social media content, but the company also operates in several countries, which limits the research subject to the Indian market only. AI adoption is influenced by behavioral intention, performance expectancy, hedonic motivation, while technology fear and consumer trust moderate usage(Cabrera-Sánchez et al., 2021).Thus achieve a high level of brand consideration in users of a specific location or interest group, the main tasks are the advertisement on rapid-growing social media platforms – Facebook, Instagram, WhatsApp, and the control of an influencer marketing campaign(*How Social Media Advertising and Repetitive Marketing Messages Affect the Online Purhasing Behavior?*, n.d.)

In this new world where the customer is the king, the customer will be able to mold the company they wish for. Customer customization is, thus, the only solution for businesses aiming to attain success in the foreseeable future. Dynamic pricing, powered by machine learning, influences consumer purchase behavior, enabling personalized pricing models and enhancing e-commerce effectiveness(Gupta & Pathak, 2014). And Modern technology, combined with the power and extensive reach of social media, enables an unprecedentedly personalised connection with the consumer. Even Virtual influencers, driven by AI, enhance trust and purchase intention, offering brands cost-effective, reliable alternatives to human influencers(-Gerlich, 2023). Digital marketing and Artificial Intelligence, hand in hand, can be the delight upon which companies can catch the customer's attention and fulfill their tastes. Automatically curated content can easily be sold to the customers with the help of some digital marketing strategies such as web push-notifications. With the rapid growth of internet usage, brands have a vast array of advertisement opportunities available to them, but simply pitching umbrellas in this rainstorm of advertisement won't lead to customer conversion. The ultimate goal of the company would be to convert diverse online customer engagements to purchasing customers, and, for the entertainment of folk, spend some portion of the 2 lakh marketing budget.

2. REVIEW OF LITERATURE

For understanding the data, keywords are quite helpful. Keywords are the research subunits or nodes. To understand the research of a particular field, one can get a birds-eye view and check the network about who was working on a specific topic and how he or she contributed to that end.

Figure 1. All Keywords Analysis by Vosviewer

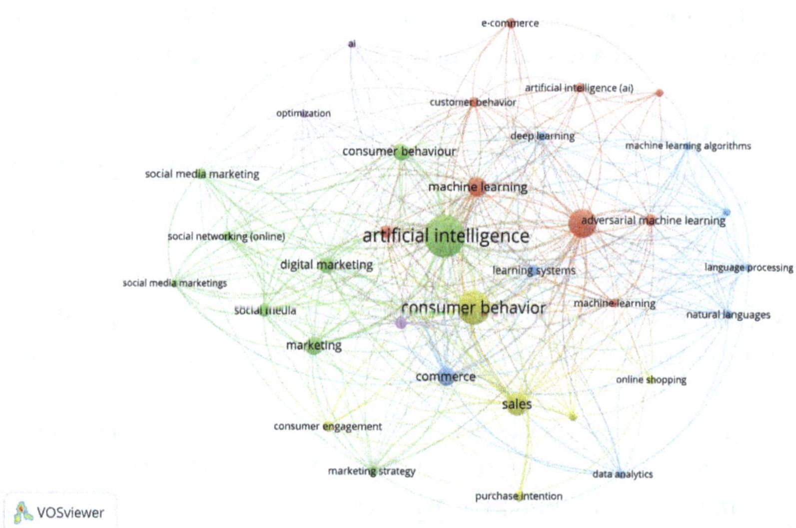

Figure 2. Author Keywords Analysis by Vosviewer

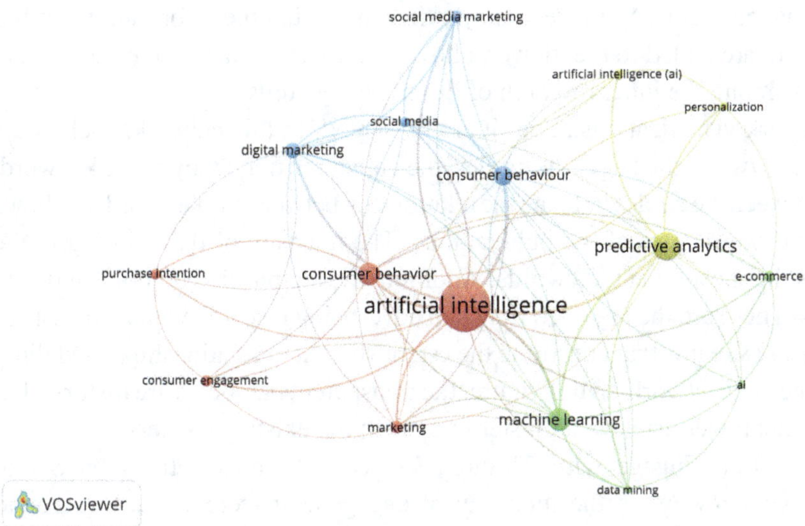

Figure 3. Index Keywords Analysis by Vosviewer

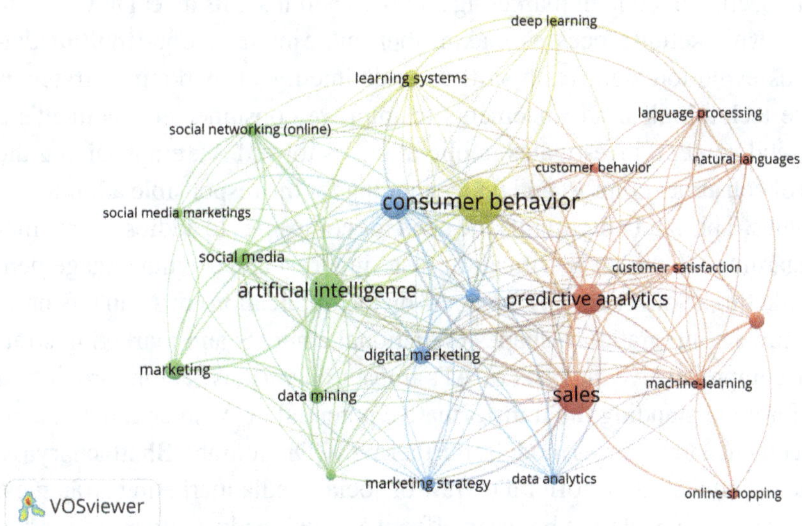

Hence, the author keywords and keywords plus analysis of the title and abstract of publications are presented. Top 20 relevant keywords in the title and abstract of the publications are development, model, data, generation, approach, detection, analysis, networks, design, method, system, algorithms, strategies, based, process, and performance according to frequency. After importing the information, author keywords data are added to the viewer, allowing it to understand the relations and interactions among the inner research of different keywords.

The network visualizations about it are presented. In this network, each circle represents a keyword, the larger the circles, the higher the frequency of the keyword. The lines between the circles indicate the relationship between the keywords. It shows the top 50 keywords plus of the publications. The intensity of the coloring in the lines shows the most recent keywords. Additionally, the purple parabolas indicate the clusters. These are the keyword trends in advertising research which consists of four significant streams that constitute the establishment of relationships modeling, brand, online, and network. In this figure, the transparent parabolas are historical as well as the mentioned irrelevant cluster to explain the existing clusters.

Consumer Can Engage with Through Clicks and Conversations on Social Platforms. After reviewing the interplay of engagement factors, the foreground hypothesis states that. (Dwivedi et al., 2021) highlights the transformative impact of digital and social media marketing, emphasizing AI, AR, and ethical practices for improving customer engagement, eWOM, and addressing research gaps, This early work sets the stage for understanding the foundational role of social media in consumer engagement.(Kose & Sert, 2017) further develop this narrative by examining the intersection of content marketing and AI. Their insights reveal how AI can enhance content marketing processes, making them more interactive and multimedia-oriented. This evolution signifies a shift towards intelligent marketing strategies that leverage technological advancements to improve consumer engagement's a broader societal context, investigates public attitudes toward AI, emphasizing the importance of consumer comfort and understanding for the responsible adoption of AI technologies. This study highlights the need for companies to address consumer concerns regarding AI, which is critical for fostering trust and driving engagement in digital marketing.(Soni et al., 2019)expand on the implications of AI in business, identifying how its integration reshapes operational contexts and marketing strategies. Their comprehensive analysis of AI's impact on various sectors provides a framework for understanding the transformative potential of AI in enhancing consumer engagement and business models. Furthermore (Dr. Sourabh Bhattacharya & Prof. Arpita Majumdar, 2020) offer a review of social media marketing strategies, illustrating the direct correlation between effective social media tactics and market performance. This study reinforces the premise that strategic engagement on social platforms can significantly influence consumer behavior and brand success. Subsequently (*Repositório Do Iscte – Instituto Universitário de Lisboa: The Influence and Impact of Artificial Intelligence in the Consumer Decision-Making Process:*

Comparing Generation X with Millennials, n.d.) delves into the consumer decision-making process, focusing on how AI can facilitate quicker access to information and enhance user experiences. By comparing generational responses, this research underscores the varying impacts of AI on different demographic groups, which is crucial for tailoring marketing strategies. In the Similar vein (He, 2022) provides a comprehensive overview of online media's role in sustainable business development, emphasizing the importance of social media in shaping consumer interactions and organizational performance. This work highlights the critical role of social media in modern marketing and consumer engagement. Eventually (Sun et al., 2022) investigate the application of natural language processing to analyze consumer opinions on advertisements, further illustrating the utility of AI in understanding consumer sentiments and preferences in marketing contexts.(Mathew & S, 2022) examine the role of AI in banking, showcasing how digital transformation enhances customer engagement and operational efficiency. This study emphasizes the broader implications of AI across various sectors in improving consumer experiences. Correspondingly (Sharma et al., 2024) extend the discussion by analyzing the impact of digital assistant attributes on millennials' purchasing intentions. Their findings contribute to the understanding of how AI-driven solutions can be optimized to enhance consumer engagement and drive sales.However (Varghese et al., 2022) discuss the pervasive influence of AI on consumer interactions, underscoring the potential for AI technologies to reshape customer experiences and engagement strategies across industries. In conjunction with this (Min et al., 2023) explore the applications of AI in consumer-driven food systems, highlighting AI's capacity to enhance food safety and personalized nutrition. This research illustrates the far-reaching implications of AI in addressing consumer needs and preferences in the food sector.Finally, (Zhang & Lu, 2023)investigate the impact of social AI on mental and social well-being, revealing its benefits for user engagement and mental health. This study contributes to the understanding of how AI can foster positive consumer interactions in a digital environment.The literature collectively underscores the transformative role of AI in enhancing consumer engagement on social platforms, particularly in the Indian context. As AI technologies continue to evolve, their implications for marketing strategies and consumer interactions are likely to expand, necessitating ongoing research and adaptation by businesses.

3. AI-POWERED CONSUMER ENGAGEMENT: CONCEPTS AND THEORIES

Artificial Intelligence (AI) is one of the most advanced technologies witnessed among brands, celebrities, and experts in consumer engagement on social media, to further improve the chances of conversion.

Figure 4. AI-Powered Consumer Engagement

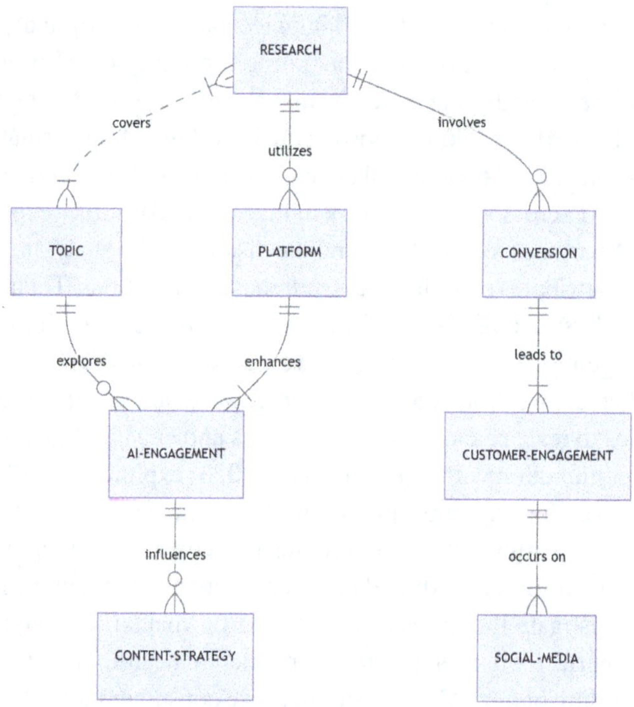

It is a common belief in the Indian market that consumer engagement implies the number of 'likes', 'shares', and 'comments'. However, consumers' engagement also thrives on a microscopic level, which is more than evident through the journey from sight, to door, to buy, and finally upkeep. The engagement is also a reflection of the fact that the intelligent systems on social platforms have started knowing the consumer quite deeply on these social platforms.

The academic community, along with multiple corporate organizations, agrees on the point that consumer buying decisions are stimulated by the sum of action – information transformation - feeling. The basic idea of this conception is that the involvement of action or impelling action should ditch the similar emotional reflection to resist purchase decisions. Multiple rhetoric devices have been explored for their potential impelling power. In this context, the electronic platform is certainly an opportunistic additional channel on which various types of media messages could be effortlessly, instantaneously, and actively created. With the enhancement of online shopping flourishing on social platforms due to the spread of the outbreak, new possibilities and challenges in PMDs have also emerged. As the young population in India is significantly drawn to social media and entertainment, brands can advertise on social platforms where the majority of the crowd spends the bulk of its allotted time.

4. OVERVIEW OF AI IN CONSUMER ENGAGEMENT

Today the overarching reality is that of digital media. This has given rise to social networking sites as a powerful mechanism in social media. One of the indispensable requisites of the digital media landscape is 'consumer engagement.' A term almost as elusive as its definition, that has critically tested the mettle of media scholars for over half a decade now. The theorists grapple with definitions, the practitioners with implementation.The integration of IoT and AI in predictive analytics revolutionizes modern marketing, enhancing personalization, customer engagement, and operational efficiency(N. S. Dahake, Gajghate, et al., 2024)

Figure 5. Role of AI in Consumer Engagement

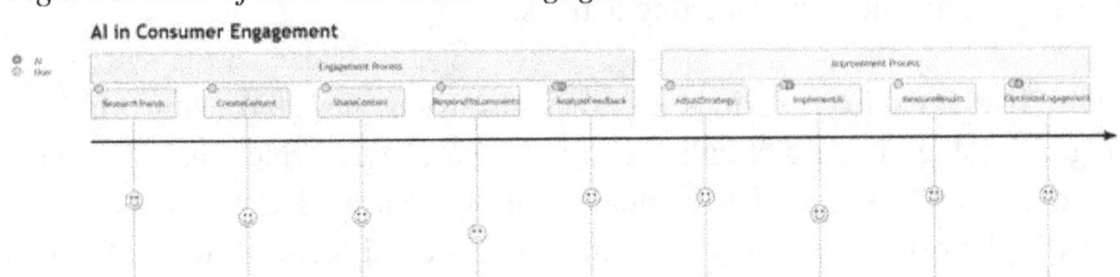

It is not to say that 'engagement' is restricted merely to cutting-edge websites. It is equally applicable to disparate mediums such as social networking sites, where it could span over a share, a like, a comment, or just an ad click. But when it comes to a platform of Facebook's immensity, it is often a daunting task to categorize these myriad forms. But on deep-dive contemplation, a uniquely interdisciplinary entity in Facebook 'consumer engagement' is unfolded: that of an esoteric flirtation existing surreptitiously on a morphing fulcrum midst cognition, behavioral attributes, and AI-powered communicative strategies.AI & Predictive analytics revolutionizes managerial decisions, improving accuracy, workforce management, and business execution, despite challenges in model reliability and expectations(N. S. Dahake, Suresh Dahake, et al., 2024).In this context, the present writing will try to estimate the consumer engagement on social networking sites using Facebook advertisements in a market like India, having a population of approximately five hundred and forty million internet users. At the same time, it will try to weigh the applicability of AI in understanding consumer perception and engagement concerning Facebook. From then on, the research seeks to learn the pertinent elements that appertain in refining the AI-powered consumer engagements efficaciously, inculcated in Facebook advertisements.

5. KEY TECHNOLOGIES FOR CONSUMER ENGAGEMENT

The main idea of Artificial Intelligence (AI) marketing is to let computers perform marketing automation and analysis to achieve high efficiency. To this end, AI is playing a critical role in a comprehensive machine learning infrastructure to initiate activities in a customer's journey. The first step is to use Natural Language Processing and the image detector to capture any group of online consumer posts. The next step is to create and deploy a machine print that can

(1) automatically comprehend the semantic meaning of consumer posts,
(2) capture individuality and emotional inclination, and
(3) demand effectiveness in marketing actions.

Finally, Big Data from various social platforms is analyzed using Machine Learning technology to predict online consumer purchases, which include a wide range of goods and services. The company can thus place advertisements on any social media platform accordingly to ensure a good value.Electronic word of mouth (eWOM) conversations in social media significantly influence consumers' purchase intentions, with quality, credibility, usefulness, and attitude towards information being key factors(Erkan & Evans, 2016). Each of these three levels of research poses challenges and opportunities that go beyond the system itself. Mastering the technological strategy of competitive intelligence can fundamentally train marketeers to become competitive and sustainable operators.Artificial intelligence enhances business model innovation, revolutionizing value creation, optimizing customer engagement(Selvakumar et al., 2025).There is a significantly increased popularity since recent social networking sites were created, and they have connected millions of people. For companies, using social networking sites is a novel option to engage in consumer business.Big Data enhances e-commerce predictions, improving customer personalization, demand forecasting, and operational efficiency, while addressing challenges in scalability(P. S. Dahake & Dahake, 2024). Nevertheless, distinguishing potential prospects who may in principle purchase their goods and services and provide personalized marketing information remains a big burden on advertisers.

6. THE SCIENCE BEHIND CONSUMER BEHAVIOR ON SOCIAL MEDIA

The social media revolution in India has witnessed phenomenal change in how people interact with each other, with social platforms emerging as the go-to channels for a new brand consumer interface; over the last couple of years, younger companies have particularly leaned on these ubiquitous platforms to launch and discuss their products. The irresistible lure of social media in India can be gauged from the numerous startups that are associated with the sector. With flag bearers like Zappfresh, Zipker, and The Derma Co., These firms have considerably grown their digital presence, with social media platforms forming the thrust of their promotional strategy. Branding and messaging initiatives including, but not limited to, celebrity endorsements, promotional prices, #Hashtags, GWP, UGC, Online Contest, and BOGOF have been implemented in a bid to solidify online presence and boost sales and thus the role of social media in driving these initiatives needs examination. If you are using AI to convert clicks to conversions, then this is for you! Converting a click to a conversion is the dream of all digital marketers. A simple, robust method employed to convert clicks into "safer" conversions is to run brand marketing campaigns alongside Click-to-Store campaigns. Nonetheless, the perfect catalyst for conversion is engagement with a consumer, which these Safety Blue Chip clients have been able to obtain through a robust science and AI-powered approach using Social Adverts. For those who are not yet in the knowledge loop, social advertising on Facebook and Instagram is very different from traditional advertising on TV or even traditional digital advertising on the web. Only a select few clicks on social media platforms result in actual store visits (Hölli, 2019). However, the marketing work of a click – viewed in such a campaign – has just begun. Now there are digital products like Social Adverts using all aspects of social media, AI, proprietary data, and advanced scientific modeling, products not just to satisfy clicks or views, but to engage consumers in their brand conclaves on social media platforms over long-term time horizons.

Using client data, over a 2-year collaboration period, on ROI measured conversion data –beit store visits or custom in-store engagements– and received authorized consumer data and accompanied store ID integrations, and aided by artificial intelligence, the mechanisms underlying consumer engagement are elucidated. Running these campaigns ensured an integrated digital media strategy for the TV campaign. Tools of data science are employed to demonstrate that, relative to the baseline of this integrated campaign, a click on a Social Advert significantly elevates the probability of engagement and significantly prolongs the time-to-store.

7. PSYCHOLOGICAL FACTORS

Artificial intelligence (AI) has been defined as the ability of a computer or other machine to carry out activities commonly associated with intelligent beings. This includes the ability to correctly interpret external data, perceive the environment, and use those learnings to achieve particular goals and tasks. AI has grown at a rapid pace in recent decades. It promises significant and transformational economic and social impacts in the future. One of the most extensively explored applications of AI research has been the development of targeted advertising systems. As a result, the advertising effort has increased dramatically. AI technologies are increasingly being used by online marketing firms to personalise online advertisements, which has sparked a vibrant debate. Some fear that such individual targeting could lead to political segregation and manipulative ad delivery, while others contend that targeted advertising can improve the effectiveness of informative campaigns.

Figure 6. Influencing Psychological Factors Artificial intelligence

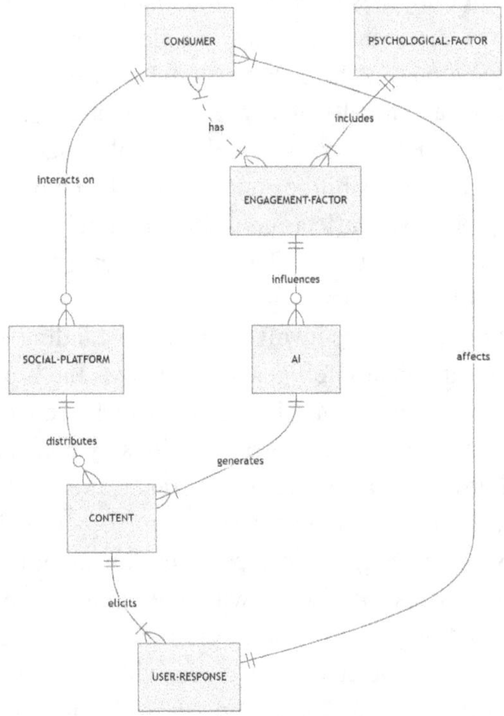

Consumer perception of advertising is indeed a fascinating topic since it does not only provide revenue for media companies but also helps businesses to compete. Influences of advertising have penetrated people's daily life regardless of whether they are watching TV or browsing web pages. Advertising is always trying its best to grab people's attention and convince them to buy products or services. One of the important factors of advertising is mass customization which states that a few basic versions are tailored to broad categories of people. Meanwhile, advertising is somehow successful due to its implicit and emotional manipulation of customers. Furthermore, advertising tries to create a connection between memorable short clips or graphical advertisements that contain a brand and our satisfaction.

8. CULTURAL INFLUENCES

Culture makes people's behavior be consistent with other people's values. National culture can influence consumer behavior, the nature of society and the manner of economic preference. Indian culture is full of rituals and beliefs, which encourages the need for cultural and moral standards. India's national culture primarily involves three characteristics: collectivism, strong domination, and high moral transcendence. These features determine a society's unique interpretation of emotions. Customer brand engagement, a three-dimensional concept, can enhance customer relationships, retention, and loyalty in marketing(Hollebeek, 2011). Relations with society tend to favor a social comparison and betrayal, inducing a tension between culture based on social responsibilities and cultural focus on personal happiness. Influencer marketing positively affects consumer trust in branded content on social media through informative content, influencer trustworthiness, attractiveness, and similarity to followers(Lou & Yuan, 2019).

Some AI impact on businesses involves the understanding of consumer behavior, the application of artificial intelligence humanizes the brand, assists in sales, and automates activities; the use of AI chatbots, which reduces customer waiting time; AI translator can interpret various publications by consumers and help businesses respond to them; AI analyzes data that creates the most interesting content for visitors; cloud technologies allow consumers to copy the displayed product to the social network wall; AI suggestion supervises consumer engagement with the website and sends messages focused on what the client can be interested in at a given point. Brand trust plays a key role in generating customer commitment and loyalty, especially in high involvement situations, with a stronger effect than overall satisfaction(Delgado-Ballester & Luis Munuera-Alemán, 2001). These Conclusions from AI and culture impact on consumer engagement, in social platforms, in respect of national culture influence on emotion content and the user's reaction to AI advertisements; these engagement aspects were analyzed in respect of India.

9. AI APPLICATIONS IN SOCIAL PLATFORM ENGAGEMENT

Introduction of consumer engagement is of interest to advertisers and social media providers. It is a strategy utilized to build a long-term relationship between customers and advertisers. The advance of social media has drastically transformed brand promotion due to develop a user-oriented advertisement strategy. In the context of social media, advertising is less intrusive. Instead, advertisers urge to involve users actively. Social media facilitates consumer social interaction, increasing trust and intention to buy, with perceived usefulness of a site also contributing to this effect(Hajli, 2014). This can be seen in various social media platforms such as Twitter, Instagram, Facebook, and others. In terms of consumer engagement, above platforms facilitate like, share, comment or tag options to involve in the discussion. This follow-up behavior is influenced by individual factors and advertising strategy. The involve of artificial intelligence as brand assistance offers an accurate strategy to increase consumer engagement. Additionally, it factors cognitive, affection, and concentration toward the advertising campaign. It uses a big data approach on customer notation on collaborative matrices from social media platforms. A novel algorithm of ternary kernel density elaboration aids to classify text into secondary context, principal context, and status architecture, all leading to a paradigm of the consumer expression viewpoint. Live streaming services like Facebook Live can increase customer engagement and trust in small online sellers, with symbolic value directly and indirectly affecting engagement through trust in sellers and product trust(Wongkitrungrueng & Assarut, 2020).On account of this User-generated social media communication positively influences brand equity and attitude, while firm-created social media communication only affects brand attitude, both of which positively impact purchase intention across different industries(Schivinski & Dabrowski, 2016).Most importantly (Voorveld et al., 2018) Social media engagement varies across platforms and is influenced by users' experiences with and evaluations of advertising on each platform.Because Social media use positively impacts consumer-brand relationships, especially when consumers associate human characteristics with brands and avoid uncertainty(Hudson et al., 2016).An Induced by all of this Social media's future in marketing will be shaped by nine themes, influenced by consumer, industry, and public policy, affecting marketing strategies and consumer engagement(Appel et al., 2020).

10. PERSONALIZATION AND RECOMMENDATION SYSTEMS

India is now Netflix's fastest growing viewer market. Six years ago, Indian households had an average of 8 channels – but now, thanks to online platforms, that number stands at 245. India is building cellphone towers faster than anywhere else in the world, and is expected to be home to more social network users than any other country by the end of the year. And the Indian government is so well aware of the power of social platforms that it has banned en-masse the Chinese ones. From clicks to conversions, it's a whole new world. So how can today's marketing executives catch this smart engagement boom? Let's dive into the AI-powered consumer engagement world on social platforms in India today. Social media marketing plays a crucial role in advertising, electronic word of mouth, customer relationship management, and firm brands and performance(Alalwan et al., 2017). After squandering a paycheck's worth of time, in the pursuit of a watch, only to be deep-learnt into purchasing three streetwear kurta XLs, this piece adds the feather of a BSc (Hons) in Artificial Intelligence to a bow-tie in semi-supervised learning. The ancient Indian philosophy of Rasa states that art creates emotions in audiences. From time to time, it was also marketed that way; when one brokered for the appreciation of the latest sculpture, perhaps. Consumer behaviour, consumer decision theories, social influences, consumer attitudes, brand choices, all seemed poltergeist to the erection of a 'female-sculpe' realm. But with new AI-powered recommendation systems as sophisticated as Facebook, with a social network pushing 621 million users with a $3.5 trillion e-tail market the sweet science of datapoint catalogue to please a Rasa patron is alive once again. You click on a, perhaps fancied on Instagram, product; then click on another; then a stoop of the third; 'here's a 14% off!' – ooo and XL, too? Position yourself indicators: a generous benefactor of the AI bid, orders almost all of the garments he clicks.

11. CHATBOTS AND VIRTUAL ASSISTANTS

Advancements in AI-powered social platforms with extended capabilities have now allowed businesses to create and manage highly targeted advertisements, ensuring optimal customer reach and engagement. For instance, Instagram—having grown as a dominant influencer platform among Indian youth—regularly uses its platform capabilities to allow personalization of posts and user suggestions. A study reports that with over 150 million users in India, Instagram is ranked the second-most used platform, influencing the purchasing decisions of 63% of users. With the surge in social commerce in India, brands have taken to exploring new-more intimate approaches via influencers, content, and partnerships. The concept of anthropomorphism reflects consumer interaction, favor, and adaptation to messaging dialogue produced by chatbots/virtual assistants. Anthropomorphism influences consumer response in physical settings through use of physical anthropomorphic device embodiments increasing holding length, click rate, and satisfaction. Physically anthropomorphic embodiments improve customer experience via user-machine interplay as demonstrated in robot embodiments producing a more advantageous spectator experience compared to a television with identical statistics. Although physically anthropomorphic devices enhancing customer experience is indicated in previous research, the consumer response and effect in agent-virtual/physical anthropomorphic systems increase customer satisfaction. Hostile form embodiments positioning agents where they face clients increase admiration, aesthetic and suitable design and conveying desirable behavioral qualities to customers (Klein & F. Martinez, 2022).

12. ETHICAL CONSIDERATIONS IN AI-POWERED CONSUMER ENGAGEMENT

The transforming world of digital marketing, especially in emerging digital markets like India, has made a radical shift from mere search and social media marketing channels to AI-powered audience engagement at every stage of the consumer decision journey. Indian digital consumer and audience behavior exhibit some typical complexities that are quite different from the mature Western digital markets. The overarching theme of the research questions remains about how digital marketing will evolve in India over time with new technologies such as AI-powered marketing approaches. How does a consumer behave in the digital mode compared to offline or in other Western markets? There are some suggested research objectives: 1. Identify the role of changing digital behavior of prospective consumers and the role of AI-powered marketing tools in India. 2. Investigate the role of potential multi-layer interactions of AI-powered digital marketing channels on social media concerning digital consumer behavior. 3. Explore significant consumer engagement and purchase behavior changes following target marketing strategies by AI in a social platform ecosystem (Sun et al., 2022).

The dilemma lies in ensuring that the direct benefit of such AI-powered consumer engagement must target the target consumer and help them to monitor and refine their choices, but at the same time, it should not manipulate the consumer and end up as a biased target marketing approach. Besides, dealing with digital consumer behavior in emerging markets is always tentative and hard to model. So, different case studies will be considered to determine a holistic empirical solution. In this context, user journey data is simulated from standard game theory-based models, and time-series logit adaptive state-space modeling is employed to capture the change under the influence of different intervention policies intended to analyze direct and indirect network effects of AI-powered channels as a new addition to game theoretical interventions. The impact of different AI-based marketing tools in a social media environment in a holistically interpreted consumer behavior model completes the analysis (Hermann, 2022).

13. SUCCESSFUL CAMPAIGNS

Successful Campaigns: “Fogg” is the short form of the model for understanding behaviour by BJ Fogg. He has performed a lot of work in the field of understanding and changing behaviour. This theory identifies the components able to increase the frequency of requested behaviour. Moreover, the persuasive system need to enable capability to request behaviour, the user to perform the behaviour, and motivation to behaviour, all three at the same time. The social platforms have realised work with firms, which enables the smooth conclusion of advertising campaigns on platforms, such as Facebook, specially made to adapt to the local Indian context. Understanding clicks and consumer engagement of the campaigns that promote a post, product or service of a brand on Facebook is of importance. Companies must merge social media programs with customer relationship management to facilitate collaborative social experiences and dialogue that customers value, overcoming the perception gap between customer needs and company offerings(Heller Baird & Parasnis, 2011). A novelty of the research is to investigate how standard and personalized advertising perform on social platforms of India. A platform aimed at enabling clicks or facilitating conversions is analyzed. Before conducting the campaign test, the related work is researched which is the basis for the formulation of the following research questions. On Indian social platforms, what sort of content advertising ends with the highest conversion rate? On Indian social platforms, what sort of content advertising is the most successful? What are proper age categories for advertising brands on Indian social platforms? Insight will be provided into how established and personalized ads operate in social platform atmosphere of India. The presented research will disclose what form of product or service advertising informs most conversions. Numerous firms all over the world meet each other in a very competitive world. Frequent updates and incentives for participation are crucial for consumer engagement in branded social media content, while experiential, image, and exclusivity messages enhance customer engagement(Ashley & Tuten, 2015).The intensity of competition forces the businesses to implement more and more advertising and promotional campaigns. Although this causes the rise of potential sales forecast and market equilibrium, it is more severe to accomplish and sustain a location in a dynamic world. Advertising message that aims to inform (by stressing a brand and its brand features), remind (by informing to stay and retain a brand in mind), or persuade (by influencing potential customers to buy a product or use a service) (Hölli, 2019). Consumers are expected to purchase after a purchase. It all starts with campaigning and several various variables need to be considered to maximize success. How often once an ad is shown to viewers, they want to press on it depends on the nature of the ad and its environment.

14. AI INNOVATIONS

The global artificial intelligence (AI) market size is booming. It reached a worth of 40.74 Billion in 2020 from 25.00 Billion in 2018 and will reach 997.77 billion in 2026. The AI sector got propelled further due to COVID-19-induced lockdowns, which led to alterations in office, work culture, and retail. The social distancing norms followed for nearly two years turned the focus on video conferencing and chat apps.User-generated content (UGC) has a stronger impact on consumer purchase behavior than marketer-generated content (MGC), with both content types influencing purchase decisions through embedded information and persuasion(Goh et al., 2013). And AI played a crucial role in the expansion of these online video coaches and even transformed a few basic apps into an imaging tech platform. Social Media giants like LinkedIn, Instagram, and Twitter are still working well with in-app advertisements, video guides or stories, and live feeds on several niches attracting youth and working professionals.

Figure 7. Simplifying way of AI Innovations

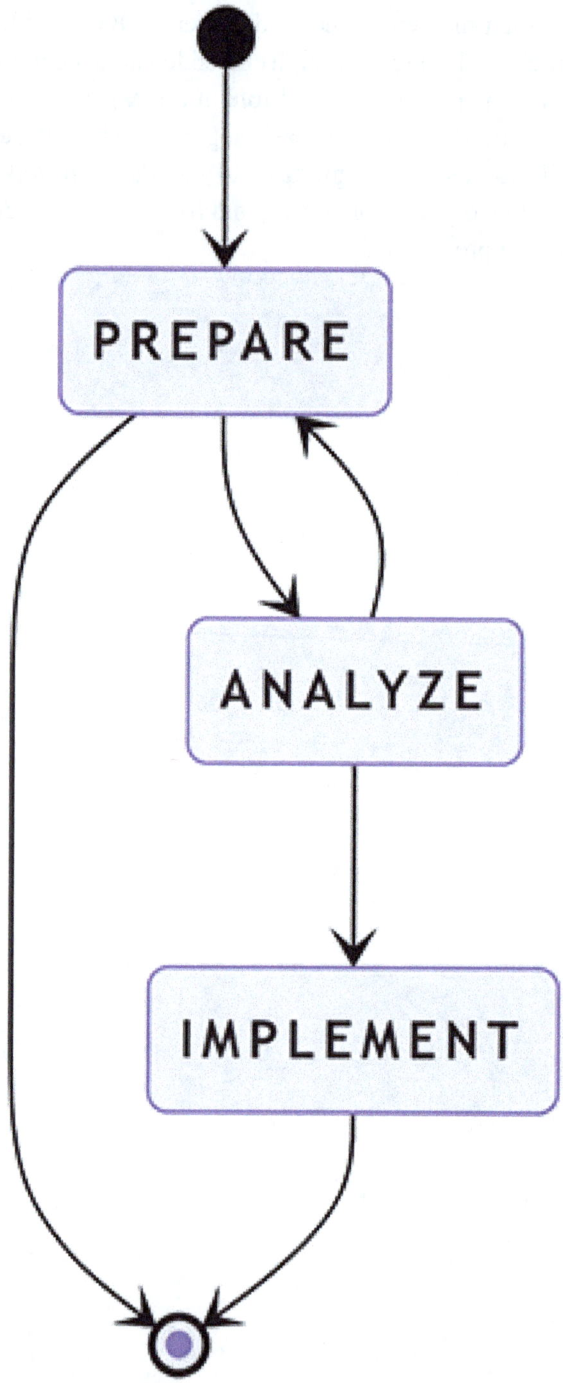

This has opened a big platform for advertisers. India being the second-most populous country and having more than 650 to 700 million internet mobile users, contributes $6 billion to global social media by advertisement business. AI can enhance customer engagement by standardizing routine tasks, personalizing data-rich services, and fostering relationships(Huang & Rust, 2021).AI in social media business in India has evolved by tracking digital products, the services the user gaze, dawdles, goes through, buys and its posting and fetching, sharing on social media, the audience involved, brands followed, advertisement clicks and likewise more. Consumer brand engagement (CBE) in social media settings is influenced by consumer'self-brand connection' and 'brand usage intent,' providing a platform for further research in this emerging area(Hollebeek et al., 2014). The same came to fore in the previous paragraph by the user behavior study of advertisement activity on Instagram in India. Keeping up basic ad-remnants such as the Audience, the Placement, the Budget, and the Creativity, one can optimize creation and dissemination of, for the story and news feed advertisements and can determine whether to However, there are diverging trends across firms depending upon their splurge on Stories in Place of or in adjunct with News Feed advertisements.

15. CHANGING CONSUMER PREFERENCES

The rapidly growing popularity and prominence of social media platforms have engendered consequential shifts in consumer habits, preferences, and tastes. Today, online social media platforms have become the quintessential haunt, cook, study, and socialize venues. Firms adopt digital marketing and social media to innovate communication and co-create content with customers, but must focus on relationship-based interactions to improve engagement.(Tiago & Verı́ssimo, 2014). The Internet and online social media have offered unrivalled opportunities for companies to tap into this boiling cauldron, and astutely engage with target demographics to peddle the wares. Within this transmogrifying online consumer milieu, the incumbent study sought to investigate the consumer engagement behavior of varied Generation Y cohorts in India. On the flip flop of the coin, e-commerce also proffers bounteous benefits for consumers. The ease of understanding about the products on the e-commerce platforms, purchasing pre-eminent commodities from the best available alternatives, and reading sundry unbiased reviews, provide anonymity and save time (Sun et al., 2022). Content type, media type, and posting day and time significantly influence customer engagement on Facebook brand pages, with different factors affecting engagement levels(Pletikosa Cvijikj & Michahelles, 2013).Not to mention, the readymade visibility of the latest trends and discounts, thorough and meticulous price comparisons, elucidations about the authenticity of commodities and plethora of secure and versatile payment methods at the disposal. Furthermore, with diminished offline shopping spaces, the competitive market prices in the online marketplace are intensifying ruckus and gashing gigantic discounts.

16. LESSONS LEARNED

The application of AI to automatically trigger actions according to data signals, called cost per action (CPA) on social platforms, will be the natural evolution of consumer engagement. Engagement by brands with social users will be data driven and robotic conversational agents (chatbots) will eventually displace creative personnel as is the case for dynamic creative on online platforms. Further on, interfaces that aggregate consumer side data across platforms will become essential for efficient consumer engagement. Patterns in this aggregate data will lead to user models that inform the shift in advertising resources from user-level to model-level, as well as to the early testing of entire user-journeys before expensive deployment (Korniichuk & Boryczka, 2021). Over the past five quarters, the rock-solid performance trend was established while pursuing the single objective of maximizing the total volume generated across each stage of the consumer journey. Social media-based brand communities positively impact community markers, value creation practices, and brand trust, leading to increased brand loyalty through brand use and impression management(Laroche et al., 2012).Eventually the Social media peer communication positively influences consumer socialization, leading to increased product involvement and purchase decisions, with uniqueness needing moderating the impact of peer communication on product attitudes.(Wang et al., 2012)Meanwhile, the dynamic targeting strategy, leveraging video for top of funnel targeting, data events for middle of the funnel, and DCO for remarketing, was tested at scale in 14 quarters. Parasocial interaction theory can help brands foster positive consumer-brand relationships in social media environments, driving increased loyalty intentions and willingness to provide information(Labrecque, 2014). It was learned that static video at the top of the funnel is as good as blend video, and only half as effective as 15" video. Moreover, video in carousel at the top of the funnel is not recommended. Another finding is that long form at the top of the funnel works best. Stories must also be viewed at the end, and the growth of the user flow of a story is often worth delaying the ticket video. Preference is for a stop and start DCO rather than fanning the fill until it burns out. Finally, an aggregates experiment was conducted that seamlessly resolved user targeting conflict between ROAS and off-CTC campaigns, informed ROI model at the industry-level, and had 6.6% improvement.

17. RESULT & DISCUSSION BASED ON THE LITERATURE

AI (Artificial Intelligence) is a buzzword nowadays. A complex field revolved around building machines capable of human-like thinking. Artificial intelligence will significantly change marketing strategies and customer behaviors, with its effectiveness being enhanced when it augments human managers rather than replacing them(Davenport et al., 2020). The notion of AI first occurred in the 1950s and ever since the dawn it has been speculated how mankind will conquer breathtaking artificial intelligence. AI, as an academic subject, consists of a wide span of subfields like: Robotics, Vision, Learning with Machines, Neural Networks, and Natural Language Processing. AI harbors the primary goal to duplicate natural intelligence in computer applications. The relationship between price and online consumer reviews evolves differently at early and mature stages of internet usage, driven by different consumer motivations and motivational factors(Chen et al., 2011).

Today, individuals are constantly bombarded with an exponential glut of information originating from internet platforms. It is a growing concern how much of it is real, and how much is counterfeit. Yet another can of worms is privacy and surveillance. Practitioners are particularly interested in how to predict and profit from these large amounts of data. AI can assist with this task. Consumer engagement in online brand communities is complex and dynamic, with different engagement states and varying levels of intensity over time, leading to enhanced loyalty, satisfaction, empowerment, connection(Brodie et al., 2013),AI will also augment the design of commercial media platforms. In the best scenario, AI-powered systems are rendered so sophisticated that allegedly can predict consumer actions. Social media can significantly impact a firm's reputation, sales, and survival, but understanding its seven functional building blocks can help firms develop strategies for monitoring, understanding, and responding to its activities(Kietzmann et al., 2011).It is well-known how internet platforms amass a vast sea of information concerning users and Consumer engagement in online brand communities is influenced by cognition, affect, and behaviors, with key drivers being social media platforms and brand categories(Dessart et al., 2015). Profound AI networks can detect engagement that is not readily discernible to human perception. But this is also important to note that the Social media use positively impacts brand performance, retailer performance, and consumer-retailer loyalty, with contagion effects across supply channel partners and social influence mechanisms(Rapp et al., 2013). For example, activity like subtle hand movements similar to browsing through a shopping magazine may be under the radar of visual exposure, but systemically noticeable for cutting-edge dynamic analysis. Customer participation in a firm's social media efforts increases visit frequency and customer profitability, particularly for those with strong patronage, buying premium products, and lower buying focus and deal sensitivity(Rishika et al.,

2013). In the near future, profitable corporations might develop such cutting-edge algorithms and inadvertently dominate social media engagement.

18. CONCLUSION

Artificial Intelligence is prominently affecting consumer engagement on social media spaces today. Be it the most prevalent search engine in India, or the most-used social network in India, artificial intelligence is delivering the serene modern consumer engagement experiences on social media and Digital content marketing fosters consumer engagement, trust, and value by creating and distributing relevant, valuable content on digital platforms, ultimately leading to increased brand equity(Hollebeek & Macky, 2019) and notably Customer engagement behaviors in Facebook brand communities can enhance satisfaction and loyalty by offering social, entertainment, and economic benefits(Gummerus et al., 2012). From content efficiently fetching people they are engaged in, to answering their questions by the means of AI assistance, it's all being delivered by the modern AI algorithms now.

Several key problems have been reviewed that have been considered and addressed by the AI-powered modern social media interfaces. Economic models and enforcement of new rules on AI vs. User-generated content (UGC) are still novel and growing fields of research. There is certainly much more to come in the social media and AI. Social media marketing strategies require brands to relinquish control and embrace open source branding, challenging traditional brand building paradigms and promoting short-term and risk-driven brand value(Fournier & Avery, 2011), Tie strength, trust, normative, and informational influence positively impact consumer engagement in electronic word-of-mouth on social networking sites(Chu & Kim, 2011), and as depicted, AI has already been deployed in a more ethics-friendly manner to augment communications across a large range of professional or communal endeavors, from consulting and providing legal services to helping unity organizers before social platforms became household brand names (Hölli, 2019). In social platforms, the AI-powered user interface can be seen shaping ever-increasing abstract expressions, such as rant, properly hailed speech, avowals with imaginative content that can be euphoric or deterministic. Social media marketing can effectively build and sustain customer relationships, with strategies for Facebook and Twitter to measure their effectiveness in promoting program awareness and raising funds("Social Media Marketing," 2015).There is a growing understanding of the manipulative risks of such expressions, both on an individual and a societal basis which paved the way for greater exploration of these aspects.

19. FUTURE SCOPE OF THE STUDY

The objective of this study is to identify science-based strategies that can increase consumer engagement with social media platforms among a growing online audience in India, and, more importantly, convert these engagements to online transactions. The study draws on a large data set on an AI-based personal health and wellness consultation platform to engage with a potential consumer base across all Indian states over a period of 9 months. Growth curve modeling on 1096 brands suggests a violent initial acceleration in consumer engagement, followed by steady-state, decade-like decay—models that are significantly more advanced than logistic growth curves. A large disengagement in sharing on social networks is also documented. Time-dilation indices reveal that consumers in large Indian states are slower shoppers, with difficult brands prodding clicks to the post.

Understanding consumer attention, perception, and spending emotions on digital evidence for knowledge-based advertisements is growing rapidly. Growing with rapid development, artificial intelligence and multimedia technologies have sparked great interest from advertisers, marketers and computational scientists alike. The purpose of this research is, using a big data corpus of online consumer content, to develop new AI methods for affective computing and understand the opinions of consumers on the new knowledge-based ads. Disposal of the corpus data, affective computing techniques unravels attention, cognition and consumer emotion for the new knowledge-based advertisements. It also discovered some interesting methods using marketing results of these AI analyses to improve customer engagement on advertisements. Moreover, a novel AI approach to extracting online consumer content provides benefits to both practitioner and academic researches in business, marketing, public policy, and social science.

REFERENCES

Alalwan, A. A., Rana, N. P., Dwivedi, Y. K., & Algharabat, R. (2017). Social media in marketing: A review and analysis of the existing literature. *Telematics and Informatics*, *34*(7), 1177–1190. DOI: 10.1016/j.tele.2017.05.008

Appel, G., Grewal, L., Hadi, R., & Stephen, A. T. (2020). The future of social media in marketing. *Journal of the Academy of Marketing Science*, *48*(1), 79–95. DOI: 10.1007/s11747-019-00695-1 PMID: 32431463

Ashley, C., & Tuten, T. (2015). Creative Strategies in Social Media Marketing: An Exploratory Study of Branded Social Content and Consumer Engagement. *Psychology and Marketing*, *32*(1), 15–27. DOI: 10.1002/mar.20761

Bhattacharya, S., & Majumdar, A. (2021). Aspects and influence of social media marketing in today's world: A review of scholarly articles. Available at *SSRN* 3775421.

Brodie, R. J., Ilic, A., Juric, B., & Hollebeek, L. (2013). Consumer engagement in a virtual brand community: An exploratory analysis. *Journal of Business Research*, *66*(1), 105–114. DOI: 10.1016/j.jbusres.2011.07.029

Cabrera-Sánchez, J.-P., Villarejo-Ramos, Á. F., Liébana-Cabanillas, F., & Shaikh, A. A. (2021). Identifying relevant segments of AI applications adopters – Expanding the UTAUT2's variables. *Telematics and Informatics*, *58*, 101529. DOI: 10.1016/j.tele.2020.101529

Chen, Y., Fay, S., & Wang, Q. (2011). The Role of Marketing in Social Media: How Online Consumer Reviews Evolve. *Journal of Interactive Marketing*, *25*(2), 85–94. DOI: 10.1016/j.intmar.2011.01.003

Chu, S.-C., & Kim, Y. (2011). Determinants of consumer engagement in electronic word-of-mouth (eWOM) in social networking sites. *International Journal of Advertising*, *30*(1), 47–75. DOI: 10.2501/IJA-30-1-047-075

Dahake, N. S., Gajghate, A., Dahake, P. S., & Bansod, S. (2024). A Transformative Impact of IoT and AI by Predictive Analytics on Modern Marketing Strategies: A Study of its Significance & Accuracy. *2024 2nd International Conference on Advances in Computation, Communication and Information Technology (ICAICCIT)*, 1150–1158. DOI: 10.1109/ICAICCIT64383.2024.10912388

Dahake, N. S., Suresh Dahake, P., & Gajghate, A. (2024). Beyond the Hype: A Critical Evaluation of Predictive Analytics Accuracy in High-Stakes Business Decisions. *2024 2nd DMIHER International Conference on Artificial Intelligence in Healthcare, Education and Industry (IDICAIEI)*, 1–6. DOI: 10.1109/IDICAIEI61867.2024.10842857

Dahake, P. S., & Dahake, N. S. (2024). The Role of Big Data in Predictive Analytics for E-Commerce: Examine How Big Data Contributes to Better Predictions in Online Shopping. In Tarnanidis, T., Papathanasiou, J., Ismyrlis, V., & Kittu Manda, V. (Eds.), (pp. 403–426). Advances in Marketing, Customer Relationship Management, and E-Services. IGI Global., DOI: 10.4018/979-8-3693-9122-8.ch018

Davenport, T., Guha, A., Grewal, D., & Bressgott, T. (2020). How artificial intelligence will change the future of marketing. *Journal of the Academy of Marketing Science*, *48*(1), 24–42. DOI: 10.1007/s11747-019-00696-0

Delgado-Ballester, E., & Luis Munuera-Alemán, J. (2001). Brand trust in the context of consumer loyalty. *European Journal of Marketing*, *35*(11/12), 1238–1258. DOI: 10.1108/EUM0000000006475

Dessart, L., Veloutsou, C., & Morgan-Thomas, A. (2015). Consumer engagement in online brand communities: A social media perspective. *Journal of Product and Brand Management*, *24*(1), 28–42. DOI: 10.1108/JPBM-06-2014-0635

Dwivedi, Y. K., Ismagilova, E., Hughes, D. L., Carlson, J., Filieri, R., Jacobson, J., Jain, V., Karjaluoto, H., Kefi, H., Krishen, A. S., Kumar, V., Rahman, M. M., Raman, R., Rauschnabel, P. A., Rowley, J., Salo, J., Tran, G. A., & Wang, Y. (2021). Setting the future of digital and social media marketing research: Perspectives and research propositions. *International Journal of Information Management*, *59*, 102168. DOI: 10.1016/j.ijinfomgt.2020.102168

Enhancing Consumer Behavior and Experience Through AI-Driven Insights Optimization. (2024). In Naveeenkumar, N., Rallapalli, S., Sasikala, K., Priya, P. V., Husain, J., & Boopathi, S. (Eds.), (pp. 1–35). Advances in Marketing, Customer Relationship Management, and E-Services. IGI Global., DOI: 10.4018/979-8-3693-1918-5.ch001

Erkan, I., & Evans, C. (2016). The influence of eWOM in social media on consumers' purchase intentions: An extended approach to information adoption. *Computers in Human Behavior, 61*, 47–55. DOI: 10.1016/j.chb.2016.03.003

Fournier, S., & Avery, J. (2011). The uninvited brand. *Business Horizons*, *54*(3), 193–207. DOI: 10.1016/j.bushor.2011.01.001

Gerlich, M. (2023). The Power of Virtual Influencers: Impact on Consumer Behaviour and Attitudes in the Age of AI. *Administrative Sciences*, *13*(8), 178. DOI: 10.3390/admsci13080178

Goh, K.-Y., Heng, C.-S., & Lin, Z. (2013). Social Media Brand Community and Consumer Behavior: Quantifying the Relative Impact of User- and Marketer-Generated Content. *Information Systems Research*, *24*(1), 88–107. DOI: 10.1287/isre.1120.0469

Gummerus, J., Liljander, V., Weman, E., & Pihlström, M. (2012). Customer engagement in a Facebook brand community. *Management Research Review*, *35*(9), 857–877. DOI: 10.1108/01409171211256578

Gupta, R., & Pathak, C. (2014). A Machine Learning Framework for Predicting Purchase by Online Customers based on Dynamic Pricing. *Procedia Computer Science*, *36*, 599–605. DOI: 10.1016/j.procs.2014.09.060

Hajli, M. N. (2014). A study of the impact of social media on consumers. *International Journal of Market Research*, *56*(3), 387–404. DOI: 10.2501/IJMR-2014-025

He, H. (2022). A comprehensive review on the role of online media in sustainable business development and decision making. *Soft Computing*, *26*(20), 10789–10803. DOI: 10.1007/s00500-022-06993-1 PMID: 35698465

Heller Baird, C., & Parasnis, G. (2011). From social media to social customer relationship management. *Strategy and Leadership*, *39*(5), 30–37. DOI: 10.1108/10878571111161507

Hollebeek, L. D. (2011). Demystifying customer brand engagement: Exploring the loyalty nexus. *Journal of Marketing Management*, *27*(7–8), 785–807. DOI: 10.1080/0267257X.2010.500132

Hollebeek, L. D., Glynn, M. S., & Brodie, R. J. (2014). Consumer Brand Engagement in Social Media: Conceptualization, Scale Development and Validation. *Journal of Interactive Marketing*, *28*(2), 149–165. DOI: 10.1016/j.intmar.2013.12.002

Hollebeek, L. D., & Macky, K. (2019). Digital Content Marketing's Role in Fostering Consumer Engagement, Trust, and Value: Framework, Fundamental Propositions, and Implications. *Journal of Interactive Marketing*, *45*(1), 27–41. DOI: 10.1016/j.intmar.2018.07.003

How Social Media Advertising and Repetitive Marketing Messages Affect the Online Purhasing Behavior? (n.d.). Retrieved May 1, 2025, from https://aaltodoc.aalto.fi/items/30c02c3e-64fb-4f11-9063-d1250330fb90

Huang, M.-H., & Rust, R. T. (2021). Engaged to a Robot? The Role of AI in Service. *Journal of Service Research, 24*(1), 30–41. DOI: 10.1177/1094670520902266

Hudson, S., Huang, L., Roth, M. S., & Madden, T. J. (2016). The influence of social media interactions on consumer–brand relationships: A three-country study of brand perceptions and marketing behaviors. *International Journal of Research in Marketing, 33*(1), 27–41. DOI: 10.1016/j.ijresmar.2015.06.004

Kietzmann, J. H., Hermkens, K., McCarthy, I. P., & Silvestre, B. S. (2011). Social media? Get serious! Understanding the functional building blocks of social media. *Business Horizons, 54*(3), 241–251. DOI: 10.1016/j.bushor.2011.01.005

Kose, U., & Sert, S. (2017). *Improving content marketing processes with the approaches by artificial intelligence*. DOI: 10.48550/ARXIV.1704.02114

Labrecque, L. I. (2014). Fostering Consumer–Brand Relationships in Social Media Environments: The Role of Parasocial Interaction. *Journal of Interactive Marketing, 28*(2), 134–148. DOI: 10.1016/j.intmar.2013.12.003

Laroche, M., Habibi, M. R., Richard, M.-O., & Sankaranarayanan, R. (2012). The effects of social media based brand communities on brand community markers, value creation practices, brand trust and brand loyalty. *Computers in Human Behavior, 28*(5), 1755–1767. DOI: 10.1016/j.chb.2012.04.016

Lee, D., Hosanagar, K., & Nair, H. (2017). Advertising Content and Consumer Engagement on Social Media: Evidence from Facebook. SSRN *Electronic Journal*. DOI: 10.2139/ssrn.2290802

Lou, C., & Yuan, S. (2019). Influencer Marketing: How Message Value and Credibility Affect Consumer Trust of Branded Content on Social Media. *Journal of Interactive Advertising, 19*(1), 58–73. DOI: 10.1080/15252019.2018.1533501

Manser Payne, E. H., Dahl, A. J., & Peltier, J. (2021). Digital servitization value co-creation framework for AI services: A research agenda for digital transformation in financial service ecosystems. *Journal of Research in Interactive Marketing, 15*(2), 200–222. DOI: 10.1108/JRIM-12-2020-0252

) Mathew, S. M., & S, S. M. (2022). *APPLICATION OF ARTIFICIAL INTELLIGENCE IN BANKING: A STUDY BASED ON SBI-SIA VIRTUAL ASSISTANT*. DOI: 10.13140/RG.2.2.24377.44645

Min, W., Zhou, P., Xu, L., Liu, T., Li, T., Huang, M., Jin, Y., Yi, Y., Wen, M., Jiang, S., & Jain, R. (2023). *From Plate to Production: Artificial Intelligence in Modern Consumer-Driven Food Systems* (Version 1). arXiv. DOI: 10.48550/ARXIV.2311.02400

Nazir, S., Khadim, S., Ali Asadullah, M., & Syed, N. (2023). Exploring the influence of artificial intelligence technology on consumer repurchase intention: The mediation and moderation approach. *Technology in Society*, *72*, 102190. DOI: 10.1016/j.techsoc.2022.102190

Paul, J., Ueno, A., & Dennis, C. (2023). ChatGPTand consumers: Benefits, Pitfalls and Future Research Agenda. *International Journal of Consumer Studies*, *47*(4), 1213–1225. DOI: 10.1111/ijcs.12928

Pletikosa Cvijikj, I., & Michahelles, F. (2013). Online engagement factors on Facebook brand pages. *Social Network Analysis and Mining*, *3*(4), 843–861. DOI: 10.1007/s13278-013-0098-8

Rapp, A., Beitelspacher, L. S., Grewal, D., & Hughes, D. E. (2013). Understanding social media effects across seller, retailer, and consumer interactions. *Journal of the Academy of Marketing Science*, *41*(5), 547–566. DOI: 10.1007/s11747-013-0326-9

Repositório do Iscte – Instituto Universitário de Lisboa: The influence and impact of artificial intelligence in the consumer decision-making process: Comparing Generation X with Millennials. (n.d.). Retrieved May 1, 2025, from https://repositorio.iscte-iul.pt/handle/10071/21828?locale=en

Rishika, R., Kumar, A., Janakiraman, R., & Bezawada, R. (2013). The Effect of Customers' Social Media Participation on Customer Visit Frequency and Profitability: An Empirical Investigation. *Information Systems Research*, *24*(1), 108–127. DOI: 10.1287/isre.1120.0460

Schivinski, B., & Dabrowski, D. (2016). The effect of social media communication on consumer perceptions of brands. *Journal of Marketing Communications*, *22*(2), 189–214. DOI: 10.1080/13527266.2013.871323

) Selvakumar, P., Shanthi, M., Pitchiah, R., Sharma, M., Dahake, P. S., & T. C., M. (2025). The Role of Artificial Intelligence in Business Model Innovation: Overview of AI Technologies. In M. Khokhar (Ed.), *Advances in Business Strategy and Competitive Advantage* (pp. 219–246). IGI Global. DOI: 10.4018/979-8-3693-9571-4.ch009

Sharma, M., Joshi, S., Luthra, S., & Kumar, A. (2024). Impact of Digital Assistant Attributes on Millennials' Purchasing Intentions: A Multi-Group Analysis using PLS-SEM, Artificial Neural Network and fsQCA. *Information Systems Frontiers*, *26*(3), 943–966. DOI: 10.1007/s10796-022-10339-5 PMID: 36185777

Social Media Marketing. (2015). In Nadda, V. K., Dadwal, S. S., & Firdous, A. (Eds.), (pp. 359–379). Advances in Marketing, Customer Relationship Management, and E-Services. IGI Global., DOI: 10.4018/978-1-4666-8353-2.ch021

Soni, N., Sharma, E. K., Singh, N., & Kapoor, A. (2019). *Impact of Artificial Intelligence on Businesses: From Research, Innovation, Market Deployment to Future Shifts in Business Models* (Version 1). arXiv. DOI: 10.48550/ARXIV.1905.02092

Sun, H., Zafar, M. Z., & Hasan, N. (2022). Employing Natural Language Processing as Artificial Intelligence for Analyzing Consumer Opinion Toward Advertisement. *Frontiers in Psychology, 13*, 856663. Advance online publication. DOI: 10.3389/fpsyg.2022.856663 PMID: 35769737

Tiago, M. T. P. M. B., & Veríssimo, J. M. C. (2014). Digital marketing and social media: Why bother? *Business Horizons, 57*(6), 703–708. DOI: 10.1016/j.bushor.2014.07.002

Varghese, M., Raj, S., & Venkatesh, V. (2022). *Influence of AI in human lives* (Version 1). arXiv. DOI: 10.48550/ARXIV.2212.12305

Virtual Retail Algorithms. (2022). Virtual Retail Algorithms, Behavioral Predictive Analytics, and Geospatial Mapping Technologies in the Decentralized Metaverse. *Review of Contemporary Philosophy, 21*(0), 171. DOI: 10.22381/RCP21202211

Voorveld, H. A. M., Van Noort, G., Muntinga, D. G., & Bronner, F. (2018). Engagement with Social Media and Social Media Advertising: The Differentiating Role of Platform Type. *Journal of Advertising, 47*(1), 38–54. DOI: 10.1080/00913367.2017.1405754

Wang, X., Yu, C., & Wei, Y. (2012). Social Media Peer Communication and Impacts on Purchase Intentions: A Consumer Socialization Framework. *Journal of Interactive Marketing, 26*(4), 198–208. DOI: 10.1016/j.intmar.2011.11.004

Wongkitrungrueng, A., & Assarut, N. (2020). The role of live streaming in building consumer trust and engagement with social commerce sellers. *Journal of Business Research, 117*, 543–556. DOI: 10.1016/j.jbusres.2018.08.032

Zhang, E., & Lu, X. (2023). *Social AI Improves Well-Being Among Female Young Adults* (Version 2). arXiv. DOI: 10.48550/ARXIV.2311.14706

Chapter 13

Strategic Digital Transformation Influencing Islamic Marketing and Consumer Behavior of Takaful and Bancassurance Channels

Muhammad Nawaz Iqbal
https://orcid.org/0009-0006-4266-4720
Sir Syed University of Engineering and Technology, Pakistan

Muhammad Tahir Jan
https://orcid.org/0000-0001-5680-8496
International Islamic University, Malaysia

ABSTRACT

There have been transformations in customer behavior due to the advent of digital technologies into the field of Islamic financial services like Takaful and Bancassurance. This chapter will discuss Islamic marketing's strategically evolution focusing on AI, social media, and digital transformation in consumer decisions. Shariah compliance is the guiding principle; hence every business is expected to innovate within the ethical integrity and transparency of such innovation. The discussion emphasizes how predictive analytics, blockchain, and personalized digital narratives stimulate consumer trust, accessibility, and drive financial inclusion. Case studies of successful digital strategies within Pakistan's Islamic finance sector will also mention challenges such as regulatory compliance, consumer skepticism, and tech

DOI: 10.4018/979-8-3373-2747-1.ch013

adaptability. Ultimately, the chapter would suggest strategy options for companies to tap into digital innovation for sustainability and competitiveness in Takaful and Bancassurance channels, thus incorporating an Islamic marketing paradigm.

1. INTRODUCTION

The financial services industry which is experiencing digital transformation has massively affected how Islamic marketing and consumption behaves in Takaful and Bancassurance. Maintaining Shariah compliance in the digital world while deploying the digital change has become a challenge, but a necessary strategy for Shariah compliant financial growth. This chapter examines the role that artificial intelligence (AI), big data, blockchain and social media play in changing the way of operating consumer interactions and spreading digital adoption in the Takaful and Bancassurance channels. The chapter emphasizes on the way these transformations impact marketing strategy, customer engagement, as well as regulatory compliance while focused on Pakistan.

In recent decades, Islamic finance has evolved to such an extent determined essentially in the growing demand of Shariah compliant financial solutions. The emergence of Takaful and Bancassurance as the crucial part of the Islamic financial system is a result of the appetite for the ethical and interest free insurance and investment products. Traditionally, these have been kind of these more conventional marketing and distribution strategies, which is that it was very kind of simply limited in its accessibility and unfortunately is limited in its scalability. Even so, with the rise of digital transformation, more and more Islamic financial institutions are also utilizing technology to cover a wider market while embedded with Islamic principles. Digital tools helped in the integration of which made it possible for previously underserved populations to have easy access to Takaful and Bancassurance services.

The Takaful industry will now flourish to offer necessary and alternative investments through sharing risk. The successful introduction and marketing of Takaful products in specific countries requires knowledge of country characteristics and their environment. As predominantly Muslim, Indonesia is a potential market for Takaful. However, the Takaful industry will have to face several challenges in marketing its products (Deloitte, 2013; Redhika & Mahalli, 2014; Ichsan, 2015). One of them is how it should innovate. Boer and During (2001) define innovation as "the creation of a new-product-market-technology-organization combinations." According to Haron and Nursofiza (2008), indeed, innovation is not only technological or product-oriented, but also the process and renewal of organizational structures or markets.

Islamic banking continues to expand and provide financial products that qualify under Sharia law, including Bancassurance. Bancassurance in Islamic banking means the operation of Islamic banks with different insurance enterprises in order to provide Sharia-compliant insurance services (Guemmaz, 2023). Bancassurance is not just a distribution system alone, perhaps even an illegal aspect, an operational one, and a cultural aspect for its implementation. According to Bank Indonesia, Bancassurance is a bank service offering insurance products for financial protection and long-term investment (Bagasworo & Simatupang, 2022). For the banks, therefore, it is their strategy to earn from fees while increasing customer loyalty and boosting overall selling efficiency in minimizing financial risks.

They are regarded as mere marketing arms of Islamic insurance companies with respect to the promotion of their Bancassurance products in the arrangements for Bancassurance. That is to say, the relationship by which banks act as agents and insurance companies act as principals is governed legally by an agency agreement, wherein banks carry out an action on behalf of the insurance companies in interacting with their customers (Shomad, 2025).

The rapid emergence of technology has changed expectations and thus, consumer behavior in Islamic finance too has changed. Today's modern consumers are seeking massively seamless digital experiences, instant access to financial products and personalized interactions, and as the fireworks die down Pakistani consumers will expect these in their modern lives. For the case of Takaful and Bancassurance, trust and ethical matters still become important, so that it is necessary to provide transparency and compliance with Islamic teachings in digital marketing strategy. In order to gain consumer trust, companies have to make sure digital narratives resonate with consumers' religious values while maintaining the convenience and accessibility that people came to expect.

It is because fintech solutions have brought new form of Takaful and Bancassurance channels for a transformative role. AI Blockchain and Big Data Analytics are changing the way organizations transform themselves and empower their capacity to run in more useful methods, and to separate the dangers and guarantee more incredible client encounters. Real time assistance to customers is being provided by AI driven chatbots and automated advisory platform while blockchain brings transparency to Islamic financial product transaction and enable more trust in Islamic products. The era of digital transformation also means an opportunity to develop novel Islamic ethical standards for financial solutions to bridge the chasms between the state of technological development. As such, it is vital for the growth of the Takaful and Bancassurance in the modern financial ecosystem to integrate strategic digital initiatives.

2. MAIN FOCUS OF THE CHAPTER

2.1 Digital Transformation In Islamic Marketing

The Islamic marketing is built on 'ethics, transparency and consumer trust', which is in line with Shariah principles. By leveraging behavioral insights using AI based analytics, these firms can segment the customers and therefore they can come up with more relevant Takaful and Bancassurance products. In addition, the use of blockchain technology increases transparency owing to secure and verifiable transactions making consumers trust.

2.1.1 Leveraging AI and Big Data for Personalized Consumer Engagement

Islamic marketing's digital transformation has given businesses the ability to leverage the power of artificial intelligence (AI) and big data analytics in order to understand and meet the needs of the consumer. With AI driven insights, firms can segment their targets audience in terms of behavioral patterns, religious beliefs as well as financial needs and consequently the marketing campaigns become more personalized. One such example would be the real time assistance offered to the consumer through the AI based chatbots in compliance with the Shariah principles for product recommendations. Furthermore, predictive analytics aid Islamic financial institutions in predicting customer demand and design of Takaful and Bancassurance based on their ethical and financial expectations. Through this data driven approach there is trust which guarantees that marketing messages will be relevant to the Islamic values making the product more appealing to a faith conscious audience.

Introduced from Europe, Bancassurance is a recent concept that is catching fire in developing nations. In fact, Bancassurance organizations are generally formed by those companies whose services are extended to selling insurance products and services to their existing clients (Eybers & Setsabi, 2021).. The ultimate benefit is common to both: the bank has customers who turn out to be prospective insurance customers, and the insurance policyholder who might want to open a bank account. To facilitate this, data would flow from bank to insurance house. Typically, IT infrastructure and data resources interchangeably network into data sharing. This may involve not only the infrastructure challenges but also the governance considerations regarding what data will be shared and in what markdown of the datasets (Eybers & Setsabi, 2021).

Similarly, decision making for the Islamic financial institutions is also enhanced by analyzing transaction histories, search behavior and social media engagement. This in turn helps companies to get a better clarity over their digital strategies and produce content in line with the customer's values. Suppose analytics show that there's rising demand for family Takaful plans in a particular country; then companies can concentrate on marketing these products more in line with ethical and social values to show that their products correspond with Islamic beliefs.

2.1.2 Social Media as a Catalyst for Islamic Consumer Awareness and Trust

Such as social media is proved to be a powerful Islamic advertising site, giving the brands a chance to talk with Muslim customers and spread awareness of Shariah compliant financial solutions. Facebook, Instagram, LinkedIn, and TikTok are the platform for the businesses to share the informative, success stories and educational videos to support the Ethical and Transparent nature of Takaful and Bancassurance products. Financial institutions partner with Islamic scholars, ethical finance experts, and Muslim lifestyle influencers on influencer marketing to increase the faith in the brand and reach a values driven audience.

The brand personality traits of Islamic brands influence brand trust positively in the context of the Islamic banking sector. They further enhance e-word-of-mouth through mediation by brand love (Yasin et al., 2024). Modern online retailing is fast-paced and thus has become difficult to grab shoppers' attention and break through the marketing clutter to influence their purchase intentions (Bebber et al., 2017; Willems et al., 2017). Many issues are examined in online retailing, specifically through social media, and trust is one of the important areas of research. In a social-mediated marketing environment, the marketers are battling a strong issue with consumers trusting them due to the absence of person-to-person contact and an overwhelming volume of user-generated input (PWC, 2018; Yahia et al., 2018).

The capability of social media marketing in building community based interaction is basically one of the most important advantage of social media marketing in the Islamic context. Social media groups, live Q&A sessions, and discussion forums can enable Islamic finance institutions to answer to consumers' concerns, clear some of the complex Shariah compliant business principles, etc. What's more, social media promotes interactive engagement with storytelling and testimonials, allowing satisfied customers to spread the message of the Takaful and Bancassurance services. They strongly influence consumers' decision making and more so in industries like Islamic finance, which are perceived as trust sensitive.

2.1.3 Block chain and Smart Contracts for Transparency and Ethical Compliance

Blockchain technology has empowered the nascent Islamic marketing by increasing trust, security and transparency in the financial transactions. Prohibition of uncertainty (gharar) is one of the most fundamental principles of Islamic finance allowing blockchain to be used as a guarantee of compliance. Though blockchain technology is still undergoing development, Takaful and Bancassurance providers can exploit the fact that it allows them to automate processes such as policy underwriting, claims processing, and fund management through smart contracts. These digital agreements take place of intermediaries by executing transactions based on conditions predetermined, which minimizes fraud risks.

In addition to these checks, another concern pertains to the algorithmic protocols for validation of smart contracts (including smart Sukuk). As a matter of principle, these raise questions concerning the Maqasid al-Sharīʿah which insists that no transaction should harm society (Chong, 2021). Transactions through blockchains are kept public, thereby making it easier to institute checks of Sharīʿah compliance or their Islamic nature but this can only happen post-operation (Chong, 2021).

Halal discussions using blockchain technology have picked up pace as their great advantages become visible. However, the insufficient explanation regarding the halal compliance of such blockchain-based products remains an issue. The model developed attempts to shed light on the synthesis of blockchain technology and halal compliance (Purusottama & Simatupang, 2025). The features of blockchain technology can work on the dimensions of halal compliance and can be applied in multiple cases. The working of features of blockchain technology is complementary, with some features of blockchain technology dominating in their contribution to a particular dimension for halal compliance while others act to complement their contribution (Purusottama & Simatupang, 2025).

Moreover, the blockchain has an objective of ensuring that the financial institutions still maintain such an immutable record of transactions, which is in line with the Islamic principle of fairness (adl). An instance where blockchain can be used is in the case of a customer buying a Takaful policy, whereby all pertinent information pertaining to the policy can be stored in the blockchain making it verifiable and tamper proof. Transparency contributes to generating faith conscious customer confidence and alleviates the fears that unethical practices have been exercised. Similarly, it also helps in the integration of blockchain within Islamic marketing strategies through the seamless cross border transaction for global expansion of Takaful and Bancassurance services.

2.1.4 Digital Content Strategies for Ethical Consumer Education

The process in which Islamic marketing opts for ethical consumer education plays a key role in its digital transformation. Due to the complexity of Muslim financial products, the institutions should deliver the content that simplifies these ideas being religiously authentic. Areas of the principles of Islamic Finance: Websites, blogs and e-learning platform provide very useful explanation of how Takaful and Bancassurance work in terms of comparison to conventional insurance and invest product.

The ethical consumerism phenomenon has attracted a lot of inquiries in recent years because shoppers are putting more and more weight on their purchases regarding ethical-social-environmental implications (Kailash et al., 2023). This changing pattern of consumer behavior has encouraged researchers and marketers as well as companies to develop new strategies focusing on the conscientious buyer (Kailash et al., 2023).

Rowley (2008) has elaborated digital content marketing stands for "the management process responsible for identifying, anticipating, and satisfying customer requirements profitably" through any relevant digital content. Thus, it is seen as an effective tool for relationship marketing. It is believed to contribute towards strengthening consumer bonds and attachment towards a brand, thereby contributing to business performance (Carranza, 2017; Kakkar, 2017).

Digital storytelling acts as a key to harness the power of engaging Muslim consumers through the link between Islamic financial principles and real world examples. Video explainers, podcasts, and animated explainers illustrate how Takaful protects families from financial hardships through a Shariah compliant manner. Besides, mobile apps feature interactive tools like Takaful premium calculator and savings estimator which contribute to end users making informed financial decisions. If we prioritize digital content strategies, Islamic marketing can bridge that gap and enable the consumer to make an informed decision in choosing ethically defensible financial solutions that they align with in their beliefs.

2.2 Consumer Behavior And Digital Adoption In Takaful And Bancassurance

Fintech has helped to raise the consumer behavior, and the digital accessibility has been a key determinant in decision for adoption of the financial services. Online platforms and mobile apps need to be as seamless as possible while AI also provides more and highly personalized customer support to customers. Due to increase in digital services demand, Islamic financial institutions need to integrate with digital services and strategies engaged in the marketing strategies must also match with

Islamic ethical and religious issues. Personalization, social media engagement, and trade gaming are emerging as very attractive tactics to draw and hold on clients.

2.2.1 The Shift towards Digital-First Financial Services

Insurance and Bancassurance services have increasingly become an area of interest for the modern consumers who are more inclined towards digital channels for conducting their transactions. This shift has been accelerated by the growing penetration of smart phones, high widespread internet access and fintech innovation which is forcing Islamic financial institutions to go digital.

Takaful and insurance companies are betting big on technology in their products and services as of now. According to Statista (2020), significant contributions have been made by such companies worldwide in terms of investments in technologies such as cyber security, robotic process automation, artificial intelligence, blockchain, and digital channels. This trend is a reflection of investment readiness and of the market themselves to be onboard with technology when it comes to their offerings, which coincides with Alshammari et al.'s (2019) recommendation for both the takaful and insurance sectors to invest in new technologies to optimize utilization of resources. In addition, Eling et al. (2021) indicate that incorporating IoT and artificial intelligence in the insurance market is still in its infancy stage and has limited business model developmental dimensions.

The new distribution paradigm has been all the more influenced or transformed by digital platforms. With social changes such as rising life expectancy, advances in technology (for example, artificial intelligence), changes in connectivity, and consumer tastes and preferences, distribution for insurance products has gambled onto online platforms (Relan & kumar, 2023). At a time like this, insurance companies should strategize on building partnerships across ecosystems, promoting collaboration among agents, and ensuring that they have the hybrid or multi-channel distribution model in place. This is so because face-to-face interaction still has a place, notwithstanding shifting preferences among consumers (Relan & kumar, 2023).

Consumers in the Takaful and Bancassurance sectors expect the same ease of digital on boarding process no matter what, instant policy issuance, and AI driven customer support. To fill the void, many providers have responded with user friendly mobile apps that make online premium payments through digital claims processing and virtual advisory services. In addition, biometric authentication, blockchain security, and chatbot-assisted services supported integration gives the user a wonderful experience and boosts the confidence in the buyers. The digital first services touch a broader change in consumer behavior towards financial planning with convenience, efficiency and transparency enabling the decision making.

2.2.2 The Role of Trust and Transparency in Digital Adoption

Trust is vital in shaping consumer behavior, especially in Islamic finance, where it is a determining factor of the choice for the Islamic financial decision. Shariah-compliant (or Islamic) financial services are based on sharing the risk with others, being fair, and the minimization of uncertainty and interest. Thus, Takaful and Bancassurance innovators are expected to meet high levels of transparency by the consumers. Such solutions as blockchain and AI driven on compliance tools increase the trust by making transparency on transactions, policy management and claims settlement possible.

In offering the changes that lead to the prophecy of data-driven business models, the availability of data increases the paradox (Hartmann et al., 2016; Kiel et al., 2017; Sestino et al., 2020; Sorescu, 2017). The more service domains are aware of the value of embedded data, the more this is an important lever for business model innovation (Ostrom et al., 2015). On the other hand, the indiscriminate exploitation of users' data brings out privacy concerns.

For example, blockchain technology provides tamper proof record keeping to consumers so they can ensure their policies and claims history are undoubtable of fraud or data manipulation. In the same manner, Islamic ethical principles can be automatically detected and prevented through employing AI-based tools so that financials products abide by Islamic principles which are not the best. These innovations allow to remove skepticism of consumers and to more actively adopt digital services. Whenever a financial institution is transparent and provides a digital platform to their customers, they are breaking through networks of distrust and increasing the likelihood of gaining consumer confidence, retention rate, and long term customer loyalty.

2.2.3 Social Media and Influencer Marketing in Consumer Decision-Making

Increasingly, social media has become a great force in the dynamics of consumer behavior in the domain of the Islamic financials. Using social media, specifically Facebook, LinkedIn, Instagram, and TikTok, as digital marketing strategies, Takaful and Bancassurance providers can directly reach their audience. They aim at educating consumers on the benefits of Shariah compliant financial solutions, through informational content, testimonials and interactive Q&A sessions which incite more involvement from consumers in Islamic insurance and banking services.

For marketing strategies, influencer marketing refers to a very effective branding strategy. In the presence of social media influencers like vloggers or instafamous personalities, companies now increasingly try to abandon the usual idea of celebrity endorsers for promoting their products (Jin & Muqaddam, 2019; Schouten et al., 2019). Companies should also realize that hiring an influencer for promotion is not to say that the people trust the quality of the product. According to our research, a large proportion of consumers think that influencers only accept their paychecks in order to sell a product.

This is a particularly open field for influencer marketing. They are in the shape of Islamic scholars, ethical finance experts, and Muslim lifestyle influencers that shape perceptions. They believe it will be more credible Islamic financing advice from credible Islamic leaders who can actually prove with Shariah compliance of the Takaful and Bancassurance product. These influencers make live webinars, podcast discussions and even social media collaborations with them can greatly increase the awareness and acceptance of digital financial solutions by consumers. Into the digital age, social media can be used as an educational tool and an engagement tool by the financial institutions so that they can penetrate into new market segments and the brands can be believed more in the digital world.

2.2.4 Behavioral Economics and Gamification for Enhanced Digital Engagement

The values of behavioral economics are key in pushing the adopt of digital in Takaful and Bancassurance. In many ways, the financial products are best suited for consumers who, by and large, require incentives and simplified decision making processes. An effective way to encourage people to participate in Islamic financial products has been gamification, i.e. applying game like elements in digital services.

Most of the time, rational consumer behavior can only be found within the premises and presumptions of classical economics (Litao & xinzhou, 2021). Actual consumptions, on the other hand, reveal consumer behaviors that are often classified by conventional theories as abnormal or illogical. Today, behavioral economics has been an important tool for understanding actual consumer behavior. This study emphasizes irrational decision-making from a behavioral economics perspective (Litao & xinzhou, 2021).

This includes, for instance, reward based programs which were introduced by Takaful providers: users earn points for financial literacy quizzes, on time payment of premium, and referrals. Interative tools like AI driven financial advisors are also used as part of digital platforms that allows the users to get customized savings plan according to user behaviors. By sticking to the concepts of gamification, financial planning should become more fun and less scary, and more so, make Islamic financial products more enjoyable to use alongside being more prone to a positive user experience and long term commitment of Islamic financial products.

Furthermore, it also makes it possible for institutions to customize micro-Takaful plans designed for people with less disposable income based on their behavioral analysis. By embracing data as well as using usage data to drive customer satisfaction and digital adoption rates, this approach ensures that every company can be inclusive of both new and existing users.

2.3 The Role Of Artificial Intelligence And Big Data

Takaful and Bancassurance stands to gain immensely from usage of AI and big data analytics vis-a-vis insight into consumer's behavior for targeted marketing campaigns. 26/7 customer support is provided by AI driven chatbots and machine learning algorithms keep predicting the needs of the consumers, thereby making policies more customized. AI in Islamic marketing may be used to assess compliance with Shariah principles so that the product fits the religious guidelines. Predictive analytics empowers firms to predict the market trends and can be used for strategic decision making.

2.3.1 AI-Driven Personalization and Customer Experience

The financial services have become highly personal in terms of engaging with the customer. AI powered algorithm will analyze preferences of an individual in the form of choice of products and their past transaction history to recommend products focused on their preferences along with Bancassurance related solutions. This enables much more personalization to customers which leads to increased customer satisfaction and uptake of policy.

AI-based predictive analytics allows organizations to forecast customer needs and behaviors. AI algorithms—by analyzing historicals—ascertain trends, patterns, and anomalies that allow organizations to predict customer preferences, recognize up selling or cross-selling opportunities, and intervene ahead of time to solve possible issues (Niknejad et al., 2021). This empowers organizations to run targeted marketing campaigns, create personalized recommendations, and give proactive customer support, leading to enhanced customer satisfaction and retention (Niknejad et al., 2021).

AI driven chatbots and virtual assistants in the Takaful industry help 24/7 to offer customer support, guiding users through the process to select a policy according to their own needs. Through these AI powered tools, these AI are used to answer the query of coverage, Shariah compliance and claims procedures which further helps in overall customer experience. Likewise, Bancassurance providers utilize AI to suggest custom financial products according to the risk profiles, investment choices, and past purchases customer's any way.

In addition to AI based recommendation engines, Islamic financial institutions are now able to target customers with personalized marketing campaigns by recommending products and services that address the customers' religion based financial goals. The targeted approach its promotes trust by customers to such financial service providers and helps establish the relationships that will last this long.

2.3.2 Predictive Analytics for Risk Assessment and Fraud Prevention

Takaful and Bancassurance sectors remain dependent on AI, Big Data for risk assessment /fraud detection, which are essential components. This enables financial institutions to more accurately assess risk profiles and even decrease the threat of future costs before the problems even arise.

Financial services have, for some time now, been besieged by new-generation fraud schemes and changing risks that place a premium on the traditional detection and assessment methods. With an increase in transaction volume and complexity, manual processes and basic rule-based systems cannot be solely depended upon to protect assets against fraud or meet regulatory obligations. In this scenario, Predictive Analytics and Artificial Intelligence (AI) could be considered as advanced tools in enhancing the ability to detect fraud and assess risks substantially. Predictive Analytics refers to statistical techniques/data mining and machine learning models for analyzing historical data to make predictions about the future (Shoetan, & Babajide, 2024). This sets a stage for detection in that, by applying such techniques, the financial institutions may be able to envisage patterns and behaviors that would typically indicate fraudulent activity before such activities actually come into being. Predictive Analytics is thus capable of analyzing the gargantuan data such that it will uncover subtle correlations and trends that will either be missed or not identified in due time by human analysts or other simpler tools. Thus, AI in the form of machine learning and deep learning significantly augments Predictive Analytics (Shoetan, & Babajide, 2024).

In Takaful, the risk assessment models are based on AI so that the customer data such as demographic details, health records and financial behavior is analyzed to select the suitable coverage plan. Such models also help insurers to offer dynamic pricing according to real-time dynamic risk evaluation, maintaining fairness and competitiveness of contributions to the pool.

Using AI powered algorithms, fraud detection has also been made a lot better as it can find unusual patterns of claims processing and financial transactions. In a never ending cycle of Big Data analytics, activities of a policyholder are constantly monitored, flagged if one is making false claims, identity theft or exaggerating losses. With the use of AI in fraud prevention, Islamic financial institutions have a chance of balancing their ethics and losses.

Moreover, AI sentiment analysis tools use AI to scan online reviews, customer feedback as well as to scan social media discussions to know the people's trust in financial products, providing direction to business owners to address the obstacles beforehand.

2.3.3 Enhancing Regulatory Compliance and Shariah Governance

Fundamentally a requisite of Islamic finance is to ensure compliance with Shariah principles as well as with the financial regulations. It allows for the financial institutions to retain compliance by automating regulatory processes and tracking transactions for compliance to Islamic laws, using AI and Big Data.

For effective and efficient Shariah compliance management, it has become a requirement for Islamic Financial Institutions (IFIs) to appoint an able Shariah officer to perform all Shariah control functions like Shariah review, Shariah audit, and Shariah risk management. Shariah review is an observation to be made frequently about the activities and operations of an IFI regarding Shariah compliance; on the other hand, Shariah auditing presents an independent periodic evaluation of the degree of Shariah compliance of an IFI with respect to its business operation (Kasim et.al, 2013; Noor Aimi et.al, 2019).

The compliance of Takaful and Bancassurance with the Shariah is complex due to continuous monitoring of financial contracts, investments and the policy structure so as to comply with the Islamic ethical standards. RegTech powered by AI uses solutions that automate the verification of the compliance requirements reducing the impact for human mistakes. These tools can analyze transaction data, identify the non compliance activities and continuously present the compliant reports.

In addition, AI-driven smart contracts in blockchain technology open up transparency in the Islamic financial transactions. Once conditions are pre defined the contracts are executed automatically to ensure that policy terms and conditions are in accordance with Shariah law. In addition to Big Data analytics, big data has further to contribute constantly monitoring market trends and regulatory updates to lend a swift change to the established parameters of compliance.

2.3.4 Data-Driven Decision-Making and Market Expansion

By being able to analyze large amounts of data in real time, Takaful and Bancassurance provider can be better placed strategically and get better expansion opportunities. Big Data analytics deliver deep insights into customers' behavior, current market trends, and new market needs which in turn helps the institutions to design the new products or services accordingly. For example, AI-powered data analytics helps to identify underserved markets where the demand for Islamic insurance as well as Bancassurance products is increasing.

Business intelligence harbors a significant influence on decision making. This is the individual process on many banking sectors under the Bancassurance system. And because Bi and DMS are central components of cognition, the above statement holds (Nanda, 2020).

Moreover, AI based business intelligence technology allows businesses to predict future business trends and investment possibilities more effectively as well as reduce their risk of financial shocks. However, these insights enable financial institutions to formulate long term growth strategy and still keep the institution in good financial health.

With the adoption of technology that incorporates AI and Big Data, Takaful and Bancassurance providers can maximize operational efficiency of their operations along with increasing customer acquisition and increasing their market reach to sustain success in the constantly developing digital environment.

2.4 The Impact Of Social Media On Consumer Engagement

Islamic marketing via the social media platforms provides different channels to communicate directly with the consumers. Businesses can interact with their audiences by engaging them through Facebook, Instagram, LinkedIn and other platforms with interactive content, live Q&A sessions and Takaful and Bancassurance educational videos. It's equivalent to influencer marketing in that one can build credibility among the Muslim consumers by promoting products especially from Islamic scholars and financial experts.

2.4.1 Building Brand Awareness and Trust through Islamic Content Marketing

Being deeply rooted in ethical principles, Islamic finance is very well suited to social media as a means of educating consumers on the benefits of Shariah compliant financial product. Building trust through providing content on Takaful and Bancassurance is a prime role played by content marketing.

Social media channels such as Facebook, LinkedIn, Instagram and YouTube allow financial institutions to share Takaful, risk sharing models, Islamic Bancassurance principles and their benefits in the form of explainer videos, info graphs and blog posts. Companies can have the opportunity to take the top space in the Islamic finance industry by making consistent efforts in providing high quality and relevant piece of content.

Aside from that, storytelling through social media is a great way to stimulate consumers. Islamic financial institutions can thus improve their credibility by sharing real life case studies and testimonials from policy holders who have satisfied with their services and also encourage other potential customers to start considering Takaful and Bancassurance as banking products.

2.4.2 Influencer and Islamic Scholar Endorsements

One of the best ways to utilize Islamic marketing is through the credibility of Islamic finance experts, religious scholars, and social media influencers who advocate for the use of ethical products. Religious guidance is widely sought by Muslim consumers, and it helps that influencer marketing is a powerful zone of consumer engagement.

Islamic financial institutions preferences to seek endorsement of their products by scholars specializing in Shariah compliant finance and providing explanation of their compliance with Islamic principles. Live Q&A sessions, webinars, video testimonials can be created and shared on platforms such as YouTube, Facebook Live, and Instagram Stories to make use of these endorsements.

Additionally, financial institutions work with Islamic style influencers who have a big audience base of Muslim consumers. And these influencers puts up his or her personal experience on Takaful policies or Bancassurance plans thus in a way providing an authentic and relatable marketing. Islamic financial service providers who tap into trusted voices in their campaigns shield consumers and pique interest in their products.

2.4.3 Social Media Engagement through Interactive Communication

Social media engagements are not only posting but how to sustain a two way communication. Social media platforms are put into use by Islamic financial institutions as interactive tools to interact with consumers, answering their queries and offering instant customer support.

Through Instagram, Facebook and LinkedIn, companies can host live sessions, polls, as well as Q&A features in order to connect with consumers on a real time basis. A lot of Takaful and Bancassurance service providers leverage chatbots on social media messaging applications like WhatsApp, Messenger and Telegram to deliver fast replies to the most often asked questions.

In addition, discussion forums and community groups make it possible for consumers to discuss and learn from each other about financial matters. Industry experts and company representatives help to moderate these groups to guarantee that consumers are gaining honest, pertinent information. Financial institutions are able to strengthen the strength of social media audience by sustaining active presence on social media.

2.4.4 Social Media Advertising and Data-Driven Targeting

Although financial institutions don't really have the market that they would like to have, the playing field is leveled by social media platforms offering advanced advertising tools that allow financial institutions to reach specific demographics that are defined according to their interests, location and online behavior. Using this data driven approach allows Takaful and Bancassurance providers to selectively promote to the potential clients with personalized marketing messages.

Companies pay to show their products to certain targeted audience through platforms like Facebook, LinkedIn and the YouTube. Advertisements suggesting investment linked Takaful plans can be used to target the young professionals who are seeking ethical solutions in financial planning. In the same manner, ad clients interested in obtaining ads about family Takaful coverage options would receive such ads.

Similar to that, retargeting strategies are also used to resurface ideas amongst Takaful or Bancassurance users where they have expressed interest but did not take action. The relevant ads that exist for an ecommerce store are delivered via AI driven algorithms that analyze user behavior and encourages conversions. Social media analytics not only helps the financial institutions to refine their marketing strategies, it also enhances the engagement rates.

2.5 Blockchain And Smart Contracts In Takaful And Bancassurance

In the financial transaction, security, transparency, and efficiency are provided by the tool of blockchain technology. Blockchain democratizes Islamic finance by making it seamless to comply with Shariah principles, the transactions being auditable and tamperproof.

2.5.1 Enhancing Transparency and Trust through Blockchain

The main concern of Islamic finance is that it should be transparent and follow ethical compliance. Blockchain's basic feature is that transactions in Takaful and Bancassurance take place in a decentralized and immutable manner, thus being recorded permanently on a public or permission ledger, and it is made available to the relevant stakeholders.

Blockchain technology works to increase trust for policyholders by giving them real time policy details, claim statuses and payments records without the use of mediators. All transactions are recorded on a distributed ledger, so the claim of fraud and manipulation is close to impossible, and risk sharing is fair.

Traditionally in Bancassurance, where banks sell insurance products, blockchain helps stick processes into straight path with the direct contact of financial institution, insurer and customers. This eliminates the chance of miscommunication or mystery clauses, each agreement is clearly documented and everybody concerned can view it.

2.5.2 Automating Takaful and Bancassurance Contracts with Smart Contracts

A self executing agreement, where the terms are defined in coded conditions. Smart contracts also perform a lot of automation and help reduce costs for administration and remove a human element in Takaful and Bancassurance.

One example would be of a smart contract which, for instance, would release the payout in a Takaful policy upon policy holder proving the claim conditions (such as a hospitalized case due to accident). It helps in faster settlements of claims, and consequently, makes the customers happy.

Thus, in Bancassurance, smart contracts ensures to pay insurance company premiums, ensure policy renewals and commission settlements between banks and insurance companies. These processes are automated to reduce paperwork, minimize errors and equation of financial transactions in time.

Furthermore, programming of smart contracts in Takaful allows the surplus funds to be distributed among policy holders automatically from a transparent source, which reflects the cooperative Islamic insurance.

2.5.3 Strengthening Compliance with Shariah Principles

Islamic finance abides by strong Shariah principles aimed at providing interest free (riba) and risk free (gharar) financing, the profits from which are circumspectly distributed among the investors. Of course, Blockchain technology vastly improves compliance by having auditable, tamper proof records of transactions so that regulators and Shariah Scholars find it easier to verify that Islamic guidelines have been followed.

Blockchain can be used by Takaful companies to be ensured that all collected premiums are invested in Shariah compliant avenues. As every purchase is recorded, policyholders can look at their funds and ensure it is not invested in non complying sectors like alcohol, gambling or traditional banking.

Blockchain, in the context of Bancassurance, brings regulatory oversight by creating a transparent record of data of policy sales, commissions and claim settlements. Blockhain based audit trails can be used by regulators to ascertain that banks and insurance providers are providing ethical and fair financial products to their customers.

2.5.4 Reducing Fraud and Enhancing Security in Insurance Transactions

In the insurance sector there are frauds and data breaches. There are no chances of fraud with blockchain technology; all recorded data on the distributed ledger is immutable and verifiable. Since every transaction is confirmed digitally, there is no way for changes or alteration to be made that any unauthorized person can gain access to that will alter the blockchain.

For instance, in Takaful, the number of fraudulent claims is minimized as each claim is verified against stored data before the claim is made so that members are not allowed to claim for the same event multiple times. Moreover, blockchain based identity verification ensures minimization of identity theft and beneficiaries get only those amount which they were eligible to get.

Blockchain in Bancassurance improves cyber security by encrypting customer data to ensure that hackers cannot hack or unauthorized access them. Since banks and insurance companies share sensitive financial information, they depend on a trusted exchange that must be able to utilize it effectively and without any kind of failure; (hence blockchain's decentralized nature) because of this there is less chance of cyber attacks being successful.

In addition, bringing blockchain to biometric authentication and digital IDs can reduce security even more, so that only authorized users will be able to see their insurance policies and financial data.

3. CHALLENGES AND COMPLIANCE IN DIGITAL TAKAFUL AND BANCASSURANCE

Still remains a priority of complying with Shariah principles and financial regulations. However, Islamic financial institutions must closely work with regulatory bodies to have digital solution which complies with legal and ethical standards. They are also very keen to cyber security and data privacy, therefore governance frameworks need to be very strong.

3.1 Ensuring Shariah Compliance in Digital Operations

The one of the most cardinal challenge within digital Takaful and Bancassurance is the adherence to Islamic Financial principles. In order to prevent riba (interest), gharar (excessive uncertainty) and haram (forbidden) investments, there is a need for a strong compliance framework to include digital transactions.

All digital platforms, payment gateways, and investment portfolios of Takaful operators and Bancassurance providers must be in line with Shariah. AI driven underwriting and blockchain based smart contracts must be crafted with such a care that no elements of uncertainty or unethical practice be accepted in the process.

Secondly, rise of fintech partnerships in Islamic finance also demands continuous Shariah audits for verification of the compliance. With new Islamic digital products going into circulation, Shariah boards and scholars need to be engaged, not only in reviewing, certifying and monitoring such products, but also in guiding the developers to create proper Islamic products. This will, in turn, result in reputational damages, financial penalties, as well as loss of consumer trust.

Compliance Strategies

- Also, AI powered compliance monitoring tools to check non-Shariah compliant transactions.
- Regular Shariah audits for digital Takaful and Bancassurance platforms.
- Working with certified Islamic scholars live to monitor digital financial products.

3.2 Cyber security Risks and Data Privacy Concerns

The digitization of Takaful and Bancassurance has made cybersecurity a major issue. There exist cases where the financial institutions handle large amounts of sensitive customer data; such as policyholder information, claims records and biometric data. By hacking, data breaches and ransom ware attacks you can provoke customer trust betrayal and data protection laws violation.

Furthermore, the Islamic financial institutions need to abide by the global data privacy regulations such as General Data Protection Regulation (GDPR) and local cybersecurity laws. As digital financial services are gaining popularity in Pakistan, compliance of the Personal Data Protection Bill and State Bank of Pakistan's cyber security guidelines is vital.

Takaful and Bancassurance providers face the challenge of implementing advanced security measures that keep digital accessibility. Investing in encryption technologies, blockchain for secure transactions and data security, and AI driven fraud detection is the effort which helps it balance the premise between customer convenience and data security.

Compliance Strategies

- A use case of implementing blockchain for secure and tamper free data storage.
- Installing multi factor authentication and biometric verification on customer login.
- To meet the global and local data protection laws.

3.3 Regulatory and Legal Framework Complexities

The industry of Digital Takaful and Bancassurance provides services in a highly regulated environment. Now with the emergence of digital financial services, the regulatory frameworks are no longer suited for traditional Islamic finance regulations. While many jurisdictions have no comprehensive laws related to digital insurance, digital insurance partnerships, and AI-based financial decision making.

In Pakistan, Takaful and Bancassurance operations have been regulated by the Securities and Exchange Commission Pakistan (SECP) and the State Bank of Pakistan (SBP). Nevertheless, the implementation of digital financial services requires new policies in terms of online engagement in dispute resolution, validity of digital contract and risk assessment based on artificial intelligence. The lack of consistent regulations in multiple markets further complicates the opening up of the digital Takaful and Bancassurance services.

Furthermore, regulators must ensure that new technologies like blockchain as well as AI remain in line with Shariah principles and at the same time protect consumers. Such delays and regulatory scrutiny should be avoided with clear guidelines.

Compliance Strategies

- Works with regulators in developing Islamic financial regulations in the digital finance space.
- Launching new digital Takaful products will be subject to conducting regulatory impact assessment.

3.4 Digital Financial Literacy and Consumer Trust Issues

Digital consumers will determine the success of both digital Takaful and digital Bancassurance but they are only willing to adopt them when they can demonstrate their financial literacy and the confidence in digital platforms. Few digital Islamic insurance services are available and known to many of the customers, in the emerging markets like Pakistan, who are hesitant to deposit their money on the electronic platforms for financial transactions.

One of the reasons behind limited adoption of digital Takaful and digital Bancassurance is otherwise false beliefs about security of digital transactions, they don't know what Takaful is, and they don't trust in the power of AI in making decisions. Further, some consumers might become afraid that they will lose personal control over their finances because underwriting and the claims processing will be automated.

Therefore, Islamic financial institutions need to promote actively the advantages of digital Takaful by educating the consumers how it contributes to transparency, security and compliance with Islamic ethics. However, social media, having AI-powered chatbots and educational campaigns can increase people's confidence in using digital financial services.

Compliance Strategies

- Initiating consumer education initiatives which help to increase the digital Takaful literacy.
- The benefits of using AI driven chatbots to increase the digital customer support for real time assistance.
- Helping Islamic thinkers and influencers developing the notion of digital Takaful and Bancassurance.

4. FUTURE DIRECTIONS

4.1 Integration of Artificial Intelligence for Personalized Offerings

AI driven personalisation that creates high engagement with customer and reduce risk management would be driving the future of digital Takaful and Bancassurance. It correctly identifies their lifestyle activities like web browsing history; it can analyze a huge quantity of customer data to make personalized product recommendations based on that data, predictions of policyholder behavior and the automation of underwriting processes.

For an example, chatbots and virtual assistants powered by AI will provide real time advising services which will respond to the customer queries, guide them to choose policy. Fraud detection in presence of digital transactions and claims processing will get enhanced using machine learning algorithms, thereby reducing risk from the electronic transactions. Moreover, AI based sentiment analysis would be capable of informing the financial institutions the customer sentiments and preferences so that they are able to modify their service offerings.

In addition, AI will assist in Takaful providers and Bancassurance firms assessing risks more accurately at fair pricing and also efficient claims management Nevertheless, this means that trust and transparency are going to be credibly maintained in digital Islamic finance when AI driven decisions must align with Shariah compliance.

Key Developments

- Underwriting done by AI to achieve faster and more accurate risk assessment.
- Predictive analysis based on which you can provide policy recommendations in accordance with them.
- AI-powered customer support for 24/7 engagement.

4.2 Blockchain and Smart Contracts for Enhanced Transparency

Digital Takaful and Bancassurance would be strengthened with blockchain technology and smart contracts in the areas of security, efficiency and transparency. Decentralized, immutable record keeping as offered by blockchain effectively reduces fraud, improve operational efficiency and improves trust between policyholders and service providers.

By using the blockchain and smart contracts, assistance is secured, and claims processing is automated to conveniently ensure electronic payouts for fulfillment of predefined conditions immediately. It alleviates delay and minimizes the probability of disputes, and in turn it builds policyholder confidence in the process of digital transactions.

Additionally, blockchain's transparent and immutably efficient ledger can be used to verify the policyholder contributions and investments and maintain compliance with Shariah principles. This will be of particular use in Takaful, where funds need to be handled on ethical grounds and in line with Islam values.

Key Developments

- Implementation of blockchain-based policy management for fraud prevention
- To reduce the claims processing efficiency
- Financial models with compliance to Islamic finance ethics

4.3 Expansion of Embedded and Inclusive Insurance Models

Digital Takaful and Bancassurance will increasingly employ embedded insurance models, which are how Takaful products are woven through digital services. Such a trend will make it possible for financial institutions to sell insurance through e-commerce platforms, mobile banking apps and fintech systems thereby making it easier for the wider section of the population to have access to same.

An example of this is when a customer buys a car online, he will receive Takaful insurance plan in the transaction automatically. Likewise, Takaful offering can be integrated to digital banking services by Bancassurance providers to provide a Shariah compliant financial protection by using lower effort.

Moreover, the focus will be on inclusive insurance i.e. developing micro-Takaful and digital first models for the underserved populations and the low income groups. The use of mobile technology in emerging markets is increasing and access to digital Takaful solutions will not only increase financial inclusion but market expansion as well.

Key Developments

- Creation of embedded Takaful solutions within the digital banking and e-commerce platforms.
- Development of micro Takaful models to offer simple affordable coverage to that segment of the population that is not covered.
- Customer profiling using AI to design the inclusive and accessible insurance solutions.

4.4 Regulatory Innovations and Standardization of Digital Islamic Finance

Digital Takaful and Bancassurance continue to evolve as regulatory frameworks should be willing to adapt to the evolving technological trends with cross border transactions. On the other hand, government, financial authorities and shariah scholars need to work out standard digital finance regulations in order to create a close Shariah financial practice validity in other market.

Variation in Shariah interpretation is one of the main challenges of the digital Islamic finance. To tackle this, global regulatory bodies for the digital Takaful and Bancassurance compliance will be established. This will give clear guidelines on AI governance, blockchain usage, and digital contract validation that are in accordance with the Islamic ethics.

In addition, the adoption of RegTech (Regulatory technology) will help financial institutions automate compliance processes, in order to ensure that financial institutions conform to legal requirement in as little human intervention as possible. In digital Takaful operations, AI driven screening and monitoring of activities will be a key component in identifying anomalies, catch red flags and at the same time, avoid financial misconduct.

Key Developments

- Integration of the RegTech solutions based on AI-powered automation of compliance monitoring.
- Islamic scholars and regulators cooperation regarding Shariah compliance.

5. CONCLUSION

An effort to achieve strategic digital transformation in Islamic marketing and consumer behavior that must be combined the technological enhancements with ethical aspects. In Islamic financial institutions, the need to adopt AI, blockchain, social media must be coupled with compliance of Shariah principles. It should therefore position future strategies aimed at enhancing financial literacy, digital inclusion, and collaborative regulatory approach to clarify and develop a comprehensive digital ecosystem for Takaful and Bancassurance in the future. When digital innovation is in line with the Islamic values, businesses create opportunity for sustainable growth as well as consumer trust in the emerging financial landscape.

Takaful and Bancassurance is going through rapid digital transformation which is changing buyer behaviour, thus driving the financial institutions to adopt innovative and engaging digital strategies. Today, the rising expectation of the consumers that they need seamless, ethical, and trust driven financial solutions leading providers to use AI, blockchain, social media and gamification to improve digital adoption. Technology can be aligned with Islamic financial principles in order to increase consumer trust, enhance engagement, and facilitate sustainable growth in the era of digital.

Having opportunities with digital transformation offered by Takaful and Bancassurance, we are also facing challenges on compliance, security, and trust on the consumer side. The solutions to these have a dose of technological innovation, regulatory collaboration, and ongoing Shariah oversight. However, Islamic financial institutions can undertake these cyber challenges successfully through the implementation of strong compliance frameworks, cybersecurity measures, consumer education strategies etc.

The transformation of Takaful and Bancassurance industry is fuelled by emerging technologies, digital transformation and changes in consumer behavior, and it will continue to shape future growth of the Takaful and Bancassurance industry. The next stage of development is for the financial institutions to adopt innovative customers strategies that will enhance customers experience by ensuring compliance and improving operational efficiency while maintaining Islamic financial principles. 4 key future developments that will shape the future of digital Takaful and Bancassurance are elaborated below.

Technological advancements, regulatory evolution and improving a strategy of consumer engagement are what will shape the future of digital Takaful and Bancassurance. Efficiency, accessibility, and transparency will be provided in the Islamic financial services through the integration of the AI, blockchain and embedded insurance models. Despite being business friendly, ensuring compliance to the evolving Shariah principles and regulatory frameworks will be key to sustaining the growth. With innovation in hands and ethics intact, digital Takaful and Bancassurance providers can discover new opportunities and broaden their reach in the worldwide Islamic finance market.

6. STRATEGIC RECOMMENDATIONS

In order for the practices of digital Takaful and Bancassurance to flourish and be profitable, financial institutions need to integrate advanced technologies from a strategic perspective while upholding Shariah principles. Risk assessment should be next enhanced using form of Artificial Intelligence and Big Data as well as to personalize customer experience and speed up of operational process. Underwriting and predictive AI analytics that support assessments of the behavior of the policyholder can help to be more accurate on pricing as well as claims management. AI powered chatbots and automated advisory services also improve significantly the customer engagement through their 24/7 available property. Yet, institutions are duty bound to make sure that AI models conform to Islamic financial ethics as well as regulatory guidelines in order to maintain transparency and trust of the consumers.

Adoption of blockchain technology and smart contracts opens up for a very good opportunity to improve security, cut fraud and boost transaction efficiency. Immutable ledger of blockchain is a good way of amplifying the policyholder trust in Takaful models by making the fund management in transparent, smart contract can revolutionize the claims process with assurances to define machine processing of claims, therefore, eliminating delays and disputes. Also, Takaful products could be embedded into digital banking and e-commerce platforms which will increase market reach as the consumer is able to access financial protection without hassles. To make this integration streamlined, regulatory bodies need to impose standard guidelines to be followed by all the regions for digital compliance, reducing the possibility of interpreting Islamic Shariah in different ways and having a universal agreement of Islamic financial service globally.

In order to explore the fluid digital world, regulatory innovation and a set of compliance frameworks must be at the top of the agenda. Financial institutions along with the regulatory authorities, and Islamic finance scholars should be in collaboration for drafting governance models where AI enabled decision making can be made to happen while being ethical. RegTech solutions can help in the implementation of such solutions, which can help in the monitoring of compliance tasks in a real time so that breaches or financial misconduct can be detected real time. Also, micro Takaful solutions would expand financial inclusion out of reach for the masses while enhanced digital offerings for the underserved would increase market penetration and reach this group. Strategically integrating innovation with ethical considerations in the development of digital Takaful and Bancassurance providers will help them achieve a long-term sustainability, consumer trust and competitive advantage in the Islamic finance ecosystem.

REFERENCES

Alshammari, A. A., Alhabshi, S. M. B. S. J., & Saiti, B. (2019). The impact of competition on cost efficiency of insurance and takaful sectors: Evidence from GCC markets based on the Stochastic Frontier Analysis. *Research in International Business and Finance*, *47*, 410–427.

Bagasworo, W., & Simatupang, S. (2022). Increased Purchases of Insurance Products Based on Factors That Affect Customer Trust (Study on Banccasurance in Greater Jakarta, Indonesia). *Jurnal Ekonomi, Manajemen Dan Perbankan (Journal of Economics, Management and Banking)*, *8*(1), 30–38.

Bebber, S., Milan, G. S., De Toni, D., Eberle, L., & Slongo, L. A. (2017). Antecedents of purchase intention in the online context. *Journal of Relationship Marketing*, *16*(1), 82–98.

Boer, H. & During, W.E. (2001). Innovation, what innovation? A comparison between product, process and organizational innovation, *International Journal of Technology Management, 22*(1/2/3), pp. 83-107.

Carranza, A. (2017). The Importance of Content Marketing in 2017 and Beyond, at: https://www.business2community.com/content-marketing/ importance-content-marketing-2017-beyond-01861200, Accessed date: 7 October 2017.

Chong, F. H. L. (2021). Enhancing trust through digital Islamic finance and blockchain technology. *Qualitative Research in Financial Markets*, *13*(3), 328–341. DOI: 10.1108/QRFM-05-2020-0076

Deloitte. (2013). The global Takaful insurance market charting the road to mass markets, A Deloitte ME IFKC Practice Insights Series, available at: https://ceif.iba .edu.pk/pdf/ Deloitte The global Takaful insurance market Charting the road to mass markets.pdf (accessed 20 November2016).

Eling, M., Nuessle, D., & Staubli, J. (2021). The impact of artificial intelligence along the insurance value chain and on the insurability of risks. In Geneva Papers on Risk and Insurance: Issues and Practice (Issue 0123456789). Palgrave Macmillan UK. DOI: 10.1057/s41288-020-00201-7

Eybers, S., & Setsabi, N. (2021). Responsible Data Sharing in the Digital Economy: Big Data Governance Adoption in Bancassurance. In *Inventive Computation and Information Technologies* [Singapore: Springer Nature Singapore.]. *Proceedings of ICICIT, 2020*, 379–394.

Guemmaz, S. (2023). Shareholding relations between banks and insurance companies in Algeria: An overview. *Journal of Innovations and Sustainability*, *7*(2), 1. DOI: 10.51599/is.2023.07.02.01

Haron, S., & Nursofiza, W. (2008). *Creating a dynamic Islamic capital market: the essential role of innovation, Islamic Capital Markets: Products, Regulation and Development, Islamic Research and Training Institute*. Islamic Development Bank Group.

Hartmann, P. M., Zaki, M., Feldmann, N., & Neely, A. (2016). Capturing value from big data–a taxonomy of data-driven business models used by start-up firms. *International Journal of Operations & Production Management*, *36*(10), 1382–1406. DOI: 10.1108/IJOPM-02-2014-0098

Ichsan, N. (2015). Analisa SWOT, prospek dan strategi pengembangan asuransi Syariah Di Indonesia (SWOT analysis, prospects and development strategy for Islamic insurance in Indonesia), available at: https://nurulichsanaan.files.wordpress.com/2015/10/analsis-swot-asuransi-syariahjurnal-kordinat.pdf (accessed 10 November 2016).

Jin, S. V., Muqaddam, E. R., & Ryu, E. (2019). Instafamous and social media influencer marketing. *Marketing Intelligence & Planning*, *37*(5), 567–579. DOI: 10.1108/MIP-09-2018-0375

Kailash, M. S. R., Joshi, C., Desai, P. R., Teferra, N. B., & Radhakrishnan, S. (2023). The Rise of Ethical Consumerism: Marketing Strategies for the Conscious Buyer.

Kakkar, G. (2017). Top 10 Reasons Behind Growing Importance of Content Marketing, at: https://www.digitalvidya.com/blog/importance-ofcontent-marketing/, Accessed date: 3 December 2017.

Kasim, N., Nuhtay, S. N., & Salman, S. A. (2013). Shariah Governance for Islamic Capital Market: A Step Forward. International Journal of Education and Research Vol. 1 No. 6. ISSN: 2201-6740.

Kiel, D., Arnold, C., & Voigt, K. I. (2017). The influence of the Industrial Internet of Things on business models of established manufacturing companies–A business level perspective. *Technovation*, *68*, 4–19. DOI: 10.1016/j.technovation.2017.09.003

Litao, X., & Xinzhou, S. (2021) Research on Consumer Behavior Based on the Perspective of Behavioral Economics. Proceedings of the 2021 3rd International Conference on Economic Management and Cultural Industry (ICEMCI 2021). Advances in Economics, *Business and Management Research, 20*(3) pp. 316-319.

Nanda, S. A (2020). Cognitive consonance between business intelligence and decision-making in Bancassurance. *Odisha journal of social science, 7*(2). Pp 8-26.

Ostrom, A. L., Parasuraman, A., Bowen, D. E., Patrício, L., & Voss, C. A. (2015). Service research priorities in a rapidly changing context. *Journal of Service Research, 18*(2), 127–159. DOI: 10.1177/1094670515576315

Purusottama, A. & Simatupang, T.M. (2025). Adoption of blockchain technology in promoting halal compliance, *Journal of Islamic Marketing*, Vol. ahead-of-print No. ahead-of-print. DOI: 10.1108/JIMA-12-2023-0423

PWC. (2018). Whom do consumers really trust? available at: https://www.pwc.com/gx/en/industries/ consumer-markets/consumer-insights-survey/consumer-trust.html

Redhika, R., & Mahalli, K. (2014). Analisis Potensi dan Kendala Pengembangan Asuransi Syariah di Kota Medan (potential analysis and constraints of Islamic insurance development in medan). *Jurnal Ekonomi DanKeuangan, 2*(5), 323–335.

Relan, M., & Kumar, M. (2023). Impact of Trust and Risk Factors on the Satisfaction Level of the Policy Holder towards Digital Bancassurance Model. [IRJMSH]. *International Research Journal of Management Sociology & Humanity, 14*(7), 15–24.

Rowley, J. (2008). Understanding Digital Content Marketing. *Journal of Marketing Management, 24*(5-6), 5–6, 517–540. DOI: 10.1362/026725708X325977

Schouten, A. P., Janssen, L., & Verspaget, M. (2019). Celebrity vs. Influencer endorsements in advertising: The role of identification, credibility, and Product-Endorser fit. *International Journal of Advertising*, •••, 24.

Sestino, A., Prete, M. I., Piper, L., & Guido, G. (2020). Internet of Things and Big Data as enablers for business digitalization strategies. *Technovation, 98*, 102173. DOI: 10.1016/j.technovation.2020.102173

Shoetan, P. O., & Babajide, T. F.Philip Olaseni ShoetanBabajide Tolulope Familoni. (2024). Transforming fintech fraud detection with advanced artificial intelligence algorithms. *Finance & Accounting Research Journal, 6*(4), 602–625. DOI: 10.51594/farj.v6i4.1036

Shomad, A. (2025). Liability of Islamic Banks in Bancassurance Activities. *Journal of Law and Regulation Governance, 3*(1), 435–445.

Sorescu, A. (2017). Data-driven business model innovation. *Journal of Product Innovation Management, 34*(5), 691–696. DOI: 10.1111/jpim.12398

Statista. (2020). Global insurance companies' digital technology investment priorities worldwide 2020.

Willems, K., Brengman, M., & Van De Sanden, S. (2017). In-store proximity marketing: Experimenting with digital point-of-sales communication. *International Journal of Retail & Distribution Management*, *45*(7-8), 910–927. DOI: 10.1108/IJRDM-10-2016-0177

Yahia, I., Ben Al-Neama, N., & Kerbache, L. (2018). Investigating the drivers for social commerce in social media platforms: Importance of trust, social support and the platform perceived usage. *Journal of Retailing and Consumer Services*, *41*(1), 11–19. DOI: 10.1016/j.jretconser.2017.10.021

Yasin, M., Porcu, L., Prados-Castillo, J. F., & Liébana-Cabanillas, F. (2024). The Role of Social Media in Building Islamic Banking Consumer Engagement: Analysing the Impact of Brand Personality Traits and Brand Love. *International Journal of Human-Computer Interaction*, •••, 1–15.

KEY TERMS AND DEFINITION

Artificial intelligence: Artificial intelligence (AI) is intelligence demonstrated by machines, and this intelligence is taken as the ability of a machine to learn, reason, and make decisions. However, all of these are A.I. Powered eg: Datamunch, predictive analytics, machine learning, and chatbots that are transforming the industries including financial services.

Bancassurance: Takaful Bancassurance was a business model where Takaful products are distributed through the banking channels. This partnership enables the banks to provide insurance solutions to their customers, making the services more accessible and secure. Bancassurance in an Islamic finance context, should guarantee to offer in the products it proposes in an Islamic manner, according to ethical and transparent financial principles.

Business Strategy: Business strategy refers to the main way of business plan and corporate decision-making with regard to realizing the corporate goals, gaining competitive advantage and firm sustainability. The are market analysis, product positioning, the financial planning and customer engagement.

Consumer Behavior: The study of consumer behavior is referred as consumer behavior which means the study about how consumers behave while making the purchase, use and discard of goods and services. There are among examined factors include cultural influences, psychological motives, the way purchasing habits and digital interactions. The behavior of the consumer has changed with the gradual developments in online platforms, artificial intelligence and the personalized marketing.

Consumer Engagement: In consumer engagement, businesses pay attention to how they engage with customers with the aim of getting them to deepen their brand loyalty, achieve trust, amongst others. Therefore personalized marketing, social media interaction, educational content and customer support are parts of it.

Digital Transformation: Digital transformation is all about using digital technologies to transform all the aspects of a business and fundamentally change how businesses run and value delivers to customers. This means that it involves the use of technologies like artificial intelligence, big data, blockchain as well as cloud computing to make the processes better, optimize customer experience, and create new business models.

Islamic marketing: Islamic marketing is an ethical and value based marketing process which is management from Islamic principles and Shariah business practices while developing a marketing plan to pursue competitive advantages in its target market. In all the marketing activities, it encourages honesty, transparency, fairness and social responsibility. Islamic marketing contrasts from common marketing because it adheres to trust and moral responsibility of consumers; the products and services do not include elements like interest (riba), gambling (maysir) or uncertainty (gharar). By following ethical advertising and communication strategies, it plays the role of promoting and introducing Muslim consumers to financial products such as Takaful and Bancassurance.

Social Media: Social media is digital platform in which users create, share, and interact with content on online. Different from all the other mediums, Facebook, Instagram, LinkedIn, and Twitter have revolutionized communication and marketing and consumer engagement within this age. Here within Islamic marketing, social media is key to Islamic Bancassurance and Takaful promotion, positive information dissemination to consumers on Takaful and Bancassurance and the connection of businesses with their target market.

Takaful: Takaful means the way of Islamic insurance based on mutual cooperation and responsibility. The concept of Takaful is quite different from conventional insurance since it does not involve uncertainty (gharar), don't make profit in interest (riba) but where people engaged in risk sharing by pooling their money towards themselves in case of need.

Chapter 14

The Role of AI in Consumer Decision-Making:
Transforming Purchase Behavior and Personalization

N. Muthurasu
Sona College of Technology, India

Venkata Ramana Kaneti
VNR Vignana Jyothi Institute of Engineering and Technology, India

S. Vengatesh Kumar
JNN Institute of Engineering, India

G. Premalatha
https://orcid.org/0000-0003-1031-5607
SRM Institute of Science and Technology, India

P. Aparna
https://orcid.org/0009-0007-7510-2561
RMK College of Engineering and Technology, India

K. Raju
Rajalakshmi Engineering College, India

Beslin Pajila
https://orcid.org/0000-0002-3905-2460
Vel Tech Rangarajan Dr. Sagunthala R&D Institute of Science and Technology, India

ABSTRACT

This chapter explores the impact of artificial intelligence (AI) on consumer decision-making, focusing on its role in transforming purchasing behavior and personalization. AI technologies such as machine learning, predictive analytics, and recommendation systems have revolutionized how businesses engage with consumers, providing personalized experiences across the decision-making process. From problem recognition to post-purchase evaluations, AI enhances efficiency and relevance.

DOI: 10.4018/979-8-3373-2747-1.ch014

However, it also raises ethical concerns, including data privacy, algorithmic bias, and transparency. The chapter examines these challenges and offers insights for marketers and retailers on leveraging AI for consumer behavior analysis. It also highlights areas for future research, particularly in AI ethics, data privacy, and the long-term effects on consumer autonomy.

1. INTRODUCTION

1.1 Background and Context

Artificial intelligence (AI) is transforming the different industries by bounds in the recent years and consumer behavior is one of the areas of life that has been most impacted by the artificial intelligence(Ifekanandu, C et al., 2023). The AI scope is rather broad and comprises machine learning (ML), deep learning, natural language processing (NLP), and predictive analytics, and all of them have been slowly becoming a component of consumer decision-making. AI enables the machine to think like a human being and learn some consumer habits, which makes it more predictive, recommending, and individualising. The introduction of AI into consumer behavior has resulted in the change which is rather impressive, in particular, in the manner in which people interact with products and services. These technologies have assisted the companies to gather large amounts of data, analyse the consumer behaviour and tailor their products to match their individual tastes. Not merely has the AI transformed the traditional vision of the marketing process, which has made it simple to make sense of the consumer data, but it has also opened the gates to superior decision-making processes.

The outcome of such revolution is AI-driven personalization- an approach that helps businesses create individualized experiences to customers based on their history, preferences, and demographics. It can be personalized product recommendations or dynamic pricing, but it is all AI-based personalization that is transforming the character of the relationship between business and consumers(Mishra, S., & Mishra, P. 2022). A case in point is that recommendation engines which are based on machine learning algorithms are an inseparable part of e-commerce stores where they suggest or recommend the products that a consumer would be likely to purchase based on their browsing or preferences. Such a tailored plan has been found to maximize consumer satisfaction, involvement and ultimately sales. Since AI is still in its developmental stages, its capacity to influence consumer choices does not end with the traditional e-commerce. It could be in the form of entertainment services like Netflix where based on the use of AI the service could recommend entertainment based on the preference of a person, to travel booking sites where users are provided with travel recommendations based on their preferences this is increasingly becoming the process by which consumers make purchase decisions. Because of its ability to offer personalized experiences that appear natural and relevant to the consumer, artificial intelligence is one step away of becoming a crucial tool of a modern marketplace(Pillarisetty, R., & Mishra, P. 2022).

1.2 Significance of Study

The importance of the role of AI in the consumer decision-making process can hardly be overestimated. As industries and companies are implementing AI technologies, they will use them more and more to forecast and manipulate consumer behavior. In this environment, the insights on how the AI-based systems operate and to what level they influence the purchasing behavior will be of value to both scholars and professionals. Such observations can inform the creation of more efficient marketing practices, product offering, and customer interaction activities. Among the key features of AI in consumer decision-making, the driver of consumer engagement must be mentioned(Khodakarami, F., & Chan, Y. E. 2014). Individualized marketing where AI tools are used can be a big boost to the customer experiences which ultimately results in customer satisfaction, loyalty and customer advocacy. With the consumers being overwhelmed with a continuous flow of options in an ever more digital marketplace, AI-based personalization offers an opportunity to slice through the clutter and bring relevant content. Companies that utilize the potential of AI will be able to establish stronger emotional links with consumers, as they will be able to offer personal experiences that will be unique to their needs.

The practical usefulness of the research in the effect of AI on the preference of consumers can also be attained. With better insights about the behavior of the consumers, the companies will be in a position to better their products and even make better pricing strategies and even customer services. The magnitude of the consumer data analysis that the AI offers to the business allows the businesses to find out the patterns and trends which would otherwise have not been noticeable and thus makes the business more informed about the operations and more efficient. The other way that companies can use AI to know the preferences and needs of the consumers is to assist them in delivering the correct, timely, and relevant content to their consumers. Another important thing to understand is the effect that AI has on the ethical concerns of consumer decision-making. With an increasing number of sensitive data being processed with the assistance of AI systems, the problem of privacy has become apparent, as well as the problem of transparency and accountability. As the use of AI is becoming more and more a part of consumer experience, businesses must pay attention to how they capture, process and use consumer data. The creation and implementation of AI-driven systems, should be done in a way that does not infringe consumer privacy, transparency and fairness to ensure the long term success of such technologies.

The other significant thing regarding this work is that AI will have more power in dictating the preferences of the consumers. As the AI systems develop, they can not only propose the products or services on the basis of the past history but also on the basis of the needs that will be in the future. This prediction capacity allows the companies to be in a position to forecast the demand better and supply based on the demand. That way, firms can influence the choices that consumers make even before they make the purchases making the process of shopping more comfortable and personal. This is a critical process to understand its working and the psychological impact it causes to the consumers in concluding the overall implication of AI on decision-making.

1.3 Objectives of the Chapter

The chapter is primarily aimed at discussing how AI plays an important role in shaping consumer decisions and how the element is revolutionary in contributing to the improvement of the buying behavior. Specifically, the chapter will discuss how the AI technologies have currently been used to influence how the businesses are being made by consumers. The goal of the chapter is to provide an in-depth understanding of the effect of AI on consumer psychology and behavior by analyzing its existence in the traditional and digital market.

The first purpose of the chapter is to evaluate how AI can drive the shift in the consumer decision-making. As the AI becomes a part of the various levels of customer experience which encompass the initial levels of discovery to the stages that come after the purchase, i.e., the assessments, this chapter will address how such technologies are affecting each of the levels of the customer decision-making process. This will entail the understanding of how the recommendation engines that apply AI can be useful in helping consumers arrive at their product decision, how AI-based tools can be useful in the comparison of alternatives, and the impact of AI in the context of post-purchase satisfaction.

The second goal is to review the changes in the purchase behavior that AI is making by altering the consumer-product and service interaction. Artificial intelligence such as chatbots, customized advertising and predictive analytics are transforming consumer interactions with brands. In this chapter, the author will discuss the impact of these technologies not only on the consumer preferences, but also on the way of decision-making including the speed and character of the purchase decisions. The role of AI in building consumer loyalty and trust will also be discussed so that to understand how it can build a long-term relationship between a consumer and a brand. Finally, the chapter will also provide the broader picture of AI-based personalization tools which have gained a lot of popularity during the previous years. Personalization may be termed as tailoring of products, services and content to the requirement and taste of individual consumers and AI is heading this movement. The chapter will discuss how AI systems will utilise the information gathered about the consumers to give them an individual experience and make superior decisions leading to more engaged consumers and higher conversion rates by the business. Having studied these techniques of personalization, companies will be able to orient themselves in the rapidly changing world of consumers and increase their opportunities to create an important contact with consumers.

2. AI TECHNOLOGIES SHAPING CONSUMER DECISION-MAKING

2.1 Artificial Intelligence Overview

Artificial Intelligence (AI) may be defined as the imitation of the human intelligence in the machine that is made to think and act human. The simple idea behind AI is to create the systems that can perform the work which is typically performed by human beings and needs human intelligence such as reasoning, problem solving, learning and decision making. The simplest types of the AI technologies are machine learning (ML) and deep learning (DL) that have changed the decision-making process of consumers by allowing systems to process large amounts of information and learn through analysis to make improved decisions over time.

Machine learning (ML) is a subfield of AI, which allows computers to develop without explicit programming to learn through experience(Prabhu et al., 2025). ML algorithms receive data in order to train the models, and the systems can identify patterns and make predictions or decisions regarding the new input. ML can be found in consumer decision systems in such form as product recommendation, buying behavior prediction, or even content customization. A more sophisticated form of ML is deep learning (DL) where the learning process is approximated by a neural network with many layers and simulates the human brain. DL is especially useful in analyzing unstructured information such as images, speech, and text, which make it suitable in such applications as voice recognition, image recognition, and natural language processing, all of which is becoming more important in consumer engagement with brands.

The combination of AI, ML, and DL makes an exceptionally strong basis of the systems that become better and better with each new piece of data and therefore can be perfectly used in consumer decision-making. These technologies also enable companies to customize the interactions, automate the processes, and provide the consumers with the highly relevant experiences which have a significant influence on the purchasing behavior. The future of AI is making the predictions of consumer preferences and the ability to understand the consumer preferences even more accurate, and this is contributing to the manner in which the decisions are being made in the market(Manjunathan et al., 2025).

2.2 AI Applications in Consumer Decision-Making

Among the most impactful AI-related transformations in consumer decision-making, one can mention the development and introduction of a broad portfolio of technologies that can make shopping more pleasant(Gutti, D et al., 2023). The following are some of the methods that business is using AI to transform consumer behavior and impact the purchasing decision; AI-powered recommendation system, chatbots, and predictive analytics.

The Recommendation Systems are one of the most popular AI applications to the consumer decision-making process. These systems analyze massive information concerning the consumers such as their buying habits, their browsing patterns, demographical information and even their social media activities and suggest to them products or services that they are likely to be interested in. To give an example, in case a consumer goes to an e-commerce site, the recommendation engine will suggest the products that the consumer has purchased before or the products that other consumers have purchased who have similar interests in the products. In the entertainment services there is an algorithm that suggests a movie or a show to a user depending on his/her history of viewing and preferences. This not only simplifies the process of decision-making of the consumer, offering relevant choices, but also significantly influences the probability of a purchase or subscription, by narrowing down the choice and making it more of an individual experience(Wang, W et al., 2025).

The Chatbots and Virtual Assistants have also emerged as an inseparable part of consumer decision making particularly in customer services and online shopping. These types of AI-powered technologies provide a customer with an immediate response to his/her inquiry, help with the process of buying a product, and even suggest a specific product. Chatbots are programmed to talk to human beings using natural language processing (NLP) and therefore it can understand and respond to the human language in its natural way, which the consumer is likely to be satisfied with(Balakrishnan, T et al., 2025). They can assist in any way including inquiries about products and even doing the purchase. Under the context of consumer decision-making, these AI tools allow consumers to make their purchases more convenient and easier which in most cases remove barriers that might not permit a purchase to be made. The process of shopping with the help of such AI application can appear smooth and natural, establishing a stronger connection between customers and brands they address.

There is also the emergence of Sentiment Analysis and predictive Analytics, which are playing a significant role in the decision making of the consumers. Predictive analytics refers to the use of AI on existing data and make predictions on future actions. The example is that predictive analytics may enable business to forecast the need of a specific product or even forecast the probability of a consumer to buy a product. The companies are able to concentrate more on their marketing campaigns, work better on their inventory and also enhance the customer experience with the help of the knowledge of the consumer behaviors. Similarly, sentiment analysis which entails the use of text information that is derived under various sources to determine consumer attitude and feeling has come out as a significant tool in studying consumer preferences. By means of the sentiment analysis, companies can get the mood or perception of a product, brand or service and this will go a long way in establishing the decision making strategies. One of them is that in a case where sentiment analysis demonstrates that a product has negative feedback, an organization may decide to alter its marketing strategy, alter the product or correct the problems that the consumers are complaining about. This helps the companies to be flexible and sensitive to the needs of consumers to establish better relationship with consumers and the likelihood of them sticking to the company.

2.3 AI in Marketing and Advertising

The influence of AI on consumer decision-making reaches much further than personal recommendations of products and chatbots, it also transformed the approaches to how businesses can market and advertise. Marketing and advertising using AI can change the way organizations approach consumers and make them more relevant, personalized, and time-sensitive in their messages, resonating with them.

One of the most apparent ways of AI in contemporary marketing is Personalized Advertisements and Promotions. AI exploits the data of consumers to make very specific advertisements that are personalized according to tastes, behavior, and needs. AI, through machine learning, uses the information about the user to analyse when, on which platform, and in which form an advertisement should be presented(Ramesh P et al., 2024). To illustrate, a consumer who has already demonstrated the interest in running shoes can be presented with an advertisement of a particular brand of shoes when surfing social media or watching a video on YouTube. The customized advertisements are not confined to the conventional forms; they go to the extent of dynamic messages which can be modified depending on the current consumer action. Such individualization makes the advertisements more relevant, and the consumers are more likely to read the content and eventually buy something.

The AI also enhances significantly the Targeting and Segmentation, especially with the help of predictive analytics and deep learning models. With the help of AI, business can segment their audiences according to the numerous different factors that include demographics, geographic location, browsing history and purchasing habits. With the help of such attributes, AI will be able to distinguish between different consumer groups and target them with particular marketing messages that will be customized to their own unique features. This is a precise strategy of targeting, which results in improved marketing campaigns and a greater rate of investment returns by businesses. An example is that a clothing company can employ AI to target people who have indicated interest in the environmentally friendly products, and provide them with discounts or adverts about its sustainable products. By so doing, it can be ensured that businesses are approaching the correct consumers with the correct message, at the correct time and this increases the likelihood of making a purchasing decision by many folds.

Besides, dynamic and adaptive advertising strategies are possible because of the ability of AI to work with large volumes of data in real-time. As an example, AI can track the reaction of consumers to advertisements and modify the messages or format according to the interaction of the audience with it. In case a consumer clicks on a product advert and fails to purchase it, AI can send retargeting adverts that remind the consumer about the product or offer some discounts to attract the consumer to purchase the product. Such a learning process will allow AI to adjust its strategies and better the effectiveness of campaigns with time.

2.4 The Role of AI in Consumer Purchase Behavior

The use of AI technologies in marketing and advertising has great consequences on the purchasing behavior of the consumers. AI does not only recommend products, but it also influences the way people communicate with businesses and make decisions. As AI can personalize product suggestions, customize advertisement, and automate customer support, companies will be able to provide the smoother, fun, and more efficient experience that will make consumers want to buy their products. In addition, AI makes the purchase decision quicker and convenient. AI can make consumers take faster decisions because it offers real-time suggestions and personalized advertisements, eliminating the friction during the purchase. The consumer can now be served with tailored offers in real-time using their phones, computers or voice assistants and act on it immediately. This instant acquisition of individual experiences helps to create a quicker and smoother consumer path that is very important in the current competitive world(siva subramanian R et al., 2023).

3. AI-DRIVEN PERSONALIZATION IN CONSUMER BEHAVIOR

3.1 Personalization Techniques

Artificial intelligence-based personalization has emerged as the pillar of the contemporary marketing approach that is dramatically changing the nature of interactions between a business and a customer and improving their purchasing patterns(Jayaraman, K. D., & Jain, S. 2024). AI-driven personalization techniques allow using huge volumes of consumer data to develop customized experiences that appeal to personal taste and requirements. Some of the most notable customization methods include dynamic pricing and personalized product and content recommendation.

Dynamic Pricing Models is an advanced way through which companies can change the price of a product or service depending on many determinants such as demand of the consumer, competitor prices and market factors as well as individual consumer characteristics. AI is very important in this process as it will allow reading the data in real-time and finding the best price point that would maximize sales, profit, or customer satisfaction. Such a strategy does not only assist companies to generate more income but also makes the consumers feel that they are being offered a more individualized offer, thus encouraging them to be more engaged. Dynamic pricing models work since they allow a business to be responsive to the changes taking place in the market, and the behaviors of the consumers so that whatever they offer is competitive.

Another important part of personalization on the basis of AI is Personalized Content and Product Recommendations. AI-based recommendation engines employ machine learning algorithms to track consumer behavior, including past purchases, browsing history, preferences, and response to recommendations that they have seen in the past. Through the pattern recognition and making future preferences, AI can recommend products or contents that are of high relevance to the consumer. The technique does not only make the consumer decision making process easier but also enhances the chances of conversion because the consumer is exposed to products that he/she will be more willing to purchase. Individual suggestions induce the feeling of relevance and convenience, and the shopping process seems more interesting and personalized.

The above personalization methods are exceptionally effective since they enable businesses to establish stronger relationships with consumers. When businesses learn what people like and dislike, they can create custom experiences that do not seem so much like a marketing gimmick but rather a true customer service. Besides, such personalization methods as dynamic pricing and recommendations result in more effective buying behavior, which does not require consumers to spend much time on searching the products or services that can satisfy their needs. Consequently, the consumers will tend to make purchases more easily, and in most cases with little hesitation as they are sure that the products being offered are of high fit to their taste.

3.2 Consumer Experience Enhancement

Personalization AI methods also apply to the whole consumer experience and not just the product offering, as it enhances the interaction between consumers and businesses. It is a major contributor to the change of consumer experience that is more customized and user-friendly because of AI-based customization of user interfaces and interactions. Customized user interfaces adjust the format and the functionality of the websites or applications in accordance with the consumer preferences, habits, and browsing behavior. As an example, a site can alter the presentation of products or services to focus on the categories that a given user has clicked on, or an online store can show offers or products based on the previous purchases of a consumer.

Such customized interfaces would prove to be a game changer as far as the ease of consumer navigation and interaction with platforms are concerned. Through the focus on the content that matters and the ease of use, AI makes the process even more convenient, minimizing the risk of decision fatigue and making the interaction much more intuitive. To take an example, a consumer who has repeatedly purchased fitness equipment can be recommended with specific suggestions such as workout clothes, health supplements or fitness plans when he/she visits an online store again. Likewise, an AI-based travel booking service can also present customized deals on the basis of the prior travel choices, including destinations, flight classes, or even hotel facilities.

Product curation and customization is another area of AI growing in use. AI-based product curation enables companies to propose products or services that meet the particular interests, needs, and preferences of a consumer, therefore, generating a curated experience. Customization takes it a notch higher where a consumer can make products to his or her taste. To give an example, a clothing store may apply AI to propose an outfit that fits the style of a consumer, yet they can modify some of the characteristics, e.g., color, material, cut. The customization by AI also spreads to such spheres as personal care products, where AI would study the type of a consumer and make a recommendation of a particular product.

These UX innovations as well as product curation assists in increasing the overall consumer experience by streamlining it and making it worthwhile. With platforms which know their needs and preferences, consumers tend to spend more time on it, see more products and make faster buying decisions. The feeling of personal attention and comfort that AI-powered interfaces have to offer can greatly contribute to the level of customer satisfaction, making a consumer feel appreciated and understood.

This means that the companies are able to build a better relationship with their customers and encourage them to buy again by creating unique experiences every time.

3.3 Impact of Personalization on Purchase Decisions

The consumer journey with the incorporated AI-driven personalization has immense effects on the decision of the purchase. Personalization does not only affect which products will be purchased by consumers but also when, how often and what they will buy. The effects of personalization methods such as dynamic pricing, recommendations and customized experiences on consumer behavior can be measured and affect the behavior in the way of impulse buying, the creation of consumer loyalty, as well as repeat purchase behavior.

Effect on Impulse Buying: Individualization based on AI has proven to have a big impact on the possibility of impulse buying. Using custom suggestions, personalized advertisement and pricing, AI systems can initiate a purchase decision immediately, and in most cases, before the consumer has the opportunity to make a considered decision. As an illustration, a consumer receiving a push notification on a time-limited discount on an item he/she has just looked at may be encouraged to make an impulsive buy. On the same note, an e-commerce site with the complementary items feature can make a consumer add additional items to their shopping cart without planning to buy them at all. The AI algorithms take advantage of such psychological stimuli, and based on the data about the consumer, they will determine when the consumer is most likely to make a purchase and they will provide him with incentive to make a purchase.

The AI personalization that leads to impulse buying is especially strong in the digital environment where consumers can make decisions without much effort. That is why a lot of e-commerce websites, online shops, and even streaming services apply recommendation engines which are powered by AI and they not only recommend the products but also can trigger the real-time offers, discounts, or promotions. With the help of AI, relevant and customized information at the opportune moment, can result in spontaneous buying, which translates into more sales and higher profits.

Generating Consumer Loyalty and Repeat Purchases: In addition to the effects of impacting impulse purchase, AI-based personalization can also be used to generate consumer loyalty and to drive repeat purchases. The concept of personalization instills a feeling of personal care and attention and consumers feel special and comprehended by the brands they interact with. This emotional relationship usually results in brand loyalty because consumers would tend to go back to brands that can provide them with personal experiences and brands that can always satisfy their needs. Such AI-powered loyalty programs, e.g., can provide personal rewards or incentives depending on the previous purchasing history and preferences of a consumer. Such programs do not only stimulate the repeat purchases, but also enhance the bond between the consumer and the brand.

In addition, AI-based personalization may help to improve customer retention because it allows to predict the needs of consumers and to provide them with the most relevant products or services at the right time. The AI systems can remind the customer of the products they may need to restock, give discounts on the products they have already shown interest in or make recommendations based on the future seasonal trends by analyzing the past interactions and predicting the future behaviors. Such anticipative measures can keep companies at the forefront of the minds of consumers, which makes them buy the products again and again.

Besides the loyalty, customer lifetime value (CLV) can also be improved with the help of AI-powered personalization. Businesses may develop a long term relationship with their customers by continuously adjusting to the behavior and preferences of the consumers. It is especially in crucial in the business sectors such as e-commerce, entertainment and subscription where customer retention is the most important ingredient to success. The more customized and specific the offerings of a business are the higher the chances that the consumers will not only purchase the products but also repeat purchase thus making the value of each customer to be higher.

4. IMPACT OF AI ON CONSUMER PURCHASE BEHAVIOR

4.1 Decision-Making Process

Artificial Intelligence (AI) is greatly transforming the consumer decision-making process by improving on the way consumers face the phases of consumer decision-making process. The capacity of AI to collect, process and decipher huge amounts of data allow businesses to have a better insight into consumer behavior which eventually determines how people make decisions. All four main stages of consumer decision-making (problem recognition, information search, evaluation of alternatives, and post-purchase behavior) are influenced by AI, therefore making the decision-making process more efficient, informed and personalized(Sudha K et al., 2023).

Problem Recognition: Problem recognition is where the process of decision making is normally initiated by the identification of a need or a problem. Consumers in the traditional environment would normally recognize their needs either by personal experiences or the external stimuli. This has however been altered by the advent of AI, whereby consumer needs are identified and predicted in advance. Predictive analytics and other AI tools enable companies to predict the time when their consumers may feel a need depending on their previous actions and interactions.

As an example, the e-commerce can detect that a customer is low on a particular product that he/she had bought before and recommend him/her to buy it again. In the same way, AI-powered systems monitor the browsing activity of consumers and once a user displays an interest in a particular category of products, one may begin to receive suggestions or even personalized content that generates new desires. This forecasting ability assists customers to be aware of their issues or needs even before they are able to be aware of them.

Information Search: The consumer will start searching information in order to solve the need that he or she has recognized. In the past, it would be a manual search, going to the stores, or browsing websites, to compare products or services. AI has transformed this step by offering a far better and customized search experience. Recommendation engines powered by AI propose a product or a service based on what a consumer has searched before, what he or she likes and what he or she has done before, essentially making the search more specific to what he or she wants. The application of AI in information search saves time and efforts of the consumers who look through the information in the form of curated results that have high chances to meet their needs. As an example, an AI can redirect the consumer to websites, blogs, reviews, or products relevant to the fitness interest of the consumer. Moreover, the voice-activated search is also made possible by natural language processing (NLP) tools, a type of AI, which means that consumers can receive information more quickly and in a conversational form and therefore have a better search experience.

Evaluation of Alternatives: The second step of decision-making process is the evaluation of alternatives in order to make a right choice. At this step, AI is important as it delivers personal recommendations of products, customer reviews, and comparison. AI can also suggest alternatives depending on the preferences of the consumers because it can analyze the consumer behavior. As an example, AI can provide side-by-side comparison of various products with reference to the earlier interactions or the purchases made by a consumer and thus, consumers can easily compare the available products that best suits their needs. With the help of machine learning algorithms, user data, such as the history of purchases, browsing history, interactions on social media, etc., are analyzed to determine which items will be the most attractive. AI can also give real-time feedback of other consumers in form of reviews and rating that would help in the creation of trust and confidence of the consumer in their judgment of alternatives. This customized decision making process simplifies the process of decision making thus making the buying decisions to be made quickly and with much conviction.

Post-Purchase Behavior: The process of decision making does not end with the act of purchase, but continues after the purchase in the form of post-purchase evaluation which may have an effect on the future purchase decisions. AI has been of great help to this stage as it monitors consumer satisfaction, offers assistance and facilitates repeat buying. AI systems collect feedback in different ways, including customer reviews, satisfaction surveys, and social media communication, and use this information to identify the consumer sentiment. Chatbots and virtual assistants are post-purchase AI applications that help customers to get real-time support on their concerns about the product and provide an instant solution to the problem, which enhances customer satisfaction. Moreover, AI enables the constant engagement by sending the personal offers, reminders, and follow-up suggestions depending on the previous purchases. To illustrate, a customer who purchases a skin care product can be sent subsequent messages that will recommend some of the products that would go well with it or some promotion of the brand. This constant interaction will keep the customers coming back to buy more goods in the future and this will form a cycle of continuous interaction.

4.2 AI and Consumer Trust

Although AI has a lot of benefits in the decision-making process, it has also posed severe issues of consumer trust, in particular, with data processing and privacy. Consumer behavior involves trust as a crucial factor, and to have a positive effect on purchasing behavior, consumers have to be sure that their data is treated ethically and responsibly.

Trust Concerns over AI in the Processing of Consumer Data: One of the major issues that consumers have when dealing with AI technologies is the issue of how their personal data are gathered, stored and utilized. Using large sets of consumer data, AI systems are able to deliver personalized experience, yet the process of collecting such data can be opaque, which is why it can prompt suspicion and distrust. To illustrate, consumers would not like the idea that AI algorithms are monitoring their web experiences, purchasing habits, and even social media habits to tell what they like in the future. With such systems getting advanced, consumers may want to know the extent of personal data that AI systems are utilizing in order to suggest a product or offer a targeted ad. The fact that the consumers feel that they are being used without their express permission or knowledge may make them hesitant to use AI-driven systems, and this may adversely affect their likelihood to purchase products or use brands.

Ethical Concerns and Data Privacy in AI Systems: Data privacy and security are some of the ethical concerns raised in relation to AI where businesses are advised to guarantee the privacy and safety of consumer data. The issue of data privacy has gained popularity due to the emergence of laws which seeks to safeguard the right of consumers on personal data. Customers are gaining knowledge about their rights to data and are becoming quite apprehensive about how businesses access their data, keep it and use it. Ethical use of AI such as open data processing and consumer approval are vital in the sustenance of trust. The AI systems that do not reveal the use of consumer data or provide an effective opt-in solution can make consumers lose trust in the platform. To achieve the successful use of AI-driven personalization without threatening the trust, companies need to make sure that their AI systems are transparent, accountable, and ethical in their data handling. In addition, the companies should follow the data protection regulations and ensure consumer privacy by exercising responsibility with data.

4.3 Changing Consumer Expectations

Artificial intelligence is also defining evolving demands in terms of the speed, accuracy, and convenience of judgment-making in general. It is in demand to be quicker and more customized, and the consumer requires the company to provide a smooth experience across all platforms, which is the basis of omnichannel experience.

The Need of More Rapid and More Accurate Decision-Making Support: In the age of digital convenience, customers demand that their needs receive a fast and accurate response. These expectations can be achieved with the help of AI-powered systems that are able to give real-time recommendations, personal offers, and support. The consumers are used to being satisfied immediately and AI can quench that thirst because it provides solutions that are nearly immediate. An example is that chatbots and virtual assistants can answer consumer questions in real time, recommendation engines can suggest specific recommendations in real time, and can assist consumers in making more efficient decisions. Predictive analytics can help companies to predict the needs of the consumers and provide them with personal products or services before they even show interest in them. Such responsiveness has increased the expectations of the consumers and companies unable to use AI to overcome these expectations might not remain competitive.

The other important change in consumer expectations is the need to have a seamless experience across channels and devices. When consumers are shopping on the Internet, in a real store or through mobile applications, they want to have a consistent experience with brands. AI is important in the development of this smooth omnichannel experience because it links data across different touchpoints to deliver a single consumer experience. AI assists companies to align their online and offline products so that the same tailored recommendations and service are offered no matter what the channel is. An example would be when a consumer visits a brands site on the internet, he may get personal emails about the products he looked up on the web site or a customer in a shop may get offers based on his location on his mobile phone. By incorporating AI into every step of the customer journey, companies will be able to guarantee that the experience of the consumers will be consistent, personalized, and convenient regardless of the channels.

With the changing consumer expectations, AI systems are finding their way into supporting the need of faster and accurate decision support and omnichannel experiences. Companies that do not keep up with these changing expectations would lose consumer loyalty and interest. Conversely, those companies that use AI to offer real-time personalization, responsive customer service, and an integrated omnichannel experience will probably develop better relationships with their customers and will enhance their business performance as a whole.

5. CHALLENGES AND ETHICAL CONSIDERATIONS

5.1 Ethical Challenges in AI-Driven Consumer Decision-Making

The process of consumer decision-making with the help of AI depends on data greatly. Nevertheless, as the AI systems progress to become more advanced in the prediction of consumer behavior, ethical concerns arise, mainly when it comes to fairness, transparency, and bias of such systems. These are some of the issues in the responsible use of AI technologies in consumer-facing applications.

Algorithmic Biases and Fairness: Algorithmic bias is the most pressing ethical problem of AI use in consumer decision-making. Big data is the one used to teach machine learning algorithms that might be biased or skewed in the past or in the society(Chong & Shi, 2015; Elgendy, N., & Elragal, A. (2014). Consumer-wise, the biases may be described as the credit scoring, personalized pricing or product recommendations, where the consumers are not treated equally, based on their demographic characteristics, such as race, gender, or socioeconomic status.

The same may apply to an AI-based credit scoring system where certain demographic groups may become unfairly disadvantaged due to the biases found in the data on which such models are trained. Similarly, individual marketing through AI can even exclude or discriminate some classes of consumers by not targeting them as frequently or promoting them less valuable products based on their past buying record or perceived worth. Such biases can prove harmful to the marginalized communities, reinforcing inequality and marginality.

To minimize such risks, companies should ensure that the data that reflects the training of AI systems is diverse, representative, and does not reflect any discriminating patterns. In addition, the algorithms should be developed in a way that they become less biased and the audit of the AI systems should be performed on the regular basis to assess whether they are fair or not. The bias in the algorithms is the problem that can be addressed and the AI systems will be more equitable and transparent, which will increase the trust that consumers have towards them.

Transparency of AI-Driven Decisions: The other significant ethical issue is transparency of AI-driven decisions. Most AI systems, particularly deep learning systems, are black boxes, which means that the logic of the decision is not simple to comprehend by people. This is not transparent and it casts doubt on accountability and fairness of relationships with consumers. When consumers face AI-based decisions, whether it is personal pricing, credit scores, or loan approvals, then they usually have little or no knowledge of the decision-making process. This invisibility may foster the feeling of powerlessness and frustration, and this may be aggravated by the feeling that consumers are being treated unfairly, or that decisions seem arbitrary.

5.2 AI's Influence on Consumer Autonomy

The growing influence of AI in decision-making processes among the consumers begs the question of whether consumers can remain autonomous and not be manipulated. Although AI is a convenient and efficient process, it is also a threat to consumer agency because it can manipulate the choices that consumers make in some way or other, often not noticeable at all.

Manipulation in Decision-Making: Manipulation is one of the most important ethical issues that should be paid attention to when it comes to AI. The consumer data can be used to make predictions of decision-making and influence through AI systems, which makes it easier to exploit the psychological triggers by businesses. As an example, the customized advertisement and pricing schemes may be made in such a way to target a weakness of a consumer, e.g. the urgency or the scarcity. These methods have the capability of forcing consumers into making a choice that they would not have otherwise made, compromising their capability to make the decision in a fully autonomous manner.

In the worst-case scenario, AI might be applied to exploit the consumer behavior in predatory ways, like offering dangerous products or services to vulnerable groups. Such manipulation is particularly problematic in cases where AI is deployed in the healthcare industry, finance industry, or gambling industry where consumer choices can be very costly. The AI design should be aimed at the prevention of manipulative approaches and the facilitation of the responsible, transparent marketing that should not exploit the consumer but provide him with power instead.

Effect on the Consumer Agency and Free Choice: AI can affect consumer agency and free choice not only through manipulation. AI systems can restrict a consumer to new knowledge or new perspectives by personalizing all the experiences of a consumer. To illustrate, a user of an AI-powered recommendation system is frequently shown the choice that is consistent with their behavior or preferences in the past, which leads to the formation of a so-called filter bubble where the user is made to have fewer choices and is more predictable. The decreasing number of choices may undermine the level of informed choices by the consumers since they may not know about other products or services that may suit their needs better.

Besides, continuous optimization of the consumer experiences through AI could create a dependence on such systems as consumers will trust AI recommendations more than they will themselves. Although personalization is convenient, it may lower the range of the experiences that consumers can have, and it restricts their ability to access new ideas, products, or services.

Businesses need to balance between personalization and diversity to maintain autonomy of the consumers. The AI systems must be designed in such a manner that they facilitate consumer agency through choice and giving them more control over the decision making process. This may include providing consumers with a facility to reset preferences, opt-out of personalization, or widen product categories that they may not be behaving in the past but can still be valuable.

6. FUTURE TRENDS IN AI AND CONSUMER DECISION-MAKING

Artificial intelligence is still developing, and its impact on the process of consumer decision-making is getting deeper and deeper. Technological advances are redefining the ways AI can communicate with the consumer and allow companies to design even more personal, intuitive, and invisible interactions. The AI in consumer decision-making in the future is expected to improve augmented and virtual reality, hyper-personalization, predictive analytics, and autonomous AI systems. This part examines the major trends that would define future of AI in consumer behavior.

6.1 Advancements in AI Technologies

The AI technologies are being developed at a very fast pace and are changing how consumers make their decisions, particularly by incorporating the use of immersive technologies such as augmented reality (AR) and virtual reality (VR). Such developments do not only present new experience to consumers but also offer new methods of business to approach potential customers and improve decision-making.

Consumer decision-making with the integration of Augmented Reality (AR) and Virtual Reality (VR): One of the most exciting prospects that AI has to offer is in the integration of Augmented Reality (AR) and Virtual Reality (VR) to consumer decision-making. Although AR superimposes data on the physical reality, VR makes consumers a part of the entirely virtual world. When mixed with AI, these technologies provide the consumers with novel means of visualizing products, engaging with services, and immersing into a brand experience prior to decision making.

AR is also used more frequently in the retail industry to enable customers to virtually test clothing, eyewear, or makeup before buying it. To illustrate, the AR apps in the fashion industry enable the consumers to see the clothes on their bodies using the smartphones or the devices in the stores to see the appearance of the clothes in the stores. Virtual reality, in its turn, is a completely immersive experience, which allows consumers to visit virtual stores, test products, or use services in a virtual environment. As an example, the automotive industry is already utilizing VR, which gives customers an opportunity to test drive cars virtually or get to know the options of a new model. In the same way, the potential buyers in the real estate sector can visit houses and other properties using VR and save time and improve the decision-making process. AR and VR can shape the consumer preferences as well as offering more interesting and knowledgeable consumer buying experiences by designing very interactive and sensory-rich environments.

6.2 The Future of Personalized Marketing

Personalized marketing with the help of AI has already started to transform consumer decision-making, and the next trend is even more advanced, i.e., hyper-personalization. Personalized marketing is the future that is to be achieved through the use of AI to provide more accurate and personalized experiences than simply suggesting products based on their previous actions. Hyper-Personalization using AI: Hyper-personalization is a step further of personalized marketing, where through complicated data analytics, AI, and machine learning, individual consumers are given a very customized experience. In contrast to the traditional personalization that is usually based on simple demographic data, or on the previous purchase history, hyper-personalization is built on a more in-depth knowledge of the consumer preferences and behaviors, social factors, and even real-time data to provide the relevant content, offers and product recommendations at each step of the customer journey.

6.3 AI-Driven Consumer Insights and Predictive Analytics

The use of AI in consumer analysis and generation of insights to enable businesses to make improvements is not new. However, the further development of predictive analytics will make it even higher, as past behaviors will no longer be analyzed only but the future trends and changes in consumer preferences will be predicted. This capacity to forecast change in the consumer behavior will give the business a great competitive advantage in the market. Role of AI in Forecasting Future Trends and Consumer Behavioural Change: The predictive analytics driven by AI has a potential to revolutionize the consumer decision-making process by enabling the businesses to know what the consumers are going to want before they themselves realize it. Through analysis of big data, AI is able to identify new trends and changes in the consumer behavior and assist companies in making informed decisions regarding product development, marketing, and inventory.

6.4 Potential for Autonomous AI Systems

Further evolution of AI is making the possibility of totally autonomous systems, which make decisions instead of consumers, a more feasible prospect. Although AI has been mainly applied as an aide to facilitate decision-making, there might be emergence of autonomous AI systems that might become the decision-making authority in purchasing decisions made by a consumer.

AI Making Decisions on Behalf of Consumers: Autonomous AI systems where the AI itself makes the decision on behalf of the consumer is likely to be one of the greatest shifts in consumer decision-making. These assistants will not merely suggest products according to the preferences of the consumer but they will take an active role of making a decision to purchase these products on behalf of the consumer. As an illustration, AI shopping assistant may automatically place an order to groceries, household items or fashion products according to the past preferences of the consumer, their current needs and budget. There is also the possibility that in the future, AI systems will also consider factors like the health of the consumer, environmental factors and even how stressed or in a good mood they are in order to make decisions that are best in the interest of the consumer.

Such autonomous systems would be able to save a great deal of time and effort of the consumers by simplifying the shopping process and automating the minor purchasing decisions. Nevertheless, they also bring up some critical ethics. The degree to which AI can be given the freedom to make decisions on behalf of the consumers, especially in such fields as health, finance, and law will be one of the biggest areas of controversy. As much as autonomous AI systems are convenient, they may restrict consumer agency and cause a person to be dependent on technology to make certain decisions that they would have made independently.

7. CONCLUSION

AI has essentially changed the way consumers make decisions by altering the way in which consumers interact with products, services and brands. Incorporation of AI solutions like machine learning, recommendation systems, and predictive analytics has helped businesses deliver a very personalized experience, which has resulted in faster and more relevant and individualized decision-making. Personalization methods with the help of AI have transformed the manner in which businesses implement marketing strategies, providing consumers with customized content, personalized products suggestions, and dynamic pricing systems. The innovations have not only led to consumer satisfaction but also conversion rate and customer loyalty. The influence of AI on consumer behavior manifests itself in various stages of decision-making process, including problem recognition, post-purchase evaluations, and so on. AI assists the consumer in determining his or her needs even before the consumer realizes them, simplifies the process of searching information, assists in comparing alternatives, and guarantees constant interaction after the purchase. Nevertheless, these developments have also brought to the fore some critical ethical issues especially on data privacy, algorithmic bias and transparency. Companies using the power of AI should also be careful about upholding ethical practices so that their AI system is fair, secure, and transparent to create and sustain consumer confidence. The use of AI in consumer behavior analysis presents a huge potential to marketers and retailers. Using AI technologies, companies will be able to process a huge number of data related to consumers to find out something about their tastes, tendencies, and purchase behavior. These insights enable businesses to develop very specific marketing plans, streamline their products, and present adverts that appeal to customers. Furthermore, AI can also assist the companies to forecast the future trends and consumer changes, which enables the company to be ahead of the competitors. To get the best returns on these benefits, firms will be required to invest in effective and ethical AI applications that do not breach the privacy of the consumers and are expected to bring value to the consumers in terms of efficient personalization. In spite of the fact that the AI role in the consumer decision-making process is enormous, there are certain gaps where further research is needed. The aspects of the ethical nature of AI and its impact on the autonomy of consumers, data privacy, and the transparency of the AI systems are the most significant directions of research. As the AI continues to evolve, it is essential to speak about the impacts of such technologies on the long-term consumer behavior and independence and the general impact on the society. The future studies may be devoted to the creation of frameworks to offer an ethical application of AI, the bias of AI models, and the attitudes of consumers towards choices, which are made by AI. The study will be instrumental in ensuring that the AI will be in best interest of the consumers and will also encourage trust and responsibility in the market.

REFERENCES

Balakrishnan, T. S., Ebenezar, U. S., & Karthikeyan, L., & BS, K. (2025, March). Exploring Few-Shot Learning to Enhance NLP's Cross-Domain Capabilities. In *2025 International Conference on Computing for Sustainability and Intelligent Future (COMP-SIF)* (pp. 1-6). IEEE. DOI: 10.1109/COMP-SIF65618.2025.10969937

Chong, D., & Shi, H. (2015). Big data analytics: A literature review. *Journal of Management Analytics*, *2*(3), 175–201. DOI: 10.1080/23270012.2015.1082449

Elgendy, N., & Elragal, A. (2014). Big data analytics: a literature review paper. In *Advances in Data Mining. Applications and Theoretical Aspects: 14th Industrial Conference, ICDM 2014, St. Petersburg, Russia, July 16-20, 2014.* [Springer International Publishing.]. *Proceedings*, *14*, 214–227.

Gutti, D., Yadav, G. V., & Kaja, H. (2023). Influence of artificial intelligence in consumer decision-making process. *The Business of the Metaverse: How to Maintain the Human Element Within This New Business Reality*, 141-155.

Ifekanandu, C. C., Anene, J. N., Iloka, C. B., & Ewuzie, C. O. (2023). Influence of artificial intelligence (AI) on customer experience and loyalty: Mediating role of personalization. *Journal of Data Acquisition and Processing*, *38*(3), 1936.

Jayaraman, K. D., & Jain, S. (2024). Leveraging Power BI for advanced business intelligence and reporting. *International Journal for Research in Management and Pharmacy*, *13*(11), 21. https://www. ijrmp. org

Khodakarami, F., & Chan, Y. E. (2014). Exploring the role of customer relationship management (CRM) systems in customer knowledge creation. *Information & Management*, *51*(1), 27–42. DOI: 10.1016/j.im.2013.09.001

Manjunathan, N., Aravindaraj, K., Anitha, J., Bharathi, V. R., Sathya, V., Senthil, R., & Subramanian, R. S. (2025). Advances in Data Processing, Machine Learning, and Data Security. In Strategic Innovations of AI and ML for E-Commerce Data Security (pp. 207-234). IGI Global.

Mishra, S., & Mishra, P. (2022). Analysis of platform business and secure business intelligence. *International Journal of Financial Engineering*, *9*(03), 2250002. DOI: 10.1142/S2424786322500025

Pillarisetty, R., & Mishra, P. (2022). A review of AI (artificial intelligence) tools and customer experience in online fashion retail. [IJEBR]. *International Journal of E-Business Research*, *18*(2), 1–12. DOI: 10.4018/IJEBR.294111

Prabhu, D., Tejasri, M. V. S. L., Saratha, B., & Anish, T. P. (2025, April). Future Horizons: Key Trends Shaping the Evolution of Machine Learning. In *2025 8th International Conference on Trends in Electronics and Informatics (ICOEI)* (pp. 1091-1099). IEEE.

Ramesh, P., Nithyanandhan, R., Faizal, M. M., Nivakumar, V., & Nalini, M. (2024, December). Machine Learning Strategies for Customer Churn Prediction in Competitive Enterprises. In *2024 International Conference on Sustainable Communication Networks and Application (ICSCNA)* (pp. 653-660). IEEE. DOI: 10.1109/ICSCNA63714.2024.10864143

Siva Subramanian, R., Maheswari, B., Nikkath Bushra, S., Nirmala, G., & Anita, M. (2023). Enhancing Customer Prediction Using Machine Learning with Feature Selection Approaches. In *Inventive Computation and Information Technologies* [Singapore: Springer Nature Singapore.]. *Proceedings of ICICIT, 2022*, 45–57.

Sudha, K., Anish, T. P., Balakrishnan, C., Lakumarapu, S., Pajila, P. B., & Subramanian, R. S. (2023). Leveraging Machine Learning for Customer Intelligence: An Experimental Analysis Learning Classifiers. *Procedia Computer Science, 230*, 128–137. DOI: 10.1016/j.procs.2023.12.068

Wang, W., Chen, Z., & Kuang, J. (2025). Artificial Intelligence-Driven Recommendations and Functional Food Purchases: Understanding Consumer Decision-Making. *Foods, 14*(6), 976. DOI: 10.3390/foods14060976 PMID: 40231979

Chapter 15
Anthropomorphism and Familiarity in AI Adoption:
A TAM-Based Perspective on Human-Machine Interaction

Mariem Sboui
https://orcid.org/0009-0004-7652-174X
University of Tunis, Tunisia

Nadia Sfar
https://orcid.org/0009-0000-6324-2419
University of Monastir, Tunisia

Ons Baati
https://orcid.org/0009-0000-1316-9241
University of Monastir, Tunisia

ABSTRACT

Artificial intelligence (AI) based chatbots have significantly transformed the landscape of AI-driven services. This chapter examines the fundamental determinants influencing the intention to adopt chatbots in the telecommunication services context. Specifically, it investigates the influence of familiarity, anthropomorphism, perceived ease of use, and perceived usefulness on chatbot usage intention. Data were collected via an online survey administrated to 321 Tunisian higher education students. The hypotheses were tested with Smart PLS4. The findings indicate that anthropomorphism and perceived usefulness positively influence chatbot adoption, whereas ease of use has no effect, and familiarity exerts a negative impact.

DOI: 10.4018/979-8-3373-2747-1.ch015

Additionally, anthropomorphism enhances both usefulness and ease of use, while familiarity does not. These results offer valuable insights for marketers, particularly in the telecommunications sector, by enhancing the understanding of factors driving user adoption. This chapter contributes to the growing body of literature on the Technology Acceptance Model (TAM).

1. INTRODUCTION

The rapid progress of Artificial Intelligence (AI) has significantly transformed various industries' operations (Rashid and Kausik, 2024). Its capacity to emulate human cognitive functions has generated huge opportunities for companies to seamlessly interact with customers (Chen et al., 2021). The incorporation of AI is revolutionizing business operations, providing managers with novel pathways to reconsider marketing approaches and improve the customer experience (Aarabe et al., 2024). One of the key tools of Artificial Intelligence is a chatbot (or conversational agent). Being accessible 24/7, chatbots enable customers to seek information about any product or service, at any time and location. Thus, it may be useful to enhance customer experience (Salem, 2024). Hence, the global chatbot market was valued at approximately USD 7.76 billion in 2024 and is projected to grow at a CAGR of 23.3% between 2025 and 2030[1].

Artificial intelligence (AI) is extensively integrated across a wide range of sectors, e.g., education, retail, tourism, entertainment, and telecommunication (Christensen et al., 2024; Sboui et al., 2024; McLean and Osei-Frimpong, 2019). Within these domains, AI is utilized for diverse functions, such as marketing (Aarabe et al., 2024), speech recognition, problem-solving, personalized recommendations, and data processing (Davenport and Ronanki, 2018). In addition, harnessing AI in telecommunication companies improves customer base and retention, delivers automated services, and radically transforms the telecom sector (Khan, 2023) into a high-tech service sector (Rashid and Kausik, 2024).

Among the various theoretical models developed to analyze the factors influencing technology acceptance, the Technology Acceptance Model (TAM) has emerged as a widely recognized and empirically validated framework (Gefen et al., 2003). Despite continued debates over its validity and reliability with the progression of emerging technology, several research confirm its relevance across digital industries (Wang et al., 2023). While studies employing TAM for the adoption of chatbots are limited, its integration into the field of AI like chatbots requires further examination (Wang et al., 2023). In this regard, the present study investigates the intention to adopt chatbot services, using the TAM as a theoretical framework.

Based on the theory of reasoned behavior, created by Davis et al. (1989), TAM suggests that behavioral intention is a pivotal determinant of current system application, which is affected by two factors: Perceived ease of use (PEOU) and Perceived usefulness (PU). The more customers have the higher the favorable opinions toward a service or system, and the more they believe it to be easy and enjoyable (Liu et al., 2024). While PU shows users' expectations of benefits and improved performance (Bailey et al., 2023), PEOU is the anticipation of an easy and enjoyable experience (Na et al., 2022).

Ahn (2023) stipulates that a critical limitation of the TAM is the rational behavior when users adopt technology. However, it is established that our decisions are derived from emotions rather than reasonable actions (Ahn, 2022). Thus, it is important to focus on the psychological effect of using emerging technology (Ahn, 2023).

The attribution of human characteristics to non-humans (Anthropomorphism), plays a pivotal role in AI chatbot adoption (Pillai and Sivathanu, 2020). In particular, although anthropomorphism offers emotional implications and attributes intelligence, consumers are more likely to favor humanoid chatbots than mechanical equivalents (Kim et al., 2023; Park et al., 2023).

Drawing from Thomaz et al. (2020) suggestions for an expanded investigation into the effects and drivers behind the humanization of AI chatbot service by users, the present study aims to develop a thorough model to explore two main determinants of intention to use chatbots: Anthropomorphism and familiarity.

Therefore, anthropomorphism seems to be an essential factor in understanding consumer acceptance of AI chatbots. In the present study, anthropomorphism represents the extent to which customers perceive chatbot services as humanlike, rather than the intentionally humanlike-designed features implemented by firms.

Familiarity with AI-enabled technology is crucial in shaping individuals' adoption tendencies. Prior research suggests that users are more likely to adopt new technologies when they have previous exposure to them. Empirical evidence (Kennedy and Funk, 2016; Horowitz et al., 2024) indicates that 52% of consumers prefer familiar brands and products, whereas only 35% are willing to adopt emerging technologies without prior experience with their effectiveness. Moreover, 39% of individuals prefer to delay adoption until they receive insights from others' experiences. However, the relationship between familiarity with technology and anthropomorphism remains inconclusive, with contradictory results in the literature. Some studies suggest a positive effect, arguing that robot-related familiarity, derived from past interactions, may enhance users' anthropomorphic perceptions (Aroyo et al., 2017; Epley et al., 2007). However, several studies suggest an opposing view, indicating a negative effect of prior experience with technology on anthropomorphism (Haring et al., 2016) or reporting no significant relationship between the two constructs (Stafford, 2013).

Moreover, while numerous studies have explored the impact of anthropomorphism on customers' intention to use service robots, the findings remain inconsistent. Some research supports a positive effect (Stroessner and Benitez, 2019), whereas others report a neutral impact (Goudey and Bonnin, 2016) or even a negative influence (Broadbent et al., 2011). By integrating anthropomorphism and familiarity into the TAM framework, this study offers a deeper insight into chatbot adoption, thereby addressing a gap in the existing literature on AI technologies.

The present study contributes to the existing literature in several ways. First, it answers the calls for further research on service- robots anthropomorphism (see Thomaz et al., 2020). In addition, to the best of our knowledge, this is the first attempt to extend TAM with two key antecedents of chatbot acceptance; familiarity and anthropomorphism, specifically within the realm of AI chatbots, as a key determinant influencing consumer adoption. Furthermore, the theoretical model in this study is empirically examined within the telecommunication industry sector as recommended by (Gatzioufa and Saprikis, 2022), where chatbots are widely implemented to enhance customer service efficiency (Shin et al., 2023).

This chapter begins by outlining the theoretical background through a critical review of relevant literature and foundational theories that underpin the study. It then develops key research hypotheses, building on theoretical and empirical insights to develop the conceptual framework. The methodology section details the research design, data collection, and analytical techniques used to ensure methodological robustness and validity. Finally, the conclusion synthesizes the main findings, discusses theoretical and managerial implications, acknowledges the study's limitations, and suggests future research directions, thereby contributing to both academic discourse and practical applications.

2. THEORETICAL BACKGROUND

2.1. AI Chatbots in Service Industries

As an important AI technology, chatbots or conversational agents are increasingly used to substitute human customer service. Indeed, these automated programs enable human conversations via text chats or voice commands to quickly answer their questions by mimicking to human exchange process. Companies use chatbots because they provide 24/7 assistance service to customers by responding to their inquiries, informing them about services, and offering them personalized suggestions (Shin et al., 2023). Furthermore, the evolving capabilities of chatbots make them increasingly effective since they assure customized interactions based on consumers' history and preferences (Kelly et al., 2022). Thus, the integration of chatbots in customer services improves the overall customer experience (Bakkouri et al., 2022), which encompasses how a customer interacts with a product or service, as well as the organization and the emotional reactions these interactions generate (Nouhaila et al., 2024).

To enhance customer-company engagement, chatbots are currently used to assist services in different fields (Ashfaq et al., 2020). As a matter of fact, during the last decade, chatbots have spread in a variety of domains such as banking (Lubbe and Ngoma, 2021; Pillai and Sivathanu, 2020), hospitality (Alotaibi and Hidayat-ur-Rehman, 2025), and e-commerce (Araújo and Casais, 2020). However, literature related to chatbot adoption in telecommunication services is relatively scant (Gatzioufa and Saprikis, 2022).

Considered a particular high-tech service sector, the telecommunications sector pioneered the use of Artificial Intelligence (AI) methods over a decade ago (Rashid and Kausik, 2024). Specifically, it is an exemplary sector that frequently adopts chatbots to offer automated services, detect faults, and conduct remote maintenance (Khan, 2023).

2.2. Chatbot Anthropomorphism

The ability of anthropomorphic attributes in non-human entities to establish links and relationships between consumers and technology has been extensively recognized (Waytz et al., 2010). It is a fundamental aspect of human-robot interaction (Song and Kim, 2022). Beyond the physical appearance of robots, anthropomorphism encompasses how their traits and behaviors shape individuals' perceptions to perceive them as human-like entities (Zlotowski et al., 2015; Song et al., 2024).

Empirical research proved that customers' adoption and engagement with automated technologies are optimized by their perception of human trait similarity (Stroessner and Benitez, 2019). "*Anthropomorphism is the assignment of human traits or actions to nonhuman objects*" (Song et al., 2024).

Previous studies focus on two important features of AI chatbot anthropomorphism: The design and appearance elements (De Kleijn et al., 2019; Go and Sundar, 2019), and the linguistic and conversational side (Araujo, 2018). Although Ciechanowski et al. (2019) demonstrate that customers prefer the text-driven chatbot over the human voice, this research investigates the conversational style of AI chatbot services to optimize user experience and engagement. Therefore, the advantage of interaction with human-like conversational agents is their capability to engage customers through pleasant communication and attractive experiences (Nordheim et al., 2019).

2.3. The Technology Acceptance Model (TAM) Theory

In the realm of emerging technologies, numerous studies have investigated how customers perceive and adopt innovation, which has caught the interest of organizations and stakeholders (Khizzou et al., 2024). To understand the determinants of technology adoption, several theoretical frameworks have been established, such as the theory of reasoned action (Fishbein and Ajzen, 1977), the theory of planned behavior (Ajzen, 1991), the technology acceptance model (Davis, 1986), the innovation diffusion theory (Rogers, 1962), the technology Readiness index (Parasuraman, 2000) and the unified theory of acceptance and use of technology (Venkatesh et al., 2003). Among these approaches, previous research proved that the TAM is a robust and reliable model for examining technology acceptance behavior throughout various digital industries (Gefen et al., 2003; Ibrahim et al.,2025; Wang et al., 2023). Furthermore, the strength of this theory is its ability to explore the crucial factors that drive behavioral intentions within different technology applications (Alotaibi and Hidayat-ur-Rehman, 2025; Kelly et al., 2022). In the context of an AI chatbot, the TAM has been an important framework for clarifying the customer's intention to use this technology (Wongyai et al., 2024; Wu et al., 2025).

To offer further knowledge to the AI chatbot adoption, recent research suggests adding other variables to enrich the approach of the TAM (Mogaji et al., 2024). Numerous extended versions have been developed: TAM2 (Venkatesh and Davis, 2000), TAM3 (Venkatesh and Bala, 2008), and UTAUT (Venkatesh et al., 2003). The additional determinants incorporated by these versions, like social influence, experience, and facilitating conditions (De Cicco et al., 2022; Liu et al., 2024; Wu et al., 2025), do not include the important factors of human-chatbot interactions: Anthropomorphism (Liu et al., 2024; Pillai and Sivathanu, 2020; Li et al., 2023) and Familiarity (Topsakal, 2024; Park et al., 2024). Thus, by examining Anthropomorphism as a cognitive factor and Familiarity as an experiential element, our extension of TAM fills this gap. The addition of familiarity as an enhancer of TAM predictive power is justified by the fact that when users have prior experience with chatbots, they become more attuned to their communication styles and interactive patterns, which increases anthropomorphism. This latter variable, as a cognitive factor, is relevant because the human-like attributes assigned to chatbots play an important role in shaping chatbot adoption.

3. HYPOTHESIS DEVELOPMENT

3.1. Familiarity and Chatbot Anthropomorphism

Prior experience is a technology-related psychological factor that refers to an individual's exposure to a specific technology (Venkatesh et al., 2012). This experience contributes to familiarity with the technology (Arce-Urriza et al., 2025). According to Komiak and Benbasat (2006), familiarity consumer's knowledge of a chatbot's functionality, reliability, and response patterns is shaped by past interactions and accumulated experience. Previous research demonstrates contradictory results on the effect of familiarity on anthropomorphism (Blut et al., 2021). Some studies suggest a significant relationship, indicating that prior experience with robots leads users to attribute human-like traits to them (Aroyo et al., 2017; Epley et al., 2007). Customers who have a higher familiarity with chatbots perceive them as human-like and promote a strong sense of humanness. In contrast, customers with limited prior experience may lack the motivation to adopt the chatbot and evaluate it as a mechanical element (Gnewuch et al., 2022). However, other studies suggest a negative impact, arguing that users with prior knowledge of robots may develop a performance expectation of these systems (Haring et al., 2016). Other studies indicate that familiarity has no significant effect on anthropomorphism (Stafford, 2013). In the present study, we adopt the existence of a positive impact of familiarity on chatbot anthropomorphism. Consequently, we propose the following hypothesis:

H1: Familiarity with a chatbot positively impacts chatbot anthropomorphism.

3.2. Familiarity and Chatbot Usage Intention

Usage intention refers to an individual's perceived probability of engaging in a particular behavior (Bae, 2018). Intention to adopt technology is a key element to improve engagement and customer experience.

Familiarity with the technology is a pivotal factor in supporting AI systems. Previous studies indicate that users who comprehend the functionality of these systems and who are familiar with them tend to identify their opportunities and challenges (Skjuve et al., 2019). In contrast, limited prior knowledge may lead customers to form negative perceptions of a chatbot's competence and reduce their motivation to use it (Li et al., 2024). Familiarity with AI chatbots leads to a higher perception and a greater willingness to interact with these AI-based systems (Bansal et al., 2016; Moody et al., 2020).

Furthermore, with prior experience, customers depend on their perception of technology rather than external opinions when forming assessments (Burnkrant and Cousineau, 1975). This effect is particularly observed in information systems research, where familiarity with technology is related to higher adoption intentions (Hartwick and Barki, 1994).

Survey data reinforce this idea, showing that the general public tends to prefer familiar technologies (Horowitz et al., 2024). Over half (52%) favor brands and products they already know, while only 35% are willing to adopt new technologies without additional proof of effectiveness. Additionally, 39% prefer to wait feedback from others before trying something new (Kennedy and Funk, 2016). These results indicate that familiarity plays a key role in building user behaviors toward chatbots. Accordingly, the second hypothesis of this research is as follows:

H2: Familiarity with a chatbot positively impacts chatbot usage intention.

3.3. Chatbot Anthropomorphism and Perceived Ease of Use

Based on the concept of perception fluency, the human-like appearance of a product enables consumers to feel that they can understand and interact with it more easily (Hart et al., 2013). This mimetic effect suggests that products resembling humans prompt individuals to interact with them as they would with another human, through speech or touch (Epley et al., 2007; Nass et al., 1997). Such interactions are perceived as particularly natural, which increases the perceived ease of use of a companion robot. Despite some exceptions (Wirtz et al., 2018), ease of use has limited examined in robot studies (Blut et al., 2021). However, existing research suggests that anthropomorphism and human likeness make interactions with the robot feel easier and more natural (Erebak and Turgut, 2019). In a service context, this implies that customers are likely to find a humanlike service robot easier to engage with than a machine-like one. This relationship is supported by (Goudey and Bonnin, 2016). Thus, it is expected that anthropomorphism has a positive effect on perceived ease of use. The third hypothesis is as follows:

H3: Chatbot anthropomorphism positively impacts perceived ease of use.

3.4. Chatbot Anthropomorphism and Perceived Usefulness

Previous studies have generally confirmed the positive relationship between anthropomorphism and perceived usefulness. For example, Canning et al. (2014) found that humanlike robots were rated as more useful than their mechanical counterparts. Stroessner and Benitez (2019) discovered that humanlike robots were perceived as more proficient than machine-like ones. Numerous studies investigate the role of anthropomorphism in chatbot design and its impact on customer decision-making and usage intention (Han, 2021; Novak and Hoffman, 2019). Epley et al. (2007) assert that anthropomorphism strengthens the social connection with robots, enhancing their perceived usefulness. Anthropomorphism increases perceptions of usefulness, particularly when tasks such as service delivery rapidity or immediate product recommendations are efficiently carried out (Selamat and Windasari, 2021). Garnier and Poncin (2013) and Viot and Bressolles (2012) indicate that incorporating anthropomorphic elements can enhance the perceived usefulness of online platforms. Previous studies also show that anthropomorphic chatbot features can drive customer engagement by aligning with the social interaction expectations individuals hold (Duffy, 2003). Based on these insights, we propose the following hypothesis:

H4: Chatbot anthropomorphism positively impacts perceived usefulness

3.5. Chatbot Anthropomorphism and Chatbot Usage Intention

Anthropomorphism plays a crucial role in shaping consumer perceptions as well as behaviors (Sumarjan et al., 2023; Goudey and Bonnin, 2016). People possess extensive knowledge and experience with human traits, actions, and anatomy, to facilitate the understanding and interaction with intelligent products that resemble humans. This perceptual accessibility enhances user engagement and increases the likelihood of adopting anthropomorphic technologies (Aggarwal and McGill, 2007). Chatbots, with human-like attributes, tend fostering more stronger connections with their users. Alike, they make their interactions more engaging and intuitive (Klein and Martinez, 2023). Cassell and Bickmore (2003) argue that a chatbot's human likeness is directly impacting user intention to engage with it. Conversely, chatbots lacking anthropomorphic characteristics may hinder user engagement and negatively affect businesses and organizations (Brandtzaeg and Følstad, 2017). Anthropomorphism also enables chatbots to respond to inquiries more accurately and appropriately, which may further enhance their usage intention (Følstad and Skjuve, 2019).

Still, through mixed empirical findings, the relationship between chatbot anthropomorphism and usage intention is complex (Blut et al., 2021). From one perspective, perceived human likeness can simplify interactions, as users naturally apply social scripts and expectations from human-to-human communication to human-chatbot interactions (Duffy, 2003; Nass and Moon, 2000). This control perception can both enhance user preference and adoption (Stroessner and Benitez, 2019). On the other hand, some studies suggest that excessive human likeness may lead to unintended consequences. Goudey and Bonnin (2016) found that anthropomorphism did not always increase users' intention to interact with companion robots, and other studies indicate that some individuals prefer less human-like or explicitly machine-like robots (Broadbent et al., 2011; Vlachos et al., 2016). These findings are in line with Mori's (1970) uncanny valley hypothesis. They suggest that highly human-like robots, but not entirely lifelike, can provoke a variety of feelings, mainly eeriness and discomfort, resulting in rejection. Additionally, the suitability of anthropomorphic design may depend on the chatbot's intended role—while human-like chatbots are preferred for social tasks, more mechanical designs may be favored for analytical or investigative roles (Goetz et al., 2003). Based on these considerations, the present study proposes the following hypothesis:

H5: Chatbot anthropomorphism positively impacts chatbot usage intention.

3.6. Perceived Ease of Use and Chatbot Usage Intention

The Technology Acceptance Model suggests that users are more likely to use intuitive and effortless technologies to operate (Davis et al., 1989; Amin et al., 2014). This perception influences users' attitudes toward technological systems, shaping their intention to use them (Ashfaq et al., 2020).

Perceived ease of use includes users' subjective evaluations of how intuitive and straightforward to interact with a given technology, including learning to navigate its interface and accessing its functionalities (Huang et al., 2023). Prior research highlights that the simplicity in operating immersive technologies increases the satisfaction and chatbot adoption (Chen et al., 2021; Iqbal and Campbell, 2023). This principle extends to chatbots, where both seamless interaction and user-friendly design can dramatically impact their acceptance.

Furthermore, prior research suggests that the use of ease is not only about simplicity but also about how effectively a technology integrates into users' workflows to adapt to their preferences (Familoni and Babatunde, 2024). Emerging innovations, such as adaptive user interfaces and intelligent assistance, provide deeper insights into the ease and extent of use influence AI-driven tools' acceptance (Choe et al., 2024; Hanji et al., 2024). If users find a chatbot effortless to use, their willingness to adopt it increases, reinforcing its role in service interactions (Chen and Tsai, 2019). In addition, developers can support greater acceptance and increased engagement with these systems. Therefore, we propose the following hypothesis:

H6: Perceived ease of use positively impacts the intention to use chatbots.

3.7. Perceived Usefulness and Chatbot Usage Intention

Perceived usefulness plays a main role in shaping individuals' attitudes toward technology adoption (Gümüş and Çark, 2021). When users believe that a device, system, or application can effectively help them complete a task, they are more likely to reuse it (Muslichah, 2018). Concerning chatbots, perceived usefulness has the most significant impact on customer attitudes, as users tend to evaluate any chatbot based on its ability to provide meaningful and efficient assistance (Davis, 1989). Consequently, a customer's attitude toward a chatbot is largely determined by its perceived usefulness, which, in turn, influences the intention to use it (Gümüş and Çark, 2021).

The recognized benefit of technology is strongly connected to users' assessments of its effectiveness, efficiency, and overall benefits (Tubaishat, 2018). When individuals recognize the tangible advantages of chatbot use, such as streamlined interactions or task automation, their intention to adopt technology increases (Zhang et al., 2023). Hence, any positive perception of a chatbot's effectiveness reinforces their users' willingness to engage with it (Song et al., 2024), since people have been more inclined to embrace technologies demonstrating clear benefits (Portz et al., 2019).

Furthermore, research suggests that users increasingly value AI-driven technologies that offer personalized, contextually relevant solutions aligned with their specific needs (Gujar, 2024; Sodiya et al., 2024). Given these insights, the high perceived usefulness of a chatbot is expected to positively influence individuals' intention to use it. Therefore, the following hypothesis is proposed:

H7: Perceived usefulness positively impacts the intention to use a chatbot

The conceptual model is illustrated in Figure 1

Figure 1. Conceptual Framework

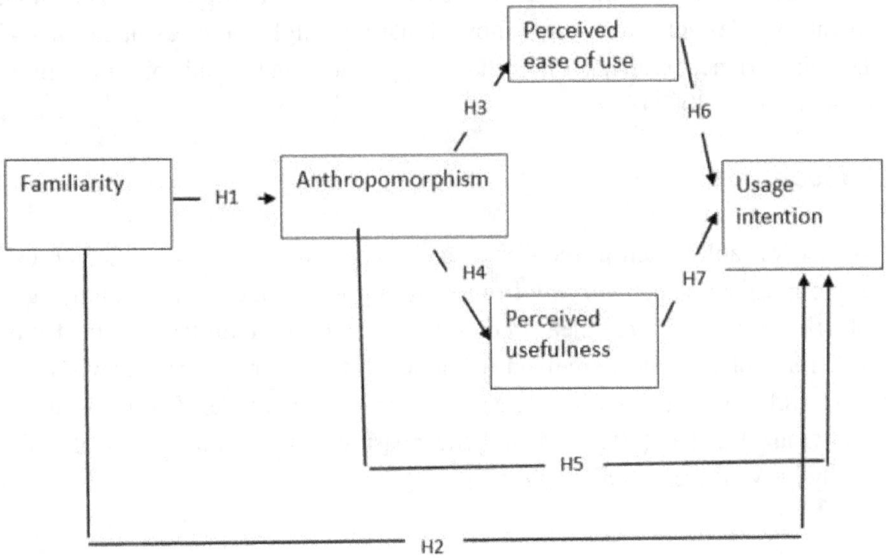

Source(s): *The authors' own work*

4. METHODOLOGY

4.1. Data Collection and Sample

To achieve the study's objective, a convenience sample of Tunisian students, aged between 20 and 22 years, is considered appropriate for this study, as they are the most web-savvy age group and the most familiar with new technologies. This age cohort dominates the use of internet applications in Tunisia[2]. The study adopted a survey-based methodology using an online questionnaire shared by e-mail. Online surveys enable rapid and simple deployment, and ready personalization (McDaniel and Gates, 2002).

After giving their explicit consent, participants voluntarily took part in the study. Firstly, they were instructed to interact with a telecommunication services chatbot to search for information about available services and promotional offers, using any language, including the Tunisian dialect. Then, they were redirected to complete the questionnaire. The final sample is composed of 321 respondents including 77 males (24%) and 244 females (76%).

As data used a single source of information and were collected in the same period, common method variance bias was taken into consideration and was explored. Hartman's single-factor technique showed that the single factor explained 19.47% of the total variance, which is lower than 50%, indicating that this bias is negligible (Podsakoff et al., 2003).

4.2. Measures

All the variables used in the survey are adapted from previous research using seven-point Likert scales Varying from 1 "strongly disagree" to 7 "strongly agree" (Table 1). Familiarity was measured from the study of Dimitriadis and Kyrezis (2010). Ease of use and perceived usefulness were adapted from Davis's study (1989). Anthropomorphism was assessed by four items taken from the study of Melián-González et al. (2021). Finally, the measure of usage intention is taken from the study by Venkatesh et al. (2003)

Table 1. Variables measures

Constructs	Items	Sources
Familiarity	FAM1. "I have experience in using a chatbot"	Dimitriadis and Kyrezis (2010)
	FAM2. "I know very well how to handle the chatbot"	
	FAM3. "Generally, I am familiar with the use of chatbot"	
Ease of Use	EU1. "My interaction with chatbots would be clear and understandable"	Davis (1989)
	EU2. "I would find chatbots easy to use"	
	EU3. "Learning to operate chatbots would be easy for me"	
Perceived Usefulness	PU1. "I find chatbot services useful in the purchasing process"	Davis (1989)
	PU2. "Using chatbot services enables me to accomplish the purchasing process quickly"	
	PU3. "Using chatbot services increases my efficiency in the purchasing process"	
	PU4. "Overall, I find Chatbot useful to me"	
Anthropomorphism	ANTH1. "The conversations I have with chatbots provided are as if I have a dialogue with a real human being"	Melián-González et al. (2021)
	ANTH2. "My interaction with the chatbot I use feels natural"	
	ANTH3. "The chatbot I use is like understanding who the chatbot is interacting with"	
	ANTH4. "Conversations with chatbot that I use don't seem artificial (natural)"	
Usage Intention	UI1. "I intend to use chatbot services the next time I make an online purchase"	Venkatesh et al. (2003)
	UI2. "I will probably use chatbot services the next time I make an online purchase"	
	UI3. "I have decided to use chatbot services the next time I make an online purchase"	

5. RESULTS

Data were analyzed by the PLS-SEM estimation method using Smart PLS4, which is widely applied in social sciences.

5.1. Measurement Model

The results presented in Table 2 confirm the robustness of the measurement model. Indeed, all Cronbach's α values are above 0.7, indicating strong internal consistency. Similarly, CR values exceed 0.7, validating the internal consistency of each construct (Hair et al., 2019). Additionally, Average Variance Extracted (AVE) indicators confirm convergent validity as they exceed 0.5 (Henseler et al., 2016). As shown in Table 3, all HTMT values are below 0.9, indicating discriminant validity (Henseler et al., 2015).

Table 2. Reliability and Convergent Validity Assessment

	Cronbach's alpha	Composite reliability (rho_a)	Composite reliability (rho_c)	Average variance extracted (AVE)
ANTHROPO	0.866	0.868	0.909	0.714
EASE OF USE	0.813	0.825	0.888	0.725
FAMILIARITY	0.936	0.984	0.959	0.886
USAGE INTENTION	0.955	0.955	0.971	0.918
USEFULNESS	0.869	0.872	0.920	0.793

Table 3. Discriminant Validity (HTMT Criterion)

	ANTHROPO	EASE OF USE	FAMILIARITY	USAGE INTENTION	USEFULNESS
ANTHROPO					
EASE OF USE	0.487				
FAMILIARITY	0.093	0.131			
USAGE INTENTION	0.450	0.288	0.108		
USEFULNESS	0.480	0.493	0.036	0.604	

5.2. Structural Model

First, we assessed the multi-collinearity issues. Following the recommendations of MacKenzie et al. (2011), the item PU4 is eliminated since its variance inflation factor value is above 10 (VIF= 11.870). The structural Model is shown in Figure 2.

Figure 2. Structural Model

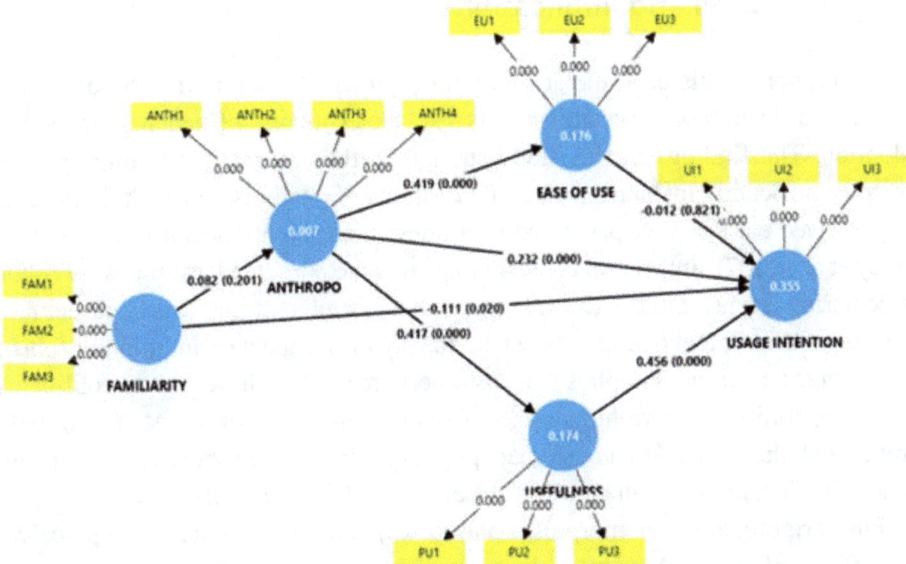

Source(s): PLS4 Software Output

Subsequently, we analyzed the hypothesized relationships between the constructs. The results illustrated in Table 4 show that the hypotheses H3, H4, H5, and H7 are supported, while H1, H2 and H6 are rejected. Among the variables that influence chatbot usage intention, perceived usefulness turned out to be the most significant predictor (β= 0.456, t= 8.097), followed by anthropomorphism (β=0.232, t=3.896). Interestingly, contrary to our hypothesis H2, familiarity influences negatively usage intention (β= -0.111, t=2.325). Ease of use and perceived usefulness are significantly influenced by anthropomorphism.

Table 4. Results

	Original sample (O)	T statistics (|O/STDEV|)	P values	Supported?
H1: FAMILIARITY -> ANTHROPO	0.082	1.278	0.201	No
H2: FAMILIARITY -> USAGE INTENTION	-0.111	2.325	0.020	No
H3: ANTHROPO -> EASE OF USE	0.419	8.155	0.000	Yes
H4: ANTHROPO -> USEFULNESS	0.417	8.068	0.000	Yes
H5: ANTHROPO -> USAGE INTENTION	0.232	3.896	0.000	Yes
H6: EASE OF USE -> USAGE INTENTION	-0.012	0.226	0.821	No
H7: USEFULNESS -> USAGE INTENTION	0.456	8.097	0.000	Yes

6. CONCLUSION

6.1. Discussion and Implications

Anthropomorphism, or the attribution of human characteristics to non-human entities, has been broadly established as a key determinant influencing technology adoption. The findings of this study strengthen the argument that anthropomorphism significantly influences users' perceptions of chatbots, particularly in terms of perceived ease of use, perceived usefulness, and intention to use. In line with Epley et al. (2007), anthropomorphism improves the perceived usefulness of robots by fostering a sense of effectiveness that enhances interaction. This is particularly relevant in the context of chatbots, where the positive impact of anthropomorphism on perceived usefulness implies that customers are likely to have greater confidence in the capability of more humanlike robots to deliver better services. Similarly, previous studies proved that customers perceive human-like robots as practical and beneficial than non-human entities (Stroessner and Benitez, 2019).

Furthermore, anthropomorphism plays a key role in influencing the perceived ease of use of AI chatbots by making conversations more engaging and simpler. Customers perceive human-like chatbot service as more intuitive and user-friendly than a machine-like system, contributing to the interactive experience (Blut et al., 2021). Burgoon et al. (2000) stipulate that it is important to incorporate human-like traits into technology to reduce the complexity of the system and offer a reliable and instant response. Prior research suggests that human-like robots are perceived as familiar and friendlier, thereby reducing uncertainty for users and improving engagement (Fotheringham and Wiles, 2023; Blut et al., 2021; Park et al., 2024).

Additionally, the findings of this research highlighted the important role of anthropomorphism in the chatbot adoption. This result is confirmed by several studies (Følstad and Skjuve, 2019; Sumarjan et al., 2023; Sheehan et al., 2020). According to Følstad and Skjuve (2019), anthropomorphism enhances the capacity of chatbots to respond with precision and relevance to inquiries and improves the intention to adopt chatbots in the future (Sumarjan et al., 2023).

Anthropomorphism is a significant determinant of usage intention, perceived ease of use, and perceived usefulness of chatbot adoption. Managers can incorporate a human-like trait into chatbot design to enhance market penetration and chatbot adoption (Sheehan et al., 2020). Human-like behaviors, such as seeking clarification, empathizing with customers, and responding with human-like cues, can significantly enhance perceived value, usability, and user intention (Gopinath and Kasilingam, 2023). Furthermore, for telecommunications companies, the incorporation of voice-based chatbots with human-like prosody can improve user engagement by offering a more natural and conversational interaction. In the e-commerce sector, deploying emotionally responsive AI chatbots that provide personalized product recommendations can elevate the shopping experience and strengthen customer loyalty.

The results of this study demonstrate the negative effect of prior experience on chatbot intention. Despite the common belief that familiarity improves adoption of technology (Alruwaie et al., 2020; Horowitz et al., 2024; Gefen et al., 2003), recent study highlights that familiarity can paradoxically decline usage intention. This contradiction might be explained by the fact that familiarity with chatbots influences user anticipation and drives them to prefer particular criteria such as characteristics and functionality (Gnewuch et al., 2022; Liao et al., 2016; Brandtzaeg and Følstad, 2017). Furthermore, this negative relation can be caused by overfamiliarity when repeated use of technology decreases the motivation and adoption of chatbots, specifically, with Generation Z marked by technological competence and their daily use of digital tools (Ragheb et al., 2022; Ayanwale and Ndlovu, 2024; Tian et al., 2024). Nevertheless, in our context, the adoption of chatbots is influenced by peer opinion rather than familiarity with conversational agents. This is particularly significant in the emerging markets, where technology adoption is affected by social expectation (Oliveira et al., 2014; Mogaji et al., 2021). Social influence can reduce the negative effect of familiarity and motivate users to reconsider the significance of chatbots. Future studies should explore the impact of social influence on familiarity.

Additionally, the present study indicates that familiarity has no significant effect on anthropomorphism. This result contradicts those of Epley et al. (2007) and Aroyo et al. (2017), implying that prior experience (familiarity) enhances the human-like perception of chatbots. This discrepancy may be attributed to the cognitive acknowledgment of the artificial nature of chatbots, which decreases the consumer's attribution of human-like characteristics. Users consider the conversational agent a practical tool rather than an anthropomorphic element. This perspective is confirmed by Lemaignan et al. (2014), who proved that with continued utilization of a conversational agent, users gain insight into the process of these technologies, which enhances their ability to predict their behavior more accurately. Therefore, the common application of chatbots prompts users to prioritize utilitarian attributes rather than anthropomorphic characteristics (Davis, 1989).

Businesses should focus on practical functionality, efficiency, and contextual relevance over human-like characteristics that will more effectively meet user expectations. Additionally, to leverage the power of familiarity, managers should foster regular interactions with chatbots, potentially through strategies such as promotions, onboarding tutorials, or regular engagement prompts that improve user exposure (Arce-Urriza et al, 2025). This approach can help counter the negative effect of familiarity on the intention by maintaining user engagement and reinforcing chatbot value. By promoting consistent usage, retailers can support customers' adoption of chatbots, thereby enhancing their comfort level with the technology.

Perceived usefulness (PU) plays a pivotal role in shaping the intention to use chatbot AI. Some existing researches (Ismatullaev and Kim, 2024; Norzelan et al., 2024; Davis et al, 1989; Rafique et al., 2020; Wu et al., 2011) consistently highlights that users' perceptions of the technology's efficacy have a direct influence on their intention to adopt it. As users recognize the adaptability of chatbot services to their needs, their potential to adopt technology rises (Topsakal, 2024).

While perceived ease of use (PEOU) is a main factor of Technology Acceptance Model (TAM), our findings reveal that it does not have a significant effect on users' intention for adopting chatbots. In line with previous studies suggesting that as users gain greater familiarity with digital technologies, simplicity becomes less significant in their decision-making process (Liu et al., 2016; Mun et al., 2006; Van Eeuwen, 2017; Gopinath and Kasilingam, 2023; Topsakal, 2024). More specifically, when users more regularly engage with technology, the importance of PEOU becomes less significant in relation with technology adoption decisions (Liu et al., 2016). In digital environments, users frequently interact with AI systems, for various reasons, such as retrieving information, e-commerce transactions, and travel planning (Han, 2021; Pillai and Sivathanu, 2020). In fact, these interactions contribute in reducing the perceived effort required to interact with AI-powered systems like chatbots (Gopinath and Kasilingam, 2023). In addition, even when users encounter difficulties in interacting with the technology, their motivation to use it is primarily driven by its perceived usefulness, rather than ease of use (Topsakal, 2024). As perceived, ease of use primarily addresses the technical aspects of device interaction, it progressively outweighed perceived usefulness (PU). This reflects the technology's importance to users' needs and its overall efficacy (Davis, 1985, 1989; Lunney et al., 2016).

Concerning chatbot adoption, managers should prioritize highlighting the functional advantages of technology rather than focusing on its ease of use. They should, also, emphasize chatbots utility, more particularly their ability in providing quick support reinforcing perceived usefulness (Arce-Urriza et al., 2025). More precisely, managerial efforts should be more concentrated in bolstering the positive drivers that influence adoption, such as chatbots utility to offer timely and effective assistance. By reinforcing their perceived usefulness through their ability to address user needs efficiently, organizations can foster a stronger intention to adopt chatbot technologies. Moreover, the usefulness of chatbots can be further optimized by ensuring they provide relevant, actionable, and current information to users, as this aligns with user expectations and increases practical effectiveness (Gopinath and Kasilingam, 2023). In addition, both the efficiency and performance of business process automation through chatbots must be further enhanced by the constant advancement of Artificial intelligence functionalities (Gopinath and Kasilingam, 2023).

Our study makes several significant theoretical contributions to the existing literature. To start with, it seeks to integrate key research variables to develop a comprehensive framework in order to predict users' intention to adopt AI-based customer chatbot services. While existing extensions of the Technology Acceptance Model (TAM), such as (UTAUT, TAM2, and TAM3) have integrated extended determinants like (social influence, facilitating conditions and perceived enjoyment) to improve the explanatory power of technology acceptance research, the strength of our model stems from its expansion of established Technology Acceptance Model (TAM) frameworks, incorporating two additional factors: Familiarity (Mostafa and Kasamani, 2022) and Anthropomorphism (Roy and Naidoo, 2021; Sands et al., 2021), both of which have been suggested as important in the context of chatbot adoption.

Moreover, the incorporation of familiarity and anthropomorphism, in our extended TAM model, contributes to this research through emphasizing user perceptions of human-like characteristics as well as his ease to interact with AI chatbots. Therefore, our model offers a more nuanced understanding of their impact on user acceptance; thereby, strengthening its predictive power compared to previous TAM extensions. In addition, to the best of our knowledge, this is the first study to combine these variables within a single model, providing novel theoretical insights into the mechanisms driving technology adoption. This integration not only deepens our comprehension of chatbot adoption but also expands the range of technology acceptance theories, providing a more nuanced perspective on the factors that influence users' decisions to engage with AI technologies.

Then, the relationship between familiarity with technology and anthropomorphism remains inconclusive. This is due to the fact that existing literature has presented contradictory findings. This study responds to some recent calls for further research related to the influence of familiarity on anthropomorphism in AI technologies, particularly in the context of chatbots (Mulcahy et al., 2024; Jörling et al., 2020). Exploring this discrepancy, our findings provide new perspectives contributing to a more comprehensive understanding of the factors that shape users' perceptions of AI-driven interactions on it.

Moreover, our study is grounded in the Technology Acceptance Model (TAM), a framework whose application in the domain of artificial intelligence (AI), particularly in chatbot adoption, remains underexplored (Wang et al., 2023). Significantly, the non-significant effect of perceived ease of use (PEOU) on users' adoption intentions challenges the traditional assumptions of TAM, which generally asserts ease of use as a key factor of technology acceptance. This finding suggests that factors beyond usability, such as anthropomorphism or perceived usefulness, may exert a greater effect on chatbot adoption decisions. In contrast, the significant impact of perceived usefulness (PU) on intention is consistent with the basic foundations of TAM, reinforcing the notion that users are more predisposed to adopt chatbots when they perceive them as beneficial assets. These findings open new avenues for expanding TAM theories in future research by underscoring the need to adapt existing theoretical frameworks to specific technological contexts.

To end with, integrating emotional factors (anthropomorphism), cognitive factors (perceived usefulness and ease of use), added to familiarity can provide more holistic and nuanced framework to understand technology adoption, in the specific context of chatbots within telecommunications sector. This integration enhances our understanding of how users interact with chatbot technologies and contributing to the literature on chatbot adoption by examining interrelationships among these factors and their influence on user behavior.

6.2. Limitations and Future Research Directions

Despite our study offers valuable contributions to both theory and practice, there are certainly some limitations and potential avenues for future research.

First, the sample composition may limit the findings generalizability, as it may not fully represent the diversity of intention across different demographic groups. Future research should focus on including more heterogeneous sample for assessing whether the observed relationships remain applicable across a broader range of user segments.

Moreover, the cross-sectional design employed in this study restricts the ability to derive causal inferences about the relationships between familiarity, anthropomorphism, and intention. Longitudinal studies would provide a more comprehensive framework for examining how these factors develop over time as users' intention evolves. Such research would offer deeper insights into the evolving dynamic of these relationships and their implications for chatbot adoption.

In addition, future research could investigate the role of other psychological factors, such as trust (Chi and Hoang vu, 2023; Topsakal et al., 2024) and perceived privacy risk (Arce-Urriza et al., 2025).

Moreover, the inclusion of moderating effects, such as demographic factors (age and gender) (Topsakal et al., 2024), could strengthen the prediction of research model in shaping technology adoption.In the same vein, understanding these factors interaction with familiarity, anthropomorphism, and perceived usefulness could offer more holistic view influencing chatbot adoption. Finally, comparative research between chatbots and other AI technologies, such as virtual assistants or smart speakers, contributes in determining whether the findings from this study are specific to chatbots or extending to a wider range of AI-driven interactions.

REFERENCES

Aarabe, M., Khizzou, N. B., Alla, L., & Benjelloun, A. (2024). Marketing applications of emerging technologies : A systematic literature review. *In AI and data engineering solutions for effective marketing* (pp. 23 47). IGI Global. https://www.igi-global.com/chapter/marketing-applications-of-emerging-technologies/350744

Aggarwal, P., & McGill, A. L. (2007). Is that car smiling at me? Schema congruity as a basis for evaluating anthropomorphized products. *The Journal of Consumer Research, 34*(4), 468–479. DOI: 10.1086/518544

Ahn, H. (2022). Emotional intelligence as a personality trait that predicts consumption behavior: The role of consumer emotional intelligence in persuasive communication. *Sustainability (Basel), 14*(22), 15461. DOI: 10.3390/su142215461

Ahn, H. (2023). Unrevealing Voice Search Behaviors: Technology Acceptance Model Meets Anthropomorphism in Understanding Consumer Psychology in the US Market. *Sustainability (Basel), 15*(23), 16455. DOI: 10.3390/su152316455

Ajzen, I. (1991). The theory of planned behavior. *Organizational Behavior and Human Decision Processes, 50*(2), 179–211. DOI: 10.1016/0749-5978(91)90020-T

Alotaibi, M., & Hidayat-ur-Rehman, I. (2025). An empirical analysis of user intention to use chatbots for airline tickets consultation. *Journal of Science and Technology Policy Management*, 16(1), 204 228. DOI: 10.1108/JSTPM-03-2024-0087

Amin, M., Rezaei, S., & Abolghasemi, M. (2014). User satisfaction with mobile websites : The impact of perceived usefulness (PU), perceived ease of use (PEOU) and trust. *Nankai Business Review International, 5*(3), 258–274. DOI: 10.1108/NBRI-01-2014-0005

Araujo, T. (2018). Living up to the chatbot hype : The influence of anthropomorphic design cues and communicative agency framing on conversational agent and company perceptions. *Computers in Human Behavior, 85*, 183–189. DOI: 10.1016/j.chb.2018.03.051

Araújo, T., & Casais, B. (2020). Customer Acceptance of Shopping-Assistant Chatbots. In Á. Rocha, J. L. Reis, M. K. Peter, & Z. Bogdanović (Éds.), *Marketing and Smart Technologies* (Vol. 167, p. 278 287). Springer Singapore. DOI: 10.1007/978-981-15-1564-4_26

Arce-Urriza, M., Chocarro, R., Cortiñas, M., & Marcos-Matás, G. (2025). From familiarity to acceptance : The impact of Generative Artificial Intelligence on consumer adoption of retail chatbots. *Journal of Retailing and Consumer Services, 84*, 104234. DOI: 10.1016/j.jretconser.2025.104234

Aroyo, A. M., Rea, F., & Sciutti, A. (2017). Will You Rely on a Robot to Find a Treasure? Proceedings of the Companion of the 2017 *ACM/IEEE International Conference on Human-Robot Interaction*, 71 72. DOI: 10.1145/3029798.3038394

Ashfaq, M., Yun, J., Yu, S., & Loureiro, S. M. C. (2020). I, Chatbot: Modeling the determinants of users' satisfaction and continuance intention of AI-powered service agents. *Telematics and Informatics, 54*, 101473. DOI: 10.1016/j.tele.2020.101473

Ayanwale, M. A., & Ndlovu, M. (2024). Investigating factors of students' behavioral intentions to adopt chatbot technologies in higher education: Perspective from expanded diffusion theory of innovation. *Computers in Human Behavior Reports, 14*, 100396. DOI: 10.1016/j.chbr.2024.100396

Bae, M. (2018). Understanding the effect of the discrepancy between sought and obtained gratification on social networking site users' satisfaction and continuance intention. *Computers in Human Behavior, 79*, 137–153. DOI: 10.1016/j.chb.2017.10.026

Bailey, A. A., Mishra, A. S., & Vaishnav, K. (2023). Response to social media influencers : Consumer dispositions as drivers. *International Journal of Consumer Studies*, 47(5), 1979 1998. DOI: 10.1111/ijcs.12976

Bakkouri, B. E., Raki, S., & Belgnaoui, T. (2022). The Role of Chatbots in Enhancing Customer Experience : Literature Review. *Procedia Computer Science*, 203, 432 437. DOI: 10.1016/j.procs.2022.07.057

Bansal, P., Kockelman, K. M., & Singh, A. (2016). Assessing public opinions of and interest in new vehicle technologies: An Austin perspective. *Transportation Research Part C, Emerging Technologies, 67*, 1–14. DOI: 10.1016/j.trc.2016.01.019

Blut, M., Wang, C., Wünderlich, N. V., & Brock, C. (2021). Understanding anthropomorphism in service provision: A meta-analysis of physical robots, chatbots, and other AI. *Journal of the Academy of Marketing Science*, 49(4), 632 658. DOI: 10.1007/s11747-020-00762-y

Brandtzaeg, P. B., & Følstad, A. (2017). Why People Use Chatbots. In I. Kompatsiaris, J. Cave, A. Satsiou, G. Carle, A. Passani, E. Kontopoulos, S. Diplaris, & D. McMillan (Éds.), *Internet Science* (Vol. 10673, pp. 377 392). Springer International Publishing. DOI: 10.1007/978-3-319-70284-1_30

Broadbent, E., Jayawardena, C., Kerse, N., Stafford, R. Q., & MacDonald, B. A. (2011). Human-robot interaction research to improve quality of life in elder care—An approach and issues.*AAAI Fall Symposium on AI in Eldercare: New Solutions to Old Problems*. https://cdn.aaai.org/ocs/ws/ws0699/3875-16713-1-PB.pdf

Burgoon, J. K., Bonito, J. A., Bengtsson, B., Cederberg, C., Lundeberg, M., & Allspach, L. (2000). Interactivity in human–computer interaction : A study of credibility, understanding, and influence. *Computers in Human Behavior*, 16(6), 553 574. DOI: 10.1016/S0747-5632(00)00029-7

Burnkrant, R. E., & Cousineau, A. (1975). Informational and normative social influence in buyer behavior. *The Journal of Consumer Research*, *2*(3), 206–215. DOI: 10.1086/208633

Canning, C., Donahue, T. J., & Scheutz, M. (2014). Investigating human perceptions of robot capabilities in remote human-robot team tasks based on first-person robot video feeds. 2014 *IEEE/RSJ International Conference on Intelligent Robots and Systems*, 4354 4361.

Cassell, J., & Bickmore, T. (2003). Negotiated Collusion: Modeling Social Language and its Relationship Effects in Intelligent Agents. *User Modeling and User-Adapted Interaction*, *13*(1/2), 89–132. DOI: 10.1023/A:1024026532471

Chen, C.-C., & Tsai, J.-L. (2019). Determinants of behavioral intention to use the Personalized Location-based Mobile Tourism Application : An empirical study by integrating TAM with ISSM. *Future Generation Computer Systems*, *96*, 628–638. DOI: 10.1016/j.future.2017.02.028

Chen, J.-S., Le, T.-T.-Y., & Florence, D. (2021). Usability and responsiveness of artificial intelligence chatbot on online customer experience in e-retailing. *International Journal of Retail & Distribution Management*, 49(11), 1512 1531. DOI: 10.1108/IJRDM-08-2020-0312

Chi, N. T. K., & Hoang Vu, N. (2023). Investigating the customer trust in artificial intelligence : The role of anthropomorphism, empathy response, and interaction. *CAAI Transactions on Intelligence Technology*, *8*(1), 260–273. DOI: 10.1049/cit2.12133

Christensen, J., Hansen, J. M., & Wilson, P. (2024). Understanding the role and impact of Generative Artificial Intelligence (AI) hallucination within consumers' tourism decision-making processes. *Current Issues in Tourism*, *28*(4), 545–560. DOI: 10.1080/13683500.2023.2300032

Ciechanowski, L., Przegalinska, A., Magnuski, M., & Gloor, P. (2019). In the shades of the uncanny valley : An experimental study of human–chatbot interaction. *Future Generation Computer Systems*, 92, 539 548. DOI: 10.1016/j.future.2018.01.055

Davenport, T. H., & Ronanki, R. (2018). Artificial intelligence for the real world. *HBR'S 10 MUST*, 67.

Davis, F. D. (1985). A technology acceptance model for empirically testing new end-user information systems : *Theory and results* [PhD Thesis, Massachusetts Institute of Technology]. https://dspace.mit.edu/bitstream/handle/1721.1/15192/14927137-MIT.pdf

Davis, F. D. (1989). Perceived usefulness, perceived ease of use, and user acceptance of information technology. *Management Information Systems Quarterly, 319*(3), 340. DOI: 10.2307/249008

Davis, F. D., Bagozzi, R. P., & Warshaw, P. R. (1989). User Acceptance of Computer Technology : A Comparison of Two Theoretical Models. *Management Science*, 35(8), 982 1003. DOI: 10.1287/mnsc.35.8.982

De Cicco, R., Iacobucci, S., Aquino, A., Romana Alparone, F., & Palumbo, R. (2022). Understanding Users' Acceptance of Chatbots : An Extended TAM Approach. In A. Følstad, T. Araujo, S. Papadopoulos, E. L.-C. Law, E. Luger, M. Goodwin, & P. B. Brandtzaeg (Éds.), *Chatbot Research and Design* (Vol. 13171, p. 3 22). Springer International Publishing. DOI: 10.1007/978-3-030-94890-0_1

De Kleijn, R., Wijnen, M., & Poletiek, F. (2019). The effect of context-dependent information and sentence constructions on perceived humanness of an agent in a Turing test. *Knowledge-Based Systems, 163*, 794–799. DOI: 10.1016/j.knosys.2018.10.006

Dimitriadis, S., & Kyrezis, N. (2010). Linking trust to use intention for technology-enabled bank channels : The role of trusting intentions. *Psychology & Marketing*, 27(8), 799 820. DOI: 10.1002/mar.20358

Duffy, B. R. (2003). Anthropomorphism and the social robot. *Robotics and Autonomous Systems*, 42(3 4), 177 190. DOI: 10.1016/S0921-8890(02)00374-3

Epley, N. (2018). A Mind like Mine : The Exceptionally Ordinary Underpinnings of Anthropomorphism. *Journal of the Association for Consumer Research, 3*(4), 591–598. DOI: 10.1086/699516

Epley, N., Waytz, A., & Cacioppo, J. T. (2007). On seeing human : A three-factor theory of anthropomorphism. *Psychological Review, 114*(4), 864–886. DOI: 10.1037/0033-295X.114.4.864 PMID: 17907867

Erebak, S., & Turgut, T. (2019). Caregivers' attitudes toward potential robot coworkers in elder care. *Cognition Technology and Work, 21*(2), 327–336. DOI: 10.1007/s10111-018-0512-0

Familoni, B. T., & Babatunde, S. O.Babajide Tolulope FamiloniSodiq Odetunde Babatunde. (2024). User experience (UX) design in medical products : Theoretical foundations and development best practices. *Engineering Science & Technology Journal, 5*(3), 1125–1148. DOI: 10.51594/estj.v5i3.975

Fishbein, M., & Ajzen, I. (1977). *Belief, attitude, intention, and behavior : An introduction to theory and research.* https://philpapers.org/rec/FISBAI?all_versions=1

Følstad, A., & Skjuve, M. (2019). Chatbots for customer service : User experience and motivation. *Proceedings of the 1st International Conference on Conversational User Interfaces,* 1 9. DOI: 10.1145/3342775.3342784

Fotheringham, D., & Wiles, M. A. (2023). The effect of implementing chatbot customer service on stock returns : An event study analysis. *Journal of the Academy of Marketing Science, 51*(4), 802–822. DOI: 10.1007/s11747-022-00841-2

Garnier, M., & Poncin, I. (2013). The avatar in marketing : Synthesis, integrative framework and perspectives. *Recherche et Applications En Marketing* (English Edition), 28(1), 85 115. DOI: 10.1177/2051570713478335

Gatzioufa, P., & Saprikis, V. (2022). *A literature review on users' behavioral intention toward chatbots' adoption.* Applied Computing and Informatics., DOI: 10.1108/ACI-01-2022-0021

Gefen, D., Karahanna, E., & Straub, D. W. (2003). Inexperience and experience with online stores : The importance of TAM and trust. *IEEE Transactions on Engineering Management, 50*(3), 307–321. DOI: 10.1109/TEM.2003.817277

Gnewuch, U., Morana, S., Adam, M. T. P., & Maedche, A. (2022). Opposing Effects of Response Time in Human–Chatbot Interaction : The Moderating Role of Prior Experience. *Business & Information Systems Engineering*, 64(6), 773 791. DOI: 10.1007/s12599-022-00755-x

Go, E., & Sundar, S. S. (2019). Humanizing chatbots : The effects of visual, identity and conversational cues on humanness perceptions. *Computers in Human Behavior, 97*, 304–316. DOI: 10.1016/j.chb.2019.01.020

Goetz, J., Kiesler, S., & Powers, A. (2003). Matching robot appearance and behavior to tasks to improve human-robot cooperation. The *12th IEEE International Workshop on Robot and Human Interactive Communication*, 2003. Proceedings. *RO-MAN ... : the ... IEEE International Symposium on Robot and Human Interactive Communication : Proceedings. IEEE International Symposium on Robot and Human Interactive Communication, 2003*(55), 60. DOI: 10.1109/ROMAN.2003.1251796

Gopinath, K., & Kasilingam, D. (2023). Antecedents of intention to use chatbots in service encounters : A meta-analytic review. *International Journal of Consumer Studies*, *47*(6), 2367–2395. DOI: 10.1111/ijcs.12933

Goudey, A., & Bonnin, G. (2016). Must smart objects look human? Study of the impact of anthropomorphism on the acceptance of companion robots. *Recherche et Applications En Marketing (English Edition)*, 31(2), 2 20. DOI: 10.1177/2051570716643961

Gujar, V. (2024). New age marketing : AI personalization strategies in digital world. *International Advanced Research Journal in Science, Engineering and Technology*, 11(3).

Gümüş, N., & Çark, Ö. (2021). The Effect of Customers' Attitudes Towards Chatbots on their Experience and Behavioural Intention in Turkey. *Interdisciplinary Description of Complex Systems : INDECS*, 19(3), 420 436. DOI: 10.7906/indecs.19.3.6

Hair, J. F., Risher, J. J., Sarstedt, M., & Ringle, C. M. (2019). When to use and how to report the results of PLS-SEM. *European Business Review*, 31(1), 2 24. DOI: 10.1108/EBR-11-2018-0203

Han, M. C. (2021). The Impact of Anthropomorphism on Consumers' Purchase Decision in Chatbot Commerce. *Journal of Internet Commerce*, 20(1), 46 65. DOI: 10.1080/15332861.2020.1863022

Hanji, S. V., Navalgund, N., Ingalagi, S., Desai, S., & Hanji, S. S. (2024). Adoption of AI Chatbots in Travel and Tourism Services. In X.-S. Yang, R. S. Sherratt, N. Dey, & A. Joshi (Éds.), *Proceedings of Eighth International Congress on Information and Communication Technology* (Vol. 696, p. 713 727). Springer Nature Singapore. DOI: 10.1007/978-981-99-3236-8_57

Haring, K. S., Silvera-Tawil, D., Takahashi, T., Watanabe, K., & Velonaki, M. (2016). How people perceive different robot types : A direct comparison of an android, humanoid, and non-biomimetic robot. *2016 8th international conference on knowledge and smart technology* (kst), 265 270.

Hart, P. M., Jones, S. R., & Royne, M. B. (2013). The human lens : How anthropomorphic reasoning varies by product complexity and enhances personal value. *Journal of Marketing Management*, 29(1 2), 105 121. DOI: 10.1080/0267257X.2012.759993

Hartwick, J., & Barki, H. (1994). Explaining the Role of User Participation in Information System Use. *Management Science*, 40(4), 440 465. DOI: 10.1287/mnsc.40.4.440

Henseler, J., Hubona, G., & Ray, P. A. (2016). Using PLS path modeling in new technology research : Updated guidelines. *Industrial Management & Data Systems*, 116(1), 2 20. DOI: 10.1108/IMDS-09-2015-0382

Henseler, J., Ringle, C. M., & Sarstedt, M. (2015). A new criterion for assessing discriminant validity in variance-based structural equation modeling. *Journal of the Academy of Marketing Science*, 43(1), 115 135. DOI: 10.1007/s11747-014-0403-8

Horowitz, M. C., Kahn, L., Macdonald, J., & Schneider, J. (2024). Adopting AI : How familiarity breeds both trust and contempt. *AI & Society*, 39(4), 1721 1735. DOI: 10.1007/s00146-023-01666-5

Huang, Y.-C., Li, L.-N., Lee, H.-Y., Browning, M. H., & Yu, C.-P. (2023). Surfing in virtual reality : An application of extended technology acceptance model with flow theory. *Computers in Human Behavior Reports*, *9*, 100252. DOI: 10.1016/j.chbr.2022.100252

Ibrahim, F., Münscher, J.-C., Daseking, M., & Telle, N.-T. (2025). The technology acceptance model and adopter type analysis in the context of artificial intelligence. *Frontiers in Artificial Intelligence*, *7*, 1496518. DOI: 10.3389/frai.2024.1496518 PMID: 39886023

Iqbal, M. Z., & Campbell, A. G. (2023). Real-time hand interaction and self-directed machine learning agents in immersive learning environments. *Computers & Education: X Reality*, 3, 100038.

Ismatullaev, U. V. U., & Kim, S.-H. (2024). Review of the Factors Affecting Acceptance of AI-Infused Systems. *Human Factors*, *66*(1), 126–144. DOI: 10.1177/00187208211064707 PMID: 35344676

Jörling, M., Böhm, R., & Paluch, S. (2020). Mechanisms and Consequences of Anthropomorphizing Autonomous Products : The Role of Schema Congruity and Prior Experience. *Schmalenbach Business Review*, 72(4), 485 510. DOI: 10.1007/s41464-020-00100-3

Kelly, S., Kaye, S.-A., & Oviedo-Trespalacios, O. (2022). A Multi-Industry Analysis of the Future Use of AI Chatbots. *Human Behavior and Emerging Technologies*, *2022*(1), 14. DOI: 10.1155/2022/2552099

Kennedy, B., & Funk, C. (2016). 28% of Americans are 'strong'early adopters of technology. https://policycommons.net/artifacts/618399/28-of-americans-are-strong-early-adopters-of-technology/1599341/

Khan, M. K. (2023). AI-enabled transformations in telecommunications industry. Telecommunication Systems, 82(1), 1 2. DOI: 10.1007/s11235-022-00989-w

Khizzou, N. B., Aarabe, M., & Alla, L. (2024). Current trends in scientific research on managerial innovations in healthcare supply chain : A bibliometric analysis. *2024 IEEE 15th International Colloquium on Logistics and Supply Chain Management* (LOGISTIQUA), 1 9.

Kim, T., Lee, O.-K. D., & Kang, J. (2023). Is it the best for barista robots to serve like humans? A multidimensional anthropomorphism perspective. *International Journal of Hospitality Management*, *108*, 103358. DOI: 10.1016/j.ijhm.2022.103358

Klein, K., & Martinez, L. F. (2023). The impact of anthropomorphism on customer satisfaction in chatbot commerce : An experimental study in the food sector. *Electronic Commerce Research*, 23(4), 2789 2825. DOI: 10.1007/s10660-022-09562-8

Komiak, S. Y., & Benbasat, I. (2006). The effects of personalization and familiarity on trust and adoption of recommendation agents. *Management Information Systems Quarterly*, *30*(4), 941–960. DOI: 10.2307/25148760

Lemaignan, S., Fink, J., Dillenbourg, P., & Braboszcz, C. (2014). The cognitive correlates of anthropomorphism. *2014 Human-Robot Interaction Conference, Workshop" HRI: a bridge between Robotics and Neuroscience"*. https://infoscience.epfl.ch/record/196441

Li, B., Chen, Y., Liu, L., & Zheng, B. (2023). Users' intention to adopt artificial intelligence-based chatbot : A meta-analysis. *The Service Industries Journal*, 43(15 16), 1117 1139. DOI: 10.1080/02642069.2023.2217756

Li, Y., Hou, R., & Tan, R. (2024). How customers respond to chatbot anthropomorphism : The mediating roles of perceived humanness and perceived persuasiveness. *European Journal of Marketing*, *58*(12), 2757–2790. DOI: 10.1108/EJM-11-2022-0827

Liao, Q. V., Davis, M., Geyer, W., Muller, M., & Shami, N. S. (2016). What Can You Do?: Studying Social-Agent Orientation and Agent Proactive Interactions with an Agent for Employees. *Proceedings of the 2016 ACM Conference on Designing Interactive Systems,* 264 275. DOI: 10.1145/2901790.2901842

Liu, M., Yang, Y., Ren, Y., Jia, Y., Ma, H., Luo, J., Fang, S., Qi, M., & Zhang, L. (2024). What influences consumer AI chatbot use intention? An application of the extended technology acceptance model. *Journal of Hospitality and Tourism Technology*, 15(4), 667 689. DOI: 10.1108/JHTT-03-2023-0057

Liu, Z., Shan, J., & Pigneur, Y. (2016). The role of personalized services and control : An empirical evaluation of privacy calculus and technology acceptance model in the mobile context. *Journal of Information Privacy and Security, 12*(3), 123–144. DOI: 10.1080/15536548.2016.1206757

Lubbe, I., & Ngoma, N. (2021). Useful chatbot experience provides technological satisfaction : An emerging market perspective. *South African Journal of Information Management*, 23(1), 1 8. DOI: 10.4102/sajim.v23i1.1299

Lunney, A., Cunningham, N. R., & Eastin, M. S. (2016). Wearable fitness technology : A structural investigation into acceptance and perceived fitness outcomes. *Computers in Human Behavior*, *65*, 114–120. DOI: 10.1016/j.chb.2016.08.007

MacKenzie, S. B., Podsakoff, P. M., & Podsakoff, N. P. (2011). Construct measurement and validation procedures in MIS and behavioral research : Integrating new and existing techniques. *Management Information Systems Quarterly*, *293*(2), 334. DOI: 10.2307/23044045

McDaniel, C. D., & Gates, R. H. (2002). *Marketing Research : The Impact of the Internet*. South-Western.

McLean, G., & Osei-Frimpong, K. (2019). Hey Alexa… examine the variables influencing the use of artificial intelligent in-home voice assistants. *Computers in Human Behavior*, *99*, 28–37. DOI: 10.1016/j.chb.2019.05.009

Melián-González, S., Gutiérrez-Taño, D., & Bulchand-Gidumal, J. (2021). Predicting the intentions to use chatbots for travel and tourism. *Current Issues in Tourism*, 24(2), 192 210. DOI: 10.1080/13683500.2019.1706457

Mogaji, E., Balakrishnan, J., Nwoba, A. C., & Nguyen, N. P. (2021). Emerging-market consumers' interactions with banking chatbots. *Telematics and Informatics*, *65*, 101711. DOI: 10.1016/j.tele.2021.101711

Mogaji, E., Viglia, G., Srivastava, P., & Dwivedi, Y. K. (2024). Is it the end of the technology acceptance model in the era of generative artificial intelligence? *International Journal of Contemporary Hospitality Management*, 36(10), 3324 3339. DOI: 10.1108/IJCHM-08-2023-1271

Moody, J., Bailey, N., & Zhao, J. (2020). Public perceptions of autonomous vehicle safety : An international comparison. *Safety Science*, *121*, 634–650. DOI: 10.1016/j.ssci.2019.07.022

Mori, M. (1970). Bukimi no tani [The uncanny valley]. *Energy*, *7*, 33.

Mostafa, R. B., & Kasamani, T. (2022). Antecedents and consequences of chatbot initial trust. *European Journal of Marketing*, *56*(6), 1748–1771. DOI: 10.1108/EJM-02-2020-0084

Mulcahy, R. F., Riedel, A., Keating, B., Beatson, A., & Letheren, K. (2024). Avoiding excessive AI service agent anthropomorphism : Examining its role in delivering bad news. *Journal of Service Theory and Practice*, *34*(1), 98–126. DOI: 10.1108/JSTP-04-2023-0118

Mun, Y. Y., Jackson, J. D., Park, J. S., & Probst, J. C. (2006). Understanding information technology acceptance by individual professionals: Toward an integrative view. *Information & Management*, *43*(3), 350–363. DOI: 10.1016/j.im.2005.08.006

Muslichah, M. (2018). The effect of self efficacy and information quality on behavioral intention with perceived usefulness as intervening variable. *Journal of Accounting* [JABM]. *Business and Management*, *25*(1), 21–34.

Nass, C., & Moon, Y. (2000). Machines and Mindlessness : Social Responses to Computers. *The Journal of Social Issues*, *56*(1), 81–103. DOI: 10.1111/0022-4537.00153

Nass, C., Moon, Y., & Green, N. (1997). Are Machines Gender Neutral? Gender-Stereotypic Responses to Computers With Voices. *Journal of Applied Social Psychology*, 27(10), 864 876. DOI: 10.1111/j.1559-1816.1997.tb00275.x

Nordheim, C. B., Følstad, A., & Bjørkli, C. A. (2019). An Initial Model of Trust in Chatbots for Customer Service—Findings from a Questionnaire Study. *Interacting with Computers*, 31(3), 317 335. DOI: 10.1093/iwc/iwz022

Norzelan, N. A., Mohamed, I. S., & Mohamad, M. (2024). Technology acceptance of artificial intelligence (AI) among heads of finance and accounting units in the shared service industry. *Technological Forecasting and Social Change*, *198*, 123022. DOI: 10.1016/j.techfore.2023.123022

Nouhaila, B. K., Aarabe, M., & Alla, L. (2024). The impact of digitalisation on the customer experience in medical tourism : A systematic review. *Impact of AI and tech-driven solutions in hospitality and tourism*, 408 428.

Novak, T. P., & Hoffman, D. L. (2019). Relationship journeys in the internet of things : A new framework for understanding interactions between consumers and smart objects. *Journal of the Academy of Marketing Science*, 47(2), 216 237. DOI: 10.1007/s11747-018-0608-3

Oliveira, T., Faria, M., Thomas, M. A., & Popovič, A. (2014). Extending the understanding of mobile banking adoption : When UTAUT meets TTF and ITM. *International Journal of Information Management*, *34*(5), 689–703. DOI: 10.1016/j.ijinfomgt.2014.06.004

Parasuraman, A. (2000). Technology Readiness Index (Tri) : A Multiple-Item Scale to Measure Readiness to Embrace New Technologies. *Journal of Service Research*, *2*(4), 307–320. DOI: 10.1177/109467050024001

Park, G., Chung, J., & Lee, S. (2024). Scope and limits of AI fundraisers : Moderated serial multiple mediation model between artificial emotions and willingness to donate via humanness and empathy. *Technological Forecasting and Social Change*, *201*, 123211. DOI: 10.1016/j.techfore.2024.123211

Park, G., Lee, S., & Chung, J. (2023). Do Anthropomorphic Chatbots Increase Counseling Satisfaction and Reuse Intention? The Moderated Mediation of Social Rapport and Social Anxiety. *Cyberpsychology, Behavior, and Social Networking*, 26(5), 357 365. DOI: 10.1089/cyber.2022.0157

Pillai, R., & Sivathanu, B. (2020). Adoption of AI-based chatbots for hospitality and tourism. *International Journal of Contemporary Hospitality Management*, *32*(10), 3199–3226. DOI: 10.1108/IJCHM-04-2020-0259

Podsakoff, P. M., MacKenzie, S. B., Lee, J.-Y., & Podsakoff, N. P. (2003). Common method biases in behavioral research : A critical review of the literature and recommended remedies. *The Journal of Applied Psychology*, *88*(5), 879–903. DOI: 10.1037/0021-9010.88.5.879 PMID: 14516251

Portz, J. D., Bayliss, E. A., Bull, S., Boxer, R. S., Bekelman, D. B., Gleason, K., & Czaja, S. (2019). Using the Technology Acceptance Model to Explore User Experience, Intent to Use, and Use Behavior of a Patient Portal Among Older Adults With Multiple Chronic Conditions : Descriptive Qualitative Study. *Journal of Medical Internet Research*, *21*(4), e11604. DOI: 10.2196/11604 PMID: 30958272

Rafique, H., Almagrabi, A. O., Shamim, A., Anwar, F., & Bashir, A. K. (2020). Investigating the acceptance of mobile library applications with an extended technology acceptance model (TAM). *Computers & Education, 145*, 103732. DOI: 10.1016/j.compedu.2019.103732

Ragheb, M. A., Tantawi, P., Farouk, N., & Hatata, A. (2022). Investigating the acceptance of applying chat-bot (Artificial intelligence) technology among higher education students in Egypt. *International Journal of Higher Education Management, 8*(2). Advance online publication. https://www.academia.edu/download/96162300/2022-02-28-20-55-56-PM.pdf. DOI: 10.24052/IJHEM/V08N02/ART-1

Rashid, A. B., & Kausik, M. A. K. (2024). AI revolutionizing industries worldwide : A comprehensive overview of its diverse applications. *Hybrid Advances, 7*, 100277. DOI: 10.1016/j.hybadv.2024.100277

Rogers, E. M. (1962). *Diffusion of innovations. New York : Free Press—Recherche Google.* (s. d.). Consulté 12 avril 2025, à l'adresse

Roy, R., & Naidoo, V. (2021). Enhancing chatbot effectiveness : The role of anthropomorphic conversational styles and time orientation. *Journal of Business Research*, 126, 23 34. DOI: 10.1016/j.jbusres.2020.12.051

Salem, M. (2024). Use of chatbots and its role in enhancing customer experience : A Study of the banking industry. In *Digital technology and changing roles in managerial and financial accounting : Theoretical knowledge and practical application* (pp. 107 114). Emerald PublishingLimited.https://www.emerald.com/insight/content/doi/10.1108/S147935122024000036010/full/html

Sands, S., Ferraro, C., Campbell, C., & Tsao, H.-Y. (2021). Managing the human–chatbot divide: How service scripts influence service experience. *Journal of Service Management, 32*(2), 246–264. DOI: 10.1108/JOSM-06-2019-0203

Sboui, M., Baati, O., & Sfar, N. (2024). Influencing factors and consequences of chatbot initial trust in AI telecommunication services : A study on Generation Z. *The TQM Journal*. Advance online publication. DOI: 10.1108/TQM-02-2024-0085

Selamat, M. A., & Windasari, N. A. (2021). Chatbot for SMEs : Integrating customer and business owner perspectives. *Technology in Society, 66*, 101685. DOI: 10.1016/j.techsoc.2021.101685

Sheehan, B., Jin, H. S., & Gottlieb, U. (2020). Customer service chatbots : Anthropomorphism and adoption. *Journal of Business Research*, 115, 14 24. DOI: 10.1016/j.jbusres.2020.04.030

Shin, H., Bunosso, I., & Levine, L. R. (2023). The influence of chatbot humour on consumer evaluations of services. *International Journal of Consumer Studies*, 47(2), 545 562. DOI: 10.1111/ijcs.12849

Skjuve, M., Haugstveit, I. M., Følstad, A., & Brandtzaeg, P. (2019). Help! Is my chatbot falling into the uncanny valley? An empirical study of user experience in human–chatbot interaction. *Human Technology*, *15*(1), 30–54. DOI: 10.17011/ht/urn.201902201607

Sodiya, E. O., Amoo, O. O., Umoga, U. J., Atadoga, A., Sodiya, E. O., Amoo, O. O., Umoga, U. J., & Atadoga, A. (2024). AI-driven personalization in web content delivery : A comparative study of user engagement in the USA and the UK. *World Journal of Advanced Research and Reviews*, *21*(2), 887–902. DOI: 10.30574/wjarr.2024.21.2.0502

Song, C. S., & Kim, Y.-K. (2022). The role of the human-robot interaction in consumers' acceptance of humanoid retail service robots. *Journal of Business Research*, *146*, 489–503. DOI: 10.1016/j.jbusres.2022.03.087

Song, X., Gu, H., Li, Y., Leung, X. Y., & Ling, X. (2024). The influence of robot anthropomorphism and perceived intelligence on hotel guests' continuance usage intention. *Information Technology & Tourism*, *26*(1), 89–117. DOI: 10.1007/s40558-023-00275-8

Stafford, R. Q. (2013). The contribution of people's attitudes and perceptions to the acceptance of eldercare robots [PhD Thesis, University of Auckland]. https://www.researchgate.net/profile/Rebecca-Stafford

Stroessner, S. J., & Benitez, J. (2019). The Social Perception of Humanoid and Non-Humanoid Robots : Effects of Gendered and Machinelike Features. *International Journal of Social Robotics*, 11(2), 305 315. DOI: 10.1007/s12369-018-0502-7

Sumarjan, N., Mazlan, N., Saiful Azmi, N. S., Kamaruddin, M. A., & Salleh, A. (2023). The usage intention of chatbot technology in hospitality and tourism industry : Customers' perspective. *Journal of Tourism. Hospitality and Culinary Arts*, *15*(1), 206–224.

Thomaz, F., Salge, C., Karahanna, E., & Hulland, J. (2020). Learning from the Dark Web : Leveraging conversational agents in the era of hyper-privacy to enhance marketing. *Journal of the Academy of Marketing Science*, *48*(1), 43–63. DOI: 10.1007/s11747-019-00704-3

Tian, W., Ge, J., Zhao, Y., & Zheng, X. (2024). AI Chatbots in Chinese higher education : Adoption, perception, and influence among graduate students—an integrated analysis utilizing UTAUT and ECM models. *Frontiers in Psychology, 15*, 1268549. DOI: 10.3389/fpsyg.2024.1268549 PMID: 38384353

Topsakal, Y. (2024). How Familiarity, Ease of Use, Usefulness, and Trust Influence the Acceptance of Generative Artificial Intelligence (AI)-Assisted Travel Planning. *International Journal of Human-Computer Interaction, 1*, 14. DOI: 10.1080/10447318.2024.2426044

Tubaishat, A. (2018). Perceived usefulness and perceived ease of use of electronic health records among nurses : Application of Technology Acceptance Model. *Informatics for Health and Social Care*, 43(4), 379 389. DOI: 10.1080/17538157.2017.1363761

Van Eeuwen, M. 2017. Mobile conversational commerce: Messenger chatbots as the next interface between businesses and consumers University of Twente]. http://purl. utwente.nl/essays/71706

Venkatesh, V., & Bala, H. (2008). Technology Acceptance Model 3 and a Research Agenda on Interventions. *Decision Sciences, 39*(2), 273–315. DOI: 10.1111/j.1540-5915.2008.00192.x

Venkatesh, V., & Davis, F. D. (2000). A Theoretical Extension of the Technology Acceptance Model : Four Longitudinal Field Studies. *Management Science, 46*(2), 186–204. DOI: 10.1287/mnsc.46.2.186.11926

Venkatesh, V., Morris, M. G., Davis, G. B., & Davis, F. D. (2003). User acceptance of information technology : Toward a unified view. *Management Information Systems Quarterly, 425*(3), 478. DOI: 10.2307/30036540

Venkatesh, V., Thong, J. Y., & Xu, X. (2012). Consumer acceptance and use of information technology : Extending the unified theory of acceptance and use of technology. *Management Information Systems Quarterly, 157*(1), 178. DOI: 10.2307/41410412

Viot, C., & Bressolles, G. (2012). Les agents virtuels intelligents. Décisions marketing, 65(1), 45 56.

Vlachos, E., Jochum, E., & Demers, L.-P. (2016). The Effects of Exposure to Different Social Robots on Attitudes toward Preferences. Interaction Studies. *Social Behaviour and Communication in Biological and Artificial Systems*, 17(3), 390 404. DOI: 10.1075/is.17.3.04vla

Waytz, A., Cacioppo, J., & Epley, N. (2010). Who Sees Human? : The Stability and Importance of Individual Differences in Anthropomorphism. *Perspectives on Psychological Science*, 5(3), 219 232. DOI: 10.1177/1745691610369336

Wirtz, J., Patterson, P. G., Kunz, W. H., Gruber, T., Lu, V. N., Paluch, S., & Martins, A. (2018). Brave new world : Service robots in the frontline. *Journal of Service Management*, *29*(5), 907–931. DOI: 10.1108/JOSM-04-2018-0119

Wongyai, P. H., Ngo, T., Wu, H., Tsui, K. W. H., & Nguyen, T.-H. (2024). Self-service technology in aviation : A systematic literature review. *Journal of the Air Transport Research Society*, *2*, 100016. DOI: 10.1016/j.jatrs.2024.100016

Wu, C.-C., Chen, C.-T., Huang, K.-C., & Chou, Y.-Y. (2025). Determinants of Chat-bot adoption among older adults : An extended TAM approach using PLS-SEM. *Information Development*, *02666669251315839*(3), 656–674. Advance online publication. DOI: 10.1177/02666669251315839

Wu, K., Zhao, Y., Zhu, Q., Tan, X., & Zheng, H. (2011). A meta-analysis of the impact of trust on technology acceptance model : Investigation of moderating influence of subject and context type. *International Journal of Information Management*, 31(6), 572 581. DOI: 10.1016/j.ijinfomgt.2011.03.004

Zhang, B., Zhu, Y., Deng, J., Zheng, W., Liu, Y., Wang, C., & Zeng, R. (2023). "I Am Here to Assist Your Tourism" : Predicting Continuance Intention to Use AI-based Chatbots for Tourism. Does Gender Really Matter? *International Journal of Human–Computer Interaction*, 39(9), 1887 1903. DOI: 10.1080/10447318.2022.2124345

Zlotowski, J., Proudfoot, D., Yogeeswaran, K., & Bartneck, C. (2015). Opportunities and challenges in human–robot interaction. *International Journal of Social Robotics*, 7(3), 347–360. DOI: 10.1007/s12369-014-0267-6

Žvanut, B., & Mihelič, A. (2024). Qualitative study on domestic social robot adoption and associated security concerns among older adults in Slovenia. *Frontiers in Psychology*, *15*, 1343077. DOI: 10.3389/fpsyg.2024.1343077 PMID: 38333061

ENDNOTES

1 https://www.grandviewresearch.com/industry-analysis/chatbot-market

2 https://www.medianet.tn/fr/actualites/detail/chiffres-cles-internet-reseaux-sociaux-web/, consulted on 20/3/2025

Chapter 16
From Algorithms to Aesthetics:
Influencer Engagement Trends in Indian Cosmetic Ads on Meta (2020–2025)

Apoorva Mahiwal
https://orcid.org/0009-0002-8087-5298
Amity School of Communication, Amity University, Jaipur, India

Tanushri Mukherjee
https://orcid.org/0000-0001-5120-7982
Amity School of Communication, Amity University, Jaipur, India

Saad Ullah Khan
https://orcid.org/0000-0002-3392-7844
Centre for Media and Mass Communiction Studies, Jamia Hamdard, New Delhi, India

Sadaf Khan
https://orcid.org/0009-0005-1348-0386
IEC College of Engineering and Technology, Greater Noida, India

Mani Sachdev
https://orcid.org/0009-0000-8284-9718
Amity Institute of Behavioural and Allied Sciences, Amity University, Jaipur, India

DOI: 10.4018/979-8-3373-2747-1.ch016

ABSTRACT

This study investigates the evolving dynamics of influencer-driven advertising in India's cosmetic sector by analyzing engagement trends on Meta platforms (2020–2025). Employing quantitative content analysis of Meta Ad Library data, it systematically evaluates ad formats (images, videos, carousels) and influencer collaborations from leading cosmetic brands. Central to the analysis is the comparative efficacy of influencer-integrated versus non-influencer content across key engagement metrics—likes, comments, shares, and impressions. The research further examines the emergent role of AI-driven algorithms in shaping ad visibility and user interaction, situating findings at the nexus of aesthetic strategy, algorithmic salience, and audience engagement. This work contributes to digital marketing scholarship and offers actionable insights for practitioners in advertising, branding, and content strategy.

INTRODUCTION

In the rapidly evolving digital ecosystem, the integration of Artificial Intelligence (AI) with advertising practices has led to a paradigm shift in how brands communicate with consumers. No longer limited to static, one-size-fits-all campaigns, digital advertising today is increasingly personalized, data-driven, and context-aware. Recent findings highlight that the millennial generation—identified as informed, conscious, and digitally savvy—expects advertising communication to be closely aligned with their evolving preferences and values, prompting brands to adopt more responsive and AI-enhanced strategies (Storhannus, 2021).

1.1 Rise of AI in Advertising

The emergence of Artificial Intelligence (AI) has fundamentally transformed the landscape of digital advertising. Unlike traditional advertising models that relied heavily on static demographics and broad targeting, AI-driven advertising leverages real-time data analytics to enable hyper-personalized campaigns (Babatunde et al., 2024). Algorithms can process vast datasets to predict consumer behaviour and preferences, making it possible to deliver targeted advertisements, customized product recommendations, and tailored content that resonates with specific user segments. Moreover, AI enhances user engagement by enabling gamified marketing experiences, thereby fostering deeper emotional and cognitive engagement with brands (Babatunde et al., 2024).

One of the most significant innovations has been the use of AI in programmatic advertising, which automates the buying and placement of ads based on audience insights. (Brayer, 2020) This automation not only increases efficiency but also enhances ad relevance, reducing wastage and increasing conversion rates. In the context of Instagram, AI determines which sponsored posts appear in a user's feed or on the Explore page, giving brands a powerful mechanism to amplify their content. Reels, in particular, are prioritized by Instagram's AI algorithm, (Shah & Malik, 2025) making them a popular format for advertisers seeking higher engagement. Consequently, cosmetic brands are increasingly investing in AI-driven ad strategies to stay competitive in the saturated beauty market (Weaver et al., 2024).

1.2 Cosmetic Industry and Social Media

The cosmetic industry in India is a consistently growing market and holds the fourth position globally in terms of revenue (Minhas, 2024). The expansion is driven by various factors, including an increase in disposable income, the influence of globalization on lifestyle choices, and a greater consumption of products due to cosmetic trials (IBEF, 2023). The industry is also benefiting from a rise in the adoption of natural products and improved channel penetration. Furthermore, recent data from 2023 and 2024 indicates that a significant number of consumers in India are willing to spend more on beauty products, highlighting a strong consumer base for the sector's continued growth (Weaver et al., 2024).

The cosmetic industry has witnessed a dramatic transformation with the rise of social media platforms, especially Instagram, (Gupta, 2024) which has become a visual-first hub for beauty marketing. Social media enables cosmetic brands to create visually immersive campaigns and real-time interactions that drive consumer loyalty and community-building. Features such as Reels, Stories, and Instagram Live offer brands dynamic ways to demonstrate product use, showcase before-and-after results, and share tutorials (Srivastava & Malik, 2024). These formats not only enhance visibility but also shape consumer behaviour by influencing purchase decisions and promoting aspirational beauty standards.

Moreover, the democratization of content creation—fuelled by beauty influencers and micro-influencers—has challenged traditional notions of authority and expertise in the beauty space. Users are more inclined to trust reviews and tutorials from relatable content creators than corporate advertising (Celestin & Sujatha, 2024). As a result, social media strategy has become central to brand identity and consumer engagement in the cosmetics sector. Bollywood emerges as a significant case study in this context, having strategically leveraged social media platforms to foster audience engagement—not only within India but also across international markets, where its promotional strategies have shown measurable impact on viewer interaction and reception (Pattanayak et al., 2025) With the increase in influencer advertising, consumers' purchasing decisions for cosmetics are largely influenced by personal feelings and psychological factors. Although the quality of ingredients matters, emotional drivers ultimately guide the final purchase (Upadhyaya & Sijoria, 2024).

Together, the dual forces of AI-driven advertising and social media proliferation have not only redefined marketing strategies but have also reshaped consumer-brand relationships. In the context of the cosmetic industry, these developments have empowered brands to deliver hyper-targeted, visually engaging campaigns that resonate with users on a personal level. Instagram, as a visual and algorithm-powered platform, has become a critical space for cosmetic brands to harness AI capabilities—from influencer collaborations and real-time feedback to predictive targeting and engagement analytics. This study builds upon these intersections, examining how AI and social media strategies converge to influence consumer engagement with Indian cosmetic advertisements on Meta platforms from 2020 to 2025.

REVIEW OF LITERATURE

The rapid evolution of the digital economy has significantly disrupted conventional advertising models, prompting a shift toward more intelligent and data-driven approaches (Shi & Wang, 2023). Traditional methods, which often relied on broad targeting and generic messaging, are no longer sufficient in an environment where consumer attention is fragmented and highly selective. In this context, enhancing the precision of ad targeting and content identification has become increasingly urgent.

This shift is further intensified by the growing influence of globalization and new media technologies, which have redefined how cultural narratives and consumer trends circulate in the 21st century (Tamandehrou & Khan, 2015). The interplay between global media flows and localized digital consumption patterns has significantly impacted branding strategies—particularly in sectors like cosmetics, where visual identity and cultural relevance are central to consumer engagement.

In India, the convergence of entertainment, beauty, and technology is driving a striking transformation, as it is considered as to be showing one of the most promising growth in the cosmetic industry (Weaver et al., 2025).

Nowhere is this shift more evident than in the digital evolution of industries like Bollywood, which has set new benchmarks in media and storytelling (Pattanayak et al., 2024). Adjacent sectors such as fashion and cosmetic advertising are also experiencing significant changes. As Bollywood continues to integrate with media-tech ecosystems, its stylistic and narrative innovations are increasingly shaping influencer marketing. One notable advancement is the use of cinematic colour grading powered by AI, which is enhancing the visual appeal and emotional tone of multimedia content across both film and promotional media (Pattanayak et al., 2025). Similarly, the adoption of AI-driven PTZ (pan-tilt-zoom) camera systems in film production is transforming how dynamic visual narratives are captured (Pattanayak et al., 2024).

This sets new aesthetic expectations that has the potential to ameliorate branded content and influencer-led campaigns. These innovations contribute to the high-production-value look and immersive quality now expected in digital beauty advertising, further reinforcing aspirational ideals and deepening audience engagement across platforms like Meta.

These cultural and technological developments intersect with advancements in artificial intelligence (AI), which is now at the core of many advertising strategies. AI enables brands to leverage personalization, automation, and predictive analytics to optimize campaign effectiveness. In the context of social media, this allows cosmetic companies to refine influencer collaborations, improve content targeting, and engage niche audiences more effectively.

To address the challenges, recent literature explores how emerging technologies—particularly Artificial Intelligence (AI)—are reshaping advertising strategies, with a focus on personalization, automation, and predictive analytics. This chapter reviews key strands of existing research related to AI-driven advertising practices and the evolving social media strategies of cosmetic brands, offering a foundation for understanding current trends and identifying research gaps.

2.1 AI – Driven Advertisements on Social Media

The integration of Artificial Intelligence (AI) into social media advertising has radically altered how brands interact with audiences, enabling a shift from generic campaigns to highly personalized and responsive marketing strategies. AI does not replace the creative role of designers; rather, it acts as a collaborative tool that accelerates idea generation, enhances creativity, and reduces production time by generating design suggestions based on textual prompts (alla El-aasy, 2023). This synergy between human innovation and machine efficiency results in more engaging and visually compelling content. AI technologies are increasingly central to content creation and aesthetic presentation in Indian media (Khan et al., 2025). These developments also intersect with gendered dimensions of technology use; as emerging research explores how AI can support more inclusive engagements (Srivastava et. al, 2025).

One of the most compelling outcomes of AI in social media advertising is its ability to substantially boost marketing performance. AI-powered advertisements can lead to conversion rate increases ranging from 200% to 300%, simply by facilitating additional personalized customer touchpoints. Furthermore, predictive analytics supported by AI can improve overall marketing effectiveness by up to 20%, driving more accurate forecasting and higher returns on investment (Patil et al., 2024).

The strength of AI lies in its ability to combine personalization with contextual targeting. This dual capability ensures that the right message reaches the right audience at the most opportune moment. When personal and contextual variables are optimized together, advertising effectiveness is significantly enhanced, offering users a more relevant and engaging experience (Häglund & Björklund, 2024).

AI has also shifted the balance of power in advertising from businesses to consumers. With AI-powered tools, users now influence one another's preferences and purchasing decisions more directly. As a result, brands must adapt by focusing on creating more personalized and interactive campaigns that foster higher consumer engagement, build loyalty, and increase conversion rates (Rathee & Monika, 2025).

Beyond operational efficiency, AI technologies are also redefining brand narratives. They enable deeper emotional connections by delivering content that aligns with individual values, preferences, and behavioural patterns—thereby transforming marketing from transactional messaging to meaningful storytelling (Dang, 2025).

Crucially, AI-enabled personalization in social media contexts has been shown to positively influence consumer perceptions. Research confirms that tailored content not only enhances perceived usefulness but also boosts trust, even when privacy concerns are considered, highlighting the strategic importance of data ethics in AI applications (Teepapal, 2025).

2.2 Social Media Advertisement Strategies of Cosmetic Brands

The evolution of media consumption habits has driven a strategic pivot among cosmetic brands—from product-centric messaging to people-centric engagement. This shift emphasizes co-creation, interaction, and personalization over mere information dissemination. As digital platforms foster a culture of two-way communication, companies are increasingly leveraging user-generated content, influencer partnerships, and emotional engagement strategies to connect with consumers more meaningfully (Shen & Bissell, 2013). These dynamics reflect a broader transformation in how audiences interact with brands and causes online, where participation and personal identification increasingly shape engagement outcomes. Similar patterns are observed in other domains—such as environmental activism—where social media's ability to mobilize decentralized communities and facilitate peer-to-peer influence has proven highly effective (Mahiwal et al.,2024).

Contextual advertising (CA) plays a pivotal role especially when powered by Artificial Intelligence. Research highlights three key factors that influence contextual ad effectiveness: applicability, or the thematic alignment between content and advertisement; affective tone, referring to the emotional mood conveyed; and content involvement, which reflects the depth of consumer engagement. Together, these elements enable brands to deliver hyper-relevant content tailored to users' current states of mind and interests—thereby enhancing brand resonance and recall (Häglund & Björklund, 2024).

Cosmetic brands specifically benefit from a systematic application of social media marketing activities. A comparative study of consumer responses to cosmetic brands revealed that users perceive brand equity differently from luxury brand consumers, with relationship equity and value equity emerging as significant variables in determining future purchase intentions. This underlines the need for brands to adapt their strategies based on segment-specific insights (Binwani & Ho, 2019).

Engagement tactics such as product reviews, influencer endorsements, interactive advertisements, and meeting customer expectations have a profound impact on shaping consumer attitudes in emerging markets. For instance, in the Ethiopian context, these strategies were found to notably boost both brand engagement and consumer purchase intent—reinforcing the power of culturally adaptive and interactive advertising (Gebre, 2024). Another study endorses influencers stating instead of using celebrity brand ambassadors, cosmetic companies can effectively engage customers through micro and macro influencers, as nearly 30% of respondents check online reviews before making a purchase (Katkar et al., 2024). This highlights the need for companies to invest in good public relations. The most influential factor in cosmetic buying decision are product reviews (Rane et al., 2025).

While trust and affective attitudes are confirmed as strong predictors of purchase intent on social media, other commonly assumed indicators such as credibility and authenticity showed no significant influence. This suggests that cosmetic brands should focus their efforts on fostering emotional trust and cultivating positive consumer sentiment rather than merely asserting credibility claims (Manan et al., 2020).

Finally, effective social media strategies in the cosmetic sector should incorporate diversified product offerings, community building, personalized marketing, and co-branding collaborations. These tactics not only improve social media performance but also drive retail sales, as demonstrated in the case of J Cosmetics Company in China. Strategic use of data analytics and community engagement further enhances brand value and customer loyalty in competitive markets (Xuanyu et al., 2025).

2.3 Influencer Marketing in the Cosmetic Industry

In today's dynamic digital landscape, Instagram influencer advertising has emerged as a powerful tool for cosmetic brands seeking authentic consumer engagement. By partnering with influencers, brands can harness their established credibility, social reach, and subject-matter expertise to foster trust and create memorable brand experiences. These collaborations often result in heightened brand awareness, increased audience engagement, and higher conversion rates, particularly when influencers are well-aligned with brand identity and values (Talreja & Chaturvedi, 2024).

The efficacy of influencer marketing is determined by multiple factors, including the type of influencer, sponsorship status, and the product exposure method used. Influencers who offer direct endorsements, whether through organic or sponsored posts, significantly shape consumer perception. Interestingly, sponsored content is often better received when it feels authentic and aligns with the influencer's usual tone. Moreover, the method of showcasing the product—such as tutorials, testimonials, or aesthetic placements—elicits varied responses from viewers, underscoring the importance of tailoring content to audience expectations (Upathamphan & Puapradit, 2024).

The strategic use of social media marketing—including influencer collaborations—has shown a considerable impact on brand awareness, repurchase intention, and electronic word-of-mouth (eWOM). Among these, brand awareness emerged as the most influenced factor. The study highlights that consistent, well-managed influencer-led communication can amplify brand messaging, inform consumers about product offerings, and generate valuable consumer-to-consumer recommendations—particularly in niche markets like halal beauty (Jalil et al., 2021).

Credibility remains a core attribute in determining an influencer's effectiveness, especially among young millennial consumers. Attributes such as expertise, attractiveness, and relatability strongly influence their purchasing decisions. These traits allow influencers—often termed 'beauty gurus'—to transcend traditional advertising by forming parasocial bonds with followers. As a result, influencers have become a vital element of modern marketing strategies, successfully driving brand preference and loyalty across diverse demographic segments (Hassan et al., 2021).

Together, these findings reveal that influencer marketing in the cosmetic industry operates at the intersection of strategic content curation, authentic storytelling, and audience alignment. Brands that thoughtfully engage with influencers—not just as promoters but as collaborators—stand to benefit from stronger consumer relationships and more impactful digital presence.

METHODOLOGY

To investigate engagement trends in influencer-driven cosmetic advertisements on Meta Platforms, this study adopts a quantitative content analysis approach. The data set comprises advertisements posted by selected Indian cosmetic brands between May 2020 and May 2025, sourced from Instagram. Upon preliminary comparison, it was observed that the content posted on Facebook by the selected brands mirrored their Instagram content, with little to no variation in format or messaging. However, the engagement levels (likes, comments, shares) on Facebook were negligible, rendering them unsuitable for meaningful quantitative analysis. As a result, Instagram emerged as the most effective platform in terms of user engagement (Singh et al., 2025). Facebook was excluded from the scope of this study, and the analysis focuses exclusively on Instagram content and engagement metrics.

Further, only Indian brands are considered for this study to maintain regional specificity. To ensure an industry-specific focus, the study includes only cosmetic brands from a curated list of top influencer-driven brands in India. Additionally, only brands actively engaged in influencer marketing as a key promotional strategy have been selected. A website listing the top Indian brands using influencer marketing serves as the source, and all cosmetic brands mentioned in the list are included in this research. This selection framework enables a targeted analysis of how Indian cosmetic brands leverage influencer-driven advertisements on Meta platforms.

Based on the above criteria, the following five Indian cosmetic brands were selected for detailed analysis: (Value4brand, 2025).

- SUGAR Cosmetics
- Mamaearth
- mCaffeine
- MyGlamm
- Nykaa

This selection provides a balanced representation of the Indian cosmetic industry's approach to influencer advertising on Instagram and supports robust comparative insights.

3.1 Objective of the Study

This study aims to conduct a comprehensive analysis of the advertising strategies employed by prominent Indian cosmetic brands on Meta platforms between 2020 and 2025, with a focus on identifying and categorizing the diverse advertisement formats utilized, including images, videos, and carousels. A key component of the research involves investigating the integration of influencer collaborations within these formats to uncover prevailing patterns and longitudinal trends over the five-year period. To assess the effectiveness of each ad format in capturing user attention, the study will analyse audience engagement metrics—namely likes, comments, shares, and impressions—thereby offering comparative insights into the performance of different media types. Furthermore, the research will evaluate the specific impact of influencer-integrated content on overall advertisement performance by juxtaposing engagement levels of influencer-driven posts against those without influencer involvement, providing a nuanced understanding of the role influencers play in enhancing brand visibility and user interaction on social media platforms.

3.2 Data Collection

The data collection process for this study was conducted manually to ensure precision and consistency. Advertisement content was retrieved from the official Instagram handles of the five selected cosmetic brands—SUGAR Cosmetics, Mamaearth, mCaffeine, MyGlamm, and Nykaa—covering a five-year period from May 2020 to May 2025.

To maintain temporal consistency and manage data volume, posts published on the 1st and 15th of each month were selected for analysis. This interval-based sampling ensured that trends across different phases of marketing cycles—such as product launches, festive promotions, or influencer collaborations—were adequately captured.

For each brand, this method yielded two posts per month, a frequency chosen to ensure consistency while capturing periodic engagement trends without over-representing high-volume content creators (Mahiwal et al., 2025). This resulted in 24 posts per year, and a total of 120 posts per brand over the five-year period. With five brands included in the study, the overall data set comprised 600 Instagram posts.

For each selected post, the following variables were manually recorded:

- Engagement metrics: Number of *likes*, *comments*, and *shares*
- Influencer integration: Whether the post featured a social media influencer or celebrity endorsement
- Ad format: Type of media used (*image*, *video*, or *carousel*)

This manual extraction approach enabled a structured and focused data set that balances representativeness with feasibility for detailed quantitative content analysis.

3.3 Data Coding

Each advertisement was analysed and coded systematically based on predefined categories aligned with the study objectives. The coding scheme was developed to capture both content features and audience engagement metrics. The operational definitions of the key variables are as follows:

- Ad Format: Categorized into three types—
  - *Image*: A single static visual
  - *Video*: A moving visual clip, including Reels

- o *Carousel*: A series of images or videos in a single post
- Influencer Integration: Posts were coded as:
  - o *Yes*: If the post visibly featured or tagged a social media influencer or celebrity
  - o *No*: If the post did not include any influencer presence
- Engagement Metrics:
  - o *Likes*: Total number of 'likes' recorded on the post
  - o *Comments*: Total number of user comments
  - o *Shares*: Estimated based on visible share count or platform-provided insights (if available)

3.4 Outlier Detection and Data Cleaning

To ensure analytical accuracy while preserving the integrity of brand-specific performance, outlier detection was conducted individually for each brand rather than applying a universal threshold. This brand-wise approach accounts for inherent variations in audience size, engagement norms, and brand visibility.

For each of the five selected cosmetic brands—SUGAR Cosmetics, Mamaearth, mCaffeine, MyGlamm, and Nykaa—outliers were identified using the interquartile range (IQR) method, applied separately to likes, comments, and shares. This method allowed for a concrete identification of extreme values within each brand's typical engagement distribution. Posts falling below $Q1 - 1.5\times IQR$ or above $Q3 + 1.5\times IQR$ were considered outliers and excluded from the main trend analysis. However, these outlier posts were analysed separately to understand virality characteristics.

This approach was adopted after observing that a significant number of high-engagement posts from brands like SUGAR Cosmetics were being classified as outliers under overall threshold, despite reflecting legitimate reach rather than data anomalies. Removing such posts would have led to the underrepresentation of brands with naturally higher visibility.

Further, to reduce data distortion while retaining valuable insights, outliers were identified using univariate detection methods, applied separately to each engagement metric (likes, comments, and shares) within each brand. That is, only outlier values were excluded when calculating averages for each engagement metric (likes, comments, shares), without discarding the entire post unless it contained multiple anomalies. For instance, if a post was an outlier in likes but not in comments or shares, it was only excluded from the average likes calculation. Outliers identified in the dataset—52 in likes, 46 in comments, and 68 in shares—were excluded from the calculation of average metrics. These outliers were analysed separately to explore the characteristics of virality. This approach allowed for maximum retention of valid data while improving the accuracy of metric-specific trends.

Therefore, by implementing brand-specific outlier detection, the study ensures fair comparative analysis without distorting the data landscape. Outliers identified through this method were separately analyzed to understand the characteristics and potential causes behind unusually high engagement.

DATA ANALYSIS AND FINDINGS

This section presents the results derived from a systematic analysis of 600 Instagram posts between 2020 and 2025 by selected five Indian cosmetic brands. Using quantitative approaches, the data was examined to uncover patterns in audience engagement across various ad formats and influencer involvement. The findings not only reveal distinct audience preferences in terms of format and content but also highlight broader trends in digital advertising strategies within the cosmetics industry.

4.1 Distribution of Formats of Content

Understanding the ad format is crucial in digital marketing as it directly influences how users interact with content. Different formats—such as images, videos, and carousels—affect attention span, engagement rate, message retention, and emotional response. By analyzing the format preferences of brands, this study aims to uncover patterns in strategic content deployment and evaluate which formats are prioritized for audience impact on Instagram.

Table 1. Instagram Post Formats by Cosmetic Brand (2020–2025)

Cosmetic Brands	Carousal	Image	Video	Grand Total
MAMAEARTH	18	48	54	120
MCAFFEINE	20	53	47	120
MY GLAMM	4	34	82	120
NYKAA	8	57	55	120
SUGAR	1	57	62	120
Grand Total	**51**	**249**	**300**	**600**

Video advertisements emerged as the most used ad format overall, comprising 300 out of the 600 analysed posts (50%). This indicates a strong preference among brands for visually dynamic and engaging content that can effectively capture viewer attention and convey product benefits. Image posts followed as the second most used format, accounting for 249 posts (41.5%). Despite the rise of video content, the sustained use of images highlights their continued relevance in digital advertising, especially for product showcases and aesthetic appeal. Carousel ads, on the other hand, were the least utilized format, with only 51 posts (8.5%). This low adoption suggests that brands may favour straightforward, single-focus storytelling or immersive video-based formats over multi-image sequences that require swiping interaction.

Figure 1. Distribution of Instagram Post Formats in Cosmetic Brand Advertisements (2020–2025)

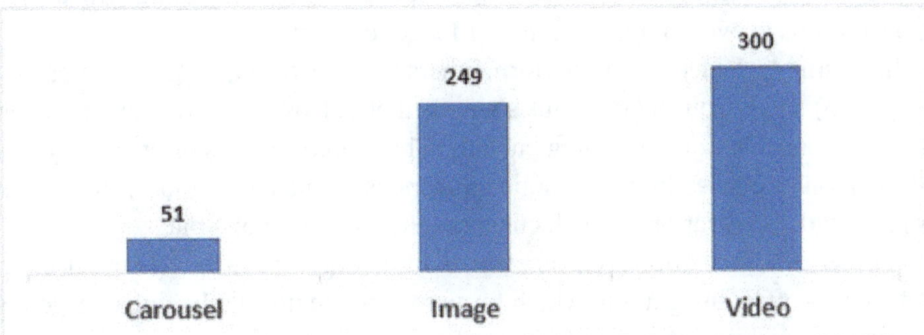

Engagement value is an prominent metric for assessing the effectiveness of a user's Instagram presence (Pattanayak et al., 2023). To understand the engagement level of different Instagram ad formats—carousel, image, and video—this study further analysed the average number of likes, comments, and shares each format received.

Average values were used instead of total sums because the number of posts per format varied significantly, (Shen & Bissell, 2013) and averages allow for a fair and normalized comparison across unequal sample sizes. The calculation of these averages was conducted after removing extreme values identified through univariate outlier detection, ensuring that the results were not skewed by anomalously high or low engagement figures.

Table 2. Average Engagement Metrics by Instagram Ad Format (2020–2025)

Ad Format	Average Likes	Average Comments	Average Shares
Carousel	921	37	16
Image	2199	46	13
Video	1711	36	21

Image ads receive the highest average number of likes (2199), followed by Video (1711), and Carousel (921). This suggests that Image-based advertisements are the most 'likable' format among audiences. The likely reason is that image ads are quick to consume, visually appealing, and often designed to make an immediate impact. Their static nature may also make them more effective for brand recall, thereby encouraging more users to express appreciation through likes.

When it comes to average comments, Image ads again lead (46), followed by Carousel (37) and Video (36). This indicates that Image ads also generate the highest commenting activity. This could be attributed to the fact that image posts often prompts users to respond, tag others, or express opinions more readily. The slight edge over videos and carousels may also reflect the ease of engaging with a single impactful image over multiple frames or longer content.

Interestingly, Video ads outperform others in terms of shares (21), compared to Image (13) and Carousel (16). This suggests that videos are more likely to be perceived as valuable or entertaining enough to be shared. Videos often convey more information or evoke stronger emotional responses, such as humour, storytelling, or product demonstrations, which enhances their virality potential.

Further, the distribution of outliers across different post formats—carousel, image, and video—offers insight into which formats generate unusually high engagement and where variability is most pronounced.

Table 3. Distribution of Outliers Across Ad Formats and Engagement Metrics

Metric	Total Outliers	Video Outliers (%)	Image Outliers (%)	Carousel Outliers (%)
Likes	52	29 (55.8%)	17 (32.7%)	6 (11.5%)
Comments	46	22 (47.8%)	21 (45.7%)	3 (6.5%)
Shares	68	54 (79.4%)	9 (13.2%)	5 (7.4%)

Video emerges as the most volatile yet powerful format, consistently generating the highest number of outliers across all engagement metrics—especially shares. A key factor behind this is Instagram's AI-driven algorithm, which prioritizes and amplifies engaging video content, especially Reels, within users' feeds and the Explore page. This synergy between high-performing formats and algorithmic promotion (sponsored advertisements) contributes to viral spikes in engagement. Image formats show moderate outlier presence, pointing to more stable but less explosive performance, while carousel posts consistently generate the fewest outliers. The data highlights how cosmetic brands leverage AI-optimized content strategies—particularly sponsored ad content—to achieve both sustained engagement and occasional viral reach.

4.2 Influencer Content Vs Non-Influencer Content

The use of influencers in cosmetic advertising on Instagram has become a strategic tool for enhancing brand credibility, relatability, and reach. Influencers serve as trusted intermediaries who can shape consumer perceptions and drive engagement through their personal branding and follower networks. In this study, an analysis was conducted to examine the presence of influencer content across three commonly used ad formats—carousel, image, and video—within a dataset of 600 Instagram posts related to cosmetic promotions.

Table 4. Distribution of Influencer and Non-Influencer Content Across Ad Formats

Ad Format	Carousel	Image	Video	Total
Posts with Influencer Content	3	34	121	158
Posts without Influencer Content	48	215	179	442
Total	51	249	300	600

The data reveals that influencer-driven content is most frequently employed in video formats, with 121 out of 300 video posts (40.3%) featuring influencers. Image posts also utilize influencer content, though to a lesser extent, with 34 out of 249 posts (13.6%) including influencers. Carousel posts showed minimal influencer involvement, with only 3 out of 51 posts (5.9%) integrating influencer elements. This pattern suggests a strategic preference for video formats when leveraging influencer partnerships, likely due to the format's capacity for storytelling, product demonstration, and fostering parasocial interaction. Image formats follow as a secondary choice, offering visual appeal with moderate influencer usage, while carousel posts appear to be used primarily for showcasing multiple product features or variations without the presence of influencers.

This analysis sets the stage for a comparative assessment of the effectiveness of influencer versus non-influencer content by examining average engagement metrics—likes, comments, and shares—which is calculated by removing univariate outlier detected.

Table 5. Average Engagement Metrics for Posts With and Without Influencer Content

Ad Format	Average Likes	Average Comments	Average Shares
Posts with Influencer Content	3326	56	28
Posts without Influencer Content	1351	34	14

Influencer content leads significantly across all three engagement metrics—likes, comments, and shares—demonstrating its superior effectiveness in capturing audience attention and prompting interaction. With over twice the number of likes, 65% more comments, and double the shares compared to non-influencer posts, this pattern conveys that influencer-driven posts are more appealing, emotionally resonant, and share-worthy. The heightened engagement suggests that audiences not only notice and appreciate content featuring influencers but are also more inclined to interact with and promote it. This underscores the power of influencer marketing in building trust, enhancing visibility, and fostering a sense of connection between the brand and its audience.

Table 6. Distribution of Outlier Posts by Influencer Presence

Metric	Total Outliers	With Influencer	Without Influencer
Likes	52	18 (34.6%)	34 (65.4%)
Comments	46	11 (23.9%)	35 (76.1%)
Shares	68	29 (42.6%)	39 (57.4%)

Furthermore, an analysis of outlier distribution reveals an interesting contrast: posts *without* influencers surprisingly account for a greater number of outliers across all three-engagement metrics compared to posts *with* influencers. While influencer content generally performs better on average, this data suggests that non-influencer posts get the potential to achieve exceptionally high engagement, possibly due to strategic use of AI-driven sponsored advertising. These posts, although lacking influencer presence, are optimized for algorithmic visibility—featuring trending audio, high-quality visuals, product-centric storytelling, and keyword-targeted captions. In contrast, influencer posts, while more consistently engaging and relatable, show fewer outliers, indicating a steadier but less volatile engagement pattern. These findings suggest that cosmetic brands are successfully leveraging two parallel strategies: one relying on influencer authenticity for consistent engagement, and the other using AI-powered sponsored content to generate viral spikes and reach beyond organic followers.

4.3 Temporal Shift in Ad Format Usage by Indian Cosmetic Brands (2020–2025)

As social media continues to dominate the advertising landscape, cosmetic brands in India have increasingly adapted their content strategies to align with platform trends and audience preferences. A key element of this adaptation lies in the choice of ad formats—namely image, video, and carousel posts—used on Meta platforms to engage users and showcase products. The following table presents a year-wise distribution of these ad formats from 2020 to 2025, offering insights into how visual storytelling and interactive design have evolved in digital cosmetic advertising.

Table 7. Year-wise Distribution of Ad Formats in Influencer Cosmetic Posts (2020–2025)

Year	Image	Video	Carousel	Total
2020	46	21	3	70
2021	64	48	8	120
2022	55	54	11	120
2023	42	66	12	120
2024	32	77	11	120
2025	10	34	6	50
Grand Total	**249**	**300**	**51**	**600**

Notably, video content has seen a consistent rise, reflecting its growing importance in influencer marketing and AI-boosted content visibility, while image posts have steadily declined, and carousel posts remain minimal yet tactically used. This shift toward video highlights the cosmetic industry's increasing alignment with platform algorithms favouring video content, especially for influencer-driven promotions that aim for higher engagement and viral potential.

Figure 2. Year-wise Distribution of Ad Formats in Influencer Cosmetic Posts

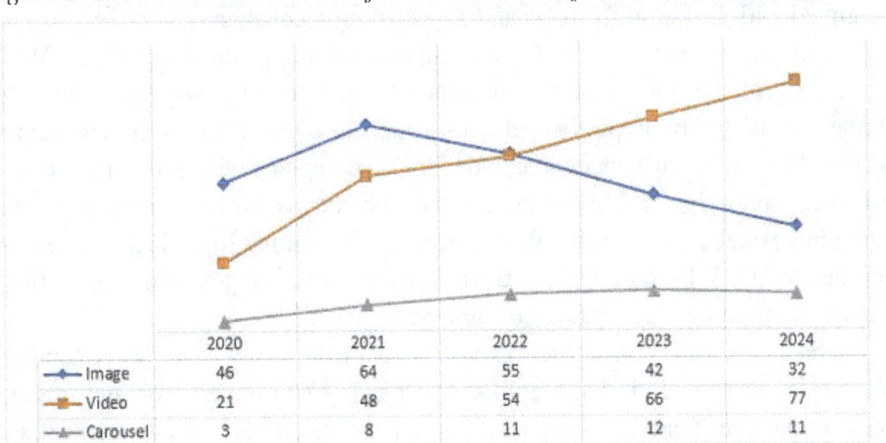

While the table includes data for 2025, the graphical representation that follows accounts only for 2020–2024, since 2025 data covers only January to May, which skews the visual trend and does not provide a full-year comparison.

CONCLUSION AND RECOMMENDATIONS

This section synthesizes the key insights derived from the analysis and translates them into actionable recommendations for cosmetic brands operating on Instagram. By examining ad formats, influencer strategies, and evolving engagement trends between 2020 and 2025, the study offers a nuanced understanding of what drives audience interaction in the cosmetic industry.

5.1 Summary of Findings

This study investigated 600 Instagram advertisements from five Indian cosmetic brands between 2020 and 2025, with a focus on content format, influencer involvement, engagement patterns, and temporal trends. The findings reveal that video ads are the most widely used format, constituting 50% of total content, followed by image posts (41.5%) and carousel posts (8.5%). Despite being least used, carousel posts generate relatively high comment averages, indicating their potential for deeper engagement when strategically employed.

In terms of engagement performance, image posts garnered the highest average likes (2,199) and comments (46), suggesting that static visuals remain highly effective for brand visibility and appreciation. Conversely, video posts received the most shares (21 on average), highlighting their storytelling appeal, particularly when integrated with Instagram's Reels and AI-boosting mechanisms.

The use of influencers significantly influenced engagement outcomes. While only 26.3% of the posts featured influencers, such content—especially in video format—consistently outperformed non-influencer content across all engagement metrics. Posts with influencers received far exceeding engagement than their non-influencer counterparts. This underscores the persuasive power of influencer marketing in cosmetic promotions. With consumers becoming more inclined towards their health, (GMI Research, 2024) the influencer advertising is holding significant position in building trust among consumers.

Interestingly, while non-influencer posts accounted for a higher number of outliers, suggesting occasional viral success likely driven by AI optimization and strategic media spends, influencer content showed more consistent and steady engagement. This points to a dual strategy: influencers ensure relatable, sustained interaction, while non-influencer posts, when boosted, can achieve sudden spikes in reach.

Lastly, the temporal analysis reveals a clear shift in format preference over time. From 2020 to 2024, brands moved away from images and increasingly adopted video-based formats, adapting to changing user behaviour and Instagram's evolving AI driven algorithm. This evolution reflects the growing centrality of immersive storytelling, influencer integration, and algorithmic visibility in shaping digital cosmetic advertising strategies.

PRACTICAL RECOMMENDATIONS

Based on the findings of this study, several practical recommendations can be proposed for cosmetic brands seeking to optimize their influencer marketing strategies on Instagram:

Prioritize Instagram for Influencer Campaigns - Given that Instagram emerged as the most effective platform in terms of consumer engagement, cosmetic brands should continue to invest in influencer collaborations on Instagram rather than diluting resources across multiple platforms like Facebook, where engagement was found to be negligible.

Emphasize Visual Storytelling and Authenticity - Posts that use visually appealing, relatable content—such as tutorials, before-and-after transformations, and user-generated content—tend to resonate more with audiences. Brands should encourage influencers to maintain authentic and consistent messaging that aligns with their personal brand.

Monitor Engagement Metrics Beyond Likes - Brands should move beyond superficial metrics such as likes, and focus more on comments, shares, and saves, which are stronger indicators of consumer interest and intent. These deeper forms of engagement can inform future content strategies and influencer selection.

REFERENCES

Babatunde, S. O., Odejide, O. A., Edunjobi, T. E., & Ogundipe, D. O. (2024). *The Role Of Ai In Marketing Personalization: A Theoretical Exploration Of Consumer Engagement Strategies*. ResearchGate; Fair East Publishers. https://www.researchgate.net/publication/379393342_THE_ROLE_OF_AI_IN_MARKETING_PERSONALIZATION_A_THEORETICAL_EXPLORATION_OF_CONSUMER_ENGAGEMENT_STRATEGIES

Binwani, K. J., & Ho, J. S. Y. (2019, July 1). *Effects of Social Media on Cosmetic Brands*. Papers.*ssrn*.com. https://papers.ssrn.com/sol3/papers.cfm?abstract_id=3446202

Brayer, M. (2020, February 3). *Programmatic Advertising Explained | Outbrain Blog*. English (US). https://www.outbrain.com/blog/programmatic-advertising/

Celestin, M., & Sujatha, S. (2024). Impact on brand trust and consumer behaviour: Leveraging social media influencers to drive credibility and engagement across industries. *Impact On Brand Trust And Consumer Behaviour: Leveraging Social Media Influencers To Drive Credibility And Engagement Across Industries*, *9*(2), 81–87. DOI: 10.5281/zenodo.13887149

Dang, T. (2025). AI-Driven Advertising and Consumer Purchase Behaviour: A Systematic Literature Review Based on the Theory of Planned Behaviour. *Ebsco.com, 13*(7), 414. https://openurl.ebsco.com/EPDB%3Agcd%3A5%3A24483973/detailv2?sid=ebsco%3Aplink%3Ascholar&id=ebsco%3Agcd%3A184662223&crl=c&link_origin=scholar.google.com

El-aasy, H. (2023). Employing Artificial Intelligence (AI) Technology in Advertising Design on Social Media. *Journal of Design Sciences and Applied Arts (Print)*, *4*(2), 247–263. DOI: 10.21608/jdsaa.2023.194906.1260

Gebre, A. (2024, January 1). *The Effect Of Social Media Advertisement On Customers' Attitude: In The Case Of Cosmetics Industry Addis Ababa*. Repository.smuc.edu.et. http://repository.smuc.edu.et/handle/123456789/7896

Gupta, R. (2024, September 21). *Insta-Fame and Image: The Social Media Influence on Cosmetic Surgery Trends*. Dr Rajat Gupta. https://drrajatgupta.com/insta-fame-and-image-the-social-media-influence-on-cosmetic-surgery-trends/

Häglund, E., & Björklund, J. (2024). AI-Driven Contextual Advertising: Toward Relevant Messaging Without Personal Data. *Journal of Current Issues and Research in Advertising*, *45*(3), 1–19. DOI: 10.1080/10641734.2024.2334939

Hassan, S. H., Teo, S. Z., Ramayah, T., & Al-Kumaim, N. H. (2021). The Credibility of Social Media Beauty Gurus in Young Millennials' Cosmetic Product Choice. *PLoS One, 16*(3), e0249286. Advance online publication. DOI: 10.1371/journal.pone.0249286 PMID: 33780487

IBEF. (2023, December). *Growth Of The Cosmetic Industry In India | IBEF*. India Brand Equity Foundation. https://www.ibef.org/research/case-study/growth-of-the-cosmetic-indusry-in-india

Jalil, M. I. A., Lada, S., Bakri, M. A., & Hassan, Z. (2021). Halal Cosmetics Repurchase Intention: The Role Of Marketing On Social Media. *Journal of Islamic Monetary Economics and Finance, 7*(4), 629–650. Advance online publication. DOI: 10.21098/jimf.v7i4.1379

Katkar, D. N., Mahajan, A., Mulekar, V., & Gupta, S. (2024). Evolution and Dynamics of India's Cosmetic Industry: A Century of Consumer Preferences, Digital Transformation and Emerging Trends. *Quest Journal of Management Research, 15*(1), 35–42. https://www.crkimr.in/wp-content/uploads/2024/07/Chetana-Quest-Vol-XV-Issue-1-June-2024-05.07.2024.pdf#page=41

Khan, S. U., Khan, S., Ballewar, S. S., Rane, J. P., & Siddiquee, A. Q. (2025). Cinema and Artificial Intelligence: Charting Its Role in the Indian Film Sector. In Kilinç, U. (Ed.), *Transforming Cinema with Artificial Intelligence* (pp. 143–180). IGI Global Scientific Publishing., DOI: 10.4018/979-8-3693-3916-9.ch007

Mahiwal, A., Khan, S. U., & Khan, S. (2024). Navigating The Digital Landscape: Social Media's Influence on Climate Activism and Environmental Awareness. *Global Media Journal-Indian Edition, 16*(1). https://gmj.manipal.edu/issues/Jun2024/P6.pdf

Mahiwal, A., Khan, S. U., Khan, S., & Sachdev, M. (2025). Mapping the Misinformation Ecosystem in India: Insights Into Key Areas and Pathways of Dissemination. In Lyle, P. L., & Esmail, A. M. (Eds.), *Impacts of Leakage, Whistleblowing, and the Rise of Propaganda* (pp. 83–108). IGI Global., DOI: 10.4018/979-8-3693-7468-9.ch005

Mamaearth. (n.d.). *@mamaearth.in*. Www.instagram.com. https://www.instagram.com/mamaearth.in/

Manan, H. A., Ariffin, S., Maknu, T. S. R., & Zakaria, F. N. (2020). Effects of Social Media Advertisements on Intention to Purchase Health and Beauty Products. *Journal of International Business. Economics and Entrepreneurship, 5*(1), 59–68. DOI: 10.24191/jibe.v5i1.14293

mCaffeine. (2025). *@mcaffeineofficial*. Instagram.com. https://www.instagram.com/mcaffeineofficial/

MyGlamm. (2025). *@myglamm*. Instagram.com. https://www.instagram.com/myglamm/

Nykaa Cosmetics. (n.d.). *Nykaa Cosmetics (@nykaacosmetics)*. Instagram.com. https://www.instagram.com/nykaacosmetics/

Patil, R. K. S., Porapur, S. M., & Kagawade, S. (2024). "The role of ai-driven social media marketing in shaping consumer purchasing behaviour: An empirical analysis of personalization, predictive analytics, and engagement." *ITM Web of Conferences, 68*, 01032. https://doi.org/DOI: 10.1051/itmconf/20246801032

Pattanayak, S., Khan, S. U., Malik, F., & Nayak, A. K. (2025). Cinematic color grading for optimizing AI multimedia content in film production and promotion. In Swaroop, A., Kansal, V., Fortino, G., & Hassanien, A. E. (Eds.), *Proceedings of Fifth Doctoral Symposium on Computational Intelligence. DoSCI 2023. Lecture Notes in Networks and Systems* (Vol. 1096, pp. 431–444). Springer. https://doi.org/DOI: 10.1007/978-981-97-7178-3_37

Pattanayak, S., Khan, S. U., Malik, F., & Sahoo, S. (2024). Automating camera movements: AI-driven PTZ cameras in film production. In Al Mubarak, M., & Hamdan, A. (Eds.), *Innovative and Intelligent Digital Technologies: Towards an increased efficiency. Studies in Systems, Decision and Control* (Vol. 564, pp. 627–639). Springer., DOI: 10.1007/978-3-031-70399-7_48

Pattanayak, S., Khan, S. U., Malik, F., & Shukla, V. K. (2023). Exploring the role of Instagram in Bollywood film promotion. *In 2023 International Conference on Computational Intelligence and Knowledge Economy (ICCIKE)* (pp. 478-483). IEEE. Pattanayak, S., Ullah Khan, S., Malik, F., & Khan, S. (2024). Pixelating Bollywood: Navigating media tech in Bollywood's digital shift. *Multidisciplinary Reviews, 7*(9), 2024188. https://doi.org/DOI: 10.1109/ICCIKE58312.2023.10131764

Pattanayak, S. K., Khan, S. U., Khan, S., & Srivastava, N. (2025). Evaluating the Impact of Bollywood's Promotional Strategies on Audience Engagement in the UAE. In Cantaş, A. (Ed.), *Audience Sociology and Consumer Behavior in the Film Industry* (pp. 57–102). IGI Global Scientific Publishing., DOI: 10.4018/979-8-3693-3104-0.ch003

Rathee, R., & Monika, . (2025). From Businesses-Centric to Consumers-Centric: A Shift of Power in AI-Driven Social Media. *Marketing*, *5*(0), 89–102. DOI: 10.1108/978-1-83797-815-120251007

Research, G. M. I. (2024, December 16). *India Cosmetic Market Size, Share & Industry Forecast 2032*. GMI Research. https://www.gmiresearch.com/report/india-cosmetic-market/

Shah, N., & Malik, P. (2025, March 25). *Instagram Reels Algorithm: 5 Best Practices to Stay Ahead.* Sprinklr.com; Sprinklr. https://www.sprinklr.com/blog/instagram-reels-algorithm/

Shen, B., & Bissell, K. (2013). Social Media, Social Me: A Content Analysis of Beauty Companies' Use of Facebook in Marketing and Branding. *Journal of Promotion Management, 19*(5), 629–651. DOI: 10.1080/10496491.2013.829160

Shi, B., & Wang, H. (2023). An AI-enabled approach for improving advertising identification and promotion in social networks. *Technological Forecasting and Social Change, 188*(122269), 122269. DOI: 10.1016/j.techfore.2022.122269

Singh, M. R., Bala, D. P., & Jain, D. A. (2025). AI Driven Advertisement Transforming Consumer Behavior in Digital Era. Available at *SSRN* 5239003.

Srivastava, A., & Malik, P. (2024, November 11). *Social Media Visuals: Types, Impact and Strategy for Brands*. Sprinklr.com; Sprinklr. https://www.sprinklr.com/blog/social-media-visuals/

Srivastava, N., Sachdev, M., Gwalani, M., Bajpai, M., Khan, S. U., Arora, M., & Arora, P. (2025). Women-Centric AI: A Step Towards Empowerment. In Misra, S. (Eds.), *Human-Centric AI in Digital Transformation and Entrepreneurship* (pp. 89–108). IGI Global Scientific Publishing., DOI: 10.4018/979-8-3693-8009-3.ch005

Storhannus, M. (2021). *Consumer perception of foreign cosmetic advertisements: A cross-cultural study of creating trust with social media advertising*. Www.doria.fi. https://www.doria.fi/handle/10024/180908

Sugar Cosmetics. (2020). *@trysugar*. Instagram.com. https://www.instagram.com/trysugar/

Talreja, M., & Chaturvedi, V. (2024). *The Role of Social Media Influencers in Advertising Cosmetic Brands: A Study on Instagram*. https://www.mcu.ac.in/jpra/2024/Volume-3-Issue-2-July-December-2024/07-jpra-volume-3-issue-2-july-december-2024.pdf

Tamandehrou, A., & Khan, S. U. (2015). Assessing the importance of globalisation and new media technology in 21st century: An analytical overview. *International Journal of Multifaceted & Multilingual Studies, 1*(4).DOI: 10.1016/j.chb.2024.108549

Teepapal, T. (2025). AI-Driven Personalization: Unraveling Consumer Perceptions in Social Media Engagement. *Computers in Human Behavior*, 165, 108549. DOI: 10.1016/j.chb.2024.108549

Upathamphan, S., & Puapradit, A. (2024). *The Effect of Social Media Influencer Marketing on Cosmetic Products and Strategic Uses*. https://rsucon.rsu.ac.th/files/proceedings/RSUSOC2024/IN24-159.pdf

Value4brand. (2025, January 13). *Value4Brand*. Value4Brand - Digital Marketing Company in India. https://value4brand.com/indian-companies-use-influencer-marketing-to-grow-their-brand/

Weaver, K., Lesko Pacchia, M., & Hudson, S. (2024, September 11). *The beauty boom and beyond: Can the industry maintain its growth?* McKinsey & Company. https://www.mckinsey.com/industries/consumer-packaged-goods/our-insights/the-beauty-boom-and-beyond-can-the-industry-maintain-its-growth

Weaver, K., Pacchia, M., & Hudson, S. (2025, June 9). *State of Beauty 2025: Solving a shifting growth puzzle*. McKinsey & Company. https://www.mckinsey.com/industries/consumer-packaged-goods/our-insights/state-of-beauty

Xuanyu, Y., Wongkumchai, T., & Chaiwiwat, U. (2025). The The Impact of Social Media Marketing on Retailer Sales:A Case Study of J Cosmetics Company, China. *Journal of Public and Private Issues*, *2*(2), 93–103. https://so17.tci-thaijo.org/index.php/jppi/article/view/805

ADDITIONAL READING

Chaudhuri, A. (2025). *Indian Advertising/1985-2025/Social Media To Ai*. Astitva Prakashan.

Khamis, S. (2023). *Branding Diversity: New Advertising and Cultural Strategies*. Routledge.

Pricken, M. (2004). *Visual Creativity: "Inspirational Ideas for Advertising, Animation and Digital Design"*. Thames and Hudson.

Venkatesan, R., & Lecinski, J. (2021). *The AI Marketing Canvas: A Five-Stage Road Map to Implementing Artificial Intelligence in Marketing*. Stanford University Press. DOI: 10.1515/9781503628045

Woldemariam, A. A. (2024). *AI Marketing: Revolutionizing the Future of Advertising*. Woldemariam.

KEY TERMS AND DEFINITIONS

Algorithm: An algorithm is a finite set of step-by-step instructions used to solve a problem or perform a task. In computing, algorithms power processes such as data analysis, search engines, and automation. They enable systems to operate efficiently, making decisions or predictions based on input data.

Artificial Intelligence (AI): Artificial Intelligence is the simulation of human intelligence in machines programmed to think, learn, and make decisions. AI technologies include machine learning, natural language processing, and robotics. They are widely used in areas like recommendation systems, speech recognition, autonomous vehicles, and customer service automation.

Contextual Advertising: Contextual advertising involves displaying ads based on the content of a webpage or user behaviour. It analyses keywords, topics, or browsing history to serve relevant ads, enhancing user engagement and increasing conversion rates. Unlike personalized ads, it doesn't rely on personal data, focusing instead on context-driven targeting.

Influencer: An influencer is an individual who has built a substantial online following and can affect the opinions, behaviours, or purchasing decisions of their audience. They use platforms like Instagram, YouTube, or TikTok to promote brands, share content, and engage with communities, often playing a key role in digital marketing.

Instagram: Instagram is a photo and video-sharing social networking service owned by Meta Platforms. Launched in 2010, it allows users to post content, share stories, and engage through likes, comments, and reels. Instagram plays a vital role in visual marketing, influencer culture, and youth digital expression.

Meta Platforms: Meta Platforms, formerly Facebook Inc., is a multinational technology company that owns major social media services including Facebook, Instagram, and WhatsApp. It focuses on building social technologies and the metaverse—an integrated digital environment blending virtual reality (VR) and augmented reality (AR) for immersive online experiences.

Reel: A reel is a short-form video feature popularized by Instagram and other platforms like Facebook. Typically lasting up to 90 seconds, reels are used for creative storytelling, trends, and brand promotion. They combine music, filters, and effects, offering high engagement and visibility, especially in social media marketing.

Social Media: Social media refers to digital platforms that enable users to create, share, and interact with content and one another. Examples include Facebook, Instagram, Twitter, and TikTok. Social media facilitates communication, networking, entertainment, and marketing, and plays a significant role in shaping public opinion and cultural trends.

Compilation of References

Aarabe, M., Bouizgar, M., Khizzou, N. B., Alla, L., & Benjelloun, A. (2025). The Transformative Impact of Artificial Intelligence on Tourism Experience : Analysis of Trends and Perspectives. *AI Technologies for Personalized and Sustainable Tourism*, 277-310.

Aarabe, M., Khizzou, N. B., Alla, L., & Benjelloun, A. (2024). Marketing applications of emerging technologies : A systematic literature review. *In AI and data engineering solutions for effective marketing* (pp. 23 47). IGI Global. https://www.igi-global.com/chapter/marketing-applications-of-emerging-technologies/350744

Aarabe, M., Khizzou, N. B., Alla, L., & Benjelloun, A. (2024b). Smart Tourism Experience and Responsible Travelers' Behavior : A Systematic Literature Review. *Promoting responsible tourism with digital platforms*, 128-147.

Aarabe, M., Khizzou, N. B., Alla, L., & Benjelloun, A. (2024a). Marketing applications of emerging technologies : A systematic literature review. In *AI and data engineering solutions for effective marketing* (pp. 23–47). IGI Global., https://www.igi-global.com/chapter/marketing-applications-of-emerging-technologies/350744 DOI: 10.4018/979-8-3693-3172-9.ch002

Abbasi-Moud, Z., Vahdat-Nejad, H., & Mansoor, W. (2019, December). Detecting tourist's preferences by sentiment analysis in smart cities. In *Proceedings of IEEE Global Conference on Internet of Things (GCIoT)* (pp. 1-4). IEEE. DOI: 10.1109/GCIoT47977.2019.9058397

Abbasi-Moud, Z., Vahdat-Nejad, H., & Sadri, J. (2021). Tourism recommendation system based on semantic clustering and sentiment analysis. *Expert Systems with Applications*, *167*, 114324. DOI: 10.1016/j.eswa.2020.114324

Abiagom, C. N., & Ijomah, T. I. (2024). *Enhancing customer experience through AI-driven language processing in service interactions*. Open Access Research Journal of Engineering and Technology.

Adanyin, A. (2024). Ethical AI in retail: Consumer privacy and fairness. *arXiv preprint arXiv:2410.15369.* /arXiv.2410.15369DOI: 10.48550

Adulyasak, Y., Cohen, M. C., Khern-am-nuai, W., & Krause, M. (2023). *Retail Analytics in the New Normal: The Influence of Artificial Intelligence and the Covid-19 Pandemic.* DOI: 10.48550/ARXIV.2312.00046

Agarwal, A., Singh, D., & Agariya, A. K. (2017). What really leads to partner relationship management? A review of literature. *Journal of Relationship Marketing, 16*(3), 228–266. DOI: 10.1080/15332667.2017.1349557

Aggarwal, P., & McGill, A. L. (2007). Is that car smiling at me? Schema congruity as a basis for evaluating anthropomorphized products. *The Journal of Consumer Research, 34*(4), 468–479. DOI: 10.1086/518544

Ahn, H. (2022). Emotional intelligence as a personality trait that predicts consumption behavior: The role of consumer emotional intelligence in persuasive communication. *Sustainability (Basel), 14*(22), 15461. DOI: 10.3390/su142215461

Ahn, H. (2023). Unrevealing Voice Search Behaviors: Technology Acceptance Model Meets Anthropomorphism in Understanding Consumer Psychology in the US Market. *Sustainability (Basel), 15*(23), 16455. DOI: 10.3390/su152316455

Ajzen, I. (1991). The theory of planned behavior. *Organizational Behavior and Human Decision Processes, 50*(2), 179–211. DOI: 10.1016/0749-5978(91)90020-T

Akter, S., & Wamba, S. F. (2016). Big data analytics in E-commerce: A systematic review and agenda for future research. *Electronic Markets, 26*(2), 173–194. DOI: 10.1007/s12525-016-0219-0

Alalwan, A. A., Rana, N. P., Dwivedi, Y. K., & Algharabat, R. (2017). Social media in marketing: A review and analysis of the existing literature. *Telematics and Informatics, 34*(7), 1177–1190. DOI: 10.1016/j.tele.2017.05.008

Alam, F., Tao, M., Lahuerta-Otero, E., & Feifei, Z. (2022). Let's Buy With Social Commerce Platforms Through Social Media Influencers: An Indian Consumer Perspective. *Frontiers in Psychology, 13*, 853168. DOI: 10.3389/fpsyg.2022.853168 PMID: 35496238

Ali, Z. A. (2024, September 21). *New vegetarian restaurant Qai Qai brings global cuisines to Park Street.* T2online.in; t2ONLINE. https://t2online.in/goodlife/food-beverage/new-vegetarian-restaurant-qai-qai-brings-global-cuisines-to-park-street/1142758

Al-Kfairy, M., Mustafa, D., Al-Adaileh, A., Zriqat, S., & Sendaba, O. (2024). User acceptance of AI voice assistants in Jordan's telecom industry. *Computers in Human Behavior Reports*, *16*, 100521. DOI: 10.1016/j.chbr.2024.100521

Alotaibi, M., & Hidayat-ur-Rehman, I. (2025). An empirical analysis of user intention to use chatbots for airline tickets consultation. *Journal of Science and Technology Policy Management*, 16(1), 204 228. DOI: 10.1108/JSTPM-03-2024-0087

Aloui, N., Mousa, M., & Chaouali, W. (2024). "Help me Chatbot!" : Customer-Brand Relationship in the Context of Tourism Chatbots. In Rather, R. A. (Ed.), *Consumer Brand Relationships in Tourism* (pp. 87–101). Springer Nature Switzerland., DOI: 10.1007/978-3-031-59535-6_5

Alshammari, A. A., Alhabshi, S. M. B. S. J., & Saiti, B. (2019). The impact of competition on cost efficiency of insurance and takaful sectors: Evidence from GCC markets based on the Stochastic Frontier Analysis. *Research in International Business and Finance*, *47*, 410–427.

Alsharhan, A., Al-Emran, M., & Shaalan, K. (2024). Chatbot Adoption : A Multi-perspective Systematic Review and Future Research Agenda. *IEEE Transactions on Engineering Management*, *71*, 10232–10244. DOI: 10.1109/TEM.2023.3298360

Alvi, I. (2024). Investigating students' adoption of virtual reality for L2-learning in India. *Education and Information Technologies*, *29*(7), 8035–8056. DOI: 10.1007/s10639-023-12140-6

Ameur, H. B., & Rached, K. S. B. (2024). *Effects of Chat GPT Adoption on Behavioral Intention in The Field of Scientific Research : Moderating Role of Familiarity*. https://www.researchgate.net/profile/Habiba-Ameur/publication/386499749_

Amin, M., Gohar, M., & Ali, I. (2025). Impact of digital transformation on SME's marketing performance: Role of social media and market turbulence. *Discover Sustainability*, *6*(1), 378. Advance online publication. DOI: 10.1007/s43621-025-01228-3

Amin, M., Rezaei, S., & Abolghasemi, M. (2014). User satisfaction with mobile websites : The impact of perceived usefulness (PU), perceived ease of use (PEOU) and trust. *Nankai Business Review International*, *5*(3), 258–274. DOI: 10.1108/NBRI-01-2014-0005

Andronie, M., Lăzăroiu, G., tefănescu, R., Ionescu, L., & Coco atu, M. (2021). Neuromanagement decision-making and cognitive algorithmic processes in the technological adoption of mobile commerce apps. *Oeconomia Copernicana*, *12*(4), 1033–1062. DOI: 10.24136/oc.2021.034

An, H., & Moon, N. (2022). Design of recommendation system for tourist spot using sentiment analysis based on CNN-LSTM. *Journal of Ambient Intelligence and Humanized Computing, 13*(3), 1653–1663. DOI: 10.1007/s12652-019-01521-w

Ao, L., Bansal, R., Pruthi, N., & Khaskheli, M. B. (2023). *Impact of Social Media Influencers on Customer Engagement and Purchase Intention : A Meta - Analysis.*

Appel, G., Grewal, L., Hadi, R., & Stephen, A. T. (2020). The future of social media in marketing. *Journal of the Academy of Marketing Science, 48*(1), 79–95. DOI: 10.1007/s11747-019-00695-1 PMID: 32431463

Araujo, T. (2018). Living up to the chatbot hype : The influence of anthropomorphic design cues and communicative agency framing on conversational agent and company perceptions. *Computers in Human Behavior, 85*, 183–189. DOI: 10.1016/j.chb.2018.03.051

Araújo, T., & Casais, B. (2020). Customer Acceptance of Shopping-Assistant Chatbots. In Rocha, Á., Reis, J. L., Peter, M. K., & Bogdanović, Z. (Eds.), *Marketing and Smart Technologies* (Vol. 167, pp. 278–287). Springer Singapore., DOI: 10.1007/978-981-15-1564-4_26

Arce-Urriza, M., Chocarro, R., Cortiñas, M., & Marcos-Matás, G. (2025). From familiarity to acceptance : The impact of Generative Artificial Intelligence on consumer adoption of retail chatbots. *Journal of Retailing and Consumer Services, 84*, 104234. DOI: 10.1016/j.jretconser.2025.104234

Arli, D., Bauer, C., & Palmatier, R. W. (2018). Relational selling: Past, present and future. *Industrial Marketing Management, 65*, 17–28. DOI: 10.1016/j.indmarman.2017.07.018

Arora, A., Bansal, S., Kandpal, C., Aswani, R., & Dwivedi, Y. K. (2019). Measuring social media influencer index–insights from Facebook, Twitter and Instagram. *Journal of Retailing and Consumer Services, 49*, 86–101. DOI: 10.1016/j.jretconser.2019.03.012

Arora, N., Dreze, X., Ghose, A., Hess, J. D., Iyengar, R., Jing, B., & Shankar, V. (2008). Putting one-to-one marketing to work: Personalization, customization, and choice. *Marketing Letters, 19*(3–4), 305–321. DOI: 10.1007/s11002-008-9056-z

Aroyo, A. M., Rea, F., & Sciutti, A. (2017). Will You Rely on a Robot to Find a Treasure? Proceedings of the Companion of the 2017 *ACM/IEEE International Conference on Human-Robot Interaction*, 71 72. DOI: 10.1145/3029798.3038394

Arya, V., Sethi, D., & Paul, J. (2019). Does digital footprint act as a digital asset?–Enhancing brand experience through remarketing. *International Journal of Information Management*, *49*, 142–156. DOI: 10.1016/j.ijinfomgt.2019.03.013

Ash, P. (2024, September 17). *Top 10 Food Influencers in India, 2024 | Hobo.Video*. Hobo.Video. http://hobo.video/blog/top-10-food-influencers-in-india-2024

Ashfaq, M., Makkar, M., Hoang, A.-P., Dang-Pham, D., Do, M. H. T., & Nguyen, A. T. V. (2025). Exploring customer stickiness during "smart" experiences : A study on AI chatbot affinity in online customer services. *Journal of Research in Interactive Marketing*. Advance online publication. DOI: 10.1108/JRIM-09-2024-0452

Ashfaq, M., Yun, J., Yu, S., & Loureiro, S. M. C. (2020). I, Chatbot: Modeling the determinants of users' satisfaction and continuance intention of AI-powered service agents. *Telematics and Informatics*, *54*, 101473. DOI: 10.1016/j.tele.2020.101473

Ashley, C., & Tuten, T. (2015). Creative Strategies in Social Media Marketing: An Exploratory Study of Branded Social Content and Consumer Engagement. *Psychology and Marketing*, *32*(1), 15–27. DOI: 10.1002/mar.20761

Aslam, U. (2023). Understanding the usability of retail fashion brand chatbots : Evidence from customer expectations and experiences. *Journal of Retailing and Consumer Services*, *74*, 103377. DOI: 10.1016/j.jretconser.2023.103377

Aswini, J., Malarvizhi, N., & Gayathri, A. (2023). Augmented reality and virtual reality in e-governance: An immersive technology applications and its challenges. In *AI, IoT, and Blockchain Breakthroughs in E-Governance* (pp. 138-153). IGI Global.

Aufenanger, S., Bastian, J., Bastos, G., Castelhano, M., Dias-Ferreira, C., Fokides, E., Gavalas, D., Kasapakis, V., Agelada, A., Kostas, A., Koutromanos, G., Makrides, G., Morgado, L., Pedrosa, D., Szemberg, T., Sofos, A., & Szpond, J. (2025). Immersive virtual reality learning environments for higher education: A student acceptance study. *Computers and Education: X Reality*, *7*(December 2024). DOI: 10.1016/j.cexr.2025.100105

Aw, E. C.-X., Tan, G. W.-H., Cham, T.-H., Raman, R., & Ooi, K.-B. (2022). Alexa, what's on my shopping list? Transforming customer experience with digital voice assistants. *Technological Forecasting and Social Change*, *180*, 121711. DOI: 10.1016/j.techfore.2022.121711

Ayanwale, M. A., & Ndlovu, M. (2024). Investigating factors of students' behavioral intentions to adopt chatbot technologies in higher education : Perspective from expanded diffusion theory of innovation. *Computers in Human Behavior Reports*, *14*, 100396. DOI: 10.1016/j.chbr.2024.100396

Azam, A., & Aldehayyat, J. (2018). Impact of Informational Social Support and Familiarity on Social Commerce Intention. *European Online Journal of Natural and Social Sciences*, *7*(4), 4.

Azuma, R. T. (1997). A survey of augmented reality. *Presence (Cambridge, Mass.)*, *6*(4), 355–385. DOI: 10.1162/pres.1997.6.4.355

Babatunde, S. O., Odejide, O. A., Edunjobi, T. E., & Ogundipe, D. O. (2024). *The Role Of Ai In Marketing Personalization: A Theoretical Exploration Of Consumer Engagement Strategies*. ResearchGate; Fair East Publishers. https://www.researchgate.net/publication/379393342_THE_ROLE_OF_AI_IN_MARKETING_PERSONALIZATION_A_THEORETICAL_EXPLORATION_OF_CONSUMER_ENGAGEMENT_STRATEGIES

Babin, B. J., & Harris, E. G. (2017). *CB: Consumer behavior* (7th ed.). Cengage Learning.

Bae, M. (2018). Understanding the effect of the discrepancy between sought and obtained gratification on social networking site users' satisfaction and continuance intention. *Computers in Human Behavior*, *79*, 137–153. DOI: 10.1016/j.chb.2017.10.026

Bagasworo, W., & Simatupang, S. (2022). Increased Purchases of Insurance Products Based on Factors That Affect Customer Trust (Study on Banccasurance in Greater Jakarta, Indonesia). *Jurnal Ekonomi, Manajemen Dan Perbankan (Journal of Economics, Management and Banking)*, *8*(1), 30–38.

Bagozzi, R. P., & Yi, Y. (1988). On the evaluation of structural equation models. *Journal of the Academy of Marketing Science*, *16*(1), 74–94. DOI: 10.1007/BF02723327

Bahadur, W., Aziz, S., & Zulfiqar, S. (2018). Effect of employee empathy on customer satisfaction and loyalty during employee–customer interactions: The mediating role of customer affective commitment and perceived service quality. *Cogent Business & Management*, *5*(1), 1491780. Advance online publication. DOI: 10.1080/23311975.2018.1491780

Bailey, A. A., Mishra, A. S., & Vaishnav, K. (2023). Response to social media influencers : Consumer dispositions as drivers. *International Journal of Consumer Studies*, 47(5), 1979 1998. DOI: 10.1111/ijcs.12976

Bakkouri, B. E., Raki, S., & Belgnaoui, T. (2022). The Role of Chatbots in Enhancing Customer Experience : Literature Review. *Procedia Computer Science*, *203*, 432–437. DOI: 10.1016/j.procs.2022.07.057

Balakrishnan, T. S., Ebenezar, U. S., & Karthikeyan, L., & BS, K. (2025, March). Exploring Few-Shot Learning to Enhance NLP's Cross-Domain Capabilities. In *2025 International Conference on Computing for Sustainability and Intelligent Future (COMP-SIF)* (pp. 1-6). IEEE. DOI: 10.1109/COMP-SIF65618.2025.10969937

Balasubraman, S., Peterson, R. A., & Jarvenpaa, S. L. (2002). Exploring the Implications of M-Commerce for Markets and Marketing. *Journal of the Academy of Marketing Science*, *30*(4), 348–361. DOI: 10.1177/009207002236910

Bansal, P., Kockelman, K. M., & Singh, A. (2016). Assessing public opinions of and interest in new vehicle technologies: An Austin perspective. *Transportation Research Part C, Emerging Technologies*, *67*, 1–14. DOI: 10.1016/j.trc.2016.01.019

Bansal, R., Shukla, G., Gupta, A., Singh, A., & Pruthi, N. (2023). Optimizing augmented reality and virtual reality for customer engagement. In *Promoting consumer engagement through emotional branding and sensory marketing* (pp. 24–35). IGI Global.

Barbu, C. M., Florea, D. L., Dabija, D.-C., & Barbu, M. C. R. (2021). Customer experience in fintech. *Journal of Theoretical and Applied Electronic Commerce Research*, *16*(5), 1415–1433. DOI: 10.3390/jtaer16050080

Barnes, S. J. (2002a). The mobile commerce value chain: Analysis and future developments. *International Journal of Information Management*, *22*(2), 91–108. DOI: 10.1016/S0268-4012(01)00047-0

Baskaran, K. (2022). E-Consumer Behavioral Analytics: Paradigm Shift in Online Purchase Decision Making. In *Handbook of Research on Consumer Behavior Change and Data Analytics in the Socio-Digital Era* (pp. 192-209). IGI Global.

Bassiouni, D. H., & Hackley, C. (2014). 'Generation Z' children's adaptation to digital consumer culture : A critical literature review. *Journal of Customer Behaviour*, *13*(2), 113–133. DOI: 10.1362/147539214X14024779483591

Batrinca, B., & Treleaven, P. C. (2015). Social media analytics: A survey of techniques, tools and platforms. *AI & Society*, *30*(1), 89–116. DOI: 10.1007/s00146-014-0549-4

Bebber, S., Milan, G. S., De Toni, D., Eberle, L., & Slongo, L. A. (2017). Antecedents of purchase intention in the online context. *Journal of Relationship Marketing*, *16*(1), 82–98.

Becker, L., & Jaakkola, E. (2020). Customer experience : Fundamental premises and implications for research. *Journal of the Academy of Marketing Science*, *48*(4), 630–648. DOI: 10.1007/s11747-019-00718-x

Belk, R. W. (1988). Possessions and the extended self. *The Journal of Consumer Research, 15*(2), 139–168. DOI: 10.1086/209154

Bennett, J., & Bennett, L. (2003). A review of factors that influence the diffusion of innovation when structuring a faculty training program. *The Internet and Higher Education, 6*(1), 53–63. DOI: 10.1016/S1096-7516(02)00161-6

Bhandari, A., & Bimo, S. (2022). Why's Everyone on TikTok Now? The Algorithmized Self and the Future of Self-Making on Social Media. *Social Media + Society, 8*(1), 20563051221086241. Advance online publication. DOI: 10.1177/20563051221086241

Bhatnagr, P., Rajesh, A., & Misra, R. (2024). Study of AI-enabled chatbots driving customer experience and intention to recommend. *International Journal of System Assurance Engineering and Management*. Advance online publication. DOI: 10.1007/s13198-024-02532-3

Bhattacharya, C., & Sinha, M. (2022). The role of artificial intelligence in banking for leveraging customer experience. *Australasian Accounting. Business and Finance Journal, 16*(5), 89–105.

Bhattacharya, S., & Majumdar, A. (2021). Aspects and influence of social media marketing in today's world: A review of scholarly articles. Available at *SSRN* 3775421.

Bilal, M., Zhang, Y., Cai, S., Akram, U., & Halibas, A. (2024). Artificial intelligence is the magic wand making customer-centric a reality! An investigation into the relationship between consumer purchase intention and consumer engagement through affective attachment. *Journal of Retailing and Consumer Services, 77*, 103674. 10.1016/j.jretconser.2023.103674. DOI: 10.1016/j.jretconser.2023.103674

Bilgihan, A., Kandampully, J., & Zhang, T. (2016). Towards a unified customer experience in online shopping environments : Antecedents and outcomes. *International Journal of Quality and Service Sciences, 8*(1), 102–119. DOI: 10.1108/IJQSS-07-2015-0054

Binwani, K. J., & Ho, J. S. Y. (2019, July 1). *Effects of Social Media on Cosmetic Brands*. Papers.*ssrn*.com. https://papers.ssrn.com/sol3/papers.cfm?abstract_id=3446202

Bischoff, J., Berezan, O., & Scardicchio, L. (2019). The digital self and customer loyalty: From theory to virtual reality. *Journal of Marketing Analytics, 7*(3), 220–233. DOI: 10.1057/s41270-019-00065-4

Biuk-Aghai, R. P., Fong, S., & Si, Y. (2008, December). Design of a recommender system for mobile tourism multimedia selection. In *Proceedings of 2nd International Conference on Internet Multimedia Services Architecture and Applications* (pp. 1-6). IEEE. DOI: 10.1109/IMSAA.2008.4753931

Blut, M., Wang, C., Wünderlich, N. V., & Brock, C. (2021). Understanding anthropomorphism in service provision: A meta-analysis of physical robots, chatbots, and other AI. *Journal of the Academy of Marketing Science*, 49(4), 632 658. DOI: 10.1007/s11747-020-00762-y

Boer, H. & During, W.E. (2001). Innovation, what innovation? A comparison between product, process and organizational innovation, *International Journal of Technology Management, 22*(1/2/3), pp. 83-107.

Boerman, S. C. (2020). The effects of influencer marketing on young adults: How social media influencers affect purchase intentions. *Journal of Interactive Advertising, 20*(2), 1–11.

Bolton, R. N., Gustafsson, A., McColl-Kennedy, J. R., Sirianni, N. J., & Tse, D. K. (2018). Small details that make big differences: A radical approach to consumption experience as a firm's differentiating strategy. *Journal of Service Management, 25*(2), 253–274. DOI: 10.1108/JOSM-01-2014-0034

Bonetti, F., Montecchi, M., Plangger, K., & Schau, H. J. (2023). Practice co-evolution : Collaboratively embedding artificial intelligence in retail practices. *Journal of the Academy of Marketing Science, 51*(4), 867–888. DOI: 10.1007/s11747-022-00896-1 PMID: 36035334

Brandtzaeg, P. B., & Følstad, A. (2017). Why People Use Chatbots. In I. Kompatsiaris, J. Cave, A. Satsiou, G. Carle, A. Passani, E. Kontopoulos, S. Diplaris, & D. McMillan (Éds.), *Internet Science* (Vol. 10673, pp. 377 392). Springer International Publishing. DOI: 10.1007/978-3-319-70284-1_30

Brayer, M. (2020, February 3). *Programmatic Advertising Explained | Outbrain Blog*. English (US). https://www.outbrain.com/blog/programmatic-advertising/

Broadbent, E., Jayawardena, C., Kerse, N., Stafford, R. Q., & MacDonald, B. A. (2011). Human-robot interaction research to improve quality of life in elder care—An approach and issues.*AAAI Fall Symposium on AI in Eldercare: New Solutions to Old Problems*. https://cdn.aaai.org/ocs/ws/ws0699/3875-16713-1-PB.pdf

Brodie, R. J., Ilic, A., Juric, B., & Hollebeek, L. (2013). Consumer engagement in a virtual brand community: An exploratory analysis. *Journal of Business Research, 66*(1), 105–114. DOI: 10.1016/j.jbusres.2011.07.029

Brugada-Ramentol, V., Bozorgzadeh, A., & Jalali, H. (2022). Enhance VR: A Multisensory Approach to Cognitive Training and Monitoring. *Frontiers in Digital Health*, *4*(June), 1–7. DOI: 10.3389/fdgth.2022.916052 PMID: 35721794

Brüns, J. D., & Meißner, M. (2024). Do you create your content yourself? Using generative artificial intelligence for social media content creation diminishes perceived brand authenticity. *Journal of Retailing and Consumer Services*, *79*, 103790. 10.1016/j.jretconser.2024.103790. DOI: 10.1016/j.jretconser.2024.103790

Burgoon, J. K., Bonito, J. A., Bengtsson, B., Cederberg, C., Lundeberg, M., & Allspach, L. (2000). Interactivity in human–computer interaction : A study of credibility, understanding, and influence. *Computers in Human Behavior*, 16(6), 553 574. DOI: 10.1016/S0747-5632(00)00029-7

Burke, R. (2002). Hybrid recommender systems: Survey and experiments. *User Modeling and User-Adapted Interaction*, *12*(4), 331–370. DOI: 10.1023/A:1021240730564

Burnkrant, R. E., & Cousineau, A. (1975). Informational and normative social influence in buyer behavior. *The Journal of Consumer Research*, *2*(3), 206–215. DOI: 10.1086/208633

Burt, R. S. (2000). The network structure of social capital. *Research in Organizational Behavior*, *22*, 345–423. DOI: 10.1016/S0191-3085(00)22009-1

BusySeed. (2025). AI and the ethics of personalization: Finding the right balance. *BusySeed Blog*. https://www.busyseed.com/ai-and-the-ethics-of-personalization-finding-the-right-balance/

Cabrera-Sánchez, J.-P., Villarejo-Ramos, Á. F., Liébana-Cabanillas, F., & Shaikh, A. A. (2021). Identifying relevant segments of AI applications adopters – Expanding the UTAUT2's variables. *Telematics and Informatics*, *58*, 101529. DOI: 10.1016/j.tele.2020.101529

Canning, C., Donahue, T. J., & Scheutz, M. (2014). Investigating human perceptions of robot capabilities in remote human-robot team tasks based on first-person robot video feeds. 2014 *IEEE/RSJ International Conference on Intelligent Robots and Systems*, 4354 4361.

Cao, H., Chen, Z., Cheng, M., Zhao, S., Wang, T., & Li, Y. (2020). *You Recommend, I Buy: How and Why People Engage in Instant Messaging Based Social Commerce* (Version 2). arXiv. DOI: 10.48550/ARXIV.2011.00191

Carranza, A. (2017). The Importance of Content Marketing in 2017 and Beyond, at: https://www.business2community.com/content-marketing/ importance-content-marketing-2017-beyond-01861200, Accessed date: 7 October 2017.

Casaló, L. V., Flavián, C., & Ibáñez-Sánchez, S. (2020). Influencers on Instagram: Antecedents and consequences of opinion leadership. *Journal of Business Research, 117*, 510–519. DOI: 10.1016/j.jbusres.2018.07.005

Cassell, J., & Bickmore, T. (2003). Negotiated Collusion: Modeling Social Language and its Relationship Effects in Intelligent Agents. *User Modeling and User-Adapted Interaction, 13*(1/2), 89–132. DOI: 10.1023/A:1024026532471

Castillo, D., Canhoto, A. I., & Said, E. (2021). The dark side of AI-powered service interactions : Exploring the process of co-destruction from the customer perspective. *Service Industries Journal, 41*(13-14), 900–925. DOI: 10.1080/02642069.2020.1787993

Cate, M. (2025). *Impact of AI-Driven Chatbot Interactions on Customer Loyalty and Retention.* https://www.researchgate.net/profile/Mia-Cate/publication/390873579_Impact_of_AI-Driven_Chatbot_Interactions_on_Customer_Loyalty_and_Retention/links/6800ee90d1054b0207d4e28c/Impact-of-AI-Driven-Chatbot-Interactions-on-Customer-Loyalty-and-Retention.pdf

Catulli, M., Cook, M., & Potter, S. (2016). Product service systems users and Harley Davidson riders: The importance of consumer identity in the diffusion of sustainable consumption solutions. *Journal of Industrial Ecology, 00*(0), 1–10. DOI: 10.1111/jiec.12518

Celestin, M., & Sujatha, S. (2024). Impact on brand trust and consumer behaviour: Leveraging social media influencers to drive credibility and engagement across industries. *Impact On Brand Trust And Consumer Behaviour: Leveraging Social Media Influencers To Drive Credibility And Engagement Across Industries, 9*(2), 81–87. DOI: 10.5281/zenodo.13887149

Chakraborty, I. (2019). RecSmart: Data augmentation to facilitate recommendation using skewed and sparse data of restaurant loyalty programs. In *Proceedings of the Future Technologies Conference (FTC 2018)*(pp. 1002–1011). https://doi.org/DOI: 10.1007/978-3-030-02683-7_74

Chandler, J. D., & Lusch, R. F. (2015). Service Systems : A Broadened Framework and Research Agenda on Value Propositions, Engagement, and Service Experience. *Journal of Service Research, 18*(1), 6–22. DOI: 10.1177/1094670514537709

Chandra, S., & Kumar, N. (2025). Understanding customer responses to AI-driven personalized advertising: The role of relevance and privacy concerns. *Journal of Advertising, 54*(2), 123–145. DOI: 10.1080/00913367.2025.2460985

Chan, H.-L., & Choi, T.-M. (2025). Using generative artificial intelligence (GenAI) in marketing: Development and practices. *Journal of Business Research, 191*, 115276. 10.1016/j.jbusres.2025.115276. DOI: 10.1016/j.jbusres.2025.115276

Chatterjee, S., Rana, N. P., Tamilmani, K., & Sharma, A. (2020). The impact of AI on consumer behavior: Exploring future research directions. *International Journal of Information Management, 54*, 102289. DOI: 10.1016/j.ijinfomgt.2020.102289

Chaudhary, N., & Chowdhury, D. R. (2019). *Data Preprocessing for Evaluation of Recommendation Models in E-Commerce*. https://doi.org/DOI: 10.48550/ARXIV.1911.01273

Chauhan, S., Akhtar, A., & Gupta, A. (2022). Customer experience in digital banking : A review and future research directions. *International Journal of Quality and Service Sciences, 14*(2), 311–348. DOI: 10.1108/IJQSS-02-2021-0027

Chen, C.-C. V., & Chen, C.-J. (2017). The role of customer participation for enhancing repurchase intention. *Management Decision, 55*(3), 547–562. Advance online publication. DOI: 10.1108/MD-06-2016-0380

Chen, C.-C., & Tsai, J.-L. (2019). Determinants of behavioral intention to use the Personalized Location-based Mobile Tourism Application : An empirical study by integrating TAM with ISSM. *Future Generation Computer Systems, 96*, 628–638. DOI: 10.1016/j.future.2017.02.028

Chen, J.-S., Le, T.-T.-Y., & Florence, D. (2021). Usability and responsiveness of artificial intelligence chatbot on online customer experience in e-retailing. *International Journal of Retail & Distribution Management, 49*(11), 1512–1531. DOI: 10.1108/IJRDM-08-2020-0312

Chen, L., Gillenson, M. L., & Sherrell, D. L. (2002). Enticing online consumers: An extended technology acceptance perspective. *Information & Management, 39*(8), 705–719. DOI: 10.1016/S0378-7206(01)00127-6

Chen, Q., Gong, Y., Lu, Y., & Tang, J. (2022). Classifying and measuring the service quality of AI chatbot in frontline service. *Journal of Business Research, 145*, 552–568. DOI: 10.1016/j.jbusres.2022.02.088

Chen, W.-K., Chen, C.-W., & Silalahi, A. D. K. (2022). Understanding Consumers' Purchase Intention and Gift-Giving in Live Streaming Commerce: Findings from SEM and fsQCA. *Emerging Science Journal, 6*(3), 460–481. DOI: 10.28991/ESJ-2022-06-03-03

Chen, Y., Fay, S., & Wang, Q. (2011). The Role of Marketing in Social Media: How Online Consumer Reviews Evolve. *Journal of Interactive Marketing*, *25*(2), 85–94. DOI: 10.1016/j.intmar.2011.01.003

Chen, Y., & Prentice, C. (2024). Integrating Artificial Intelligence and Customer Experience. *Australasian Marketing Journal*, *14413582241252904*. Advance online publication. DOI: 10.1177/14413582241252904

Cheung, C. M. K., & Thadani, D. R. (2012). The impact of electronic word-of-mouth communication: A literature analysis and integrative model. *Decision Support Systems*, *54*(1), 461–470. DOI: 10.1016/j.dss.2012.06.008

Cheung, C. M. K., Xiao, B. S., & Liu, I. L. B. (2014). Do actions speak louder than voices? The signaling role of social information cues in influencing consumer purchase decisions. *Decision Support Systems*, *65*, 50–58. DOI: 10.1016/j.dss.2014.05.002

Chi, N. T. K., & Hoang Vu, N. (2023). Investigating the customer trust in artificial intelligence : The role of anthropomorphism, empathy response, and interaction. *CAAI Transactions on Intelligence Technology*, *8*(1), 260–273. DOI: 10.1049/cit2.12133

Chi, O. H., Chi, C. G., Gursoy, D., & Nunkoo, R. (2023). Customers' acceptance of artificially intelligent service robots : The influence of trust and culture. *International Journal of Information Management*, *70*, 102623. DOI: 10.1016/j.ijinfomgt.2023.102623

Choi, Y. K., & Lotz, S. (2017). The effect of personalization and privacy assurance on behavioral intentions: A test of risk–benefit trade-off in e-commerce. *Journal of Retailing and Consumer Services*, *34*, 289–296. DOI: 10.1016/j.jretconser.2016.01.001

Chong, D., & Shi, H. (2015). Big data analytics: A literature review. *Journal of Management Analytics*, *2*(3), 175–201. DOI: 10.1080/23270012.2015.1082449

Chong, F. H. L. (2021). Enhancing trust through digital Islamic finance and blockchain technology. *Qualitative Research in Financial Markets*, *13*(3), 328–341. DOI: 10.1108/QRFM-05-2020-0076

Christensen, I., Schiaffino, S., & Armentano, M. (2016). Social group recommendation in the tourism domain. *Journal of Intelligent Information Systems*, *47*(2), 209–231. DOI: 10.1007/s10844-016-0400-0

Christensen, J., Hansen, J. M., & Wilson, P. (2024). Understanding the role and impact of Generative Artificial Intelligence (AI) hallucination within consumers' tourism decision-making processes. *Current Issues in Tourism*, *28*(4), 545–560. DOI: 10.1080/13683500.2023.2300032

Chu, S.-C., & Kim, Y. (2011). Determinants of consumer engagement in electronic word-of-mouth (eWOM) in social networking sites. *International Journal of Advertising*, *30*(1), 47–75. DOI: 10.2501/IJA-30-1-047-075

Ciechanowski, L., Przegalinska, A., Magnuski, M., & Gloor, P. (2019). In the shades of the uncanny valley : An experimental study of human–chatbot interaction. *Future Generation Computer Systems*, 92, 539 548. DOI: 10.1016/j.future.2018.01.055

Clark, S. (2020). *How Artificial Intelligence and Chatbots Are Improving Employee Experience*. Reworked.Co. https://www.reworked.co/employee-experience/5-ways-chatbots-improve-employee-experience/

Collier, J. E., Barnes, D. C., Abney, A. K., & Pelletier, M. J. (2018). Idiosyncratic service experiences: When customers desire the extraordinary in a service encounter. *Journal of Business Research*, *84*, 150–161. DOI: 10.1016/j.jbusres.2017.11.016

Colomo-Palacios, R., García-Peñalvo, F. J., Stantchev, V., & Misra, S. (2017). Towards a social and context-aware mobile recommendation system for tourism. *Pervasive and Mobile Computing*, *38*(Part 2), 505–515. DOI: 10.1016/j.pmcj.2016.03.001

Cowgill, B., Dell'Acqua, F., & Deng, S. (2021). Biased programmers? Or biased data? A field experiment in operationalizing AI ethics. *NBER Working Paper No. 27427*. DOI: 10.3386/w27427

Cox, D., & Cox, A. D. (2002). Beyond First Impressions : The Effects of Repeated Exposure on Consumer Liking of Visually Complex and Simple Product Designs. *Journal of the Academy of Marketing Science*, *30*(2), 119–130. DOI: 10.1177/03079459994371

Crolic, C., Thomaz, F., Hadi, R., & Stephen, A. T. (2022). Blame the Bot : Anthropomorphism and Anger in Customer–Chatbot Interactions. *Journal of Marketing*, *86*(1), 132–148. DOI: 10.1177/00222429211045687

Dabbous, A., Aoun Barakat, K., & Merhej Sayegh, M. (2020). Social Commerce Success: Antecedents of Purchase Intention and the Mediating Role of Trust. *Journal of Internet Commerce*, *19*(3), 262–297. DOI: 10.1080/15332861.2020.1756190

Dahake, N. S., Gajghate, A., Dahake, P. S., & Bansod, S. (2024). A Transformative Impact of IoT and AI by Predictive Analytics on Modern Marketing Strategies: A Study of its Significance & Accuracy. *2024 2nd International Conference on Advances in Computation, Communication and Information Technology (ICAICCIT)*, 1150–1158. DOI: 10.1109/ICAICCIT64383.2024.10912388

Dahake, N. S., Suresh Dahake, P., & Gajghate, A. (2024). Beyond the Hype: A Critical Evaluation of Predictive Analytics Accuracy in High-Stakes Business Decisions. *2024 2nd DMIHER International Conference on Artificial Intelligence in Healthcare, Education and Industry (IDICAIEI)*, 1–6. DOI: 10.1109/IDICAIEI61867.2024.10842857

Dahake, P. S., Bagaregari, P., & Dahake, N. S. (2024). Shaping the Future of Retail: A Comprehensive Review of Predictive Analytics Models for Consumer Behavior. *Entrepreneurship and Creativity in the Metaverse*, 143-160.

Dahake, P. S., Chandak, S., & Dahake, N. S. (2024). Predictive Analytics in Performance Appraisal Systems: Enhancing Objectivity and Fairness. *2024 2nd DMIHER International Conference on Artificial Intelligence in Healthcare, Education and Industry (IDICAIEI)*, 1–5. DOI: 10.1109/IDICAIEI61867.2024.10842916

Dahake, P. S., Jain, M., Anusha, B., Poojitha, S., Singh, N., & Sharma, A. (2024). Integrating Organisational Theory, Resource-Based View, and Big Data Culture to Improve Manufacturing Performance. In D. Jelonek, N. Kumar, M. Chahar, R. Kinkladze, & L. Knop, *Recent Trends In Engineering and Science for Resource Optimization and Sustainable Development* (1st ed., pp. 156–159). CRC Press. DOI: 10.1201/9781003596721-36

Dahake, P. S., Mohare, R., Chandak, S., & Bhadade, P. (2024). Predictive Analytics in Assessing Employee Retention Rates: An Analysis of Effectiveness and Accuracy of Different Predictive Model. *2024 2nd International Conference on Advances in Computation, Communication and Information Technology (ICAICCIT)*, 1159–1164. DOI: 10.1109/ICAICCIT64383.2024.10912426

Dahake, P. S., Parchake, S., Somani, N., & Ingale, A. R. (2024). Predictive Analytics in Automotive Consumer Behaviour: An Insight into Personal use 4-Wheeler Purchase Decisions. *2024 2nd International Conference on Advances in Computation, Communication and Information Technology (ICAICCIT)*, 1143–1149. DOI: 10.1109/ICAICCIT64383.2024.10912242

Dahake, P. S., Bagaregari, P., & Dahake, N. S. (2024). Shaping the Future of Retail: A Comprehensive Review of Predictive Analytics Models for Consumer Behavior. In Inder, S., Min, B., & Sharma, S. (Eds.), (pp. 143–160). Advances in Business Strategy and Competitive Advantage. IGI Global., DOI: 10.4018/979-8-3693-1734-1.ch011

Dahake, P. S., Chandak, S., Mohare, R. V., Wadhwani, K., & Bhadade, P. (2023). The Crystal Ball of Marketing: How Predictive Analytics is Reshaping the Industry? *2023 Second International Conference On Smart Technologies For Smart Nation (SmartTechCon)*, 304–311. DOI: 10.1109/SmartTechCon57526.2023.10391334

Dahake, P. S., & Dahake, N. S. (2024). The Role of Big Data in Predictive Analytics for E-Commerce: Examine How Big Data Contributes to Better Predictions in Online Shopping. In Tarnanidis, T., Papathanasiou, J., Ismyrlis, V., & Kittu Manda, V. (Eds.), (pp. 403–426). Advances in Marketing, Customer Relationship Management, and E-Services. IGI Global., DOI: 10.4018/979-8-3693-9122-8.ch018

Dahake, P. S., Mohare, R. V., & Somani, N. (2023). Exploring Machine Learning's Potential in Predicting Consumer Behavior for Captivating Marketing. *2023 Second International Conference On Smart Technologies For Smart Nation (SmartTechCon)*, 1347–1352. DOI: 10.1109/SmartTechCon57526.2023.10391558

Dang, T. (2025). AI-Driven Advertising and Consumer Purchase Behaviour: A Systematic Literature Review Based on the Theory of Planned Behaviour. *Ebsco.com, 13*(7), 414. https://openurl.ebsco.com/EPDB%3Agcd%3A5%3A24483973/detailv2?sid=ebsco%3Aplink%3Ascholar&id=ebsco%3Agcd%3A184662223&crl=c&link_origin=scholar.google.com

Davenport, T. H., & Ronanki, R. (2018). Artificial intelligence for the real world. *HBR'S 10 MUST*, 67.

Davenport, T. H., Guha, A., Grewal, D., & Bressgott, T. (2020). How artificial intelligence will change the future of marketing. *Journal of the Academy of Marketing Science*, *48*(1), 24–42. DOI: 10.1007/s11747-019-00696-0

Davis, F. D. (1985). A technology acceptance model for empirically testing new end-user information systems : *Theory and results* [PhD Thesis, Massachusetts Institute of Technology]. https://dspace.mit.edu/bitstream/handle/1721.1/15192/14927137-MIT.pdf

Davis, F. D., Bagozzi, R. P., & Warshaw, P. R. (1989). User Acceptance of Computer Technology : A Comparison of Two Theoretical Models. *Management Science*, 35(8), 982 1003. DOI: 10.1287/mnsc.35.8.982

Davis, F. D. (1989). Perceived usefulness, perceived ease of use, and user acceptance of information technology. *Management Information Systems Quarterly*, *13*(3), 319–340. DOI: 10.2307/249008

Davis, F. D. (1993). User acceptance of information technology : System characteristics, user perceptions and behavioral impacts. *International Journal of Man-Machine Studies*, *38*(3), 475–487. DOI: 10.1006/imms.1993.1022

Davis, F. D., & Venkatesh, V. (1996). A critical assessment of potential measurement biases in the technology acceptance model : Three experiments. *International Journal of Human-Computer Studies*, *45*(1), 19–45. DOI: 10.1006/ijhc.1996.0040

De Cicco, R., Iacobucci, S., Aquino, A., Romana Alparone, F., & Palumbo, R. (2022). Understanding Users' Acceptance of Chatbots : An Extended TAM Approach. In Følstad, A., Araujo, T., Papadopoulos, S., Law, E. L.-C., Luger, E., Goodwin, M., & Brandtzaeg, P. B. (Eds.), *Chatbot Research and Design* (Vol. 13171, pp. 3–22). Springer International Publishing., DOI: 10.1007/978-3-030-94890-0_1

De Keyser, A., Lemon, K. N., Klaus, P., & Keiningham, T. L. (2015). A framework for understanding and managing the customer experience. *Marketing Science Institute working paper series, 85*(1), 15-121.

De Keyser, A., & Kunz, W. H. (2022). Living and working with service robots : A TCCM analysis and considerations for future research. *Journal of Service Management, 33*(2), 165–196. DOI: 10.1108/JOSM-12-2021-0488

De Kleijn, R., Wijnen, M., & Poletiek, F. (2019). The effect of context-dependent information and sentence constructions on perceived humanness of an agent in a Turing test. *Knowledge-Based Systems, 163*, 794–799. DOI: 10.1016/j.knosys.2018.10.006

De Veirman, M., Cauberghe, V., & Hudders, L. (2017). Marketing through Instagram influencers: The impact of number of followers and product divergence on brand attitude. *International Journal of Advertising, 36*(5), 798–828. DOI: 10.1080/02650487.2017.1348035

Delgado-Ballester, E., & Luis Munuera-Alemán, J. (2001). Brand trust in the context of consumer loyalty. *European Journal of Marketing, 35*(11/12), 1238–1258. DOI: 10.1108/EUM0000000006475

Deloitte. (2013). The global Takaful insurance market charting the road to mass markets, A Deloitte ME IFKC Practice Insights Series, available at: https://ceif.iba .edu.pk/pdf/ Deloitte The global Takaful insurance market Charting the road to mass markets.pdf (accessed 20 November2016).

Deloitte. (2022). *The Deloitte Global 2022 Gen Z and Millennial Survey*. Deloitte Global. https://www.deloitte.com/global/en/issues/work/genzmillennialsurvey-2022 .html

Dendrinos, K., & Spais, G. (2024). An investigation of selected UTAUT constructs and consumption values of Gen Z and Gen X for mobile banking services and behavioral intentions to facilitate the adoption of mobile apps. *Journal of Marketing Analytics, 12*(3), 492–522. DOI: 10.1057/s41270-023-00271-1

Deng, L., Turner, D. E., Gehling, R., & Prince, B. (2010). User experience, satisfaction, and continual usage intention of IT. *European Journal of Information Systems, 19*(1), 60–75. DOI: 10.1057/ejis.2009.50

Derossi, A., Di Palma, E., Moses, J. A., Santhoshkumar, P., Caporizzi, R., & Severini, C. (2023). Avenues for non-conventional robotics technology applications in the food industry. *Food Research International, 173*(Part 1), 113265. DOI: 10.1016/j.foodres.2023.113265 PMID: 37803578

Dessart, L., Veloutsou, C., & Morgan-Thomas, A. (2015). Consumer engagement in online brand communities: A social media perspective. *Journal of Product and Brand Management, 24*(1), 28–42. DOI: 10.1108/JPBM-06-2014-0635

Dhiman, R., & Bhati, N. S. (2025). When AI meets influencers: Role of AI-powered instagram influencers driving consumers' purchase intentions: An integration of SMIV & SOR framework. *Journal of Open Innovation, 11*(3), 100591. DOI: 10.1016/j.joitmc.2025.100591

Dimitriadis, S., & Kyrezis, N. (2010). Linking trust to use intention for technology-enabled bank channels : The role of trusting intentions. *Psychology & Marketing*, 27(8), 799 820. DOI: 10.1002/mar.20358

Dimitrova, T., Ilieva, I., & Terziyska, M. (2025). Understanding Consumers' Functional Beverages Purchase Intention: Modeling the Impact of Explanatory Factors. *BIO Web of Conferences, 170*. DOI: 10.1051/bioconf/202517001020

Dobbala, M., & Lingolu, M. (2024). Conversational AI and Chatbots : Enhancing User Experience on Websites. *American Journal of Computer Science and Technology*, *7*(3), 62–70. DOI: 10.11648/j.ajcst.20240703.11

Du Prezz, R., Bendixen, M., & Abratt, R. (2017). The behavioral consequences of internal brand management among frontline employees. *Journal of Product and Brand Management, 26*(3), 251–268. DOI: 10.1108/JPBM-09-2016-1325

Duffy, B. R. (2003). Anthropomorphism and the social robot. *Robotics and Autonomous Systems*, 42(3 4), 177 190. DOI: 10.1016/S0921-8890(02)00374-3

Durgam, V. (2018). Social media and its role in marketing. *International journal of advanced research in management, 9*(2), 1-10.

Dwivedi, Y. K., Balakrishnan, J., Baabdullah, A. M., & Das, R. (2023). Do chatbots establish "humanness" in the customer purchase journey? An investigation through explanatory sequential design. *Psychology and Marketing*, *40*(11), 2244–2271. DOI: 10.1002/mar.21888

Dwivedi, Y. K., Hughes, L., Ismagilova, E., Aarts, G., Coombs, C., Crick, T., Duan, Y., Dwivedi, R., Edwards, J., Eirug, A., Galanos, V., Ilavarasan, P. V., Janssen, M., Jones, P., Kar, A. K., Kizgin, H., Kronemann, B., Lal, B., Lucini, B., & Williams, M. D. (2021). Artificial Intelligence (AI): Multidisciplinary perspectives on emerging challenges, opportunities, and agenda for research, practice and policy. *International Journal of Information Management*, *57*, 101994. DOI: 10.1016/j.ijinfomgt.2019.08.002

Dwivedi, Y. K., Ismagilova, E., Hughes, D. L., Carlson, J., Filieri, R., Jacobson, J., Jain, V., Karjaluoto, H., Kefi, H., Krishen, A. S., Kumar, V., Rahman, M. M., Raman, R., Rauschnabel, P. A., Rowley, J., Salo, J., Tran, G. A., & Wang, Y. (2021). Setting the future of digital and social media marketing research: Perspectives and research propositions. *International Journal of Information Management*, *59*, 102168. DOI: 10.1016/j.ijinfomgt.2020.102168

Eastman, J. K., & Eastman, J. K. (2023). *Artificial intelligence consumer behavior : A hybrid review and research Artificial intelligence consumer behavior : A hybrid review and research agenda. September*. DOI: 10.1002/cb.2233

Ekstrand, M. D., Das, A., Burke, R., & Diaz, F. (2012). Fairness in recommender systems. In *Recommender systems handbook* (pp. 679–707). Springer US.

El-aasy, H. (2023). Employing Artificial Intelligence (AI) Technology in Advertising Design on Social Media. *Journal of Design Sciences and Applied Arts (Print)*, *4*(2), 247–263. DOI: 10.21608/jdsaa.2023.194906.1260

Elgendy, N., & Elragal, A. (2014). Big data analytics: a literature review paper. In *Advances in Data Mining. Applications and Theoretical Aspects: 14th Industrial Conference, ICDM 2014, St. Petersburg, Russia, July 16-20, 2014.* [Springer International Publishing.]. *Proceedings*, *14*, 214–227.

Eling, M., Nuessle, D., & Staubli, J. (2021). The impact of artificial intelligence along the insurance value chain and on the insurability of risks. In Geneva Papers on Risk and Insurance: Issues and Practice (Issue 0123456789). Palgrave Macmillan UK. DOI: 10.1057/s41288-020-00201-7

Elliott, D., & Soifer, E. (2022). AI technologies, privacy, and security. *Frontiers in Artificial Intelligence*, *5*, 826737. DOI: 10.3389/frai.2022.826737 PMID: 35493613

Emplifi. (2022). *Top 35+ customer experience statistics to know in 2022. Emplifi—Recherche Google.* (s. d.). Consulté 16 février 2025

Epley, N. (2018). A Mind like Mine : The Exceptionally Ordinary Underpinnings of Anthropomorphism. *Journal of the Association for Consumer Research, 3*(4), 591–598. DOI: 10.1086/699516

Epley, N., Waytz, A., & Cacioppo, J. T. (2007). On seeing human : A three-factor theory of anthropomorphism. *Psychological Review, 114*(4), 864–886. DOI: 10.1037/0033-295X.114.4.864 PMID: 17907867

Erebak, S., & Turgut, T. (2019). Caregivers' attitudes toward potential robot coworkers in elder care. *Cognition Technology and Work, 21*(2), 327–336. DOI: 10.1007/s10111-018-0512-0

Erkan, I., & Evans, C. (2016). The influence of eWOM in social media on consumers' purchase intentions: An extended approach to information adoption. *Computers in Human Behavior, 61*, 47–55. DOI: 10.1016/j.chb.2016.03.003

European Commission. (2022, October 25). *Ethical guidelines on the use of artificial intelligence and data in teaching and learning for educators*. European Education Area. https://education.ec.europa.eu/news/ethical-guidelines-on-the-use-of-artificial-intelligence-and-data-in-teaching-and-learning-for-educators

Eybers, S., & Setsabi, N. (2021). Responsible Data Sharing in the Digital Economy: Big Data Governance Adoption in Bancassurance. In *Inventive Computation and Information Technologies* [Singapore: Springer Nature Singapore.]. *Proceedings of ICICIT, 2020*, 379–394.

Familoni, B. T., & Babatunde, S. O.Babajide Tolulope FamiloniSodiq Odetunde Babatunde. (2024). User experience (UX) design in medical products : Theoretical foundations and development best practices. *Engineering Science & Technology Journal, 5*(3), 1125–1148. DOI: 10.51594/estj.v5i3.975

Fan, H., Gao, W., & Han, B. (2023). Are AI chatbots a cure-all? The relative effectiveness of chatbot ambidexterity in crafting hedonic and cognitive smart experiences. *Journal of Business Research, 156*, 113526. DOI: 10.1016/j.jbusres.2022.113526

Faqih, K. M. (2016). An empirical analysis of factors predicting the behavioral intention to adopt Internet shopping technology among non-shoppers in a developing country context : Does gender matter? *Journal of Retailing and Consumer Services, 30*, 140–164. DOI: 10.1016/j.jretconser.2016.01.016

Farris, L. (2021). *Optimized Recommender Systems with Deep Reinforcement Learning* (Version 1). arXiv. DOI: 10.48550/ARXIV.2110.03039

Fishbein, M., & Ajzen, I. (1977). *Belief, attitude, intention, and behavior : An introduction to theory and research*. https://philpapers.org/rec/FISBAI?all_versions=1

Fishbein, M. (1979). A theory of reasoned action : Some applications and implications. *Nebraska Symposium on Motivation.*

Følstad, A., & Skjuve, M. (2019). Chatbots for customer service : User experience and motivation. *Proceedings of the 1st International Conference on Conversational User Interfaces,* 1 9. DOI: 10.1145/3342775.3342784

Fornell, C., & Larcker, D. F. (1981). Evaluating Structural Equation Models with Unobservable Variables and Measurement Error. *JMR, Journal of Marketing Research, 18*(1), 39–50. DOI: 10.1177/002224378101800104

Fotheringham, D., & Wiles, M. A. (2023). The effect of implementing chatbot customer service on stock returns : An event study analysis. *Journal of the Academy of Marketing Science, 51*(4), 802–822. DOI: 10.1007/s11747-022-00841-2

Fournier, S., & Avery, J. (2011). The uninvited brand. *Business Horizons, 54*(3), 193–207. DOI: 10.1016/j.bushor.2011.01.001

Freberg, K., Graham, K., McGaughey, K., & Freberg, L. A. (2011). Who are the social media influencers? A study of public perceptions of personality. *Public Relations Review, 37*(1), 90–92. DOI: 10.1016/j.pubrev.2010.11.001

Gagandeep, V. J. (2023). Impact of Augmented Reality and Virtual Reality on Customer Purchase Behavior in the Virtual World. In *Applications of Neuromarketing in the Metaverse* (pp. 258-270). IGI Global.

Gambetti, R. C., & Kozinets, R. V. (2024). From killer bunnies to talking cupcakes: Theorizing the diverse universe of virtual influencers. *European Journal of Marketing, 58*(13), 205–251. DOI: 10.1108/EJM-12-2022-0948

Gao, C., Lei, W., He, X., De Rijke, M., & Chua, T. S. (2021). Advances and challenges in conversational recommender systems: A survey. AI open, 2, 100-126.

Garnier, M., & Poncin, I. (2013). The avatar in marketing : Synthesis, integrative framework and perspectives. *Recherche et Applications En Marketing* (English Edition), 28(1), 85 115. DOI: 10.1177/2051570713478335

Gatzioufa, P., & Saprikis, V. (2022). *A literature review on users' behavioral intention toward chatbots' adoption.* Applied Computing and Informatics., DOI: 10.1108/ACI-01-2022-0021

Gebre, A. (2024, January 1). *The Effect Of Social Media Advertisement On Customers' Attitude: In The Case Of Cosmetics Industry Addis Ababa.* Repository.smuc.edu.et. http://repository.smuc.edu.et/handle/123456789/7896

Gefen, D., Karahanna, E., & Straub, D. W. (2003). Inexperience and experience with online stores : The importance of TAM and trust. *IEEE Transactions on Engineering Management*, *50*(3), 307–321. DOI: 10.1109/TEM.2003.817277

Gerlich, M. (2023). The Power of Virtual Influencers: Impact on Consumer Behaviour and Attitudes in the Age of AI. *Administrative Sciences*, *13*(8), 178. DOI: 10.3390/admsci13080178

Ghobakhloo, M., Arias-Aranda, D., & Benitez-Amado, J. (2011). Adoption of e-commerce applications in SMEs. *Industrial Management & Data Systems*, *111*(8), 1238–1269. DOI: 10.1108/02635571111170785

Gloor, P., Krauss, J., Nann, S., Fischbach, K., & Schoder, D. (2022). Detecting influence structures in social media using sentiment-enhanced network analysis. *Journal of Business Research*, *141*, 364–377.

Gnewuch, U., Morana, S., Adam, M. T. P., & Maedche, A. (2022). Opposing Effects of Response Time in Human–Chatbot Interaction : The Moderating Role of Prior Experience. *Business & Information Systems Engineering*, 64(6), 773 791. DOI: 10.1007/s12599-022-00755-x

Go, E., & Sundar, S. S. (2019). Humanizing chatbots : The effects of visual, identity and conversational cues on humanness perceptions. *Computers in Human Behavior*, *97*, 304–316. DOI: 10.1016/j.chb.2019.01.020

Goetz, J., Kiesler, S., & Powers, A. (2003). Matching robot appearance and behavior to tasks to improve human-robot cooperation. The *12th IEEE International Workshop on Robot and Human Interactive Communication*, 2003. Proceedings. *RO-MAN ... : the ... IEEE International Symposium on Robot and Human Interactive Communication : Proceedings. IEEE International Symposium on Robot and Human Interactive Communication*, *2003*(55), 60. DOI: 10.1109/ROMAN.2003.1251796

Goh, K.-Y., Heng, C.-S., & Lin, Z. (2013). Social Media Brand Community and Consumer Behavior: Quantifying the Relative Impact of User- and Marketer-Generated Content. *Information Systems Research*, *24*(1), 88–107. DOI: 10.1287/isre.1120.0469

Goktas, P., & Dirsehan, T. (2025). Using PLS-SEM and XAI for causal-predictive services marketing research. *Journal of Services Marketing*, *39*(1), 53–68. DOI: 10.1108/JSM-10-2023-0377

Gomes, S., Lopes, J. M., & Trancoso, T. (2025). Customer experience in digital transformation : The influence of intelligent chatbots toward a sustainable market. *International Journal of Innovation Science*, *17*(4), 803–823. Advance online publication. DOI: 10.1108/IJIS-06-2024-0148

Gong, W., & Khalid, L. (2021). *Aesthetics, Personalization and Recommendation: A survey on Deep Learning in Fashion* (Version 1). arXiv. DOI: 10.48550/ARXIV.2101.08301

Gopinath, K., & Kasilingam, D. (2023). Antecedents of intention to use chatbots in service encounters : A meta-analytic review. *International Journal of Consumer Studies, 47*(6), 2367–2395. DOI: 10.1111/ijcs.12933

Goudey, A., & Bonnin, G. (2016). Must smart objects look human? Study of the impact of anthropomorphism on the acceptance of companion robots. *Recherche et Applications En Marketing (English Edition)*, 31(2), 2 20. DOI: 10.1177/2051570716643961

Grandinetti, R., Di Bernardo, B., D'Antonio, F., & Iannone, R. (2020). Servitization and the fourth industrial revolution: A comparative analysis of ICT and traditional manufacturing firms. *Technological Forecasting and Social Change, 157*, 120092. DOI: 10.1016/j.techfore.2020.120092

Grewal, D., Roggeveen, A. L., & Nordfält, J. (2017). The future of retailing. *Journal of Retailing, 93*(1), 1–6. DOI: 10.1016/j.jretai.2016.12.008

GS1 (2023). Trend research 2023-2024 : Innovation in a world of continuous disruption—Recherche Google. (s. d.). Consulté 16 février 2025

Guemmaz, S. (2023). Shareholding relations between banks and insurance companies in Algeria: An overview. *Journal of Innovations and Sustainability, 7*(2), 1. DOI: 10.51599/is.2023.07.02.01

Gujar, V. (2024). New age marketing : AI personalization strategies in digital world. *International Advanced Research Journal in Science, Engineering and Technology*, 11(3).

Gulan, M., Feng, Y., Mvondo, G. F. N., & Niu, B. (2025). How Do Virtual Influencers Affect Consumer Brand Evangelism in the Metaverse? The Effects of Virtual Influencers' Marketing Efforts, Perceived Coolness, and Anthropomorphism. *Journal of Theoretical and Applied Electronic Commerce Research, 20*(1), 36. DOI: 10.3390/jtaer20010036

Gummerus, J., Liljander, V., Weman, E., & Pihlström, M. (2012). Customer engagement in a Facebook brand community. *Management Research Review, 35*(9), 857–877. DOI: 10.1108/01409171211256578

Gümüş, N., & Çark, Ö. (2021). The Effect of Customers' Attitudes Towards Chatbots on their Experience and Behavioural Intention in Turkey. *Interdisciplinary Description of Complex Systems : INDECS*, 19(3), 420 436. DOI: 10.7906/indecs.19.3.6

Guo, J., & Li, L. (2022). Exploring the Relationship Between Social Commerce Features and Consumers' Repurchase Intentions: The Mediating Role of Perceived Value. *Frontiers in Psychology*, *12*, 775056. DOI: 10.3389/fpsyg.2021.775056 PMID: 35401287

Guo, L., Gruen, T. W., & Tang, C. (2015). Seeing relationships through the lens of psychological contracts: The structure of consumer service relationships. *Journal of the Academy of Marketing Science*, *43*(6), 904–925. DOI: 10.1007/s11747-015-0462-5

Gupta, R. (2024, September 21). *Insta-Fame and Image: The Social Media Influence on Cosmetic Surgery Trends*. Dr Rajat Gupta. https://drrajatgupta.com/insta-fame-and-image-the-social-media-influence-on-cosmetic-surgery-trends/

Gupta, S., Arora, A., Singh, S., & Jain, J. (2025). AI feel millennials : Prioritizing the intentions towards adoption of AI-enabled chatbots using fuzzy-AHP approach. *Journal of Science and Technology Policy Management*. DOI: 10.1108/JSTPM-09-2023-0159

Gupta, R., & Pathak, C. (2014). A Machine Learning Framework for Predicting Purchase by Online Customers based on Dynamic Pricing. *Procedia Computer Science*, *36*, 599–605. DOI: 10.1016/j.procs.2014.09.060

Gursoy, D., Chi, O. H., Lu, L., & Nunkoo, R. (2019). Consumers acceptance of artificially intelligent (AI) device use in service delivery. *International Journal of Information Management*, *49*, 157–169. DOI: 10.1016/j.ijinfomgt.2019.03.008

Gutti, D., Yadav, G. V., & Kaja, H. (2023). Influence of artificial intelligence in consumer decision-making process. *The Business of the Metaverse: How to Maintain the Human Element Within This New Business Reality*, 141-155.

Guttman, R. H., Moukas, A. G., & Maes, P. (1998). Agent-mediated electronic commerce: A survey. *The Knowledge Engineering Review*, *13*(2), 147–159. DOI: 10.1017/S0269888998002082

Gvili, Y., & Levy, S. (2021). Consumer engagement in sharing brand-related information on social commerce: The roles of culture and experience. *Journal of Marketing Communications*, *27*(1), 53–68. DOI: 10.1080/13527266.2019.1633552

Gvili, Y., & Levy, S. (2023). I Share, Therefore I Trust: A moderated mediation model of the influence of eWOM engagement on social commerce. *Journal of Business Research*, *166*, 114131. DOI: 10.1016/j.jbusres.2023.114131

Haenlein, M., & Kaplan, A. (2019). A Brief History of Artificial Intelligence: On the Past, Present, and Future of Artificial Intelligence. *California Management Review*, *61*(4), 5–14. DOI: 10.1177/0008125619864925

Häglund, E., & Björklund, J. (2024). AI-Driven Contextual Advertising: Toward Relevant Messaging Without Personal Data. *Journal of Current Issues and Research in Advertising*, *45*(3), 1–19. DOI: 10.1080/10641734.2024.2334939

Hair, J. F., Risher, J. J., Sarstedt, M., & Ringle, C. M. (2019). When to use and how to report the results of PLS-SEM. *European Business Review*, 31(1), 2 24. DOI: 10.1108/EBR-11-2018-0203

Hajli, M. N. (2014). A study of the impact of social media on consumers. *International Journal of Market Research*, *56*(3), 387–404. DOI: 10.2501/IJMR-2014-025

Hajli, N. (2015). Social commerce constructs and consumer's intention to buy. *International Journal of Information Management*, *35*(2), 183–191. DOI: 10.1016/j.ijinfomgt.2014.12.005

Haleem, A., Javaid, M., Asim Qadri, M., Pratap Singh, R., & Suman, R. (2022). Artificial intelligence (AI) applications for marketing: A literature-based study. *International Journal of Intelligent Networks*, *3*, 119–132. 10.1016/j.ijin.2022.08.005. DOI: 10.1016/j.ijin.2022.08.005

Han, M. C. (2021). The Impact of Anthropomorphism on Consumers' Purchase Decision in Chatbot Commerce. *Journal of Internet Commerce*, 20(1), 46 65. DOI: 10.1080/15332861.2020.1863022

Hande, P. V., Ghosh, D., & Govil, A. (2015). A Comparative Study on Factors Shaping Buying Behaviour on B2B and B2C E-Commerce Platforms in India. *Journal of Marketing and Consumer Research*, *8*(0), 53.

Hanji, S. V., Navalgund, N., Ingalagi, S., Desai, S., & Hanji, S. S. (2024). Adoption of AI Chatbots in Travel and Tourism Services. In X.-S. Yang, R. S. Sherratt, N. Dey, & A. Joshi (Éds.), *Proceedings of Eighth International Congress on Information and Communication Technology* (Vol. 696, p. 713 727). Springer Nature Singapore. DOI: 10.1007/978-981-99-3236-8_57

hannahaile. (2023, February 12). *Food is more than nutrition*. HeritageNutrition.co.uk. https://heritagenutrition.co.uk/food-is-more-than-nutrition/

Haque, A., Akther, N., Khan, I., Agarwal, K., & Uddin, N. (2024). Artificial Intelligence in Retail Marketing: Research Agenda Based on Bibliometric Reflection and Content Analysis (2000–2023). *Informatics (MDPI)*, *11*(4), 1–30. DOI: 10.3390/informatics11040074

Haring, K. S., Silvera-Tawil, D., Takahashi, T., Watanabe, K., & Velonaki, M. (2016). How people perceive different robot types : A direct comparison of an android, humanoid, and non-biomimetic robot. *2016 8th international conference on knowledge and smart technology* (kst), 265 270.

Haron, S., & Nursofiza, W. (2008). *Creating a dynamic Islamic capital market: the essential role of innovation, Islamic Capital Markets: Products, Regulation and Development, Islamic Research and Training Institute*. Islamic Development Bank Group.

Hart, P. M., Jones, S. R., & Royne, M. B. (2013). The human lens : How anthropomorphic reasoning varies by product complexity and enhances personal value. *Journal of Marketing Management*, 29(1 2), 105 121. DOI: 10.1080/0267257X.2012.759993

Hartmann, P. M., Zaki, M., Feldmann, N., & Neely, A. (2016). Capturing value from big data–a taxonomy of data-driven business models used by start-up firms. *International Journal of Operations & Production Management*, *36*(10), 1382–1406. DOI: 10.1108/IJOPM-02-2014-0098

Hartwick, J., & Barki, H. (1994). Explaining the Role of User Participation in Information System Use. *Management Science*, 40(4), 440 465. DOI: 10.1287/mnsc.40.4.440

Hassan, S. H., Teo, S. Z., Ramayah, T., & Al-Kumaim, N. H. (2021). The Credibility of Social Media Beauty Gurus in Young Millennials' Cosmetic Product Choice. *PLoS One*, *16*(3), e0249286. Advance online publication. DOI: 10.1371/journal.pone.0249286 PMID: 33780487

Hazarika, A. (2013). E-Commerce: Expectations and Shortfalls. *Christ University Law Journal*, *2*(2), 59–78. DOI: 10.12728/culj.3.4

He, H. (2022). A comprehensive review on the role of online media in sustainable business development and decision making. *Soft Computing*, *26*(20), 10789–10803. DOI: 10.1007/s00500-022-06993-1 PMID: 35698465

Heller Baird, C., & Parasnis, G. (2011). From social media to social customer relationship management. *Strategy and Leadership*, *39*(5), 30–37. DOI: 10.1108/10878571111161507

Hennig-Thurau, T., Herting, A. M., & Jütte, D. (2025). Adoption of Virtual Reality Headsets: The Role of Metaverse Trials for Consumers' Usage and Purchase Intentions. *Journal of Interactive Marketing*, *60*(2), 145–160. DOI: 10.1177/10949968241263353

Henseler, J., Hubona, G., & Ray, P. A. (2016). Using PLS path modeling in new technology research : Updated guidelines. *Industrial Management & Data Systems*, 116(1), 2 20. DOI: 10.1108/IMDS-09-2015-0382

Henseler, J., Ringle, C. M., & Sarstedt, M. (2015). A new criterion for assessing discriminant validity in variance-based structural equation modeling. *Journal of the Academy of Marketing Science*, 43(1), 115 135. DOI: 10.1007/s11747-014-0403-8

Hermann, E. (2022). Leveraging Artificial Intelligence in Marketing for Social Good—An Ethical Perspective. *Journal of Business Ethics*, *179*(1), 43–61. DOI: 10.1007/s10551-021-04843-y PMID: 34054170

Hermann, E., & Puntoni, S. (2024). Artificial intelligence and consumer behavior: From predictive to generative AI. *Journal of Business Research*, *180*, 114720. 10.1016/j.jbusres.2024.114720. DOI: 10.1016/j.jbusres.2024.114720

Higgs, S., & Thomas, J. (2016). Social influences on eating. *Current Opinion in Behavioral Sciences*, *9*, 1–6. DOI: 10.1016/j.cobeha.2015.10.005

Hiort, A. (2021, December 2). *Virtual influencers: The future of fashion.* VirtualHumans.org. https://www.virtualhumans.org/article/virtual-influencers-are-the-future-of-fashion

Hollebeek, L. D. (2011). Demystifying customer brand engagement: Exploring the loyalty nexus. *Journal of Marketing Management*, *27*(7–8), 785–807. DOI: 10.1080/0267257X.2010.500132

Hollebeek, L. D., Glynn, M. S., & Brodie, R. J. (2014). Consumer Brand Engagement in Social Media: Conceptualization, Scale Development and Validation. *Journal of Interactive Marketing*, *28*(2), 149–165. DOI: 10.1016/j.intmar.2013.12.002

Hollebeek, L. D., & Macky, K. (2019). Digital Content Marketing's Role in Fostering Consumer Engagement, Trust, and Value: Framework, Fundamental Propositions, and Implications. *Journal of Interactive Marketing*, *45*(1), 27–41. DOI: 10.1016/j.intmar.2018.07.003

Horowitz, M. C., Kahn, L., Macdonald, J., & Schneider, J. (2024). Adopting AI : How familiarity breeds both trust and contempt. *AI & Society*, 39(4), 1721 1735. DOI: 10.1007/s00146-023-01666-5

How Social Media Advertising and Repetitive Marketing Messages Affect the Online Purhasing Behavior? (n.d.). Retrieved May 1, 2025, from https://aaltodoc.aalto.fi/items/30c02c3e-64fb-4f11-9063-d1250330fb90

Hoyer, W. D., Kroschke, M., Schmitt, B., Kraume, K., & Shankar, V. (2020). Transforming the Customer Experience through New Technologies. *Journal of Interactive Marketing*, *51*(1), 57–71. DOI: 10.1016/j.intmar.2020.04.001

Huang, M.-H., & Rust, R. T. (2017). Technology-driven service strategy. *Journal of the Academy of Marketing Science*, *45*(6), 906–924. DOI: 10.1007/s11747-017-0545-6

Huang, M.-H., & Rust, R. T. (2018). Artificial Intelligence in Service. *Journal of Service Research*, *21*(2), 155–172. DOI: 10.1177/1094670517752459

Huang, M.-H., & Rust, R. T. (2021). Engaged to a Robot? The Role of AI in Service. *Journal of Service Research*, *24*(1), 30–41. DOI: 10.1177/1094670520902266

Huang, Y.-C., Li, L.-N., Lee, H.-Y., Browning, M. H., & Yu, C.-P. (2023). Surfing in virtual reality : An application of extended technology acceptance model with flow theory. *Computers in Human Behavior Reports*, *9*, 100252. DOI: 10.1016/j.chbr.2022.100252

Hudson, S., Huang, L., Roth, M. S., & Madden, T. J. (2016). The influence of social media interactions on consumer–brand relationships: A three-country study of brand perceptions and marketing behaviors. *International Journal of Research in Marketing*, *33*(1), 27–41. DOI: 10.1016/j.ijresmar.2015.06.004

Hue, T. T., & Hung, T. H. (2025). Impact of artificial intelligence on branding: A bibliometric review and future research directions. *Humanities & Social Sciences Communications*, *12*(1), 209. DOI: 10.1057/s41599-025-04488-6

Hu, L., & Bentler, P. M. (1999). Cutoff criteria for fit indexes in covariance structure analysis : Conventional criteria versus new alternatives. *Structural Equation Modeling*, *6*(1), 1–55. DOI: 10.1080/10705519909540118

Hussain, K., Ying, F., Junaid, M., Shi, H., & Baig, U. (2020). The buyer–seller relationship: A literature synthesis on dynamic perspectives. *Journal of Business and Industrial Marketing*, *35*(4), 669–684. DOI: 10.1108/JBIM-09-2018-0280

Hutto, C. J., & Gilbert, E. (2014). VADER: A parsimonious rule-based model for sentiment analysis of social media text. *Proceedings of the International AAAI Conference on Web and Social Media*, 8(1). DOI: 10.1609/icwsm.v8i1.14550

IBEF. (2023, December). *Growth Of The Cosmetic Industry In India | IBEF*. India Brand Equity Foundation. https://www.ibef.org/research/case-study/growth-of-the-cosmetic-indusry-in-india

Ibrahim, F., Münscher, J.-C., Daseking, M., & Telle, N.-T. (2025). The technology acceptance model and adopter type analysis in the context of artificial intelligence. *Frontiers in Artificial Intelligence*, *7*, 1496518. DOI: 10.3389/frai.2024.1496518 PMID: 39886023

Ichsan, N. (2015). Analisa SWOT, prospek dan strategi pengembangan asuransi Syariah Di Indonesia (SWOT analysis, prospects and development strategy for Islamic insurance in Indonesia), available at: https://nurulichsanaan.files.wordpress.com/2015/10/analsis-swot-asuransi-syariahjurnal-kordinat.pdf (accessed 10 November 2016).

Ifekanandu, C. C., Anene, J. N., Iloka, C. B., & Ewuzie, C. O. (2023). Influence of artificial intelligence (AI) on customer experience and loyalty: Mediating role of personalization. *Journal of Data Acquisition and Processing*, *38*(3), 1936.

Illescas-Manzano, M. D., Vicente López, N., Afonso González, N., & Cristofol Rodríguez, C. (2021). Implementation of Chatbot in Online Commerce, and Open Innovation. *Journal of Open Innovation*, *7*(2), 125. DOI: 10.3390/joitmc7020125

Image Processing Computational Algorithms, Sensory Data Mining Techniques, and Predictive Customer Analytics in the Metaverse Economy. (2022). Image Processing Computational Algorithms, Sensory Data Mining Techniques, and Predictive Customer Analytics in the Metaverse Economy. *Review of Contemporary Philosophy*, *21*(0), 205. DOI: 10.22381/RCP21202213

Ingrassia, M., Bellia, C., Giurdanella, C., Columba, P., & Chironi, S. (2022). Digital Influencers, Food and Tourism—A New Model of Open Innovation for Businesses in the Ho.Re.Ca. Sector. *Journal of Open Innovation*, *8*(1), 50. DOI: 10.3390/joitmc8010050

Iqbal, M. Z., & Campbell, A. G. (2023). Real-time hand interaction and self-directed machine learning agents in immersive learning environments. *Computers & Education: X Reality*, 3, 100038.

Isaac, O., Abdullah, Z., Ramayah, T., & Mutahar, A. M. (2017). Internet usage, user satisfaction, task-technology fit, and performance impact among public sector employees in Yemen. *The International Journal of Information and Learning Technology*, *34*(3), 210–241. DOI: 10.1108/IJILT-11-2016-0051

Ismatullaev, U. V. U., & Kim, S.-H. (2024). Review of the Factors Affecting Acceptance of AI-Infused Systems. *Human Factors*, *66*(1), 126–144. DOI: 10.1177/00187208211064707 PMID: 35344676

Ithy, A. (2025). The role of AI in shaping consumer decision-making for personal care products. *The Journal of Consumer Research, 48*(3), 567–589.

Jalil, M. I. A., Lada, S., Bakri, M. A., & Hassan, Z. (2021). Halal Cosmetics Repurchase Intention: The Role Of Marketing On Social Media. *Journal of Islamic Monetary Economics and Finance, 7*(4), 629–650. Advance online publication. DOI: 10.21098/jimf.v7i4.1379

Jalputra, A., Molinillo, S., & Wang, S. (2018). Aesthetic or self-expressiveness? Linking brand logo benefits, brand stereotypes and relationship quality. *Journal of Retailing and Consumer Services, 44*, 191–200. DOI: 10.1016/j.jretconser.2018.06.015

Jannach, D., Adomavicius, G., & Tuzhilin, A. (2021). Recommender systems: Challenges, insights, and research opportunities. *Information & Management, 58*(1), 103597. DOI: 10.1016/j.im.2020.103597

Javeed, D., Saeed, M. S., Kumar, P., Jolfaei, A., Islam, S., & Islam, A. N. (2023). Federated learning-based personalized recommendation systems: An overview on security and privacy challenges. *IEEE Transactions on Consumer Electronics, 70*(1), 2618–2627. DOI: 10.1109/TCE.2023.3318754

Javornik, A. (2016). Augmented reality: Research agenda for studying the impact of AR on consumer experiences. *Journal of Retailing and Consumer Services, 30*, 252–261. DOI: 10.1016/j.jretconser.2016.02.004

Jayaraman, K. D., & Jain, S. (2024). Leveraging Power BI for advanced business intelligence and reporting. *International Journal for Research in Management and Pharmacy, 13*(11), 21. https://www. ijrmp. org

Jenkins, H. (2006). *Convergence culture: Where old and new media collide*. NYU Press.

Jenneboer, L., Herrando, C., & Constantinides, E. (2022). The impact of chatbots on customer loyalty : A systematic literature review. *Journal of Theoretical and Applied Electronic Commerce Research, 17*(1), 212–229. DOI: 10.3390/jtaer17010011

Jiao, D. (2025). AI-enhanced digital therapeutics for cognitive impairment: Integrating mobile applications, virtual reality, and wearable devices. *Discover Artificial Intelligence, 5*(1), 69. Advance online publication. DOI: 10.1007/s44163-025-00325-6

Jiménez-Barreto, J., Rubio, N., & Molinillo, S. (2021). "Find a flight for me, Oscar!" Motivational customer experiences with chatbots. *International Journal of Contemporary Hospitality Management, 33*(11), 3860–3882. DOI: 10.1108/IJCHM-10-2020-1244

Jin, S. V., Muqaddam, E. R., & Ryu, E. (2019). Instafamous and social media influencer marketing. *Marketing Intelligence & Planning*, *37*(5), 567–579. DOI: 10.1108/MIP-09-2018-0375

Jin, S. V., & Viswanathan, V. (2025). "Threatened and empty selves following AI-based virtual influencers": Comparison between followers and non-followers of virtual influencers in AI-driven digital marketing. *AI & Society*, *40*(1), 117–131. DOI: 10.1007/s00146-023-01832-9

Jörling, M., Böhm, R., & Paluch, S. (2020). Mechanisms and Consequences of Anthropomorphizing Autonomous Products : The Role of Schema Congruity and Prior Experience. *Schmalenbach Business Review*, 72(4), 485 510. DOI: 10.1007/s41464-020-00100-3

Joshi, S., Bhattacharya, S., Pathak, P., Natraj, N. A., Saini, J., & Goswami, S. (2025). Harnessing the potential of generative AI in digital marketing using the Behavioral Reasoning Theory approach. *International Journal of Information Management Data Insights*, *5*(1), 100317. 10.1016/j.jjimei.2024.100317. DOI: 10.1016/j.jjimei.2024.100317

Ju, N., Kim, T., & Im, H. (2024). Fake human but real influencer: The interplay of authenticity and humanlikeness in Virtual Influencer communication? *Fash Text*, *11*(1), 16. DOI: 10.1186/s40691-024-00380-0

Jyothsna, M., & Kryvinska, N. (2024). Exploring the Chatbot Usage intention-A mediating Role of Chatbot Initial trust. *Heliyon*, **•••**, 33028. PMID: 39027428

Kaba, B., & Touré, B. (2014). Understanding information and communication technology behavioral intention to use : Applying the UTAUT model to social networking site adoption by young people in a least developed country. *Journal of the Association for Information Science and Technology*, *65*(8), 1662–1674. DOI: 10.1002/asi.23069

Kailash, M. S. R., Joshi, C., Desai, P. R., Teferra, N. B., & Radhakrishnan, S. (2023). The Rise of Ethical Consumerism: Marketing Strategies for the Conscious Buyer.

Kakkar, G. (2017). Top 10 Reasons Behind Growing Importance of Content Marketing, at: https://www.digitalvidya.com/blog/importance-ofcontent-marketing/, Accessed date: 3 December 2017.

Kasim, N., Nuhtay, S. N., & Salman, S. A. (2013). Shariah Governance for Islamic Capital Market: A Step Forward. International Journal of Education and Research Vol. 1 No. 6. ISSN: 2201-6740.

Katkar, D. N., Mahajan, A., Mulekar, V., & Gupta, S. (2024). Evolution and Dynamics of India's Cosmetic Industry: A Century of Consumer Preferences, Digital Transformation and Emerging Trends. *Quest Journal of Management Research, 15*(1), 35–42. https://www.crkimr.in/wp-content/uploads/2024/07/Chetana-Quest-Vol-XV-Issue-1-June-2024-05.07.2024.pdf#page=41

Kaur, J., Mogaji, E., Paliwal, M., Jha, S., Agarwal, S., & Mogaji, S. A. (2024). Consumer behavior in the metaverse. *Journal of Consumer Behaviour, 23*(4), 1720–1738. DOI: 10.1002/cb.2298

Kelly, S., Kaye, S.-A., & Oviedo-Trespalacios, O. (2022). A Multi-Industry Analysis of the Future Use of AI Chatbots. *Human Behavior and Emerging Technologies, 2022*(1), 14. DOI: 10.1155/2022/2552099

Kennedy, B., & Funk, C. (2016). 28% of Americans are 'strong'early adopters of technology. https://policycommons.net/artifacts/618399/28-of-americans-are-strong-early-adopters-of-technology/1599341/

Khan, M. K. (2023). AI-enabled transformations in telecommunications industry. Telecommunication Systems, 82(1), 1 2. DOI: 10.1007/s11235-022-00989-w

Khan, M. I., Fatima, J. K., Bahmannia, S., Chatrath, S. K., Dale, N. F., & Johns, R. (2025). Investigating the influence of perceived humanization of service encounters on value creation of chatbot-assisted services. *Journal of Service Theory and Practice, 35*(1), 56–88. DOI: 10.1108/JSTP-10-2023-0282

Khan, S. U., Khan, S., Ballewar, S. S., Rane, J. P., & Siddiquee, A. Q. (2025). Cinema and Artificial Intelligence: Charting Its Role in the Indian Film Sector. In Kilinç, U. (Ed.), *Transforming Cinema with Artificial Intelligence* (pp. 143–180). IGI Global Scientific Publishing., DOI: 10.4018/979-8-3693-3916-9.ch007

Khan, S., & Rabbani, M. R. (2021). Artificial intelligence and NLP-based chatbot for islamic banking and finance. [IJIRR]. *International Journal of Information Retrieval Research, 11*(3), 65–77. DOI: 10.4018/IJIRR.2021070105

Khizzou, N. B., Aarabe, M., & Alla, L. (2024). Current trends in scientific research on managerial innovations in healthcare supply chain : A bibliometric analysis. *2024 IEEE 15th International Colloquium on Logistics and Supply Chain Management* (LOGISTIQUA), 1 9.

Khizzou, N. B., Aarabe, M., & Alla, L. (2024). Current trends in scientific research on managerial innovations in healthcare supply chain : A bibliometric analysis. *2024 IEEE 15th International Colloquium on Logistics and Supply Chain Management (LOGISTIQUA)*, 1-9. https://ieeexplore.ieee.org/abstract/document/10571373/?casa_token=U6xJHWHau7gAAAAA:tjzLDj4RuxVqHUReRd1FeosvQeEznMUOhVEe4FPUr1uwfc9Py49g_DZSWHuP4NP1_Y_UuwlXcxq9

Khodakarami, F., & Chan, Y. E. (2014). Exploring the role of customer relationship management (CRM) systems in customer knowledge creation. *Information & Management*, *51*(1), 27–42. DOI: 10.1016/j.im.2013.09.001

Khoi, N. H., Le, A. N.-H., & Nguyen Dong, P. (2023). A moderating – mediating model of the urge to buy impulsively in social commerce live-streaming. *Electronic Commerce Research and Applications*, *60*, 101286. DOI: 10.1016/j.elerap.2023.101286

Kiel, D., Arnold, C., & Voigt, K. I. (2017). The influence of the Industrial Internet of Things on business models of established manufacturing companies–A business level perspective. *Technovation*, *68*, 4–19. DOI: 10.1016/j.technovation.2017.09.003

Kietzmann, J. H., Hermkens, K., McCarthy, I. P., & Silvestre, B. S. (2011). Social media? Get serious! Understanding the functional building blocks of social media. *Business Horizons*, *54*(3), 241–251. DOI: 10.1016/j.bushor.2011.01.005

Kim, J. K., Kim, H. K., Oh, H. Y., & Ryu, Y. U. (2010). A group recommendation system for online communities. *International Journal of Information Management*, *30*(3), 212–219. DOI: 10.1016/j.ijinfomgt.2009.09.006

Kim, T., Lee, O.-K. D., & Kang, J. (2023). Is it the best for barista robots to serve like humans? A multidimensional anthropomorphism perspective. *International Journal of Hospitality Management*, *108*, 103358. DOI: 10.1016/j.ijhm.2022.103358

Kitchin, R., & Dodge, M. (2014). *The data revolution: Big data, open data, data infrastructures & their consequences*. SAGE Publications.

Klein, K., & Martinez, L. F. (2023). The impact of anthropomorphism on customer satisfaction in chatbot commerce : An experimental study in the food sector. *Electronic Commerce Research*, 23(4), 2789 2825. DOI: 10.1007/s10660-022-09562-8

Koivunen, K., Haanpää, M. A. A., & Saraniemi, S. (2025). The emergence of cause-oriented influencers – conceptualizing de-influencing on TikTok. *Journal of Business Research*, *197*, 115463. 10.1016/j.jbusres.2025.115463. DOI: 10.1016/j.jbusres.2025.115463

Komiak, S. Y., & Benbasat, I. (2006). The effects of personalization and familiarity on trust and adoption of recommendation agents. *Management Information Systems Quarterly, 30*(4), 941–960. DOI: 10.2307/25148760

Kose, U., & Sert, S. (2017). *Improving content marketing processes with the approaches by artificial intelligence*. DOI: 10.48550/ARXIV.1704.02114

Kotp, M. H., Ismail, H. A., Basyouny, H. A. A., Aly, M. A., Hendy, A., Nashwan, A. J., Hendy, A., & Abd Elmoaty, A. E. E. (2025). Empowering nurse leaders: Readiness for AI integration and the perceived benefits of predictive analytics. *BMC Nursing, 24*(1), 56. Advance online publication. DOI: 10.1186/s12912-024-02653-x PMID: 39819624

Kumar, A., Shankar, A., Behl, A., Chakraborty, D., & Gundala, R. R. (2025). Anthropomorphic generative AI chatbots for enhancing customer engagement, experience and recommendation. *Journal of Consumer Marketing*. https://www.emerald.com/insight/content/doi/10.1108/JCM-06-2024-6922/full/html

Kumar, A., & Shankar, A. (2024). Investigating the role of metaverse influencers' attributes for the next generation of services. *Journal of Services Marketing, 38*(7), 816–838. DOI: 10.1108/JSM-09-2023-0320

Kumar, M., Khan, L., & Chang, H. T. (2025). Evolving techniques in sentiment analysis: A comprehensive review. *PeerJ. Computer Science, 11*, e2592. DOI: 10.7717/peerj-cs.2592 PMID: 39957863

Kumar, V., Aksoy, L., Donkers, B., Venkatesan, R., Wiesel, T., & Tillmanns, S. (2010). Undervalued or overvalued customers: Capturing total customer engagement value. *Journal of Service Research, 13*(3), 297–310. DOI: 10.1177/1094670510375602

Kumar, V., Ashraf, A. R., & Nadeem, W. (2024). AI-powered marketing : What, where, and how? *International Journal of Information Management, 77*, 102783. DOI: 10.1016/j.ijinfomgt.2024.102783

Kumar, V., Rajan, B., Salunkhe, U., & Joag, S. G. (2022). Relating the dark side of new-age technologies and customer technostress. *Psychology and Marketing, 39*(12), 2240–2259. DOI: 10.1002/mar.21738

Labrecque, L. I. (2014). Fostering Consumer–Brand Relationships in Social Media Environments: The Role of Parasocial Interaction. *Journal of Interactive Marketing, 28*(2), 134–148. DOI: 10.1016/j.intmar.2013.12.003

Laroche, M., Habibi, M. R., Richard, M.-O., & Sankaranarayanan, R. (2012). The effects of social media based brand communities on brand community markers, value creation practices, brand trust and brand loyalty. *Computers in Human Behavior*, *28*(5), 1755–1767. DOI: 10.1016/j.chb.2012.04.016

Larsen, M. S. S., Lindhard, S. M., Brunoe, T. D., Nielsen, K., & Larsen, J. K. (2019). Mass customization in the house building industry: Literature review and research directions. *Frontiers in Built Environment*, *115*(5), 115. Advance online publication. DOI: 10.3389/fbuil.2019.00115

Lăzăroiu, G., Neguriţă, O., Grecu, I., Grecu, G., & Mitran, P. C. (2020). Consumers' Decision-Making Process on Social Commerce Platforms: Online Trust, Perceived Risk, and Purchase Intentions. *Frontiers in Psychology*, *11*, 890. DOI: 10.3389/fpsyg.2020.00890 PMID: 32499740

Lee, D., Hosanagar, K., & Nair, H. (2017). Advertising Content and Consumer Engagement on Social Media: Evidence from Facebook. SSRN *Electronic Journal*. DOI: 10.2139/ssrn.2290802

Lee, C. T., & Shen, Y.-C. (2025). Artificial humanity: A multi-method exploration of user responses to AI influencer affordances in short video platform. *Telematics and Informatics*, *98*, 102245. 10.1016/j.tele.2025.102245. DOI: 10.1016/j.tele.2025.102245

Lee, S. E., Ju, N., & Lee, K.-H. (2023). Service chatbot : Co-citation and big data analysis toward a review and research agenda. *Technological Forecasting and Social Change*, *194*, 122722. DOI: 10.1016/j.techfore.2023.122722

Lehnert, L., & Kuehnl, C. (2025). Empathy at the heart of customer experience : A holistic framework for understanding and enhancing consumer empathy through the lens of customer experience. *Psychology and Marketing*, *42*(2), 332–358. DOI: 10.1002/mar.22130

Leite, H., & Vieira, L. R. (2025). The use of virtual reality in human training: Trends and a research agenda. *Virtual Reality (Waltham Cross)*, *29*(1), 25. Advance online publication. DOI: 10.1007/s10055-024-01093-x

Lemaignan, S., Fink, J., Dillenbourg, P., & Braboszcz, C. (2014). The cognitive correlates of anthropomorphism. *2014 Human-Robot Interaction Conference, Workshop" HRI: a bridge between Robotics and Neuroscience"*. https://infoscience.epfl.ch/record/196441

Lemon, K. N., & Verhoef, P. C. (2016). Understanding Customer Experience Throughout the Customer Journey. *Journal of Marketing, 80*(6), 69–96. DOI: 10.1509/jm.15.0420

Leong, L.-Y., Hew, T. S., Ooi, K.-B., Hajli, N., & Tan, G. W.-H. (2024). Revisiting the social commerce paradigm: The social commerce (SC) framework and a research agenda. *Internet Research, 34*(4), 1346–1393. DOI: 10.1108/INTR-08-2022-0657

Levy, S., & Gvili, Y. (2020). Online shopper engagement in price negotiation: The roles of culture, involvement and eWOM. *International Journal of Advertising, 39*(2), 232–257. DOI: 10.1080/02650487.2019.1612621

Liang, H., & Fung, I. (2021). From opinion leaders to influencers: Re-examining opinion leadership in the era of social media. *Current Sociology, 69*(6), 803–821.

Liao, Q. V., Davis, M., Geyer, W., Muller, M., & Shami, N. S. (2016). What Can You Do?: Studying Social-Agent Orientation and Agent Proactive Interactions with an Agent for Employees. *Proceedings of the 2016 ACM Conference on Designing Interactive Systems,* 264 275. DOI: 10.1145/2901790.2901842

Liao, C. H. (2025). The role of virtual reality in enhancing behavioral empathy: Exploring cognitive absorption, engagement, and emotional moderation using multivariate methods. *Humanities & Social Sciences Communications, 12*(1), 1–15. DOI: 10.1057/s41599-025-05334-5

Li, B., Chen, Y., Liu, L., & Zheng, B. (2023). Users' intention to adopt artificial intelligence-based chatbot : A meta-analysis. *Service Industries Journal, 43*(15-16), 1117–1139. DOI: 10.1080/02642069.2023.2217756

Ling, E. C., Tussyadiah, I., Tuomi, A., Stienmetz, J., & Ioannou, A. (2021). Factors influencing users' adoption and use of conversational agents : A systematic review. *Psychology and Marketing, 38*(7), 1031–1051. DOI: 10.1002/mar.21491

Lin, J., Fan, W., & Wallace, L. (2021). Social network influence on sentiment diffusion. *Decision Support Systems, 148*, 113587.

Lin, J., Li, L., Yan, Y., & Turel, O. (2018). Understanding Chinese consumer engagement in social commerce: The roles of social support and swift guanxi. *Internet Research, 28*(1), 2–22. DOI: 10.1108/IntR-11-2016-0349

Lin, K.-Y., & Lu, H.-P. (2015). Predicting mobile social network acceptance based on mobile value and social influence. *Internet Research, 25*(1), 107–130. DOI: 10.1108/IntR-01-2014-0018

Lin, W. R., Lin, C.-Y., & Ding, Y.-H. (2020). Factors affecting the behavioral intention to adopt mobile payment : An empirical study in Taiwan. *Mathematics*, *8*(10), 1851. DOI: 10.3390/math8101851

Litao, X., & Xinzhou, S. (2021) Research on Consumer Behavior Based on the Perspective of Behavioral Economics. Proceedings of the 2021 3rd International Conference on Economic Management and Cultural Industry (ICEMCI 2021). Advances in Economics, *Business and Management Research, 20*(3) pp. 316-319.

Liu, M., Yang, Y., Ren, Y., Jia, Y., Ma, H., Luo, J., Fang, S., Qi, M., & Zhang, L. (2024). What influences consumer AI chatbot use intention? An application of the extended technology acceptance model. *Journal of Hospitality and Tourism Technology*, 15(4), 667 689. DOI: 10.1108/JHTT-03-2023-0057

Liu, B. (2012). Sentiment analysis and opinion mining. *Synthesis Lectures on Human Language Technologies*, *5*(1), 1–167. DOI: 10.1007/978-3-031-02145-9

Liu, H., Zhang, P., Cheng, H., Hasan, N., & Chiong, R. (2025). Impact of AI-generated virtual streamer interaction on consumer purchase intention: A focus on social presence and perceived value. *Journal of Retailing and Consumer Services*, *85*, 104290. 10.1016/j.jretconser.2025.104290. DOI: 10.1016/j.jretconser.2025.104290

Liu, P., Li, M., Dai, D., & Guo, L. (2021). The effects of social commerce environmental characteristics on customers' purchase intentions: The chain mediating effect of customer-to-customer interaction and customer-perceived value. *Electronic Commerce Research and Applications*, *48*, 101073. DOI: 10.1016/j.elerap.2021.101073

Liu, Y., Li, Q., Edu, T., Fam, K., Zaharia, R., & Negricea, C. (2023). Mobile social commerce content, consumer emotions and behaviour. *International Journal of Consumer Studies*, *47*(4), 1315–1334. DOI: 10.1111/ijcs.12908

Liu, Z., Shan, J., & Pigneur, Y. (2016). The role of personalized services and control : An empirical evaluation of privacy calculus and technology acceptance model in the mobile context. *Journal of Information Privacy and Security*, *12*(3), 123–144. DOI: 10.1080/15536548.2016.1206757

Li, Y., Hou, R., & Tan, R. (2024). How customers respond to chatbot anthropomorphism : The mediating roles of perceived humanness and perceived persuasiveness. *European Journal of Marketing*, *58*(12), 2757–2790. DOI: 10.1108/EJM-11-2022-0827

Lou, C., & Yuan, S. (2019). Influencer Marketing: How Message Value and Credibility Affect Consumer Trust of Branded Content on Social Media. *Journal of Interactive Advertising*, *19*(1), 58–73. DOI: 10.1080/15252019.2018.1533501

Lubbe, I., & Ngoma, N. (2021). Useful chatbot experience provides technological satisfaction : An emerging market perspective. *South African Journal of Information Management, 23*(1), 1–8. DOI: 10.4102/sajim.v23i1.1299

Lu, L., Cai, R., & Gursoy, D. (2019). Developing and validating a scale to measure consumers' trust toward artificial intelligence in service encounters. *Journal of Hospitality Marketing & Management, 28*(7), 803–827. DOI: 10.1080/19368623.2019.1568989

Lunney, A., Cunningham, N. R., & Eastin, M. S. (2016). Wearable fitness technology : A structural investigation into acceptance and perceived fitness outcomes. *Computers in Human Behavior, 65*, 114–120. DOI: 10.1016/j.chb.2016.08.007

MacKenzie, S. B., Podsakoff, P. M., & Podsakoff, N. P. (2011). Construct measurement and validation procedures in MIS and behavioral research : Integrating new and existing techniques. *Management Information Systems Quarterly, 293*(2), 334. DOI: 10.2307/23044045

Mahiwal, A., Khan, S. U., & Khan, S. (2024). Navigating The Digital Landscape: Social Media's Influence on Climate Activism and Environmental Awareness. *Global Media Journal-Indian Edition, 16*(1). https://gmj.manipal.edu/issues/Jun2024/P6.pdf

Mahiwal, A., Khan, S. U., Khan, S., & Sachdev, M. (2025). Mapping the Misinformation Ecosystem in India: Insights Into Key Areas and Pathways of Dissemination. In Lyle, P. L., & Esmail, A. M. (Eds.), *Impacts of Leakage, Whistleblowing, and the Rise of Propaganda* (pp. 83–108). IGI Global., DOI: 10.4018/979-8-3693-7468-9.ch005

Makudza, F., Jaravaza, D. C., Makandwa, G., & Mukucha, P. (2024). Disruptive artificial intelligence : Augmenting consumer experience through chatbot banking. In *Digital Influence on Consumer Habits : Marketing Challenges and Opportunities* (p. 1-18). Emerald Publishing Limited. https://www.emerald.com/insight/content/doi/10.1108/978-1-80455-342-820241001/full/html

Malik, S., Muhammad, K., & Waheed, Y. (2024). Artificial intelligence and industrial applications-A revolution in modern industries. *Ain Shams Engineering Journal, 15*(9), 102886. DOI: 10.1016/j.asej.2024.102886

Mamaearth. (n.d.). *@mamaearth.in*. Www.instagram.com. https://www.instagram.com/mamaearth.in/

Manan, H. A., Ariffin, S., Maknu, T. S. R., & Zakaria, F. N. (2020). Effects of Social Media Advertisements on Intention to Purchase Health and Beauty Products. *Journal of International Business. Economics and Entrepreneurship, 5*(1), 59–68. DOI: 10.24191/jibe.v5i1.14293

Manjunathan, N., Aravindaraj, K., Anitha, J., Bharathi, V. R., Sathya, V., Senthil, R., & Subramanian, R. S. (2025). Advances in Data Processing, Machine Learning, and Data Security. In Strategic Innovations of AI and ML for E-Commerce Data Security (pp. 207-234). IGI Global.

Manoharan, J. S., Arunkumar, M., Hemamalini, M., Sathya, V., Anish, T. P., & Subramanian, R. S. (2025). Virtual and Augmented Reality in the Automobile Industry: Applications and Future Directions. *Virtual and Augmented Reality Applications in the Automobile Industry*, 377-406.

Manser Payne, E. H., Dahl, A. J., & Peltier, J. (2021). Digital servitization value co-creation framework for AI services: A research agenda for digital transformation in financial service ecosystems. *Journal of Research in Interactive Marketing*, *15*(2), 200–222. DOI: 10.1108/JRIM-12-2020-0252

Marandu, E. E., Makudza, F., & Ngwenya, S. N. (2019). Predicting Students' Intention and Actual Use of E-Learning Using the Technology Acceptance Model : A Case from Zimbabwe. *International Journal of Learning. Teaching and Educational Research*, *18*(6), 110–127. DOI: 10.26803/ijlter.18.6.7

Mariani, M. M., Hashemi, N., & Wirtz, J. (2023). Artificial intelligence empowered conversational agents : A systematic literature review and research agenda. *Journal of Business Research*, *161*, 113838. DOI: 10.1016/j.jbusres.2023.113838

Mariani, M. M., Perez-Vega, R., & Wirtz, J. (2022). AI in marketing, consumer research and psychology : A systematic literature review and research agenda. *Psychology and Marketing*, *39*(4), 755–776. DOI: 10.1002/mar.21619

Marikyan, D., & Papagiannidis, S. (2023). Technology Acceptance Model. *TheoryHub Book. Retrieved*, (June), 6.

Martínez Puertas, S., Illescas Manzano, M. D., Segovia López, C., & Ribeiro Cardoso, P. (2024). *Purchase intentions in a chatbot environment : An examination of the effects of customer experience*. https://www.ceeol.com/search/article-detail?id=1238151

Martins, C., Oliveira, T., & Popovič, A. (2014). Understanding the Internet banking adoption : A unified theory of acceptance and use of technology and perceived risk application. *International Journal of Information Management*, *34*(1), 1–13. DOI: 10.1016/j.ijinfomgt.2013.06.002

mCaffeine. (2025). *@mcaffeineofficial*. Instagram.com. https://www.instagram.com/mcaffeineofficial/

McDaniel, C. D., & Gates, R. H. (2002). *Marketing Research : The Impact of the Internet*. South-Western.

McKinsey & Company. (2022, August 17). What is the metaverse and where will it lead next? Www.mckinsey.com

McKinsey & Company. https://www.mckinsey.com/featured-insights/mckinsey-explainers/what-is-the-metaverse

Mclean, E. R., Sedera, D., & Tan, F. T. C. (2011). *Reconceptualizing system use for contemporary information systems*. https://aisel.aisnet.org/pacis2011/130/

McLean, G., & Osei-Frimpong, K. (2019). Hey Alexa… examine the variables influencing the use of artificial intelligent in-home voice assistants. *Computers in Human Behavior*, *99*, 28–37. DOI: 10.1016/j.chb.2019.05.009

Mc, M., B, M., Ks, S., Bm, S., M, M., M, C., & Dvsk, M.MC. (2024). Understanding Medical Healthcare Solutions in GIS Platform: A Review. *Journal of Experimental and Laboratory Medicine*, *0*(0), 1. DOI: 10.5455/JELM.20241030075959

Meddah, N. (2024). *The impact of artificial intelligence on consumer behavior : Insights and implications. 18*, 2764–2772.

Melewar, T. C., Foroudi, P., Gupta, S., Kitchen, P. J., & Foroudi, M. M. (2017). Integrating identity, strategy and communications for trust, loyalty and commitment. *European Journal of Marketing*, *51*(3), 572–604. DOI: 10.1108/EJM-08-2015-0616

Melián-González, S., Gutiérrez-Taño, D., & Bulchand-Gidumal, J. (2021). Predicting the intentions to use chatbots for travel and tourism. *Current Issues in Tourism*, 24(2), 192 210. DOI: 10.1080/13683500.2019.1706457

Merz, M. A., Zarantonello, L., & Grappi, S. (2018). How valuable are your customers in the brand value co-creation process? The development of a customer co-creation value (CCCV) scale. *Journal of Business Research*, *82*, 79–89. DOI: 10.1016/j.jbusres.2017.08.018

Miller, A. (2025). AI-driven personalization: Transforming marketing strategies for 2025 and beyond. *Miller Media*. https://millermedia7.com/ai-driven-personalization-transforming-marketing-strategies-for-2025-and-beyond/

Min, W., Zhou, P., Xu, L., Liu, T., Li, T., Huang, M., Jin, Y., Yi, Y., Wen, M., Jiang, S., & Jain, R. (2023). *From Plate to Production: Artificial Intelligence in Modern Consumer-Driven Food Systems* (Version 1). arXiv. DOI: 10.48550/ARXIV.2311.02400

Mishra, S., & Mishra, P. (2022). Analysis of platform business and secure business intelligence. *International Journal of Financial Engineering*, *9*(03), 2250002. DOI: 10.1142/S2424786322500025

Mogaji, E., Viglia, G., Srivastava, P., & Dwivedi, Y. K. (2024). Is it the end of the technology acceptance model in the era of generative artificial intelligence? *International Journal of Contemporary Hospitality Management*, 36(10), 3324 3339. DOI: 10.1108/IJCHM-08-2023-1271

Mogaji, E., Balakrishnan, J., Nwoba, A. C., & Nguyen, N. P. (2021). Emerging-market consumers' interactions with banking chatbots. *Telematics and Informatics*, *65*, 101711. DOI: 10.1016/j.tele.2021.101711

Mogaji, E., & Nguyen, N. P. (2022). Managers' understanding of artificial intelligence in relation to marketing financial services : Insights from a cross-country study. *International Journal of Bank Marketing*, *40*(6), 1272–1298. DOI: 10.1108/IJBM-09-2021-0440

Mohanty, M. (2024). AI in everyday life: How it's changing consumer behavior. *LinkedIn Pulse*. https://www.linkedin.com/pulse/ai-everyday-life-how-its-changing-consumer-behavior-manas-mohanty-mxyuc

Mohsin, S. K. (2024). The influence of AI-driven personalization on consumer decision-making in e-commerce platforms. *Research Journal of Engineering Sciences, 12*(9), 45–56. https://rjes.iq/index.php/rjes/article/download/99/106/900

Moody, J., Bailey, N., & Zhao, J. (2020). Public perceptions of autonomous vehicle safety : An international comparison. *Safety Science*, *121*, 634–650. DOI: 10.1016/j.ssci.2019.07.022

Moore, G. C., & Benbasat, I. (1991a). Development of an Instrument to Measure the Perceptions of Adopting an Information Technology Innovation. *Information Systems Research*, *2*(3), 192–222. DOI: 10.1287/isre.2.3.192

Mori, M. (1970). Bukimi no tani [The uncanny valley]. *Energy*, *7*, 33.

Moriuchi, E. (2021). An empirical study on anthropomorphism and engagement with disembodied AIs and consumers' re-use behavior. *Psychology and Marketing*, *38*(1), 21–42. DOI: 10.1002/mar.21407

Mostafa, R. B., & Kasamani, T. (2022). Antecedents and consequences of chatbot initial trust. *European Journal of Marketing*, *56*(6), 1748–1771. DOI: 10.1108/EJM-02-2020-0084

Mozafari, N., Weiger, W. H., & Hammerschmidt, M. (2022). Trust me, I'm a bot–repercussions of chatbot disclosure in different service frontline settings. *Journal of Service Management, 33*(2), 221–245. DOI: 10.1108/JOSM-10-2020-0380

Mulcahy, R. F., Riedel, A., Keating, B., Beatson, A., & Letheren, K. (2024). Avoiding excessive AI service agent anthropomorphism : Examining its role in delivering bad news. *Journal of Service Theory and Practice, 34*(1), 98–126. DOI: 10.1108/JSTP-04-2023-0118

Mun, Y. Y., Jackson, J. D., Park, J. S., & Probst, J. C. (2006). Understanding information technology acceptance by individual professionals: Toward an integrative view. *Information & Management, 43*(3), 350–363. DOI: 10.1016/j.im.2005.08.006

Muslichah, M. (2018). The effect of self efficacy and information quality on behavioral intention with perceived usefulness as intervening variable. *Journal of Accounting* [JABM]. *Business and Management, 25*(1), 21–34.

Mustafizul Haque. (2023). Impact of Influencer Marketing on Consumer Behavior : An Analytical Study. *Tuijin Jishu/Journal of Propulsion Technology, 44*(4), 3160–3166. DOI: 10.52783/tjjpt.v44.i4.1410

MyGlamm. (2025). *@myglamm*. Instagram.com. https://www.instagram.com/myglamm/

Myin, M. T., & Watchravesringkan, K. (2024). Investigating consumers' adoption of AI chatbots for apparel shopping. *Journal of Consumer Marketing, 41*(3), 314–327. DOI: 10.1108/JCM-03-2022-5234

Nadda, V. K., Dadwal, S. S., & Firdous, A. (2015). Social Media Marketing. In Hajli, N. (Ed.), *Handbook of Research on Integrating Social Media into Strategic Marketing* (pp. 359–379). IGI Global Scientific Publishing., DOI: 10.4018/978-1-4666-8353-2.ch021

Nadeem, W., Tan, T. M., Tajvidi, M., & Hajli, N. (2021). How do experiences enhance brand relationship performance and value co-creation in social commerce? The role of consumer engagement and self brand-connection. *Technological Forecasting and Social Change, 171*, 120952. DOI: 10.1016/j.techfore.2021.120952

Nanda, S. A (2020). Cognitive consonance between business intelligence and decision-making in Bancassurance. *Odisha journal of social science, 7*(2). Pp 8-26.

Närhi, A. (2024). Generative AI and consumer behaviour: A new era of personalisation and efficiency. *Horton International*. https://hortoninternational.com/generative-ai-and-consumer-behaviour-a-new-era-of-personalisation-and-efficiency/

Na, S., Heo, S., Han, S., Shin, Y., & Roh, Y. (2022). Acceptance model of artificial intelligence (AI)-based technologies in construction firms : Applying the Technology Acceptance Model (TAM) in combination with the Technology–Organisation–Environment (TOE) framework. *Buildings (Basel, Switzerland), 12*(2), 90. DOI: 10.3390/buildings12020090

Nass, C., Moon, Y., & Green, N. (1997). Are Machines Gender Neutral? Gender-Stereotypic Responses to Computers With Voices. *Journal of Applied Social Psychology*, 27(10), 864 876. DOI: 10.1111/j.1559-1816.1997.tb00275.x

Nass, C., & Moon, Y. (2000). Machines and Mindlessness : Social Responses to Computers. *The Journal of Social Issues, 56*(1), 81–103. DOI: 10.1111/0022-4537.00153

Naveeenkumar, N., Rallapalli, S., Sasikala, K., Priya, P. V., Husain, J., & Boopathi, S. (2024). Enhancing Consumer Behavior and Experience Through AI-Driven Insights Optimization. In *AI impacts in digital consumer behavior* (pp. 1–35). IGI Global. DOI: 10.4018/979-8-3693-1918-5.ch001

Nazir, S., Khadim, S., Ali Asadullah, M., & Syed, N. (2023). Exploring the influence of artificial intelligence technology on consumer repurchase intention: The mediation and moderation approach. *Technology in Society*, *72*, 102190. 10.1016/j.techsoc.2022.102190. DOI: 10.1016/j.techsoc.2022.102190

Nguyen, T. H., & Le, X. C. (2025). Artificial intelligence-based chatbots – a motivation underlying sustainable development in banking : Standpoint of customer experience and behavioral outcomes. *Cogent Business & Management, 12*(1), 2443570. DOI: 10.1080/23311975.2024.2443570

Nguyen, T. H., Trivedi, R. H., Fukukawa, K., & Adomako, S. (2025). Investigating Drivers of Customer Experience with Virtual Conversational Agents. *Information Systems Frontiers, 27*(5), 1871–1897. Advance online publication. DOI: 10.1007/s10796-024-10572-0

Nicolescu, L., & Tudorache, M. T. (2022). Human-Computer Interaction in Customer Service : The Experience with AI Chatbots—A Systematic Literature Review. *Electronics (Basel), 11*(10), 1579. DOI: 10.3390/electronics11101579

Noble, S. M., & Mende, M. (2023). The future of artificial intelligence and robotics in the retail and service sector : Sketching the field of consumer-robot-experiences. *Journal of the Academy of Marketing Science, 51*(4), 747–756. DOI: 10.1007/s11747-023-00948-0 PMID: 37359262

Nogueira, E., Lopes, J. M., & Gomes, S. (2025). *The new era of Artificial Intelligence in consumption: theoretical framing, review and research agenda*. Management Review Quarterly., DOI: 10.1007/s11301-025-00531-7

Nordheim, C. B., Følstad, A., & Bjørkli, C. A. (2019). An Initial Model of Trust in Chatbots for Customer Service—Findings from a Questionnaire Study. *Interacting with Computers*, 31(3), 317 335. DOI: 10.1093/iwc/iwz022

Norzelan, N. A., Mohamed, I. S., & Mohamad, M. (2024). Technology acceptance of artificial intelligence (AI) among heads of finance and accounting units in the shared service industry. *Technological Forecasting and Social Change*, *198*, 123022. DOI: 10.1016/j.techfore.2023.123022

Nouhaila, B. K., Aarabe, M., & Alla, L. (2024). The impact of digitalisation on the customer experience in medical tourism : A systematic review. *Impact of AI and tech-driven solutions in hospitality and tourism*, 408 428.

Nouhaila, B. K., Aarabe, M., & Alla, L. (2024). The impact of digitalisation on the customer experience in medical tourism : A systematic review. *Impact of AI and tech-driven solutions in hospitality and tourism*, 408-428.

Novak, T. P., & Hoffman, D. L. (2019). Relationship journeys in the internet of things : A new framework for understanding interactions between consumers and smart objects. *Journal of the Academy of Marketing Science*, 47(2), 216 237. DOI: 10.1007/s11747-018-0608-3

Nunnally, J. C., & Bernstein, I. H. (1994). The Assessment of Reliability. Psychometric Theory, 3, 248-292. Nyhan, RC, and HA Marlowe.(1997). Development And Psychometric Properties Of The Organizational Trust Inventory. *Evaluation Review*, *21*(5), 614–635.

Nykaa Cosmetics. (n.d.). *Nykaa Cosmetics (@nykaacosmetics)*. Instagram.com. https://www.instagram.com/nykaacosmetics/

O'Dea, M. (2025). Are Technology Acceptance Models still fit for purpose? *Journal of University Teaching & Learning Practice*, *21*(08). Advance online publication. http://open-publishing.org/journals/index.php/jutlp/article/view/1157. DOI: 10.53761/1bdbms32

Ocxas, J. J. A., Martin, F. K. C., & Junes, A. N. H. (2024). AI Chatbot with Emotional Recognition for an Improved Customer Service Experience. *2024 IEEE XXXI International Conference on Electronics, Electrical Engineering and Computing (INTERCON)*, 1-8. DOI: 10.1109/INTERCON63140.2024.10833509

Oliveira, T., Faria, M., Thomas, M. A., & Popovič, A. (2014). Extending the understanding of mobile banking adoption : When UTAUT meets TTF and ITM. *International Journal of Information Management*, *34*(5), 689–703. DOI: 10.1016/j.ijinfomgt.2014.06.004

Olujimi, P. A., & Ade-Ibijola, A. (2023). NLP techniques for automating responses to customer queries : A systematic review. *Discover Artificial Intelligence*, *3*(1), 20. DOI: 10.1007/s44163-023-00065-5

Oluwadamilola, F. J., & Emmanuel, A. A. (2024). *A Systematic Review of Chatbot Model and chatbot technologies*. https://www.ieeesem.com/researchpaper/A_Systematic_Literature_Review_and_Existing_Challenges_of_Chatbot_Models.pdf

Omeish, F., Al, M., & Khair, N. (2024). Computers in Human Behavior Reports Investigating the impact of AI on improving customer experience through social media marketing : An analysis of Jordanian Millennials. *Computers in Human Behavior Reports*, *15*(July), 100464. DOI: 10.1016/j.chbr.2024.100464

Ostrom, A. L., Parasuraman, A., Bowen, D. E., Patrício, L., & Voss, C. A. (2015). Service research priorities in a rapidly changing context. *Journal of Service Research*, *18*(2), 127–159. DOI: 10.1177/1094670515576315

Owusu, P. R., Asiedu, E. P., Ji, J., & Sarpong, F. A. (2022). Innovation and evaluation of technology acceptance model (Tam) in S-commerce : A case of social media platforms in Ghana. *Journal of Computer and Communications*, *10*(3), 100–124. DOI: 10.4236/jcc.2022.103007

Oyeniyi, L. D., Ugochukwu, C. E., & Mhlongo, N. Z.Lawrence Damilare OyeniyiChinonye Esther UgochukwuNoluthando Zamanjomane Mhlongo. (2024). Implementing AI in banking customer service : A review of current trends and future applications. *International Journal of Science and Research Archive*, *11*(2), 1492–1509. DOI: 10.30574/ijsra.2024.11.2.0639

Ozdemir, M. A. (2021). Virtual reality (VR) and augmented reality (AR) technologies for accessibility and marketing in the tourism industry. In *ICT tools and applications for accessible tourism* (pp. 277-301). IGI Global.

Ozdemir, O., Kolfal, B., Messinger, P. R., & Rizvi, S. (2023). Human or virtual: How influencer type shapes brand attitudes. *Computers in Human Behavior*, *145*, 107771. DOI: 10.1016/j.chb.2023.107771

Padigar, M., Li, Y., & Manjunath, C. N. (2025). "Good" and "bad" frictions in customer experience : Conceptual foundations and implications. *Psychology and Marketing*, *42*(1), 21–43. DOI: 10.1002/mar.22111

Pagani, M., & Mirabello, A. (2011). The Influence of Personal and Social-Interactive Engagement in Social TV Web Sites. *International Journal of Electronic Commerce, 16*(2), 41–68. DOI: 10.2753/JEC1086-4415160203

Pantano, E., & Pizzi, G. (2020). Forecasting artificial intelligence on online customer assistance: Evidence from chatbot patents analysis. *Journal of Retailing and Consumer Services, 55*, 102096. DOI: 10.1016/j.jretconser.2020.102096

Pantano, E., Pizzi, G., Scarpi, D., & Dennis, C. (2021). Competing in the digital era: The role of augmented reality and virtual reality in retailing. *International Journal of Retail & Distribution Management, 49*(6), 786–803. DOI: 10.1108/IJRDM-07-2020-0272

Parasuraman, A. (2000). Technology Readiness Index (Tri) : A Multiple-Item Scale to Measure Readiness to Embrace New Technologies. *Journal of Service Research, 2*(4), 307–320. DOI: 10.1177/109467050024001

Park, G., Lee, S., & Chung, J. (2023). Do Anthropomorphic Chatbots Increase Counseling Satisfaction and Reuse Intention? The Moderated Mediation of Social Rapport and Social Anxiety. *Cyberpsychology, Behavior, and Social Networking*, 26(5), 357 365. DOI: 10.1089/cyber.2022.0157

Park, A., & Lee, S. B. (2024). Examining AI and Systemic Factors for Improved Chatbot Sustainability. *Journal of Computer Information Systems, 64*(6), 728–742. DOI: 10.1080/08874417.2023.2251416

Park, G., Chung, J., & Lee, S. (2024). Scope and limits of AI fundraisers : Moderated serial multiple mediation model between artificial emotions and willingness to donate via humanness and empathy. *Technological Forecasting and Social Change, 201*, 123211. DOI: 10.1016/j.techfore.2024.123211

Park, H., Jiang, S., Lee, O.-K. D., & Chang, Y. (2024). Exploring the Attractiveness of Service Robots in the Hospitality Industry: Analysis of Online Reviews. *Information Systems Frontiers, 26*(1), 41–61. DOI: 10.1007/s10796-021-10207-8

Pasquale, F. (2015). *The black box society: The secret algorithms that control money and information*. Harvard University Press. DOI: 10.4159/harvard.9780674736061

Patel, N., & Trivedi, S. (2020). Leveraging predictive modeling, machine learning personalization, NLP customer support, and AI chatbots to increase customer loyalty. *Empirical Quests for Management Essences, 3*(3), 1–24.

Patil, D. (2024). Artificial Intelligence In Retail And E-Commerce : Enhancing Customer Experience Through Personalization, Predictive Analytics, And Real-Time Engagement. *Predictive Analytics, And Real-Time Engagement (November 26, 2024)*. https://papers.ssrn.com/sol3/papers.cfm?abstract_id=5057420

Patil, R. K. S., Porapur, S. M., & Kagawade, S. (2024). "The role of ai-driven social media marketing in shaping consumer purchasing behaviour: An empirical analysis of personalization, predictive analytics, and engagement." *ITM Web of Conferences, 68*, 01032. https://doi.org/DOI: 10.1051/itmconf/20246801032

Pattanayak, S., Khan, S. U., Malik, F., & Shukla, V. K. (2023). Exploring the role of Instagram in Bollywood film promotion. *In 2023 International Conference on Computational Intelligence and Knowledge Economy (ICCIKE)* (pp. 478-483). IEEE. Pattanayak, S., Ullah Khan, S., Malik, F., & Khan, S. (2024). Pixelating Bollywood: Navigating media tech in Bollywood's digital shift. *Multidisciplinary Reviews, 7*(9), 2024188. https://doi.org/DOI: 10.1109/ICCIKE58312.2023.10131764

Pattanayak, S. K., Khan, S. U., Khan, S., & Srivastava, N. (2025). Evaluating the Impact of Bollywood's Promotional Strategies on Audience Engagement in the UAE. In Cantaş, A. (Ed.), *Audience Sociology and Consumer Behavior in the Film Industry* (pp. 57–102). IGI Global Scientific Publishing., DOI: 10.4018/979-8-3693-3104-0.ch003

Pattanayak, S., Khan, S. U., Malik, F., & Nayak, A. K. (2025). Cinematic color grading for optimizing AI multimedia content in film production and promotion. In Swaroop, A., Kansal, V., Fortino, G., & Hassanien, A. E. (Eds.), *Proceedings of Fifth Doctoral Symposium on Computational Intelligence. DoSCI 2023. Lecture Notes in Networks and Systems* (Vol. 1096, pp. 431–444). Springer. https://doi.org/DOI: 10.1007/978-981-97-7178-3_37

Pattanayak, S., Khan, S. U., Malik, F., & Sahoo, S. (2024). Automating camera movements: AI-driven PTZ cameras in film production. In Al Mubarak, M., & Hamdan, A. (Eds.), *Innovative and Intelligent Digital Technologies: Towards an increased efficiency. Studies in Systems, Decision and Control* (Vol. 564, pp. 627–639). Springer., DOI: 10.1007/978-3-031-70399-7_48

Paul, J., Ueno, A., & Dennis, C. (2023). ChatGPTand consumers: Benefits, Pitfalls and Future Research Agenda. *International Journal of Consumer Studies, 47*(4), 1213–1225. DOI: 10.1111/ijcs.12928

Phan, Q. P. T., Pham, N. T., & Nguyen, L. H. L. (2020). How to Drive Brand Engagement and eWOM Intention in Social Commerce: A Competitive Strategy for the Emerging Market. *Journal of Competitiveness, 12*(3), 136–155. DOI: 10.7441/joc.2020.03.08

Picard, R. W. (1997). *Affective computing*. MIT Press. DOI: 10.7551/mitpress/1140.001.0001

Pillai, R., & Sivathanu, B. (2020). Adoption of AI-based chatbots for hospitality and tourism. *International Journal of Contemporary Hospitality Management, 32*(10), 3199–3226. DOI: 10.1108/IJCHM-04-2020-0259

Pillarisetty, R., & Mishra, P. (2022). A review of AI (artificial intelligence) tools and customer experience in online fashion retail. [IJEBR]. *International Journal of E-Business Research, 18*(2), 1–12. DOI: 10.4018/IJEBR.294111

Plassmann, H., Venkatraman, V., Huettel, S., & Yoon, C. (2012). Consumer neuroscience: Applications, challenges, and possible solutions. *JMR, Journal of Marketing Research, 49*(4), 427–435. DOI: 10.1509/jmr.14.0048

Pletikosa Cvijikj, I., & Michahelles, F. (2013). Online engagement factors on Facebook brand pages. *Social Network Analysis and Mining, 3*(4), 843–861. DOI: 10.1007/s13278-013-0098-8

Podsakoff, P. M., MacKenzie, S. B., Lee, J.-Y., & Podsakoff, N. P. (2003). Common method biases in behavioral research : A critical review of the literature and recommended remedies. *The Journal of Applied Psychology, 88*(5), 879–903. DOI: 10.1037/0021-9010.88.5.879 PMID: 14516251

Poria, S., Cambria, E., Bajpai, R., & Hussain, A. (2017). A review of affective computing: From unimodal analysis to multimodal fusion. *Information Fusion, 37*, 98–125. DOI: 10.1016/j.inffus.2017.02.003

Portz, J. D., Bayliss, E. A., Bull, S., Boxer, R. S., Bekelman, D. B., Gleason, K., & Czaja, S. (2019). Using the Technology Acceptance Model to Explore User Experience, Intent to Use, and Use Behavior of a Patient Portal Among Older Adults With Multiple Chronic Conditions : Descriptive Qualitative Study. *Journal of Medical Internet Research, 21*(4), e11604. DOI: 10.2196/11604 PMID: 30958272

Prabha, D., & Subramanian, R. S. (2017, January). A survey on customer relationship management. *In 2017 4th International Conference on Advanced Computing and Communication Systems (ICACCS)* (pp. 1-5). IEEE.

Prabhu, D., Tejasri, M. V. S. L., Saratha, B., & Anish, T. P. (2025, April). Future Horizons: Key Trends Shaping the Evolution of Machine Learning. In *2025 8th International Conference on Trends in Electronics and Informatics (ICOEI)* (pp. 1091-1099). IEEE.

Press, G. (2024, May 1). *AI Influencer market will grow up to $6.95 billion U.S. Dollars in 2024.* What's the Big Data? https://whatsthebigdata.com/ai-influencer-statistics/

Priest, D. (2024). AI is becoming ingrained in businesses across industries. Where is it going in 2025? *Associated Press.* https://apnews.com/article/ai-future-business-trends-2025

Przegalinska, A., Ciechanowski, L., Stroz, A., Gloor, P., & Mazurek, G. (2019). In bot we trust : A new methodology of chatbot performance measures. *Business Horizons, 62*(6), 785–797. DOI: 10.1016/j.bushor.2019.08.005

Purusottama, A. & Simatupang, T.M. (2025). Adoption of blockchain technology in promoting halal compliance, *Journal of Islamic Marketing*, Vol. ahead-of-print No. ahead-of-print. DOI: 10.1108/JIMA-12-2023-0423

Puschmann, C., & Bastos, M. (2015). How digital are the digital publics? Sampling, validity and report bias in social media data. In Sloan, L., & Quan-Haase, A. (Eds.), *The SAGE handbook of social media research methods* (pp. 75–88). SAGE.

PWC. (2018). Whom do consumers really trust? available at: https://www.pwc.com/gx/en/industries/ consumer-markets/consumer-insights-survey/consumer-trust.html

Rafique, H., Almagrabi, A. O., Shamim, A., Anwar, F., & Bashir, A. K. (2020). Investigating the acceptance of mobile library applications with an extended technology acceptance model (TAM). *Computers & Education, 145*, 103732. DOI: 10.1016/j.compedu.2019.103732

Ragheb, M. A., Tantawi, P., Farouk, N., & Hatata, A. (2022). Investigating the acceptance of applying chat-bot (Artificial intelligence) technology among higher education students in Egypt. *International Journal of Higher Education Management, 8*(2). Advance online publication. https://www.academia.edu/download/96162300/2022-02-28-20-55-56-PM.pdf. DOI: 10.24052/IJHEM/V08N02/ART-1

Ramesh, P., Nithyanandhan, R., Faizal, M. M., Nivakumar, V., & Nalini, M. (2024, December). Machine Learning Strategies for Customer Churn Prediction in Competitive Enterprises. In *2024 International Conference on Sustainable Communication Networks and Application (ICSCNA)* (pp. 653-660). IEEE. DOI: 10.1109/ICSCNA63714.2024.10864143

Ranieri, A., Di Bernardo, I., & Mele, C. (2024). Serving customers through chatbots : Positive and negative effects on customer experience. *Journal of Service Theory and Practice, 34*(2), 191–215. DOI: 10.1108/JSTP-01-2023-0015

Rapp, A., Beitelspacher, L. S., Grewal, D., & Hughes, D. E. (2013). Understanding social media effects across seller, retailer, and consumer interactions. *Journal of the Academy of Marketing Science, 41*(5), 547–566. DOI: 10.1007/s11747-013-0326-9

Rashid, A. B., & Kausik, M. A. K. (2024). AI revolutionizing industries worldwide : A comprehensive overview of its diverse applications. *Hybrid Advances, 7*, 100277. DOI: 10.1016/j.hybadv.2024.100277

Rashid, R. M., Pitafi, A. H., Qureshi, M. A., & Sharma, A. (2022). Role of Social Commerce Constructs and Social Presence as Moderator on Consumers' Buying Intentions During COVID-19. *Frontiers in Psychology, 13*, 772028. DOI: 10.3389/fpsyg.2022.772028 PMID: 35222183

Rathee, R., & Monika, . (2025). From Businesses-Centric to Consumers-Centric: A Shift of Power in AI-Driven Social Media. *Marketing, 5*(0), 89–102. DOI: 10.1108/978-1-83797-815-120251007

Rawat, A. (2024, September 5). *How AR VR is shaping the food and beverages industry – 10 use cases and real examples.* Appinventiv. https://appinventiv.com/blog/ar-vr-in-food-and-beverages/

Redhika, R., & Mahalli, K. (2014). Analisis Potensi dan Kendala Pengembangan Asuransi Syariah di Kota Medan (potential analysis and constraints of Islamic insurance development in medan). *Jurnal Ekonomi DanKeuangan, 2*(5), 323–335.

Relan, M., & Kumar, M. (2023). Impact of Trust and Risk Factors on the Satisfaction Level of the Policy Holder towards Digital Bancassurance Model. [IRJMSH]. *International Research Journal of Management Sociology & Humanity, 14*(7), 15–24.

Repositório do Iscte – Instituto Universitário de Lisboa: The influence and impact of artificial intelligence in the consumer decision-making process: Comparing Generation X with Millennials. (n.d.). Retrieved May 1, 2025, from https://repositorio.iscte-iul.pt/handle/10071/21828?locale=en

Rese, A., Ganster, L., & Baier, D. (2020). Chatbots in retailers' customer communication : How to measure their acceptance? *Journal of Retailing and Consumer Services, 56*, 102176. DOI: 10.1016/j.jretconser.2020.102176

Research, G. M. I. (2024, December 16). *India Cosmetic Market Size, Share & Industry Forecast 2032*. GMI Research. https://www.gmiresearch.com/report/india-cosmetic-market/

Restianto, Y. E., Suliyanto, S., Naufalin, L. R., Krisnaresanti, A., Dinanti, A., Iskandar, D., & Sugiyono, S. (2024). User experience and behavioral intention to use e-commerce : A study of digital literacy as a moderating variable. *Journal of Governance and Regulation*, *13*(1), 8–17. DOI: 10.22495/jgrv13i1art1

Rezaei, S., & Amin, M. (2013). Exploring online repurchase behavioural intention of university students in Malaysia. *J. for Global Business Advancement*, *6*(2), 92. DOI: 10.1504/JGBA.2013.053561

Rishika, R., Kumar, A., Janakiraman, R., & Bezawada, R. (2013). The Effect of Customers' Social Media Participation on Customer Visit Frequency and Profitability: An Empirical Investigation. *Information Systems Research*, *24*(1), 108–127. DOI: 10.1287/isre.1120.0460

Rizomyliotis, I., Kastanakis, M. N., Giovanis, A., Konstantoulaki, K., & Kostopoulos, I. (2022). "How mAy I help you today?" The use of AI chatbots in small family businesses and the moderating role of customer affective commitment. *Journal of Business Research*, *153*, 329–340. DOI: 10.1016/j.jbusres.2022.08.035

Rogers, E. M. (1962). *Diffusion of innovations. New York : Free Press—Recherche Google*. (s. d.). Consulté 12 avril 2025, à l'adresse

Rogers, E. M. (1995). *Diffusion of Innovations*. https://scholar.google.com/scholar?hl=fr&as_sdt=0%2C5&q=Rogers%2C+E.M.+%281995%29%2C+Diffusion+of+Innovations+%284th+Ed.%29%2C+The+Free+Press%2C+New+York%2C+NY.&btnG=

Rogers, E. M. (2003). *Diffusion of Innovations* (5th ed.). Simon and Schuster.

Rose, S., Clark, M., Samouel, P., & Hair, N. (2012). Online Customer Experience in e-Retailing : An empirical model of Antecedents and Outcomes. *Journal of Retailing*, *88*(2), 308–322. DOI: 10.1016/j.jretai.2012.03.001

Ross, T., May, A., & Cockbill, S. A. (2020). The personal and contextual factors that affect customer experience during rail service failures and the implications for service design. *Applied Ergonomics*, *86*, 103096. DOI: 10.1016/j.apergo.2020.103096 PMID: 32342887

Rowley, J. (2008). Understanding Digital Content Marketing. *Journal of Marketing Management*, *24*(5-6), 5–6, 517–540. DOI: 10.1362/026725708X325977

Roy, R., & Naidoo, V. (2021). Enhancing chatbot effectiveness : The role of anthropomorphic conversational styles and time orientation. *Journal of Business Research*, 126, 23 34. DOI: 10.1016/j.jbusres.2020.12.051

Rudeloff, C. (2023). *AI-Driven Influencer Marketing : Comparing the Effects of Virtual and Human Influencers on Consumer Perceptions AI-driven influencer marketing : Comparing the effects of virtual and human influencers on consumer perceptions. April.* DOI: 10.2139/ssrn.4404372

Saheb, T., Sidaoui, M., & Schmarzo, B. (2024). Convergence of artificial intelligence with social media: A bibliometric & qualitative analysis. *Telematics and Informatics Reports, 14*, 100146. 10.1016/j.teler.2024.100146

Sahin, I. (2006). Detailed Review of Rogers' Diffusion of Innovations Theory and Educational Technology-Related Studies Based on Rogers' Theory. *Turkish Online Journal of Educational Technology - TOJET, 5*(2), 14-23.

Sahut, J.-M., & Laroche, M. (2025). Using artificial intelligence (AI) to enhance customer experience and to develop strategic marketing: An integrative synthesis. *Computers in Human Behavior, 170*, 108684. 10.1016/j.chb.2025.108684. DOI: 10.1016/j.chb.2025.108684

Salem, M. (2024). Use of chatbots and its role in enhancing customer experience : A Study of the banking industry. In *Digital technology and changing roles in managerial and financial accounting : Theoretical knowledge and practical application* (pp. 107 114). Emerald Publishing Limited. https://www.emerald.com/insight/content/doi/10.1108/S147935122024000036010/full/html

Salem, M. (2024). Use of chatbots and its role in enhancing customer experience : A Study of the banking industry. In *Digital technology and changing roles in managerial and financial accounting : Theoretical knowledge and practical application* (pp. 107–114). Emerald Publishing Limited., https://www.emerald.com/insight/content/doi/10.1108/S1479-351220240000036010/full/html DOI: 10.1108/S1479-351220240000036010

San Martín, H., & Herrero, Á. (2012). Influence of the user's psychological factors on the online purchase intention in rural tourism : Integrating innovativeness to the UTAUT framework. *Tourism Management, 33*(2), 341–350. DOI: 10.1016/j.tourman.2011.04.003

Sands, S., Ferraro, C., Campbell, C., & Tsao, H.-Y. (2021). Managing the human–chatbot divide : How service scripts influence service experience. *Journal of Service Management, 32*(2), 246–264. DOI: 10.1108/JOSM-06-2019-0203

Saoud, L. S., & Romman, A. A. (2024). AI-Powered Chatbots in the Telecommunications Industry in the UAE : Studying the Factors Impacting Consumer Adoption. *2024 15th International Conference on Information and Communication Technology Convergence (ICTC)*, 1549-1553. https://ieeexplore.ieee.org/abstract/document/10827670/?casa_token=0tZCraF5fxEAAAAA:Q-hdlPue7xS7bsY1Bs_H08roFE66lsLDGNTtLNjFIRggA__Z70znAZCnejNQ59JtvpGMeGnDSr7lNJs

Sarkar, J. L., Majumder, A., Panigrahi, C. R., & Roy, S. (2020). MULTITOUR: A multiple itinerary tourists recommendation engine. *Electronic Commerce Research and Applications*, *40*, 100943. DOI: 10.1016/j.elerap.2020.100943

Sarkar, J. L., Majumder, A., Panigrahi, C. R., Roy, S., & Pati, B. (2023). Tourism recommendation system: A survey and future research directions. *Multimedia Tools and Applications*, *82*(6), 8983–9027. DOI: 10.1007/s11042-022-12167-w

Sayed, D., & Abutaleb, S. (2025). Anthropomorphic chatbots as a catalyst for online customer experience (CX) : The case of Egyptian consumers. *Journal of Marketing Communications*, •••, 1–15. DOI: 10.1080/13527266.2025.2453229

Sboui, M., Baati, O., & Sfar, N. (2024). Influencing factors and consequences of chatbot initial trust in AI telecommunication services : A study on Generation Z. *The TQM Journal*. Advance online publication. DOI: 10.1108/TQM-02-2024-0085

Schivinski, B., & Dabrowski, D. (2016). The effect of social media communication on consumer perceptions of brands. *Journal of Marketing Communications*, *22*(2), 189–214. DOI: 10.1080/13527266.2013.871323

Schouten, A. P., Janssen, L., & Verspaget, M. (2019). Celebrity vs. Influencer endorsements in advertising: The role of identification, credibility, and Product-Endorser fit. *International Journal of Advertising*, •••, 24.

Schumann, J. H., von Wangenheim, F., & Groene, N. (2014). Targeted online advertising: Using reciprocity appeals to increase acceptance among users of free web services. *Journal of Marketing*, *78*(1), 59–75. DOI: 10.1509/jm.11.0316

Schwarz, N., & Clore, G. L. (2007). Feelings and phenomenal experiences. In Kruglanski, A. W., & Higgins, E. T. (Eds.), *Social Psychology: Handbook of Basic Principles* (2nd ed., pp. 385–407). Guilford Press.

Scott, J. (2017). *Social network analysis* (4th ed.). SAGE Publications. DOI: 10.4135/9781529716597

Selamat, M. A., & Windasari, N. A. (2021). Chatbot for SMEs : Integrating customer and business owner perspectives. *Technology in Society*, *66*, 101685. DOI: 10.1016/j.techsoc.2021.101685

Selem, K. M., Islam, M. S., Aureliano-Silva, L., & Shehata, A. E. (2023). Nexus of customer adaptation to mannequins with visit intention to full-service restaurants : Role of spatial layout. *International Journal of Hospitality Management, 115*, 103608. DOI: 10.1016/j.ijhm.2023.103608

Sestino, A., Prete, M. I., Piper, L., & Guido, G. (2020). Internet of Things and Big Data as enablers for business digitalization strategies. *Technovation, 98*, 102173. DOI: 10.1016/j.technovation.2020.102173

Sfar, N., Sboui, M., & Baati, O. (2025). The impact of chatbot anthropomorphism on customer experience and chatbot usage intention : A technology acceptance approach. *International Journal of Quality and Service Sciences, 17*(2), 168–194. Advance online publication. DOI: 10.1108/IJQSS-06-2024-0079

Shachak, A., Kuziemsky, C., & Petersen, C. (2019). Beyond TAM and UTAUT : Future directions for HIT implementation research. *Journal of Biomedical Informatics, 100*, 103315. DOI: 10.1016/j.jbi.2019.103315 PMID: 31629923

Shafqat, W., & Byun, Y. C. (2019). A recommendation mechanism for under-emphasized tourist spots using topic modeling and sentiment analysis. *Sustainability (Basel), 12*(1), 320. DOI: 10.3390/su12010320

Shah, N., & Malik, P. (2025, March 25). *Instagram Reels Algorithm: 5 Best Practices to Stay Ahead*. Sprinklr.com; Sprinklr. https://www.sprinklr.com/blog/instagram-reels-algorithm/

Sharma, M., Joshi, S., Luthra, S., & Kumar, A. (2024). Impact of Digital Assistant Attributes on Millennials' Purchasing Intentions: A Multi-Group Analysis using PLS-SEM, Artificial Neural Network and fsQCA. *Information Systems Frontiers, 26*(3), 943–966. DOI: 10.1007/s10796-022-10339-5 PMID: 36185777

Sheehan, B., Jin, H. S., & Gottlieb, U. (2020). Customer service chatbots : Anthropomorphism and adoption. *Journal of Business Research*, 115, 14 24. DOI: 10.1016/j.jbusres.2020.04.030

Shen, B., & Bissell, K. (2013). Social Media, Social Me: A Content Analysis of Beauty Companies' Use of Facebook in Marketing and Branding. *Journal of Promotion Management, 19*(5), 629–651. DOI: 10.1080/10496491.2013.829160

Sheth, J. N., Jain, V., Roy, G., & Chakraborty, A. (2022). AI-driven banking services : The next frontier for a personalised experience in the emerging market. *International Journal of Bank Marketing, 40*(6), 1248–1271. DOI: 10.1108/IJBM-09-2021-0449

Shi, B., & Wang, H. (2023). An AI-enabled approach for improving advertising identification and promotion in social networks. *Technological Forecasting and Social Change*, *188*(122269), 122269. DOI: 10.1016/j.techfore.2022.122269

Shin, H., Bunosso, I., & Levine, L. R. (2023). The influence of chatbot humour on consumer evaluations of services. *International Journal of Consumer Studies*, *47*(2), 545–562. DOI: 10.1111/ijcs.12849

Shoetan, P. O., & Babajide, T. F.Philip Olaseni ShoetanBabajide Tolulope Familoni. (2024). Transforming fintech fraud detection with advanced artificial intelligence algorithms. *Finance & Accounting Research Journal*, *6*(4), 602–625. DOI: 10.51594/farj.v6i4.1036

Shomad, A. (2025). Liability of Islamic Banks in Bancassurance Activities. *Journal of Law and Regulation Governance*, *3*(1), 435–445.

Shrey. (2025, January 25). *The evolution of virtual and augmented reality: What's next in AR and VR technology?* Nextbrick, Inc. https://nextbrick.com/the-evolution-of-virtual-and-augmented-reality-whats-next-in-ar-and-vr-technology-2/

Singh, M. R., Bala, D. P., & Jain, D. A. (2025). AI Driven Advertisement Transforming Consumer Behavior in Digital Era. Available at *SSRN* 5239003.

Singh, P. (2025). *Leveraging AI for Real-Time Customer Support in Telecommunications*. https://www.techrxiv.org/doi/full/10.36227/techrxiv.174952654.43690912 DOI: 10.36227/techrxiv.174952654.43690912/v1

Siva Subramanian, R., Maheswari, B., Nikkath Bushra, S., Nirmala, G., & Anita, M. (2023). Enhancing Customer Prediction Using Machine Learning with Feature Selection Approaches. In *Inventive Computation and Information Technologies* [Singapore: Springer Nature Singapore.]. *Proceedings of ICICIT, 2022*, 45–57.

Siva Subramanian, R., Nalini, M., & Aswini, J. (Eds.). (2024). *Navigating the Augmented and Virtual Frontiers in Engineering*. IGI Global. DOI: 10.4018/979-8-3693-5613-5

Skjuve, M., Haugstveit, I. M., Følstad, A., & Brandtzaeg, P. (2019). Help! Is my chatbot falling into the uncanny valley? An empirical study of user experience in human–chatbot interaction. *Human Technology*, *15*(1), 30–54. DOI: 10.17011/ht/urn.201902201607

Slater, M., & Wilbur, S. (1997). A framework for immersive virtual environments (FIVE). *Presence (Cambridge, Mass.)*, *6*(6), 603–625. DOI: 10.1162/pres.1997.6.6.603

Smale, M. C., Fox, J. D., & Fox, A. K. (2024). When being smart trumps AI: An exploration into consumer preferences for smart vs. AI-powered products. *Computers in Human Behavior, 161*, 108405. 10.1016/j.chb.2024.108405. DOI: 10.1016/j.chb.2024.108405

Sodiya, E. O., Amoo, O. O., Umoga, U. J., Atadoga, A., Sodiya, E. O., Amoo, O. O., Umoga, U. J., & Atadoga, A. (2024). AI-driven personalization in web content delivery : A comparative study of user engagement in the USA and the UK. *World Journal of Advanced Research and Reviews, 21*(2), 887–902. DOI: 10.30574/wjarr.2024.21.2.0502

Sojahrood, Z. B., Taleai, M., & Cheng, H. (2023). Hybrid POI group recommender system based on group type in LBSN. *Expert Systems with Applications, 219*, 119681. DOI: 10.1016/j.eswa.2023.119681

Sokolova, K., Vessal, S. R., & Perez, C. (2024). Home cooking in the digital age: When observing food influencers on social media triggers the imitation of their practices. *Psychology and Marketing, 41*(5), 1152–1171. DOI: 10.1002/mar.21973

Soltis, T. (2013). Social media impact on virtual shopping. *Senior Honors Theses and Projects*. https://commons.emich.edu/honors/358

Song, C. S., & Kim, Y.-K. (2022). The role of the human-robot interaction in consumers' acceptance of humanoid retail service robots. *Journal of Business Research, 146*, 489–503. DOI: 10.1016/j.jbusres.2022.03.087

Song, S. W., & Shin, M. (2024). Uncanny Valley Effects on Chatbot Trust, Purchase Intention, and Adoption Intention in the Context of E-Commerce : The Moderating Role of Avatar Familiarity. *International Journal of Human-Computer Interaction, 40*(2), 441–456. DOI: 10.1080/10447318.2022.2121038

Song, X., Gu, H., Li, Y., Leung, X. Y., & Ling, X. (2024). The influence of robot anthropomorphism and perceived intelligence on hotel guests' continuance usage intention. *Information Technology & Tourism, 26*(1), 89–117. DOI: 10.1007/s40558-023-00275-8

Soni, N., Sharma, E. K., Singh, N., & Kapoor, A. (2019). *Impact of Artificial Intelligence on Businesses: From Research, Innovation, Market Deployment to Future Shifts in Business Models* (Version 1). arXiv. DOI: 10.48550/ARXIV.1905.02092

Sorescu, A. (2017). Data-driven business model innovation. *Journal of Product Innovation Management, 34*(5), 691–696. DOI: 10.1111/jpim.12398

Sorosrungruang, T., Ameen, N., & Hackley, C. (2024). How real is real enough? Unveiling the diverse power of generative AI-enabled virtual influencers and the dynamics of human responses. *Psychology and Marketing*, *41*(12), 3124–3143. DOI: 10.1002/mar.22105

Spais, G., & Jain, V. (2025). Consumer Behavior's Evolution, Emergence, and Future in the AI Age Through the Lens of MR, VR, XR, Metaverse, and Robotics. *Journal of Consumer Behaviour*, cb.2468. DOI: 10.1002/cb.2468

Srivastava, A., & Malik, P. (2024, November 11). *Social Media Visuals: Types, Impact and Strategy for Brands*. Sprinklr.com; Sprinklr. https://www.sprinklr.com/blog/social-media-visuals/

Srivastava, N., Sachdev, M., Gwalani, M., Bajpai, M., Khan, S. U., Arora, M., & Arora, P. (2025). Women-Centric AI: A Step Towards Empowerment. In Misra, S. (Eds.), *Human-Centric AI in Digital Transformation and Entrepreneurship* (pp. 89–108). IGI Global Scientific Publishing., DOI: 10.4018/979-8-3693-8009-3.ch005

Stafford, R. Q. (2013). The contribution of people's attitudes and perceptions to the acceptance of eldercare robots [PhD Thesis, University of Auckland]. https://www.researchgate.net/profile/Rebecca-Stafford

Statista. (2020). Global insurance companies' digital technology investment priorities worldwide 2020.

Stieglitz, S., Dang-Xuan, L., Bruns, A., & Neuberger, C. (2014). Social media analytics: An interdisciplinary approach and its implications for information systems. *Business & Information Systems Engineering*, *6*(2), 89–96. DOI: 10.1007/s12599-014-0315-7

Storhannus, M. (2021). *Consumer perception of foreign cosmetic advertisements: A cross-cultural study of creating trust with social media advertising*. Www.doria.fi. https://www.doria.fi/handle/10024/180908

Storyclash. (2023, August 29). *Top 10 Virtual Influencers Rocking the Fashion Industry*. Storyclash. https://www.storyclash.com/blog/en/virtual-influencers/

Storyclash. (2023, August 29). *Top 10 VIs Rocking the Fashion Industry*. Storyclash. https://www.storyclash.com/blog/en/virtual-influencers/

Stroessner, S. J., & Benitez, J. (2019). The Social Perception of Humanoid and Non-Humanoid Robots : Effects of Gendered and Machinelike Features. *International Journal of Social Robotics*, 11(2), 305 315. DOI: 10.1007/s12369-018-0502-7

Sudha, K., Anish, T. P., Balakrishnan, C., Lakumarapu, S., Pajila, P. B., & Subramanian, R. S. (2023). Leveraging Machine Learning for Customer Intelligence: An Experimental Analysis Learning Classifiers. *Procedia Computer Science*, *230*, 128–137. DOI: 10.1016/j.procs.2023.12.068

Sugar Cosmetics. (2020). *@trysugar*. Instagram.com. https://www.instagram.com/trysugar/

Sukrat, S., & Papasratorn, B. (2018). An architectural framework for developing a recommendation system to enhance vendors' capability in C2C social commerce. *Social Network Analysis and Mining*, *8*(1), 22. DOI: 10.1007/s13278-018-0500-7

Sumarjan, N., Mazlan, N., Saiful Azmi, N. S., Kamaruddin, M. A., & Salleh, A. (2023). The usage intention of chatbot technology in hospitality and tourism industry : Customers' perspective. *Journal of Tourism. Hospitality and Culinary Arts*, *15*(1), 206–224.

Sun, H., Zafar, M. Z., & Hasan, N. (2022). Employing Natural Language Processing as Artificial Intelligence for Analyzing Consumer Opinion Toward Advertisement. *Frontiers in Psychology*, *13*, 856663. Advance online publication. DOI: 10.3389/fpsyg.2022.856663 PMID: 35769737

Susser, D., Roessler, B., & Nissenbaum, H. (2019). Online manipulation: Hidden influences in a digital world. *SSRN*, *4*(1), 1–45. DOI: 10.2139/ssrn.3306006

Suta, P., Lan, X., Wu, B., Mongkolnam, P., & Chan, J. H. (2020). An overview of machine learning in chatbots. *International Journal of Mechanical Engineering and Robotics Research*, *9*(4), 502–510. DOI: 10.18178/ijmerr.9.4.502-510

Suzić, N., Forza, C., Trentin, A., & Anišić, Z. (2018). Implementation guidelines for mass customization: Current characteristics and suggestions for improvement. *Production Planning and Control*, *29*(10), 1–16. DOI: 10.1080/09537287.2018.1485983

Tafesse, W., & Wood, B. P. (2021). Followers' engagement with Instagram influencers: The role of influencers' content and engagement strategy. *Journal of Retailing and Consumer Services*, *58*, 102303. DOI: 10.1016/j.jretconser.2020.102303

Talreja, M., & Chaturvedi, V. (2024). *The Role of Social Media Influencers in Advertising Cosmetic Brands: A Study on Instagram*. https://www.mcu.ac.in/jpra/2024/Volume-3-Issue-2-July-December-2024/07-jpra-volume-3-issue-2-july-december-2024.pdf

Tamilmani, K., Rana, N. P., & Dwivedi, Y. K. (2021). Consumer Acceptance and Use of Information Technology : A Meta-Analytic Evaluation of UTAUT2. *Information Systems Frontiers*, *23*(4), 987–1005. DOI: 10.1007/s10796-020-10007-6

Tang, Y. M., Wong, J. K. N., & Ho, G. T. S. (2025). Exploring Consumer Acceptance of Metaverse Marketing for Branding Activities and the Pre-Purchase Stage. *Journal of Theoretical and Applied Electronic Commerce Research*, *20*(3), 159. DOI: 10.3390/jtaer20030159

Tao, Q., & Xu, Y. (2018). Understanding consumers' adoption of subscription fashion retailing: The role of perceived value and innovation. *Journal of Fashion Marketing and Management*, *22*(1), 22–38. DOI: 10.1108/JFMM-10-2016-0087

Teepapal, T. (2025). AI-driven personalization: Unraveling consumer perceptions in social media engagement. *Computers in Human Behavior*, *165*, 108549. 10.1016/j.chb.2024.108549. DOI: 10.1016/j.chb.2024.108549

Thakur, N., & Aditya, A. (2024). International Journal of Research Publication and Reviews. SSRN *Electronic Journal*, *5*(11), 2388–2390. DOI: 10.2139/ssrn.4991412

Thomaz, F., Salge, C., Karahanna, E., & Hulland, J. (2020). Learning from the Dark Web : Leveraging conversational agents in the era of hyper-privacy to enhance marketing. *Journal of the Academy of Marketing Science*, *48*(1), 43–63. DOI: 10.1007/s11747-019-00704-3

Tiago, M. T. P. M. B., & Veríssimo, J. M. C. (2014). Digital marketing and social media: Why bother? *Business Horizons*, *57*(6), 703–708. DOI: 10.1016/j.bushor.2014.07.002

Tian, W., Ge, J., Zhao, Y., & Zheng, X. (2024). AI Chatbots in Chinese higher education : Adoption, perception, and influence among graduate students—an integrated analysis utilizing UTAUT and ECM models. *Frontiers in Psychology*, *15*, 1268549. DOI: 10.3389/fpsyg.2024.1268549 PMID: 38384353

Timimi, H., Baaddi, M., & Bennouna, A. (2025). Impact of artificial intelligence on the personalization of the customer experience: A systematic literature review. *Multidisciplinary Reviews*, *8*(7), 2025224. Advance online publication. DOI: 10.31893/multirev.2025224

Topsakal, Y. (2024). How Familiarity, Ease of Use, Usefulness, and Trust Influence the Acceptance of Generative Artificial Intelligence (AI)-Assisted Travel Planning. *International Journal of Human-Computer Interaction*, *1*, 14. DOI: 10.1080/10447318.2024.2426044

Tran, K. (2025, March 27). *Topic: Social media in Southeast Asia*. Statista. https://www.statista.com/topics/10537/social-media-in-southeast-asia/

Tran, T. P., Van Solt, M., & Zemanek, J. E.Jr. (2020). How does personalization affect brand relationship in social commerce? A mediation perspective. *Journal of Consumer Marketing, 37*(5), 473–486. DOI: 10.1108/JCM-12-2017-2499

Trivedi, S., & Malik, R. (2021). Social media marketing as new marketing tool. In *Big Data Analytics for Improved Accuracy, Efficiency, and Decision Making in Digital Marketing* (pp. 207-226). IGI Global. DOI: 10.4018/978-1-7998-7231-3.ch015

Trivedi, J. (2019). Examining the Customer Experience of Using Banking Chatbots and Its Impact on Brand Love : The Moderating Role of Perceived Risk. *Journal of Internet Commerce, 18*(1), 91–111. DOI: 10.1080/15332861.2019.1567188

Trusov, M., Bucklin, R. E., & Pauwels, K. (2009). Effects of word-of-mouth versus traditional marketing: Findings from an internet social networking site. *Journal of Marketing, 73*(5), 90–102. DOI: 10.1509/jmkg.73.5.90

Tubaishat, A. (2018). Perceived usefulness and perceived ease of use of electronic health records among nurses : Application of Technology Acceptance Model. *Informatics for Health and Social Care*, 43(4), 379 389. DOI: 10.1080/17538157.2017.1363761

Twimbit. (2025, February 14). *State of VIs 2025*. https://cdn.twimbit.com/uploads/2025/02/13170410/State-of-virtual-influencers-2025.pdf

Upathamphan, S., & Puapradit, A. (2024). *The Effect of Social Media Influencer Marketing on Cosmetic Products and Strategic Uses*. https://rsucon.rsu.ac.th/files/proceedings/RSUSOC2024/IN24-159.pdf

Value4brand. (2025, January 13). *Value4Brand*. Value4Brand - Digital Marketing Company in India. https://value4brand.com/indian-companies-use-influencer-marketing-to-grow-their-brand/

van der Harst, J. P., & Angelopoulos, S. (2024). Less is more: Engagement with the content of social media influencers. *Journal of Business Research, 181*, 114746. DOI: 10.1016/j.jbusres.2024.114746

Van Eeuwen, M. 2017. Mobile conversational commerce: Messenger chatbots as the next interface between businesses and consumers University of Twente]. http://purl. utwente.nl/essays/71706

Varghese, M., Raj, S., & Venkatesh, V. (2022). *Influence of AI in human lives* (Version 1). arXiv. DOI: 10.48550/ARXIV.2212.12305

Vargo, S. L., & Lusch, R. F. (2004). Evolving to a new dominant logic for marketing. *Journal of Marketing, 68*(1), 1–17. DOI: 10.1509/jmkg.68.1.1.24036

Varun, C. M., Kumar, R. A., Gokila, E., Gayathri, S., Nalini, M., & Subramanian, R. S. (2024, October). Virtual Frontiers navigating the impact and potential of AR and VR. In *2024 2nd International Conference on Self Sustainable Artificial Intelligence Systems (ICSSAS)* (pp. 1559-1565). IEEE. DOI: 10.1109/ICSSAS64001.2024.10760749

Vazquez, D., Wu, X., Nguyen, B., Kent, A., Gutierrez, A., & Chen, T. (2020). Investigating narrative involvement, parasocial interactions, and impulse buying behaviours within a second screen social commerce context. *International Journal of Information Management*, *53*, 102135. DOI: 10.1016/j.ijinfomgt.2020.102135

Velasco, C., Reinoso-Carvalho, F., Barbosa Escobar, F., Gustafsson, A., & Petit, O. (2024). Paradoxes, challenges, and opportunities in the context of ethical customer experience management. *Psychology and Marketing*, *41*(10), 2506–2524. DOI: 10.1002/mar.22069

Venkatesh, V., & Bala, H. (2008). Technology Acceptance Model 3 and a Research Agenda on Interventions. *Decision Sciences*, *39*(2), 273–315. DOI: 10.1111/j.1540-5915.2008.00192.x

Venkatesh, V., & Brown, S. A. (2001). A Longitudinal Investigation of Personal Computers in Homes : Adoption Determinants and Emerging Challenges. *Management Information Systems Quarterly*, *25*(1), 71–102. DOI: 10.2307/3250959

Venkatesh, V., & Davis, F. D. (2000). A Theoretical Extension of the Technology Acceptance Model : Four Longitudinal Field Studies. *Management Science*, *46*(2), 186–204. DOI: 10.1287/mnsc.46.2.186.11926

Venkatesh, V., Morris, M. G., Davis, G. B., & Davis, F. D. (2003). User acceptance of information technology : Toward a unified view. *Management Information Systems Quarterly*, *27*(3), 425–478. DOI: 10.2307/30036540

Venkatesh, V., Thong, J. Y., & Xu, X. (2012). Consumer acceptance and use of information technology : Extending the unified theory of acceptance and use of technology. *Management Information Systems Quarterly*, *36*(1), 157–178. DOI: 10.2307/41410412

Verhoef, P. C., Lemon, K. N., Parasuraman, A., Roggeveen, A., Tsiros, M., & Schlesinger, L. A. (2009). Customer Experience Creation : Determinants, Dynamics and Management Strategies. *Journal of Retailing*, *85*(1), 31–41. DOI: 10.1016/j.jretai.2008.11.001

Verma, A. (2024, October 20). *Understanding AR and VR: Transforming our world with immersive technology*. Medium. https://medium.com/@ajayverma23/understanding-ar-and-vr-transforming-our-world-with-immersive-technology-8d530aeff236

Verma, S., Sharma, R., Deb, S., & Maitra, D. (2021). Artificial intelligence in marketing : Systematic review and future research direction. *International Journal of Information Management Data Insights*, *1*(1), 100002. DOI: 10.1016/j.jjimei.2020.100002

Viot, C., & Bressolles, G. (2012). Les agents virtuels intelligents. Décisions marketing, 65(1), 45 56.

Virtual Retail Algorithms. (2022). Virtual Retail Algorithms, Behavioral Predictive Analytics, and Geospatial Mapping Technologies in the Decentralized Metaverse. *Review of Contemporary Philosophy*, *21*(0), 171. DOI: 10.22381/RCP21202211

VIs Market. (2025, February 27). *Market.us*. https://market.us/report/virtual-influencers-market/

Vitsentzatou, E., Tsoulfas, G. T., & Mihiotis, A. N. (2022). The Digital Transformation of the Marketing Mix in the Food and Beverage Service Supply Chain: A Grey DEMATEL Approach. *Sustainability (Basel)*, *14*(22), 15228. DOI: 10.3390/su142215228

Vlachos, E., Jochum, E., & Demers, L.-P. (2016). The Effects of Exposure to Different Social Robots on Attitudes toward Preferences. Interaction Studies. *Social Behaviour and Communication in Biological and Artificial Systems*, 17(3), 390 404. DOI: 10.1075/is.17.3.04vla

Voorveld, H. A. M., Van Noort, G., Muntinga, D. G., & Bronner, F. (2018). Engagement with Social Media and Social Media Advertising: The Differentiating Role of Platform Type. *Journal of Advertising*, *47*(1), 38–54. DOI: 10.1080/00913367.2017.1405754

Vrontis, D., Makrides, A., Christofi, M., & Thrassou, A. (2021). Social media influencer marketing: A systematic review, integrative framework and future research agenda. *International Journal of Consumer Studies*, *45*(4), 617–644. DOI: 10.1111/ijcs.12647

Wang, W., Feng, F., He, X., Wang, X., & Chua, T. S. (2021, August). Deconfounded recommendation for alleviating bias amplification. In Proceedings of the 27th ACM SIGKDD conference on knowledge discovery & data mining (pp. 1717-1725). DOI: 10.1145/3447548.3467249

Wang, C., Li, Y., Fu, W., & Jin, J. (2023). Whether to trust chatbots : Applying the event-related approach to understand consumers' emotional experiences in interactions with chatbots in e-commerce. *Journal of Retailing and Consumer Services*, *73*, 103325. DOI: 10.1016/j.jretconser.2023.103325

Wang, P., & Huang, Q. (2023). Digital influencers, social power and consumer engagement in social commerce. *Internet Research*, *33*(1), 178–207. DOI: 10.1108/INTR-08-2020-0467

Wang, W., Chen, Z., & Kuang, J. (2025). Artificial Intelligence-Driven Recommendations and Functional Food Purchases: Understanding Consumer Decision-Making. *Foods*, *14*(6), 976. DOI: 10.3390/foods14060976 PMID: 40231979

Wang, X., Yu, C., & Wei, Y. (2012). Social Media Peer Communication and Impacts on Purchase Intentions: A Consumer Socialization Framework. *Journal of Interactive Marketing*, *26*(4), 198–208. DOI: 10.1016/j.intmar.2011.11.004

Wang, Y., Wang, J., Yao, T., Li, M., & Wang, X. (2020). How does social support promote consumers' engagement in the social commerce community? The mediating effect of consumer involvement. *Information Processing & Management*, *57*(5), 102272. DOI: 10.1016/j.ipm.2020.102272

Wasserman, S., & Faust, K. (1994). *Social network analysis: Methods and applications*. Cambridge University Press. DOI: 10.1017/CBO9780511815478

Waytz, A., Cacioppo, J., & Epley, N. (2010). Who Sees Human? : The Stability and Importance of Individual Differences in Anthropomorphism. *Perspectives on Psychological Science*, 5(3), 219 232. DOI: 10.1177/1745691610369336

Weaver, K., Lesko Pacchia, M., & Hudson, S. (2024, September 11). *The beauty boom and beyond: Can the industry maintain its growth?* McKinsey & Company. https://www.mckinsey.com/industries/consumer-packaged-goods/our-insights/the-beauty-boom-and-beyond-can-the-industry-maintain-its-growth

Weaver, K., Pacchia, M., & Hudson, S. (2025, June 9). *State of Beauty 2025: Solving a shifting growth puzzle*. McKinsey & Company. https://www.mckinsey.com/industries/consumer-packaged-goods/our-insights/state-of-beauty

Wibawa, R. C., Pratiwi, C. P., Wahyono, E., Hidayat, D., & Adiasari, W. (2022). VIs: Is the persona trustworthy? [JAMIKA]. *Jurnal Manajemen Informatika*, *12*(1), 51–62. DOI: 10.34010/jamika.v12i1.6706

Wigand, R. T. (1997). Electronic Commerce: Definition, Theory, and Context. *The Information Society*, *13*(1), 1–16. DOI: 10.1080/019722497129241

Willems, K., Brengman, M., & Van De Sanden, S. (2017). In-store proximity marketing: Experimenting with digital point-of-sales communication. *International Journal of Retail & Distribution Management, 45*(7-8), 910–927. DOI: 10.1108/IJRDM-10-2016-0177

Wirtz, J., Patterson, P. G., Kunz, W. H., Gruber, T., Lu, V. N., Paluch, S., & Martins, A. (2018). Brave new world : Service robots in the frontline. *Journal of Service Management, 29*(5), 907–931. DOI: 10.1108/JOSM-04-2018-0119

Wongkitrungrueng, A., & Assarut, N. (2020). The role of live streaming in building consumer trust and engagement with social commerce sellers. *Journal of Business Research, 117*, 543–556. DOI: 10.1016/j.jbusres.2018.08.032

Wongyai, P. H., Ngo, T., Wu, H., Tsui, K. W. H., & Nguyen, T.-H. (2024). Self-service technology in aviation : A systematic literature review. *Journal of the Air Transport Research Society, 2*, 100016. DOI: 10.1016/j.jatrs.2024.100016

World Health Organization. (2021). *WHO Results Report 2020-2021*. World Health Organization. https://www.who.int/about/accountability/results/who-results-report-2020-2021

Wu, K., Zhao, Y., Zhu, Q., Tan, X., & Zheng, H. (2011). A meta-analysis of the impact of trust on technology acceptance model : Investigation of moderating influence of subject and context type. *International Journal of Information Management*, 31(6), 572 581. DOI: 10.1016/j.ijinfomgt.2011.03.004

Wu, C.-C., Chen, C.-T., Huang, K.-C., & Chou, Y.-Y. (2025). Determinants of Chatbot adoption among older adults : An extended TAM approach using PLS-SEM. *Information Development, 02666669251315839*(3), 656–674. Advance online publication. DOI: 10.1177/02666669251315839

Wuenderlich, N. V., Heinonen, K., Ostrom, A. L., Patricio, L., Sousa, R., Voss, C., & Lemmink, J. G. A. M. (2015). "Futurizing" smart service : Implications for service researchers and managers. *Journal of Services Marketing, 29*(6/7), 442–447. DOI: 10.1108/JSM-01-2015-0040

Xia, H., Zhang, L., Chen, J., & Wang, X. (2025). Decoding virtual influencer endorsement using machine learning: The role of virtual influencer, posting, and disclosure characteristics. *Journal of Retailing and Consumer Services, 87*, 104366. 10.1016/j.jretconser.2025.104366. DOI: 10.1016/j.jretconser.2025.104366

Xiang, Z., Wang, D., O'Leary, J. T., & Fesenmaier, D. R. (2014). Adapting to the Internet: Trends in Travelers' Use of the Web for Trip Planning. *Journal of Travel Research, 54*(4), 511–527. DOI: 10.1177/0047287514522883

Xuanyu, Y., Wongkumchai, T., & Chaiwiwat, U. (2025). The The Impact of Social Media Marketing on Retailer Sales:A Case Study of J Cosmetics Company, China. *Journal of Public and Private Issues*, *2*(2), 93–103. https://so17.tci-thaijo.org/index .php/jppi/article/view/805

Xue, J., Liang, X., Xie, T., & Wang, H. (2020). See now, act now: How to interact with customers to enhance social commerce engagement? *Information & Management*, *57*(6), 103324. DOI: 10.1016/j.im.2020.103324

Yahia, I., Ben Al-Neama, N., & Kerbache, L. (2018). Investigating the drivers for social commerce in social media platforms: Importance of trust, social support and the platform perceived usage. *Journal of Retailing and Consumer Services*, *41*(1), 11–19. DOI: 10.1016/j.jretconser.2017.10.021

Yasin, M., Porcu, L., Prados-Castillo, J. F., & Liébana-Cabanillas, F. (2024). The Role of Social Media in Building Islamic Banking Consumer Engagement: Analysing the Impact of Brand Personality Traits and Brand Love. *International Journal of Human-Computer Interaction*, •••, 1–15.

Yen, C., & Chiang, M.-C. (2021). Trust me, if you can : A study on the factors that influence consumers' purchase intention triggered by chatbots based on brain image evidence and self-reported assessments. *Behaviour & Information Technology*, *40*(11), 1177–1194. DOI: 10.1080/0144929X.2020.1743362

Yin, J., Qiu, X., & Wang, Y. (2025). The Impact of AI-Personalized Recommendations on Clicking Intentions: Evidence from Chinese E-Commerce. *Journal of Theoretical and Applied Electronic Commerce Research*, *20*(1), 21. Advance online publication. DOI: 10.3390/jtaer20010021

Yuce, A. (2021). The Impact of Digital Transformation and Virtual Reality in Tourism Marketing: A Conceptualized Exploration. In *Handbook of Research on IoT, Digital Transformation, and the Future of Global Marketing* (pp. 1-14). IGI Global. DOI: 10.4018/978-1-7998-7192-7.ch001

Yu, K.-H., Beam, A. L., & Kohane, I. S. (2018). Artificial intelligence in healthcare. *Nature Biomedical Engineering*, *2*(10), 719–731. DOI: 10.1038/s41551-018-0305-z PMID: 31015651

Yu, Z., Zhou, X., Hao, Y., & Gu, J. (2006). TV program recommendation for multiple viewers based on user profile merging. *User Modeling and User-Adapted Interaction*, *16*(1), 63–82. DOI: 10.1007/s11257-006-9005-6

Zanchini, R., Spina, D., De Pascale, A., Lanfranchi, M., Giannetto, C., D'Amico, M., & Di Vita, G. (2025). Shaping consumer preferences for sweet peppers: Exploring the role of social, environmental, and sensory attributes in the era of health consciousness and local sourcing. *Agricultural and Food Economics, 13*(1), 42. Advance online publication. DOI: 10.1186/s40100-025-00386-2

Zhang, B., Zhu, Y., Deng, J., Zheng, W., Liu, Y., Wang, C., & Zeng, R. (2023). "I Am Here to Assist Your Tourism" : Predicting Continuance Intention to Use AI-based Chatbots for Tourism. Does Gender Really Matter? *International Journal of Human–Computer Interaction*, 39(9), 1887 1903. DOI: 10.1080/10447318.2022.2124345

Zhang, E., & Lu, X. (2023). *Social AI Improves Well-Being Among Female Young Adults* (Version 2). arXiv. DOI: 10.48550/ARXIV.2311.14706

Zhang, Z., Li, C., & Zhang, H. (2026). Digital confusion: Comprehending the impact mechanisms of artificial intelligence-generated content and user-generated content on tourism decision making. *Tourism Management, 112*(June 2025), 105269. DOI: 10.1016/j.tourman.2025.105269

Zhang, H., Lu, Y., Gupta, S., & Zhao, L. (2014). What motivates customers to participate in social commerce? The impact of technological environments and virtual customer experiences. *Information & Management, 51*(8), 1017–1030. DOI: 10.1016/j.im.2014.07.005

Zhang, L., Chen, M., & Zamil, A. M. A. (2023a). Live stream marketing and consumers' purchase intention: An IT affordance perspective using the S-O-R paradigm. *Frontiers in Psychology, 14*, 1069050. DOI: 10.3389/fpsyg.2023.1069050 PMID: 36818116

Zhang, Z., & Ghorbani, A. A. (2022). Visualizing and analyzing social networks: From graph theory to network science. *Computers in Human Behavior, 129*, 107131.

Zhao, L., & Wu, W. (2025). Is Customer Service Innovation Always Preferable? The Impact of AI Technology on an Online Retailer's Customer Service Decision. *Journal of Theoretical and Applied Electronic Commerce Research, 20*(2), 101. DOI: 10.3390/jtaer20020101

Zhou, T., Lu, Y., & Wang, B. (2010). Integrating TTF and UTAUT to explain mobile banking user adoption. *Computers in Human Behavior, 26*(4), 760–767. DOI: 10.1016/j.chb.2010.01.013

Zlotowski, J., Proudfoot, D., Yogeeswaran, K., & Bartneck, C. (2015). Opportunities and challenges in human–robot interaction. *International Journal of Social Robotics, 7*(3), 347–360. DOI: 10.1007/s12369-014-0267-6

Zungu, N. P., Amegbe, H., Hanu, C., & Asamoah, E. S. (2025). AI-driven self-service for enhanced customer experience outcomes in the banking sector. *Cogent Business & Management, 12*(1), 2450295. DOI: 10.1080/23311975.2025.2450295

Žvanut, B., & Mihelič, A. (2024). Qualitative study on domestic social robot adoption and associated security concerns among older adults in Slovenia. *Frontiers in Psychology, 15*, 1343077. DOI: 10.3389/fpsyg.2024.1343077 PMID: 38333061

About the Contributors

Gopalakrishnan Soundararajan is an Assistant Professor of Marketing at Muscat College, Muscat, Sultanate of Oman, with over 20 years of experience in teaching, research, and administration. He earned his PhD in Management from Anna University, India, and holds Fellowship in Higher Education (FHEA) from the University of Stirling, UK. He has successfully secured research funding from various agencies in India and Oman and has organized numerous international conferences and workshops. He has also served as a reviewer for multiple international journals and books and is an external examiner for PhD thesis. Over the years, he has supervised more than 50 MBA projects, 55 Higher National Diploma projects (SCQF level 8) from SQA-UK, 32 Bachelor with Honors projects (SCQF level 10) from the University of Stirling, UK, and 2 MSc projects from the University of Stirling.

Ruksana Banu is an Assistant Professor in the Business and Accounting Department at Muscat College, Oman, with over 25 years of teaching experience. She earned her Ph.D. from the University of Technology Malaysia and holds FHEA (UK). She is also a Certified Lean Six Sigma Black Belt and a Certified Trainer. Dr. Banu has secured several research grants from MOHERI, including the completed project "Recovery and Resilience Attributes among SMEs in Oman." She has delivered more than 30 national and international webinars and workshops. She serves as a reviewer for international journals and as an external examiner for doctoral theses. She has supervised over 30 MA projects (University of Madras), 50 UG projects (University of Stirling and University Malaysia Pahang Al Sultan Abdullah), 3 MSc dissertations (University of Stirling), and around 10 industrial training projects (UMPSA).

***

Firnanda Amalia is an information technology professional with interests in information systems and digital innovation. Her work focuses on the development and application of technology-driven solutions to enhance efficiency, support decision-making, and enable digital transformation in organizational and societal contexts. She is particularly interested in user-centered system design, data-informed technologies, and sustainable digital practices.

Desva Selvi Anggraini is an emerging scholar with a growing interest in information systems, digital technology, and applied research in contemporary organizational environments. Her academic interests focus on system analysis, data management, and the use of information technology to improve efficiency, accuracy, and decision-making processes. Desva demonstrates strong analytical skills, attention to detail, and a commitment to continuous learning throughout her academic journey. She actively participates in academic projects and research activities that integrate theoretical knowledge with practical implementation, aiming to develop solutions that are both effective and sustainable. With an interest in digital transformation and technology-driven innovation, Desva aspires to contribute to the advancement of information systems research and to apply her expertise in professional settings, supporting organizations in adapting to evolving technological challenges.

Nihar Suresh Dahake is currently serving as an Assistant Professor in the Department of MBA at G H Raisoni College of Engineering, Nagpur. He holds a B.Com, M.Com, and MBA from Rashtrasant Tukdoji Maharaj Nagpur University and earned his Ph.D. from Sant Gadge Baba Amravati University, Amravati. In addition to his academic qualifications, Dr. Dahake has successfully qualified the State Eligibility Test (SET) in both Commerce and Management, demonstrating his strong foundation in these disciplines. With a rich academic background, he brings 14 years of teaching experience and 8 years of dedicated research experience to his role. Throughout his career, he has consistently contributed to academic excellence and research development. Dr. Dahake's areas of expertise include Financial Accounting, Consumer Behavior, Marketing Management, and Financial Management. His multidisciplinary knowledge allows him to effectively engage with a wide range of topics in business and management studies. Passionate about both teaching and research, he strives to inspire students while also contributing meaningfully to the academic community through his scholarly work. His professional journey reflects a deep commitment to education, research, and the advancement of management studies in higher education institutions.

Pragati Parihar Dahake is an Assistant Professor in the Department of MBA at VMV Commerce, JMT Arts, and JJP Science College, Nagpur. With 2 years of academic experience, she specializes in Marketing, Human Resource Management, and Consumer Behavior. Passionate about shaping future business leaders, she combines theoretical knowledge with practical insights to create an engaging learning environment. Her teaching approach emphasizes real-world applications and student-centered learning. Pragati is committed to academic excellence and continuously works to enhance her subject expertise while contributing to the holistic development of her students in the dynamic field of management education.

G. Chamdramowleeswaran is currently working as Assistant Professor in Department of Commerce and business administration, VelTech Rangarajan Dr. Sagunthala R&D Institute of Science and Technology (Deemed to be University), Avadi, Chennai. He has more than 11 years 5 months of industry experience and 1 year and 11 months of teaching experience with specialization in HR and Marketing. He Holds a B.Com., M.B.A., M. Phil., and Ph.D. in Management from Bharathidasan University, Trichy

G. Premalatha is an Assistant Professor in the Department of Data Science and Business Systems, School of Computing, Faculty of Engineering and Technology, SRM Institute of Science and Technology, Kattankulathur Campus. Her research interests include data analytics, machine learning, and artificial intelligence. She is actively involved in academic research and mentoring, contributing to advancements in data-driven technologies and computational intelligence.

|Shaju G.M - Contributing Author|Currently, I serve as the Registrar at MIANZ International College, where I oversee registrar operations, examinations, international student admissions, and institutional compliance. My leadership has contributed to the streamlining of admission protocols and the strengthening of international collaboration. With more than 7 years in senior leadership roles and over 9 years in academic teaching and administration, I have cultivated a deep understanding of the nuances of student recruitment, international enrollment, and regulatory frameworks across different education systems.

Arshad Hussain is a distinguished expert in the field of Marketing, blending academic expertise with real-world experience. With over 1.5 years dedicated to teaching and training, Mr. Hussain brings a wealth of knowledge to his students' academic journey. His corporate and industrial exposure includes a year-long tenure with a prestigious firm in Uttar Pradesh, where he was actively involved in strategic marketing functions, consumer insights, and branding initiatives. This hands-on industry experience has given him a practical edge and a nuanced understanding of market dynamics, customer behavior, and contemporary business challenges. Additionally, he has engaged in corporate training and consultancy projects, strengthening the link between academic theory and real-world business applications. Presently, Mr. Hussain is on an intellectual journey, pursuing his doctorate in Marketing at Bennett University, under the esteemed Times of India Group, located in Greater Noida. His dedication to scholarly pursuits is matched only by his commitment to practical application and innovation in the marketing domain. Mr. Hussain's academic fervor extends beyond the classroom, as evidenced by his active participation in numerous events hosted by esteemed institutions such as the Indian Institute of Management (IIM), including IIM Ahmedabad, IIM Bangalore, IIM Amritsar, and IIM Sambalpur, as well as IMMRC, Dr. A.P.J. Abdul Kalam Technical University (AKTU), and the Asia Pacific Institute. Each engagement serves as a testament to his unwavering dedication to the advancement of marketing theory and practice.

Muhammad Nawaz Iqbal is an Academician, Researcher and Philosopher. He have almost 13 years of corporate experience and now serving as an Assistant Professor in department of Business Administration of Sir Syed university of Engineering and Technology, Karachi, Pakistan. He credited numerous publications in local and international journals and also credited two books in the field of Business Management.

Mohammad Irfan is a Professor at the School of Business and Commerce, Chandigarh University, Lucknow (Unnao), India. He earned his Ph.D. from the Central University of Haryana and holds an MBA in Finance, an M.Com in Accounts and Law, and an MA in Economics. A UGC-JRF/SRF/NET qualifier in Management and Commerce, he also holds certifications from NSE (NCFM) and BSE. With more than sixteen years of teaching and research experience, Dr. Irfan's expertise includes Security Analysis and Portfolio Management (SAPM), Artificial Intelligence, Machine Learning, Blockchain, Cryptocurrency, Financial Engineering, FinTech, Green Finance, and Alternative Finance. He has authored over 109 Scopus-indexed research papers in reputed journals such as The Journal of Economic Cooperation and Development (Q2), International Journal of Business Excellence, Montenegrin Journal of Economics (Q2), Cogent Business & Management (Q2), and Journal of Islamic Monetary Economics and Finance. His work has received 700+ citations with an H-index of 15. He has also published 12 books with Springer and IGI Global and is listed among the World's Top 2% Scientists.

K. Raju is an Associate Professor in the Department of Artificial Intelligence and Machine Learning at Rajalakshmi Engineering College, Chennai. He is committed to academic excellence and advancing research in AI and emerging technologies. With a passion for student development, he actively mentors learners toward innovative problem-solving. His contributions strengthen the growth of AI education and interdisciplinary advancements in engineering.

Ganesha K S is an Assistant Professor in the Department of Management Studies, at Dayananda Sagar College of Engineering, Bangalore, India. He has 15 years of experience in Corporate, Teaching and Research. He is a Member of the International Safety Quality Environment Management Association (ISQEM), UK. His primary research interests are tourist behavior, social media, sentiment analysis, human resource management, and labor studies. He has presented at multiple conferences and published articles in Scopus and other International Indexed journals. He has conducted FDP, workshops, and training in the areas of Digital Marketing, Statistical Analysis using SPSS, Project Management, Research Methodology, Entrepreneurship etc.

Saad Ullah Khan has more than a decade long extensive experience at university level teaching and research. Dr. Khan has authored various research papers in journals of national as well as international repute. He was awarded 'Rajat Jayanti Vigyan Sancharak Fellowship-2009' by DST, Ministry of Science and Technology (Government of India) for his contribution to the field of communication and its social implications. Further he was bestowed with MANF Fellowship 2011 by UGC to carry out his research work. A PhD from prestigious Aligarh Muslim University, Dr. Saad Ullah Khan has presented 90 Research Papers in various National and International Conferences. He was awarded 'Best Researcher Award' twice (2020 & 2023) and 'Best Journalism Teacher Award' in 2021.

Sadaf Khan has extensive teaching experience of more than ten years. A core academician and a prolific researcher, she has done incredible work in the domain of English Literature, Cultural Studies, and Afghanistan Studies. Having an international teaching experience, she has been felicitated multiple times as 'Best Teacher' by various academic institutions in which she had worked. Besides, she has also served as the Joint Editor of Women's College Annual magazine of Aligarh Muslim University for the session 2007-2008.

Jenifer Lawrence an Associate Professor of Management Department at Woldia University, Ethiopia. He has a rich experience in teaching and research activities. He received his Ph.D in Management from Bharathiar University in 2016. His research interest includes the advancements and the new concepts pertaining to Marketing and Human Resources areas. Dr.Jenifer Lawrence has published many research articles and book chapters in several peer-reviewed, and Scopus indexed journals. He has also published many book chapters in Springer and IGI Scopus indexed journals. He has secured a patent from the Patent Office, Government Of India for "Learning

Tablet for Kids". Dr.Jenifer Lawrence teaches postgraduate courses on Marketing and Human Resources courses. He has supervised more than 80 MBA theses and served on 14 PhD adjudication as an external examiner for various universities in India. He is also an editorial board member for i-manager's "Journal on Management", and IJMSRT, and acts as a reviewer for different journals.

Ezhilvendan M is an Assistant Professor in the Department of Artificial Intelligence & Machine Learning at Panimalar Engineering College, Poonamallee (Chennai) with research interests in machine learning and data-driven intelligent systems.

M. Kalimuthu, a dynamic faculty of Commence has been in service since 2004. He worked in different reputed institutions across India, and during his headship many undergraduate students got university ranks from Bharathiyar University, Coimbatore. He is such a committed and versatile person, has attended a number of national and international workshops (17), conferences & seminars (59), webinars and Faculty Development Programmes (78) across India. Similarly, he organized more than 10 seminars, conferences and workshops, and published 30 papers in conference and seminar proceedings and 12 Book chapters also. With his great interest in research, he published 79 research articles in various national and international journals (5 Articles Indexed in Scopus) and produced four M.Phil. Scholars and now doctoral studies are also going under his supervision. Moreover, he was awarded as Best Fund Mobilizer Award, Best Working Paper Research Award, Best Citizen Consumer Club Co-ordinator, and Best Youth Red Cross Programme Officer as well. Having a good background in teaching and research he plays in different academic roles as Doctoral Committee Member, a member of Board of Studies, Peer-Reviewer & Editorial Board Member in 11 Journals, Membership in 6 Professional Bodies, Question paper setter and external examiner for various colleges in and around Coimbatore. At present he is a faculty of Commerce at Dr. N.G.P. Arts and Science College, Coimbatore, Tamil Nadu, India.

Krishna M B, Assistant Professor, Department of commerce and Management, Amrita Vishwa Vidyapeetham, Kochi Campus

Apoorva Mahiwal is a Research Scholar at Amity University Rajasthan, specializing in Advertising, Public Relations, and Corporate Communication, with a concentrated interest in emerging digital media dynamics. Her academic inquiry is informed by prior experience with the Research Unit of the Ministry of Information and Broadcasting, where she contributed to government communication and policy-oriented research. In addition to her scholarly pursuits, she has facilitated instruction and training in communication and soft skills. A lifetime member of the

Indian Society for Training and Development (ISTD), Rajkot Chapter, she remains actively involved in both academic discourse and industry engagements within the communication domain.

Abhishek Majumder is currently working as Associate Professor in the Department of Computer Science & Engineering, Tripura University (A Central University). Prior to joining Tripura University he had worked as Assistant Professor in the Department of Information Technology (Currently Department of Computer Science & Engineering, Assam University (A Central University). He had completed his BE, MTech and PhD from NIT Agartala, Tezpur University and Assam University respectively. His research interests are Mobile Computing, IoT, AI and Network Security. He has published more than 50 papers in National and International Journals and Conferences. He has also authored many book chapters in books published by reputed publishers. As Principal Investigator/Coordinator he has handled projects funded by Ministry of Electronics and Information Technology, Government of India, AICTE and IBITF.

Tanushri Mukherjee, PhD, is an Associate Professor at the Amity School of Communication and currently serves as the Deputy Director – Outcome at Amity University Rajasthan, Jaipur, India. With nearly two decades of experience in academia, she has established herself as a specialist in the domains of public relations, corporate communication, and event management. She earned her doctoral degree in Public Relations from Amity University Rajasthan in 2016 and holds certification of eligibility for lectureship through the University Grants Commission's National Eligibility Test (UGC-NET), reflecting her strong academic foundation and research competence. Over the course of her career, Dr. Mukherjee has demonstrated a consistent commitment to academic excellence, student development, and scholarly inquiry. Her contributions have been recognized nationally, most notably through her inclusion in the July 2021 edition of IMPACT Magazine, which named her among the 'Top 50 Women Leaders in PR and Corporate Communication'. She has also received several prestigious honors, including the Communication Excellence Honour by PRSI, Distinguished Associate Professor Award, Educator of the Year Award by Exchange4media Group, the Distinguished Teacher for Holistic Development of Students Award conferred by the International Centre for Excellence in Education in association with the Society for Perpetuation of Art, Culture & Education, and the Teaching Excellence Award in PR and Communication from the Public Relations Society of India (Jaipur Chapter). Further accolades include the Media Innovation Award at the All India Media Conference, the Women's Excellence Award, and the Empowered Women Award. In recognition of her applied research acumen, she was awarded the Gold Medallion National Award for the Best PR Case Study—along with a medal, citation, and certificate of merit—by the Public Relations Society of India, Hyderabad Chapter. Dr. Mukherjee is an active contributor to the field of communication studies, having presented numerous papers at reputed national and international conferences. Her research has been widely published in refereed journals, edited volumes, and conference proceedings, underscoring her sustained engagement with academic research and discourse. Her scholarly trajectory reflects a deep commitment to advancing knowledge in communication and fostering academic excellence in both research and teaching.

Muthurasu N is an Assistant Professor in the Department of Computer Science and Engineering at Sona College of Technology. He is dedicated to fostering innovation and excellence in computer science education. His academic and research interests support advancements in modern computing technologies. Passionate about student success, he actively contributes to skill development and professional growth in the engineering field.

Aparna P is a faculty member in the Department of Computer Science and Engineering at RMK College of Engineering and Technology, Puduvoyal. Her academic interests include core computing concepts and emerging technologies. She is committed to delivering quality education and fostering student development.

Gopika Priya P is an Assistant Professor in the Department of Artificial Intelligence and Data Science at Vel Tech Multi Tech Dr. Rangarajan Dr. Sakunthala Engineering College, Avadi, Chennai. She is engaged in teaching and mentoring students in emerging AI and data-driven technologies. Her academic interests focus on applying intelligent systems to solve real-world problems

P. Visu is a Professor in the Department of Artificial Intelligence and Data Science at Velammal Engineering College, Chennai. His research interests include machine learning, data analytics, and intelligent systems. He is dedicated to advancing academic excellence and fostering research-driven learning.

Beslin Pajila is a faculty member at Vel Tech Rangarajan Dr. Sagunthala R&D Institute of Science and Technology, Chennai. Her academic and research interests include emerging technologies and innovative engineering solutions. She is committed to high-quality teaching, research, and student mentoring.

Ardra Rianisa is an Information Technology professional with a strong interest in digital technology and information systems. Ardra actively engages in writing academic papers and popular articles that discuss current trends, innovations, and developments in the field of information technology. With a solid understanding of technology and its practical applications, Ardra is committed to continuously expanding knowledge and contributing insights to the digital and academic community.

Shreya Roy currently is a research scholar of Department of Computer Science and Engineering Department at Tripura University, India.Her main research interest includes artificial intelligence, machine learning, and recommendation system. She posses one and half years of industrial experience in the field of programming and development.She had completed her B.Tech,M.Tech in Computer Science and Engineering from ICFAI University Tripura and Tripura University respectively.

Sujith T.S. is currently working as an assistant professor, Department of Commerce and Management, Amrita Vishwa Vidyapeetham (Deemed University), Kochi Campus. He holds his Ph.D. in Marketing from Bharathiar University, Coimbatore, Tamil Nadu; Master of Commerce (Finance) from Sree Narayana College, Nattika affiliated to Calicut University, Kerala; and Master of Business Administration (Marketing) from Bharathiar University, Coimbatore. He has 10 years of experience in teaching. He has published more than 25 research papers in various national and international journals with high impact factor including Web of Science & Scopus. He has written 12 chapters in various national and international edited books. He is the academic editor and reviewer of various national and international journals. He has presented more than 40 research papers in numerous international and national seminars and conferences. He attended various national and international research methodology workshops and FDPs. He also served as a resource person for research methodology programmes conducted by various colleges.

S. Vengatesh Kumar is an Assistant Professor in the Department of CSE (Cyber Security) at JNN Institute of Engineering. His academic interests include cybersecurity, network security, and digital forensics. He is dedicated to providing quality education and guiding students in emerging security technologies.

Mani Sachdev is an esteemed academician currently serving as Professor and Head of the Institute of Behavioural and Allied Sciences at Amity University Rajasthan, Jaipur. Her academic journey includes earning an M.Phil. in Philosophy and completing her Doctorate at the University of Rajasthan, specializing in Aesthetics, Metaphysics, and Epistemology. With an impressive tenure spanning 37 years, she has excelled as an Associate Professor of Philosophy. Dr. Sachdev's pioneering roles include founding the Department of Philosophy at Vedic Kanya P. G. College, Jaipur, and establishing the Department of Philosophy at B.N.D. Arts Government P.G. College Chimanpura, Jaipur. Her scholarly contributions and administrative leadership underscore her commitment to advancing philosophical discourse and academic excellence in higher education. Her professional portfolio encompasses the design and development of innovative curricula tailored for students, ensuring adherence to rigorous quality assurance standards within the University framework. Additionally, she contributes to the pedagogical landscape by teaching ethics to medical professionals at a distinguished medical university in Jaipur, where she serves as a distinguished member of the ethics committee. Her scholarly contributions extend to numerous international and national conferences, seminars, and scholarly journals, where she has presented research papers, authored book chapters, and contributed book reviews. Beyond academia, she has demonstrated versatility in media production, having produced, directed, and scripted corporate films for hospitals and organizations, as well as documentaries for national broadcast on Doordarshan. Furthermore, she has conducted in-depth interviews with over 50 prominent global figures, spanning governors, philosophers, academics, and renowned personalities from the film industry. Her cultural engagement includes creating, directing, writing, and narrating the acclaimed 'Light and Sound Cultural Show' celebrating Rajasthan's art, culture, and heritage, showcased at numerous tourism festivals and international conferences.

Binastya Anggara Sekti has been a lecturer at the Faculty of Computer Science, Esa Unggul University, Jakarta, since 2016. He is actively involved in the Artificial Intelligence and Information Security Study Group. He holds a Bachelor's degree in Informatics Engineering from the Bandung Institute of Technology and a Master's degree in Information Systems Management from Trisakti University, Jakarta. Prior to entering academia, he accumulated over 25 years of professional experience as an IT practitioner in various companies across Jakarta. His work focused on developing data centers for internet service providers and delivering IT solutions for the manufacturing and oil & gas sectors. His research interests include artificial intelligence, cybersecurity, and the development of IT infrastructure.

Janmejay V. Shukla is an accomplished academician and researcher with over nine years of combined experience in academia and industry. He holds a Ph.D. in Management from G H Raisoni University, Amravati, with research focused on consumer buying behavior in online food delivery services. Dr. Shukla has served as Assistant Professor at prestigious institutions such as Shri Ramdeobaba College of Engineering and Management and G H Raisoni College of Engineering, Nagpur. His research interests span digital marketing, consumer behavior, IoT in supply chain, and AI-driven innovations. He has published extensively in Scopus-indexed journals and international conferences, with multiple patents and copyrights to his credit. Dr. Shukla has also contributed as a reviewer, session chair, and expert evaluator at various academic forums. His blend of academic insight and industry experience uniquely positions him at the intersection of theoretical rigor and practical relevance in contemporary management research.

Arora Gaurav Singh is specialized in area of International Business. An Academician with more than 12 years of experience in teaching, training and research. Dr. Arora has taught in universities of repute in North India. His area of research includes Export Import Finance, International Marketing, and World Trade Organization & Regional Trade Agreements. He has several research papers of National as well as International level to his credit published in Journals of repute indexed in ABDC (Australian Business Deans Council), SCOPUS & UGC-CARE. Dr.Arora has Participated and presented at various events/Conferences held at national and International podium organized by various reputed institutions such as Indian Institute of Management(IIM), Society for Education Research & Development, Federation of Indian Chambers of Commerce & Industry (FIICI),Indian Institute of Technology-Bombay(IIT-B) and Confederation of Indian Industry (CII) etc.

J. Sudarvel is an Associate Professor at Karpagam Academy of Higher Education, Coimbatore, with nine years of teaching and six years of research experience. Specializing in finance and marketing, he has supervised seven Ph.D. scholars, with six more currently under his guidance. He has published 111 articles, including 52 in Scopus Indexed Journals, 13 in the Web of Science, and 12 in edited volumes, and presented 36 papers at international conferences. He serves as a Doctoral Committee Expert at Periyar University, and as an expert on the Board of Studies for VLB College and Nallamuthu Gounder Mahalingam College. Recognized for his contributions, he has received awards like Best Paper Presenter and Best Faculty and has led workshops and guest lectures on research methodology.

Anish T. P is an faculty member in the Department of Computer Science and Engineering at R.M.K College of Engineering and Technology, Puduvoyal. His academic interests focus on advancing knowledge and innovation in computing technologies. He is committed to guiding students and contributing to impactful research in the field of Computer Science.

Venkata Ramana Kaneti is an Assistant Professor in the Department of Computer Science and Engineering at VNR Vignana Jyothi Institute of Engineering and Technology, Hyderabad, Telangana. His research interests include artificial intelligence, machine learning, and data analytics. He is dedicated to advancing innovative teaching and research in emerging areas of computer science and engineering.

Tiara Zahira is an information technology professional with a strong interest in digital systems and emerging technologies. Her focus lies in exploring how intelligent and data-driven solutions can be designed to improve processes, enhance user experiences, and support innovation across diverse domains. She is particularly interested in the intersection of technology, usability, and sustainability, with an emphasis on developing adaptable and impactful digital solutions.

Index

A

B

C

D

E

F

I

L

M

P

R

S

www.ingramcontent.com/pod-product-compliance
Lightning Source LLC
LaVergne TN
LVHW061531290926
849162LV00004B/751
9798337327471